LITERATURE IN REVOLUTION

Literature in Revolution

EDITED BY
GEORGE ABBOTT WHITE
AND CHARLES NEWMAN

HOLT, RINEHART AND WINSTON
TriQuarterly Book
New York · Chicago · San Francisco

Published simultaneously in Canada by Holt, Rinehart
and Winston of Canada, Limited.

Library of Congress Catalog Card Number: 75-155537

First Edition

ISBN:0-03-086661-8

Designer: Lawrence Levy

Printed in the United States of America

To the memory of F. O. Matthiessen (*1902–1950*)
teacher, scholar, critic

III
POPULAR CULTURE

IV
CRITICAL CONSCIOUSNESS

I
THE RESPONSIBILITY
OF LITERATURE

. . . the advantage of the new movement is that
we do not want to anticipate the world
dogmatically, but only to discover the new by
way of the criticism of the old world. Until now,
philosophers kept the solution of all mysteries
inside their desks, and the stupid uneducated
world merely had to open its mouth and the
fried dove of absolute knowledge would fly in.
Philosophy is now secular, for which the best proof
is that philosophical consciousness itself feels the
pain of the struggle not merely externally, but
also internally. It is not our task to construct the
future and to deal with everything once and for
all, but it is clear what we have to do at present—
I am thinking of the merciless criticism of
everything that exists—merciless criticism in the
sense that it is not afraid of its findings, and just
as little afraid of conflict with the existing
powers. . . It will be found that what is involved
is not to draw a large dash between past and
future, but to realize the ideas of the past . . . it
will be found that humanity does not start a new
task, but consciously carries through the old.
Marx to Rugé, 1843

There is no revolutionary art as yet.
Leon Trotsky, 1924

Introductions

In *Literature and Revolution,* Leon Trotsky defined two kinds of revolutionary art—those works "whose themes reflect the Revolution, and the works which are not connected with the Revolution in theme, but are thoroughly imbued with . . . the new consciousness arising out of the Revolution." He differed from most revolutionary reformers in his belief that artistic creation springs from the same sources as social rebellion—that the hatred of injustice and a love of beauty were not necessarily contradictory, as they appear in cruder Leninism. He probably would never have agreed with Camus, in many ways a polar temperament, that "the revolution and art of the 20th century are tributaries of the same nihilism and live in the same contradiction [in that] both try to find a solution through terror." But he believed, at least in 1924, that the same revolutionary spirit which had triumphed politically would produce a revolutionary art in its own image and for its own needs. However implicitly, he rejected the vulgar Hegelian notion—recently resurfaced on the mystical Left of advanced capitalist societies—that there would be no need for art in a future society of reconciliation and solidarity. Trotsky saw art as the organic culmination of, rather than a simple service to, the revolution, and thus he could make the distinction between art with a revolutionary subject matter (and "appropriate" form) and that motivated by a new consciousness—a distinction which totalitarians of both the Left and Right tend to ignore in their allegiance to a reality of conventional wisdom.

However, does not an excess of solidarity, as the Nietzscheans fear, threaten to degenerate man into a sentimental, passive herd animal? Not at all. The powerful force of competition which, in bourgeois society, has the character of market competition, will not disappear in a Socialist society, but, to use the language of psycho-analysis, will be sublimated, that is, will assume a higher and more fertile form. There will be the struggle for one's opinion, for one's project, for one's taste. In the measure in which political struggles will be eliminated—and in a society where there will be no classes, there will be no such struggles—the liberated passions will be channelized into technique, into construction which also includes art. Art then will become more general, will mature, will become tempered, and will become the most perfect method of the progressive building of life in every field. It will not be merely "pretty" without relation to anything else . . . Art, therefore, will not suffer the lack of any such collective psychic impulses which make for the creation of new artistic tendencies and for changes in style . . . In a struggle so disinterested and tense, which will take place in a culture whose foundations are steadily rising, the human personality, with its invaluable basic trait of continual discontent, will grow and become polished at all its points. In truth, we have no reason to fear that there will be a decline of individuality or an impoverishment of art in a Socialist society . . . (*Literature and Revolution*)

That these words still retain a power beyond their irony in a society in which the word "revolution" has been so debased that it can hardly be used unself-consciously (even in titles for anthologies) is almost a miracle in itself. We continue to honor such utopian possibilities, but without Trotsky s faith in the existence of revolutionary man, nor with any clear notion of the historical situation which predicates his existence. Our society—the best part of it, one is tempted to say—is characterized by an utter confusion between avant garde art, bohemian life style, and radical politics, and more often than not these quite disparate phenomena serve as surrogates for one another. In the wake of the sixties —that "slum of the decade" as Benjamin DeMott has called it—the consensus of the Left seems to be that whereas Trotsky at first doubted the existence of a truly historical revolutionary *situation,* he never doubted for a moment the existence of a truly revolutionary psychology and requisite strategy—while, on the other hand, we assume a revolutionary situation, but wonder if we have genuine revolutionaries or an ideology/tactics equal to it.

In such a time, literature in particular comes under peculiar stress and scrutiny. For of all the arts, literature is closest to ideology, and more than any other art, it is both created and consumed in privacy. In periods of crisis, it therefore suffers both from the Right—if not from classical censorship then from its debasement as a commodity (censorship at the distribution point)—and from the Left's demands for objective relevance (criticism from "within" the revolution). The conventional response to both forms of pressure has historically been a kind of premeditated linear realism, which reconfirms reality for the Right by witless entertainment, or serves the Left in overthrowing reality by didacticism. A further effect, in much serious literature, is the direction of social loathing and paranoia upon itself—social impotence expressed increasingly as aesthetic involution, irony as its own subject—art which relinquishes its prophetic role and tends to grasp, however tenuously, at the traditional notions of the sanctity—hence apoliticality—of isolated genius. It is no accident that the notions of both "avant garde art" and "art for posterity" parallel the rise of the bourgeoisie, and perhaps the contemporary artist tends to exaggerate the fear that revolutionary art must be art by proscription, or based on reactionary aesthetics. There is, after all, a crucial difference between the Philistine's question, "What good is it?" and the revolutionary question, "What is it for?"

Camus acknowledges such aesthetic self-consciousness in order to dismiss it:

The trial of art has been opened definitively and is continuing today with the embarrassed complicity of artists and intellectuals dedicated to calumniating both their art and their intelligence. We notice, in fact, that in the contest between Shakespeare and the shoemaker, it is not the shoemaker who maligns Shakespeare or beauty but, on the contrary, the man who continues to read Shakespeare and who does not choose to make shoes—which he could never make, if it comes to that. The artists of our time resemble the repentant noblemen of nineteenth-century Russia; their bad conscience is their excuse. But the last emotion that an artist can experience, confronted with his art, is repentance. It is going far beyond simple and necessary humility to pretend to dismiss beauty, too, until the end of time, and meanwhile to deprive all the world, including the shoemaker, of this additional bread of which one has taken advantage oneself. (*The Rebel*)

3

One could also answer that for the practitioner the distinction between the active and autonomous artist is really a false one. Every writer thinks he is a realist, as Robbe-Grillet has said, and contingently, every writer believes himself to be "committed". It is really a reductive or at least a *post-festum* question, and one which can only be answered discursively, historically, and not by premeditated aesthetic strategies. As the neo-Marxist philosopher Leszek Kolakowski points out, "One can bed down just as comfortably on the idea of tragedy as on the (Christian) idea of eternal salvation, or the (Marxist) idea that consciousness is determined by being."

The question is whether those literary experiments which innovate our verbal world and linguistic perception can also be said to delineate the social struggle at any discrete moment, and whether such innovative literature clarifies or activates the social passions which historically parallel it. Even in hindsight, this is the most difficult of analytical questions and the one which this collection confronts: To what extent does the study and practice of literature in a particular time relate to contingent current social and political upheaval, and, conversely, to what extent do such events (or, in fact, their absence) influence the way we *do* literature?

It should be pointed out, I think, that whatever their viewpoint, tone, or methodology, no matter how topical or traditional the subject matter, these contributors would not have written what they have here without having lived through the particular social upheaval of the last three or four years. If that seems a banal statement now, it would have been an unlikely and probably insupportable one in 1967. There is a sense here not only of unease, but rather of a desperate attempt to re-establish a constituency—an audience, in a word. And as much as the collection as a whole is a lament for the consequences of radical protest of the last few years, there is very little "repentance" here.

Section One attempts to set up a context for the debate, long dormant in this country, concerning the responsibility of literary

4

people as practicing citizens. It also raises some of the uneasy relationships between practitioners, critics, and publishers; i.e., what gets published, taught, read, written, and why? It is the traditional debate as to whether "relevance" is established by personal choice or dictated by social forces. As might be expected, there remains little consensus on this point.

Section Two offers a series of textual analyses, in which various "classical" or established writers are examined in the context of the social revolution of their times. The basic question again is most pithily formulated by Trotsky: "Can we christen revolutionary art with any of the names that we have?"

Section Three extends the debate beyond traditional or classical literature to the popular media: To what extent is revolutionary change cultural rather than political, symbolic rather than actual, and to what extent is it initiated in popular expression, rather than by the intelligentsia? Is the medium the message?

Section Four offers four generalistic, speculative essays, which in their concern and methodology militate explicitly against the recently popularized notion of "new consciousness" as an ahistorical, spontaneous, and anti-rational phenomenon.

Some of the contributors would call themselves Marxists; others would simply say they find Marxist methodology useful. Some are well-established, preeminent in their fields; others just beginning to become known. There is a considerable range in age, background, methodology, and a good deal of interior polemic, and I see no evidence of the rigid ideological polarization, at least regarding the function and uses of literature, which is often attributed to the Left. For my part, the collection confirms the fact that any political debate requires a fully realized language—a literature—to take dimension, and that no amount of "position-taking" and action can substitute for serious analysis and reflection. Literature, as it is discussed here, is truly an instrument which allays the professional division of labor and general social weariness; literature is an attack on the established language of the

5

moment, a process in which language is the medium of whatever new consciousness we are to have, and that consciousness is, as in early Marx, "the realization of the past," re-thinking and re-feeling of the thoughts of man. This is offered as a collective enterprise, certainly not in terms of unanimity, or even less so in the current fashion of anonymity, but in the sense that literature, for all the contributors, means a truly reorientive enterprise; a belief that a reflective, autonomous language has an organic and supra-historical relation with things as they are, and as they should be. Literature *in* revolution, then, functions as both counterweight to, and energizer of, everyday speech, reflecting what Marx calls, in one of his few lyrical sentences, the "sensuous expression of estranged human life," continually renewing the possibility of "self-consciousness" as *positive* human nature, and not the latest excuse for silence.

The collection has no definitive pretensions, and in the end economic determinism played its usual role in our selection. Indeed, the essays which were ultimately rejected for the collection might well make an interesting sequel: We don't pretend to have represented all points of view which we can identify, any more than we can identify with all of the points of view we've included. My only consistent principle of rejection is that while I encourage authors to repeat themselves in the hope of amplification, I tried to avoid having the authors repeat one another. Among the most obvious omissions are essays written from black and feminist points of view. Hopefully, entire future issues of *TriQuarterly*, as well as *TriQuarterly* books, will concern themselves with such work. In the meantime, neither by way of justification nor apology, let me offer a small theory. Given the deserved pre-eminence of the black and feminist movements, it becomes very difficult to find statements which haven't already been articulated elsewhere, particularly when the major energies of the respective movements have been expended in establishing the *legitimacy* of the viewpoint in question. This is certainly a categorical oversimplification, but

I sense that after the first breakthrough of a new consciousness (what might be called its *legitimizing* phase) after it has been repackaged and fed back to us through bureaucratic rhetoric and the commercial media, there is an increasing reluctance among serious writers to repeat themselves, to trade off a voice, an image already stereotyped by media exposure. Hence the response of a prominent poetess, deeply involved in Women's Lib before it was called that, to our offer of a commission: ". . . I suppose I write as a woman, I certainly want to write for women, but I'm increasingly becoming uncomfortable with the idea that I should write 'like a liberated woman should'." In short, at the very moment a new political consciousness acquires a public force and common rhetoric, there is a natural resistance on the part of writers against the very voice which insures them a new audience, a constant questioning of their own means of expression as well as their public roles. No wonder the traditional hostility of reformers to poets. But if the 20th century has taught us anything, it is that such a centripetal motion within the larger movement is the lifeblood of any continuing revolution.

Otherwise, it is difficult to categorize the furious motion of the collection as a whole; most of the individual pieces are tentative, open-ended, a mixture of strict analysis and personal speculation. Without exception, they cry out for book length treatment more than a conventional periodical article—but this reflects our normal editorial policy, as well as the nature of the investigations themselves. In other words, the contributors have put a severe strain on our original rubrics, and we don't pretend that we've made them conform—which is, in the end, to everyone's advantage. And this is as it should be—for this is no minority report, with a program and resolutions, but simply a current record of a number of professional writers, trying to divine the relationship between their highly sophisticated literary expertise, language at its most liberating and complex intensity, and those embryonic, still dimly perceived, and inarticulate forces which affect their social relations and their daily lives.

We hope that our readers will find themselves drawn into this
continuing debate, and that we will hear from them.

CHARLES NEWMAN
Budapest, Hungary
December 1971

*   *   *

In the spring of 1969 I was invited to give a course on "Politics
and Literature" at Harvard University in the Department of
Social Relations. For my part, this collection had its origins in that
course.

It was all very informal, very enthusiastically a part of those
dark, yet optimistic times, and very much a part of the work I had
been doing for the past three years: a critical biography of F. O.
Matthiessen. The course was to be part of the now-famous "Soc
Rel 148–149," a lecture-recitation survey of the problems facing
America in the political, economic, and social sectors, from a
radical perspective. 148 was modest in most respects: Its instructors were young, bright, committed, but not too vocal; the problem
of social change was examined in more-or-less traditional ways
using the disciplines of sociology, psychology, economics, and
history; students were closely graded; and enrollment was no more
than three hundred students. An average Harvard course, one
might think, a little *too* committed and perhaps too explicit in its
ethics, though still an acceptable Harvard course.

149 rode the roller-coaster of history that by the spring of 1969
saw eruptions on every major (and most minor) campus across
the country, centered around the issue of the Vietnam War, but
also, and significantly, around student rights and "relevancy,"
community control, open enrollments, black studies, and everything that fell under the rubric of "student power." Where 148
had had perhaps 25 or 30 section leaders, 149 had over a hundred
and more seemed to be added each day. By the first week over
1,100 students had signed to take the course—classes were held
all over Cambridge, morning, afternoon, evening. 149, as 148,

looked at American economics and American history, but it also studied "Sex Role Oppression in the United States," "Existential Psychology," "What Road for Black Power?" (closed to whites), "Survival in the American Maelstrom," and, of course, "Politics and Literature."

Where 148 was seen by its founders and most of the campus as a way of merely introducing new critical concepts into the University, challenging the hegemony of the existing academic priesthood in concept and methodology, and offering no specific, *a priori* critique, 149 quickly became a most politically-kicked football, surrounded by myth and misconception.

The University, to say nothing of the Social Relations Department (with more than its share of the unorthodox), perceived 149 as a locus for a number of long-repressed issues: the nature and direction of the University, for a start, as well as the specific content of numberless programs and courses. It was not as though 148–149 made overtly threatening gestures—what was rapidly understood by many Harvard undergraduates was: Here is a place where there are interesting and excited professors and instructors; here is a place where *how* I learn is taken as seriously as *what* I learn; here is a place where disciplines are interrelated and socially responsible; here is a place where I have as much a voice in the direction of my study as my instructor; in short, here is a place where I can begin to participate as a human being in the decisions that affect my life.

148–149 attracted support from older faculty both within and without the Department who, for years, had been looking for ways of rescuing their own disciplines from enervation, desiccation, and the extremes of professionalism. *Cf.* Robert Coles' moving account of Anna Freud's April 1968 lecture on what psychoanalysis had become as the generation of intellectual gadflies gave way to the people engineers. "They were the unconventional ones," she says, "the doubters, those who were dissatisfied with the limitations imposed on knowledge ... the dreamers"—they had given way to those "hardworking enough to wish to better their professional efficiency" inasmuch as "psy-

9

choanalytic training has become institutionalized and appeals in this stricter form to a different kind of personality." (*Erik H. Erikson: The Growth of His Work,* 1970, lxxvii.)

In other words, these people were looking for ways of relating what had happened to their discipline to what had happened to the University as it became uncritically wedded to the state. Sadly, support came from only a few, and a very quiet few at that. In this respect, Harvard did neither better nor worse than its counterparts.

In addition, every faction of the New Left—which included joyriders, independents, liberals, anarchists, and varying shades of Marxists, in varying shades of organization—had an interest in the content and direction of the course. If it could continue, some said, then there was hope for the University; Harvard was not impervious to change. If they smashed it, others said, it would only demonstrate, here at home, the repressiveness of the University administration in its relationship with the government. The two major factions were "independent" *Students for a Democratic Society* (SDS) and the more tightly organized *Worker-Student Alliance* (WSA), which was closely aligned with the Marxist-Leninist-Maoist *Progressive Labor Party* (PLP). These distinctions, an anagrammatic regression to the thirties, one might think, were crucial to the massive strike at the University that spring but, more specifically, greatly affected the relationship between the course organizers and the Social Relations Department when it came time to decide the course's fate in mid-March of 1969.

It goes without saying that the course was popular with the students. The reasons for faculty opposition against continuing the course were categorized in three ways: (1) purely administrative problems—span of control and unification of content; (2) educational policy problems—recruitment, certification, and grading; and (3) "radical problems"—an instructor's clear commitment to an ideology. Various student factions had their reasons for opposition as well. Among these were that the course was patently "too liberal"; that merely teaching people "new

10

concepts" was ineffective (roughly translated as an unreconstructed Marxist attitude toward base/superstructure—a change in the structure of consciousness—arguing that such an approach was unidirectional and irreversible); and also that fighting for the retention of the course drained energies from two crucial struggles on campus: the University's insensitive expansion into lower income areas of the city of Cambridge, and its support of the Reserve Officer Training Corps (ROTC).

The rather ironic point of all this in terms of this collection was that not only was the "Politics and Literature" seminar the object of slightly-raised eyebrows within the Department (none other than the *New York Times* reported it linked with, I believe, "questionable" seminars on education and women), but within liberal and radical ranks it was the subject of both structural and textual concern; did we really belong in Soc Rel? One could have argued that my students were eagerly reading a backbreaking load to satisfy the traditionalists, and raising significant questions about their relationship to society to satisfy the radicals, yet it was sad to have to justify it in such a way. The more painful political differences are perhaps best illustrated by the fact that the seminar, originally quite large, broke in two—one beginning its term with Chairman Mao's "Talks at the Yenan Forum on Literature and Art," mine with Richard Wright's *Native Son*.

Everyone seemed strangely self-conscious about the ways in which they had been taught to perceive, the slick, neutral ways they had learned to "open" the text, like Andy cracking another shell at the Union Oyster House. We tried to get alternate angles of vision by reading Trotsky, Caldwell, and Lukács, but we found entry difficult and no "introductory" material seemed suitable, if in fact available.

When I think about that seminar and what I still consider, in retrospect, its radiant success, I remember people and the great variety of unexamined and naive positions they held, all in search of something at once more useful, more responsible, more true to experience as they knew it.

I remember Steve Likosky, a graduate student with an intimate knowledge of Slavic literature, shyly reading before an audience for the first time—Mayakovsky, in the Russian—and later, with more confidence but still with great love, arguing with a young psychologist, Matt Lincoln, about Pasternak's *Dr. Zhivago* and Yuri's mixed feelings about the revolution. There was Jim Gray, now a laywer, talking about Ralph Ellison as an artist—not a "Negro" or a "black" artist, but a man who utilized with skill and honesty the black experience closest to him. And Stewart Barnes, now a priest, with Dick Tyner, challenging Mark Mazer—fresh from a seminar with Robert Coles on "Photography in the Thirties" or something like that—on what *Let Us Now Praise Famous Men* was all about, whether or not it was exploitive, or uncritically celebrative, or simply sprawling. And Spencer Marx, quietly talking about a discovery in James, honestly attempting to plumb the relationship between, say, Pound's translations and his politics; and Carlos Joly, introducing us to existentialism in Sartre's *The Words* and, when we were ready, sharing Octavio Paz and Pablo Neruda in the Spanish. Marion Weil questioned us all on Mailer, and when I praised him for his vision in *Armies of the Night,* she could only bring us all to a fuller truth in reminding us that his lust for power was of a piece with his destructiveness toward people, little people. Each with his or her pasts, experiences, questions, needs, gave shape to what a critical literature might be.

Had we a critical literature, something like this collection that raised the questions it took the duration of the course to raise, how much richer our experience would have been. As it was, we had the great good fortune of encountering one another. And our lives were changed.

GEORGE ABBOTT WHITE
Cambridge, Mass.
December 1971

12

Language and freedom

NOAM CHOMSKY

As a preliminary, let me say just a word about the contemporary study of language, as I see it. There are many aspects of language and language use that raise intriguing questions, but—in my judgment—only a few have so far led to productive theoretical work. In particular, our deepest insights are in the area of formal grammatical structure. A person who knows a language has acquired a system of rules and principles—a "generative grammar," in technical terms—that associates sound and meaning in some specific fashion. There are many reasonably well-founded and rather enlightening hypotheses as to the character of such grammars for quite a number of languages. Furthermore, there has been a renewal of interest in "universal grammar," interpreted now as the theory that tries to specify the general properties of languages that can be learned in the normal way by humans. Here too, significant progress has been achieved. The subject is of

This article appears by generous permission of the editors of *Abraxas,* where it was first published. It was originally a lecture delivered at Loyola University in Chicago. It will appear, along with the complete symposium of which it is a part, in *Studies in Contemporary Thought* (Waner & Breech, Inc.).

particular importance. It is appropriate to regard universal grammar as study of one of the essential faculties of mind. It is, therefore, extremely interesting to discover that the principles of universal grammar are rich, abstract and restrictive, and can be used to construct principled explanations for a variety of phenomena. At the present stage of our understanding, if language is to provide a springboard for the investigation of other problems of man, it is these aspects of language to which we will have to turn our attention, for the simple reason that it is only these aspects that are reasonably well-understood. In another sense, the study of formal properties of language reveals something of the nature of man in a negative way; it underscores, with great clarity, the limits of our understanding of those qualities of mind that are apparently unique to man and that must enter into his cultural achievements in an intimate, if still quite obscure, manner.

In searching for a point of departure, one turns naturally to a period in the history of Western thought when it was possible to believe that "the thought of making freedom the sum and substance of philosophy has emancipated the human spirit in all its relationships, and . . . has given to science in all its parts a more powerful reorientation than any earlier revolution."[1] The word "revolution" bears multiple associations in this passage, for Schelling also proclaims that "man is born to act and not to speculate"; and when he writes that "the time has come to proclaim to a nobler humanity the freedom of the spirit, and no longer to have patience with men's tearful regrets for their lost chains," we hear the echoes of the libertarian thought and revolutionary acts of the late 18th century. Schelling writes that "the beginning and end of all philosophy is—Freedom." These words are invested with meaning and urgency at a time when men are struggling to cast off their chains, to resist authority that has lost its claim to legitimacy, to construct more humane and more democratic social institutions. It is at such a time that the philosopher may be driven to inquire into the nature of human freedom and its limits, and perhaps to conclude, with Schelling, that with respect to the human ego, "its essence is freedom"; and with respect to

14

philosophy, "the highest dignity of Philosophy consists precisely therein, that it stakes all on human freedom."

We are living, once again, at such a time. A revolutionary ferment is sweeping the so-called "Third World," awakening enormous masses from torpor and acquiescence to traditional authority. There are those who feel that the industrial societies as well are ripe for revolution—and I do not refer only to representatives of the "New Left." For example, Paul Ricoeur, in the wake of the May events in Paris, wrote in *Le Monde* that the West too is entering a period of revolutionary change; a revolution which "attacks capitalism not only because it fails to bring about social justice but also because it succeeds too well in deluding men by its own inhuman commitment to quantitative well-being; it attacks bureaucracy not only because it is burdensome and ineffectual, but because it places men in the role of slaves in relation to the totality of powers, of structures and hierarchical relations from which they have become estranged; finally it attacks the nihilism of a society which, like a cancerous tissue, has no purpose beyond its own growth."

The threat of revolutionary change brings forth repression and reaction. Its signs are evident in varying forms, in France, in the Soviet Union, in the United States. It is natural, then, that we should consider, abstractly, the problems of human freedom, and turn with interest and serious attention to the thinking of an earlier period when archaic social institutions were subjected to critical analysis and sustained attack. It is natural and appropriate, so long as we bear in mind Schelling's admonition, that man is born not merely to speculate, but also to act.

One of the earliest and most remarkable of the 18th century investigations of freedom and servitude is Rousseau's *Discourse on Inequality* (1755), in many ways a revolutionary tract. In it, he seeks to "set forth the origin and progress of inequality, the establishment and abuse of political societies, insofar as these things can be deduced from the nature of man by the light of reason alone . . ." His conclusions were sufficiently shocking so that the judges of the prize competition of the Academy of Dijon, to whom the work was originally submitted, refused to hear the manuscript through.[2] In it, Rousseau challenges the legitimacy of virtually every social institution, as well as individual control of property and wealth. These are "usurpations . . . established only on a precarious and abusive right . . . having been acquired only by force, force could take them away without [the rich] having grounds for complaint." Not even property acquired by personal industry is held "upon better titles." Against such a claim, one might object: "Do you not know that a multitude of your brethren die or suffer from need of what you have in excess, and that you needed express and unanimous consent of the human race to appropriate for yourself anything from common subsistence that exceeded your own?" It is contrary to the law of nature that "a handful of men be glutted with superfluities while the starving multitude lacks necessities."

Rousseau argues that civil society is hardly more than a conspiracy by the rich to guarantee their plunder. Hypocritically, the rich call upon their neighbors to "institute regulations of justice and peace to which all are obliged to conform, which make an exception of no one, and which compensate in some way for the caprices of fortune by equally subjecting the powerful and the weak to mutual duties"—those laws which, as Anatole France was to say, in their majesty deny to the rich and the poor equally the right to sleep under the bridge at night. By such arguments, the poor and weak were seduced: "All ran to meet their chains thinking they secured their freedom . . ." Thus society and laws "gave new fetters to the weak and new forces to the rich, destroyed natural freedom for all time, established forever the law of property and inequality, changed a clever usurpation into an irrevocable right, and for the profit of a few ambitious men henceforth subjected the whole human race to work, servitude and misery." Governments inevitably tend towards arbitrary power, as "their corruption and extreme limit." This power is "by its nature illegitimate . . . ," and new revolutions must

dissolve the government altogether or bring it closer to its legitimate institution . . . The uprising that ends by strangling or dethroning a sultan is as lawful an act as those by which he

16

disposed, the day before, of the lives and goods of his subjects. Force alone maintained him, force alone overthrows him.

What is interesting, in the present connection, is the path that Rousseau follows to reach these conclusions "by the light of reason alone," beginning with his ideas about the nature of man. He wants to see man "as nature formed him." It is from the nature of man that the principles of natural right and the foundations of social existence must be deduced.

This same study of original man, of his true needs, and of the principles underlying his duties, is also the only good means one could use to remove those crowds of difficulties which present themselves concerning the origin of moral inequality, the true foundation of the body politic, the reciprocal rights of its members, and a thousand similar questions as important as they are ill explained.

To determine the nature of man, Rousseau proceeds to compare man and animal. Man is "intelligent, free . . . the sole animal endowed with reason." Animals are "devoid of intellect and freedom."

In every animal I see only an ingenious machine to which nature has given senses in order to revitalize itself and guarantee itself, to a certain point, from all that tends to destroy or upset it. I perceive precisely the same things in the human machine, with the difference that nature alone does everything in the operations of a beast, whereas man contributes to his operations by being a free agent. The former chooses or rejects by instinct and the latter by an act of freedom, so that a beast cannot deviate from the rule that is prescribed to it even when it would be advantageous for it to do so, and a man deviates from it often to his detriment . . . it is not so much understanding which constitutes the distinction of man among the animals as it is his being a free agent. Nature commands every animal, and the beast obeys. Man feels the same impetus, but he realizes that he is free to acquiesce or resist; and it is above all in the consciousness of this freedom that the spirituality of his soul is shown. For physics explains in some way the mechanism of the senses and the formation of ideas; but in the power of willing, or rather of choosing, and in the sentiment of this power are found only purely spiritual acts about which the laws of mechanics explain nothing.

Thus the essence of human nature is man's freedom and his consciousness of his freedom. So Rousseau can say that "the jurists, who have gravely pronounced that the child of a slave would be born a slave, have decided in other terms that a man would not be born a man."[3]

Sophistic politicians and intellectuals search for ways to obscure the fact that the essential and defining property of man is his freedom: ". . . they attribute to men a natural inclination

17

to servitude, without thinking that it is the same for freedom as for innocence and virtue—their value is felt only as long as one enjoys them oneself and the taste for them is lost as soon as one has lost them." In contrast, Rousseau asks rhetorically "whether, freedom being the most noble of man's faculties, it is not degrading one's nature, putting oneself on the level of beasts enslaved by instinct, even offending the author of one's being, to renounce without reservation the most precious of all his gifts and subject ourselves to committing all the crimes he forbids us in order to please a ferocious or insane master"—a question that has been asked, in similar terms, by many an American draft resister in the last few years, and by many others who are beginning to recover from the catastrophe of 20th century Western civilization, which has so tragically confirmed Rousseau's judgment:

Hence arose the national wars, battles, murders, and reprisals which make nature tremble and shock reason, and all those horrible prejudices which rank the honor of shedding human blood among the virtues. The most decent men learned to consider it one of their duties to murder their fellowmen; at length men were seen to massacre each other by the thousands without knowing why; more murders were committed on a single day of fighting and more horrors in the capture of a single city than were committed in the state of nature during whole centuries over the entire face of the earth.

The proof of his doctrine that the struggle for freedom is an essential human attribute, that the value of freedom is felt only as long as one enjoys it, Rousseau sees in "the marvels done by all free peoples to guard themselves from oppression." True, those who have abandoned the life of a free man

do nothing but boast incessantly of the peace and repose they enjoy in their chains . . . But when I see the others sacrifice pleasures, repose, wealth, power, and life itself for the preservation of this sole good which is so disdained by those who have lost it; when I see animals born free and despising captivity break their heads against the bars of their prison; when I see multitudes of entirely naked savages scorn European voluptuousness and endure hunger, fire, the sword, and death to preserve only their independence, I feel that it does not behoove slaves to reason about freedom.

Rather similar thoughts were expressed by Kant, forty years later. He cannot, he says, accept the proposition that certain people "are not ripe for freedom," for example, the serfs of some land-lord.[4]

If one accepts this assumption, freedom will never be achieved; for one cannot arrive at the maturity for freedom without having already acquired it; one must be free to learn how to make use of one's powers freely and usefully. The first attempts will surely be brutal and will lead to a state of affairs more painful and dangerous than the former condition under the dominance but also the protection of an external authority. However, one can achieve reason only through one's own experiences and one must be free to be able to undertake them ... To accept the principle that freedom is worthless for those under one's control and that one has the right to refuse it to them forever is an infringement on the rights of God himself, who has created man to be free.

The remark is particularly interesting because of its context. Kant was defending the French Revolution, during the terror, against those who claimed that it showed the masses to be unready for the privilege of freedom. Kant's remarks have contemporary relevance. No rational person will approve of violence and terror. In particular, the terror of the post-revolutionary state, fallen into the hands of a grim autocracy, has, more than once, reached indescribable levels of savagery. Yet no person of understanding or humanity will too quickly condemn the violence that often occurs when long-subdued masses rise against their oppressors, or take their first steps towards liberty and social reconstruction.

Let me return now to Rousseau's argument against the legitimacy of established authority, whether that of political power or of wealth. It is striking that his argument, up to this point, follows a familiar Cartesian model. Man is uniquely beyond the bounds of physical explanation; the beast, on the other hand, is merely an ingenious machine, commanded by natural law. Man's freedom and his consciousness of this freedom distinguish him from the beast-machine. The principles of mechanical explanation are incapable of accounting for these human properties, though they can account for sensation and even the combination of ideas, in which regard "man differs from a beast only in degree."

To Descartes and his followers, such as Cordemoy, the only sure sign that another organism has a mind, and hence also lies beyond the bounds of mechanical explanation, is its use of language in the normal, creative human fashion, free from control by identifiable stimuli, novel and innovative, appropriate to situations, coherent and engendering in our minds new thoughts and ideas.[5] To the Cartesians, it is obvious by introspection that each man possesses a mind, a substance whose essence is thought;

19

his creative use of language reflects this freedom of thought and conception. When we have evidence that another organism too uses language in this free and creative fashion, we are led to attribute to it as well a mind like ours. From similar assumptions regarding the intrinsic limits of mechanical explanation, its inability to account for man's freedom and consciousness of his freedom, Rousseau proceeds to develop his critique of authoritarian institutions, which deny to man his essential attribute of freedom, in varying degree.

Were we to combine these speculations, we might develop an interesting connection between language and freedom. Language, in its essential properties and the manner of its use, provides the basic criterion for determining that another organism is a being with a human mind and the human capacity for free thought and self-expression, and with the essential human need for freedom from the external constraints of repressive authority. Furthermore, we might try to proceed from the detailed investigation of language and its use to a deeper and more specific understanding of the human mind. Proceeding on this model, we might further attempt to study other aspects of that human nature which, as Rousseau rightly observes, must be correctly conceived if we are to be able to develop, in theory, the foundations for a rational social order.

I will return to this problem, but first I would like to trace further Rousseau's thinking about the matter. Rousseau diverges from the Cartesian tradition in several respects. He defines the "specific characteristic of the human species" as man's "faculty of self-perfection," which, "with the aid of circumstances, successively develops all the others, and resides among us as much in the species as in the individual." The faculty of self-perfection and of perfection of the human species through cultural transmission is not, to my knowledge, discussed in any similar terms by the Cartesians. However, I think that Rousseau's remarks might be interpreted as a development of the Cartesian tradition in an unexplored direction, rather than as a denial and rejection of it. There is no inconsistency in the notion that the essential

20

attributes of mind underlie a historically evolving human nature that develops within the limits that they set; or that these attributes of mind provide the possibility for self-perfection; or that, by providing the consciousness of freedom, these essential attributes of human nature give man the opportunity to create social conditions and social forms to maximize the possibilities for freedom, diversity, and individual self-realization. To use an arithmetical analogy, the integers do not fail to be an infinite set merely because they do not exhaust the rational numbers. Analogously, it is no denial of man's capacity for infinite "self-perfection" to hold that there are intrinsic properties of mind that constrain his development. I would like to argue that in a sense the opposite is true, that without a system of formal constraints there are no creative acts; specifically, in the absence of intrinsic and restrictive properties of mind, there can be only "shaping of behavior" but no creative acts of self-perfection. Furthermore, Rousseau's concern for the evolutionary character of self-perfection brings us back, from another point of view, to a concern for human language, which would appear to be a prerequisite for such evolution of society and culture, for Rousseau's perfection of the species, beyond the most rudimentary forms.

Rousseau holds that "although the organ of speech is natural to man, speech itself is nonetheless not natural to him . . ." Again, I see no inconsistency between this observation and the typical Cartesian view that innate abilities are "dispositional," faculties that lead us to produce ideas (specifically, innate ideas) in a particular manner under given conditions of external stimulation, but that also provide us with the ability to proceed in our thinking without such external factors. Language too, then, is natural to man only in a specific way. This is an important and quite fundamental insight of the rationalist linguists that was disregarded, very largely, under the impact of empiricist psychology in the 18th century and since.[6]

Rousseau discusses the origin of language at some length, though he confesses himself to be unable to come to grips with the problem in a satisfactory way. Thus if men needed speech in order to learn to think, they had even greater need of knowing how to think in order to discover the art of speech . . . So that one can hardly form tenable conjectures about this art of communicating thoughts and establishing intercourse between minds: a sublime art which is now very far from its origin . . .

He holds that "general ideas can come into the mind only with the aid of words, and the understanding grasps them only through propositions"—a fact which prevents animals, devoid of reason, from formulating such ideas or ever acquiring "the perfectibility which depends upon them." Thus he cannot conceive of the means by which "our new grammarians began to extend their ideas and to generalize their words," or to develop the means "to express all the thoughts of men": "numbers, abstract words, aorists, and all the tenses of verbs, particles, syntax, the linking of propositions, reasoning, and the forming of all the logic of discourse." He does speculate about later stages of the perfection of the species, "when the ideas of men began to spread and multiply, and when closer communication was established among them, [and] they sought more numerous signs and a more extensive language. . . ." But he must, unhappily, abandon "the following difficult problem: which was most necessary, previously formed society for the institution of languages, or previously invented languages for the establishment of society?"

The Cartesians cut the Gordian knot by postulating the existence of a species-specific characteristic, a second substance that serves as what we might call a "creative principle" alongside of the "mechanical principle" that determines totally the behavior of animals. There was, for them, no need to explain the origin of language in the course of historical evolution. Rather, man's nature is qualitatively distinct: there is no passage from body to mind. We might reinterpret this idea in more current terms by speculating that rather sudden and dramatic mutations might have led to qualities of intelligence that are, so far as we know, quite unique to man, possession of language, in the human sense, being the most distinctive index of these qualities.[7] If this is correct, as at least a first approximation to the facts, the study of language might be expected to offer an entering wedge, or perhaps a model, for an investigation of human nature that would provide the grounding for a much broader theory of human nature.

To conclude these historical remarks, I would like to turn, as I have elsewhere,[8] to Wilhelm von Humboldt, one of the most stimulating and intriguing thinkers of the period. Humboldt was, on the one hand, one of the most profound theorists of general linguistics, and on the other an early and forceful advocate of libertarian values. The basic concept of his philosophy is *Bildung,* by which, as J.W. Burrows accurately expresses it, "he meant the fullest, richest and most harmonious development of the potentialities of the individual, the community or the human race."[9] His own thought might serve as an exemplary case. Though he does not, to my knowledge, explicitly relate his ideas about language to his libertarian social thought, there is, quite clearly, a common ground from which they develop, a concept of human nature that inspires each. Mill's essay *On Liberty* takes as its epigraph Humboldt's formulation of the "leading principle" of his thought: "the absolute and essential importance of human development in its richest diversity." Humboldt concludes his critique of the authoritarian state by saying: "I have felt myself animated throughout with a sense of the deepest respect for the inherent dignity of human nature, and for freedom, which alone befits that dignity." Briefly put, his concept of human nature is this:[10]

The true end of Man, or that which is prescribed by the eternal and immutable dictates of reason, and not suggested by vague and transient desires, is the highest and most harmonious development of his powers to a complete and consistent whole. Freedom is the first and indispensable condition which the possibility of such a development presupposes; but there is besides another essential—intimately connected with freedom, it is true—a variety of situations.

Like Rousseau and Kant, he holds that:

nothing promotes this ripeness for freedom so much as freedom itself. This truth, perhaps, may not be acknowledged by those who have so often used this unripeness as an excuse for continuing repression. But it seems to me to follow unquestionably from the very nature of man. The incapacity for freedom can only arise from a want of moral and intellectual power; to heighten this power is the only way to supply this want; but to do this presupposes the exercise of the power, and this exercise presupposes the freedom which awakens spontaneous activity. Only it is clear we cannot call it giving freedom, when bonds are relaxed which are not felt as such by him who wears them. But of no man on earth—however neglected by nature, and however degraded by circumstances—is this true of all the bonds which oppress him. Let us undo them one by one, as the feeling of freedom awakens in men's hearts, and we shall hasten progress at every step.

Those who do not comprehend this "may justly be suspected of misunderstanding human nature, and of wishing to make men into machines."

Man is fundamentally a creative, searching, self-perfecting being: "to inquire and to create—these are the centres around which all human pursuits more or less directly revolve." But freedom of thought and enlightenment are not only for the elite. Once again echoing Rousseau, Humboldt states: "There is something degrading to human nature in the idea of refusing to any man the right to be a man." He is, then, optimistic about the effects on all of "the diffusion of scientific knowledge by freedom and enlightenment." But "all moral culture springs solely and immediately from the inner life of the soul, and can only be stimulated in human nature, and never produced by external and artificial contrivances." "The cultivation of the understanding, as of any man's other faculties, is generally achieved by his own activity, his own ingenuity, or his own methods of using the discoveries of others . . ." Education, then, must provide the opportunities for self-fulfillment; it can at best provide a rich and challenging environment for the individual to explore, in his own way. Even a language cannot, strictly speaking, be taught, but only "awakened in the mind: one can only provide the thread along which it will develop of itself." I think that Humboldt would have found congenial much of Dewey's thinking about education. And he might also have appreciated the recent revolutionary extension of such ideas, for example, by the radical Catholics of Latin America who are concerned with the "awakening of consciousness," referring to "the transformation of the passive exploited lower classes into conscious and critical masters of their own destinies"[11] much in the manner of "Third World" revolutionaries elsewhere. He would, I am sure, have approved of their criticism of schools which are[12]

more preoccupied with the transmission of knowledge than with the creation, among other values, of a critical spirit. From the social point of view, the educational systems are oriented to maintaining the existing social and economic structures instead of transforming them.

24

But Humboldt's concern for spontaneity goes well beyond educational practice in the narrow sense. It touches also the question of labor and exploitation. The remarks just quoted about the cultivation of understanding through spontaneous action continue as follows:

man never regards what he possesses as so much his own, as what he does; and the labourer who tends a garden is perhaps in a truer sense its owner, than the listless voluptuary who enjoys its fruits . . . In view of this consideration,[13] it seems as if all peasants and craftsmen might be elevated into artists; that is, men who love their labour for its own sake, improve it by their own plastic genius and inventive skill, and thereby cultivate their intellect, ennoble their character, and exalt and refine their pleasures. And so humanity would be ennobled by the very things which now, though beautiful in themselves, so often serve to degrade it . . . But, still, freedom is undoubtedly the indispensable condition, without which even the pursuits most congenial to individual human nature can never succeed in producing such salutary influences. Whatever does not spring from a man's free choice, or is only the result of instruction and guidance, does not enter into his very being, but remains alien to his true nature; he does not perform it with truly human energies but merely with mechanical exactness.

If a man acts in a purely mechanical way, reacting to external demands or instruction rather than in ways determined by his own interests and energies and power, "we may admire what he does, but we despise what he is."[14]

On such conceptions Humboldt grounds his ideas concerning the role of the state, which tends to "make man an instrument to serve its arbitrary ends, over-looking his individual purposes." His doctrine is classical liberal, strongly opposed to all but the most minimal forms of state intervention in personal or social life.

Writing in the 1790's, Humboldt had no conception of the forms that industrial capitalism would take. Hence he is not overly concerned with the dangers of private power:

But when we reflect (still keeping theory distinct from practice) that the influence of a private person is liable to diminution and decay, from competition, dissipation of fortune, even death; and that clearly none of these contingencies can be applied to the State; we are still left with the principle that the latter is not to meddle in anything which does not refer exclusively to security . . .

He speaks of the essential equality of the condition of private citizens, and of course has no idea of the ways in which the notion "private person" would come to be reinterpreted in the era of corporate capitalism. He did not foresee that "Democracy with its motto of *equality of all citizens before the law* and Liberalism with its *right of man over his own person* both [would be] wrecked on realities of capitalist economy."[15] He did not foresee that in a predatory capitalist economy, State intervention would be an absolute necessity to preserve human existence and to prevent the destruction of the physical environment—I am being optimistic. As Karl Polanyi, for one, has pointed out, the self-adjusting market "could not exist for any length of time without annihilating the human and natural substance of society; it would have physically destroyed man and transformed his surroundings into a wilderness."[16] Humboldt did not foresee the consequences of the commodity character of labor, the doctrine (in Polanyi's words) that: "It is not for the commodity to decide where it should be offered for sale, to what purpose it should be used, at what price it should be allowed to change hands, and in what manner it should be consumed or destroyed." But the commodity, in this case, is a human life, and social protection was therefore a minimal necessity to constrain the irrational and destructive workings of the classical free market. Nor did Humboldt understand that capitalist economic relations perpetuated a form of bondage which, as early as 1767, Simon Linguet had declared to be even worse than slavery.[17]

It is the impossibility of living by any other means that compels our farm laborers to till the soil whose fruits they will not eat, and our masons to construct buildings in which they will not live. It is want that drags them to those markets where they await masters who will do them the kindness of buying them. It is want that compels them to go down on their knees to the rich man in order to get from him permission to enrich him . . . What effective gain has the suppression of slavery brought him? . . . He is free, you say. Ah! That is his misfortune. The slave was precious to his master because of the money he had cost him. But the handicraftsman costs nothing to the rich voluptuary who employs him . . . These men, it is said, have no master —they have one, and the most terrible, the most imperious of masters, that is *need*. It is this that reduces them to the most cruel dependence.

If there is something degrading to human nature in the idea of bondage, then a new emancipation must be awaited, Fourier's "third and last emancipatory phase of history"[18]—the first having made serfs out of slaves, and the second wage-earners out of serfs, the third which will transform the proletariat to free men by eliminating the commodity character of labor, ending wage-slavery, and bringing the commercial, industrial, and financial institutions under democratic control.

Perhaps Humboldt might have accepted these conclusions. He does agree that State intervention in social life is legitimate if "freedom would destroy the very conditions without which not only freedom but even existence itself would be inconceivable"— precisely the circumstances that arise in an unconstrained capitalist economy. In any event, his criticism of bureaucracy and the autocratic State stands as an eloquent forewarning of some of the most dismal aspects of modern history, and the basis of his critique is applicable to a broader range of coercive institutions than he imagined.

Though expressing a classical liberal doctrine, Humboldt is no primitive individualist in the style of Rousseau. Rousseau extols the savage who "lives within himself"; he has little use for "the sociable man, always outside of himself, [who] knows how to live only in the opinion of others . . . from [whose] judgment alone . . . he draws the sentiment of his own existence."[19] Humboldt's vision is quite different:

the whole tenor of the ideas and arguments unfolded in this essay might fairly be reduced to this, that while they would break all fetters in human society, they would attempt to find as many new social bonds as possible. The isolated man is no more able to develop than the one who is fettered.

Thus he looks forward to a community of free association without coercion by the State or other authoritarian institutions, in which free men can create and inquire, and achieve the highest development of their powers—far ahead of his time, he presents an anarchist vision that is appropriate, perhaps, to the next stage of industrial society. We can, perhaps, look forward to a day when these various strands will be brought together within the framework of libertarian socialism, a social form that barely exists today though its elements can perhaps be perceived: in the guarantee of individual rights that has achieved its highest form—though still tragically flawed—in the Western democracies; in the Israeli Kibbutzim; in the experiments with workers' councils in Yugoslavia; in the effort to awaken popular consciousness and create a new involvement in the social process which is a fundamental element in the "Third World" revolutions, coexisting uneasily with indefensible authoritarian practice.

A similar concept of human nature underlies Humboldt's work on language. Language is a process of free creation; its laws and principles are fixed, but the manner in which the principles of generation are used is free and infinitely varied. Even the interpretation and use of words involves a process of free creation. The normal use of language and the acquisition of language depend on what Humboldt calls the fixed form of language, a system of generative processes that is rooted in the nature of the human mind and constrains but does not determine the free creations of normal intelligence or, at a higher and more original level, of the great writer or thinker. Humboldt is, on the one hand, a Platonist who insists that learning is a kind of reminiscence in which the mind, stimulated by experience, draws from its own internal resources and follows a path that it itself determines; and he is also a romantic, attuned to cultural variety and the endless possibilities for the spiritual contributions of the creative genius. There is no contradiction in this, any more than there is a contradiction in the insistence of esthetic theory that individual works of genius are constrained by principle and rule. The normal, creative use of language, which to the Cartesian rationalist is the best index of the existence of another mind, presupposes a system of rules and generative principles of a sort that the rationalist grammarians attempted, with some success, to determine and make explicit.

The many modern critics who sense an inconsistency in the belief that free creation takes place within—presupposes, in fact—a system of constraints and governing principles are quite mistaken; unless, of course, they speak of "contradiction" in the loose and metaphoric sense of Schelling, when he writes that "without the contradiction of necessity and freedom not only philosophy but every nobler ambition of the spirit would sink to that death which is peculiar to those sciences in which that contradiction serves no function." Without this tension between necessity and freedom, rule and choice, there can be no creativity, no communication, no meaningful acts at all.

28

I have discussed these traditional ideas at some length not out of antiquarian interest, but because I think that they are valuable and essentially correct, and that they project a course that we can follow with profit. Social action must be animated by a vision of a future society, and by explicit judgments of value concerning the character of this future society. These judgments must derive from some concept of the nature of man, and one may seek empirical foundations by investigating man's nature as it is revealed by his behavior and his creations, material, intellectual, and social. We have, perhaps, reached a point in history when it is possible to think seriously about a society in which freely constituted social bonds replace the fetters of autocratic institutions, rather in the sense conveyed by the remarks of Humboldt that I quoted, not to speak of a rich tradition of libertarian socialism in the years that followed.

Predatory capitalism created a complex industrial system and an advanced technology; it permitted a considerable extension of democratic practice and fostered certain liberal values, but within limits that are now being pressed and must be overcome. It is not a fit system for the mid-20th century. It is incapable of meeting human needs that can be expressed only in collective terms, and its concept of competitive man who seeks only to maximize wealth and power, who subjects himself to market relationships, to exploitation and external authority, is anti-human and intolerable in the deepest sense. An autocratic State is no acceptable substitute; nor can the militarized state capitalism evolving in the United States or the bureaucratized, centralized welfare State be accepted as the goal of human existence. The only justification for repressive institutions is material and cultural deficit. But such institutions, at certain stages of history, perpetuate and produce such a deficit, and even threaten human survival. Modern science and technology can relieve men of the necessity for specialized, imbecile labor. They may, in principle, provide the basis for a rational social order based on free association and democratic control, if we have the will to create it.

A vision of a future social order is in turn based on a concept of human nature. If, in fact, man is an indefinitely malleable, completely plastic being, with no innate structures of mind and no intrinsic needs of a cultural or social character, then he is a fit subject for the "shaping of behavior" by the State authority, the corporate manager, the technocrat, or the central committee. Those with some confidence in the human species will hope this is not so and will try to determine the intrinsic human characteristics that provide the framework for intellectual development, the growth of moral consciousness, cultural achievement, and participation in a free community. In a partly analogous way, a classical tradition spoke of artistic genius acting within, and in some ways challenging, a framework of rule. Here we touch on matters that are little understood. We must break away, sharply and radically, from much of modern social and behavioral science if we are to move towards a deeper understanding of these matters.

Here too I think that the tradition I have briefly reviewed has a contribution to offer. As I have already observed, those who were concerned with human distinctiveness and potential repeatedly were led to a consideration of the properties of language. I think that the study of language can provide some glimmerings of understanding of rule-governed behavior and the possibilities for free and creative action within the framework of a system of rules that in part, at least, reflect intrinsic properties of human mental organization. It seems to me fair to regard the contemporary study of language as in some ways a return to the Humboldtian concept of the form of language: a system of generative processes rooted in innate properties of mind but permitting, in Humboldt's phrase, an infinite use of finite means. Language cannot be described as a system of organization of behavior. Rather, to understand how language is used, we must discover the abstract Humboldtian form of language—its generative grammar, in modern terms. To learn a language is to construct for oneself this abstract system, of course unconsciously. The linguist and psychologist can proceed to study the use and acquisition of language only insofar as he has some grasp of the properties of the system that has been mastered by the person who knows the language. Furthermore, it seems to me that a good case can be made in support of the empirical claim that such a system can be acquired, under the given conditions of time and access, only by a mind that is endowed with certain specific properties that we can now tentatively describe in some detail. As long as we restrict ourselves, conceptually, to the investigation of behavior, its organization, its development through interaction with the environment, we are bound to miss these characteristics of language and mind. Other aspects of human psychology and culture might, in principle, be studied in a similar way.

Conceivably, we might in this way develop a social science based on empirically well-founded propositions concerning human nature. Just as we study the range of humanly attainable languages, with some success, we might also try to study the forms of artistic expression or, for that matter, scientific knowledge that humans can conceive, and perhaps even the range of ethical systems and social structures in which humans can live and function, given their intrinsic capacities and needs. Perhaps one might go on to project a concept of social organization that would—under given conditions of material and spiritual culture—best encourage and accommodate the fundamental human need—if such it is—for spontaneous initiative, creative work, solidarity, pursuit of social justice.

I do not want to exaggerate, as I no doubt have, the role of investigation of language. Language is the product of human intelligence that is, for the moment, most accessible to study. A rich tradition held language to be a mirror of mind. To some extent, there is surely truth and useful insight in this idea.

I am no less puzzled by the topic "language and freedom" than when I began—and no less intrigued. In these speculative and sketchy remarks there are gaps so vast that one might question what would remain, when metaphor and unsubstantiated guess are removed. It is sobering to realize how little we have progressed in our knowledge of man and society, or even in formulating clearly the problems that might be seriously studied. But there are a few footholds that seem fairly firm. I like to believe that the intensive study of one aspect of human psychology—the study of human language—may contribute to a humanistic social science that will serve, as well, as an instrument for social action. It must, needless to say, be stressed that social action cannot await a firmly established theory of man and society, nor can the validity of the latter be determined by our hopes and moral judgments. The two—speculation and action—must progress, as best they can, looking forward to the day when theoretical inquiry will provide a firm guide to the unending, often grim, but never hopeless struggle for freedom and social justice.

Notes

1. F.W.J. Schelling, *Philosophical Inquiries into the Nature of Human Freedom,* 1809, translated and edited by James Gutmann (Chicago: Open Court, 1936).
2. R.D. Masters, ed., Rousseau, *First and Second Discourses* (New York: St. Martin's Press, 1964), introduction.
3. Compare Proudhon a century later: "No long discussion is necessary to demonstrate that the power of denying a man his thought, his will, his personality, is a power of life and death, and that to make a man a slave is to assassinate him."
4. Cited in M. Bakounine, *Étatisme et anarchie,* edited by Arthur Lehning (Leiden: E.J. Brill, 1967), editor's note 50, from P. Schrecker, "Kant et la révolution française," *Revue philosophique,* Sept.–Dec., 1939, 397–398.
5. I have discussed this matter in *Cartesian Linguistics* (New York: Harper and Row, 1966) and *Language and Mind* (New York: Harcourt Brace, 1968).
6. See the references of note 5, and also my *Aspects of the Theory of Syntax* (Cambridge, Mass.: M.I.T. Press, 1969), Chapter 1, section 8.
7. I need hardly add that this is not the prevailing view. For discussion, see E.H. Lenneberg, *Biological Foundations of Language,* 1967; my *Language and Mind;* E.A. Drewe, G. Ettlinger, A.D. Milner, and R.E. Passingham, "A comparative review of the results of behavioral research on man and monkey," Institute of Psychiatry, London S.E. 5, unpublished draft, 1969; P. Lieberman, "Vocal Tract Limitations on the Vowel Repertoires of Rhesus Monkey and Other Nonhuman Primates," *Science,* Vol. 164, June 6, 1969, 1185–1188, and "Primate Vocalizations and Human Linguistic Ability," *Journal of the Acoustical Society of America,* Vol. 44, note 6, December, 1968, 1574–1584.
8. In the books cited above, and in *Current Issues in Linguistic Theory* (The Hague: Mouton, 1964).
9. Introduction to his edition of W. von Humboldt, *The Limits of State Action* (London: Cambridge University Press, 1969), from which most of the following quotes are taken.
10. Compare the remarks of Kant, quoted above. Kant's essay appeared in 1793. Humboldt's was written in 1791–1792. Parts had already appeared. It did not appear in full during his lifetime. See Burrows, *The Limits of State Action,* for details.
11. Thomas G. Sanders, "The Church in Latin America," *Foreign Affairs,* January, 1970.
12. *Ibid.* The source is said to be the ideas of Paulo Freire. Similar criticism is widespread in the student movement in the West. See, for example, M. Cohen and D. Hale, eds., *The New Student Left* (Boston: Beacon Press, 1967), Chapter 3.
13. Namely, that a man "only attains the most matured and graceful consummation of his activity, when his way of life is harmoniously in keeping with his character"—i.e., when his actions flow from inner impulse.

14. The latter quote is from Humboldt's comments on the French Constitution, 1791–1792, parts translated in M. Cowan, ed., *Humanist Without Portfolio* (Detroit: Wayne State University Press, 1963).

15. Rudolf Rocker, "Anarchism and Anarcho-syndicalism," reprinted in P. Eltzbacher. ed., *Anarchism* (London: Freedom Press). In his book *Nationalism and Culture* (London: Freedom Press, 1937), Rocker describes Humboldt as "the most prominent representative in Germany" of the doctrine of natural rights and of the opposition to the authoritarian State. Rousseau he regards as a precursor of authoritarian doctrine, but he considers only the *Social Contract*, not the far more libertarian *Discourse on Inequality*. Burrows observes that Humboldt's essay anticipates "much nineteenth century political theory of a populist anarchist and syndicalist kind" and notes the hints of the early Marx. See also my *Cartesian Linguistics* for some comments.

16. *The Great Transformation* (Boston: Beacon Press, 1957).

17. Cited by Paul Mattick, "Workers' Control," *The New Left*. P. Long, ed. (Boston: Porter Sargent, 1969).

18. Cited in M. Buber, *Paths in Utopia* (New York: Macmillan, 1950).

19. Yet Rousseau dedicates himself, as a man who has lost his "original simplicity" and can no longer "do without laws and chiefs" to "respect the sacred bonds" of his society and "scrupulously obey the laws, and the men who are their authors and ministers," while scorning "a constitution that can be maintained only with the help of so many respectable people . . . and from which, despite all their care, always arise more real calamities than apparent advantages."

Offing culture: literary study and the movement

FREDERICK CREWS

"To ignore the fact that each thing has a
character of its own and not what we wish
to demand of it is in my opinion the real
capital sin . . ." Ortega y Gasset

Everyone knows that the study of literature, along with the
universities that harbor it, is suffering a protracted crisis of
confidence. It is now common for professors to announce that
they can't understand why they have spent decades in the library
when life is so much more interesting than books, or when the
draft has made a mockery of the academic cloister, or when the
old should be learning from the young. The familiar genteel
claims for literary study as fostering an aristocracy of taste and
sophistication no longer sound plausible after the student revolts
of the later sixties, and no other claims have filled their place.
Yet most professors feel uneasy with the main line of attack that
has been launched against their field. They wonder whether the
charges of "irrelevance," "sellout," and "brainwashing" have
been triggered by misdeeds of theirs or by a general cultural
eruption that happened to intersect their sleepy outpost of
knowledge.

Those of us who have been most appalled and angered by the Vietnam war have tended to shy away from this question and, if anything, to add our own complaints to those of activists. The New Left, which was or seemed to be the most courageous faction of peace, has also been the main source of anti-academic sentiment, and it did succeed in linking the universities to the war machine. For a while the revelations of hypocrisy and complicity were impressive enough to put in abeyance whatever doubts we may have felt about the Movement's own nature and purpose. Even though literary study looked to be one of the fields least worth corrupting for official ends, and even though a turn toward "relevance" never seemed quite the right prescription, we shared the Movement's sense that something was drastically missing.

Now, however, the New Left has lost much of its impetus and credibility. "What was once good propaganda," according to Andrew Kopkind, "became bad rhetoric," and as the Movement failed to adapt to a changing situation it "began visibly to disintegrate."[1] The New Left now looks less like a force for rational analysis than a breakthrough of feeling, a historical mobilization of guilt and penance. If so, then the shortcomings of literary study have to be considered apart from the activist perspective. Yet not entirely apart, for the cultural strain that produced the New Left is also felt by critics and teachers of literature. To grasp the New Left's meaning as a cultural enterprise is also to reopen the question of whether literary study deserves to survive, for the New Left has been, all along, an embodied rejection of the assumptions of academic humanism.

By the Movement or the New Left I refer to the amorphous group of mostly youthful, white, middle-class Americans who developed solidarity around the issues of civil rights (and later Black Power), war protest, and the rights of students, and who exhibit a suspicion of formal ideology, a belief in mass-participatory, confrontational action, a disdain for consumerism and for liberal institutions, and a feeling of brotherhood with foreign and domestic victims of capitalism.[2] Although they regard themselves as revolutionaries, their politics are for the most part a series of improvisations in response to outrages. From the very beginning, even before Tom Hayden's Port Huron Statement of 1962, the Movement has insisted on *feeling* its way toward an appropriate style, and different factions have been at odds with regard to violence or nonviolence, single-issue or global-issue orientation, opposition to the Cold-War university or to rational knowledge in general. As a result, it is hard to discern "the Movement position" on any topic. It may nevertheless be possible to isolate a core of Movement sentiment that has survived all the mergers, defections, and contradictions of a decade's experience, and which manifests itself quite distinctly when cultural and literary matters are debated.

The pivotal question for anyone attempting to characterize the New Left is whether it began as an upwelling of revulsion against unusual episodes of war and racism or as an expression of the anxieties and unmet needs of young people in a time of prosperity. Those who share the Movement's moral passion automatically favor the first view, while conservatives and disillusioned liberals take the latter, often explaining away objective grievances in the process. Now, in the Movement's evident decline, we can perhaps accept the "conservative" case without the politics that accompanied it.

The Movement's campaign against segregation began after the Supreme Court had undertaken the most dramatic gain for Civil rights since Emancipation, and in those days the Vietnam war was of no concern to activists. The possibility that the war "caused" the Movement is belied not only by chronology but by the striking absence of any such response to a similar war in the early fifties. And if we read the Port Huron Statement attentively we cannot fail to see that its emphasis falls on problems of collegiate identity and on distaste with the apathetic bourgeois millions. Here was a dissatisfaction *in search of* issues that would allow a stifled idealism to burst forth. The New Left was given its issues, it tried vainly to fashion a stable identity around them, and it spun apart as activists learned one by one that politics could not contain their clamorous feelings.

Although some of the New Left's most fervent apologists have been middle-aged, its psychology has been unmistakably adolescent, with all that this implies about vague yearnings and resentment, loneliness, egoistic thinking, identification with the victimized, and uncertainty of role. Not a radical's age but his degree of participation in this psychology tells us whether he belongs within the Movement. Many student radicals of the sixties, especially among the orthodox Marxists, were relatively exempt from Movement style. The mere fact of having an articulated political vision set the Marxists apart, and their vision was pointedly antipathetic to the visceral politics practiced on the campuses. Where the Movement trusts instinct, Marxists trust theory, acquaintance with the masses, and tactical experience. Marxism's notion of history fosters patience; the Movement is apocalyptic and opposed on principle to postponement of action. The Movement's appropriation of Marx's terms often blurs these distinctions, but radicals who learned their politics from the classic Marxist texts or from scholars such as Mandel, Deutscher, Mills, Williams, Baran and Sweezy, and Magdoff generally lack the Movement's habit of treating personal and public issues as if they were interchangeable.

The New Left as I construe it has always trafficked primarily in symbolism. This fact is clear to anyone who studies Mitchell Goodman's documentary compendium of the Movement, and it is recognized (and instanced) by Peter Marin in the essay that Goodman takes to be the quintessential Movement utterance. "Their specific grievances," says Marin of the young, "are incidental; their real purpose is to make God show his face, to have whatever pervasive and oppressive force makes us perpetual children reveal itself, declare itself, commit itself at last."[3] Those who have worked alongside the Movement for concrete ends, always hoping in vain that activists would learn to keep their hostility focused on the larger issues, will know what Marin means. When the task is to make God show his face the nearest surrogate will do, and it usually turns out to be some hapless college president or dean.

I vividly recall hearing Noam Chomsky plead with Berkeley leftists, in January 1967, to bear in mind the difference between their situation as privileged students and the plight of the decimated Vietnamese. The students listened politely but they were already tired of the "liberal" peace movement and absorbed in fighting imperialism at home by protesting campus rules. A year and a half later Chomsky was shouted down by the striking students at Columbia, who by then were losing all willingness to attach their impulses to commonly accepted goals. In the Weatherman an ultimate disgust with politics emerged. "What was significant for them as revolutionaries," says the Marxist David Horowitz, "was not the political consequence of the deed, but its *karma*. What was important was the *will* to bomb. Revolution here has almost ceased to be a strategy for social change and has become instead a yoga of perfection."[4]

If the Movement makes little sense as politics, it is at least coherent as therapy. What Marin says of himself holds for the New Left at large: "What I am after is an alternative to separation and rage, some kind of connection to things to replace the system of dependence and submission—the loss of self—that now holds sway, slanted toward violence" ("The Open Truth," p. 10). The complaint is not against the oppression and imperialism that form the Movement's manifest concerns, but against bad feelings, "separation and rage" and an anxiety about one's identity. That anxiety is all too plausible in our automated, overorganized age, with its ethic of greed and its humiliation of individuals, not before tyrants and robber barons, but before random stimuli, impersonal procedures, invisible bureaucracies. The Movement shares Ahab's wish to strike through the mask, to locate the absent father and charge him with having caused the unhappiness that now seems to hang in the air without a reason. It is to this end that the *tangibly* oppressed must be courted and mimicked; to feel oneself a part of their cause, to trade one's anxiety for their just anger, is to come into the presence of reality at last. And once one has succeeded in feeling despised rather than simply ignored, one can begin to conceive of a glorious and apocalyptic change of fortune.

Only if we recognize the New Left as a religious venture, "a psychic revolution" as Susan Sontag has called it, can we explain its enthusiasm for thinkers who are, in Sontag's phrase, "not very political"; she lists them as Herbert Marcuse, Norman O. Brown, Norman Mailer, R.D. Laing, Wilhelm Reich, and, on a lesser level of influence, "such openly apolitical, or even reactionary, types as Alan Watts, Leary and McLuhan."[5] These figures share a millenarian style and an absence of definite revolutionary content. The Movement seems scarcely bothered by Reich's veering into McCarthyism or by Brown's explicit anti-Marxism; what counts is the air of drawing up an omnibus indictment of authority.[6] If Marcuse remains the Movement's godfather it is because he has taken the most pains to becloud his misgivings about the juvenile left, yet even thinkers who ignore the Movement altogether can win its sympathy merely by adopting an antinomian and utopian manner. The Movement's taste is for intellectually careless ideologues who diagnose society's neurosis in such drastic terms that no political cure is really imaginable, and word-magic becomes the only recourse. What is required above all is an appearance of proof that the repression of instinct coincides with the repressiveness of capitalist institutions, for then the activist can feel that he is making revolution in the very process of shedding his bourgeois traits.

Radicals sometimes decry this weakness for intellectual sleight-of-hand, yet the Movement as a whole cannot overcome it. To grasp the limitations of the revolutionary quietists is to be thrown back upon traditional structures of knowledge, methodological scruples, and argumentative restraint; but these are exactly what Romantic activists are trying to avoid. "At every step," says Goodman, "we are asked to explain ourselves 'rationally.' That is, we are asked to think in a language—a vocabulary—of rationality that denies feeling—a language eroded and deformed by misuse, and which was formulated by a non-culture that has never undergone our experience" (*The Movement*, p. ix). Rationality is the language of the fathers, the enemies of instinct; in Theodore Roszak's words, "there *must* be an appeal from this reductive rationality which objective consciousness dictates."[7]

Anti-intellectualism, then, is not one of the activists' handicaps but one of their fundamental aims. The Movement strikes Goodman as nothing less than "a force, coming up out of the unconscious, from the gods" (*The Movement*, p. viii), and this force is pitted against an oppressive majority consciousness embracing science, technology, tradition, even logic. According to Roszak the counter culture's project is "to proclaim a new heaven and a new earth so vast, so marvelous that the inordinate claims of technical expertise must of necessity withdraw in the presence of such splendor to a subordinate and marginal status in the lives of men" (*Counter Culture*, p. 240). The mere fact that students find no satisfaction in school suggests to Roszak that the revolution is already at hand, and Susan Sontag too cites "the revolutionary implications of dropping out—of taking drugs (thereby reducing efficiency, clarity, productivity), of disrupting the school system (which furnishes the economy with docile, trained personnel), of concentrating on unproductive hedonistic activities like sex and listening to music" ("Some Thoughts," p. 16). Here is a virtual equation between sabotaging one's intellect and making history. It would be hard to imagine a more patent departure from the coldly rational revolutionism of Marx, Lenin, and Fanon.[8]

It was Marcuse, with his vulgar-Hegelian notion of historical transformation, who most encouraged the Movement to overrate its countercultural style.[9] Defining the existing system only in terms of its puritanical ideals, he could consider every instance of deviance as at once a negation of the negation, a return of the repressed, and a concrete argument against his *bête noire,* scientific positivism. At various points in the sixties Marcuse dallied with the hope that long hair, rock lyrics, homosexuality, even psychosis were signs of capitalism's imminent demise. By combining pedantry, sophistry, and avuncular charm he succeeded in making the rebellious late adolescence of the well-to-do look like a world-historical program instead of a phase. Revolutionism in his hands became a bizarre mixture of ambiguously worded militancy and Romantic hedonism. (The park benches in Hanoi, he gaily observed, are just wide enough to accommodate two lovers.) Reading Marcuse, a young leftist could allow himself to forget the antithesis between the Marxist example of hard work, respect for science and technology, and ideological orthodoxy and the Movement's own blend of libidinal anarchism and "existential" self-absorption.

The New Left's divergence from Marxism is nowhere more apparent than in its thinking about culture. A Marxist such as Lukács or Trotsky regards culture as a product of arduous development, and he sees the revolution's long-run problem as being how to surpass capitalist culture while correcting the injustice that underlies it. One of the classic issues in Marxist social theory is whether the proletariat, having been vaulted to power without any cultural preparation, can achieve a high level of culture before its historical task is finished. No one, however, doubts that the transfer of power and the making of culture are two distinct stages. "We must, first of all," wrote Trotsky, "take possession, politically, of the most important elements of the old culture, to such an extent, at least, as to be able to pave the way for a new culture."[10] The fully human culture predicted by Marx will come into existence when equality, material abundance, and universal education have provided the necessary base.

New Leftists sometimes refer honorifically to such a future, but they are far more interested in undoing their complicity in the existing capitalist culture. The Oedipal politics that enables an activist to feel sorry for himself in the projected form of a ghetto dweller or a Vietnamese peasant also tells him that culture is a burdensome legacy of the ancestors, a junkpile standing between him and his liberation. Sometimes he expresses this view directly, attacking the threat to spontaneity posed by high culture and its spokesmen, who are felt to be snuffing out youthful rebelliousness by enforcing their doctrines of aesthetic distance, objective contemplation, and a classless, Arnoldian pantheon of master-pieces. More often, the activist tells himself that culture is prevent-ing someone else's liberation—the ghetto dweller's and the peasant's. "Even when the humanities and the high culture to which they are devoted are most radical in content," says one New Leftist, "they are essentially a leisure-class luxury and an

41

enticement away from the necessity for radical political action."[11] There is so much penance to be done for "our ineradicable bourgeois upbringing"; we had best "absent ourselves from cultural felicity awhile" and try to become more like "Huey Newton or Regis Debray" ("Down with Culture", p. 32). Or perhaps like Savonarola.

There is, however, a rival notion of culture that catches the activists' enthusiasm. "We appear to have forgotten in our schools," says Peter Marin, "what every primitive tribe with its functional psychology knows: allegiance to the tribe can be forged only at the deepest levels of the psyche and in extreme circumstance demanding endurance, daring, and awe; that the participant must be given *direct* access to the sources of cultural continuity—by and in himself; and that only a place in a coherent community can be exchanged for a man's allegiance" ("The Open Truth," p. 4). By seeking out "extreme circumstance" and courting danger among a few like-minded friends, the activist can form a magnetic field of meaning around his deeds. Instead of abasing himself before objects and ideas he will be caught up in the energies of his own psyche and feel himself part of "a live organism" (*The Movement*, p. viii). The Movement itself will be his culture.

This immersion in the Movement should not be confused with another project that some radicals find appealing, the rediscovery of folk subcultures that capitalism has bypassed or nearly eradicated. From the New Left standpoint this is just another form of antiquarianism. As Louis Kampf explains,

the rediscovery of a natural culture cannot provide a cure for the individual's [i.e., the New Leftist's] sense of separation from society. However, given the movement's stress on community, intellectuals may be able to plant their roots in the movement itself. This implies that the movement must become a culture—that is, a way of life. The very forces which have brought about the alienation of intellectuals and the young have propelled us toward that historical moment appropriate for creating a radical culture.[12]

There is thus no need to look anywhere for a culture, provided you belong to the Movement; you yourself will "renovate ways of thinking, feeling, looking and, ultimately, acting"

("Notes," p. 423) in the historical moment that is just arriving, and others can presumably follow along.

As a cultural enterprise, then, the New Left exists not in order to effect political changes, and assuredly not to prepare a base for cultural progress as the Marxists conceive it, but for the sake of its own vitality and emotion. Activists must of course persuade themselves that they are "sharpening contradictions" and "polarizing the masses," but meanwhile they compose what Kampf frankly calls an "elect" with a "secret language" ("Notes," p. 420) that sustains them. Those who know what the Movement is, says Kampf, "are already a part of this culture: they know its private—and rapidly shifting—language; they understand its physical mannerisms; they are wise to its tensions, loves, divisions, and hatreds" ("Notes," p. 420). Feeling oneself to be a member, recognizing one's brothers and sisters by their most up-to-date affectations, appears to have largely replaced political success as a focus of satisfaction.

"The radical Movement of the '60's," as Andrew Kopkind has perceived, "developed a kind of Ptolemaic theory of the political universe: everything is in orbit around *my* movement, around *my* politics, around *my* collective" ("The Greening," p. 52). The Movement renders cultural issues invisible by admitting them only as future tasks for its members to work out within their lives. In place of dead objects we will have live actions, and those actions can symbolically expiate "the crimes, the human suffering" ("Notes," p. 424) that have buttressed the specious official culture. "Not a performance should go by without disruption," says Kampf of Lincoln Center. "The fountains should be dried with calcium chloride, the statuary pissed on, the walls smeared with shit" ("Notes," p. 426). Lincoln Center will still be surrounded by a ghetto but Movement activists will be doing their thing, and *that* is genuine culture.

If New Left fraternalism is an end in itself, we can appreciate why activists find much to engage them in their home base, the university. Just about every aspect of the academic environment impresses them as an attempt to rob them of brotherhood, and chief among such devices are the repressive ideals of disinterestedness and rational debate. The ideals themselves—not merely the Cold-War perversion of them—are felt to threaten the Movement by proposing a rival basis of association and belief. An instrumental organization like ROTC can be met on its own ground, for the Movement shares its conception of the university's purpose; but what can be done about "self-selected authorities" (*Counter Culture*, p. 263) who claim that scientific logic stands above all organizations? The community of scholars, even radical scholars, reeks of paternal authoritarianism and must be replaced by a community of activists who already know the necessary truths about genocide and resistance, liberal fascism and freedom, the pigs and the people.[13]

There are obvious limits to the candor an activist can exercise in writing, or even thinking, about the egoistic basis of his culture. To realize that he has joined a vanguard without any possibility of a following would abruptly end his revolutionary dream. Simply to be a pisser of statues is not enough. The most admired Movement documents are therefore those that exhort activists to take their message to the people, who have been numbed and harangued by the ruling class's media and do not yet understand that student leftists are their friends. Even the despised bourgeoisie, say these documents, is suffering amid its surfeit of gadgets and will benefit from learning about consumerism, surplus repression, and repressive desublimation. The better Movement essays have a Grecian-urn quality: the activists and the masses are always just about to embrace.

Hence the appeal of the most famous New Left cultural manifesto, John McDermott's "The Laying On of Culture."[14] Universities, says McDermott, are prime reinforcers of the "hierarchic tendencies implicit in the social and economic system" (p. 299), and one of their chief instruments is the idea of culture—specifically, the belief that culture "includes the Western Heritage, the Western Tradition, the Literary Tradition, the traditions of reason and civility, etc., and that these are most fully embodied in the profession of academe and the written treasures of which academe is priestly custodian and inspired interpreter" (p. 300). Before this sentence is halfway finished we have realized that "culture" is an unspeakable affront to the people. But McDermott is politic. He is not, he says, attacking Western culture and scholarship, but only their implications for working-class students who are being systematically humiliated by their teachers in community colleges. These students are essentially colonials, destined to fill deadening jobs near the base of the technocracy, and their introduction to cultural masterpieces is really intended to strip them of local and class pride. To avoid this fate they will require "critical universities, liberation courses, seminars in local and working-class history" (p. 301), and similar measures which, as McDermott implies, can be stimulated by the Movement teachers who are fanning across the country from their graduate schools.

The beauty of this argument is its semblance of egalitarianism. McDermott has found a real phenomenon that bears scrutiny, the use of community colleges as implements of social channeling, and he seems eager to help a neglected group of citizens become whatever they please. Oddly, however, his harshest comments are directed not against policies but against diffuse "hierarchic tendencies" that are chiefly instanced in the teaching of literature. Like all New Left anti-authoritarianism, McDermott's is at once global and parochial, challenging all oppression everywhere (in the capitalist world) while coming down hardest on the relatively insignificant abuses that are closest to home. What he has brought to the academic hinterlands is simply his concern to put down the English professors back at the university.

I doubt whether much animus against hierarchy as such is harbored by the upwardly mobile working people who have made their way into the community colleges; this passion is restricted to disaffected intellectuals in search of proletarian moorings. A leftist who pondered such a difference of outlook and admitted the class basis of his own unfocused rage would immediately graduate from the Movement, but McDermott's course is rather to consider how the children of workers can be brought around to his sophomoric ideas about liberation. These students are, for the duration of his essay, not real people but agents of a shadowy campaign against power. The abstract severity of the analysis forecloses any possibility that some of them might *want* to expose themselves to non-local culture or to occupy a different social class. They are domestic "natives" one and all, and if they are reluctant to resent this status it must be because they have not yet found their Che Guevaras, namely McDermott and the other radicals he is addressing. McDermott encourages the knowledgeable activist to become a missionary, bringing Samuel Gompers and John L. Lewis to the unwashed while casting out the heathen idol Shakespeare. Who, then, is laying what on whom?

When the New Left trains its attention directly on literature and literary study, the result is a combination of Lawrentian and moralistic demands. What we require from art, according to Theodore Roszak, is "the white-hot experience of authentic vision that might transform our lives and, in so doing, set us at warlike odds with the dominant culture" (*Counter Culture,* p. 257).[15] The implication is that without such a boost from the arts we will be left immobile. The point, as always with the New Left, is to sustain the Movement's own spirit—"a spirit," Mitchell Goodman explains, "that inter-plays in many bodies, that come together as they move and touch, and give one another warmth, hope" (*The Movement,* p. vii). Hence the importance of keeping clear of the literary professors, whose specialty is draining away the vital juices from everything they touch, and hence too the necessity of avoiding those works that are sedative to begin with. The more politically minded wing of the Movement puts the matter in ideological terms borrowed from conventional revolutionism: we need books that were written from a liberated perspective, books that side unambiguously with the oppressed.

Unfortunately, not many works can be found to pass this test. Some of the promising candidates are tainted by their membership in that abomination, the Western Heritage, and they generally smack of "ruler morality."[16] "Whom did the values represented by Homer's Achilles serve?" asks Louis Kampf. "Are we to take the reactionary and mercenary objectives of Balzac [Marx's favorite novelist: F. C.] as merely an adjunct to his artistry? We take the concept of tragedy to represent the West's most profound understanding of man's place in the world. Yet is its counter-revolutionary acceptance of fate something we are supposed to teach as a received value?"[17]

It would be pointless to reply that these questions confound literature with propaganda and teaching with indoctrination, for Kampf wants to be disburdened of all such nice distinctions. The ego functions that might enable him to grasp that a work of art is only a hypothetical world, and a potential occasion for exercising the mind rather than brutalizing it, have been exposed and denounced as part of the capitalist apparatus of thought control. Literature is now regarded as a set of land mines, nearly all of which have been laid in the Movement's path by the ruling class, which is considered to have preserved its reactionary continuity from Homer's day to the present. In his search for acceptable texts Kampf is finally reduced to proposing Chairman Mao's poems about the Long March and even his "political formulas," which "may be simple, naïve, unsubtle, devoid of tragic doubt— but they happen to be true" ("The Trouble," p. 32).

There are, naturally, various possible attitudes for a radical to take toward literature. Marxists have their own, rather jesuiti-cal, excuse for reading the classics as part of their prehistory. Some radicals take an interest in the efforts of Artaud, Brecht, and the Surrealists to help smash the bourgeoisie by alarming its sensibility. Others, including Marcuse, justify eclecticism by pleading that the classics are more rebellious than you might suppose.[18] And some leftists, concurring with Marx himself in this regard, actually think that literature is one thing and revolution another. But none of these attitudes, least of all Marx's, captures the New Left program of *replacing* literary culture with activism. Louis Kampf (currently President of the Modern Language Association) thus spoke for much of the Movement when he proclaimed that "the *study* of literature—the voyeurism implicit in this—must really come to an end if all of us are to be full participants in the making of our culture" ("The Trouble," p. 34). The New Left view of literary criticism, though it follows logically from Kampf's position, may seem incomprehensible unless we bear in mind the Movement's belief that everything is either part of the solution or part of the problem. That is, propositions about literature are really attempts to subvert or enhance social change. The modern shibboleths of irony, complexity, and ambiguity are thus exposed as devices for downgrading revolutionary authors and for inculcating resignation. The matter is settled as soon as the conservative and agrarian leanings of some of the founders of New Criticism have been cited, for a critic's class affiliation is considered the most reliable clue to the meaning of his remarks about poetry. New Criticism, says Bruce Franklin, triumphed along with McCarthyism and represented an attempt to "sweep the field of literary study of any relevance to contemporary life."[19] Viewed in the light of Vietnam—and the New Left views everything in this light—the New-Critical attempt to reconcile tensions amounts to "murder" (DiSalvo, "This Murder" p. 11). And the same judgment applies to all other schools of commentary that dwell on form and value instead of on the relevant social issues.[20] Criticism is worse than superfluous anyway, for we already know that real (collective) creativity aims not at producing beautiful artifacts but at liberating people from the bourgeois mentality; and the latter is typified precisely in the fussiness of "critical insights."

The aesthetic and political implications of this attitude come across vividly in an essay on Cuban literature by Roberta Salper, who was recently elected to the Executive Council of the MLA.[21] Her argument is framed with sayings of Marcuse's from *An Essay on Liberation* and "Repressive Tolerance," and she adopts Marcuse's view that freedom of imagination in our time is threatened, not by anything so crude as censorship, but by rationality in the service of profit, by consumerism, by the near-impossibility of mounting an effective political protest, and by tolerance itself. Tolerance, she has learned from Marcuse, is the principle under which "a magazine prints both a negative and positive report on the FBI" (p. 29) and thereby disguises its oneness with that very organization. "In aesthetic terms," she explains, "this ethic of objectivity or 'benevolent neutrality' has meant an ability to absorb and neutralize even the most radical of formal experiments. Socialist Realism is an overreaction to this liberal tolerance and credo of 'impartiality'" (p. 29).

Socialist Realism, which became the Union of Soviet Writers' fearsome theme in 1932, happened in fact to be a bureaucratic "overreaction" to the last vestiges of artistic freedom in Russia. It is strange to find this doctrine, under which thousands of writers and artists were exiled and murdered, interpreted as a wholesome though possibly imprudent reply to Western eclecticism.[22] What the author means, however, is that she herself is prepared to overreact to the maddening blandness of American policy toward dissent. True aesthetic freedom as expounded by Marcuse, she says, is simply the freedom to imagine a society entirely different from our own—but how can we realize such freedom when our government refuses to manifest its essential bias? ". . . A free society in Marcuse's terms," explains Salper, "demands a sensitivity free from the repressive satisfactions of the unfree societies . . ." (p. 17). Still following Marcuse, she concludes that left-propagandistic art is really the freest sort because it helps us to picture a better social order.

With her definitions thus squared away, Salper can give an unclouded survey of the Cuban literary scene. She finds it heartening that Cuban writers are sometimes forced to work in the factories and fields "so they will learn what needs to be communicated and to whom" (p. 30n.); she marvels at Fidel's magnanimity in proposing not to suppress any books that are loyal to the revolution (no others can be published); she sympathetically explains the Culture Council's objections to Heberto Padilla's scandalous "concern with 'individualism' and 'liberty' in a pre-revolutionary sense" (p. 24); and she hails Cuban censorship for its hearty openness, so unlike the "more or less hidden censorship" (p. 30) which, in our own country, takes the insidious form of protecting dissident statements without offering them prime media time. "Censorship in Cuba still serves to protect and preserve society," she concedes, "but it is not a repressive society, vitiating life instincts and isolating human beings from one another, from their political existence" (p. 30). Unlike Castro himself, who until recently was apologetic about the need for any anti-libertarian measures, the author is thus disposed to favor them on principle as constituting part of a thoroughgoing antithesis to her surroundings. No one actually living under a dictatorship could imagine that official control over the arts is a boon to the life instincts. This soap bubble can only be lofted in a climate of bourgeois individualism, when radicals have begun to confound freedom with the overcoming of loneliness.

A casual reader of Salper's essay might miss her Romantic emphasis on the buried self and conclude that she is an outright Stalinist; careless or disingenuous analysts have made just that misjudgment of the New Left as a whole. The point of worshiping Cuba's fraternal politicization of literature is simply to arm one's mind against the suffocating pluralism under which one continues to live at home. The literary leftist's conduct in his university sufficiently reveals that, far from being a Stalinist, he is obsessed with the contaminating effect of all power, including his own as a teacher.

There are, to be sure, scattered bits of contrary evidence. Our students, says Louis Kampf, "*will have to* oppose the system of acculturation and spiritual servitude which our colleges encourage."[23] As for his colleagues, Kampf in an early essay envisioned a lockstep faculty of leftists who would implement the Movement line: "Departments of literature will have to look on themselves as . . . part of a front dedicated to the human ends of poetry. . . . Their critical function will be to expose the enemies of literature with the light of reason and to destroy them with the passion of moral concern."[24] This, however, was only a passing Zhdanovite dream, out of keeping not only with the New Left's political weakness but also with its anarchism. The Movement professor more typically uses his limited academic authority to undermine the university's legitimacy in minor ways (giving all students the

50

same grade, cancelling classes to honor leftist festivals, substituting Movement topics for the announced subject-matter, joining sit-ins against the president, etc.), always in the expectation that "repression" will ensue and that everyone standing between him and his persecutors will have to choose sides. The activist embarks on these struggles half-knowing that he is going to lose. Whatever else this is, it isn't Stalinism.

Only while standing at the students' side, it would seem, can the activist professor feel untroubled by his own authority. The teacher-student relationship in its ordinary form floods him with guilt. Kampf reports that he, like his students, can only tolerate his own teaching when a creative disruption occurs—as, for example, when a two-hour debate about why one student was sitting on the floor without any clothes on provided "the only lively discussion we had all semester," or when, in a dreary seminar on Proust, the students "decided" participatorily to reconvene at the M.I.T. Student Center which had been unilaterally "declared" a sanctuary for a military deserter, and suddenly "Proust's sensibility became politicized for us" ("The Trouble," pp. 33, 34). (It is a shame that Proust, with his supreme taste for incongruities, could not have lived to see his languors so improved.) In both cases tedium was conquered by a nullifying of the teacher-student hierarchy and the formation of a community of people who were all, for a brief period, upset about the same thing. Literature is useful to such a a community only insofar as it bolsters morale, and perhaps the worst thing for that morale would be overscrupulous regard for what an author actually wrote.

There remains the problem of what to do with literature between demonstrations. The New Left can't dwell on the superiority of one work to another, for, says Kampf, all such judgments derive from competition and commerce. The very circulation of literature, to say nothing of its publication, strikes him as a step toward commodity fetishism ("The Trouble," p. 34). Even the seemingly innocent fact that novels have usually been "written by one individual working in isolation for the consumption of another individual, likewise reading in the isolation of his or her room" ("The Trouble," p. 30), violates the necessary group spirit. The depressing thing about verbal art is that it wallows unashamedly in fantasy, turning the imagination inward "rather than outward, toward worldly activity" ("The Trouble," p. 34). The more he thinks about it, the more the activist professor feels like a preacher who finds himself married to a whore—and obliged to drum up business for her among the congregation. No wonder Kampf is prompted to suspect that resistance to the dominant culture is "madness." Yet "the only real choice may be whether to be mad (though civilized) on society's terms, or on one's own" ("The Humanities," p. 312).

Professors who have found themselves briefly outflanked by New Leftists in their departments or in the MLA have feared a takeover of the discipline, and in the ensuing hysteria even mild criticism of "English" for its political provincialism has been greeted as advocating a Bolshevik reign.[25] What is truly worrisome is not this implausible specter but the fact that academic people continue to be dumbstruck by absurd arguments. The New Left, along with the rest of the burgeoning counter culture, has shown itself incapable of tolerating the moral indeterminacy of art and the intellectual dizziness of knowing that one doesn't know. Perhaps a decade back, when a good number of people still assumed that the criticism and teaching of literature were worthwhile activities, the irrationalist faction would simply have had to take one path and the English departments another. No one is quite so sure now; "English" has lost its nerve.

The reasons for this development are only partly known, and they probably extend to such varied and uncontrollable phenomena as the ascendancy of visual media, the enervated frivolity of much contemporary literature, the rise of the "service station" multiversity, the loss of human scale as a result of technology, and the disorientation of aesthetic and moral impulses in an age of routine terror and cosmic banality, of televised war from Asia and televised golf from the moon. Then, too, there is the counter culture itself, which has taught even some of the professors to hang loose and let it be—or at least to annotate the Beatles instead of their former texts. Their success in keeping pace with fashion has drawn them farther from their old sense of working on problems whose interest lay in their very subtlety and exactingness. To some extent the profession already shares the New Left's embarrassment in the presence of merely aesthetic issues.

No one, then, is to blame for the apparent decline of literary study. The right question to ask is whether we ought to care. The standard academic reply to utilitarian detractors, that objective knowledge is a sufficient end in itself, doesn't carry much conviction in this instance. No one really thinks that new outpourings of fact and opinion about the dog-eared classics will be valuable simply because they are knowledge, and there is nothing precious about a person's ability to be unprejudiced about works that have long since ceased to interest him. Nor, of course, are most professors so politically neutral as they think. Lacking awareness of their politics as readers, they cannot refute the New Left's wild assertion that literary study is all politics anyway—first yours and now ours.

There is probably no way to make a convincing defense of any of the humanities except by showing, through committed practice, that the discipline is still meaningful to oneself. The question of whether the results of this practice are needed can only be parried: what we emphatically don't need is a society in which somebody's politicized idea of need determines whether a given activity is allowed to continue. Having made that minimal stand, we could add that the humanities are precisely those disciplines that search for value. The effective disappearance of literary study would imply that the society no longer sought value from literature; people would have decided that all the relevant norms were fully known or not worth knowing in view of our helplessness before events. Such a society could no longer be called free.

Literary study, then, may not yield especially useful findings, but at its best it fosters an important kind of engagement, a disposition to risk being changed by lending oneself to a problematic experience. This quality is what Sartre means by "generosity":

Reading is an exercise in generosity, and what the writer requires of the reader is not the application of an abstract freedom but the gift of his whole person, with his passions, his prepossessions, his sympathies, his sexual temperament, and his scale of values. . . . But he does not stop there; he also requires that [readers] recognize his creative freedom, and that they in turn solicit it by a symmetrical and inverse appeal.[26]

Where such generosity is lacking we find either pedantry or its left-wing counterpart, relevance. That is, we find one way or another of ensuring that nothing will be learned but inessential reinforcements of what one already knows, or thinks he knows.

If English studies remain more than superficially alive, it is because people still feel a challenge to test their evolving sensibilities, including their sense of politics, against works that can answer—not simply confirm—whatever expectations are brought to them. Literary study at its best sharpens our awareness of the boundaries between literature and our predispositions, enabling us to have a colloquy with sources of meaning that will never be fully assimilated. Both the pedant and the activist abolish one of the parties to this colloquy. The irony in the activist's case is that his hope in removing boundaries is to feel less severed from meaning, less alone. What he finds instead is that his remedy for separation and rage is worse than the disease: he has turned the world into an echo chamber resounding with slogans. Then his complaints about oppression, though still misplaced, are finally commensurate with the gravity of his plight, for a man who can no longer respond to the freedom of others has lost his own freedom as well.

Notes

1. Andrew Kopkind, "The Greening of America: Beyond the Valley of the Heads," *Ramparts,* March 1971, p. 52.

2. I am excluding some elements often considered to be part of the New Left, chiefly the ethnic minorities and women who have sought power on their own behalf. The Movement as I construe it has shared tactics with these groups but has differed from them in its psychology and goals.

3. Peter Marin, "The Open Truth and Fiery Vehemence of Youth: A Sort of Soliloquy," in Mitchell Goodman, ed., *The Movement Toward a New America: The Beginnings of a Long Revolution* (Philadelphia and New York, 1970), p. 9.

4. Susan Sontag, "Revolutionary Karma vs. Revolutionary Politics," *Ramparts,* March 1971, p. 29.

5. "Some Thoughts on the Right Way (for us) to Love the Cuban Revolution," *Ramparts,* April 1969, p. 10.

6. Both Marcuse and Reich are praised for their very extravagance in Paul A. Robinson, *The Freudian Left: Wilhelm Reich, Geza Roheim, Herbert Marcuse* (New York, Evanston, and London, 1969). "All three thinkers," says Robinson appreciatively, "are eminently injudicious; they harbor only contempt for the pluralistic tolerance of the liberal imagination" (p. 6). Whether any of them made plausible statements about the world is of only fleeting concern to Robinson. For an illuminating discussion of Laing's politics see David Martin, "R. D. Laing: Psychiatry and Apocalypse," *Dissent,* June 1971, 235–251.

7. *The Making of a Counter Culture: Reflections on the Technocratic Society and Its Youthful Opposition* (Garden City, N.Y., 1969), p. 240. Roszak's appeal is made not only to Marcuse, Brown, and Watts, but to "oracles, dervishes, yogis, sibyls, prophets, druids, etc.–the whole heritage of mystagoguery toward which the beat-hip wing of our counter culture now gravitates" (p. 247).

8. Sontag, to her credit, draws attention to the differences between the Cuban revolutionary outlook and the counter culture's. Her essay tactfully advises young leftists to avoid superimposing one situation on the other—which is exactly what they do.

9. Marcuse's mechanistic application of Hegel's Absolutism to history is discussed by Alasdair MacIntyre, *Herbert Marcuse: An Exposition and a Polemic* (New York, 1970), pp. 21–41.

10. *Literature and Revolution,* Rose Strunsky, tr. (Ann Arbor, 1960), p. 191.

11. Donald Lazere, "Down With Culture?" *Village Voice,* September 11, 1969, p. 28.

12. Louis Kampf, "Notes Toward a Radical Culture," *The New Left: A Collection of Essays,* Priscilla Long, ed., (Boston, 1969), p. 422.

13. An instructive example of the Movement's attitude toward radical scholarship is a review in *Ramparts* of Alvin W. Gouldner's *The Coming Crisis of Western Sociology,* a book which, in reducing all Establishment sociology to Talcott Parsons, ought to have satiated anyone's taste for anti-pluralism. The reviewer praised Gouldner's book for demolishing sociology but added resentfully that it was, after all, only a presentation of ideas and not the fruit of revolutionary praxis in the streets. At a certain point Movement *machismo* had to be invoked and turned against the left-wing academic who seemed to take sociology too seriously as an autonomous discipline. Debate was thus shifted from the arena of rival ideas to that of rival postures, with the young reviewer and his brothers emerging as the true militants.

14. John McDermott, *The Nation,* March 10, 1969, pp. 296–301.

15. Cf. Jackie Di Salvo, "This Murder: New Criticism and Scholarship," *NUC-MLC Newsletter,* I, no. 3 (n.d.), 11: "The poet, according to William Blake, is imprisoned like the rest of us but he serves us by singing about that cage. Having heard his song we must turn our energies to the bastille itself."

16. Katherine Ellis, "The Function of Northrop Frye at the Present Time," *College English,* XXXI (March 1970), p. 544.

17. Louis Kampf, "The Trouble with Literature . . . ," *Change,* May–June 1970, p. 30.

18. In a lecture, "The Arts," delivered at the New School in October 1970, Marcuse extended his equation of deviance and revolution to the literary realm. It is true, he said, that the bourgeois classics superficially encourage a resigned affirmation, but they are negative at the core. As an example he mentioned the theme of the noble prostitute in Balzac. Nothing could better epitomize bourgeois sentimentalism than that theme, but by Marcuse's neo-Hegelian scorekeeping it constituted an item of negation and hence a point for the

revolution. The unstated, but unmistakable, purpose of his lecture was to dissociate himself from the New Left's windmill-tilting campaign against literature—without, however, challenging the New Left's habit of doing a security check on all authors dead and alive. Marcuse simply proposed that the standards be relaxed to allow an imprimatur for his favorite texts.

19. Bruce Franklin, "The Teaching of Literature in the Highest Academies of the Empire," *College English,* XXXI (March 1970), p. 556. Franklin adds that the professors' strategy—to assign tepidly quietistic works and reinforce their oppressive influence by diverting conscious attention to their formal properties—failed to pacify the politically awakened students:

So it was necessary to find less subtle vehicles of counter-revolutionary ideology. Alexander Pope and the metaphysical poets, Nathaniel Hawthorne and the Romantics, could hardly lure many students away from the contradictions of their own society or lead them into a reactionary view of them. Stronger medicine was needed, outright reactionary tracts written by contemporaries, works like *Lord of the Flies* **and** *Animal Farm,* **which come right out and say in terms that everyone can understand: Man is nothing but a pig.** (p. 556)

20. See also Barbara Bailey Kessel, "Free, Classless, and Urbane?", *College English,* XXXI (March 1970), 531–540.

21. Roberta Salper, "Literature and Revolution in Cuba," *Monthly Review,* XXII (October 1970), 15–30.

22. Before telling us more about Socialist Realism Professor Salper might want to look at Edward J. Brown, *The Proletarian Episode in Russian Literature 1928–1932* (New York, 1953); Herman Ermolaev, *Soviet Literary Theories 1917–1934: The Genesis of Socialist Realism* (Berkeley and Los Angeles, 1963); and for the human interest angle, Nadezhda Mandelstam, *Hope Against Hope: A Memoir* (New York, 1970).

23. Louis Kampf, "The Humanities and Inhumanities," *The Nation,* September 30, 1968; the quotation, lacking italics, is on p. 312.

24. Louis Kampf, "The Scandal of Literary Scholarship," *Harper's,* CCXXXV (December 1967), 89.

25. My own essay, "Do Literary Studies Have an Ideology?", *PMLA,* LXXXV (May 1970), 423–428, met with such a reception; see the letters in the January 1971 *PMLA.*

26. Jean-Paul Sartre, *What is Literature?,* Bernard Frechtman, tr. (New York, 1965), p. 45.

Tom Eliot meets the hulk at Little Big Horn: the political economy of poetry

MARGE PIERCY
and DICK LOURIE

We as poets† have become workers in a specialized discipline which commands the attention only of other specialists. It has been so in this country for at least fifty years, maybe longer. We are not going to say, on the one hand, that "the poets are at fault, they're deliberately elitist" or, on the other, that "this is a natural condition for art, high art—it is by definition available only to a small cultural minority in any society." We are going to say that the ultimate reasons for this specialization are political and economic, and that the technological/sociological/intellectual reasons are largely political and economic functions. And we're going to say that just as drastic, radical, revolutionary change is needed in the political and economic structure of this country—and that struggle has begun— so also drastic, radical, and revolutionary change is needed in our

† We are aware some of the poets we quote would disagree with our ideas. We have used quotations to illustrate points and have tried not to wrench them out of context. We do *not* write as objective observers, but as participants. We both worked on the whole but have signed the parts we each wrote.

habits, attitudes, and practices in poetry. This struggle too has already begun, and is related to the other.

Regis Debray has written:

Militant also is he who in his own intellectual work ideologically combats the class enemy, he who, in his work as an artist, roots out the privilege of beauty from the ruling class. (From a letter to Enrique de la Osa, published in *Bohemia*, July 22, 1966, quoted in *Ikon* # 6, Nov.-Dec., 1968)

DICK LOURIE:

I have participated in programs, financed by the federal government through the New York City Board of Education, where poets are sent to public (usually ghetto) high schools to read their poems and talk with the students. Which is OK, except that you do have to be cool, or get fired for controversy; and except that the whole thing is laying poetry on someone who didn't ask for it.

But I know of other, more hopeful things: in a high school in the Bronx (mostly black and Puerto Rican) there is a poetry club. The members are invited to classes in the school to read their own poetry. If they are asked in advance "what kind of thing they'll be reading," they answer, "Don't worry, we'll be there." And so they don't get themselves in a bag where everything has to be cooled and non-controversial. They only go where they are asked, which is a lot of classrooms—because their constituency is interested. Another example of what I mean: a group called the Last Poets recently was on the bill at Harlem's Apollo, with all the music groups, reading their poems.

I asked a member of the high school poets' club why so many students are turning on to poetry. He said they used to think of poetry (when it was a school subject) as trees, flowers, birds, but now they're seeing that it can also be about their own lives, really relate to where they are. We are learning from our own Third World, the oppressed colonialized groups living, in Eldridge Cleaver's phrase, within the mother country. We're learning from the Third World peoples outside the U.S. And we're learning too from the tribal, so-called "primitive" cultures that poetry can be a functioning part of the society, doesn't *have* to be Specialized Culture.

We have been learning it by ourselves as well; that is part of the change we're undergoing, already begun. In his Commentaries on the "primitive" poems he has collected in his anthology, *Technicians of the Sacred,* Jerome Rothenberg notes some "intersections and analogies" between primitive and modern poetry. He parallels "Lorca's duende" and "beat poetry" with

the poet as shaman, or primitive shaman as poet and seer . . . an open "visionary" situation prior to all system-making (priesthood) . . .

and "surrealism," "deep image," "composition by field," with

a highly-developed process of image-thinking: concrete or non-causal thought in contrast to the simplifications of Aristotelian logic . . . creation through dream, etc. . . . (p. xxiii)

In Rothenberg's words, this analogy

shows some of the ways in which primitive poetry & thought are close to an impulse toward unity in our own time of which the poets are forerunners. (p. xxii)

In our terms this impulse is related to a movement toward the kind of tribal constituency for which poetry is an important element of life; and politically, it is related to a movement toward a radical alternate culture which will oppose the oppressive system of the United States in every way.

MARGE PIERCY:

Poetry is an old habit of humans, but we found it strangely cramped in its attention and audience, a long way from its own roots. We had to ask what it was for all over again. A lot of what was handed us as our culture came to seem more of a sentence than an inheritance.

Public school history begins with strangely white-skinned Egyptians and leads inevitably to the sum of all good, the greatest nation on earth and the Pledge to the Flag. Except perhaps for the sciences, our education emphasized a static world. Sociology treated society as if it had evolved to *stasis,* a final norm from which one could measure deviations. Psychology focused on adjustment to roles seen almost as absolutes. Political science preached an end to ideology, the arrival at a pluralistic open society which needed only minor tinkering to perpetuate itself. The rest of the world was seen optimistically as emerging toward the American condition, or pessimistically as damned and plotting like the fallen angels cast out of heaven to bring down Paradise.

The New Critical training we received in Departments of English taught us to view the art work as existing in a Platonic dimension coeval with all other works in a grand hierarchy. But such pretensions went with the fact that the dead had better be reading it, because the living weren't. Now in a society where the means of production and economic (and thus political) power belong to a few hundred families and corporations, everything done must show a profit to those folks or, once in a while, secure profits through acting as a tax loss. The publishing companies have not figured out how to make a killing on poetry, except in textbooks. Textbooks are a booming industry. Therefore poetry was pushed out of the central market economy.

Poetry survived as an academic discipline: something you could take a PhD in and teach. You were expected to write frequent critical pieces and might write occasional poems in journals or quarterlies often published at and subsidized by universities. Clearly an attitude which maintains that the essence of poetry is oral, or one which says that art is inspired and that it is the quality of what Lorca called "duende," that daemonic underlay that makes it great, is just not going to catch on in English Departments, because you can't write papers for the PMLA about the psychedelic *wow.*

Poetry which can support a large critical apparatus (thus keeping, in a minor way, the wheels of the economy turning) tends to have at least one of two properties: either it was written far enough into the past (*Beowulf*) or enough embedded in its own time and place and politics (Dante) to acquire or excuse an army of companion volumes explaining the references and context of the work. Or, the poem must be dense enough in its symbols and language and structure and difficult and ambiguous enough in its meaning to enable a complicated system to be erected on or alongside it.

Some poetry being written now is oblique, complicated, dense enough to be useful to the people applying academic critical standards; but much is not. Poetry has developed its own means

60

of getting about outside the dominant economy: a counter-culture where people live in part by taking in each other's washing. The mimeograph revolution, underground papers, small presses, circuits of readings in universities, lofts, and coffee houses, and the writing of poems to be chanted or sung with music have created poetry with its own sets of standards, as has the growth of enclaves of alternate cultures.

DICK LOURIE:

In terms of poetry, what is an "alternate culture" alternate to? Over the last fifty years or so, how *have* poets been fitted into our society?

Teaching has become increasingly tempting. The work week these days is nine to twelve class hours, and even if you double that for preparation and grading (unlikely), you still have something which beats insurance or the Post Office. Not to mention those long summers. Writer-in-residence is even better. Another factor bringing poets on campus is the recent proliferation of MFA programs, writers' workshops, etc.—which could be called generically the "Gradcreate Programs."

Years ago, if you wanted a poet, your best bet was to hire a famous one—then you knew what you were getting. But if you couldn't get a clearly prominent practitioner, you were stuck; how does one find a good poet who isn't well-known, except by slogging through books of poetry, actually *reading* poems, and trying to evaluate them, in terms of—hireability? Or you could get a famous poet to recommend someone else. At any rate, the whole business of hiring poets (painters, etc., same problems) has a lot of loose ends, when what you're trying to do is run a good tight ship with everything in its proper place. Better to hire English teachers and not mess with poets. At least with an English teacher, you could check his ID and his PhD.

So what the Gradcreate Program does, as an improvement, is to provide a species of *licensing*—you want to be part of the new Creative College trend? listen to and channel the voices of the student creative generation? Go hire a bona fide MFA.

The analogy can go further: what this kind of licensing mentality does in poetry is just what happens with PhDs. One poet reads another's work and likes it and maybe encourages him to get into a Gradcreate Program, where other poets read his work and influence and help him, and where he gets a diploma so he can get a job where he then reads and shows his work to all those people in that particular school who are potential future poets and whom he can help and influence in his turn. In other words, it is nearly as specialized as, let's say, "Military History of Sweden in the 17th Century"—where any number of scholars in the field will read one another's work (because who outside the field is interested?), and will also pass judgment on and argue about one another's stature and prominence (who outside "the field" is qualified to judge?).

Here is an example of an unhealthy sign—quoting from a column in a publication which aims to keep little presses/magazines (hence poets) in touch with one another:

Most poetry activity in Bloomington centers around Indiana University, either officially or unofficially, and it would appear the situation gets better and better, or such has been my experience in my eight years enrolled here. The School of Letters . . . the Writers' Conference . . . the Creative Writing Seminars . . . and other activities provide a unique opportunity for the study of poetry. Some poets here are on the faculty, some visit for periods of time as teachers or readers, most are students, and a smaller number maintain distant but cordial relationships with academia. The University remains one of the best places to study poetry in the country. (*Small Press Review,* Jan. 1970, p. 25)

The Gradcreate Programs—which tend to center poets on university islands (how many poets are there in the countryside fifty miles from Bloomington?)—have helped to get us into this situation where poetry's audience is nearly exclusively poets.

A related tendency of the Gradcreate Programs is for them to become reputation mills: it is not so much a matter of getting work published, but what happens to it after it's published. Does it get reviewed in "important" places? Does it get considered for a literary prize or grant of one sort or another? If you are associated with, or graduated from, a Gradcreate Program, you know people there; it helps. People will put in the good word.

That is logical. If you teach, and if your reputation depends not only on your own work but also on the students you turn out, then obviously anything you can do to help them get published and well-known is going to be good for you. Besides, you thought all the time they were good poets, or else you wouldn't have admitted them to the program; so you're only telling the truth when you help them get established. This is basically a guild system in operation. This is what the Gradcreate Programs are about, and poetry readings too, to the (large) extent they depend on an established reputation as criterion for hiring.

In other words, evaluations are made, and hierarchy established, from within the profession itself. So poets evaluate other poets, and act as guides to whomever is doing the hiring or the spending. This is true also of the grant business: how does Guggenheim know whom to give all that money to? By asking some other poets, well-known ones, to choose a worthy recipient. They are authorities because their own reputations have been long established through previous appeals to *other* well-known poets.

We are inbred, ingrown. We belong to a profession in which only an infinitesimal number of practitioners can make a living. This makes competition heavy, which makes a hierarchy of choosers useful and convenient. And we have tended, over the last, say, fifty years, to write for each other because we are the ones who can help each other out—not only with professional criticism, etc., but with jobs, with making that scarce living (I write for you, you for me, because we *understand* each other, in ways the non-poets know not of).

Could it be also that the shortage of poet-jobs (and the oddness of the idea of working as a poet) is partly an effect, as well as a cause, of our profession being so ingrown? Would more public schools hire poets to teach children if they thought poetry was something simple, as well as something which specialists with special skills specialize in writing and showing to each other in specialized magazines? How did people get this "specialist" idea in their heads? Would more people buy poetry in stores if they thought it related directly to their own selves as well as to art-as-complexity-of-ideas?

Reaction away from specialization and toward an alternate

culture has already begun. For example, the 1970 annual meeting of COSMEP, a kind of trade association for little magazines, featured a discussion of just this point.

At the start, a noted critic and professional academic wildman told the assembled editors (which means about 97% poets) what he thought their true significance is. The "littles" are in effect a training ground for the "bigs." The best or most prominent of the little magazine editors eventually work their way (up, presumably) into things like *NAR, Harper's,* etc. His argument was that the big magazines relied on the little ones to tell them about new trends.

Several people took exception. Their point was that there's a *choice* involved here, as to the role of the little magazine. Historically what he described may well have taken place, but it doesn't have to. You can see yourself as: (1) taste-maker for the culture, or (2) representative/interpreter/member of an alternate one. It is the difference in conception, as Allen Ginsberg pointed out in the same discussion, between an avant-garde and an underground. We all have that choice to make, as artists; it is becoming increasingly difficult to ignore. The critic in his argument used *Partisan Review* as an example, perhaps unaware of how long it had been not quite what anyone would call a "little" magazine. He was surrounded by editors and publishers of little magazines and small presses he had probably never heard of, some of whom already represent the kind of alternate culture they were talking about as a choice to be made. Then there were some who were not there, as Susan Sherman noted. Where were the editors of black magazines? Why didn't they come to our conference to talk about directions and future in little magazines? Perhaps they had already made their choices, and didn't have the time to come and tell us about it.

Not that this day, at this particular conference was *the* decisive moment of the conflict, but Ginsberg's terminology is exact and accurate: it is a conflict between leading the changes in society's taste, and being part of an alternate culture, a counter-culture.

During the discussion Robert Creeley affirmed his debt to the little magazines and small presses as a publishing medium. No large publisher would touch his poetry; his work appeared in the "little" world first; only later when he was more widely recognized, well-known, would a large publisher touch it. The same could be said of many poets who began their careers in the late '40s and '50s. It's linear—the small press books and magazines in front, the larger commercial publishers behind. And as always, the big publishers who make profits wait to see what will sell or what they can push. In the case of poetry, what's involved is small profits anyway, so there's really no hurry to rush into print with what's new. This is one of the reasons why "younger poets" in this country has come to mean anyone up to fifty. Schools, in what they teach, have naturally kept pace with the big publishers, who supply their texts.

The conflict we're talking about must happen over and over. In my memory it began with the Beats. They were showing us (college students) a life and a life style that was exciting and freer than ours. We used to wear ties to dinner. They showed us a sweep of life across America, the kind of sweep and feel some of us were getting also from traditional folk music, but we weren't acquainted with any folksingers (except ourselves picking it up). They showed us immediate poetry—the great work obviously was *Howl*. Astonishing—poetry in the coffee house, poetry you didn't have to be a specialist to read and write.

Of course most of what we wrote was terrible, but that didn't matter. We did it, and we read it to people. I remember standing up in the Deux Magots Coffee House in the East Village (1959? 60?) and reading a poem. Well, I was a poet too, nobody could say I wasn't. That was a true experience, is still true in fact.

We were experiencing the beginning of a counter-culture, or more precisely, the widening and strengthening of what had been known as Bohemia to include a lot more people. What has been turning it from a specialized artists' culture to a viable broad culture is related to politics. Protest in the early sixties was a first step, like dropping out—though, unlike the drop-out, the protesters may think of themselves as members of society. But as with dropping out, if you move beyond protest it's into the realization that the system needs to be changed and can't be changed by "working within it." You figure that what you're protesting against (the war, militarism) is not an aberration of the system but its logical extension.

What's been forming over these last fifteen years is a culture alternate/counter, in political, artistic, and life-style terms. Life style: we begin to live in modes different from prevailing oppressive American culture. Politics: we make an underground, to attack, disrupt and change the system. Poetry (and other arts): we look at our work as celebration/extension/ritual of the counter culture, not the prevailing one.

The Wobblies said, "Build the new world within the shell of the old."

MARGE PIERCY:
The counter-culture has a long way to go before it's a real counter-culture for women. Playing the role of poet, like that of revolutionary, often involves machismo, abusing women and setting up a fief with good old number one on top. The Beats too were guilty of all this. Dropping out, digging the primitive and the tribal too often goes along with women as beasts of burden and a whole ragbag of patriarchal myth and heaviness, the creation of a hierarchy outside the mainstream that is even a bit cruder and meaner and more ruthless.

DICK LOURIE:
No thank you, we prefer not to become editors at Grove Press. No thank you, we prefer not to have our books done by the Doubledeal Series of Younger Poets. We'll print them ourselves, sell them at our prices, and give the reprint rights away for free if we want to. We prefer not to be poets writing for poets as a class, but poets as members of a tribe, where we speak to/celebrate/ give visions to our sisters and brothers, and to those in the old society we hope to persuade to join us.

An important distinction between avant garde and underground is in attitudes toward style. We see that in a couple of years the most difficult/freaky/experimental style you can invent will be accepted, coopted, eaten up and we'll see it in the

66

New Yorker, Esquire, Saturday Review. Ginsberg's work was at one time avant garde, but only as long as it was *the* new experiment. It is still part of the counter-culture, not because of *how* it talks, but because of what it says to us. The avant garde, after digesting *Howl,* has gone on to newer, stranger things—if that's your bag, you can buy *Evergreen Review* served up with sadism. What we are into in style is sometimes new and strange, sometimes not.

In the introduction to *Word Alchemy,* Lenore Kandel puts it this way: "Craft is valuable insofar as it serves as a brilliant midwife for clarity, beauty, vision . . . The aim is toward the increase of awareness." Leroi Jones was convicted by a Newark court because of *what* a poem says. His style is not what anyone would call avant garde. Revolutionary poems come in all styles.

A change must occur in little magazines, as it's put in *Poems of the People†* in "the convention that a poem may appear in only one little magazine of limited circulation." I suppose this convention happened because first of all the whole idea of a magazine is to publish new things, right? Every poetry magazine in its first issues gives you this:

SEEDS ON THE WIND (or whatever) has been created to publish new and exciting poems. Unlike other poetry magazines, we do not favor any particular style, school, or clique. We are just interested in Good Poetry. There is in this country a crying need for a poetry magazine like ours which is not a creature of the Literary Establishment and which yata yata yata—

So almost by definition you proudly present *new,* previously unpublished poems. Your magazine will be read by . . . 100 people? 500 is good for a little magazine; then it's the end unless a particular poem is anthologized or used in the poet's next book.

Figure this too: it may take an editor (not a sloppy one) three to five months to decide he wants my poem, then print it. By that time I'm tired of looking at it; a ghost from the past. Some poems I don't care if they get a rest like that, but most of them I want

† *Poems of the People,* Eric and Paula Torgersen, Box 324, Mt. Pleasant, Michigan 48858. They send out free to more than 200 underground papers monthly a mimeo'd sheaf of poems and some small press reviews for all to reprint. You can subscribe as an individual or magazine for $5 a year. Any poetry magazines can reprint from POTP; and they will, when they see things they like, ask permission to reprint.

out of my hands—I want people reading them now, as many people as possible, because I want them to help shape our movement, our culture.

This poetry magazine convention we're talking about, it is the old way, the concept of rarity = value. That's acceptable and appropriate if you figure you are writing for other poets, and many of them have magazines themselves which will exchange copies with the one your poem is in, so they will read it. And if the poem isn't trying to speak to people *immediately* about something important for them *now,* then you can let it wait till your next book. This convention is one of the things that needs changing because our poetry & its aims & its thrust have changed. So have the magazines. There are at least three hundred poetry magazines in the country right now. There is simply not enough virginally unpublished and at the same time good and exciting poetry to fill them all. They exchange copies, why not poems too?

Why couldn't I send out my poem to a dozen magazines (letting them each know that I've done so) and send the poem to underground newspapers too? Why couldn't a poetry magazine have one-quarter or one-third of its pages given over to stuff that's good but which has appeared elsewhere? Easy enough to make correspondence convenient by printing poets' addresses with their poems. *Hanging Loose* has made a practice of printing poets' addresses for ten issues, and no complaints yet.

MARGE PIERCY:
Along with publishing habits, we must change our aesthetics. Propaganda is still a dirty word. We were trained to divorce our politics from our aesthetics and cautioned that to confuse them produced dreadful proletarian drivel like the thirties.

The poet Jerry Badanes, who was active in SDS for years, edited *CAW!* and was with Burning City Theater, was the first person I met who said bluntly that an individual's aesthetics had to belong to the same world view as his politics: it was senseless to have Che's politics and Eliot's poetics. Equally, I might add, you shouldn't adopt socialist realism unless you dig Stalin's politics too. The great grizzly grandfathers we had loved, in their erudition and their elegance and their religions and their class identifications were of a piece, and we couldn't be revolutionaries while writing allusive poems for the leisured and academic Establishment. The reaction of most hearers was that there was only one God, only one aesthetics, and that politics was a matter of whom you voted for and need not—should not—soil the purity of your other ideas.

> Have I become an apologist for some quaint aesthetic?
> How is it 7 years ago, when I was first advised of insurrection
> My thoughts were all of metre and the New Criticism?
> At heart, I tell myself, I am an arsonist.
> Yet last evening in the firehouse I was reading aloud
> from the selected poems
> of Benito Mussolini . . .
> (Robert Sward, "Dreams")

a poem which ends:

> All my poems are burning
> And the cities are burning.

For an example of continuing schizophrenia, look at the *New York Review of Books*. Often the political articles are useful. Often reportage on foreign events, the Indo-China War, Black Panther trials are on the mark. But let them review a book which has any relevance to my generation, and invariably they can't see it. Invariably they put it down. I have never yet read a review of a novel which moved me that meant anything to their reviewers except what a state cop sees when you go 90 down the expressway. And they never review the poetry I read. As soon as they start dealing with literature, they are the enemy. The dead hand of the Cold War Intellectual shows.†

It is just no longer possible for many of us to take an innocent and individualistic view of what we're doing as writers. The political is not alien but inherent. We tend to define "political" only as that which asks for change, which demands something

---

† Please observe this was written six months before they attacked me. Answering reviews is an elitist game. But I'm not about to change what I said.

new. Poetry which upholds the status quo is considered apolitical. Poetry which embodies the present hierarchies, traditional family structure, male supremacy, mysticism about woman as Other, racism is seen as outside the realm of politics. Poetry which incorporates the values of the ruling class and the oppressors, whether white or male or landlords, is not political. Only poetry which embodies the values of those fighting their oppression is considered political. Writing which looks at society from the viewpoint of aroused minorities (or majorities) is political. Writing from a black point of view is political. Recently Phyllis Chesler had poems rejected by a New York poetry magazine with a long letter about how bad the poems were because they expressed attitudes of women's liberation and thus were not properly literature; yet that magazine has often published poems vaunting male supremacy without considering whether they were "political" or not. To those who judge literature, putting down women is a traditional genre, but caricaturing men is polemical. But we cannot see why a traditional poem which uses white to represent good and purity and godliness, and black to represent evil and chaos and the devil, is less political than a poem which says black is beautiful. We have come to be mistrustful of the whole way that "political" is used as a judgment in criticism.

For this country, with 5 per cent of the world's people, to use up 50 per cent of the world's resources is political. How can we ignore what we are eating and who? Drink your coffee: in northern Brazil hundreds of thousands are wandering through the countryside starving and homeless. We control the economy of Brazil. The lettuce we eat is picked by wetback laborers who die of the poisons sprayed in the fields. The tin in that can comes from Bolivian miners shot down when protesting the conditions of their virtual slavery in mines controlled by U.S. corporations. To sit and eat is political. To drive away merrily polluting the air with carbons and lead is political.

We cannot swallow assumptions that what is social is less primary than what is private. A feral child is simply an upright anthropoid. Communication at once makes us social and human,

70

and we are enabled to survive (and perhaps condemned to destruction) by the culture that is our unique invention. Men and women don't learn by instinct, but by chattering together.

To survive, we need to evolve a new consciousness. Poetry reflects our laboring toward that. Most poems of the sort we're talking about are unfinished. How can we write poems of the new consciousness when we are old men and old women? The poetry we grope toward will be illuminated by the consciousness of the 21st century man Che talked about, but there will be no 21st century if we take that long to give birth to him.

We are all babies delivered by Dr. Williams' bag, and we are obsessed with writing and talking and being American. Eliot called himself Anglo-Catholic and was more British than Trollope. Pound spoke of America as the Great Occidental Desert. Auden and Yeats, Europeans by birth. That whole generation always seems to be sitting around Paris. If we feel international, it is not toward Europe that we turn, but toward Asia and the Third World. Neruda and Vallejo were important voices of utter contrast to anything happening here when Bly and the other fifties-sixties people began to translate them. Snyder studied in Japan, Ginsberg in India. We have all been studying at Vietnam. Cuba looms larger in our consciousness than France or Italy. From Edward Field and Lawrence Ferlinghetti on, how many poems to Fidel, how many tons of poems for Che? And our martyrs. We are always writing memorials and elegies because we are always getting killed: poems for James Rector shot in Berkeley, poems for Schwerner and Goodman and Chaney, for Teddy Gold and Diana Oughton and Terry Robbins, for Malcolm X, the Kent State 4, the Vietnamese millions.

Still we end up obsessed with our nationality, our version of original sin. Our sin of birth is to have come out in the center of an empire. It is seldom without a long fascinated struggle with where we were spawned that some of us come at last to identify ourselves as Indians, as tribesmen, as Third World revolutionaries—the present horrors of imperialism gone mad to its beginnings, as in "Hatred of Men with Black Hair":

I hear voices praising Tschombe, and the Portuguese
In Angola, these are the men who skinned Little Crow!
  and
Underneath all the cement of the Pentagon
  There is a drop of Indian blood preserved in snow . . .
(Robert Bly, "The Light Around the Body")

At one point in *Portrait of the Artist,* Joyce has Stephen talk of proper art as static, evoking ideal pity and terror in contemplation, and improper art as kinetic: pornographic or didactic, for instance. Perhaps in the push and pull of history, writers are always veering between viewing their output as object or as utterance. Utterances occur in time and are aimed at some end: evoking, propitiating, doing good or harm, changing someone's mind or mood, destroying or embalming or explaining a past, creating a specific future, justifying, threatening, coaxing, seducing, mourning, all the reasons somebody has for speaking to others, whether in his own voice or through the mouths of characters or myths or masks.

Maybe we could say that the grandfathers and those who came in between were men of letters, while we are people of the voice. Poetry is an old habit, as we remarked, and much poetry being produced now is more "primitive" than has been customary in Anglo-American verse. The kid writing poems for his high school underground paper, the Bronx poetry club, the black student who comes into class with a poem instead of a paper (George Abbott White, from a letter: "A friend of mine . . . writes me that in his history classes the young blacks just read their poems rather than write his papers. He feels good about it, the whites gets blasted off their chairs, and the poems often are good, powerful and sensitive") is closer in some ways to the Omaha warrior who made his poem as part of his identity than to the poet writing for the *Partisan Review* in 1952 about paintings seen in Italy on a Fulbright trip. Poetry is in the process—which maybe began in the middle fifties on both coasts—of going back to its own roots and trying to locate what is still vital in the long itch to make poems and to hear them. We must take poetry back and unprivatize it, despecialize it, undo some of what happened during its long capture by the bourgeoisie.

All of this is not to say that our poetry is better than the early moderns. Neither were the poets of the forties and fifties who imitated them. What we are saying is that we cannot go on writing those kinds of poems. The early moderns assumed an orderly existence, a life with a fair amount of leisure and a cultivated class who could reread them and understand their learned references.

We cannot even assume a posterity, except for cockroaches and a few invertebrate mutants.

> **The ones who camped on the slopes, below the bare summit,**
> **saw differently from us, who breathed thin air and kept walking . . .**
> **Do we still have to feel jealous of our creations?**
>
> **Once they might have outlived us; in this world, we'll die together.**
> (Adrienne Rich, "Ghazals: Homage to Ghalib," *Leaflets*)

The Western vision of more and more has run dry. We must assume a world of scarce resources and billions of people. The allocation of resources for the profit of the few, and the use of the schools as channeling devices to impress social class and keep the proles down, prevents us from being able to count on even a crudely educated public. We may often be reading our poems to audiences that can never read them or any other books. We are not members of an aristocracy of talent. We have no desire to rise through merit proved in print to serve the ruling class or on occasion hobnob with them. We want to stay with our constituency and create a counter-culture.

Radical poetry does *not* mean poetry which is harnessed to the needs and desires of a particular set of activists who cannot, by the nature of the fight and the survival through repression, see further than the next crisis or remember clearly past two crises ago. Further, people who serve the Movement full time have a natural tendency to confuse their own career lines with larger priorities, and to think that whatever they are presently doing or about to do is objectively the most important act available to mankind at that moment. The poet has to have a long memory, back to Neolithic experience. (The poet and the activist are often the same person.)

Radical art falls in three rough categories by intent. *Agitprop* is created by the needs of the moment. It may last and last, like a pitcher made by a woman 4,000 years ago to carry water, or the posters of the Russian revolution. It may age at once and seem quaint by the next demonstration. Its purpose is to move, immediately. It must be clear. It must be grasped by the eye or ear. Many poems about the Vietnam war fall in this category. Anyone who sneers at agitprop should try making some. It requires stamina, compression and an ideograph mentality.

The next categories overlap. Both may or may not seem overtly political. This classifying isn't meant to be all-inclusive, and we wouldn't claim all poetry is political, even in our broad sense. A poet may still write an ode to a birch tree with no social implications. But, for instance, it would be hard to find poetry about love or sex which doesn't contain political assumptions: about the nature and proper roles of women and men and the divvying up of power to be wrestled for or granted or dangled in couplings. Statements about possession always concern power, and women and children were the original private property.

Our second type might be called poetry of influence or transformation, aimed at people not yet in motion, aimed at increasing awareness or changing consciousness. Often militants dismiss such art because it's not overtly radical, while they may have forgotten how to talk to people who do not yet share their assumptions. But the view of society which such a poem embodies criticizes the existing set-up; or envisions another more just, more beautiful, more humane; or attacks lethal myths about history or such institutions as the courts or the family. Thus a science fiction tale about a planet of furry green blobs who absorb each other might be such an object, as is William Carlos Williams' poem about what a funeral should be ("Tract") addressed to his townspeople. Or Philip Levine's "Animals Are Passing from Our Lives":

> I'm to market. I can smell
> the sour, grooved block. I can smell
> the blade that opens the hole
> and the pudgy white fingers
>
> that shake out the intestines
> like a hankie. In my dreams

the snouts drool on the marble,
suffering children, suffering flies . . .
(Not This Pig)

Or Victor Contoski's poem about money which ends:

Then one day when you think
you are its master
it will turn its head
as if for a kiss
and bite you gently
on the hand.

There will be no pain
but in thirty seconds
the poison will reach your heart.
(*Hanging Loose* # 3)

. . . burn through the veil that blinds
those who do not imagine the burned bodies
of other people's children.
(Denise Levertov, *Relearning the Alphabet*)

Revolutionary art is art with a sense of constituency, of tribe.
It wants to raise the consciousness of those involved in struggle,
to unify them against the thrust of their prickly egos, to purge
relationships of lies and bad habits and power plays. In truth-
telling often comes criticism, which can bring down the charge
of attacking one's brothers.

Contradiction in essence
i
met
a
part
time
re
vo
lu
tion
ist
to-
day
        (natural hair, African dressed,
        always angry, in a hurry &c.)
talk
ing
black
&
sleep
ing
whi
te   (Don L. Lee, *Black Pride*, Broadside Press)

Lenore Kandel says in a poem called "Age of Consent": "I require answers for which I have not yet learned the questions." Revolutionary poetry is truly social. But we are not. We are alienated, dispossessed, fragmented, stupefied, humiliated, and ever ready to fight our brother. Thus at this moment revolutionary poetry is a contradiction and an act of magic: it aims to produce that which it must come out of. It embodies a coherent world view or a coherent tribal view. I am not using revolutionary in a yardstick Marxist sense: the revolutionary poetry of red power will be quite different from the revolutionary poetry of the women's movement. At least there is seldom a problem of material. I know that in my own movement, the women's movement, there is a crying need for ritual, for that kind of public articulation of defined-in-struggle selfhood and emerging sisterhood that black poets are giving their people. When a poem is read which speaks to people, it is immediately gobbled up and handed around and reprinted. Thus, revolutionary poetry in this sense is not addressed to God or the muse or English majors.

> Having long ago dispersed
> from the valley home of our sources
> we are only now looking to come together again.
> And who can forget the first time
> he visioned the people
> marching through his mouth?
> (Todd Gitlin, "Who Are the People?")

Diana di Prima's *Revolutionary Letters* may seem prosy, even clumsy, until you hear the speaking voice in them. For me they have emerged as a genuine voice of our proverbs, our survival wisdom. The idiom is exact, always.

> we are
> endless as the sea, not separate, we die
> a million times a day, we are born
> a million times . . .
> get up, put on your shoes, get
> started, someone will finish.
> (No. 2)

> not to 'trust'
> even your truelove, that is
> lay no more knowledge on him than he needs
> to do his part of it, a kindness
> we must extend to each other in this game.
> (No. 14)

This sort of poetry may attempt to cleanse the language and raise the awareness of people toward the words they use. Here is an example where Denise Levertov examines our political counters:

> **Robert reminds me** *revolution*
> **implies the circular: an exchange**
> **of position, the high**
> **brought low, the low**
> **ascending, a revolving,**
> **an endless rolling of the wheel. The wrong word.**
> **We use the wrong word. A new life**
> **isn't the old life in reverse, negative of the same photo.**
> **But it's the only**
> **word we have . . .**
> ("From the Notebook: October '68–May '69," *Relearning the Alphabet*)

Revolutionary poems are not poems of protest. A protester is a member of society who wants to reform it. These are poems of a society struggling to birth. If any are universal, it is not because they are written for the ages or to a set of standards conceived of as transcendent to the struggle. When Nikki Giovanni says, "The only thing universal about me is that I am a black unwed mother," she is rejecting the whole notion that what makes a poet good is his freedom from the limitations of place and time.

> **the red sun's sword**
> **slashes my soul**
> **and black blood**
> **flows from my darkness**
> **i am the sun**
> **of an ancient**
> **people**
> **i cry tears**
> **of blood**
> **and fire**
> **during the day**
> **i hunt**
> **and at night**
> **i carry mountains**
> **on my**
> **back.**
> (Manuel Gomez)

Aside from racism—a goddamn big aside—white critics and white poets don't seem able to see black poetry because they do not comprehend what the poets are doing. Yet black poetry is begin-

77

ning to approach being a functional part of the culture of black nationalism, is near the heart of that consciousness and speaking to its people and getting response back in a vital way that other poets can only daydream about when near delirium. It should occur to us that they are doing something right which we must learn—not directly, because we would produce the worst sort of minstrel show parody. Black poets have the disadvantage that just about every way to print and distribute is in the hands of whites; they have the advantage of a live oral art which is not a tradition learned in folklore classes but still going on: the blues, the dirty dozens, the oral forms of the black churches, and the central charismatic spokesmen-figures of the bluesman and the preacher, to which is now added the poet.

Black poetry often has ritual and magic and drama beating purposefully through. One of the aims of much black poetry is to change the people who read it and who hear it from ashamed niggers into proud, fighting black people. It is magic, then, but no more so than the society's weapons that persuaded them they were ugly, stupid, and without history. Black poetry aims to create a nation on the spot, to create an "Us" sense in the oppressed which, at that moment, welds them into a strong force. Repeated rituals of unity and pride help accomplish a strength that the people can carry back into the streets.

When a people are building themselves, poetry must write the history at the same time that it evokes it. The vernacular must be turned into a vehicle capable of embodying the new self-perceptions pushing their way out and the myths and legends vital to the sense of self and brother and sister.

Hell, Mary your womb
Bell Jones Willie Lee,
full of groans as it was
the slum lord in 1619
is on you and ever
Cursed are you shall be
among women SHIT
and cursed is without end
the fruit of Amen

(John Eckles, *Home is Where the Soul Is*, Broadside)

Parodying the white words, this is close enough to white idioms to make it easy for us. This isn't:

> his tikis were hand carved
> out of ivory
> & came express from the motherland.
> he would greet u in swahili
> & say good-by in yoruba.
> woooooooooooo-jim he bes so cool & ill tel li gent
>   cool-cool is so cool he was un-cooled by
>   other niggers' cool
>   cool-cool ultracool was bop-cool/ice box
>   cool so cool cold cool
>   his wine didn't have to be cooled, him was
>   air conditioned cool
>   cool-cool/real cool made me cool/now
>   ain't that cool
>   cool-cool so cool him was nick-named refrig-
>   erator
> cool-cool so cool
> he didn't know,
> after detroit, newark, chicago &c.,
> we had to hip
>   cool-cool/   super-cool/   real cool
>   that
>   to be black
>   is
>   to be
>   very-hot.
> ("But He Was Cool or: he even stopped for green lights,"
> Don L. Lee, *Don't Cry, Scream,* Broadside Press)

A number of black poets (and Puerto Rican poets: there are clean separations and there are overlaps: Felipe Luciano of the Young Lords, who often reads his poems as part of his speeches to the people, also reads with the Last Poets and Concept East) have developed methods of delivery and styles of oral poems that represent technical breakthroughs. Sonia Sanchez chanting with a drummer and the Last Poets with their dramatic use of different voices, sometimes at once in counterpoint, are making poetry oral again in exciting ways.

DICK LOURIE:

If we are to understand what black poets are doing and to learn from them, we must re-examine and change our attitudes.

During the school year 1958–59, a white suburban middle-class Ivy League undergraduate sat down to write an essay entitled "American Negro Poets," thinking that as well as being interesting and educational, it would in some vague way be socially useful. He found a lot of scholarly sources, and some texts, from Phyllis Wheatly (contemporary with General Washington) to Langston Hughes and Gwendolyn Brooks; but these two were the only well-known black poets around in the late fifties, or at least the only ones whose reputations had reached into the Ivy League. Leroi Jones was a *beat* poet, right? and one did not write Ivy League essays on such things. Hence the chapters on contemporary poets were thin and tacked on to the vast bulk and wealth of scholarship about earlier figures.

The same young man today, if he were still in the essay-writing business, would obviously have his hands full, and anyway he would probably decide the whole idea would be better left to a black man. How times have changed.

Langston Hughes was a man of letters really, a literary man. That is, he wrote plays, newspaper columns, poems, and in fact Stood for Something. For whites, perhaps he stood for (it is not to our credit) something like "You See, They Can So." For blacks—I don't know, you would have to ask them. Hughes anyway kept something alive himself.

Gwendolyn Brooks, still very much alive, won a Pulitzer Prize in the late forties. She probably wouldn't now—I think the Prize Committee's reaction would be, "There are after all so many black poets nowadays; how can we choose the right one to give our prize to?" Also, this kind of poem from a 1968 pamphlet of hers is not likely to meet with literary committee approvals:

. . . John Cabot
itched instantly beneath the nourished white
that told his story of glory to the World.
"Don't let It touch me! the blackness! Lord!"
        he whispered
to any handy angel in the sky . . .

John Cabot went down in the smoke and fire
and broken glass and blood, and he cried "Lord!
Forgive these nigguhs that know not what they do."
(*Riot,* p. 9–10, Broadside)

Don L. Lee, a younger black poet, says in a poem titled "Gwendolyn Brooks":

> and everywhere the
> lady "negro poet"
> appeared the poets were there.
> they listened & questioned
> & went home feeling uncomfortable/unsound & so-
> untogether
> they read/re-read/wrote & re-wrote
> & came back the next time to tell the
> lady "negro poet"
> how beautiful she was/is & how she had helped them
> & she came back with:
>   how necessary they were and how they've helped her.
> (*Black Pride*, p. 23)

What she says about Lee in her introduction to his book is that he ". . . has no patience with black writers who do not direct their blackness toward black audiences." (p. 9)

She says something in the same place about black poetry:

Sometimes there is a quarrel. "Can poetry be 'black'? Isn't all poetry just POETRY?" . . . The juice from tomatoes is not called merely *juice*. It is always called TOMATO juice . . . The poetry from black poets is black poetry. Inside it are different nuances AND outright-nesses.

(pp. 12–13)

Since at least the early sixties, black poets' consciousness has been changing to a more definitely revolutionary one—they are much more than before writing purely *for* black people to read. The change can be seen happening in Gwendolyn Brooks' work from the late forties to the present.

This is the kind of art Marge Piercy talked about, tribal/revolutionary/constituency/for a people. This has happened before (Claude McKay earlier, and the Black Renaissance of Harlem in the thirties), but not so strongly. Take a look at the list of books published by Dudley Randall's black Broadside Press (in our bibliography), and those from the Third World Press—their brochure says, "We publish black energy for black people."

This is not to say whites can't read black poetry; but we have to be aware of it as black poetry and not "just poetry." For example, what would our friend the undergraduate essay writer do with this from Nikki Giovanni's "Of Liberation"?

We have tried far too long to ally with whites
Remember the rule of thumb:
WILD ANIMALS CAN BE TRAINED BUT NEVER TAMED
The honkie is in this category
Like any beast he can be trained with varying degrees of excellence to
1) eat from a table   2) wash his hands
(*Black Judgment,* p. 3, Broadside)

He would say, "Hmm . . . , very hard to evaluate this as a work of literature since it is so prejudiced against me." Yes, of course. What did you expect? How about Lindsay's poem "The Congo"? Is that hard to evaluate? What could you write about it "as literature" if you were black? It would be difficult, because it is treating you as an object, not as a potential reader of the poem. So I'm saying that my reaction to the Giovanni poem must be a reaction to the truth in the poem, to the emotional and political reality of it. I react by saying if this is so, then I am not a honky; and am I sure I'm not and can I prove it; and if I can't I better start finding out how to change.

The progression is a natural one in black literature from, say, *Native Son,* to the black poets of today. Wright was aiming at least in part to awaken the white consciousness; the black poets of today are fully revolutionary, fully committed to the consciousness of their own people. Our white American literature has either treated blacks as objects or ignored them into invisibility; it should not be surprising to us to see black poets engaged in an effort to cleanse themselves and their constituency of the effects of white literature by doing something similar in reverse. This is a part of creating themselves and their readers as a nation/tribe/people and of seizing all power including spiritual power from the hands of their oppressors.

We are beginning to see the same consciousness among Indian and Chicano communities, which already have the long tradition of poetry as an integral part of the community life that marks what we in this culture refer to as "primitive" societies, and which are struggling to retain that tradition, transform it, and continue to speak within it.

And we are ourselves making a poetry for our revolution, built on ourselves. Our style is experimental, momentarily avant-garde,

82

or transparent as newspapers, or anything that we've found works. We develop for ourselves what we have learned from our immediate poetic forebears. Some of us call ourselves surrealists, or choose to go by other names, rough indications of style or ideas, or no name at all. The point is that we are beginning to understand, partly through seeing what is happening in the U.S.A. Third World communities, that we *can* have a broader constituency for poetry, we don't need to distinguish ourselves from one another in terms of schools or styles, poetry *is* capable of functioning as an element in a community, a movement like the one we are part of. And over the last fifteen or twenty years our poetry itself has been changing, in a number of important ways.

MARGE PIERCY:

Changes in sensibility, in notions of the good, in language and syntax, in rhythm and in structure all interact in a way I doubt can be expressed this side of 3-dimensional computer-aided modeling. But relate they do. I can still remember hearing Ginsberg read for the first time in Chicago and coming unstuck. He made me realize my poetry was not real. I had started out in high school writing crudely about my life and Detroit and my grandfather and my anger and my hunger and my doubts, and had gone to college and learned a permissible set of emotions and masks and a body of conventional languages for writing about them: an educated Amer-English. This education outlawed most of my own experiences. At that time I read my poems aloud in a high rapid monotone carefully pronouncing every syllable and giving each T and D loving enunciation. I read as if my poems were a liturgy in another language, one I did not understand but had laboriously learned to pronounce. I imagined that this behavior was pure. I imagined that any attempt to read with emotion was corrupt and smelled of the stage. Ginsberg knocked that and a whole lot else out of my head. What he was writing about was my world too: but I was living in it and writing as if I were Yeats in Dublin.

In the false gentility of English Departments there was an

understanding sub rosa about the thoughts and emotions proper to a gentleman. Anger did not belong in literature. They were all gentlemen, all Anglican gentlemen, in the middle of an America as gentle as a gang-bang.

Paranoia is one of the prevailing modes of sensibility useful to us now, because it apprehends reality. That is, the phone *is* tapped, the FBI is at the door, the army is keeping a dossier on me, the air is toxic, there are poisons in the water, and someone is trying to entrap us in their wars all of the time. What we mean by the sensibility of paranoia can be seen in a poem by Robert Hershon, "German Eyes," which starts:

> german eyes are counting your teeth
> quickly in the pumpernickel   too late

and finishes:

> you have been warned   i have warned you
> you have been watched   i have watched you
> they'll hang us all
> you first

(*Swans Loving, Bears Burning, The Melting Deer*, Newbooks)

although the end has a certain optimism not wholly characteristic of the genre.

Extreme paranoia is not equal to the truth. As a literary mode, often combined with techniques descended from the surrealists, it tries to render not even the exotic in human experience but the daily humdrum newspaper: the army has accidentally given bubonic plague to half of Arizona; cop shoots six-year-old black girl in self-defense; calcium propionate, added to bread to retard spoilage, has been proved to cause mental deterioration, and the average IQ in America is now -17; the Shah of Glovinda has just invited the U.S. to come in and exterminate the peasant population of his country in the interests of peace and the free world. They *are* trying to kill us!

Our sensibility has also been stretched by the use of drugs, and drugs have produced both new genres of poems and the widespread use of another set of surrealist techniques—a whole coloring of modes and moods and images most commonly called psychedelic.

84

Further, the collage—violent juxtapositions, quotes and fragments
—is a natural form for people growing up in a media-bombarded
culture.

> Pay cashier. Pay when served
> Oh, before you go. When you get a chance.
> You're tardy!—again.
> The sun shines here an hour a day.
> On Friday, at five, it rains.
> The bottom rung
> on the ladder of success
> is temporarily broken.
> Power is progress.
> There will be a slight delay.
> I'll never, ever take you out again.
> We turned the switch, but nothing happened . . .
> (Kirby Congdon, "Chorus for Photograph")

Kids who hear or read or write poems now are generally less
discursive and less expectant that there be transitions and connections and linear structure. They are more open to the oblique,
explosive, and irrational.

We are talking now about changes in sensibility and changes in
notions of what is appropriate in a poem that have happened over
thirty years, that were already in motion long before the political
ice began to break. The Beat poets were using poems to talk about
the very personal psychic events of their lives and the bomb and
other social problems, to talk about their subculture and to
insist on using its language over the taboos against street language
imposed from one direction by the educational system and from
the other by the courts and jails. The reaction that some people
still have to street language, that writers must be using the simpler
words because of some assumed shock values, is a class reaction.
I knew what "fuck" meant years before I learned to say "sexual
intercourse" or "the act of love," and it is still the basic verb and
noun to me for which I seek synonyms consciously or not at all.
If all city kids at any rate speak two languages, one on the streets
and one in the classroom under threat, then obviously it is the
emotional, relational language that is the basic language of poetry,
not the teacher-taught English.

From Williams on through some of the "domestic" poets like

W. D. Snodgrass and on through Frank O'Hara in New York, the limit of what could go into poems was being forced back. O'Hara was particularly important in eroding the line between what is poetic and what isn't. Whom he had dinner with, what he was reading, which parties he went to and who else was there, going to the movies and writing poems about movie stars, all went in, attacking too the line between pop culture and High Kulchur. This is part of a continuing assault on any notion of the poetic that doesn't include shit and cigarette packs. Once again, it is anti-aristocratic and anti-universalist.

Finally, political poems were being written by people like Kenneth Patchen, Kenneth Rexroth, Walter Lowenfels, and Thomas McGrath all through the Ice Age. I have sometimes seen in Left mags of the forties poems of Thomas McGrath that are perfect still.

Then there are the changes in language. Once again there is an important lineage out of Williams through Olson and Creeley and the Black Mountain people: poetry of the voice. The attention to breath moved the poem closer to American speech. It was not possible to change the concept and the use of rhythm without making changes in syntax. We are leaving behind extreme compression: what we were taught characterized poetry (think of the Robert Lowell of *Lord Weary's Castle*) as something made to be spoken. We might think of poetry very crudely as moving in two directions: toward the short line conversational and toward the long line chant. Tom Parkinson's "A Litany for the American People" has a biblical sound, but not King James: Bible Belt biblical.

> *The Governing Forces of the United States:*
> We will farm our forests and use the trees for
>   packages that contain packages that contain
>   packages that contain packages that contain
>   objects that do not have to be packaged,
>   and we will use the trees for newspapers
>   and magazines that fight the truth with
>   every device of libel and untruth developed
>   through all the centuries of human misery,
>   and we will let the forest lands erode
>   and the deer drop with starvation and hunt

the puma and wolf and every bird until
these pests are gone and nothing is left
but a great void on the face of the earth.

The People of the United States:
COUNT ME OUT, COUNT ME OUT, COUNT ME OUT.
(*Green Flag*/ anthology)

or Lew Welch's "The Song Mt. Tamalpais Sings" with its refrain *"This is the last place. There is nowhere else to go."* Incidentally, these are People's Park poems, coming out of that community struggle.

We know that language must be made new. Ginsberg's effort in WITCHITA VORTEX SUTRA to resurrect it through mantra is one attempt among many. The shock of Americans at four-letter words in poetry best expresses the profound rudeness felt in a society at calling anything by its right name, a society in which public and private acts of violence and robbery and murder are justified by such names as pacification and stabilization.

"I am not a lady/I live in an elevator"

Once every three months,
solstice and equinox,
a cop comes and clubs me a little,
The man from TIME says
I articulate my generation something
wobble squeegy squiggle pop pop.

(Jean Tepperman in *The Whites of Their Eyes*/Anthology)

'It became necessary
to destroy the town to save it,'
A United States major said today.
He was talking about the decision
by allied commanders to comb and shell the town
regardless of civilian casualties,
to rout the Vietcong

O language, mother of thought,
are you rejecting us as we reject you?

Language, coral island
accrued from human comprehensions,
human dreams,

you are eroded as war erodes us.

(Denise Levertov, "An Interim," *Relearning the Alphabet*)

87

The language of radical politics tends to jargon. We have few words to describe our world, and the neologisms we invent are patterned on the bureaucratic mumblings we have heard all our lives, words like politicization and desanctification. (When I was making notes for this essay, I kept talking about the debourgoization of poetry—a word I cannot even spell.) As in any group feeling the weight of repression, radicals need fashionable clichés for use as passwords and talismans. In an attempt to be relevant, and because in nervous fatigue one comes to talk in counters rather than living words, whole poems get written in blocks of rhetoric and the current slogans out of the slot machine of that season: right on, the streets belong to the people, rip off imperialism, off the pigs, etc. The trouble with such poetry is that it exploits the haste and aridity of the political culture rather than enriching it. Both black and white militant poets write at times in compendiums of street clichés. Such poems attempt to sound current by aping currency, rather than giving to the people a new living image and form of political reality.

Radical poets have ways of defending bad verse. Writers sometimes assume you can only write for people without a college education if your language exactly conforms to their ordinary spoken language: an assumption they would never make about college people. Often those who have left suburban abundance for the Movement create a snobbish romanticism about poor people whom they imagine to be simpler because their vocabulary is smaller and their culture more meager. Yet the relationships between members of a poor family may be more complicated, denser, and more rococo than the families of the upper middle class. The simplicity is imposed by the onlooker, who imagines what he has not the sensitivity to register does not exist: someone from a verbal subculture passing judgment on a less verbal one.

Other writers feel any marked attention to language or form is a squandering of energies and is decadent and bourgeois. It is only needful to set down any which way exemplary anecdotes or statements, and the job is done. Yet all peoples have art. All peoples decorate themselves, sing and dance their lives. Only the robbed, the colonialized who have had their culture stolen, only the thoroughly proletarianized penned in cities and manipulated by the media have no native art. Part of regaining a sense of self and pride in one's being, which is part and parcel of fighting to end oppression, is to begin again to make songs and images of the beauty and bravery of our brothers and sisters and ourselves.

> *The permanent revolutionary*
> **liberates framed-up words**
> **from library death cells/**
> **frees grammar**
> **from university tombs/**
> **marries verbs**
> **to rhythms in the streets/**
> **each poem**
> **the death of a definition**
> **Walter Lowenfels,**
> (From *Only Humans with Songs to Sing/* anthology)

Freud and other students of the psyche taught us that the irrational and apparently trivial components of a person's daily life are important, and poets have been insisting on putting more much of that dailiness into their poems. When we are mystics, we are not transcendent but immanent:

> **The world is holy! The soul is holy! The skin is holy!**
> **The nose is holy! The tongue and cock and hand**
> **and asshole holy!**

Whether Blakean visionaries or drug-based in-sighters, it starts with the senses.

The humor of the oppressed is a funky thing that runs slantwise through sorrow and self-pity, a funny sideways nuance of irony and self-mockery: coming out of the black community, descending too from the remains of the East European Yiddish ghettos. Nobody writes "light verse" any more. But there is humor and play and mockery and exaggeration in the most serious poems. Because if you are trying to write in some way of your whole life with the whole person . . . well, it's pretty absurd. You have to dig yourself: your own absurdity.

Trying to write with the whole person? Why, we're all little

Eichmanns. We bottle napalm all day long and go home to barbe-cue with the family. How many of us believe what we do is truly good and useful and necessary? We compartmentalize. We sell ourselves as commodities and choose and reject others as com-modities and work to buy commodities that will improve our commodity-image.

The urge to communicate, the urge to create beauty out of our short sloppy lives for each other, is a kind of love which has much in common with the love which Che pointed out is the basis for action of the revolutionary who stays in touch with what he is about. Which is why I think it is no coincidence that many revolutionaries in this century have been poets; and why I think that if many poets could strip away the media lies and the obfusca-tions, more would be revolutionaries.

We would be making, anyhow, that world which exists in our best poems, as it does in our best music. If we fail, who is to read our poems? Starving millions scrabbling about the shit heap of decaying cities poisoned and stupefied? Robots of the ultimate systems analysis rationalized corporation? The officers of Standard Oil and IT&T and Boeing? Other poets and seven generations of graduate students in Departments of English?

We must fight for the liberated ground on which poetry, as the other human gentlenesses and creations, can naturally flourish between people.

COLLABORATION

The list here is not only of sources quoted from the essay, but also other books and poets that have helped us in the shaping and writing of it, and others we think especially important in the light of this essay. As usual, an incomplete list.

Jack Anderson: *The Invention of New Jersey*, University of Pittsburgh Press
Robert Bly: *The Light Around the Body*
Gwendolyn Brooks: *Riot*, Broadside Press
Jon Eckels: *Home Is Where the Soul Is*, Broadside
Allen Ginsberg
Nikki Giovanni: *Black Judgment*, Broadside
Robert Hershon: *Swans Loving, Bears Burning, The Melting Deer*, New Books
Leroi Jones
Don L. Lee: *Don't Cry, Scream*, Broadside
Denise Levertov: *Relearning the Alphabet*, New Directions

Philip Levine: *Not This Pig*, Wesleyan University Press
Walter Lowenfels
Charles Olson
Adrienne Rich: *Leaflets*, Norton
Jerome Rothenberg: *Technicians of the Sacred*, Doubleday
Sonia Sanchez: *Homecoming*, Broadside
Gary Snyder: *Earth House Hold, The Back Country*, New Directions
Robert Sward
William Carlos Williams
James Wright

El Corno Emplumado
Green Flag (The Journal for the Protection of All Beings #3)
In a Time of Revolution (ed. Walter Lowenfels)
Only Humans with Songs to Sing, Ikon, Basta Press
Radical America
The Whites of Their Eyes, Consumption Press

Other books from Broadside Press (12651 Old Mill Pl., Detroit 48238)
Black Arts: An Anthology of Black Creations, ed. Ahmed Alhamisi & Harun Kofi Wangara
Black Man Listen: Marvin X
Black Poetry: A Supplement to Anthologies Which Exclude Black Poets (ed. Dudley Randall)
Black Pride: Don L. Lee
Cities Burning: Dudley Randall
For Malcolm: Poems on the Life & Death of Malcolm X (ed. Dudley Randall & Margaret
    Danner)
Impressions of African Art: Margaret Danner
Moving Deep: Stephany
Poem Counterpoem: Dudley Randall & Margaret Danner
Poems from Prison: Etheridge Knight
The Rocks Cry Out: Beatrice M. Murphy & Nancy L. Arnez
Spirits Unchained: Keorapetse Kgosissile
Think Black: Don L. Lee
The Treehouse and Other Poems: James A. Emanuel
We Walk the Way of the New World: Don L. Lee
The Third World Press (c/o Ellis' Book Store, 6447 S. Cottage Grove Ave., Chicago, 60637)

Publications:
Paper Soul: Carolyn M. Rodgers
Black Essence: Johari Amini (Jewel C. Lattimore)
Images in Black: Johari Amini
Portable Soul: Sterling Plump
Two Love Raps: Carolyn M. Rodgers
Folk Fable: Johari Amini
Revolution: Ebon
Songs of a Black Bird: Carolyn M. Rodgers
Let's Go Somewhere: Johari Amini
Affirmations: Ifeanyi Menkiti
For Melba: Keorapetse Kgosissile
JUJU: Askia Muhammad Tourè

91

On creating revolutionary art and going out of print

TRUMAN NELSON

As long as I can remember having any political consciousness at all, I have been shocked and obsessed by the awareness that this is not really a land of the free. Like many other innocents growing up, I began to wonder if the whole complex of libertarian ideas and promises I was told to live by and to defend with my life was not a pious fraud. If I looked on the gross corruption of the rights of man, the ground rules, supposedly, of our daily existence, with unstirred contemplation, I knew I was committing a sin against my own senses, against the light that was in me. If I accepted the disparity in the human condition existing all around me, I knew I was committing the greatest of sins: that of hypocrisy, which blinds a man to his own failings and gives him a false idea of his position and purpose in the world. Pressing forward for some answer to the accursed questions confronting every practicing citizen, I finally began to understand that a revolutionary morality is inextricably woven into the expanding network of the world's advance and that it already runs its course through the

American fabric with a greater purity and continuity than anywhere else.

Why, then, was it always blacked out, always denied—historically, juridically, politically? Why were our heroic personalities, the carriers and reinforcers of the lifeline to a future beyond the chaos of a greedy and irrational society, so denigrated, so deprinciplized that they could no longer fortify the hope that we can establish a rational world of peace and beauty. As the great names came to mind, now on far-off shores, dimly seen, the names of Sumner, Theodore Parker, Garrison, John Brown, Wendell Phillips, Frederick Douglass, Atgeld, Debs . . . I began to realize that these men have been exorcised because they understood and dramatized those crises which came at the peak of the flowering of a young and vigorous capitalist democracy, dramatized them in ways which led to the unmasking and sharpening of the very contradictions which will cause this bloom to fade and flower into yet higher social forms. The savage irony is that the contemporaries of these noble and prophetical men, most of them a hundred years dead, were better prepared to understand the multiple revolutionary crises engulfing the world presently than we are; were better fitted to keep this republic intact because they were less liable, through ignorance and apathy, to tolerate the militarist-bureaucrat assaults on colonial revolutions which could trigger the ultimate holocaust for humanity.

No one talks of this, but somewhere along the line our primary right has been taken from us: the right of revolution, of resistance to any government which is clearly destructive of all other inalienable rights of man. The proof that this is gone and that hardly anything is left of the truth between us and our revolutionary beginnings lies in the things that have been done by the white people to the black people here and all over the world . . . things that have made many of us want to secede from the white race. It is in this area that we find the historical contradictions and conflicts most clearly developed; here millions of oppressed people and the classic "one reactionary mass" generate polar tensions which can only exist in the real world when crisis is at its zenith, when political action and passion is at its most elemental and decisive stage.

My overruling purpose has been to get the greatest number of people to rethink the whole concept of revolutionary morality . . . to keep it alive as a living faith. No one will ever do this, I know, because I ask them to, although the urgency of this demand is attested by crisis after crisis in the daily press. This is a revolutionary epoch but we cannot judge it intelligently by its own day-by-day consciousness, any more than we can judge an individual by his own opinion of himself. So I turned to an intensive study of the period immediately preceding the Civil War, a massive struggle in which, willy-nilly, the fundamental interest of a huge oppressed class was realized. About ten years ago, I stumbled upon an event which, in the sharpest way imaginable, presented a view of crisis at its zenith.

What I had been looking for was a situation in which it was possible for a small number of dissenters to release, in one action, uncontrollable explosive forces which could overturn an oppressive social system. It had to be a small group in order that their personalities could be explored with enough depth to invest the affair with a credible human scale. In May, 1854, a fugitive slave, Anthony Burns, was captured in Boston and remanded by a Federal Court, in accordance with existing law, to his master in Virginia. Resistance to this was developed by a secret vigilance committee under the control of some very distinguished men: Theodore Parker, Wendell Phillips, Samuel Gridley Howe and others, ornaments of their age as they would be of any age. They decided, after the exploration of many alternatives, to hold a mass meeting in Faneuil Hall and, at a certain point, to whip the crowd into such a frenzy that they would storm the courthouse in which the fugitive was confined and rescue him by brute force. This would constitute a direct attack on the national government, which was using the rendition of Burns as a pledge to the South that their peculiar institution would be respected and enforced. Some of the men involved in the conspiracy were armed; it was patently a violent and unmanageable plan which could be represented by administration supporters as of treasonable proportions. Great personal drama was provided by the fact that Theodore Parker, the chairman of the Vigilance Committee and the man who would give the word for the assault on the courthouse, was the grandson of Captain Parker, whose shot on Lexington Green had already proven that it was possible for a handful of people to transform revolutionary impulses from potential to kinetic energy. Up to a point, Parker acted with innocence and a sense of righteousness but at the climax, his revolutionary morality broke down; he had a failure of nerve and haplessly betrayed himself and his associates and the heroic design became a fiasco.

Regardless of this unfortunate result, perhaps because of it, I felt that the episode revealed the essence of revolutionary morality, American style, so I tried to write a book about it. A quotation from Thoreau became the ideological matrix for the work. "A very few, as heroes, patriots, martyrs, reformers in the great sense, and *men,* serve the state with their consciences also, and so necessarily resist it for the most part; and they are commonly treated as enemies by it." The question then arose as to what form the book would take. To be truthful, I did not decide in advance on any form but began to set down the pre-incidents just as I thought they had happened. My first problem was to put the reader back at a stage of the event where he would not be directly conscious of what was already known to him historically, so that he would have to grope with the characters involved for the solutions necessary to advance along the chain of circumstances leading to the climax. This, I felt, would force the reader to share some of the darkness and the ambiguity the actual characters had in the beginning, some of the agony and effort of other humans striving to understand their situation and attempting to either rise above its perils or to extract from defeat the full values of a bitter and tragic experience. Michelet calls this process "humanity creating itself." I then discovered that this method created confusion in those used to reading history strictly as a series of causes leading to effects, ignorant of the elements of interaction, of contradiction . . . of dialectic. Here I had to make a choice of simplifying,

95

perhaps stereotyping, the ascent to the climax in the hope that in its emotional shock the reader would feel, even though he did not know, all that had happened (however, the more I considered this easy way out, the more abhorrent and cowardly it seemed to be) . . . or utilizing the discoveries of historical materialism to show the truth of the way things are and to recreate it as the nature of an historical event requires it should be . . . a "conflict between many individual wills, of which each again was made what it is by a host of particular conditions of life. Thus there are innumerable intersecting forces, an infinite series of parallelograms of forces, which give rise to one resultant, the historical event. For what each individual wills is obstructed by everyone else and what emerges is something that no one willed."

It was obvious that I could not make the story I wanted out of "an infinite series of parallelograms of forces." And yet I felt it was important that people should understand the peculiarly will-less motion of history. My prior experience as a writer had been as a highly unsuccessful playwright and I began to wonder if I could not utilize some of the direct perceptions of character, action and settings which adhere even to the written form of drama to solve the dilemma of developing a humanly compelling narrative line from "an endless host of accidents." There is a certain amount of stability and predictability about individuals themselves; if their immersion in the event could be made visibly plausible, I thought perhaps the reader could carry each scene intact in his mind as a picture and be able to keep the pieces in a dramatic alignment as the event developed organically, regardless of its inevitable contradictions and delays. But this meant that I would have to make a contained little drama, with its own little denouement, out of every connective incident in the event—a prodigious, an impossible task.

Again I went to historical materialism for the answer; reading in Marx's *Eighteenth Brumaire* that: "Nineteenth Century revolutions criticize themselves constantly, interrupt themselves continually in their own course, come back to the apparently accomplished in order to recommence it afresh, deride with unmerciful thoroughness the inadequacies, weaknesses of their first attempts, seem to throw down their adversary only in order that he may draw new strength from the earth and rise again more gigantic before them, recoil ever and anon from the infinite immensity of their own aims, until the situation had been created which made all turning back impossible."

The impacted drama of this protean vision of humanity creating itself really hooked me, gave me an appetite for the impossible. Moreover, it was obvious that to attempt to evoke the smallest segment of this concept as formal history would not work; for one thing, there was not a sufficient sum of empirical data available to present the characters and scenes as would be necessary for formal provable history. Furthermore, to do the job right, the disciplines of art forms would have to be utilized. Themes would have to be picked up symphonically, dropped and picked up again at intervals. The artist's eye would have to be used with its sensitivity to aspects of coloration and composition. Every mutation of ideology, of character, of taste had to be striven for, while the author's viewpoint had to constantly change focus from a close-up of an individual to the movement of this or that contending group and then to a field of vision wide enough to let the reader catch a glimpse of the whole panorama of the front. Only an egomaniac would attempt such a task . . . an egomaniac or a citizen obsessed with the need for a restatement or reaffirmation of the indigenous nature of revolutionary morality.

Working through the total data of the Anthony Burns case, I found that fortunately it took place in a very compressed time scale and was, therefore, easy to manage chronologically. Furthermore, the characters involved were prodigious writers and talkers and had made public or private statements upon every conceivable matter on which opinions might be asked. This made it possible to reconstruct their diction to a fairly close degree. And by presenting the event as it happened, with the chronology intact, it was possible to avoid those erroneously invented incidents or ideas which mar a work of art by falsifying the psychology of the characters.

While this work was in process, I was working and also functioning as a union steward at the General Electric plant in Lynn, Mass., six days a week. I had to write on Sundays only. It was a dreadful ordeal but I was greatly helped by the late Professor F.O. Matthiessen, who, although I had no passports to the academic world, not even a high school diploma, gave me the advice and encouragement that I had to have. Under his perceptive and tolerant eye, the book began to emerge in a bastard form, neither history nor fiction; its frame of reference best explained as an attempt to deal directly with the social superstructure under pressure and in line with Marx's insistence that differentiation must be made between the economic base, which can be determined with scientific accuracy, "and the juridical, political, religious, aesthetic, or philosophic—in a word, ideological forms wherein men become conscious of the conflict and fight it out."

Parker was a great man, willing to admit his failure and to pay for it. He was indicted by the courts for the rescue attempt and in a magnificent defense said this, again, through me, under the nose of McCarthy: "Let them call me a traitor. We come from a rebellious nation, our whole history was treason, our blood was tainted before we were born. Our creeds are infidelity to the mother church. Our Constitution is treason to our fatherland. What of it? Though all the rulers in the world bid us commit treason against man and set the example, let us never submit!"

Despite the book's failure on many levels, I felt that I had evolved a slightly different method of storytelling and one which could live harmoniously within the materialist conception of history. Letting the event itself come first, relentlessly exploiting and dramatizing every connection except those so remote they could not be proved, I found it did establish its own form. The incessant opposition of wills, which seemed at first to knock every attempt at forward motion so much out of line that the narrative appeared to be a vicious circle, soon began to bend under tension until the motion along the front began to spiral sharply, increasing its velocity until everything collided at the center. My necessary preoccupation with historical elements gave me an active sense of the motion inside the characters, the moments in the dialectical process of becoming. To paraphrase Marx again, as a writer I became supremely aware that it was not my consciousness that was determining the characters and the action in this book; rather, established social existences were determining both the characters and action . . . and my own consciousness as an artist.

What it revealed very sharply was the paralysis of the liberal in the face of a demand for action, for violence. This was the sin of the prophet: that men of learning and sensibility are capable of understanding the physical and political facts of their own existence, yet cannot commit the irrevocable acts needed to transform them. They proclaim what is wrong, but they hesitate to move against the wrong, and really don't want anybody else to. I have Parker trying to explain this failure in the last paragraph of the book: "This is my sin. I hated the tensions and disturbances created by the weak driven against the wall. And I must confess thinking it a pity that a people so ignorant and degraded should be the means of tearing this nation apart . . . this because of my resentment at being forced from my chosen role as a scholar and philosopher and not being able to finish and publish my book. I thought you [the slaves] were all too speechless and submissive, forgetting that your story can only be told in outbreaks and revolutions . . ."

When the book came out it had a good critical reception, but as it was in the high tide of McCarthyism, two of the largest wholesale distributors refused to handle it because it had the picture of a black man and a white man on the cover, which made it a communist book. Because I wrote, and still write, only for use, I felt that the only way to fight McCarthyism, which then threatened to destroy the entire American radical heritage as completely as the monotheism of Ikhnaton in 1354 B.C., was to form collectives and communes to create loving communities where political insult and slander were simply meaningless and all life self-sustained. I felt there was a need for a book about communes.

In that marvelous period of American history when every honest artist was ignited again and again by the struggle to abolish slavery, there was also one to abolish capitalism. There were over eighty communes established. Their economic basis was very shaky, but all of them completely understood what Marx wrote in *The Holy Family,* that capitalism brings about "the divorcement of existence and thought, consciousness and life." They knew that property, capital, money, labor and the like are far from being figments of the mind, but they are all the very practical, objective products of their own alienation, which therefore must be abolished in a practical, material way; so that not only in thinking, in consciousness, but also in his mass existence, man should become human.

The problem was which collective to choose to write about. After much research I decided to write about Brook Farm, in Wext Roxbury, Massachusetts. Perhaps the most famous, but always written about tritely because the historians persist in dealing with it in its early, transcendentalist phase, instead of later, when it was worked out from a blueprint by Charles Fourier. Georg Lukacs says of Fourier, "Despite the fantastic nature of his ideas about Socialism, and the ways to Socialism, the picture of Capitalism is shown with such overwhelming clarity in all its contradictions that the idea of the transitory nature of this society appears tangibly and plastically before us." The people at Brook Farm expressed their repugnance at the brutality and stupidity of capitalism in the early 1840's, felt it was transitory and tried to build an alternate form of society to replace it. I decided to drop the complex and laborious event structure and to impose the ideology of Fourier on the novel as relentlessly as the Brook Farmers did on their collective.

Charles Fourier was unquestionably one of the greatest of all satirists . . . Marx considered him the most brilliant . . . but his positive guidance system for the replacement of capitalism was to "utilize the passions now condemned, just as Nature has given them to us and without any way changing them. That is the whole secret of the calculus of Passionate Attraction."

Again I decided to use "real" characters who could be historically validated. The reality of their experience could not be wholly organic and personal because they were all acting under the externally imposed structure of Fourierism. They had to accept it and live with it every day. So, in the writing, I locked their total experience into a rigid form, constructing the book in twelve chapters, each having for its denouement the relationship of the life of the collective to one of the twelve passions which were the master plan of Fourier . . . sight, cabals, touch, smell, taste, hearing, variety, familism, friendship, ambition, love, composite. The total exercise of these passions and their interaction, Fourier thought, would make men and women ideal in their relationship with one another.

The leading character had to be a Unitarian minister, George Ripley, who one morning stood up in his pulpit and said, "I cannot witness the glaring inequalities of condition, the scornful apathy, the burning witness, the glaring inequalities of condition, the scornful apathy, the burning zeal with which men run the race of selfish competition with no thought for the elevation of their brethren, without the sad conviction that the spirit of Christ has well-nigh disappeared from our churches. Any defense of humanity is considered an attack on society. When a minister cannot show by his words and works that he is hostile to all oppression of man by man, and that his sympathies are with the down-trodden and suffering poor, I feel it is time to look at the foundation on which we stand and see if it does not suffer from some defect which threatens its destruction."

Ripley is a good man, now forgotten, and I do not regret that I revived him and his magnificent failure at Brook Farm, but in comparison with the drama inherent in a genuine revolutionary crisis, Brook Farm is pretty small potatoes.

My thoughts were drawn back to the failure of Theodore Parker at his moment of truth and I began to look for a man who would not fail when the chips were down and would meet his tyrannies head on. The question arises whether it is possible for a man to control or surmount a revolutionary act of violence which he himself has ordered and carried through without becoming so corrupted by it that he does lose, finally, his revolutionary morality. Meanwhile, the decade of the futile fifties began to develop a universal image of man as a helpless bundle of inexplicable ganglia, straining toward status, appetite, repletion and togetherness like a plant to the sun, with no more judgment, discrimination or control over his destiny than a puppy dog. The followers of Freud began to occupy the commanding heights of criticism and editorial taste. But there is more than one Sigmund Freud and the older and wiser one said, in *Moses and Monotheism,* after affirming the will-less nature of the historical process, "But we must keep a place for the great man in the chain, or rather the network of determining causes. His nature is not as important as the qualities by virtue of which he influences his contemporaries . . . done in two ways, by his personality and the ideas for which he stands. The great man is the image of the father; the decisiveness of thought, the strength of will, the forcefulness of his deeds, belong to the picture of the father; above all things, however, the self-reliance and independence of the great man, his divine conviction of doing right which may pass into ruthfulness."

Every American with a fair knowledge of history has to read this with a shock of recognition . . . a name sounds in his ears with the attack and timbre of a horn call . . . JOHN BROWN. Here is a man who compressed into his personality the whole image and conflict, the whole consciousness of his time, and then brought it to an end, after dying the death of a Socrates, a Jesus, with a titanic apocalypse of fire and blood such as this country had never known. Somehow he was able to work on the mass emotions of his day with the same impact of fear, pity and exultation with which the great Greek dramatists used to shock and delight the citizens of Athens in its great days. But old John Brown was a real man in a real world. He killed and got killed, and always, incredibly always, for principle. There is no question that he is the finest example of pure revolutionary morality produced in this country, perhaps in any country.

It is almost impossible for a writer of my mold of mind to

describe the point-to-point solutions of his work in process. With my decision to do a book about John Brown as a Great Man came a warning from the man who will always be my editor, regardless of who publishes my books: Angus Cameron.

" . . . as long as a single dramatic episode is employed, the reader does not miss the suspense of the novel. Now there is little suspense in John Brown if a considerable portion of his life is taken for a novel [I had decided to tell of his Kansas adventures], because we know, or we think we know, that he had a monolithic character, almost without contradictions. Brown's career was not a self-contained narrative like the Anthony Burns case Of all your writing in this new form, I find it viable when you are telling a story which contains, historically, its own form . . . beginning, middle and end, but find it difficult when the material doesn't. It is then the book is neither fish or fowl."

Characteristically, I ignored this and went ahead anyway and was wrong in the end, wasting over two years of intensive effort and having to junk a complete manuscript of a 500-page novel. My error was that I thought by putting back all the wonderful truths about Brown taken out by the latter-day deprinciplizing historians, and representing him as the man Emerson and Thoreau knew and celebrated, I would have a good book.

I was wrong in many ways. I had Brown figured for an anarchist, which he was not. I ignored his religion as something related exclusively to his time and not motivational to him. I thought I could pin the entire story on the executions or murders he had carried out at Pottawatomie . . . which I thought were in simple reprisal for five men killed by his enemies and, in anarchist terms, "propaganda of the deed." In building up a historical justification for this act, I had to include long stretches of approach which I thought were significant but which were really only background and without any organic life of their own.

I wish I could say I had this or that moment of dazzling revelation where I saw the truth and everything "started to jell," but it was nothing like that. In 1954 I went out to Kansas and poked around Brown's sites and the papers in the Kansas Historical

Society. I knew I had got it all wrong and that I had to start all over again. By this time, the advance money on the book had run out.

If there was any one turning point in my mind, it was the deep realization that what went on here was revolutionary and could be ultimately explained if I could only somehow penetrate to the historical motion underneath. I knew it could never be explained by a single episode or a single outstanding character, and that rather than a one-act play, as the Sin of the Prophet had been, this was a four-act drama of titanic proportions.

Stumbling and fumbling along, I came across some hard evidence which allowed me to begin the drama with some sense that I was entering a believable totality of human history. There was a letter at Duke University from David Atchison of Missouri, the active agent in the Southern cabal to control the western territories and enter them into the Union as satellites, to Jefferson Davis, then Secretary of War. This was my first real benchmark.

"Sept. 24, 1854. Dear Davis: We will before six months rolls around, have the Devil to pay in Kansas and this State with the Negro thieves. They are resolved, they say, to keep the slaveholder out and our people are resolved to go in and take their 'niggers' with them. We are organizing to meet their organization. We will be compelled to shoot, burn and hang, but the thing will soon be over."

I had to find out everything about this invasion and boil it down to elements of action and passion in personal interplay. There was, alas, in the congressional report on *The Troubles in Kansas,* 1206 pages of the lists of every settler in Kansas, their allegiances, their claims, their points of origin. There was the sworn testimony of their conflicts or collaborations with the various Missouri invasions. Using this for a mere starting point, I read everything available, finding the richest pay dirt in bound volumes of the *New York Times* and *Tribune* for 1855 and 1856, in my personal possession.

My next springboard was the opposite tension of what happened in the Free State resistance movement, which had agreed, in June,

1855, "to take all steps necessary to throw off the tyranny imposed upon us and form a provisional government for ourselves." There was a genuine revolution in prospect, which was changed into a "legal and peaceful one," then changed back in the face of a third Atchison invasion in May, 1856. Then, according to the diary of the former Territorial Governor of K.T. (Andrew Reeder), deposed, and going over to the Free State side:

" . . . the plans of the enemy are well laid, if they are allowed to pick up our leaders on these treason indictments, they could then take our people and break them down in detail and destroy our party. We resolved to make an open, organized resistance and to make it as effective and justifiable as it is already righteous and just, we must do it under the forms of a state government set up against the Territorial, and make the issue of force and blood in the best way we can."

That was the Free State policy around May 19, 1856. On May 24, under attack from 3,000 Missourians, it collapsed, and Brown's "Pottawatomie Policy" took over. This was discovered only after unearthing some forgotten records of a Territorial grand jury carrying out the pro-slavery master plan of indicting for treason the Free State leadership in Brown's neighborhood. Brown's policy was the bloody but enormously effective one of executing, without trial, the D. A. and some prominent members of a Territorial court . . . which plunged all other Territorial courts into such a panic that they could not go on with Atchison's and the South's grand design for the conquest of Kansas.

I will mention a final piece of evidence. There has been some awareness, historically, that Brown's deed of darkness at Pottawatomie was political, but there was an unsolved contradiction in that one of his victims was not a court official and that he had not killed the foreman of the jury . . . in short, the choice of victims was not fully consistent with political assassination. I felt I had the answer to this when I studied the original surveys of the township in which this took place. Brown was performing his action in the dead of night, on extremely rough terrain, in an area of widely scattered cabins. As surveyor, he did what was occupationally natural to him. He selected his victims from those residing on a survey line running directly north and south, which he could follow in the night by consulting his pocket compass. It was a tactic of great economy of action and he brought it off with complete success.

Naturally, I can only give a few highlights of the germinal discoveries which allowed me, I felt, to gain control over the massive complexities of the Kansas struggle. I finally boiled it down to as near as I could come to a formal narrative line in which the fusion of historical and human events began to take hold with the unity which life shows, but which is seldom achieved, or even understood, in either history or fiction.

David Atchison of Missouri, the overlord of the Southern expansionists, had led thousands of armed Missourians into Kansas at the time when the political forms of a virgin territory were to be determined by the popular vote of the settlers. By the familar tactic of seizing and controlling the election apparatus, Atchison successfully swung the plebiscite to the pro-slavery side and the permanent government of the Territory was established in such a way that it was not possible to alter its pro-slavery character by democratic means. The Free State organization decided to set up a complete rump government to actually overthrow the Atchison cabal . . . although it was not to be put into operation until appeals had been made to an ostensibly sympathetic House of Representatives in Washington. The House was petitioned to reject the Territorial government, as established by force and fraud, in favor of a Free State, based on a rump election which proved that the majority of settlers were not pro-slavery. Like all revolutionary movements, this was a very complicated sequence of events, full of betrayals and opportunisms.

John Brown, then in Kansas and living with his sons, committed the so-called Pottawatomie Massacres in May, 1856. The generally accepted authority for this period, James Malin of the University of Kansas, explains the killing of the five men who were not slaveholders and had not molested any of the Browns personally, as "the explosive self-assertion of a frustrated old man . . . a

106

means by which he might enjoy untrammeled authority and restore his confidence in himself." Professor Malin, and all the other professors who have consistently accepted his findings, ignore the revolution in process in Kansas in 1856 and that John Brown's bloody act of tyrannicide was its culmination and turning point.

Why this obvious conclusion has been evaded is somewhat strange. Perhaps it is because the traditional concept of tyranny is the oppressive government imposed by a single ruler. But modern tyranny is more often an institution, a system of impersonal pressures exerting arbitrary power. Brown's victims at Pottawatomie were all members or partisans of the pro-slavery court at the precise time when it was using its undeniable powers to indict all anti-slavery settlers as traitors. His assault was on tyranny as a system.

The two factors for re-establishing the connection were Brown's religion and politics. It is admittedly difficult to explain his pure Calvinism against the image now persisting of the Calvinist as a nay-sayer so everlastingly permeated with guilt over man's depravity that an enlightened conscience recoils in disgust from any justification of the doctrine.

Nowhere in Brown's expression do you find this rat-hole darkness and despair, the notion of God as treating man as a worm under his heel was completely irrelevant to him. Thoreau said of him, "No man has appeared in America, as yet, who loved his fellow man so well and treated him so tenderly." Brown was a "Calvinist" who so disbelieved in the "innate depravity of man" that he fought to free men often chained up like ferocious animals, who put guns in their hands and depended upon them to act toward their late oppressors with justice and mercy.

Actually all Brown took from Calvinism was its revolutionary cutting edge and its revolutionary righteousness. With it he could explain why he acted without consciousness of guilt, against the law and against the system. When in a dialogue with those who did not need God-talk, he was quite divested of his religious idiom. When he did use it, it was because, as Donald Freed pointed out, the Bible provided radicals with an acceptable vocabulary of dissent which "allows one to take extreme positions when required and yet not cede an inch of humanism or patriotism to the status quo." Whenever John Brown's revolutionary morality came into conflict with his Calvinism, it was the Calvinism and the Bible and the fear of God himself that went down, and the revolution that prevailed.

Parenthetically, in the latest book about Brown, touted as "the first based on original research to appear in sixty years," Brown is presented as a "violent old Calvinist who always exhibited a puritanical obsession with the wrongs of others and punished them with an old Testament vengeance." Needless to say, this book was received with high praise from the critics, including the super-liberals of the *New York Review of Books,* and will inevitably become the "taught" book about John Brown for the next decade or so.

John Brown's politics were concise, revolutionary, quick with innocence and righteousness. He simply believed that slavery was unconstitutional and that the founding fathers, after carrying through a liberating revolution, could not possibly have sentenced a class which had fought by their sides to eternal bondage. His theorist was the great and neglected Yankee thinker, Lysander Spooner. Spooner, the platform writer for the RADICAL ABOLITIONIST PARTY, claimed it was the constitutional duty of every citizen to go to the rescue of those enslaved; that not to was to connive at their enslavement.

He wrote that "A government, so powerful and so tyrannical as to restrain men from the performance of these primary duties of humanity and justice, ought not to be suffered to exist." To those who claimed that the democratic process allowed evils to be corrected by legal and peaceful means, he argued that once the first act of tyranny has been allowed to be enforced against the people, those in power are capable of preventing its repeal by forbidding discussion and dissent and can then impose a whole chain of oppressive laws. He said that government knows no limit but the endurance of people and their revolutionary right to resist by force when the other alternatives are closed off to them.

It was a convention of the RADICAL ABOLITIONIST PARTY which financed Brown's trip to Kansas with a wagonload of arms. It seemed obvious that he had a full awareness of political programs and that all his acts, however irrational they seemed to be, related to cold-blooded cerebration . . . (Although, as Thoreau pointed out, he never bothered to explain himself, nor had he any "organ advocating his cause.") Where Brown differed from most libertarians was that he felt that those who destroy the inalienable rights of man should be punished for it, swiftly and to make an example.

Brown's story had to come out of a matrix of months of reverberating alarms and incidents, crowded with false starts, threats that ended nowhere with plots and conspiracies that were outright crimes, ranging from the White House to the lowest of frontier post offices, in which the fate of the nation swung like a pendulum between solution and self-slaughter. I felt again that no "history" could achieve the reflected reality, the "mimesis" that should tear at the emotion of the reader; that the wholeness of it had to be felt, the peripheral whirlpools of senseless violence closing in, the sense that every alternative to blood-letting was being played out; . . . that only the "charging" of the facts and conjectures with the intangible energies of an art form could make it work.

It worked for a little over a year . . . it took six years to write . . . and then the surveyor went forever out of print, to join the two other novels in the living-dead limbo of living authors whose works are dead. They were not regarded in any realm of academia as containing any usable truths. I like to think this is because of their explicit and insistent revolutionary content but this is not really true . . . what had happened was that the political-revolutionary-historical novel was phased out of the American literary scene. No one pretended to take it seriously anymore. But it was a genre which, in the words of the great critic Georg Lukacs, "portrays the totality of history, and makes it a mass experience . . . makes it possible for men to comprehend their own existence as something historically conditioned, for them to see in history something that deeply affects their daily lives and immediately concerns them."

It is difficult to pinpoint the reason for this. Perhaps we have become too decadent to either write or read them. Trotsky says, "Literature without the power of great synthesis is the symptom of social weariness." Certainly we are all profoundly weary and hopeless about our present culture. The historical novel is a prime form of people's art; it is storytelling, it is example, it is an embodiment of our hidden continuities of hope and rage. It can be very, very revolutionary and uncontrolled by the consciousness-controllers now deprinciplizing and derevolutionizing students in the academic process . . . teaching counter-revolution.

It seems clear that these same people now control the publishing, the publicizing and the criticizing process with the same iron hand with which they control their students. It is no longer possible to circumvent them by writing revolutionary history in the form of a novel nor is it possible to attain the distribution or viability of revolutionary essays or tracts until they appear somewhere on a "reading list." The only sensible suggestion on this matter comes from Lenin. "The first thing to do is deprive capital of the possibility of hiring writers, buying up publishers and buying newspapers, and to do this the capitalists and exploiters have to be overthrown and their resistance suppressed."

The enemy: words
CARLOS FUENTES

Literature in the Spanish language is no longer produced in a vacuum. Now, it can only be understood as part of the greater and vibrant reality of words. An old positivist tradition, prevalent in Latin America (where even a national flag, the Brazilian, bears the Comtean motto: "Order and Progress") and frequently disguised as its opposite, idealism for idealism's sake, allows words a friendly function bordering on buffoonery: the writer can divert, even advert (among us, the Barons of Munchhausen are irresponsibly praised) but cannot, plain and simply, convert. But only convertive words can discolor what passes for "reality" to show us the real, what sanctified "reality" hides, the totality hidden or mutilated by conventional (not to say convenient) logic. Convertive words are the enemy, words that neither divert nor advert but, perhaps, convert. These are the words that in today's world are impossible or that, if we try to make them possible, are repressed. In recent times, an impressive number of writers and artists have suffered violent attacks, censorship, or jail: Jean Genet, Mikis Theodorakis, Regis Debray, Benjamin Spock, Susan Sontag, Norman Mailer, Leroi Jones, Alexander Solzhenitsyn, Ladislas Mnacko, Fernando Arrabal, José Revueltas, Alberto Ginastera, Harold Pinter, Sinyavsky and Daniel, Allen Ginsberg, Adam Schaff, Kolakowski, Marco

Bellochio, Jacques Rivette, Pier Paolo Passolini, Julio Le Parc, Heberto Padilla. These are only some out of many individuals, not to mention the works that have been burned or confiscated in the customhouses of various Latin American capitals: the works of C. Wright Mills dumped into the sea at Lima, a shipment of Stendhal's *The Red and the Black* seized and appropriated in Buenos Aires as suspected, by virture of the color of its title, of being Marxist propaganda, etc.

Ostensibly, the technocratic and consumer society presents a homogeneous front and absorbs all challenges. On the other hand, in the societies which still haven't achieved abundance, social heterogeneity could represent, on being expressed, a direct challenge to a more or less monolithic power. It would be worth considering to what degree the situations are diverse and at what point they regain a certain unity.

In the United States, for example, the growing concentration of power and the consequent disappearance of real political options within the established system is smoke-screened by the long-established exercise of the freedom of speech. Nevertheless, Johnson and his team didn't hesitate to call irresponsible, servile, and traitorous those intellectuals who opposed the Vietnamese venture; and Mayor Daley's police proved, in the summer of 1968, that police brutality is a universal fact, practiced uniformly and with similar sadism by all the powers, capitalist or socialist, technocratic or underdeveloped. The American status quo, however, continues to believe that the great leveling power of a comfortable and conformist society will finally dampen the powder of rebellious words. Hasn't this always happened in the United States?

The American revolution was the only one in modern times that didn't become a tragedy. In France, Russia, China, Mexico, Cuba, revolution meant both a radical break with an order and the affirmation of not only a material, but a spiritual change in men. The revolutions were not made to produce more and better, but to save men from alienation. And, above all, to make need coincide with freedom.

112

This vision and its tragic and common incarnation is the key to the greatness of those movements; in a given moment all men were able to recognize themselves in the lives of a few. Nothing like this happened in the United States. There, it wasn't a matter of destroying an order, but rather of assuring the continuity of a local democracy which the metropolis was limiting. The American revolutionaries didn't shout, "Liberty, Equality and Fraternity," "Power to the Soviets," "Land and Liberty." They were not the men who had nothing to lose but their chains. On the contrary, they only said that they wanted to earn a little more and that they didn't want taxation without representation. It had nothing to do with reforming human vision, but with obtaining certain concrete conditions that would benefit the development of the thirteen colonies. The shadow of a Robespierre or a Stalin was not cast upon the American revolution; but neither was the enlightenment of a Saint-Just or a Lenin.

However, the germ of tragedy was buried in the breast of that optimistic society. On one side, optimism itself summons its opposite: at the least failing of the founding success, a good conscience is the easy prisoner of terrible anxieties. On the other, the American revolution was organizable and optimistic only because it was the revolution of one part of the nation: the ruling, productive, expansionist, white class. The presence of the blacks in the revolution for independence might have turned it into an enterprise of a completely different significance. In reality, the first American revolution was a postponement of the total revolution, whose first battle took place one hundred years ago in the war of secession. The second phase begins now, before our very eyes (I say this in the literal sense: political assassinations and street riots are the daily bread of live television).

The blacks reveal that the American consumer society also shares in a tragic division, no matter how much its political, economical and cultural rhetoric has uselessly tried to hide it. Only one American writer in the first third of this century understood in time that a society is unrecognizable in optimism and only universal in tragic tension: William Faulkner.

Outside of him, words in the United States had been, at the most, reformist. That is to say: language had a predictable place within the utopia of unlimited progress. Dreiser and Norris, Lewis and Dos Passos criticized work conditions, Puritan morals, middle-class vulgarity, but always within the circle of optimism. Labor legislation and fiscal reforms, tolerance and the founding of a museum of fine arts in Wichita would solve the problems.

Today, for the first time, the writer's valid words prove that the words of Power are invalid. The credibility gap that pursued Lyndon Johnson, until he was forced to forgo a second chance at the presidency for the sake of maintaining the system, had no other meaning. The fact is that the head of the most powerful nation in the world was run out of his post by the students, intellectuals, journalists, writers, by men with no other weapon than words. And it is because words today do not fit within the perpetuated and re-newed foundation order of the United States. Nobody can re-member the Alamo, the *Maine,* the *Lusitania* or Pearl Harbor to justify daily murder and destruction in Vietnam. No "manifest destiny" convinces us that in order to insure the doubtful democ-racy of South Vietnam's oligarchs a country must be erased from the map with napalm and phosphorus. Similarly, nobody can be content with simply asking for proper legislation to resolve the black problem, which is not a legal problem but one of alienation and which is not a conflict of feelings but of being. In these con-ditions, words become rhetoric on the side of power and heresy on the side of dissent: words deny the orthodox position assigned to them by the Founding Fathers. The new American words indicate the breakdown of the "American dream," to its degrada-tion into grotesque or criminal nightmare. Words have become the enemy of Power: Norman Mailer, William Styron, Arthur Miller, Susan Sontag, Robert Lowell, Joan Baez . . .

The European consumer society, by attenuating or dissimu-lating class struggles, turned politics into an enormous verbal exercise. The "political" struggle (that is, within the established order: elections, parliament, executive decisions, position and "opposition") was reduced to the shades of a phrase, the possession of a slogan, the unending diffusion of words turned into invitations to consume, tranquilizers of consciences, endorsements of an unlimited well-being: nothing is oppressing you; everything is benefiting you; we live in the best of worlds— a world in which everything was an amplified, multiplied verb, a perpetually communicated verb to stop communication, loaded with all senses minus that of sense itself, words at the service of established nihilism. Everything became words but the word was nowhere. Hamlet's ironic reflection was to find its contemporary echo in Beckett: "Ce qui se passe, ce sont des mots." Words are the reality of the consumer society; a whole system is maintained upon its usage of language. The political act is language only: politics is what Pompidou, Heath, or Willy Brandt *says*. And economic life, by centering upon consumption, totally depends upon the language capable of convincing the consumer so that he will, in effect, consume. And also capable of convincing him that he is freely opting for this or that product: the sublimated message. Every word that announces a real act, every word that destroys the magic of consumption, will be the enemy word.

The strength of these societies has consisted in the fact that even enemy words are transformed into consumer goods. Rebellion degenerates into fashion; the rebel is flattered, bought, sanctified; and the iconoclast ends up an icon, imprisoned, like an ape behind the bars in the zoo, playing the electric guitar and shaking his mane in front of the satisfied consumer—animal tamers.

But Beaumarchais and Voltaire also entertained the aristocracy and perhaps tomorrow people will understand that the language of Grass and Genet, Godard and Bellochio, Beckett and Calvino, Xenakis and Nono, Adami and Dubuffet, has not been less efficient than that of Figaro and of Candide. In any case, the consumer society can flatter words instead of persecuting them, but it knows that the artist's word is an enemy, even when its meaning is (and it's enough for it to have a meaning to be an enemy: the basis of the consumer society is the loss of meaning by virtue of giving everything a false meaning; it is the lack of

115

questioning the meaning) that which, clear and precise, Engels attached to it: to affirm and reaffirm that we are not living in the best of worlds, that no society represents the culmination of history.

"L'Imagination au Pouvoir": the revolution of the European university youth, and specifically the May revolution of 1968 in France, has established that the consumer world is not the best of all possible worlds, that abundance is not enough, that there are needs which the absence of need does not satisfy. And they did it by rescuing and bringing up to date the revolutionary sense of words: the barricades of the Latin Quarter were made not only of cobblestones and burnt automobiles, but of all the words that had been sequestered by power: love, passion, responsibility, creation, brotherhood, autonomy and democracy and justice, words they put into direct, not meretricious, content. The students and workers of France gave the artist's visionary and rebellious words a grave and immediate content: man, each man, is capable of defining his own destiny as an artist defines, in the act of creating, his own work. And like a work of art, the individual responsibility is the supreme instance of the collective responsibility as, simultaneously, the reverse is also true.

The Soviet Union and the countries of its sphere of influence are not the best of worlds either, and you don't have to be anticommunist to say this. On the contrary, one of socialism's demands is that of exercising constant criticism. How can there be true dialectics if the real is only identified with the thesis? How can alienation be overcome if the very alienations of the socialist system are not admitted and challenged? Socialism was born from dissidence; consent is fatal to it. Socialism faced the optimistic lie of the bourgeoisie with a vision of the real (the total); it cannot, without negating itself in the absurd, fall in the same trap and demand that writers of the socialist world behave like writers of the Victorian world.

Neither did need coincide with freedom in the Soviet Union. But the fact of having attempted that conciliation is enough to affirm the greatness of the October revolution. The true tyranny

116

of Stalin and his grey successors consisted in again sacrificing freedom to need while propaganda was proclaiming the opposite. The true Soviet revolution was and is in the mind of those who understand that the profound revolutionary effort to reconcile historical opposites must depend upon the presence of a mask, the tragic vision which is, at once, the fact of separation and the consciousness of this fact. Fact and consciousness renew the revolutionary will; there are no free paradises.

As the consumer structures assert themselves in the USSR, the writers will probably stop suffering under the present pressures and begin to confront problems similar to those of the Western writer. If this foreseeable process (as long as nothing indicates that in the Soviet Union there will be a substantial step toward socialist democracy, but rather an assimilation of the consumer structures camouflaged by growing ideological rigidity) presents itself to the world as a revolutionary fact it will be a lie, also foreseeable, but still more unacceptable than the Western one. Words shouldn't be the enemy in socialism. They should be the bearers of freedom confronting need, provisionally represented by the State. A vision can be born from this mutual challenge that would be neither Stalinist oppression nor neocapitalist suppression. The Solzhenitsyns, Kolakowskis and Vancuras keep this hope alive. Their words offer a present way out for socialism; the words considered enemies by Novotny's Czech tyranny stopped being so in 1968 without Czechoslovakia having to stop being a socialist country; or rather, because, thanks to them, Czechoslovakia began to be a completely socialist country. But the present Soviet bureaucracy can neither accept free critical dialogue with the State, nor that the State be altered under the pressure of increasing popular initiatives. The Czech workers, students and intellectuals showed that, in a country of complete collective structuration, the critical and libertarian word is a practical need; otherwise the social groups within socialism cannot communicate, understand each other, and practice democracy at all levels, those of the State, work, thought, and representation. Without freedom of words in socialism, the

117

bureaucracy cannot know or comment on the initiatives of a communist working class, and vice versa. When, in December 1968, Julio Cortázar, Gabriel García Márquez and I visited Czechoslovakia, we were able to realize the profound need for total democracy in that country and for the precise and free function of words in a system that, for the first time, was about to fulfill the great dream of Marxism. That in the name of Communism, the Russian bureaucracy and army had tried to murder that dream, is a crime and a tragedy.

C. Wright Mills once said to us that the fate of writers in certain Latin American countries seemed enviable to him. Mills's fate, we mustn't forget, was tragic and exemplary: the last writer persecuted by the witchhunters of the fifties, his life and death were the bridge to present-day intellectual dissent in America. But in 1960, when he visited the School of Political Science at the University of Mexico, Mills was still far—and nevertheless, so close—from his meeting with Cuba that was to change his life and bring down upon his always clear head and weak heart all the furies of the State Department, the House of Representatives Committee on Un-American Activities and a cowardly academic community incapable of defending its best men. When the answer to words—Mills said then—is prison and perhaps death, this means that what is said and written counts. On the other hand, in the United States of that era, ruled by what Mills called "the cheerful robots," the dissenting writer ran the danger of becoming a TV star.

In Latin America, a long time before the invention of television, reality was already camouflaged by a false language. The Renaissance language of the conquest hides the Medieval marrow of the colonizing enterprise, like that of the Laws of the Indies, the Encomienda exploitation. The enlightened language of the Independence conceals the feudal permanence, and the positivist language of nineteenth-century liberalism, the sell-out to financial imperialism. The "liberal" language of the Alliance for Progress, finally, disguises the restructuralization of Latin America in accordance with the nature of servitude required by the neocapitalist societies. It is not necessary to talk about Mexico; the language of the revolution covers up the realities of the counterrevolution. But in each case, the origin of the deceit is the same: a concept of the world as a vertical, hierarchical order, with options and sanctions of a religious nature safely transferred to social and intellectual life. Perhaps, in the beginning, the language which translated that mental attitude was not lacking in magnificence; it was the language of conquerors, missionaries and liberators. In its present degradation, it's the jargon of corny orators, semiliterate politicians, public relations men, coarse colonels and pathological bureaucrats carried, by the miracle of our weakness and carelessness, to power. The presence of embryonic modes of consumption in some great Latin American cities has duplicated this phenomenon; masters of the false language of underdevelopment, we are also imitators of the false language of development.

The corruption of the Latin American language is such that an act of true language is in itself revolutionary. In Latin America, as in no other part of the world, every authentic writer puts complacent certitudes in crisis because he stirs the roots of something that came before them: an untouched, uncreated language. Language, for good or bad, possesses all of us. The writer is simply more possessed by language and this extreme possession forces language to unfold itself, without losing its unity, in a collective and an individual mirror. The writer and the word are the permanent intersection, the crossroads of language. Through the writer and words, talk becomes speech and speech language; but, also, the system of language turns into event and event into process. In this way, literature insures the vital circulation which structure requires so as not to become petrified and which change needs to become conscious of itself. Both movements again unite into one to affirm in language the validity of all levels of the real.

This function, the most obvious but also the most complex of literature, is possible with particular intensity in Spanish America because our true language (that of which Darío and Neruda, Reyes and Paz, Borges and Huidobro, Vallejo and Lezama Lima, Cortázar and Carpentier have had a glimpse) is in the process of

119

being discovered and created; and, in the very act of its discovery and creation, is putting in check revolutionarily a whole economic, political and social structure founded on a vertically false language. To write on Latin America, from Latin America, for Latin America, to be a witness of Latin America in action or in language is now, will be more and more, a revolutionary fact. Our societies don't want witnesses. They don't want critics. And each writer, like each revolutionary, is in some way that: a man who sees, hears, imagines and says; a man who denies that we live in the best of worlds.

One of the theses of the reactionary technocracy disguised as "progress" is that the writer is a kind of dinosaur in modern societies: an archaeological being whose reason for being has been snatched from him by the public and private articulation of the mass means of communication and by the electronic revolution in which the message is identical to the messenger, the computer.

In Latin America we lack technology. But we also lack information, in the European or American sense of the word. We lack means of social expression. We don't have real parliaments, real unions, real political parties. And the movies, television, radio, are instruments of the most despicable mercantilism.

Faced with this situation, the writer in our countries is not immune to certain challenges. His answer, perhaps, is destined to failure; his victory, it is true, may be insignificant. But these are not valid reasons for indifference or discouragement. We have already indicated some of the traditional challenges for our literature; our history has been more imaginative than our fiction; the writer has had to compete with mountains, rivers, jungles, deserts of superhuman dimensions. How can we invent more fantastical characters than Cortes and Pizarro, more sinister than Santa Anna or Rosas, more tragicomic than Trujillo or Batista? Re-invent history, tear it from the epic and transform it into personality, humor, language, myth: save the Latin Americans from abstraction and place them in the human kingdom of the accidental, variety, impurity: only the writer, in Latin America, can do this.

But if these have been the traditional challenges, the new menaces seem even more terrible. In what kind of society will Latin American literature be produced in the future? The signs are disquieting. Midway between feudalism and the consumer society, in both cases we continue to live in colonialism; if we are not always backward societies, in any case we are deformed societies. The world politics of power and the division of spheres of influence constitute an enormous obstacle for new social revolutions; a second Cuba would upset the world balance of power and would be actively crushed by the United States and passively abandoned by the Soviet Union. The Kennedy road to bourgeois reform has failed because, naïve and hypocritical at the same time, it couldn't subscribe to the transformation of the most anachronistic and most oppressive structures of Latin America without threatening the traditional interests of imperialism in our lands. Perhaps the immediate sad future of Latin America will be fascist populism, dictatorship of Peronist lineage capable of realizing some reforms in exchange for the suppression of the revolutionary impulse and public freedom.

But a much graver perspective exists: as the abyss between the geometric development of the technocratic world and the arithmetic development of our ancillary societies grows larger, Latin America becomes an *expendable* world for imperialism. Traditionally, we have been exploited countries. Soon we won't even be that; it won't be necessary to exploit us, because technology will have been able to—in great measure, it can already—substitute monoproductive offerings. Will we be then a vast continent of beggars? Will ours be the outstretched hand waiting for the crumbs of American, European and Soviet charity? Will we be the India of the western hemisphere? Will our economy be a simple fiction maintained by pure philanthropy? Or will we be capable of putting our own houses in order, of profoundly reviewing the notion of "progress" and of offering our own selves hard but viable roads, modest but sure, in any case united in the faint hope the modern world grants us? And what will be the sense, the content, the form, the demands of our literature in such a world? What

121

will we do with our words? Whose friends and whose enemies will they be?

I have insisted, in these pages, on the breakdown of the traditional insularity of our novel. Does what I have just noted go along with this thesis? I think so. The end of Latin American regionalism coincides with the end of European universalism; we are all central in the same measure that we are all eccentric. A British nuclear physicist is like a native tzotzil peasant in that both have been marginalized by the unsurpassable astronomic advance of American technology; both are ignorant—the Mexican peasant totally, the British physicist to a great extent—of the secrets which make possible a lunar landing. But both represent and centralize the aspirations that cannot be fulfilled by simple technology. That unsurpassable character of the technological vanguard forces us to review our notions about "progress" and conclude that what passes for such today—the American model—is not, will no longer be, will never be—like Tantalus' water and fruit—ours. In the impossible race toward an impossible mirage, even our language becomes expendable; Spanish will not be the tongue of that "progress"; in its presence, our language is just one more mountain of junk on the edge of the superhighway, a cemetery of obsolete automobiles.

But if we Spanish Americans are capable of creating our own model of progress, then our language will be the only vehicle capable of giving form, of proposing aims, of establishing priorities, of elaborating criticism for a certain life style, of saying all that cannot be said any other way. I believe that in Spanish America novels are being written and will go on being written so that, in the moment of achieving that consciousness, we can count on the indispensable weapons to drink the water and eat the fruit of our true identity. Then those works, those Lost Steps, those Hopscotches, those One Hundred Years of Solitude, those Green Houses, those Marks of Identity, those Gardens of Forking Paths, those Labyrinths of Solitude, those General Cantos, will appear as "the nameless mythologies . . . anticipation of our future."

122   *translated by Suzanne Jill Levine*

II
REREADINGS

Melville,
or
water consciousness
& its madness:
a fragment from
a work-in-progress

CARL OGLESBY

Imagine that these are again times of magic & captivity.

Imagine that it is once again the moment at which the young scholar at last panics and overpowers old Ahab for the false prophet he always seemed to be, underneath it all, who tumbling helter-skelter one day with his glum semi-hostage crew was killed forever like a blithering stovepipe madman by some disinterestedly passionate white snake.

Thus will chilly Elizabeth's Herman establish the first of industrial America's epics of concealed political despair. "Perhaps it is not going to work," he seems to be saying." *Are there not too many victims?* "Perhaps it is better this way," he seems to murmur. Lovers, brothers, clergy and fellow crewman, the pit photographer who hustles both sides equally, and handsome Queequeg too. Even the Compromise of 1850 will become the victim of ancient history. The ship itself—right over the edge. Everything could go:

1850. What is going to be left of human innocence if the great white Moby is provoked so close to the edge?

Yet what is this *climax* all about? White whale smites black whaling boat after long evasive action fails. White water on the high seas, careening flukes, stove bows, cracked yards: it may make sense, but it is not now a convincing political method. The metaphor sinks the craft it meant to float. Moby must be dead by now of some long ago infected harpoon scratch, and *Pequod's* daughters include a high-speed diesel-driven catcher-killer boat equipped with sonic detection and harassment equipment and bearing grenade-tipped cannon-fired harpoons rigged to explode well within the body of the whale, say an exhausted mother sperm or a big blue; then another sister to round up & buoy-mark the kill; finally the huge factory ship in which a few minutes' expert butchery chops, saws, tears, gouges, peels, strips, boils, and altogether reduces Leviathan to so much cat food and imitation butter.

On the principle that the kill must be eaten lest it self-resurrect, I assume that Melville very well knew who was crucifying whom, and that the jolly captain, the merry crew, the plucky ship, the fabled port, the storied sea, star Moby and the rest make up together Melville's mid-century estimate of the republic's position, bearing and velocity.

Recall, he composes this one a rough decade before the Civil War and at the time of the 1846 campaign against Mexico and thru the doomed Compromise of 1850. Was the very idea of a socially unified "free republic" not a tragic illusion? In the seamen's taverns of Boston and the New York proletarian saloons, who talked of honest, lasting work, calm weather and balmy skies?

In brief, it was in a season much like the apple of our own current deliberations that our abiding contemporary Melville posed in effect the following question: "Given these historical origins and social sources, these current grounds of spirit and pathways of hope, how might we secure the faith that our imperial-minded republic, unlike its ancient homologues, will commit its energies in immense genocidal gulps at the expense, one time or another, of all the major colors, types and varieties of humankind, then still find somewhere in a forgotten secret pocket the residual last-second innocence needed to fight off the final and most disastrous temptations of empire, those of a doomed defense of a cause deemed both necessary and unworthy?"

So with a subdued Melville, I ask: Given some broad estimate of the scale, tempo & rhythm at which protoimperial systems condense out and acquire historical outline and social architecture, then swell and grow fevered, finally either to hang suspended a moment before a sometimes luminously sweeping descent, or else to burst all at once and splash blood everywhere, leaving little behind besides shards, cripples, and memories that everyone who survives them pants to forget: given these choices, what is the political utility of the concept *anti-imperialism?*

Ahab

In any event, Ahab's vocation and avocation are at least all combined in the mouth of the whale. There, as a figure symbolic of the sovereignty of practical economic activity (that is, as a Faustist technician), Ahab dies a farcical death. Promptly discarded but then classicalized in the 1920s and '30s as the acute expression of an important American reality, Ahab's death stipulates:

A. The machine system of production is limited practically by the horizon of its culture's symbolic intuition. "Symbolic intuition"—that is, the capacity, linked to faith as a technique of knowledge, to conceptualize what is not yet known in such a way that knowing it will not transform it into something already familiar. Without this function, science (for example) is increasingly a quibble about procedures, and technology will in turn lead industry to the reproduction of artificial truth, false goodness and dry beauty.

B. The symbolic extrication of technical practice from economy, then the subordination of the practical technic (the factory ship, the specialist crew) to a crudely-encoded psychopathic reasoning (kill Moby = victory over nature = man's destiny), constitute together the halves of a characteristically naive American

125

Faustism. But *Moby Dick* is a critical book. It says that a ship or ship of state (a prevailing image in the mid-19th century American debate about progress, expansion and internal social structure) which long tolerates such bold-experimenter captains as fleecy Ahab will come to grief, and that the kingdom which raises its Ahabs to command will come to grief smartly.

C. The technical virtuosity of nature's self-defense is constantly advanced by culture's technical virtuosity of "natural aggression," although its instruments must become in the process even much less selective than discriminating Moby, who strategically needed only Ahab, but who for technical (and probably moral) reasons had to eliminate the whole boat. The Melvillian critique thus poses political questions about the emerging industrial order of culture, but goes beyond the customary progressivist framework, beyond economy to ecology.

Ahab's ghost then becomes a pillar of virtuosic American madness among those other incommunicable moral fugitives who remain still the better guides to the ruins of early American consciousness. Even though the images of its technology seem almost quaint a hundred years after nearly everything else has happened, *Moby Dick* is still a not-yet-contemporary novel of historical speculation. That is because Ahab is a still-developing, still-emerging force in our society, the same as in Melville's time.

Ahab's continuing energy must result in part from his voice's having come so uninventedly upon Melville, as if from his most private and reliable parts. It was not a voice to be swallowed. But what could he have hoped to do with it, this immense, half-strangled eloquence of his most natural private madness?

I am among those who have found this question menacing and have often tried to overcome it with abstract reasoning. I have said: "In this question, we meet another mirror/window surface of the inexhaustible Faustist intelligence." Or I have said: "Far out again with the haunted New England mind, we travel as of yore with mad whiskery seacaptains who plunge sideways off the slab-waterfall edge of the world in tall phosphorescent ships that slowly climb roaring through the nighttime tropical sky. Demons flicker past with scrambled messages for the possessed. Lyrical dragons drift across the blood-red evening sun of a low industrial suburb, singing of baffling triumphs over adversity. Behind so unsolvently situated an Ahab, fields of black miracles surely bloom and dissolve. New England," I let myself mumble, "one of the world's great witcheries once. Can it be as defunct as it seems?" As I recall, the secret Resolution on Genocide was debated here, officially and privately.

The problem which Ahab is set forth in order to solve, or to become the paradigmatic New World demonstration of, the technical problem of *the practical Faustist intelligence,* is this: How is Faust to control madness without defeating it, to possess it without being possessed, yet not give up his functional contempt for what he perfectly understands is only abstract sanity? How can Ahab constantly aim to deflower the virgin whale (strange duty!) without coming to lean so close into the work as to make an absurd duel over into a blunt economic necessity? But then: *Does the Great White Whale economize too?*

"No," shrieks Ahab, who panics one-leggedly on the administrative deck of the industrial *Pequod,* its simple-hearted proletarian crew amazed to see him wheel, pivot, gesticulate and salute so, then stand fascinated. "No," he appears to say, "the Great White Moby does not economize."

For economy implies the social foreknowledge of death. That establishes *whale consciousness* and *whale "culture"* within the *"human"* planet. Ahab is for a moment in danger of being reunited through these two cultures with the whale adversary. For all the overwhelming intimacy of his insults, Ahab has risked everything on the irreducible reality of the human-whale differences: Ahab (and his human economy) define Moby as *non-economic;* hence, as effectively immortal. Then since Moby must not be divine (otherwise Ahab is tricked), he must be evil. But then what could the American imagination be counted on to cull and cling to from a prospect as bleak as these New Bedford winters? Moby must be *evil,* what else? The only other high gunner in the game.

127

Economy, a distressing word. A dull mystery. What is worse? Here, reduced and flung off wildly as I try to make it do some honest ordinary work, the word *economy* is a misfit that changes often and suddenly but within this family of changes: survival, the consciousness of a species predicament, the relation of an individual to a group and a groundbase, of base to group, of culture to nature (of tune to chord) . . . thence to the question: What is the distance, and how is it measured, between the base of the species experience (base: oxygen-nitrogen, salt and stars, etc.) and the more-than-structural culture whose needs seem always to come to supersede or to compete with those of the base? The distance: how far away from the fundamental living seed is the death agenda drawn up & published? An approximation might continue: The technology that hears the whales singing their enchanted dirges is financed by the harpoon.

Thus, the technical problem of the Faustist intelligence remains that of overheating sanity without evaporating it, and yet not to curtail its imperious hostility for madness and sanity alike, two conceptions of limit; still constantly moreover to be on watch for the Whale's Far Misty Breath, to respect the Whale's Magic Tooth, but not to live forever ignorant of those powerful flukes which can only be understood by those who have already come too close. Politics.

Somewhere in the floorbottom of the sea—for so it is told still today—there is a lighted window. Through it one can see other fishes swimming, other keels, other floors and lights, then other windows and, through them, other mirrors. The Faustist always swims alone because the Faustist wants to commune with manta rays on strictly human terms. This is crazy. But the *Pequod's* crewmen are not alone in the boat with this Ahab. Consider the brilliance which academic criticism organized in the defense of Ahab, hoisting the old salt aloft myth-fashion from the *Pequod's* remains, then casting the shadow of his lunatic meanings on the whale he would not even allow to be an *economic* victim, a consciousness within a culture. Ahab loses, but narrowly. Meanwhile, the national-industrial pursuit of Moby has not been concluded.

Like Ahab on the high seas, pounding and pounding, the Faustist technician of today need only accept the solitude he may actually have been seeking. Accepting it, he inherits the earth. There is no undersea window that is not his for the breaking, and no mirror in which he will not find his confusions reversed, see his confessions praised & his prayers replied to, rejected but not refuted.

Melville

Melville too seems to have found a madness he can live with. The energetic merriment he lavishes so freely upon his portentous despair passages may imply that in him the pleasure of self-affirming madness had surpassed ecstasy already and was active now in behalf of an effort of self-repossession. In other words: When he at last fully consented to it and attempted a recomprehension of it on its own special terms, his fearful insanity was free to develop its own interests. Thus, it reintroduced the conception of *selfhood* as a purpose and *sanity* as a practical method.

Still, however, the problem is to see what is the result of Ahab unfettered when he is exposed in the free and excited state to the image of a languid, disinterested albino sperm of some 60 feet and 40 landsman's tons gliding past peacefully on the other side of the undersea window: so fine a peace, so fragile an atmosphere. Comes raving Ahab to burst the mirror through again. We critics flash our tiny windows at him as if doomed to pursue explainingly in crazy disarray no matter where Moby makes Ahab try to live. No wonder we too come to hate as the whale hates, scarcely deigning to conceal a sort of stymied metaphysical amusement for the doughty crew's plight once Moby completes his magic circles and restores peace to the ocean again. For we too are the sad proles of industrial culture & must take our masters' weary allegories as they come, exposing one and then another to their exasperatingly thin fortunes. Who dares blame us, when the proletarian can only escape his destiny by means of shipwreck, and when the stinking-with-spider-piss belowdecks of your standard operational banana galleon will still blow the stovepipes out of a normal man's character in about a few yards flat?

Yet Ahab could not have been a jolly deck captain Jonah either, happily scrubbing the oceans down from the throne-like blowhole of that hardly credible whale. That choice never came up with Ahab. He and Moby were on the outs from the first.

Contradiction—madness—therefore constantly relaunches itself against these high seas. It is already the 19th century—late for European civilization—which has decided to resume, in what its official philosophy still calls the "new world," the absurd struggle of maniacal innocence against speechless death. Melville's premonitions as to the results when some Ahab finally will return in triumph are not in the public domain and have not been straightforwardly discussed. But picture the technical, craftsmanly problem he has to face in that alternative, rejected ending: the one in which he will have to describe, finally, the face and sound of Ahab when his high foundry iron harpoon, enchanted as it has been, starts churning and churning in Moby's enormous heart, and the *Pequod* floats home triumphantly in a mask of satisfaction. In this case, Ahab himself escapes to tell thee the precious story, and Ishmael is the one who must drown.

Ishmael

Ishmael serves Melville's fascination with Ahab without disclosing much about Ahab's actual resources. Is Ahab only *too early?* He practically volunteers his death. His stranglehold on Melville is repeated in Melville's stranglehold on him. He doesn't return. He is dead at sea, lashed to the hump of a whale with lots of time. Melville snares himself too when he omits the story of Ahab's return to New Bedford, Boston, the capital of the torn republic 10 years before the Civil War.

Given Ahab's virtual suicide, Ishmael is never forced even to consider making a choice between Ahab and Moby, does not even begin to ask himself what practical meaning such a choice might have. Since Melville guarantees Ishmael's survival, Ishmael is presumably allowed to swirl away with Ahab into the last shattering consequences of this maritime Faust's reasoning. But since Ishmael only implicitly presupposes the high moral satisfaction of Moby's disdain, since in other words Ishmael must have come to regard himself as *inescapably* trapped inside a demented culture—a mad prisoner of the *Pequod*—what follows is that Ahab must be forcibly counter-explained, or mystified. And so he is. Ishmael, whose position is in fact the compromised one, presents Ahab bluntly with only the feeblest token analysis of his derangement: something about revenge for the wound— maybe the wound of history, maybe of cosmic indifference to humankind, maybe the wound of being itself: the muttering is thick & fast & you never entirely get the sovereign gist of a chapter like the celebrated "Whiteness of the Whale"—which is *pure mystification*.

Taken all together, indeed, Ishmael's full-orchestra reflections on the origin and velocity of Ahab's alleged madness are indubitable masterpieces, but they are masterpieces of the private arts of concealment more than of confrontation; more of evasion than struggle.

Ahab

Certainly Ahab is not turned around and around beneath our eyes. He is hurled upon us. We are plunged across his high-speed incoherence. Melville is dimly still visible, behind the sapphires of this plunging national catastrophe, flashing every mumbo-jumbo magic sign his sailoring among native peoples taught him, hoping to communicate. But at the same time Melville never allows Ishmael to speak of Ahab behind his back, and finally the only images of Ahab that crystallize fully are Ahab's own: the words to be charmed by, the poses to be awed by, then the action of the chase considered as a sequence of intensifyingly physical & concrete gestures.

But by accidents of birth & experience, a few farmers come to think that Ahab has no private mind at all. At least we all see that the solitary passionate struggle around grave mysterious issues that plunge to the central mirror-orifice of being is conducted foolishly and for other eyes. Ahab dies with less selfhood even than he lived with, someone with nothing to do—and who consequently does not know how to harness his madness. In short, an

131

easy adversary when the showdown he has exhausted himself to provoke finally shapes up, and Moby begins to swim with a different rhythm, then begins that broad, mountingly accelerated circling turn (so lovely, so redemptive!) that brings the sorry-looking squat satanic *Pequod* broadside to his simple, brief determination. With all his dreaming of violent metaphysical collision, it seems Ahab had left off the craft of whaling. Did Ahab think Poseidon would let a peg-legged freak from an offshoot colony of basic mistakes and useless errors simply rip away his main current whale with no more weighty a magic than that? Faust should be more professional. Think what don Juan de los Yapuis could have taught Ahab about whaling for magic animals! Far off the path of any sorcery, Ahab's intelligence is inactive or indeed defective, most disappointingly in what was given out to be its main trump suit, the technological side of Faustist nihilism.

Queequeg

It is true, I think, that Melville's characters think more and better than other characters in American fiction. Still, the American Parnassus does not know how to keep fiction distinct as art unless fiction produces *meanings instead of understandings*. The American esthetic has always been at peace about this: that if thought does appear within the artwork, then at least its status must constantly be resolved to that of a *mode of gesture among other modes of gesture* . . . This is because the most natural, basic, and indeed practically invisible epistemological assumption of American novelists, dramatists, critics, and politicians is that perception differs from and is independent of thought, while thought remains imprisoned in particulars which finally obliterate it . . . (Action "more basic than" thought, etc . . .) So that when thought does come to American fiction, it is encouraged to speak mainly through pseudo-action, i.e., *actions which are present only to symbolize what they stand for.* But in novel writing as well as in politics, *it is false to make gestures that only symbolize what they stand for.* Style thereupon falls back into a crafty stylistic crouch which the young well-provisioned adventurer critic (who holds his own madness at such a distance and in such low esteem) will hardly ever fail to recognize as *mythic* or *neomythic* or some such killer thing. Then a cloudy veil of soothing symbols will close again like the great shroud of the sea, a luminously impenetrable metaphor. Queequeg's vast silence is lost.

Starbuck

America's resulting fascination with myth (the counterweight to its fascination with technique) also seemed a confirmation of the verdict of the ages to the effect that what lasts more than Tolstoy is Homer. Apart from talent (a trifle) the reasons must be a) Homer didn't give a clear shit for the *presentation* of reality, and b) Homer didn't give another clear shit for the *interpretation* of reality. Which is to say the same thing two ways, twice backwards.

Soundly I think choosing to defend our often embarrassing modern predicaments (so disappointing in Homer's blind eyes, were he watching), we assert a belief to the effect that for Homer reality was interpreted to begin with, *before interpretation,* so to speak. And furthermore: How can it not be more difficult to endure the nonexistence than the displeasure of the gods? (The voice of flagging modernism.) Indeed, whole boulevards of gods were held to be sailing abroad in those days. The humans were this and that; so were the gods, who in aggregate summed and recapitulated the substance of human experience. Something two-way was going on and people didn't have to carry more than they believed they could bear of the burden of keeping reality real.

We know how this lovely relationship between light and shadow dissolved. What night could ever dawn again? We know how an immense grim cloud appeared on Europe's horizon one day, then drooped and stayed, and how the days continued to grow darker and the winters kept advancing, and how all the advanced architects finally decided humanity was trapped in the buried cellars of what was to be seen shortly as the incredible ancient ruins of Hegel's system. For ages no one could see or develop the

133

remarkable tourist opportunities these ruins afforded. One day people of all nations would prowl the slopes & loops of that fine abandoned logic just as we swarmers of today pant up & down the Pyramids of Toot wondering where we are, what we think we're doing & looking at. Everyone cursed but in vain, without satisfaction, and meandered through long dialectical riddles & tunnels. They gave their cellars names like Florence and Venice, then Rome and afterwards Paris, then Berlin and London, then Moscow and Washington. "Where does the Renaissance lead today?" newsmakers and analysts muttered in cellars the world over, peering sometimes at a ceiling which everyone had long before desperately agreed to call a sky—the agreement itself long forgotten, long held to have been a false historian's dismal, stupid hoax. Peking moved silently meanwhile into Pisces.

So until good times come back (and will they not?), Homer may as well have been some altogether different sort of animal, say a whale. My clarifications at least never resulted in Odysseus, or even leaned that way. I concluded and far too long believed that Ahab (a Faustist, not a Faustian) must be *like* Faust. No. That is merely what Ahab would like you to believe. You try. An act of animal friendship. Then you see how it stinks. Ahab is not the source of whatever reasoning may attach to this only seemingly "rebellious" act. Ahab is as empty and silent as stupid Iago. Trying to seem content to let the truth speak for itself, he will never let it be; and he gives you his madness in gestures which he is powerless to explain. With these Iagos, upon whom so much compassionate fellow-villainy is heaped, I was never at all sure we saw even suffering in the same place, in the same pair of eyes. What could Iago tell you about Moby, or Ahab of Desdemona? Each one intends only to leave his victim behind, a work of art. Who wants to say, then, what were the features of the world in which Iago would have pronounced himself happy & satisfied and his life's work over and his soul at peace? Could Moby have swum contentedly too, in Iago's contentment? Could Desdemona have accepted Ahab's confession? Does he think it is she who needs a specific world-historical reality with a dead white whale awash constantly on its beaches besides everything else, all the dead soldiers?

Poor Starbuck! Through whom all the good angels mobbed a worse than devil's madness with omens & warning riddles, who saw everything in advance & yet could not jump bail, who constantly found obedience as plain as good and as good as true, and for whom the fatal split between the system and the law still left no space for escape or other architectural styles. Poor Starbuck, so constant in his sorrowing liberalism there is neither remorse besides drowning nor angry gesture short of suicide. So reliable you could not trust him. "I misdoubt me that I disobey my God in obeying him!" Thus soliloquizes stouthearted Starbuck, bucksailing nigh straight on the starry wind's eye on the third day of the Vietnam war, and all the while stands coiling the new-hauled mainbrace upon the rail.

Faustism Described

Yet Ahab is reminiscent of a grandeur dissolving even then, that of Old World Faustism, the magical-technical attempt to know & then to alter the secret nature or inner structure of reality, to change thus the surface in which humanity experiences its subjectivity, its culture, its nature, and its cosmos. It seems possible to hope for a principled blasphemy as long as you can dissemble a technical-economic operation against a whale as a magical-metaphysical operation against cosmic uncertainty & the resulting disquietude of spirit. But when that illusion finds its way into the curious jaws of Moby and its gunwales get refuted, it's hard to see how philosophy can still try to look angry and act aroused. Was it not aboard that boat?

Hence the problem: "Are the logics of Faust's desire for knowledge and Ahab's for control two logics or many, if not one, and if seldom then cognate or what? Dissonant? Incommensurable? How is this to be handled? For sooner or later, someone will always think of saying, "If only one of us can truly know what eternity can do, Lord, what follows?"

In that case, what of the *Pequod,* that blunt, speechless ship?

First, it was the main contemporary result, as type, concreta and individual, of the Enlightenment Democracy and all its technical economic revolutions. Second, it comes to us prefitted with the fine magic of being the last command of a major Yankee captain, as flinty and blood-minded as that species came, and to boot a stone lunatic in a grudge fight with a mystified Seagoing Serpent. Third, Devil's Light is cast on its masts and spars. Fourth, even the wind seems to know something funny is going on. And so on.

Yet in the end, *Pequod* has no independent character. It has subtracted its sailing ship's natural & normal charm from the standard ship-to-sailor relationship equations. It no longer knows how to make a sailor treat it like an animal, furry and emotional. Remaining the single most constant voice among all the adventure's voices, it is nonetheless absent from the struggle that destroys it: seemingly. Its persisting keel is what Moby will hear coming and coming until finally he turns. Yet it is not *Pequod* which we consider Moby to have attacked. The target. we understand—even if we think Moby may not, *must* not understand this—is Yankee Ahab the Fishfreak. "*Moby's* Moby Dick," someone muses: the whale's dream of mad whaling captains, of what life means to the captain behind the barb, the blade, the hickory shaft & hempen rope . . . plus whale's intimations of lost Babylonian hanging gardens, lost memories, forgotten desires . . . what whales may make of such things, however wanton their deliberations. Oh, whales, do not think we do not see. We industrials come riding up as thoughtlessly as though we were drifters from a whole other span of dreams. Which appears to be our advantage in the economy of our relationship. We see you and are not seen. Only one of us can define—therefore, redefine—the other.

So there is my song from the *Pequod's* brig.

"If I were a whale, O Wild Powers of the Western World, I should hope to be a Giant Killer Whale, the one the sailors agreed must be the most antihuman ruthless conniving cruel & wise Great Double Giant Shark Serpent Whale of all time, of all ages, of all oceans, for fear of whom no longer shalt thou bathe in salty waters. I'd take these Atomic *Pequods* in my snout and swallow them up with all their restless captains & exasperating, weary, stupid crews, spitting out on some dry place somewhere Ishmael and lovely sweet Queequeg and perhaps the rest of the crew with a stern rebuke. All we can really do, you say, is to foist off light on the blind. I answer: Maybe; I can only do the best I can, trying to sail the *Pequod* backwards out of Moby's eternal wound."

Yet she had a builder, did the *Pequod,* who answered my prayer without having actually heard it, I think:

"You have lost faith with a captain and have called the universe bad names?"

And an owner, of course, who added:

"Surely someone saw that exquisite instrument crushed and dissolved. Baffled crew snuffed out. Sextant lost, compass fouled. And wanted to cry out: 'O Moby, stay thy wanton flukes and brow! Not these sailors in their tool that press against thee! Take old Ahab off & leave thy placid instrument ship alone. Only crazy Ahab haunts thee in particular, the others take no heed of thy race, thy creed, thy color.'"

The Crew

When did I leave Ahab's corner? I started where everyone did: The whale is Evil. Perhaps this happens because bookteachers are overwhelmed by the size of Ahab's penis, which occupies in the presence of John C. Calhoun the narrative-dramatic center of a story culminating in the War of 1845, the conquest of northern Mexico. In other words, Melville is in *Omoo* and *Typee* a radical nativist, in *Redburn* an existentialist, in *White Jacket* a left liberal reformist, in *Mardi* an anti-imperialist, and in the time of the Mexican War a madman. His Frankenstein, a pegleg boatman stalking around in the rainy-winter fog of Nantucket Sound and

137

New Bedford: Ahabian Calhoun† THROUGH WHOM THE NATION'S GENE PRIDE ADVANCES THE CONCEPTION OF A GREGORY PECK, THE RESOLUTELY EUCLIDIAN GEOMETRY HENCEFORTH OF THAT CULTURE'S HISTORICAL SPACE. Since Peck is beautiful, Ahab must be strange. So much for the rule of platonistic psychotrinitarianism.

Finally, we observe: Every *thing* is described so lovingly, every technical process in the reduction of Leviathan is so lovingly described, as if in effect we had been provided an explicit handbook which our adversaries are mentally ill-equipped to visualize or conceive of, much less to understand and appropriately react to. A handbook in the ultimate reduction of not Leviathan-Moby, who transcends Ahab's audacious effort to surmount him and make him answer to his, Ahab's, definitions, and who achieves this transcendence in fact by assuming the characteristics, then, after all, of just such a monstrous adversary as that of fierce lonely Ahab's premonitions. *Moby Dick* is named for one of its two survivors. It is a handbook in the reduction of Leviathan-state.

What else can we make of this barmy crew, which huzzahs its ridiculous way over the waterfall at the edge of worldly reality without a sigh of regret or a tear of rage, barmy to the last briny bit of it? Ishmael, too, fecundating as it were on Queequeg's true luxury-class type of coffin.

1. Ahab's solitude seems resumed & variegated in each of the sailors' lives. They never talk to one another except by feel of hands in the tubvats of the whale's quintessence & life elixir. Moby's life is never discussed from the point of view of the Vietnamese people.

2. Each of them—can we yet find grounds for the exoneration of Queequeg, harpoon extraordinaire to white commercial

† The Biblical Ahab, recall, a minor king who aggresses against his neighbor Naboth, was condemned as a result to an old-age of sackcloth and repentance. In the furious debate that tore the country in the 1840s and '50s around the issues of (imperialist) expansion, (racist) slavery, and infrequently (racist) genocide, the anti-imperialist, abolitionist, peace intellectuals, in their private discussions and their polemics & broadsides equally, established specifically the political analogy between that Biblical Ahab and this "manifest-destiny," pro-slavery Arab from Madagascar, John Whathisname the Fourth or Fifth. So much for history.

interests linked to the would-be killers of red life; of Dagoo, black giant who champions the point first of agriculture, then boxing, now the Combined Military Forces of the enslaver of black people & the single world-historical source of the would-have-been permanent ruinification of black culture; of Tashtego, wherever he's at, and so on . . . ? Each seems, *au contraire,* satisfied to have been offered so exotic & highly-refined a destiny. High Chief Harpoonist on the heaviest killing-system trip of all machine-industrial time.

Were they so crippled & forlorn, the proletarians of the middle 19th century? If they could not altogether have disposed of this presumptively chronic Sailor's Nemesis, the Mad Captain of the Four-Year Adventure Cruise, then why could they not have been shown belowdecks at least once to explain somehow why it is that they are never even going to consider raising the question of loyalty and/or obedience and/or identity (whether personally & freely defined or socially superimposed) and/or responsibility elsewhere to be felt than in their ropes & oars and otherwise expressed than in these childish fevers? Why not a belowdecks plot to ransom safety with a ruse? Ahab only has to snore once and the whole whale can be headed out for Boston as if nonstop, and the merry *Pequod* bounding along under bright billowing & towering sails and fluffy clouds of an Atlantic autumn. He would surely soon know that their eager ahoys and piercing avasts were strange, how very strange. But then . . .

But then one word from an honest Odysseus—any truly homewards-bound man—would long since have been enough. "Captain, do not suppose that you will successfully invest this ship with meanings so counter to its purpose." Not even Douglas MacArthur (of whom more dialectical gossip later) would have argued with Odysseus.

But no. Not the shallowest conception of a collective self-interest, safe in the market of objects & functions. Inseparable from *Pequod* body and soul: having no body save as the technical apparatus of shipboard economic life gave body extension,

139

rationalization & value; having no mind save where the grip mind takes of uses & intentions socially received was sufficiently plausible and/or exhausting and/or enforced with sufficient force as to make the struggle for alternative modes of self-realization seem impossible outside that system's subsystem of rewards, hence of values.

No thoughts of using the machine they live lashed to as an instrument of their own liberation. No thoughts of founding a common take in a sort of general, all-around public sanity for use day in and out.

As for crewmember Ishmael's "survivorship," that turns out to be the luck of the first-person draw (short of floating caskets &c, there's nothing else to do but bring back the narrator—"Who else should survive?" says the novelist in the corner). Ishmael's persistence is never in doubt, because he never had any. His survival is the basis of worship, not its result, in much the same way that Moby's victory is the result, not the basis, of Ahab's defeat. How could he have written, this Melville, "Humanity cannot be saved as humanity, and history cannot be justified from within by historical action"?

This is an old, old slogan. A Mediterranean or West Indian idea which even the scorn of Marx† cannot make me want to surrender. The attempt to impart meaning to history from within history, however unchallengeable its aura of necessity, succeeds for the most part only in historicizing meaning. In other words, succeeds only in changing the creature one by one into a creature of sovereign economy. No doubt the need for this economy is great. But unless politics is more than history instead of the reverse, less, how can some people ever ask other people to die?

---

† As in *The Grundrisse's* pleasantly modernistic reflections: "Is Achilles possible side by side with powder and lead? . . . The Greeks were normal children. The charm their art has for us does not conflict with the primitive character of the social order from which it had sprung. It is rather the product of the latter, and is due rather to the fact that the immature social conditions under which the art arose and under which alone it could appear can never return." (*The Grundrisse,* ed. and trans. by David McLellan [Harper & Row, 1971], pp. 45–46.)

We live in a time of whaleboats that fly faster than fifty whales. They are armed with sleepless sonar for pursuit and an underwater horn said to tear the whale's mind apart, sending it to the surface exhausted to meet the blows of the contemporary grenade-tipped harpoon, fired by cannon from high on the bow. Usually, says one source,

[such a harpoon] kills the whale in about five seconds. Often, however, the struggle between the catcher boat and a frantic whale lasts much longer. The death throes of one whale on record lasted five hours and required nine harpoons. Another whale, struggling to save itself, pulled a ninety-foot catcher boat, with its engines fully reversed, forward at five knots for eight and a half hours. (*The Whale,* based on the work of Dr. Roger S. Payne and accompanying the record *Songs of the Humpback Whale*. CRM Records, Del Mar, California.)

How can so difficult a treatise be faced? "Ahab's iron harpoons churn and churn in the deep heart of Moby Dick. The great whale spouts jets of brilliant scarlet blood. The crew of the whaleboat is drenched in these remarkable profusions, standing to their tasks all scarlet to a man, like a painted tableau. Ahab subsequently exults, and the men of the crew become special figures in the taverns of dockside Liverpool or Aberdeen or Shanghai or New Bedford." Ahab victorious.

Passion and cunning:
the politics of W. B. Yeats

CONOR CRUISE O'BRIEN

1

THE DAY THE NEWS of Yeats's death reached Dublin I was lunching with my mother's sister, Hanna Sheehy Skeffington. Hanna was the widow of Frank Skeffington, pacifist and socialist, who had been murdered on the orders of a British officer, Bowen-Colthurst, in Easter Week 1916. She was not consistently a pacifist; she was an Irish revolutionary; Madame MacBride and Countess Markievicz were among her close political friends, Countess Markievicz being, however, politically the closer. Physically she looked a little like Queen Victoria and—a comparison that would have pleased her better—a little like Krupskaya. Mentally she was extremely and variously alert. Her conversation, when politics were not the theme, was relaxed, humorous and widely tolerant of human eccentricity; when politics were the theme she always spoke very quietly and economically, with a lethal wit and a cutting contempt for 'moderates' and compromisers. Hers was the kind of Irish mind which Yeats

This article is reprinted by permission of the publisher from *In Excited Reverie*, edited by A. N. Jeffares, © 1965 by The Macmillan Co., Ltd.

could call—when he felt it to be on his side—'cold', 'detonating', 'Swiftian', or when—as in this case—it was not on his side, 'bitter', 'abstract', 'fanatical'.[1]

On this day I tried to tell her something of my generation's sense of loss by Yeats's death. I was genuinely moved, a little pompous, discussing a great literary event with my aunt, a well-read woman who loved poetry.

Her large, blue eyes became increasingly blank, almost to the polar expression they took on in controversy. Then she relaxed a little: I was young and meant no harm. She almost audibly did not say several things that occurred to her. She wished, I know, to say something kind; she could not say anything she did not believe to be true. After a pause she spoke:

'Yes', she said, 'he said, 'he was a Link with the Past.'

I had been speaking of the poet; she was thinking of the politician.

At the time I thought this attitude exasperating and even ludicrous. Who cared about Yeats the politician? What mattered was the poetry; the fact that Yeats had been at sea in politics—as I then thought—was irrelevant. Yeats the poet was all-in-all.

This opinion was characteristic of my generation—which is partly why I cite it—and, as that generation is now middle-aged, it is now perhaps the dominant one. On re-reading Yeats's poetry and some of his prose—and reading some of the prose for the first time—I no longer think this opinion quite adequate. I no longer believe Yeats's political activities to have been foolish or fundamentally inconsistent or his political attitudes to be detachable from the rest of his personality, disconnected from action, or irrelevant to his poetry. His politics were, it now seems to me, marked by a considerable degree of inner consistency between thought and action, by a powerful emotional drive, cautious experimentalism in action, and, in expression, extravagances and disengagements which succeeded one another not without calculation and not without reference to the given political conjuncture of the moment.

It is true that warrant—rather too much warrant—can be

143

found in his poetry for the conventional picture of the impractical poet drawn to politics by romantic love and generous emotion, and recoiling ruefully from each political failure to poetry, his proper sphere:

> All things can tempt me from this craft of verse:
> One time it was a woman's face, or worse—
> The seeming needs of my fool-driven land;
> (*1909*)

And again:

> I think it better that in times like these
> A poet's mouth be silent, for in truth
> We have no gift to set a statesman right;
> (*1916*)

And again:

> Dear shadows, now you know it all,
> All the folly of a fight
> With a common wrong or right.
> (*1927*)

And finally:

> I never bade you go
> To Moscow or to Rome.
> Renounce that drudgery,
> Call the Muses home.
> (*1938*)

Such apolitical or anti-political pronouncements, scattered over thirty years of Yeats's writing, represent 'the true Yeats' for three large classes of Yeats's admirers: those who are bored by Irish politics, those who are bored by all politics, and those who are frightened by Yeats's politics. 'We have no gift to set a statesman right' is particularly popular because it sets a neat and memorable dividing line between literature and politics. Yet the poet who wrote it was exercising a political choice: he was refusing to write a war-poem—probably solicited for the cause of the Allies in the First World War, a cause which did not move Yeats. He politely and elegantly refused to be drawn. That the aphorism produced in the process was not, for him, a guiding maxim he was to prove a few months later when he wrote a series of noble war-poems in a cause which did move him, that of Ireland. He who had no gift to set a statesman right was no longer troubled by this disability when he wrote after the executions of the leaders of the 1916 Rebellion:

144

> You say that we should still the land
> Till Germany's overcome;
> But who is there to argue that
> Now Pearse is deaf and dumb?
> And is there logic to outweight
> MacDonagh's bony thumb?

When the Muses came home, they came full of politics; there is a far higher proportion of poems with political themes in the last book than in any other, and the last four poems of all, when there was no longer time for politeness or pretences, carry a burden of politics. Throughout his life as a writer Yeats had abiding, and intensifying, political interests and passions. It is misleading to make him essentially non-political, on the strength of certain disclaimers, refusals and ironies. The fact that General Ludendorff carried out a number of tactical withdrawals did not necessarily make him a pacifist.

This essay is concerned, not primarily with Yeats's 'political philosophy',[2] but with the forms of his actual involvement, at certain critical times, in the political life of his own day. Yeats's biographers have recounted some of his political activities—and in some of what follows I am indebted in particular to the late J. M. Hone's *W. B. Yeats;* Dr. Richard Ellmann's *Yeats, the Man and the Masks;* and Dr. A. N. Jeffares's *W. B. Yeats, Man and Poet.* But a biographer may feel that he cannot—without toppling his book over—give the detail necessary to situate a given action, or inaction, in the political context of its time. In biographies, as in literary histories, we necessarily find, instead of the complexities of actual political conjunctures, a generalized 'political background', lacking the texture and the weight of real politics. It is often assumed, I think, that this does not matter much in the case of a writer like Yeats because his politics, if they existed, were probably rather vague and generalized themselves. In what follows I shall present some reasons for believing that Yeats's politics were less vague than is commonly supposed.

2

At the bottom of it all was the Anglo-Irish predicament. The

145

Irish Protestant stock from which Yeats came was no longer a ruling class but still a superior caste, and thought of itself in this way.[3] When he wrote towards the end of his life of 'the caste system that has saved the intellect of India'[4] he was almost certainly thinking not so much of India as of Ireland. His people were in the habit of looking down on their Catholic neighbors—the majority of those among whom they lived—and this habit Yeats never entirely lost. But when he went to school in England Yeats was to find, as Parnell and others had found, that this distinction had lost much of its validity. Unsophisticated Englishmen—including all the young—made no more distinction between 'Protestant-Irish' and 'Catholic-Irish' than they did between Brahmin and untouchable. The Irish were known by their brogue—which in Yeats's case must have been quite marked at this stage—and they were all comic, inferior and 'mad'[5] (among the sophisticated classes these same categories found gentler nuances: witty, impractical, imaginative). The Irish Protestant thus acquired two basic bits of information: the important thing about him, in relation to Ireland, was that he was a Protestant; in relation to England, that he was an Irishman. This duality was the characteristic feature of the community to which Yeats belonged. 'Everyone I knew well in Sligo', he wrote, 'despised Nationalists and Catholics but all disliked England . . .'[6]

For proud and sensitive natures, exposed at this period to the English view of the Irish, a political reaction was predictable, starting from the premises: 'I, an Irishman, am as good as any Englishman. Ireland is therefore as good as England. Yet England governs herself; Ireland is governed by England. Can this be right?'

Parnell thought not; Yeats's father thought not; Yeats thought not.

It used to be widely assumed in Ireland that Yeats became entangled in politics by Maud Gonne. This is of course wrong; Yeats had been drawn into politics before he ever heard of Maud Gonne, and the most active phases of his political life were to come after he had quarrelled with Maud Gonne. Yeats entered politics

146

under the influence of John O'Leary, the Fenian convict and exile, who returned to Ireland in 1884. Yeats now became what he was to remain all his life—as he was to repeat towards the end—'a nationalist of the school of John O'Leary'.

What was the school of John O'Leary? Its central doctrines were those of classical, uncompromising Irish Republicanism: 'the tone', as O'Leary himself said, 'of Wolfe Tone'—but scarcely less important were certain limitations placed, by O'Leary himself, on the practical application of the doctrine. 'There are things', he used to say, 'that a man ought not to do to save his country'. It was a phrase that Yeats was often to repeat. The 'certain things' included, along with some pleasant personal taboos—'a man ought not to cry in public for his country'—some of practical political importance. The school of John O'Leary withheld its endorsement from parliamentary action, frowned on agrarian agitation, and vehemently condemned acts of individual terrorism.

Now in the eighties these, and no others, were the methods effectively used to weaken the foundations of English rule. The successful application of agrarian ostracism had just given a new word—boycott—to the languages of the world, and the dynamite of the Clan na Gael had reinforced the arguments of Parnell's disciplined parliamentary party so that Englishmen were beginning, for the first time in their lives, to feel that self-government for Ireland was a question within the bounds of practical politics. 'Violence', as William O'Brien so rightly said, 'is the only way of securing a hearing for moderation'. O'Leary had little use for O'Brien's kind of moderation and no use for the kinds of violence O'Brien had in mind. The Dublin Fenians whom O'Leary led— and whom Yeats was to join—spent their time not in causing but in preventing acts of terrorism. Their task, it seems, was to keep an organization in being for the day when a general rising would become a practical possibility. The distant future was to show that their work was not in vain, but in the eighties insurrection seemed—and was—a very remote contingency. In the eighties, the people who were hanged were political and agrarian terrorists; the people who were beaten by the police and put in jail were the 'moderate' agrarian nationalists of the Plan of Campaign. O'Leary's group, shunning alike agrarian action, terrorism and moderation, was left alone by the police.

The school of John O'Leary, then, was in the eighties and nineties extreme but not dangerous. This combination has a natural appeal to two of Yeats's most enduring characteristics: his pride and his prudence. With the power he knew to be in him he had much to be both proud and prudent about. The prudent Yeats, the sound calculator of chances, is as it seems the manager of the poet. A poet, if he is to survive long enough to be recognized as a great poet, has need of such a manager. The poet is drawn to nationalism by a deep sense of injured dignity and by a hatred proportionate to his power: hatred always strong in him, and (with pride) the strongest of his political emotions. 'There are moments', he wrote, 'when hatred [of England in the context] poisons my life and I accuse myself of effeminacy because I have not given it adequate expression'.[7] Yeats the manager was always there to see that he gave it just the right degree of expression for any given time. One can imagine him saying to the poet trembling on the verge of national politics: 'Oh well, if you must you must, but for God's sake don't do anything—like getting jailed or killed —that would stop your poetry. I'll tell you what—I'll arrange an introduction to John O'Leary.'

Yet there were some things no manager could have arranged. How could it come about that the extremist politician most likely to attract the manager, should also have the magnificence—in moral stature, in style of speech and in personal appearance—which could hold the poet:

Beautiful lofty things: O'Leary's noble head;

Or what manager could have arranged that the young woman, ablaze with politics,[8] who called on him, with an introduction from the O'Leary's, on that fateful winter day in 1889 should be the most beautiful woman of her time:

Pallas Athene in that straight back and arrogant head:
All the Olympians; a thing never known again.

148

One has to remind oneself that O'Leary and Maud Gonne were historical figures and not simply invented by Yeats, like Michael Robartes and Owen Aherne:

As if some ballad-singer had sung it all.

Yeats's long and splendidly unhappy relation to Maud Gonne had, of course, profound effects on his life and work but I do not find that it had any proportionate effect, at least directly, on his political alignment. It is true that it was after he met her—and probably at her instance—that he actually joined the Fenian brotherhood, but they were O'Leary's Fenians, he was already closely associated with them, and joining them committed him, as we have seen, to little of practical consequence.[9] There was also a sound practical argument for going with the Fenians. 'In this country', O'Leary had told him, 'a man must have upon his side the Church or the Fenians, and you will never have the Church.'[10]

His letters, just after he first met Maud Gonne, do show some trace of her specific influence. He wrote to Katharine Tynan, about the murder in America of a supposed informer by members of the Clan na Gael: 'He seems to have been a great rascal. It was really a very becoming thing to remove him . . . a Spy has no rights'.[11] These ferocious sentiments are definitely not 'school of John O'Leary'; they are characteristic of Maud Gonne, whom Yeats had met six months before. The difference was that Maud Gonne perhaps meant them, and might conceivably have acted on them;[12] Yeats probably did not mean them and certainly would not have acted on them. His letter went on: 'There! You will be angry with me for all these dreadful sentiments. I may think the other way tomorrow.'

In practice, where Maud Gonne differed from O'Leary—as she did in favoring agrarian agitation—Yeats does not seem to have followed her, although he did intercede for her with O'Leary.[13]

Maud Gonne did not affect Yeats's political course at this time so profoundly as is usually assumed. What did affect it were events which took place two to three years later—the fall and death of Parnell.

149

3

'The modern literature of Ireland', Yeats told the Swedish Academy in 1925, 'and indeed all that stir of thought which prepared for the Anglo-Irish war, began when Parnell fell from power in 1891. A disillusioned and embittered Ireland turned from parliamentary politics; an event was conceived and the race began, as I think, to be troubled by that event's long gestation.'[14]

Elsewhere he speaks of Four Bells, 'four deep tragic notes' in Irish history, the first being the war that ended in the Flight of the Earls (1603), the fourth being the death of Parnell in 1891.

'I heard the first note of the Fourth Bell forty years ago on a stormy October morning. I had gone to Kingston [*sic*] Pier to meet the Mail Boat that arrived about 6 a.m. I was expecting a friend, but met what I thought much less of at the time, the body of Parnell.'[15]

The friend was, of course, Maud Gonne, who came over on the boat that brought Parnell's body back to Ireland.

Few historians, I think, would challenge Yeats's estimate, in his Swedish address, of the impact of Parnell's fall and death, or his summary account of a process in which he himself played an important part. His historical sense was keen, as his political sense also was. For he not only saw in retrospect the crucial importance of the fall and death of Parnell. He saw it *at the time,* immediately, and he saw in it his opportunity and took that opportunity. He had not been a follower of Parnell's before his fall—the 'school of John O'Leary' forbade it, and his father's influence was also against it[16]—and he does not seem to have become intensely interested in Parnell until the moment of his fall. Since, in later life, he made Parnell a symbol, almost a god indeed, in whose name he as priest excommunicated prominent public figures of the day; it is interesting that in his letters of the time there is no note of grief at his fall or even at his death. The first note is one of rather gleeful excitement at an event and an opportunity; the creation of a vacuum. 'This Parnell business', he wrote to O'Leary after the divorce case, 'is most exciting. Hope he will hold on. As it is he has driven up into dust and vacuum no end of insincerities. The whole matter of Irish politics will be the better of it'.[17] In a later letter to O'Leary Yeats expresses an optimism, which sounds a little artificial, about Parnell's chances and gives some not entirely random reasons for being on Parnell's side: the priests and the 'Sullivan gang' were on the other side. Then Parnell died. Yeats wrote a poem about him on that day for the press that evening. The poem was called 'Mourn and Then Onward'.[18] It concluded:

> Mourn—and then onward, there is no returning
> He guides ye from the tomb;
> His memory now is a tall pillar, burning
> Before us in the gloom!

There is not much gloom in the covering letter with which the poet sent this dirge to his sister:

I send you a copy of United Ireland with a poem of mine on Parnell written on the day he died to be in time for the press that evening. It has been a success.

The Funeral [which Yeats did not attend] is just over. The people are breathing fire and slaughter. The wreaths have such inscriptions as 'Murdered by the Priests' and a number of Wexford men were heard by a man I know promising to remove a Bishop and some priests before next Sunday. Tomorrow will bring them cooler heads I doubt not.[19]

Yeats, according to Dr. Ellmann, 'had grasped instinctively that the time had come for him to act'. The word 'instinctively' may be misleading. Yeats in later life, when he had no more use, for the moment, for nationalist political activity, used to write as if his political activity at this time had been a sad mistake, committed mainly because of his passion for Maud Gonne. Critics and biographers have tended to follow him in exaggerating, as I believe, the importance of the Gonne factor in his politics. This influences presentation: thus Dr. Ellmann reserves the entrance of Maud Gonne into his narrative for the moment of Parnell's death, although the natural moment to have brought her in would, one would have thought, have been the time at which Yeats first met her and fell in love with her, almost three years before. Keeping her back intensifies the drama but blurs the politics. It helps to perpetuate Yeats's myth of himself as 'a foolish passionate man', whereas the weight of the evidence suggests that he was something much more interesting: a cunning passionate

151

man.[20] In this case the cunning was more in evidence than the passion. Yeats was still almost unknown. He had been glad to get space, through O'Leary's influence, in a paper like *The Gael*—the organ of the Gaelic Athletic Association—and was sometimes in danger of being squeezed out by a big football-match. Now he had an opportunity of reaching, with powerful impact, at a time of maximum national emotion, the widest possible Irish audience. *United Ireland* was Parnell's last paper and Irish people everywhere must have fought for copies of its issue of 10 October, to see what it had to say about the death of the Chief. And they found there the poem and the name of W. B. Yeats. There can have been few—and hardly any on the Parnellite side—who were not more moved by 'Mourn and Then Onward' than Yeats was. A name almost unknown the day before became known to most of Ireland overnight.

I can see no reason to suppose that, in writing this poem and above all in getting it to the press with the necessary celerity, Yeats was just reacting instinctively or trying to please Maud Gonne. He had an eye for an opportunity—a politician's eye, and a politician's sense of timing.[21]

Some will perhaps find offensive the suggestion that Yeats used Parnell's coffin for a platform. Parnell, who made his own name out of the Manchester Martyrs, would have approved Yeats. Parnell knew, as Pearse knew, by Rossa's grave, that in Ireland there is no better platform than a hero's coffin.

Yeats had seen Parnell, after consolidating his Irish fief, impose himself on the politics of the United Kingdom. 'Mourn and Then Onward' was not exactly a bid for the mantle of Parnell—a garment which was just then, as Yeats well knew, being thoroughly torn in pieces—but may reasonably be interpreted as an attempt, by bringing poetry into the political vacuum left by Parnell's death, to become as a poet something like what Parnell had been in politics: a virtual dictator in Ireland: a power, and sometimes an arbiter, in England. If so, it was not a wild aim, and Yeats in large measure made it good. Not that power, in itself, was the object as it is for the man who is primarily a politician, but that the power already in him needed living-space. The poet Yeats wanted elbow-room and an audience, and the politician Yeats saw to it that he got them.

Ireland was now, as he said, 'like wax' and he set about shaping it. In later years—after the fighting had begun—the phrase 'the litherary side of the Movement' came to be used derisively, but in the nineties and in the early years of the new century 'the litherary side of the Movement' was the only side that was moving, and its leader was Yeats. In helping to found the Irish Literary Society in London and the National Literary Society in Dublin, and the theatre which later became the Abbey Theatre, the politician Yeats was about the poet's business, using for the ends of poetry the political energy diverted by the fall of Parnell. Later, he liked to talk as if he had been duped, and wrote bitterly of evenings spent with 'some small organizer' pouring his third glass of whisky into the spittoon.[22] One may feel that, if anyone was duped, it was more likely to be the unfortunate 'small organizer' than Yeats, the big organizer. But there is no need to speak of dupes at all; both Yeats and the 'small organizer' were serv-ing, in their different ways, the dignity of the nation to which they both belonged. For the small organizer the end was a political one, and poetry a means; for Yeats the end was a poetic one, and the means political. They had to part in the end but there is no need now to regret, or to quarrel over, the road they travelled together.

4

They parted, of course, in 1903, with the marriage of Maud Gonne to Major John MacBride. Nature, deferential to the poet, made this 'the year of the big wind' in which great trees blew down all over Ireland, including Lady Gregory's park at Coole. It was the great turning point in Yeats's life, in politics as well as in other ways. The fact that he broke—for a time and in a way—with Irish politics after Maud Gonne's marriage has naturally contributed to the romantic belief, encouraged by himself, that his politics were 'just Maud Gonne'. The evidence does not warrant this

153

conclusion. As we have seen he had made his political choice before he met Maud Gonne, and his entry into effective politics dates, not from his meeting with Maud Gonne, but from the political opportunity created by the fall of Parnell. The most that can be said of Maud Gonne—politically—is that she deepened his political involvement, and probably kept him politically involved for some time after he would otherwise have quit. For her he had written *Cathleen ni Houlihan,* and she had played the part so that a member of the audience could write this: 'The effect of *Cathleen ni Houlihan* on me was that I went home asking myself if such plays should be produced unless one was prepared for people to go out to shoot and be shot . . . Miss Gonne's impersonation had stirred the audience as I have never seen another audience stirred.'[23]

After the curtain fell on *Cathleen ni Houlihan* (1902) it could fairly be said that Yeats's work for the Irish revolution had been accomplished. It seems, in retrospect, considerate of Maud Gonne to have married in the following year.

The poet—having acquired in his political years a name, an audience and the dramatic society that was about to become the Abbey Theatre—now turned aside from Irish politics. He did not cease—he never ceased—to be an Irish nationalist but his nationalism now became aristocratic and archaizing, instead of being popular and active. Aristocratic nationalism was not, in Ireland, practical politics because the aristocracy was almost entirely Unionist, that is to say anti-national. This did not matter to Yeats, who had had enough, for the moment, of practical politics. In his new aristocratism he was releasing a part of his personality he had been forced to try to suppress during the years of political activity. In those years this Irish Protestant had necessarily emphasized his Irishness, minimizing or denying the separate and distinct tradition which the word 'Protestant' implies. The Protestant now re-emerged with an audible sigh of relief. It had been stuffy in there, and getting stuffier. For, in the first years of Yeats's involvement in active politics, there had been special circumstances making political life among Irish nationalists tolerable for a Protestant: by 1900 these special circumstances had disappeared. The fall of Parnell had produced, as well as a 'clerical' party, led by Dillon, an anti-clerical Parnellite party led by John Redmond. Parnellite circles—to which Yeats had directed his first appeal, and which probably made up the larger part of his audiences—were distinguished by a scarcity of priests and a minimum of priestly authority. The glee with which Yeats in his letters chronicles threats against priests is significant. It was not that he necessarily hated priests himself—though he certainly did not like them—but that an atmosphere of priestly authority, in which, for example, priests tended to be arbiters of taste, was inimical to Protestant and poet. This atmosphere was temporarily dissipated in a considerable part of Ireland, including Dublin, in 1891, and Yeats must have found the going relatively easy then. By 1900, however, with the reunification of the Irish party and the burying of the Parnellite hatchet—which was an anti-clerical hatchet—the clergy had recovered most of their former authority, and life among nationalists must have become proportionately depressing for Protestants.[24] It was already depressing enough, for reasons of class. Yeats has left us a collective picture of his political associates of the nineties: 'Men who had risen above the traditions of the countryman, without learning those of cultivated life, or even educating themselves and who because of their poverty, their ignorance, their superstitious piety, are much subject to all kinds of fear.'[25]

This is a classical statement of the Irish Protestant view of the rising Catholic middle-class. From this class Yeats was now recoiling and the violence of his recoil did much to determine the political direction of his later years.

'One thing that Marxist criticism has not succeeded in doing', as George Orwell pointed out, 'is to trace the connection between "tendency" and literary style'.[26] Orwell goes on, in the essay on Yeats, to reveal, unconsciously, some of the reasons for that failure. He seeks, in Yeats's work, 'some kind of connection between his wayward, even tortured, style of writing and his rather sinister vision of life'. He finds this connection, as far as he finds it at all, in Yeats's archaisms, affectations and 'quaint-ness'. This does not fit very well, for the 'quaintness' was at its

155

height in the nineties, when Yeats's vision of life was, from either an Orwellian or a Marxist point of view, at its least sinister: when he was identified with the popular cause in his own country and when, in England, he sat at the feet of William Morris and looked on Socialism with a friendly eye. Unfortunately for Orwell's thesis, it was precisely at the moment—after the turning point of 1903—when Yeats's vision of life began to turn 'sinister': aristocratic and proto-Fascist—that he began to purge his style of quaintness, and his greatest poetry was written near the end of his life when his ideas were at their most sinister. A Marxist critique which starts from the assumption that bad politics make for bad style will continue 'not to succeed'. The opposite assumption, though not entirely true, would be nearer to the truth. The politics of the left—any left, even a popular 'national movement'— impose, by their emphasis on collective effort and on sacrifice, a constraint on the artist, a constraint which may show itself in artificialities of style, vagueness or simple carelessness. Right-wing politics, with their emphasis on the freedom of the *élite,* impose less constraint, require less pretense, allow style to become more personal and direct.

It is not necessary to claim that these generalizations are universally valid; they were, I think, valid for Yeats and for many of his generation and that immediately following. Snobbery— 'abhorring the multitude'—was then a more acceptable, and therefore comfortable, attitude than it now would be. A hero of François Mauriac's, after a day spent among workers in some Christian Socialist movement, used to change into black silk pyjamas in the evening and read Laforgue, *pour se désencanailler.* Yeats after 1903 *se désencanaillait* in the company of Lady Gregory and her circle. Now that he had withdrawn for the time from active politics, politics became explicit in his poetry. His bitterness about Maud Gonne's marriage took a political form:

> Why should I blame her that she filled my days
> With misery, or that she would of late
> Have taught to ignorant men most violent ways,
> Or hurled the little streets upon the great,
> Had they but courage equal to desire?

If the snobbery endemic in his class and generation takes in his writing from now on an almost hysterical intensity, it is, I think, that he felt himself to have undergone, in his political years, a kind of contamination, a loss of caste, through 'the contagion of the throng' and that, in the end, he had suffered a deep injury to his pride. 'One must accept'—he had written to Lady Gregory near the end of his political involvement—'the baptism of the gutter'.[27] 'The foul ditch' and 'the abounding gutter' became recurring symbols of disgust in his later poetry. In the same letter in which he accepted the baptism of the gutter, he spoke of trying to get someone to resign from something 'in favour of MacBride of the Irish Brigade'—the man whom Maud Gonne was to marry three years later:

> My dear is angry that of late
> I cry all base blood down,
> As though she had not taught me hate
> By kisses to a clown.

There were moments when he felt ashamed of this hate,[28] but it proved enduring. Hatred of England had been with him early; hatred of 'the base' in Ireland now joined it. The two hates represented an abnormal intensification of the normal dualism of the Irish Protestant. They formed an unstable and potentially explosive combination: a volcanic substance which would from time to time erupt through the surface of Yeats's public life.

5

Although Yeats withdrew in a sense from Irish politics about 1903, this did not mean that Irish politics withdrew from him. His theatre, because of *Cathleen ni Houlihan,* had just become a kind of Holy Place of Irish nationalism and his new frame of mind—fortunately for the theatre—was far from that of a custodian of such a Holy Place. Militant nationalists, of whom the most vocal Dublin leader at this time was Arthur Griffith, the founder of Sinn Fein, naturally wanted the theatre to serve the cause actively, as it had done with *Cathleen ni Houlihan.* They also—and with them a wider Dublin public—insisted that it must not 'play into the enemy's hands' by presenting a 'degrading' image of Irish life. Here nationalist pressures and Catholic pressures—which often worked against each other, as Parnell and the Fenians knew—converged in turbulent menace. Plays that showed Irishmen as sinful—or even, for example, coarse in speech—were hurtful to many militant nationalists as denigrating the inherently virtuous and refined character of 'the Irish race'[29] (a phrase much in use at the time); to many militant Catholics such plays were both inherently immoral and scandalous and also offensive by the suggestion that the Catholic education of the Irishman left something to be desired. 'An insult to Ireland', cried the first set of voices, and the second set responded: 'an insult to Catholic Ireland'.

'Audience', telegraphed Lady Gregory on the first night of *The Playboy of the Western World,* 'broke up in disorder at the word *shift.*'[30]

It seems in retrospect surprising—and it is a tribute to the courage, tenacity and skill of Yeats and Lady Gregory—that the theatre should have been able to survive at all under the combined pressure—only fitfully applied it is true—of the two most powerful forces in Irish life.[31] Yeats had many battles to fight and fought them with gusto. 'Into the dozen or so fairly important quarrels in the theatre movement from 1903 to 1911 he threw himself with something like abandon. The issue was in almost every case national art versus nationalist propaganda.'[32]

The art that he defended in his theatre was that which belonged to 'life' as against, in his words, 'the desire which every political party has, to substitute for life a bunch of reliable principles and assertions'.[33]

He never, as we say in Dublin, said a truer word. He was here taking his stand as an artist, in defense of the life of art in his country. For him then—and for us now—the politics of the matter came on a much lower level. But it is with that lower level—in which he took an ever-renewed interest—that we are concerned here. On that level the defense of 'national art' against 'nationalist propaganda' represented a political shift; for Yeats, in *Cathleen ni Houlihan,* had produced one of the most powerful pieces of nationalist propaganda ever written. Yeats could be an excellent propagandist when he wanted to, and he often did want to. 'You have been liable at times, only at times', his father wrote to him anxiously, 'to a touch of the propaganda fiend'.[34] And he himself was later to affirm more sweepingly: 'I have been always a propagandist . . .'[35] Those who looked to him and his theatre for nationalist propaganda, and did not get it, had therefore some reason to feel confusion and disappointment. The fact was that their cause—the nationalist cause—did not sufficiently stir Yeats at this particular time (between 1903 and 1916) to make him write (or encourage others to write) in a way which would have had the effect they desired—as he had written before and as he was to write again. The nationalist in him was dormant, the aristocrat wide awake, dominating the mob from the stage.[36] For those in whose blood-stream *Cathleen ni Houlihan* was still working this was an unfortunate conjuncture; for those who detested all that that play stood for, it was an auspicious one. The young men from Trinity came to the Abbey to defend artistic freedom by singing *God Save the King.*[37]

There is one important apparent break in the otherwise consistently aristocratic line of thought and action which he pursued in these years and—with the partial exception of certain nationalist flare-ups—throughout his life from about 1903 to the end. This apparent break is constituted by the stand he took on the great Dublin Lock-out, when in 1913 the Dublin employers, led by William Martin Murphy, tried to starve the Dublin workers into submission[38] in order to break Jim Larkin's Irish Transport and General Workers' Union. Few who had read Yeats's writings, or considered his attitude to public questions in the preceding ten years, could have expected him to come out on the side of Larkin's men. William Martin Murphy, if he had had time for Yeats and for his poetry, might plausibly have claimed that if ever there was a man who that man was Big Jim Larkin. He could also have contended—and proved his case, certainly to the satisfaction of a Dublin court of the time—that it was actually Larkin's policy to:

. . . hurl the little streets upon the great.

For this Larkin himself, if not all his followers, had 'courage equal to desire'. 'My advice to you', Larkin had told his men, 'is to be round the doors and corners, and if one of our class should fall, then two of the others should fall for that one. We will demonstrate in O'Connell Street [Dublin's principal thorough-fare]. It is our street as well as William Martin Murphy's. We are fighting for bread and butter. We will hold our meeting in the streets, and if any one of our men fall, there must be justice. By the living God if they want war they can have it.'

A conservative admirer of Yeats could reasonably have expected to find him, in such a war, on the side of public order, the rights of property and the rule of the educated. What Yeats did, however, was to come out explicitly and vehemently against the activities of the employers' principal allies—police, press and clergy. His protest—in the form of a letter to Larkin's *Irish Worker*—is important enough, in the context of the present discussion, to be quoted in full:

I do not complain of Dublin's capacity for fanaticism whether in priest or layman, for you cannot have strong feeling without that capacity, but neither those who directed the police nor the editors of our newspapers can plead fanaticism. They are supposed to watch over our civil liberties, and I charge the Dublin Nationalist newspapers with deliberately arousing religious passion to break up the organisation of the workingman, with appealing to mob law day after day, with publishing the names of workingmen and their wives for purposes of intimidation.

And I charge the Unionist Press of Dublin and those who directed the police with conniving at this conspiracy. I want to know why the *Daily Express*, which is directly and indirectly inciting Ulster to rebellion in defence of what it calls 'the liberty of the subject' is so indifferent to that liberty here in Dublin that it has not made one editorial comment, and I ask the *Irish Times* why a few sentences at the end of an article, too late in the week to be of any service, has been the measure of its love for civil liberty?

I want to know why there were only (according to the press reports) two policemen at Kingsbridge on Saturday when Mr. Sheehy Skeffington was assaulted and a man prevented from buying a ticket for his own child? There had been tumults every night at every Dublin railway station, and I can only assume that the police authorities wished those tumults to continue.

I want to know why the mob at North Wall and elsewhere were permitted to drag children from their parents' arms, and by what right one woman was compelled to open her box and show a marriage certificate; I want to know by what right the police have refused to accept charges against rioters; I want to know who has ordered the abrogation of the most elementary rights of the citizens, and why authorities who are bound to protect every man in doing that which he has a legal right to do—even though they have to call upon all the forces of the Crown—have permitted the Ancient Order of Hibernians to besiege Dublin, taking possession of the railway stations like a foreign army.

Prime Ministers have fallen, and Ministers of State have been impeached for less than this. I demand that the coming Police Inquiry shall be so widened that we may get to the bottom of a conspiracy, whose like has not been seen in any English-speaking town during living memory. Intriguers have met together somewhere behind the scenes that they might turn the religion of Him who thought it hard for a rich man to enter into the Kingdom of Heaven into an oppression of the poor.[39]

'It may be surmised', wrote the late J. M. Hone about this letter, 'that Yeats was not actuated solely by humanitarian zeal'.[40] It may indeed—as we shall see—but Hone's comment needs itself to be treated with some reserve. Hone was a friend of Yeats, and in tune with his political views, but his conservatism was of a colder and more intellectual stamp than Yeats's. It is clear from Hone's references to the lock-out—he pays tribute to Murphy's services to 'Dublin'—that the employers, rather than the workers, commanded such store of sympathy as he possessed.[41] The very use of the words 'humanitarian zeal' conveys as much. Granted his premises this was a logical position. But Yeats was not logical in this chilly way. He was an enthusiast, in the old sense of the word; he was not only capable of generous indignation—he positively reveled in it, as he was to show again and again. We may—and I do—accept the view that Yeats on this occasion was not actuated *solely* by humanitarian zeal, but we need more stress on the 'solely' than Hone, in the context, seems to imply. The events of the Dublin Lock-out—including the events which Yeats described—aroused strong emotions and there can be no doubt that Yeats's indignation was genuine, and that it sprang, in part, from those human feelings which, when we find them inconvenient, we call 'humanitarian zeal'.

Yet, as Hone suggests, feelings of this kind would hardly by themselves explain the phenomenon of the letter. There is no reason to suppose that Yeats was either peculiarly accessible, or peculiarly resistant, to such feelings. He could, like most other politically-minded people, modulate the expression of such feelings—and perhaps even, to some extent, the feelings themselves—in accordance with his judgment of the social and political context in which the 'crimes' or 'regrettable incidents', as the case might be, occurred. Thus, in later years, Yeats did not, as we shall see, allow his humane feelings to overpower his political judgment in connection either with the repressive measures of the first Free State government, or with the penal achievements of the Fascist governments. Nor, in these later contexts, did he show the marked specific concern for civil liberties which he shows here. It is true that he became more conservative—and more than conservative—as he grew older, but a conservative, aristocratic pattern had already, by 1913, become quite distinct. The concern about the 'oppression of the poor' in this letter does not fit more easily into this pattern than the apparent Christian piety of the last sentence fits into the pattern of Yeats's religious ideas.

The explanation of the letter which Hone suggests is, as far as it goes, helpful. This is that Yeats was already violently incensed against Murphy on an artistic issue—Murphy's opposition, in his powerful paper *The Irish Independent,* to the housing, by Dublin Corporation, of the Lane collection of paintings, in the manner proposed by Lane. When Murphy attacked Lane, Larkin praised Lane. Yeats, it is hinted—no more than a hint is given— came to the support of Larkin for reasons similar to those that made Larkin come to the support of Lane. The poet was naturally no more disposed in favor of the labor leader than the labor leader was predisposed in favor of the art-connoisseur, but all three had a common enemy in the person of the arch-philistine and arch-bourgeois: William Martin Murphy. This is illuminating, and the reminder that Murphy had been a prominent anti-Parnellite is also highly relevant. If this were all, however, the letter would be little more than an incident in something like a personal feud, with little relevance to the wider pattern of Yeats's politics. I believe, however, that this is not all, and that the letter is both more relevant to that pattern and more consistent with it than appears at first sight.

'Yeats', according to Hone, 'chose to regard Martin Murphy as a representative type and leader of the middle-class which had begun to rise to power under the shadow of the Land League . . .'[42] Both Yeats and Hone are rather vague about this middle-class; it is possible to be a little more specific. The Land League (1879–81), with its successor movements, had profoundly weakened the influence, formerly overpowering, of the old Protestant landed Ascendancy, with which Yeats liked to identify himself; it threatened also the privileged social position—and sometimes directly hit the incomes—of the Protestant middle-class to which Yeats did in fact belong. The boycott, in which the people had received and absorbed effective instruction from Land League times on, was certainly not intended by its organizers as a lever to help in bringing about the emergence of a Catholic middle-class, but it is probable that that is one of the ways in which it actually worked. People who sold goods to, or had dealings with, boycotted farmers, land-agents, etc., were themselves boycotted; those who attempted to break the boycott in this way had a high propensity to be—in politics—Unionist and—in religion—Protestant. It may be imagined that a 'Nationalist' shopkeeper would not be backward in urging the boycott of a 'Unionist' competitor: in this way a socio-political movement could shade over to a communal-religious one. This process is still a reality of life, within the experience of the present writer, in parts of Northern Ireland. I remember being gently chided, by a group of nationalist friends in a Northern city, for not staying at 'the nationalist hotel'; in fact they not only chided me, but with two telephone calls neatly transferred my hotel-political allegiance.[43] These friends were quite conscious about their intent: to shift as much economic power as possible from 'their' hands into 'ours'. They had not the air of having invented the idea and I believe that it was an important, though seldom mentioned, feature of Irish life generally for many years. Conditions between the institution of the boycott and the First War—that is during the first phases of Yeats's active life—must have been particularly propitious to it. Yeats, in associating as he did—rather strangely at first sight—the 'new middle-class' with the agrarian agitation, had this set

of phenomena in mind. For the class from which Yeats had come—
Protestant merchants and professional people—'the shadow of
the Land League' meant the boycott in its wide variety of forms,
as an instrument for the transfer of economic power out of their
hands into those of the more astute, energetic and rapacious of
the conquered caste, now beginning to form a 'new middle-
class'.[44]

Yeats was not wrong in seeing in the 'Sullivan gang'—that
clan from Bantry, Co. Cork, of which the economic head was
William Martin Murphy and the political head Tim Healy—
representative leaders of this new class. The qualities of acumen
and energy all Ireland, friend and foe, conceded to them; the
quality of unscrupulous rapacity was persistently attributed to
them by their numerous enemies. They had not been particularly
closely associated with the Land League but they were associated
with the varieties of religious-communal, economic and social
activity which I have been describing as arising from the successful
operation of the boycott. The Land League itself had not been
clerically inspired or dominated—far from it—but in its successor body, the National League, the clergy began to play a direct
and recognized political part.[45] After the Parnell divorce case
the 'Sullivan gang', led by Healy and backed by Murphy's money,
emerged as the spearhead of the clerical attack on Parnell. Other,
more important, leaders who went against Parnell—John Dillon
and William O'Brien—carefully eschewed the 'moral issue'
and tried to spare Parnell. It was left to Healy and his clan, with
the active support of the clergy, to hammer away at this issue, often
in scurrilous language, and to Parnell's undoing. To the young
Yeats—whose dislike of the 'Sullivan gang' antedated these
proceedings—the spectacle of the plebeian Healy taunting the
falling aristocrat was a powerful symbol. Paradoxically, the
Parnell Split closed—for a time—the schism in his political soul
between the 'Protestant/aristocrat' and the 'Irish nationalist'.
The unified nationalist movement of 1880–90—a movement in
which the 'Sullivan gang' had followed Parnell—had been putting
pressure on England, and there Yeats approved them, but they

164

were also putting pressure on the superior caste in Ireland, and that he very much disliked. When Parnell and the 'Sullivan gang' flew apart, this tension in Yeats was relaxed. Parnell was fighting England and no longer the Ascendancy, which began to discern merits in him for the first time, but the Catholic middle-class, encouraged by the clergy and led by the 'Sullivan gang'.

We know with what intensity this struggle revived in Yeats's mind in 1913 when, in the poem 'To a Shade', he apostrophized the ghost of Parnell. The line

Your enemy an old foul mouth

refers to a collective Sullivan orifice—the tongue of Healy and the teeth of Murphy. The immediate occasion for the attack— the art-gallery controversy—was aesthetic, but the roots of the controversy, and its emotional charge, were social and political and—in the communal sense—religious. It is true that the poet attacked the 'Sullivan gang' for its philistinism—and Murphy's *Irish Independent* was indeed, and long remained, a philistine bastion—but he had hated them long before any artistic controversy arose; in any case the Sullivan clan were certainly intellectually well above the level of the Irish middle-class as a whole (both Protestant and Catholic) and, aesthetically, did not lag conspicuously behind the upper class generally.[46] It was not primarily as art critics but as representatives of a class—the new middle-class—and exponents of a method—clerical pressure— that they were obnoxious.

Yeats's intervention in the 1913 industrial conflict came just at the moment when the leader of the obnoxious class brought the obnoxious method to bear. Murphy, supported in this by Archbishop Walsh, had enlisted clerical aid to prevent children of the Dublin workers from being sent to the homes of English sympathizers. From the Archbishop's point of view the children's departure involved a danger to their faith: from Murphy's point of view it represented a danger to his economic blockade. If the children were not on hand, to go hungry—and be seen and heard to go hungry—then the men might be able to hold out and Larkin would win. So the cry 'the faith in danger' was used to starve the children.

Yeats's attack is directed first and foremost at Murphy's use of 'religion'. His first charge is against 'the Dublin nationalist newspapers'—which were led by Murphy's *Irish Independent*—for 'deliberately arousing religious passion to break up the organisation of the workingman . . .' The other charges are all ancillary to this—charges of connivance in Murphy's methods of defending the faith, and some details of these methods.

One can discern, then, in this letter, honest disgust at an odious piece of cruel hypocrisy, a human desire for a crack at Murphy, and the wish to illuminate a particularly unlovely example of the social influence of the Catholic clergy. Concern for the workers is also present, but it must be noted that this, in itself, had not been sufficient to arouse Yeats to intervene. The lock-out (of some workers) and strike (of others) and the police brutalities had begun in August, and protests began soon after. Yeats did not, however, protest until after the publication (21 October) of the letter from the Catholic Archbishop of Dublin in which he told the workers' wives that, if they allowed their hungry children to go to England to be fed, they could 'no longer be held worthy of the name of Catholic mothers'.

Yeats's indignation at the 'saving of the children' was spontaneous, comprehensible and creditable. It does not constitute—appearances to the contrary—an isolated pro-working-class outbreak, unique in his career. It was in no way inconsistent with his 'Protestant/aristocratic' position to attack the leaders of the rising Catholic middle-class, and their clerical allies, or to defend their victims. These leaders and that alliance had long inspired in him distrust and repugnance—feelings which 1913 fanned into flame. These feelings in themselves were habitual in the class from which he himself sprang. Other members of that class could, however, muffle the expression of these feelings when, as now, it suited their economic interest to do so—that is the meaning of the charge of 'connivance' which Yeats directs against the (Protestant) *Irish Times* and *Daily Express*. Yeats himself could do some muffling at times, but when the provocation was great—as now—he had to give vent to his feelings, against the formidable alliance of savings and prayers:

> What need you, being come to sense,
>   But fumble in a greasy till
> And add the halfpence to the pence
>   And prayer to shivering prayer, until
> You have dried the marrow from the bone?
>   For men were born to pray and save:
> Romantic Ireland's dead and gone,
>   It's with O'Leary in the grave.[47]
>
> (*'September 1913'*)

6

Most of the leaders who planned the Rising—which proved three years later that romantic Ireland was not yet dead and gone—belonged to the general class which Yeats distrusted; not to the climbing 'Sullivan gang' section of it, but to the 'clerks and shopkeepers' whom he thought of as 'the base'; the leaders included the basest of the base—from Yeats's point of view—Major MacBride himself. They had all been engaged for years in the kind of politics on which he had turned his back. But in 1916 they were shot by the English:

> All changed, changed utterly:
> A terrible beauty is born.

The poems 'Easter 1916', 'Sixteen Dead Men', 'The Rose Tree' and 'On a Political Prisoner' drew strength from the complexity as well as from the intensity of the emotions involved—the sense—which became explicit years after—of his own share in the 'gestation' of the event;[48] the presence in the event of the strongest love and the strongest personal hatred of his life; an old hate, and even a kind of disgust, for much of what the insurrection meant

> Blind and leader of the blind
> Drinking the foul ditch where they lie . . .

an even older and deeper hate for those who crushed the insurrection; and finally a prophetic sense of the still more bitter struggle yet to come:

167

> But who can talk of give and take,
> What should be and what not
> While those dead men are loitering there
> To stir the boiling pot?

By the time when 'Easter 1916' and 'The Rose Tree' were published, in the autumn of 1920, the pot had boiled over. The Black-and-Tan terror was now at its height throughout Ireland. To publish these poems in this context was a political act, and a bold one: probably the boldest of Yeats's career. Yeats could be fearless on issues where artistic integrity was involved—as he showed, for example, in facing the riots over *The Playboy of the Western World* in 1907—and also when clerical meddling aroused his anger. But in national politics, even where he felt passionately, he usually acted prudently. And even at this point, although he acted with unusual boldness, he did not allow himself to be carried away. What he published in 1920 concerned an historical event of four years earlier; even on that event he did not publish, in England, the poem 'Sixteen Dead Men' which, with its 'boiling pot', had the most explicit bearing on contemporary politics. He did not publish at all the poem 'Reprisals', written against the Black and Tans and addressed to the ghost of Lady Gregory's son, killed in the Great War:

> Flit to Kiltartan Cross and stay
> Till certain second thoughts have come
> Upon the cause you served, that we
> Imagined such a fine affair:
> Half-drunk or whole-mad soldiery
> Are murdering your tenants there.
> Men that revere your father yet
> Are shot at on the open plain.
> Where may new-married women sit
> And suckle children now? Armed men
> May murder them in passing by
> Nor law nor parliament take heed.
> Then close your ears with dust and lie
> Among the other cheated dead.[49]

Yeats did, however, speak, at the Oxford Union in February 1921, in favor of Sinn Fein and against the Black and Tans.

Yeats's indignation was spontaneous: his method of giving expression to that indignation in his published writings seems calculated.[50] By publishing the 1916 poems in 1920 he placed himself openly 'on Ireland's side' in the fight with England but he closed no doors in terms of contemporary politics. For it was known, in 1920, that Ireland was going to get some form of self-government. If the rebels were beaten, it would be the Home Rule (with partition) of the British Act of 1920. If the rebels won, it would be the Republic proclaimed in 1916. The two poems that Yeats chose to publish covered, as it happened, both eventualities neatly. The spirit of the Proclamation of the Republic was in them:

> 'But where can we draw water,'
> Said Pearse to Connolly,
> 'When all the wells are parched away?
> O plain as plain can be
> There's nothing but our own red blood
> Can make a right Rose Tree.'

But there were also in them the doubts and reservations which most Irishmen had felt about the Proclamation of 1916: the doubts and reservations of those for whom Home Rule and the Act of 1920 represented an acceptable settlement:

> Was it needless death after all?
> For England may keep faith
> For all that is done and said.
> We know their dream; enough
> To know they dreamed and are dead;
> And what if excess of love
> Bewildered them till they died?

In the event the Anglo-Irish Treaty brought to Ireland the realities of the Act of 1920 with some of the trappings of 1916. This treaty set up, not the Republic proclaimed in 1916, but a Free State within the Empire and without the six counties of the north-east. Many—probably more than half—of those who had been fighting the Black and Tans while Yeats had been publishing his 1916 poems felt that this was a betrayal, as Yeats's Pearse and Connolly might have felt:

> Maybe a breath of politic words
> Has withered our Rose Tree ...

Those who felt in this way tried to reject the treaty and carry on the struggle. The majority of the people, tired of war, had

169

voted, in effect, for the acceptance of the treaty. The Free State Government, with the aid of British artillery and armored cars, now set about liquidating the Republican forces. Whether it had behind it, in this effort, all of those who had given it its majority may be doubted. It certainly had behind it all the wealthier elements in the country, including almost all the Anglo-Irish, and it had W. B. Yeats, nominated by President Cosgrave to the Senate of the Irish Free State in December 1922. The Civil War had now been raging for six months.

The Free State forces, in destroying the Republican forces, were obliged to use some of the same methods as the Black and Tans (flogging, shooting of hostages), but applied these with greater efficiency, based on far better intelligence, and with proportionately less accompanying publicity.[51] It was a pattern that was to be repeated—perhaps copied—after the mid-century, in many ex-colonies, and came to be assailed as neo-colonialism. Many of those who had denounced the excesses of the Black and Tans were plunged in deeper horror by what happened during the Civil War and in its aftermath. These included Lady Gregory, whose journals tell a story:[52]

During the Civil War: Jan. 23 [1923] **These floggings in my mind. I wrote to Yeats in protest. The young men taken away were flogged, as well as those left, 'with a thonged whip'. I was not surprised to hear Hogan's house at Kilchreest has been destroyed. Hatred must grow—'death answering to death through the generations like clerks answering one another at the Mass'.**

After the Civil War: Aug. 23 **W. B. Yeats here yesterday. I say the fault of the Government is this hatred of the Republicans they show in their speeches. He says it is justified or at least excused by the information they have had from America that it is to be said, in case 'of a Republican defeat', that the elections were not carried out fairly and assassinations are threatened. But with the Republicans saying the prisoners are flogged or tortured they probably have the same hatred . . .**

Nov. 10. . . . **There had been some talk about the hunger strike, Esmonde saying the Government would not yield. And this is Yeats's view. I had some talk with him after we came home, the first time I had seen him close and again this morning. He says the Government cannot give in. That if they had let Miss MacSwiney die, when she began it, this new hunger strike would not have begun, but they had a sentimental feeling for her brother's sake.[53] We talked a long time this morning. I had had a bad night and thought it over a long time, and had come to a determination of writing to the papers about it, asking that the crime or accusation against these four hundred men remaining on [hunger] strike might be told out, that we might know if consenting to their suicide is in accordance with the conscience of Christian nations and the law of God. I meant to go and consult 'A. E.' about them. But Yeats is violently against any protest, says it is necessary to the stability of Government to hold out, says they cannot publish the accusations because many are on suspicion, or as they think certainty, but they have not evidence that can be shown. . . .**

I ask if that might not come under an amnesty at the conclusion of the war, for the Government themselves signed death sentences during it. But he says no, and he says the Government cannot publish the real reason for the detention of this thousand, they themselves are in danger of being assassinated by some among them.

I asked if they could not, on their side, try to get rid of the Oath [of allegiance to the Crown]; that would do away with the real cause of trouble, the keeping of Republicans out of the Dail. He said they cannot in the present state of English feeling, it would be useless to ask for it, and besides we may probably want English help in getting the Loan. And the Senate can make no move in the matter....

Nov. 11. . . . Went on to Jack Yeats [the painter, the poet's brother] . . . Lennox Robinson . . . said: 'Can we not do anything about the hunger strikers? Write a letter perhaps'. Strange, because I had not spoken of my own restless night or my talk with Yeats. So we walked and planned and at last went into the Arts Club and wrote a letter. We thought Stephens [James] and Jack Yeats might join in signing it. He called in Cruise O'Brien[54] from another room to ask if the *Independent* [pro-Government paper] would put it in. He thought so, made one or two slight alterations, thinking it showed a slight prepossession against the Government; then I came back to Merrion Square [to Yeats's house]. Later Lennox Robinson telephoned that Jack Yeats had refused to sign, 'he is much too red to do so', and asked if we should still send it on with our own names and Stephens' who has agreed. I said 'Yes'. It may perhaps bring letters or suggestions from others and possibly save some lives. Then I told Yeats (W. B.) what I had done and proposed leaving his house for the hotel, as he might not approve. He would not allow that and after talking for a while thought perhaps we had done right. Of course one won't have any gratitude from either side. But I slept better.

Nov. 16. On Monday night 'A.E.' and Lieutenant 'X' were with Yeats. I looked in but didn't stay. Yeats said they had talked of the prisoners. 'X' said they were not on hunger strike, were being fed. And that the stories of ill-treatment are not true—gave instances, thinks it 'likely only half a dozen men will die'. Dreadful, I think, even if that half-dozen were not of the bravest.[55]

7

Yeats was now an established public figure. Having become a Senator in December 1922, he received an honorary Doctorate from Trinity College in 1923 and the Nobel Prize for Literature in the same year. The Yeatses had now a house in Merrion Square: 'the Berkeley Square of Ireland', as he said. He was soberly pleased about his political position and prospects. 'We', he wrote of himself and his fellow Senators, 'are a fairly distinguished body and should get much government into our hands'.[56] His political ideas were now explicitly reactionary: 'Out of all this murder and rapine,' he wrote in 1922, 'will come not a demagogic but an authoritarian government'.[57] And again: 'everywhere one notices a drift towards Conservatism, perhaps towards Autocracy'.[58] His ideas for Ireland were explicitly linked with the rise of Fascism in Europe:

We are preparing here, behind our screen of bombs and smoke, a return to conservative politics as elsewhere in Europe or at least to a substitution of the historical sense for logic. The return will be painful and perhaps violent but many educated men talk of it and must soon work for it and perhaps riot for it.

A curious sign is that 'A.E.' who was the most popular of men is now suffering some slight eclipse because of old democratic speeches—things of years ago. I on the other hand get hearers where I did not get them because I have been of the opposite party. . . . The Ireland that reacts from the present disorder is turning its eyes towards individualist [i.e. Fascist] Italy.[59]

This letter was written just before Yeats's nomination to the Senate of the Free State and just after Mussolini's March on Rome (22 October 1922).

Many of Yeats's contemporaries and of his younger admirers and subsequent writers about him refused to take all this very seriously.[60] The Dublin to which Yeats belonged—in so far as he belonged to Dublin at all—the Dublin of the Arts Club, liked to treat Yeats's politics as a joke, and this tradition went a long way back. More than twenty years before, when Yeats and Maud Gonne were stirring up opinion against Queen Victoria's visit to Ireland, Percy French had made the Queen protest:

> And there must be a slate, sez she,
> Off that Willie Yeats, sez she.
> He'd be betther at home, sez she,
> Frinch-polishin' a pome, sez she,
> Than writin' letthers, sez she,
> About his betthers, sez she,
> Paradin' me crimes, sez she,
> In the Irish Times, sez she.

This mood of affectionate raillery persisted, and perhaps did something to protect Yeats from possible adverse consequences of his political involvement. My father, at the Arts Club, used to poke gentle fun at Yeats's 'Fascism', parodying him as referring in a speech to 'that very great man, Missolonghi' and then, when corrected, saying majestically: 'I am told the name is not Missolonghi but Mussolini—but, does it . . . really . . . matter'?[61]

Yeats enjoyed, and even encouraged, this kind of joke about himself and others:

> And thought before I had done
> Of a mocking tale or a gibe
> To please a companion
> Around the fire at the club,
> Being certain that they and I
> But lived where motley is worn . . .

For those who admired Yeats, but were made uneasy by his politics, the idea that his politics were vague, ill-informed and funny offered a way out: a way out, left open by Yeats himself. Yet his politics had this much serious about them: that practice and theory tended to concur. The poet admired Mussolini and his colleagues from afar:[62] the Senator admired, and worked with, Ireland's strong man, Kevin O'Higgins.[63] O'Higgins, in Irish politics—he was Minister of Justice in the Free State Government—was thought to stand for what was most ruthless and implacable in the party of property: the stern defense of seventy-seven executions. This was not repugnant to Yeats; the 'right of the state to take life in its own defence' became dear to him. O'Higgins was 'their sole statesman'; Yeats did him the honor of including him, along with Grattan, Parnell and Berkeley, in a list of great Irishmen—a list in which the sole Gaelic and Catholic name is that of O'Higgins. His portrait is among 'my friends' in 'The Municipal Gallery Revisited':

> Kevin O'Higgins' countenance that wears
> A gentle questioning look that cannot hide
> A soul incapable of remorse or rest . . .

Those who—like Yeats—admired in O'Higgins a potential autocrat would not have taken it for granted that he, as his colleagues were to do in 1932, would have tamely allowed the party defeated in the Civil War to come to power through impeccably conducted free elections. But by then O'Higgins was no longer there; he had been assassinated in 1927:

> A great man in his pride
> Confronting murderous men

'Nobody', he had said in a phrase which impressed Yeats, 'can expect to live who has done what I have'.[64] How deeply hated he was—not only by his political opponents but by some of 'his own side' including his own police—I can remember myself. I was ten years old and returning from a drive in the country—my first drive in a motor-car—with my aunt, Mrs. Skeffington, and a friend of hers. We were stopped at a road-block and the Sergeant, recognizing my aunt, smiled broadly and said: 'Ye'll be delighted to hear, Ma'am—Kevin's been shot!' My aunt did not smile; she

173

was not disposed to be amused either by murder or by policemen.

Countess Markievicz—'Madame' as she was known among the poor of Dublin who loved her—died just after O'Higgins was murdered. She had a great following among the street-traders of Moore Street; famed hecklers and the bane of every Free State politician, they were known at this time as 'Madame's wans'. About O'Higgins's death, one of them said: 'poor Madame's last wish'.

It was of her that Yeats had written:

> Did she in touching that lone wing
> Recall the years before her mind
> Became a bitter, an abstract thing,
> Her thought some popular enmity:
> Blind and leader of the blind
> Drinking the foul ditch where they lie?

All Ireland was divided by the end of that week between those who mourned Countess Markievicz and those who mourned O'Higgins. The latter were probably fewer but more 'respectable'. From a window in Parnell Square I watched O'Higgins's funeral go by. I had not imagined there were so many top-hats in the world; I was never to see so many again.[65] They were there to honor a man who had defended what they stood for, at the cost of many lives including his own. Senator Yeats must have been under one of the top-hats. The poet had stayed away from Parnell's funeral; the Senator would not, I think, have stayed away from that of Kevin O'Higgins.[66]

8

In 1928, the year after O'Higgins's death, Yeats lost his Senate seat; his term had expired and the Government made no move to renew his nomination. For some time past the going had been increasingly difficult, for similar reasons to those which had applied at the turn of the century. That is to say that the specific influence of the Catholic Church in politics was growing more palpable again. It is true that the régime to which Yeats belonged had always been supported by the Church, but in the beginning it had also needed Protestant support. When it was struggling for

174

its life, and needed money and guns from England, it had to reassure English opinion by giving places of prominence to members of the Protestant middle-class most of whom, though not Yeats, were classified as 'Southern loyalists'. When the emergency was over and 'the Loan' negotiated, the need to placate English opinion, by showing deference to Protestants, subsided. The Government no longer needed British artillery; it still needed to have its position fully covered by the Canons of the Church. The vital principle for the party now in power was one later reduced by a member of that party to a lapidary formula—never to risk 'a sthroke of a crozier'. The fact was that the 'Sullivan gang'— Yeats's old bugbears from 1890 to 1913—were an important component in the régime which had made Yeats a Senator. Healy was Governor-General and Yeats had called on him in that capacity; the Murphy press—which had called vociferously for the execution of the 1916 leaders—was a pillar of the Cosgrave régime; Kevin O'Higgins himself was a member of the clan, a nephew of Healy's, and a grandson of T.D. Sullivan, the first Irish parliamentarian to declare against Parnell after the divorce. Granted that Yeats's hostility to this clan—and the 'clerical bourgeoisie' for which it stood—was sincere, as it surely was, how did he become so easily reconciled to them in 1922? The answer is, I think, a double one. First, the Civil War had changed many things. The Protestant middle- and upper class, which had so long regarded the social and political influence of the clergy as either a baneful or a contemptible phenomenon, had now seen its advantages as a barrier against 'anarchy'; the propertied classes had been made more conscious of a common danger and common interests, less insistent on differences and group competition. Yeats—who worked in the Senate generally in concert with the representatives of the Protestant propertied classes—could also move with them in suppressing his repugnance for what 'the Bantry band' represented. Second, the reconciliation was only partial and temporary:

A patched-up affair if you ask my opinion.

As long as the 'clerical bourgeoisie' showed consideration for

175

the susceptibilities of Protestants, it was possible to work with them. When the bishops began to dictate, the strain, for Yeats, became too great. The Irish bishops, crozier-happy, now extorted the legislation they wanted, forbidding divorce and the sale of contraceptives and later setting up a censorship of publications. The government party, which Yeats had supported on all major matters, carried out the wishes of the bishops.

Irish Protestants generally did not care for the new trend but most of them now made their political choices, not as Protestants but as bourgeois. The Government was obnoxiously Papist, but it was sound on the essential: the rights of property. Nor did Protestants wish to say anything to confirm their fellow-countrymen in an opinion to which they were already too prone: that the distinguishing characteristic of Protestantism is a devotion to divorce, contraceptives and dirty books. The new legislation was, in practice, not much more than a minor irritant: Belfast is not far away.

Most Irish Protestants therefore took a guarded line in the matter. But not Yeats.[67] Yeats's aristocratic feelings, and his pride as a Senator, were hurt; the sage oligarchy to which he had felt himself to belong, the 'fairly distinguished body' which 'should get much government into its hands', was now taking its orders from a bunch of peasants in mitres.[68] The 'base' were dictating to their betters. The peroration of his speech on divorce was not a liberal one: it was the statement of the spokesman of a superior caste, denying the right of inferior castes to make laws for it: 'We against whom you have done this thing are no petty people. We are one of the great stocks of Europe. We are the people of Burke; we are the people of Grattan; we are the people of Swift, the people of Emmet, the people of Parnell. We have created most of the modern literature of this country. We have created the best of its political intelligence.'[69]

Some have felt that Yeats's own political intelligence was not at its best on this occasion. Certainly he seemed to be committing political—or at the very least parliamentary—suicide. Yet he could not do otherwise; to remain in politics he would have had to swallow his pride, and pride was essential to his political life. His dilemma—the dilemma which, happily for his work, pushed him away from the center and towards the margins of politics— was that he had become an anti-clerical conservative in a country where the clergy were an indispensable element of any practical conservative politics. Because of his conservative option in the Civil War he had cut himself off from all the forces in the country which were, in any notable degree, resistant to clerical pressure (or, for that matter, to the temptation of manipulating religious issues for their own ends). His political friends now showed themselves to be a clerical party, the direct heirs to the anti-Parnellites of the nineties. What was still living in the Parnellite tradition had gone on the Republican side in the Civil War and regarded Yeats with aversion and a sense of betrayal. He now, by openly defying the Church, cut himself off, for a time at least, from the modern 'anti-Parnellites'. Politically he had become for the moment completely isolated.

9

The year 1932 was a turning point in Irish political history. In that year the party, led by Mr. Cosgrave, which had won the Civil War and ruled the country since the foundation of the State, fell from power. The party, led by de Valera, which represented the losers in the Civil War, now won a General Election and took over the Government. The respect for democratic process shown by Mr. Cosgrave's government was, in the circumstances, rather remarkable. It was, indeed, too remarkable to please many of the members of the fallen party, and some of these now set about organizing a paramilitary movement, on the Fascist model, for the intimidation of their opponents and the recovery of power. 'They have the Black-shirts in Italy', said one of the politicians concerned, 'they have the Brownshirts in Germany, and now in Ireland we have the Blueshirts.'

Yeats took part in the launching of this movement and wrote songs for it:

What is equality? muck in the yard.

177

It was necessary, he explained, to break 'the reign of the mob' and 'if any Government or party undertake this work it will need force, marching men (the logic of fanaticism whether in a woman or a mob is drawn from a premise, protected by ignorance and therefore irrefutable); it will promise not this or that measure but a discipline, a way of life; that sacred drama must to all native eyes and ears become the greatest of the parables. There is no such government or party today; should either appear, I offer it these trivial songs and what remains to me of life' (April 1934).

Several months later he added this postscript:

P.S. Because a friend belonging to a political party wherewith I had once had some loose associations told me that it had, or was about to have, or might be persuaded to have, some such aim as mine, I wrote these songs. Finding that it neither would nor could, I increased their fantasy, their extravagance, their obscurity, that no party might sing them (August 1934).[70]

The picture presented in the postscript is that of a dreamy, unpractical poet hardly even on the fringes of politics, and innocent with regard to them, moved by an impulse, and misled by a friend, into a political gesture which he later regretted. On the whole this picture has been accepted.[71] Yet the evidence of the letters suggests that his involvement was considerably deeper, and more conscious than he found it convenient, in retrospect, to say.

At the moment [he wrote in April 1933 to Olivia Shakespear] I am trying in association with [an] ex-cabinet Minister, an eminent lawyer and a philosopher to work out a social theory which can be used against Communism in Ireland. This country is exciting. I am told that De Valera has said in private that within three years he will be torn in pieces.[72]

A few months later to the same correspondent:

Politics are growing heroic. De Valera has forced political thought to face the most fundamental issues.[73] A Fascist opposition is forming behind the scenes to be ready should some tragic situation develop. I find myself constantly urging the despotic rule of the educated classes. . . . I know half a dozen men any one of whom may be Caesar—or Catiline. It is amusing to live in a country where men will always act. Where nobody is satisfied with thought. There is so little in our stocking that we are ready at any moment to turn it inside out and how can we not feel emulous when we see Hitler juggling with his sausage of stocking. Our chosen colour is blue, and blue shirts are marching about all over the country and their organizer tells me that it was my suggestion—a suggestion I have entirely forgotten—that made them select for their flag a red St. Patrick's cross on a blue ground—all I can remember is that I have always denounced green and commended blue (the colour of my early book covers).

178

The chance of being shot is raising everybody's spirits enormously. There is some politics for you of which your newspapers know nothing.[74]

To the same, 23 July 1933:

The great secret is out—a convention of blue shirts—National Guards—have received their new leader with the Fascist salute and the new leader announces reform of Parliament as his business.

When I wrote to you, the Fascist organizer of the blue shirts had told me that he was about to bring to see me the man he had selected for leader that I might talk my anti-democratic philosophy. I was ready, for I had just rewritten for the seventh time the part of *A Vision* that deals with the future. The leader turned out to be Gen[eral] O'Duffy, head of the Irish police for twelve years and a famous organizer. . . . Italy, Poland, Germany, then perhaps Ireland. Doubtless I shall hate it (though not so much as I hate Irish democracy) but it is September and we must not behave like the gay young sparks of May or June. *The Observer*, the *Sunday Times*, the only English newspapers I see, have noticed nothing though Cosgrave's ablest ministers are with O'Duffy. O'Duffy himself is autocratic, directing the movement from above down as though it were an army. I did not think him a great man though a pleasant one, but one never knows, his face and mind may harden or clarify.[75]

To the same, 17 August 1933:

The papers will have told you of the blue shirt excitement here. The government is in a panic and has surrounded itself with armoured cars. The shirts themselves are made in batches of 600 and cannot be made fast enough. The organization is for an independent Ireland within the Commonwealth. Whether it succeeds or not in abolishing parliamentary government as we know it today it will certainly bring into discussion all the things I care for. Three months ago there seemed not a trace of such a movement and when it did come into existence it had little apparent importance until that romantic dreamer I have described to you pitched on O'Duffy for a leader. About him the newspapers have probably told you enough. He seemed to me a plastic man but I could not judge whether he would prove plastic to the opinions of others, obvious political current or his own will ('Unity of being').

To the same, 20 September 1933:

I wonder if the English newspapers have given you any idea of our political comedy. Act I. Capt. Macmanus, the ex-British officer I spoke of, his head full of vague Fascism, got probably from me, decided that Gen[eral] O'Duffy should be made leader of a body of young men formed to keep meetings from being broken up. He put into O'Duffy's head—he describes him as 'a simple peasant'—Fascist ideas and started him off to organise that body of young men. Act II. Some journalist announced that 30,000 of these young men were going to march through Dublin on a certain day (the correct number was 3,000). Government panic. Would not O'Duffy, who had once been head of the army, and more recently head of the police, march on the Government with 30,000 plus army and police? Result, martial law—in its Irish form— armoured cars in the streets, and new police force drawn from the I.R.A. to guard the Government, and O'Duffy's organization proclaimed. Act III. O'Duffy is made thereby so important that Cosgrave surrenders the leadership of his party to O'Duffy and all the opposition united under him. Two months ago he was unknown politically.

That was the climax: from then on the references to O'Duffy in Yeats's letters become much sparser and increasingly disparaging, and Yeats soon adopts an attitude of political disengagement, which becomes explicit in the poem 'Church and State' (November 1934):

> Here is fresh matter, poet,
> Matter for old age meet;
> Might of the Church and the State,
> Their mobs put under their feet.
> O but heart's wine shall run pure,
> Mind's bread grow sweet.
>
> That were a cowardly song,
> Wander in dreams no more;
> What if the Church and the State
> Are the mob that howls at the door!
> Wine shall run thick to the end,
> Bread taste sour.

It is customary to say that, at this point, Yeats had become 'disillusioned with Fascism'. One may accept this judgment, but must also remark that the principal illusion which had been dissipated was the illusion that Fascism in Ireland stood a good chance of winning. In the spring and summer of 1933, the Fascism of the Irish Blueshirts looked to many people like a possible winner and in this phase Yeats was with the Blueshirts. By the autumn and winter of 1933–34, the Government's energetic measures—described by Yeats as 'panic measures'—made it clear that de Valera was no von Papen. O'Duffy, failing to devise anything effective in reply, revealed that he was no Hitler. The blue began to fade, and Yeats's interest in it faded proportionately.[76]

Commenting on a mildly anti-Blueshirt anecdote in a letter of Yeats, Professor Jeffares says: 'This ironic attitude to the Blueshirts reveals the true Yeats, detached and merely playing with his thoughts, except for the intervals when he wanted to achieve complete directness and accuracy'.

The date of the anecdote in question is February 1934, by which date the Blueshirts were beginning to look a little silly. The thoughts Yeats had 'played with' in the days when they had looked possibly formidable were less 'detached'. I cannot see on what grounds we are to regard the Yeats who began to sneer at the Blueshirts when they proved a flop, as being more 'real' than the

Yeats who was excited about them when he thought they might win. It was the same Yeats, strongly drawn to Fascism, but no lover of hopeless causes.

In April 1934—as we have seen (p. 178)—he was still advocating 'force, marching men' to break the reign of the mob, but professing, somewhat disingenuously, that 'no such party' as would undertake this work had yet appeared. By August 1934—when the party for which he had in fact written the songs was on the verge of public disintegration—he has found that that party 'neither could nor would' do what he proposed for it. This, it will be noted, does *not* amount to a disavowal of the programme of 'force, marching men' to 'break the reign of the mob'. The irony and detachment of the poem 'Church and State' belong to the period after the final break-up of the Blueshirt movement.

Comment on the question of Yeats's attitude to Fascism has been bedevilled by the assumption that a great poet must be, even in politics, 'a nice guy'. If this be assumed then it follows that, as Yeats obviously was a great poet, he cannot *really* have favored Fascism, which is obviously not a nice cause. Thus the critic or biographer is led to postulate a 'true Yeats', so that Yeats's recorded words and actions of Fascist character must have been perpetrated by some bogus person with the same name and outward appearance.[77]

If one drops the assumption, about poets having always to be nice in politics, then the puzzle disappears, and we see, I believe, that Yeats the man was as near to being a Fascist as his situation and the conditions of his own country permitted. His unstinted admiration had gone to Kevin O'Higgins, the most ruthless 'strong man' of his time in Ireland, and he linked his admiration explicitly to his rejoicing at the rise of Fascism in Europe—and this at the very beginning, within a few weeks of the March on Rome. Ten years later, after Hitler had moved to the center of the political stage in Europe, Yeats was trying to create a movement in Ireland which would be overtly Fascist in language, costume, behavior and intent. He turned his back on this movement when it began to fail, not before. Would the irony and detachment of this phase of disillusion have lasted if a more effective Fascist leader and movement had later emerged? One may doubt it. Many in Germany who were 'disillusioned' by the failure of the Kapp *putsch* and the beer-cellar *putsch* were speedily 'reillusioned' when Hitler succeeded—and 'disillusioned' again when he lost the war.

Post-war writers, touching with embarrassment on Yeats's pro-Fascist opinions, have tended to treat these as a curious aberration of an idealistic but ill-informed poet. In fact such opinions were quite usual in the Irish Protestant middle-class to which Yeats belonged (as well as in other middle-classes), in the twenties and thirties. The *Irish Times,* spokesman of that class, aroused no protest from its readers when it hailed Hitler (4 March 1933) as 'Europe's standard bearer against Muscovite terrorism' and its references to Mussolini were as consistently admiring as those to Soviet Russia were consistently damning. But the limiting factor on the pro-Fascist tendencies of the *Irish Times* and of the Irish Protestant middle-class generally was the pull of loyalty to Britain, a factor which did not apply—or applied only with great ambivalence—in the case of Yeats. Mr. T. R. Henn is quite right when he says that Yeats was 'not alone in believing at that moment of history, that the discipline of Fascist theory might impose order upon a disintegrating world'. I cannot follow Mr. Henn, however, to his conclusion that 'nothing could be further from Yeats's mind than [Fascism's] violent and suppressive practice' (*The Lonely Tower,* p. 467). 'Force, marching men' and 'the victory [in civil war] of the skilful, riding their machines as did the feudal knights their armoured horses' (*On the Boiler*), surely belong to the domain of violent and suppressive practice.

Just as one school is led to claim that the pro-Fascist Yeats was not the 'true' Yeats, so another tries to believe that the Fascism to which Yeats was drawn was not a 'true' Fascism.

Several critics have assured us that he was drawn not really to Fascism, but to some idealized aristocracy of eighteenth-century stamp. 'In all fairness', writes Dr. Vivian Mercier, 'we should allow that his views were closer to Hamilton's or even to

Jefferson's than they were to Mussolini's'.[78] As far as political theory is concerned this is probably correct—although the name of Swift would seem more relevant than that of Hamilton or of Jefferson. But it ignores one important reality: that Yeats was interested in contemporary politics and that he was a contemporary, not of Swift's or Jefferson's, but of Mussolini's.[79]

He would certainly have preferred something more strictly aristocratic than Fascism, but since he was living in the twentieth century he was attracted to Fascism as the best available form of anti-democratic theory and practice. Mr. Frank O'Connor, who knew him well in his last years and—politics apart—greatly admired and liked him, has told us plainly that 'he was a fascist and authoritarian, seeing in world crises only the break-up of the "damned liberalism" he hated'.[80]

George Orwell, though critical, and up to a point percipient, about Yeats's tendencies, thought that Yeats misunderstood what an authoritarian society would be like. Such a society, Orwell pointed out, 'will not be ruled by noblemen with Van Dyck faces, but by anonymous millionaires, shiny-bottomed bureaucrats and murderous gangsters'. This implies a degree of innocence in Yeats which cannot reasonably be postulated. O'Higgins and O'Duffy were not 'Duke Ercole and Guidobaldo', and Yeats had considerable experience of practical politics, both in the nineties and in the early twenties. 'In the last forty years', wrote J. M. Hone in the year of Yeats's death, 'there was never a period in which his countrymen did not regard him as a public figure'.[81] When he thought of rule by an *élite* it was a possible *élite,* resembling in many ways the nominated members of the Senate in which he had sat.[82] Its membership—bankers, organizers, ex-officers—would correspond roughly to what Orwell, in more emotive language, describes. Nor should it be assumed—as Orwell with his 'murderous gangsters' seems to imply—that the sensitive nature of the poet would necessarily be revolted by the methods of rule of an authoritarian state.[83] Yeats—unlike, say, his brother, or Lady Gregory—was not, in politics, a very squeamish person. Seventy-seven executions did not repel him; on the contrary, they made him admire O'Higgins all the more. At least one of his associates of the early thirties might have been described as a 'murderous gangster'. And when, in 1936, Ethel Mannin appealed to him for a gesture which would have helped the German writer, Ossietzki, then in a Nazi concentration camp, Yeats re-refused. 'Do not', he said, 'try to make a politician of me . . .'[84]

It is true that neither Yeats nor anyone else during Yeats's lifetime knew what horrors Fascism would be capable of. But the many who, like Yeats, were drawn to Fascism at this time knew, and seemed to have little difficulty in accepting, or at least making allowances for, much of what had already been done and continued to be done. 'The Prussian police', wrote the *Irish Times* in an editorial of February 1933, 'have been authorized by Herr Hitler's Minister to shoot Communists—a term which in Germany has a wide political connotation—on sight'. The same editorial which contained this information ended with the words: 'Naturally the earlier phases of this renascence are crude, but Germany is finding her feet after a long period of political ineptitude.'[85]

Yeats read the newspapers; he also read, as Hone records, several books on Fascist Italy and Nazi Germany.[86] If, then, he was attracted to the dominant movements in these countries, and if he supported a movement in his own country whose resemblances to these Continental movements he liked to stress, it cannot be contended that he did so in ignorance of such 'crude' practices as the *Irish Times* described.[87]

Some writers—notably Professor Donald Torchiana in his well-documented study *W. B. Yeats, Jonathan Swift and Liberty*[88] —have insisted that, in spite of Yeats's authoritarian and Fascist leanings, he was essentially a friend of liberty. 'Both Swift and Yeats', Torchiana concludes, 'served human liberty'. The senses in which this is true for Yeats are important but clearly limited. He defended the liberty of the artist, consistently. In politics, true to his duality, he defended the liberty of Ireland against English domination, and the liberty of his own caste—and some-times, by extension, of others—against clerical domination.

Often these liberties overlapped, and the cause of artist and aristocrat became the same; often his resistance to 'clerical' authoritarianism (his position on the Lock-out, on divorce, on censorship) makes him appear a liberal. But his objection to clerical authoritarianism is not the liberal's objection to *all* authoritarianism. On the contrary he favors 'a despotism of the educated classes' and, in the search for this, is drawn towards Fascism. It is true that Fascism was not in reality a despotism of the educated classes, but it was a form of despotism which the educated classes in the twenties and thirties showed a disposition to settle for—a disposition proportionate to the apparent threat, in their country, of Communism or 'anarchy'. In assessing Yeats's pro-Fascist opinions, there is no need to regard these as so extraordinary that he must either not have been himself, or not have known what he was about.

10

Yet, in challenging the assumption that Yeats's pro-Fascism was either not 'truly Yeats' or not 'truly pro-Fascist', one must not overlook the intermittent character of his pro-Fascism and of all his political activity. If his pro-Fascism was real, his irony and caution were real too, and his phases of detachment not less real than his phases of political commitment. The long phase of nationalist commitment (1887–1903) was followed by a long phase (1903–16) of detachment from almost all practical politics (except those to which the theatre exposed him), by a critique of Irish nationalist politics, and by the formation of an aristocratic attitude which did not find practical political expression until after 1916 when—after a new flare-up of nationalist feeling—he re-entered Irish politics on the right, in the Free State Senate. After clerical pressures had made the Senate uncongenial to him and had extruded him from it, he withdrew again from active politics (1928–33), only returning when a situation propitious to Fascism seemed to present itself. When O'Duffy's Irish Fascists failed ignominiously he turned away from politics again, though not for ever. In the last two years of his life politics flared up again. Always, in the long phases of withdrawal, he tended to write of all politics with a kind of contempt, a plague-on-both-your-houses air.[89] In that same letter in which he refused to try to help Ossietzki he wrote, '. . . if I did what you want I would seem to hold one form of government more responsible than any other and that would betray my convictions. Communist, Fascist, nationalist, clerical, anti-clerical, are all responsible according to the number of their victims.'[90]

This was 'the true Yeats'—the true Yeats of a period of political inactivity when he watched, bitterly or sardonically, a game he had no chance of playing. But when he had a chance, when he saw political opportunities, as in 1891 or 1920, or thought he saw them, as in 1933 and again in 1938, he wrote differently, and with excitement. These 'manic' phases of political activity were no less real or important than the 'depressive' phases which followed them. And the options of the 'manic' phases were not haphazard or middle-of-the-road. They were either anti-English or—in Irish politics—aristocratic and, from the time Fascism had appeared, distinctly pro-Fascist. At the end, in the last two years, as we shall see, these two elements were beginning to combine.

It was Yeats's misfortune as a politician, and his good fortune as a poet, that his political opportunities or temptations were few and far between. Irish politics in their normal run have not, since the introduction of universal suffrage, been receptive to poets, aristocrats or Protestants—there have been distinguished exceptions, but that has been the general rule for many years. It is only in rare conjunctures, times of great national stress and division, that an Irish party is likely to find room for such exotics for, in such times, men welcome an ally with a name and voice. Such moments of excitement and emotion, which offered opportunities, were also the moments which most stirred the poet. Such times were the Parnell split of 1891 and the Sinn Fein split of 1920–22. The abortive Fascist movement of 1933 seemed to be, but was not, the opening of another profound fissure in Irish political life. In the first two cases, the world of Irish politics proved, when 'normalcy' had returned, no place for the poet.

In the third case the poet retired from a political movement which had lost momentum. It is fairly safe to say that, if it had succeeded, it would have dropped him or forced him out; not through any great aversion on his part from thugs in colored shirts, but because an Irish Fascism, to have any chance of staying in power, would necessarily have to become an intensely clerical Fascism. In fact the successor movement to the Blueshirts—the Christian Front—was a noisily Catholic clerical-Fascist movement. This was a kind of Fascism—perhaps the only kind—which Yeats could not accept or tolerate, since his authoritarian view of life derived ultimately from his concept of the caste to which he belonged, and the distinguishing mark of that caste was its Protestantism.

In the political writings of his last two years the two elements in his politics—the 'Irish' and the 'Protestant' elements—entered into a new set of relations. The 'Irish' element became more vocal than it had been since 1916 and the 'Protestant' element was obliged to break finally with the traditional right wing in Irish politics. Anti-English feeling, long dormant in Yeats, became increasingly pronounced in the period 1937–38. A series of poems, 'Roger Casement', 'The Ghost of Roger Casement', 'The O'Rahilly', 'Come Gather Round Me, Parnellites', both expressed and did much to rekindle the old pride in Irish nationalism which the cynicism that followed the Civil War had dulled. The Casement poems especially had a powerful anti-English charge:

> O what has made that sudden noise?
> What on the threshold stands?
> It never crossed the sea because
> John Bull and the sea are friends;
> But this is not the old sea
> Nor this the old seashore.
> What gave that roar of mockery,
> That roar in the sea's roar?
> *The ghost of Roger Casement*
> *Is beating on the door.*

No Irishman, reading these lines on the eve of the Second World War, had forgotten that Casement had been hanged, as well as

187

'morally assassinated' for trying, in 1916, to bring help to Ireland from Germany. And some Irishmen, at least, must have reflected that if the sea was no longer the old sea, which had been friends with John Bull, the reason for this might be that the nation from which Casement had tried to bring help now possessed a powerful air force.

Potentially, 'The Ghost of Roger Casement' was as explosive as *Cathleen ni Houlihan.*

Just at this time Yeats was writing to Ethel Mannin that, while he liked neither side in Spain, and did not want to see his old leader O'Duffy—now fighting for Franco—return to Ireland with enhanced prestige to 'the Catholic front',[91] he was attracted by the thought that a Fascist victory would weaken England.

I am an old Fenian and I think the old Fenian in me would rejoice if a Fascist nation or government controlled Spain because that would weaken the British empire, force England to be civil to India and loosen the hand of English finance in the far East of which I hear occasionally. But this is mere instinct. A thing I would never act on. Then I have a horror of modern politics— I see nothing but the manipulation of popular enthusiasm by false news—a horror that has been deepened in these last weeks by the Casement business. My ballad on that subject has had success. . . .[92]

The success of the ballad was mainly among those who had been Yeats's political enemies and against whom he had conspired: de Valera's party. It was in de Valera's paper, the *Irish Press,* that the ballad appeared. Yeats wrote:

On Feb. 2 my wife went to Dublin shopping and was surprised at the deference everybody showed her in buses and shops. Then she found what it was—the Casement poem was in the morning paper. Next day I was publicly thanked by the Vice-President of the Executive Council (Mr. de Valera's deputy in the Government), by de Valera's political secretary, by our chief antiquarian and an old revolutionist, Count Plunkett, who called my poem 'a ballad the people much needed'. De Valera's newspaper gave me a long leader, saying that for generations to come my poem will pour scorn on the forgers and their backers.[93]

There were adequate reasons for a degree of reconciliation between Yeats and his former foes. First, from Yeats's point of view, the events of the early thirties had shown that, if there was a 'strong man' in Irish politics, it was not O'Duffy but de Valera.[94] Second, five years of de Valera's government had dissipated the theory—once cherished by Yeats's former political friends—that de Valera meant Communism. Third, de Valera was the main barrier against what Yeats then saw—with considerable justice—as a rising tide of clericalist power, a tide which threatened all that Yeats had built in Ireland: 'I am convinced that if the Spanish war goes on or if [it] ceases and O'Duffy's volunteers return heroes, my "pagan" institutions, the Theatre, the Academy will be fighting for their lives against combined Gaelic and Catholic bigotry. A friar or monk has already threatened us with mob violence.'[95]

In the same letter, Yeats noted how de Valera had carried in Parliament, against a pro-Franco opposition, a measure to stop Irish volunteers from going to Spain.

The fourth reason for a *rapprochement* with de Valera's party is more complex. Just as Yeats's own mind was hopelessly divided about the Spanish War—the authoritarian and Anglophobe in him desiring a Franco victory, the Irish anti-clerical dreading the results—so the party of his former friends was also in confusion. But their confusion was almost the mirror-image, the inversion, of his. They wanted, or said they wanted, a Franco victory on Catholic grounds. But also, as the party of the Anglo-Irish treaty, the 'Commonwealth Party', they contained the most 'pro-British' elements in Irish life: the people who, in the event of Britain's going to war, would try to see to it that Ireland came in on Britain's side.

De Valera at this time was engaged, with the Chamberlain Government, in the negotiations which led to the return of the Irish ports, which the Treaty had retained under British control. Without the return of these ports Ireland's neutrality in the coming war, which it was de Valera's policy to ensure, would scarcely have been practical politics. Yeats—who, as Frank O'Connor has told us,[96] in his last years admired and defended de Valera—put his name and influence explicitly behind the recovery of the ports; implicitly but clearly behind a policy of neutrality:

Armament comes next to education. The country must take over the entire defence of its shores. The formation of military families should be encouraged. I know enough of my countrymen to know that, once democratic plausibility has gone, their small army will be efficient and self

189

reliant, highly trained though not highly-disciplined. Armed with modern weapons, officered by men from such schools as I have described, it could throw back from our shores the disciplined, uneducated masses of the commercial nations.

From the point of view of de Valera's party, Yeats's tentative overtures—for such, I believe, they were—would have presented some advantages. The patriotic poems undoubtedly struck a genuinely responsive note among most Irish people: their appearance in de Valera's newspaper was helpful, especially at this time, in Ireland; the prestige—by now great—of Yeats's name in England would be helpful there in relation to the ports and to neutrality. Yet, while there were reasons on both sides for some degree of *rapprochement,* it may be doubted whether this would ever have become close or warm. Irish political life between the wars had been too bitter for that. De Valera's memory has not the reputation of being short or inaccurate. Yeats's activities in 1922–23 and in 1933 would have been quite fresh in de Valera's mind. It is believed also that he had read, with distaste and distress, the lines:

> Had de Valera eaten Parnell's heart
> No loose-lipped demagogue had won the day,
> No civil rancour torn the land apart.

Real reconciliation had to wait for the next generation. After the war Yeats's son, Michael, joined de Valera's party and became a Senator.

11

The two main currents in Yeats's active politics—his Anglophobe Irish nationalism and his authoritarianism—necessarily converged in the years immediately before the war, thrusting him in the direction of desiring the victory of the Fascist powers. The doctrine of John O'Leary, to whose school Yeats always claimed to belong, was Tone's doctrine: that 'England's difficulty is Ireland's opportunity'. The caution and scepticism, which were also features of Yeats's personality, worked, together with his repulsion from Irish clerical Fascism, to prevent him from being carried too far by Tone and O'Leary. But an underlying wish found voice, at this time, when the prestige and authority of England

190

were lower than they had been for centuries, in an increasingly anti-English tone, in verse and prose and in his conversation. This did not happen without a violent inner struggle.

The 'Irishry' [he wrote in *A General Introduction for My Work* (1937)] have preserved their ancient 'deposit' through wars which, during the sixteenth and seventeenth centuries, became wars of extermination; no people, Lecky said at the opening of his *Ireland in the Eighteenth Century,* have undergone greater persecution, nor did that persecution altogether cease up to our own day. No people hate as we do in whom that past is always alive, there are moments when hatred poisons my life and I accuse myself of effeminacy because I have not given it adequate expression. It is not enough to have put it into the mouth of a rambling peasant poet. Then I remind myself that though mine is the first English marriage I know of in the direct line, all my family names are English and that I owe my soul to Shakespeare, to Spenser and to Blake, perhaps to William Morris, and to the English language in which I think, speak and write, that everything I love has come to me through English; my hatred tortures me with love, my love with hate. I am like the Tibetan monk who dreams at his initiation that he is eaten by a wild beast and learns on waking that he himself is eater and eaten. This is Irish hatred and solitude, the hatred of human life that made Swift write *Gulliver* and the epitaph upon his tomb, that can still make us wag between extremes and doubt our sanity.

On the Boiler, written the following year, is his last political statement: a sort of political testament. 'For the first time', he wrote to Maud Gonne about this tract, in what may be his last letter to her, 'I am saying what I believe about Irish and European politics' (16 June 1938; *Letters,* p. 910). *On the Boiler* assumes— without, however, being altogether explicit about it—that the Fascist powers are winning and England is in contemptible decline. 'The Fascist countries', he writes in the section 'To-morrow's Revolution', 'know that civilization has reached a crisis, and found their eloquence upon that knowledge'. The only fault he has to find with them is that 'perhaps from dread of attack' they encourage large families. He assumes in 'Ireland after the Revolution' that 'some tragic crisis shall so alter Europe and all opinion that the Irish government will teach the great majority of its school-children nothing but'—a list of manual and menial occupations follows.[97]

At the time when this was written, the 'tragic crisis' many expected was that which was to lead Pétain's France to adopt somewhat similar educational policies. It is hard to resist the conclusion that Yeats, when writing this, expected, and hoped, that Ireland 'after the revolution' would be a sort of satellite of a Fas-

191

cist-dominated Europe. 'The danger', he wrote in this year 1938, 'is that there will be no war, that the skilled will attempt nothing, that the European civilization, like those older civilizations that saw the triumph of their gangrel stocks, will accept decay'. The war he said he wanted was a war between the skilled and the unskilled; as types of the skilled he took the crack German submarine commanders of the First World War, and nationally-unspecified mechanized warriors of the future, 'riding their machines as did the feudal knights their armoured horses'. As regards England his contempt, in this year of Munich, is un-qualified and savage. After saying some hard things about King George V, he concludes 'Ireland After the Revolution' with the words: 'The Irish mind has still, in country rapscallion or in Bernard Shaw, an ancient cold, explosive detonating impartiality. The English mind, excited by its newspaper proprietors and its schoolmasters, has turned into a bed-hot harlot.'

Dorothy Wellesley, who was troubled by his increasingly anti-British attitude in the last years of his life, made a shrewd comment: 'Why then, in the twentieth century and when the Irish are freed from their oppressors the English, does he despise and dislike us increasingly? Because he dislikes the stuffed lion and admires the ranting, roaring oppressors.'[98]

During Yeats's life the English government gave him a Civil List pension, and offered him a knighthood, which he refused,[99] and the Athenaeum Club gave him the honor of a special election. Since his death, the British Council has presented him to the world as one of England's glories. There is therefore some irony in the thought that there was something in him that would have taken considerable pleasure—though not without a respectful back-ward glance at Shakespeare—in seeing England occupied by the Nazis, the Royal Family exiled, and the Mother of Parliaments torn down. Meanwhile in Ireland one would have expected to see him at least a cautious participant, or ornament, in a col-laborationist régime.

It is probably fortunate for his future reputation, and especially his standing with the British Council, that he died in January 1939 before the political momentum of his last years could carry him any farther than *On the Boiler*.

12

Yeats was a public figure for more than forty years; deeply immersed in political interests, politically active whenever opportunity presented itself. His best poetry—that of his maturity and old age—had often a political theme, sometimes a political intent. The argument of this essay has been that his politics deserve to be taken more seriously than they have been, were not fundamentally inconsistent, vague or irrelevant to his 'real self' and were, in his maturity and old age, generally pro-Fascist in tendency, and Fascist in practice on the single occasion when opportunity arose.

How can those of us who loathe such politics continue not merely to admire but to love the poetry, and perhaps most of all the poems with a political bearing?

An important part of the answer is supplied by the poet himself in a note on 'Leda and the Swan':

I wrote 'Leda and the Swan' because the editor of a political review asked me for a poem. I thought 'After the individualist, demagogic movement founded by Hobbes [*sic*] and popularized by the Encyclopaedists and the French revolution, we have a soil so exhausted that it cannot grow that crop again for centuries'. Then I thought 'Nothing is now possible but some movement from above preceded by some violent annunciation'. My fancy began to play with Leda and the Swan for metaphor, and I began this poem; but as I wrote, bird and lady took such possession of the scene that all politics went out of it, and my friend tells me that his 'conservative readers would misunderstand the poem'.[100]

They would have been puzzled certainly:

> A sudden blow: the great wings beating still
> Above the staggering girl, her thighs caressed
> By the dark webs, her nape caught in his bill,
> He holds her helpless breast upon his breast.
>
> How can those terrified vague fingers push
> The feathered glory from her loosening thighs?
> And how can body, laid in that white rush,
> But feel the strange heart beating where it lies?
>
> A shudder in the loins engenders there
> The broken wall, the burning roof and tower
> And Agamemnon dead.

> Being so caught up,
> So mastered by the brute blood of the air,
> Did she put on his knowledge with his power
> Before the indifferent beak could let her drop?

Very little seems to be known—and perhaps little can be known —of how this process of transformation works. How can that patter of Mussolini prose 'produce' such a poem? How can that political ugly duckling be turned into this glorious Swan? It is in a sense like the transmutation, in 'Easter 1916', of those whom Yeats had thought of as commonplace people:

> All changed, changed utterly:
> A terrible beauty is born.

Is the connection, then, between the politics and the poetry only trivial and superficial? There is, I think, a deeper connection: if the political prose and the poetry are thought of, not as 'substance' and 'metaphor', or 'content' and 'style', but as cognate expressions of a fundamental force, anterior to both politics and poetry.

That force was, I suggest, Yeats's profound and tragic intuitive—and intelligent—awareness, in his maturity and old age, of what the First World War had set loose, of what was already moving towards Hitler and the Second World War. That he is conscious of the danger a letter shows as early as 1923: 'Unless Europe takes to war again and starts new telepathic streams of violence and cruelty'.[101] But the poetry is already responding to the telepathic streams as early as 1920, when he wrote 'The Second Coming':

> Things fall apart; the centre cannot hold;
> Mere anarchy is loosed upon the world,
> The blood-dimmed tide is loosed . . .
>
> . . . .
>
> And what rough beast, its hour come round at last,
> Slouches towards Bethlehem to be born?

Years afterwards, just before the Spanish War, he drew Ethel Mannin's attention to this poem: 'If you have my poems by you look up a poem called "The Second Coming". It was written more than sixteen or seventeen years ago and foretold what is happening. I have written of the same thing again and again since.'[102]

The words 'violence', 'hatred' and 'fanaticism' became key-words in Yeats's poetry. He often uses them in condemnation of the left in Irish politics—the politics of Constance Markievicz and of Maud Gonne:

> I thought my love must her own soul destroy
> So did fanaticism and hate enslave it

But he is also increasingly conscious of these same forces in himself:

> Out of Ireland have we come:
> Great hatred, little room,
> Maimed us from the start.
> I carry from my mother's womb
> A fanatic heart.

The 'fanatic heart', an unusual capacity for hatred and an unusual experience of it, probably made him more sensitive and more responsive to the 'telepathic waves' coming from Europe than other writers in English seem to have been. The forces in him that responded to the hatred, cruelty and violence welling up in Europe produced the prophetic images of 'The Second Coming' and the last part of 'Nineteen Hundred and Nineteen':

> Violence upon the roads: violence of horses;
> Some few have handsome riders, are garlanded
> On delicate sensitive ear or tossing mane,
> But wearied running round and round in their courses
> All break and vanish, and evil gathers head:
> Herodias' daughters have returned again,
> A sudden blast of dusty wind and after
> Thunder of feet, tumult of images,
> Their purpose in the labyrinth of the wind; . . .

It may be objected that 'Nineteen Hundred and Nineteen' and 'The Second Coming' were written not about the coming of Fascism but about the Anglo-Irish War and the Black and Tans. The distinction is less than absolute: the Black and Tans were in fact an early manifestation of an outlook and methods which the Nazis were later to perfect. The *Freikorps* on the Polish-German border were at this time trying to do exactly what the Black and Tans were doing in Ireland and the *Freikorps* were the direct and proudly acknowledged predecessors of Hitler's Nazis. There is even a direct link between the Black and Tans and the

Nazis in the person of 'Lord Haw Haw'—William Joyce—who fought for the British Government in the first movement and was hanged by it for his work in the second.

Bruno Brehm, one of Hitler's novelists, made the assassination by Irish revolutionaries of Sir Henry Wilson—the principal exponent of intensified Black-and-Tan measures in Ireland—symbolic of the tragic confrontation of hero and submen. Wilson was seen in the same relation to the Irish as Hitler to Jews and Bolsheviks.

In *A General Introduction for My Work* (1937) Yeats made specific the connection between his own hatred and what was happening in Europe:

When I stand upon O'Connell Bridge in the half-light and notice that discordant architecture, all those electric signs, where modern heterogeneity has taken physical form, a vague hatred comes up out of my own dark and I am certain that wherever in Europe there are minds strong enough to lead others the same vague hatred arises; in four or five or in less generations this hatred will have issued in violence and imposed some kind of rule of kindred. I cannot know the nature of that rule, for its opposite fills the light; all I can do to bring it nearer is to intensify my hatred. I am no Nationalist, except in Ireland for passing reasons; State and Nation are the work of intellect, and when you consider what comes before and after them they are, as Victor Hugo said of something or other, not worth the blade of grass God gives for the nest of the linnet.

By the time the *General Introduction* was written, Fascist power and 'rule of kindred' were already in full swing: the length of time—'four or five generations'—is odd and perhaps calculated: it brings to mind the retrospective 'commentaries' on the songs for O'Duffy. The paragraph itself may be taken as a kind of retrospective commentary on 'The Second Coming'.

In 'The Second Coming' the poet, perhaps from the foretaste of the Black and Tans, augured the still more terrible things that were to come. The sort of 'premonitory' intuition present in 'The Second Coming' and in other poems necessarily affected Yeats in his ordinary life as well as in his poetry. Yeats the manager, the Senator, the politician, stands in a diplomatic relation to these intimations of power. His references to Fascism, though sometimes mildly critical, are never hostile, almost always respectful, often admiring, and this especially in years of Fascist victories: 1922, 1933 and 1938. Some reasons for this have already been suggested; it might be added that for Yeats a band-wagon had the same high degree of attraction that it has for other political mortals:

Processions that lack high stilts have nothing that catches the eye

If a Marxist, believing that history is going in a given direction, thinks it right to give it a good shove in the way it is going, it is natural enough that one who, like Yeats, feels that it is going in the opposite direction should accompany it that way with, if not a shove, at least a cautious tilt.

In the poetry, however, the raw intimations of what is impending—the 'telepathic waves of violence and fear'—make themselves known, not in the form of calculated practical deductions, but in the attempt to reveal, through metaphoric insight, what is actually happening and even, in a broad sense, what is about to happen.[103] The poet, like the lady, is

. . . so caught up,
So mastered by the brute blood of the air

that he does indeed take on the knowledge of what is happening with the power to make it known. The political man had his cautious understanding with Fascism, the diplomatic relation to a great force; the poet conveyed the nature of the force, the dimension of the tragedy. The impurities of this long and extraordinary life went into its devious and sometimes sinister political theories and activities. The purity and integrity—including the truth about politics as Yeats apprehended it—are in the poetry concentrated in metaphors of such power that they thrust aside all calculated intent: bird and lady take possession of the scene.

NOTES

1. An unpublished letter from Yeats to my father, dated October 1927, contains an extremely angry reference to her 'ungraciousness and injustice' in some controversy.

2. On that aspect see J. M. Hone, 'Yeats as a Political Philosopher', *London Mercury* (April, 1939); Grattan Freyer, 'The Politics of W. B. Yeats', *Politics and Letters* (Summer, 1947); Donald Torchiana, 'W. B. Yeats, Jonathan Swift and Liberty', *Modern Philosophy* (August, 1963). The last two also discuss his political activities, but the stress is more on theory and less on practical political choices—in an Irish context—than is the case with the present essay. The two lines of approach give significantly different results.

3. Yeats belonged, not to the 'Ascendancy' in the strict sense of the word, but to the

Protestant middle-class of merchants and professional people: *une famille de bonne bourgeoisie protestante*, in the words of Paul-Dubois. But, like many members of this class, he preferred, particularly in his later years, to think of himself as belonging to an aristocracy. The family tree, it seems, had been 'burnt by Canadian Indians' (*Explorations*, p. 347).

4. *On the Boiler*, Dublin, 1939.

5. See *Reveries over Childhood and Youth*, London, 1916.

6. *Ibid.*

7. *A General Introduction for My Work* (1937). The important passage from which this is taken is quoted at greater length on p. 192.

8. . . . . 'It was you was it not', Yeats wrote to O'Leary, 'who converted Miss Gonne to her Irish opinions? She herself will make many converts' (1 February 1889). *The Letters of W. B. Yeats*, ed. Allan Wade, London, 1954, p. 108.

9. He seems never to have taken the Fenian oath (Hone, *W. B. Yeats*, p. 145).

10. *Autobiographies*, p. 209.

11. To Katharine Tynan, 25 July 1889. (*Letters*, p. 151).

12. In practice, when an occasion offered, she did not.

13. Maud Gonne, *A Servant of the Queen*, pp. 206–7; *Scattering Branches*, p. 49.

14. Lecture on accepting the Nobel Prize. Text in *Autobiographies*, p. 559.

15. Commentary on the poem 'Parnell's Funeral'. Text in *The Variorum Edition*, London, 1957, p. 834.

16. J. B. Yeats admired Butt and thought Parnell 'not a great man' (*Letters*, 20 September 1915).

17. Undated letter (probably December 1890) quoted in Ellmann, p. 102. Not in the selection of *Letters* edited by Allan Wade.

18. Full text in *The Variorum Edition*, p. 737. The poem was never republished by Yeats.

19. *Letters*, p. 179.

20.   'That I may seem though I die old
                A foolish passionate man.'
The use here of the word 'seem' seems to have been overlooked by some critics.

21. Those who doubt the existence of an element of calculation in Yeats's behavior at this time should consider a sentence in a letter of his advising a young Irishwoman to write about 'Irish legends and places': 'It helps originality and makes one's verses sincere, and gives one less numerous competitors' (31 January 1889). *Letters*, p. 104.

22. *Autobiographies*, p. 355.

23. Stephen Gwynn, quoted by A. N. Jeffares, *W. B. Yeats: Man and Poet*, p. 138. This is not at all an isolated judgment: P.S. O'Hegarty stated that to him and his revolutionary contemporaries *Cathleen ni Houlihan* was 'a sort of sacrament' ('W. B. Yeats and the Revolutionary Ireland of His Time' in *Dublin Magazine*, July–September, 1939).

24. How little the trend to reconciliation between the factions was to Yeats's taste may be gathered from the following: 'John Dillon [leader of the anti-Parnellite faction] is making the first speech he has made before a popular Dublin audience since the death of Parnell . . . [he] is very nervous . . . I am almost overpowered by an instinct of cruelty: I long to cry out, "Had Zimri peace that slew his master?"' (*Autobiographies*, p. 366.) Yeats has been represented as himself seeking to make peace between Parnellite and anti-Parnellite. This is true only in the sense that he and Maud Gonne, in helping, for example, to organize the centenary commemoration of the 1798 rebellion (a commemoration in which parliamentarians of both sections took part) reflected what J. M. Hone described, I believe correctly, as an endeavor on the part of the Irish Republican Brotherhood to assume control not only of Fenian propaganda but also of the Irish Parliamentary Party which was still torn by internal dissension (*W. B. Yeats*, p. 146). The support of the former anti-Parnellites— being the majority of the Irish people—was essential to the success of any Irish movement.

198

But the quotation from the *Autobiographies* (above) shows how Yeats continued to feel about the anti-Parnellite parliamentarians—of whom Dillon was not only the most eminent but also the most moderate.

25. 'The Cutting of an Agate' (1907) in *Essays and Introductions*, p. 260.

26. 'W.B. Yeats' in *Critical Essays*, London, 1943.

27. 10 April 1900. (*Letters*, p. 338.) In later years he liked to tell the story of the speaker at the Socialist picnic: 'I was brought up a gentleman and now as you can see associate with all sorts.'

28. Cf. 'The People' (1916).

29. Those who find it hard to understand such hypersensitivity should look through the back files of *Punch*. It was natural—though silly—that some Irish people, depressed by being seen as Caliban, should insist on getting from 'our own theatre' a much more flattering reflection.

30. Hone, *W.B. Yeats*, p. 217.

31. To be fair to the much-maligned Abbey audiences the survival was also due to the recognition by small—but qualitatively significant—sections of Catholics and nationalists that the *Playboy* rioters had made fools of themselves.

32. Ellmann, p. 179.

33. Quoted in Hone, p. 194.

34. J.B. Yeats, *Letters* (11 December 1913).

35. Letter to Ethel Mannin, 4 March 1935 (*Letters*, p. 831). He added: 'though I have kept it out of my poems and it will embitter your soul with hatred as it has mine'.

36. His always latent hostility to 'the crowd', including his own audience, was generously stimulated when, on a night in 1905, some members of an Abbey audience hissed Maud Gonne on her appearance after her separation from Major MacBride. 'He felt that never again could he touch popular politics'. (Hone, p. 210.)

37. Not at all to Yeats's pleasure.

38. This is not just a rhetorical flourish. 'You will recollect, when dealing with a company of this kind', said Murphy in an address to his tramway workers on 19 July 1913, 'that every one of the shareholders, to the number of five, six or seven thousand, will have three meals a day whether the men succeed or not. I don't know if the men who go out can count on this'. (Quoted in *1913: Jim Larkin and the Dublin Lock-out*, Workers' Union of Ireland, Dublin, May, 1964.)

39. 'Dublin Fanaticism', *Irish Worker*, 1 November 1913; reprinted in *1913: Jim Larkin and the Dublin Lock-out*.

40. *W.B. Yeats*, p. 268. Hone's reference to the letter is brief and he does not quote it.

41. Typically, he refers to the events which followed the lock-out, decided on by the Dublin employers of members of the Irish Transport and General Workers' Union, as 'the great strike led by Larkin which paralysed the life of Dublin'.

42. 'This,' Hone adds rather cryptically, 'Murphy certainly was not.'

43. 'The nationalist hotel' was not a political center, but the only hotel owned by a Catholic. The owner gave no sign of objecting to the political *status quo* and even, for business reasons, kept 'Protestant Bibles' in the hotel rooms.

44. The Land League was primarily an agrarian body but it and its successor bodies extended their operations to urban areas. Michael Davitt boasted that a 'run' organized by the League broke the Munster Bank in Cork: the Plan of Campaign certainly brought economic life to a standstill in the town of Tipperary.

45. This was by decision of Parnell himself at a time when he wanted to brake the revolutionary tendencies of the movement. See the present writer's *Parnell and His Party*.

46. It is true that, as in comparable situations elsewhere, the new middle-class as a whole was inferior to the old one in education as in money. In the novels of Somerville and Ross

we catch glimpses of this new class, as they appeared to two pairs of brightly observant Ascendancy eyes.

47. John O'Leary died in 1907.

48.   'Did words of mine send out
         Certain men the English shot?'

49. Full text in *The Variorum Edition*, p. 791. It has been stated that he intended to publish this 'but cancelled the publication on hearing that it would distress Robert's widow'. (Hone, *W.B. Yeats*, p. 338.)

50. He could hardly, of course, have published any of them in the United Kingdom in wartime, but could have published at least 'Easter 1916' in America; it was written in September 1916, and the United States did not enter the war until the following April. 'Easter 1916' was printed at the time in an edition of twenty-five copies for distribution among friends, but the series was withheld from the sight of the general public until 1920. (Hone, *W.B. Yeats*, p. 301.)

51. A friend who read this in draft objected to this comparison and pointed out that the Free State forces, unlike the Black and Tans, did not use indiscriminate terror against the civilian population. This is a valid point, though even the Black-and-Tan terror was not *altogether* indiscriminate.

52. *Lady Gregory's Journals, 1916–1930,* ed. Lennox Robinson, London, 1946.

53. Mary MacSwiney was the sister of Terence MacSwiney, the famous Lord Mayor of Cork, who had died on hunger-strike as a prisoner of the British. The Government may or may not have had a sentimental feeling for her; some of its members probably had; all of them knew that to let her die as her brother had died would discredit them in the eyes of most of their countrymen.

54. Father of the present writer; at this time a leader-writer on the *Independent*.

55. While refusing to protest publicly about the Government's policy on hunger-striking, Yeats may have interceded privately. Patrick McCartan informed Mr. Terence de Vere White, many years later, that 'I got Mrs. Green, W.B. Yeats and others to intercede for them, but it was futile'. (White, *Kevin O'Higgins,* London, 1949, p. 179.)

56. To Edmund Dulac, 1 December 1922. (*Letters,* p. 694.)

57. To Olivia Shakespear, May 1922. (*Letters,* p. 682.)

58. To the same. October 1922. (*Letters,* p. 690.)

59. To H.J.C. Grierson, 6 November 1922. Dr. Ellmann quotes (pp. 248–9) a public speech in the same vein nearly two years later (2 August 1924).

60. Thus, Mr. Arland Ussher has said that 'Yeats, in spite of his desire to be a public figure, was more apolitical than any fully responsible person alive' (*Three Great Irishmen,* p. 91). Another critic has said that even his 'superficially political poems' are 'not really so'. (M. L. Rosenthal, in *The Nation,* 23 June 1956.) It is hard to see how these judgments can be reconciled with the known facts of Yeats's life and work.

61. I am not sure that it was parody. Dr. Sheehy Skeffington recalls it as an anecdote, and believes it to be true.

62. 'Students of contemporary Italy where Vico's thought is current through its influence upon Croce and Gentile think it created, or in part created, the present government of one man surrounded by just such able assistants as Vico foresaw'. (Introduction to *The Words upon the Window-pane* (1931); *Explorations,* p. 355.)

63. O'Higgins's biographer, Mr. Terence de Vere White, while noting that it became the fashion to call him 'the Irish Mussolini', maintains that he was in fact 'an intense believer in democracy'. This may well be so; as far as the subject of this essay is concerned, the important point is that it was as 'an Irish Mussolini' that Yeats rightly or wrongly saw him, and that he admired him for that.

64. To Olivia Shakespear, April 1933. (*Letters,* p. 809.)

200

65. I was not alone in being impressed by the top-hats. 'Rarely', noted the Dublin *Evening Mail*, 'has there been such a display of silk hats and frock coats'. The same paper recorded that 'the Fascisti in Dublin were present with their flag and black shirts and they were given a place in the procession by the police'. (*E. M.* 'Items of the Funeral', 13 July 1927.)

66. The Senate attended the funeral as a body: the press did not report the names of individual Senators attending. Senate records show that Yeats was present on the previous day at the meeting which unanimously decided that the Senate would attend the funeral as a body.

67. The *Irish Times*, representative of Irish Protestant opinion, editorially regretted 'the manner of Senator Yeats's intervention' on this subject (12 June 1925).

68. Yeats's growing resentment of the Irish bishops found vent, as early as 1924, in a criticism of the style of the Pastorals: 'a style rancid, coarse and vague like that of the daily papers' (leading article in *Tomorrow* quoted in Ellmann, pp. 250–1). Senator Yeats—not yet flinging prudence to the winds—did not sign this article, but got two other people to sign it.

69. 11 June 1925.

70. 'Commentary on the Three Songs', December 1934, in *The Variorum Edition*, pp. 836–7.

71. It has even been improved upon. Mr. Arland Ussher has made the remarkable claim that Yeats's 'brief flirtation with O'Duffy's "blueshirts"' was 'something of a pro-British peacemaking gesture' (*Three Great Irishmen*, p. 92). Yeats's letters to Olivia Shakespear do not suggest that affection for England or peace had anything to do with his excitement about the Blueshirts.

72. *Letters*, p. 808.

73. Earlier he had written as if he thought de Valera a Fascist. 'You are right', he wrote to Olivia Shakespear in February 1933, 'in comparing de Valera to Mussolini or Hitler. All three have exactly the same aim so far as I can judge'. (*Letters*, p. 806.) It is hard to reconcile this ambiguous and—however interpreted—untrue statement with the organization of 'a Fascist opposition' to de Valera.

74. 13 July 1933. (*Letters*, pp. 811–12.)

75. *Letters*, pp. 812–13.

76. The sequence of events described by Yeats in his September letter involved, in reality, a climb down by O'Duffy who had announced a mass parade of the Blueshirts (National Guard) for 13 August, the anniversary of Collins's death. When the National Guard was proclaimed illegal the parade was called off and 'a quiet ceremony at Cenotaph' was held instead. O'Duffy immediately became, as Yeats noted, leader of the Opposition United Party but, as a historian sympathetic to the opposition has observed: 'from the very outset the new arrangement was thoroughly unsatisfactory, it quickly became apparent that O'Duffy did not possess the special qualities that equip a man for leadership in public life'. (D. O'Sullivan, *The Irish Free State and the Senate*, p. 406.) O'Duffy resigned his chairmanship of the United Party in September 1934.

77. There is a sense of course in which the poet, actually engaged in writing his poetry, is 'the true Yeats', but that is another matter.

78. 'To pierce the dark mind', *Nation* (10 December 1960). My friend Dr. Mercier, like almost all scholars from Ireland who have written on Yeats, finds his aristocratism, as an Anglo-Irish attitude, more congenial than the aboriginal writer of the present essay can find it.

79. He had, in any case, the assurance of his friend Ezra Pound (*Jefferson and/or Mussolini*) that the Duce was translating Jeffersonian ideas into twentieth-century terms.

80. 'The Old Age of a Poet', *The Bell* (February 1941). He also mentions an Abbey

dispute over an attempt by Yeats to stage *Coriolanus* for purposes of 'fascist propaganda'. Mr. Sean O'Faoláin, a more cautious observer, who also knew Yeats at this time, speaks of his 'fascist tendencies' ('Yeats and the Younger Generation', *Horizon,* January, 1942).

81. 'Yeats as a Political Philosopher', *London Mercury* (April 1939). Hone adds that, among Yeats's fellow Senators, a banker thought the poet would have made 'an admirable banker' and a lawyer thought that 'a great lawyer' was lost in him.

82. 'In its early days', Yeats wrote of the Senate, 'some old banker or lawyer would dominate the House, leaning upon the back of the chair in front, always speaking with undisturbed self-possession as at some table in a board-room. My imagination sets up against him some typical elected man, emotional as a youthful chimpanzee, hot and vague, always disturbed, always hating something or other'. (*On the Boiler.*) In another mood, however, he wrote about these oligarchs in a more disparaging vein. (*A Packet for Ezra Pound.*)

83. The late Louis MacNeice in *The Poetry of W.B. Yeats* seems to have been the first to lay much stress on Yeats's relation to Fascism, but could not quite make up his mind what that relation was. He refers to Yeats at one point as 'the man who nearly became a fascist' (p. 174), having spoken of him earlier as having arrived at 'his own elegant brand of fascism' (p. 41).

84. To Ethel Mannin, April 1936. In fairness to Yeats it must be noted, however, that in order to help Ossietzki he would have had to recommend him to the Nobel Committee for consideration for the Nobel Prize—something which, on artistic grounds, he may well have been unwilling to do. His degree of 'toughness' on political matters, minimized as it has been by some of his admirers, should not be exaggerated either. In the Senate he supported an amendment to the Government's Public Safety Bill intended to secure in-dependent inspection of prisons (Senate Debates, I. Cols. 1440–41; 1638–9). He also sent 'warm blankets' to Maud Gonne when his government put her in jail (*Letters,* p. 696). But in all essentials he supported the Government's policy of firmness. 'Even the gentle Yeats', wrote Sean O'Casey, 'voted for the Flogging Bill' (*i.e.* the Public Safety Bill which introduced flogging as a punishment for arson and armed robbery). Yeats voted for the Second Reading (26 July 1923). This was in the aftermath of the Civil War.

85. The *Irish Times* was in no way exceptional in this kind of comment. I cite it only because it was the journal of the class to which Yeats belonged, and he read it.

86. Hone tells us (*W.B. Yeats,* p. 467) that Yeats had learned with 'great satisfaction' of a law of the Third Reich 'whereby ancient and impoverished families can recover their hereditary properties'. Professor T. Desmond Williams of University College, Dublin, tells me that 'to benefit from the hereditary law [of September 1933] you had to trace your ancestry back to 1760 and you had to be purely Aryan. There was provision for the return of land that had passed into "impure" hands as a result of mortgages.'

87. It is true that the Blueshirts did not even try to go to anything like the lengths of their Continental models. It is also true that, unlike the case of their models, the Com-munists whom the Blueshirts were fighting were, in Ireland, largely imaginary.

88. *Modern Philosophy* (August 1963).

89. 'Contempt for politics' is of course a characteristic conservative stance.

90. *Letters,* 8 April 1936. In a similar, but significantly different, mood he wrote to the same correspondent six months later: 'Some day you will understand what I see in the Irish national movement and why I can be no other sort of revolutionist—as a young man I belonged to the I.R.B. and was in many things O'Leary's pupil. Besides why should I trouble about communism, fascism, liberalism, radicalism, when all, though some bow first and some stern first but all at the same pace, all are going down stream with the artificial unity which ends every civilization'. (30 November 1938; *Letters,* p. 869.) But in his letters to Ethel Mannin, who was herself on the Left, Yeats tended to understate the specifically

right-wing elements of his thought; he more than once used John O'Leary to fend her off (cf. *Letters*, p. 921); his letters to Olivia Shakespear are in some ways more revealing.

91. His worries on this ground were needless.

92. 11 February 1937. (*Letters*, p. 881.) The occasion of the ballad was the publication of Dr. W. F. Maloney's *The Forged Casement Diaries*, which claimed that British officials had forged documents in order to impute homosexuality to Casement. Controversy on this question still continues, but Casement's remains are now in Ireland.

93. To Dorothy Wellesley, 8 February 1937. (*Letters*, p. 880.)

94. Even before his Blueshirt phase, Yeats had been impressed by de Valera at his first meeting with him: '... I was impressed by his simplicity and honesty though we differed throughout' (to Olivia Shakespear, 9 March 1933. *Letters*, p. 806).

95. To Ethel Mannin, 1 March 1937. (*Letters*, p. 885.)

96. *The Old Age of a Poet.*

97. .... 'ploughing, harrowing, sowing, curry-combing, bicycle-cleaning, drill-driving, parcel-making, bale-pushing, tin-can-soldering, door-knob-polishing, threshold-whitening, coat-cleaning, trouser-patching, and playing upon the Squiffer'. ...

98. 'Comments and Conversations', p. 195 (July 1938), in the introduction to *Letters on Poetry to Dorothy Wellesley*.

99. Hone, *W. B. Yeats*, p. 291.

100. June 1924; *The Variorum Edition*, p. 828.

101. Letter to Olivia Shakespear, 28 June 1923. (*Letters*, p. 699.)

102. 8 April 1936. (*Letters*, pp. 850–1.) This was the same letter in which he refused to help Ossietzki.

103. This continued, I believe, to the very end. Just as 'The Second Coming' contains the rise of Fascism, I think that that mysterious and beautiful poem 'Cuchulain Comforted' may contain the fall of Fascism. I hope, in a separate essay, to examine the political themes of the four last poems: the subject requires the kind of detailed—and often necessarily speculative—treatment that would be out of place in the present general review of 'Yeats's political life'.

The forging of Orc: Blake and the idea of revolution
AILEEN WARD

We think of William Blake as the most revolutionary poet in England during a great age of revolution. Political or social regeneration is a central theme of his poetry for more than a decade after 1789, and in his old age Blake liked to remember himself as a youthful "Liberty Boy," flaunting his revolutionary bonnet in the streets of London. In 1780, during the Gordon Riots in London, Blake—then twenty-two—was in the front ranks of the crowd which burned Newgate Prison and freed over a thousand prisoners—an event which reverberates in his later work as a symbol of apocalyptic liberation. In September 1792, Blake is supposed to have saved the life of his friend Tom Paine by warning him to flee to Paris to escape arrest for sedition. It now appears that this story is mostly legend; but it is a matter of record that in August 1803 Blake himself was indicted for seditious utterance, for supposedly damning the king and calling his soldiers slaves during a quarrel with a drunken trooper: a charge for which he was tried and fortunately acquitted. Three of the best modern studies of Blake, those of Bronowski, Schorer, and Erdman, document his revolutionary allegiances at length. All this makes it hardly surprising that he has become the unofficial Bard of the New Left.

In April 1969, it is reported, the Harvard students retreating from University Hall after the occupation left one of the Proverbs of Hell scrawled on the walls: "The road of excess leads to the palace of wisdom."

But this is only half of the matter. Anyone who reads beyond the early Prophetic Books knows that toward the end of the 1790's Blake became deeply disillusioned with the French Revolution and shortly thereafter experienced what can only be called a religious conversion. His withdrawal from politics has been compared with Wordsworth's—that "lost leader" whom the young Robert Browning held up to scorn. Was this shift merely "a strategic retreat," as Mark Schorer put it, during an age of harsh political repression, or was it more like a recantation—"unsaying a lifetime of hope," as Bronowski said of a passage in *Jerusalem?* Schorer has described the later prophecies as "pushing external problems back into the realm of mind"; critics such as Kathleen Raine would deny Blake had been seriously concerned with political problems even in his early work. Indeed, Foster Damon apparently disposed of the whole political theme by defining "Revolution" in Blake as the third step of the Mystic Way, preceding the Dark Night of the Soul, and cited Jesus as Blake's great example of the revolutionary. But Blake himself told Crabb Robinson in 1825 that Jesus "was wrong in suffering himself to be crucified. He should not have attacked the government. He had no business with such matters." Robinson probably missed the real point of the pronouncement; yet still it poses a problem. Did Blake finally condemn all political action? Is he simply one more example of revolutionary youth lapsing into reactionary age? Or is there some real sense in which he kept faith with the idea of revolution all his life long?

But this question raises another one: what we mean by revolution. Already it seems one of those valuable words we squander as mindlessly as our natural resources; when it is extended to the programs of a Republican President it is surely ready for the discard. In Blake's time, however, the term was just beginning to acquire the meaning that it has held in political discussion ever since.

205

Raymond Williams includes it on a long list of words such as *class, culture, industry, ideology, democracy, capitalism,* and so forth, which took on their distinctively modern meanings in the decades just before and after 1800. Up until recently, at least, this modern sense of political "revolution" was clear—the overthrow of an established government by an organized minority group, aiming at radical change in the political or social structure, and using violent or otherwise illegal means to gain power. But the term had no such meaning in England in 1789. The OED cites six different meanings current in the 17th century: the movement of celestial bodies in their orbits, the recurrence of a point or period of time, the act of turning something around, the action of a thing or person turning around, the act of turning something over in thought, and finally an instance of great change in fortune or affairs (including political affairs). Not until the middle of the 17th century was this last usage extended to the idea of a forcible replacement of one ruling body by another: but this meaning was almost invariably limited to a specific event in English history. Capitalized, "Revolution" denoted the overthrow of the Rump Parliament in 1660 and the restoration of the Stuarts; but this reference was superseded with the "bloodless," or Glorious, Revolution of 1688, which transferred the crown to William and Mary and restored Protestant and parliamentary rule, and this remained the primary meaning of "Revolution" for Englishmen throughout the 18th century.

It is curious that in all these uses the implied root meaning is "revolve," not "revolt": "revolution" thus suggests restoration, the return to a previous state of affairs, far more often than rebellion, the change to something new—a cyclical rather than a progressive theory of history. What Crane Brinton called "the English Revolution"—the deposition of Charles I and the Puritan Interregnum—was not then and seems not even now to be termed a revolution by the English; evidently the events of 1688 fixed the connotations of nonviolence for at least a century afterward. November 4, the anniversary of the Glorious Revolution, was celebrated by Whigs and Dissenters alike throughout the 18th century, and never so fervidly as in the centenary year 1788. On the following anniversary, Richard Price preached a sermon at Old Jewry to the Society for Commemorating the Revolution in Great Britain, which summed up the feelings of most Englishmen on the subject at that time: that "bloodless victory," by which "the fetters of despotism . . . were broken," "the rights of the people asserted," property secured, conscience emancipated, the bounds of free inquiry enlarged, and the fame of British liberty extended through the world.

Yet it was Price's suggestion that the work of the English Revolution was still incomplete and that Englishmen could learn from the example of the Americans and the French, that goaded Edmund Burke in 1790 to his defense of the established order in his *Reflections on the Revolution in France*. Ironically to us, Burke felt he must protect the sacred word "revolution" from contamination: he charged that the Revolution Society "abuses its name" by claiming that certain "fictitious rights" of popular government were established in 1688. By a similar reasoning the Earl of Chatham in 1775 had invoked the principles of "the ever-glorious Revolution" *against* the rebels in the American colonies. The ensuing conflict was invariably called the "American War" by the English, or else the "rebellion," the "disorders," or the "commotions" overseas. Even the Americans seemed reluctant at the time to claim the term for themselves: contemporary documents speak of a "war," a "contest," a "struggle for liberty," and so on. In fact the first book in which the term "American Revolution" appears in the title seems to have been a French work—Paul Dubuisson's *Abrégé de la révolution de l'Amérique angloise,* published in 1778. Perhaps encouraged by this example, the Americans and their sympathizers in England began to use the term "American Revolution" quite generally until the 1790's, when events in France began to prove embarrassing. So a counter-movement set in. In 1800 the German historian Friedrich Gentz published a monograph in Berlin, which John Quincy Adams liked so much that he translated it under the title *The French and American Revolutions Compared* for use in the presidential campaign of that year. Gentz, said Adams, had "rescued [our] revolution from the disgraceful imputation of having proceeded from the same principles as the French"—a point which Russell Kirk thought worth repeating in 1955, when he reprinted the book as a campaign document for the New Conservativism. American historians, from old-fashioned patriots to liberals and Marxists, are still arguing today whether the American Revolution was a "real" revolution or not, and for a variety of reasons on each side. But the very fact of the argument proves one thing: the modern conception of revolution is the product not of the American but of the French and Russian revolutions, and the term "glorious" has long since dropped out of sight.

The meaning of the word "revolution" did not change overnight, however, and the change was a painful process. We watch Burke in a parliamentary debate of February 1790 going to all possible lengths to avoid applying the word "revolution" to what he described as the spread of anarchy, fraud, violence, and atheism in France by "an irrational, unprincipled, proscribing, confiscating, plundering, ferocious, bloody and tyrannical democracy." To Burke's outburst Sheridan replied rather mildly that no man who "revered [our] revolution" could really abhor the "proceedings of the patriotic party in France," since "theirs is as just a revolution as ours." Yet even in his *Reflections* Burke preferred to describe the upheavals in France not as a revolution but as "subversion" or "anarchy," in contrast to "reformation." When he gave in to the current usage and applied the proper term "revolution" to these events, he always distinguished it as the "French" Revolution—which, it is interesting to note, he referred to as "completed" within a year of its outbreak. This is important, for the almost universal approval in England of the events of 1789 —the destruction of the Bastille, the emancipation of religious minorities, the abolition of tithes, the nationalization of Church property—was based on the widespread assumption that these achievements were the real goal of the revolution. Even after the anti-Jacobin reaction set in, most English liberals in 1791 would have agreed with Tom Paine in *The Rights of Man* when he hailed the creation of the new French Constitution as "a solemn and majestic spectacle": the term "revolution," he added, "is diminutive of its character, and it rises into a Regeneration of man." But the September Massacres of 1792 marked a turning point for English sympathizers; and with the execution of Louis XVI, the outbreak of war between France and England, and the Reign of Terror in 1793, the connotations of the word "revolution" took on a sinister cast. A few years later all the sacred implications of the term had vanished, even for Burke. In his *Letter to a Noble Lord* of 1796, he spoke with horror of the possibility that if the movement for electoral reform in the 1780's had succeeded "not France but England [might] have had the honor of leading the death-dance of democratic revolution."

Seen against this background, Blake's use of the term "revolution" is strikingly conservative: he never once used the word in the modern sense that was emerging in his time. In 1791 he entitled his first political prophecy *The French Revolution,* and referred to the specific event twice in his letters;† but the American Revolution, which he glorified, was "the American War" to him as to most Englishmen. The word "revolution" appears eleven times in his work, almost invariably in its most general sense, the action of a thing or person turning around. Yet "revolution" in this sense had no glorious or even neutral connotations to Blake; rather it suggested the hateful image of the wheel, symbol to him of all the endless recurrences of history, the tortures of punitive religion, the compulsions of "cogs tyrannic" in industrial society, the mindless orbitings of the stars—the "image of infinite / Shut up in finite revolutions." This suggests that certain of his mythological characters should not be identified, as they usually are, with our political concept of revolution, which did not exist when he first conceived them; their primary meaning lies elsewhere, and their association with the French Revolution was secondary and to a certain extent fortuitous. Nor can Blake be accused of abandoning

† The second time contemptuously: "Since the French Revolution Englishmen are all Intermeasurable One by Another, certainly a happy state of Agreement to which I for One do not Agree." (Letter to Cumberland, 12 April 1827)

the idea of revolution, since he never really subscribed to it; the idea itself was a product, not a cause, of the French Revolution, and the difficulties he encountered in shaping *Vala* (later revised as *The Four Zoas*) to shifts in political events during the time he was writing it (roughly from 1797 to 1807) suggest the dangers of contemporary "relevance."

The figure most clearly linked with the revolutionary theme in Blake's prophecies is Orc, "the new born terror" of "A Song of Liberty" who is destined to overthrow the tyrannical "starry king" of the *ancien régime*. Orc's name first occurs in *America* (1793), and it is a splendid example of Blake's Joyce-like ingenuity in naming his mythological creations. As an anagram of *cor,* Orc represents the emotions, and is born from Enitharmon's heart; but he is also a whale, the grampus or killer whale, from the Latin *orca;* a King of Hell, like the Roman Orcus; and he signifies the vitality of the genitals—from the Greek ὄρχεις. Before he received his name he appeared in *The Marriage of Heaven and Hell* as the principle of Energy, or Eternal Delight, dialectically and diabolically opposed, in Blake's marriage of contraries, to Reason, "the bound or outward circumference of Energy," who as the starry king, a figure of repressive rational order, will soon be named Urizen—a play of words on the Greek verb ὁρίζειν, to bound or limit (like a horizon), and the phrase "Your Reason?", a verbal tic of a certain philosopher-scientist in Blake's early prose satire *An Island in the Moon*. Orc is also prefigured in the concluding poem of *Songs of Innocence* in 1789, a salute to the new era that opened with the sack of the Bastille:

> Youth of delight, come hither,
> And see the opening morn,
> Image of truth new born.
> Doubt is fled, & clouds of reason,
> Dark disputes & artful teazing.
> Folly is an endless maze,
> Tangled roots perplex her ways.
> How many have fallen there!
> They stumble all night over bones of the dead,
> And feel they know not what but care,
> And wish to lead others, when they should be led.
> (*"The Voice of the Ancient Bard"*)

This "youth of delight" first appears in one of Blake's earliest designs—a naked youth with arms outstretched against the sunrise, often called "Glad Day" but properly titled "The Dance of Albion"†—a figure which Blake drew in 1780, as Erdman has suggested, in response to the apocalyptic experience of the Gordon Riots. As a principle of male fertility Orc is also glimpsed in several of Blake's early lyrics in *Poetical Sketches,* a ruddy-limbed god who descends to impregnate Earth every spring and departs, leaving his golden load of harvest, at the end of autumn. For Orc's function is not simply to oppose Urizen, whether in the realm of thought or of political action; it is also to impregnate with his energy a certain "Nameless Shadowy Female," who appears at the beginning of *America* and *Europe.* Her identity is mysterious: she is variously interpreted as the spirit of fallen and formless nature, the muse of history, "Woman at the ultimate point of her neglect," America oppressed by Britain, and humanity everywhere longing for deliverance or waiting to be roused by the revolutionary energy of a Tom Paine. To some extent the Shadowy Female is each of these things—Blake never specifies; and she serves as reminder that his mythical narrative makes sense at many levels of meaning, cosmological and psychological as well as political.

As Orc's story unfolds through the early prophetic poems, Blake's view of the transformative power of energy acting on the sterile rationalism of the 18th century and its repressive social forms is itself transformed by the experience of the French Revolution. Orc's birth, described in "A Song of Liberty," can be dated as 1762, the year of Rousseau's *Social Contract,* whose opening sentence—"Man is born free, and everywhere he is in chains"—is the text expounded in all of Blake's prophecies. Fourteen years later, as recounted in *America,* he reaches puberty

† The title comes from the legend which Blake added to the drawing when he engraved it about twenty years later:

Albion rose from where he labour'd at the Mill with Slaves:
Giving himself for the Nations he danc'd the dance of Eternal Death.

The connection with Samson underlines the theme of liberation through revolutionary violence.

Albion rose from where he labourd at the Mill with Slaves

(left, above) "The Dance of Albion." Untitled design, after Scamozzi's *Architettura Universale*, 1780. Engraved c. 1800, with added legend:
  Albion rose from where he labour'd at the Mill with Slaves:
  Giving himself for the Nations he danc'd the dance of Eternal Death.

(above) "Satan Smiting Job With Sore Boils." Original design c. 1799. Engraved as Plate VI of *Illustrations of the Book of Job*, 1823–25. Cf. *The Four Zoas*, III.79–82:
  And Luvah strove to gain dominion over the mighty Albion.
  They strove together above the Body where Vala was inclos'd
And the dark Body of Albion left prostrate upon the crystal pavement,
  Cover'd with boils from head to foot, the terrible smitings of Luvah.

(left, below) Fire.

in 1776, breaks his chains, and rapes the Shadowy Female, who in an ecstasy of pain salutes the spirit of fire striking through her frost. Orc then proclaims the downfall of tyranny and the dawn of freedom in tones of apocalypse:

> The morning comes, the night decays, the watchmen leave their stations;
> The grave is burst, the spices shed, the linen wrapped up;
> The bones of death, the cov'ring clay, the sinews shrunk and dried,
> Reviving shake, inspiring move, breathing! awakening!
> Spring like redeemed captives when their bonds & bars are burst.
> Let the slave grinding at the mill, run out into the field;
> Let him look up into the heavens & laugh in the bright air;
> Let the inchained soul shut up in darkness and in sighing,
> Whose face has never seen a smile in thirty weary years,
> Rise and look out, his chains are loose, his dungeon doors are open;
> And let his wife and children return from the oppressor's scourge.
> They look behind at every step & believe it is a dream,
> Singing, "The Sun has left his blackness, & has found a fresher morning,
> And the fair Moon rejoices in the clear & cloudless night;
> For Empire is no more, and now the Lion & Wolf shall cease."

After this Declaration of Independence (as Erdman describes it) Orc is denounced by Albion's Angel, the spirit of England, as "Blasphemous Demon, Antichrist, hater of Dignities; / Lover of wild rebellion, and transgressor of God's Law"; but Boston's Angel recognizes the falsity of that God and his Law and revolts, carrying the other thirteen Angels of the American colonies with him. In the war that follows, the flames of Orc reach across the Atlantic to stir up a new rebellious life in the cities of England (the Gordon Riots of 1780), but Urizen quenches the fires by pouring forth a vast snowstorm which saves the monarchs of Europe from revolution for another twelve years (the interval between Yorktown and the outbreak of war between France and England in 1793).

But in *Europe,* published in 1794, the end of empire predicted in *America* the year before has become problematic. The actual historical substance of the poem—the growth of anti-Jacobin repression in England in 1792 as Pitt mobilized the country for war against France—is overbalanced by the mythological framework which traces the roots of political enslavement deep into European history, back to the birth of Christ and the subversion of his promise of peace with the establishment of Christianity.

214

The reasons for this defeat are many: Blake hints in turn at the greed of men exploiting nature to their own self-indulgent ends, the perversity of women dominating men through sex and driving their frustrated energies into militarism, and the threefold tyranny of repressive religion, the mechanistic universe of Locke and Newton, and the war machine of the modern industrial state, all of which reduce the individual to helpless and lifeless passivity. Orc himself remains in the background of this long night of European history, to appear at the end glowing in the fire above the vineyards of red France: it is 1793, and England has declared war against the French Republic. But no victory for the spirit of Energy or Liberty is in sight: the burden of the poem is the universal weight of tyranny.

A crucial transformation is beginning to take place, which appears first as a shift of Blake's attention from Orc to Urizen. For in 1794 Blake began a new cycle of poems—*The Book of Urizen, The Book of Ahania, The Book of Los,* and *The Song of Los*—whose focus is not politics but cosmogony. Extending and consolidating his myth, Blake attempted in these poems to trace the present state of historical affairs back to the very origin of evil—the creation of the material world with the fall of man (or as Blake would have it, the fall of God) from Eternity into Time. Urizen figures in these poems as the false God of this world, a tyrant like Shelley's Jupiter, a Gnostic Demiurge who by separating himself from the Divine Family dragged a portion of Eternity down into the Abyss; then, to give this shapeless material world some form and life, another member of the Eternal Family is sent to bind Urizen and hammer him into shape. This is Los, whom Blake calls the Eternal Prophet; he is a kind of Holy Ghost, the Lord and giver of life, who spake by the Prophets and still speaks through the mouth of every honest man; he is a figure of creative power, the Prolific, a divine blacksmith like Hephaestus or Loki. Blake will later identify him with the poetic imagination, the spark of divine thought left to man in this fallen world; his name is an anagram of *Sol,* the sun, and perhaps also *soul,* or spirit; it also suggests the loss of Paradise or Eternity man suffers

215

in this world. For the present, Los is cast as the father of Orc, whom he begets on Enitharmon, an Eve-like figure who is born out of his own psychic division in the binding of Urizen; and Los at once proves a jealous father, for he chains the new-born Orc to a rock where he remains till he is strong enough to break free as the spirit of rebellion.

This shift in Blake's attention seems to have been caused in the first place by the unexpected endurance of the old order, religious and philosophical as well as political, which did not vanish like shadows at the dawn of the new regime, as he had earlier hoped. But Blake was no mere political enthusiast, looking for instant solutions to age-old problems; he did not lose faith in the idea of freedom, yet clearly he was troubled by the turn of events in France in late 1793 and 1794. Revolutionary violence was producing not the long-awaited reign of liberty but a new regime as repressive as the old, the Republic of Virtue dominated by Robespierre. Blake had not taken off his revolutionary bonnet after the September Massacres of 1792, as his Victorian biographer Gilchrist would have us believe; instead he went on to publish his most overtly revolutionary poem *America* in 1793—and this took courage in an England already manacled by the Proclamation Against Sedition of May 1792. Yet he must have been ironically moved by reports of the enthronement of the Goddess of Reason, replacing official Christianity, in Notre Dame at Paris in November 1793; and a greater irony was to come—the deposing of this goddess in June 1794 and the establishment of the Worship of the Supreme Being in her place. This ceremony was presided over by Robespierre, who in the following month went to the guillotine and was succeeded by the reactionary regime of the Directory. These events are reflected in *The Book of Ahania,* where Fuzon, the fiery son of Urizen (named from *feu,* fire, and φύσις, Nature) revolts against his father and sets himself up as God, "eldest of things," then is immediately slain by Urizen. Fuzon at first appearance is an Orc-figure, a Moses leading the Israelites out of bondage from the land of Egypt; yet the final result of his revolt

216

is a new enslavement of his people under the Mosaic Decalogue. Blake has already glimpsed the possibility that revolutionary violence does not in fact change the minds of men but hardens them, and so is itself changed into the repressive power it first opposed; so in *Vala* he shows the chains which first bound Orc to the rock taking root and growing into his very fibers—"a living Chain Sustained by the Demon's life" (*Vala, or The Four Zoas,* V, 170).

Thus the figure of Orc in *Vala* begins to be transformed in a way that strikingly suggests the metamorphosis of Milton's Satan from the brightest angel to the grovelling serpent. From the beginning Blake had represented Orc in the ambiguous image of the snake, which emerging from the earth each spring and casting its winter weeds symbolizes recurrent vitality, but which as the coiling serpent, the *uroboros* or the snake with the tail in its mouth, suggests mere recurrence, the endless repetition of all the fatal mistakes of history. With the French armies invading Switzerland and Italy to consolidate the power of the Directory at home, the Revolution was beginning to reveal itself as the old imperial tyranny in a new form. So Orc, like Satan in Book X of *Paradise Lost,* disappears at last into the pestilential serpent of temptation and fall, in a passage which Erdman has linked with Napoleon's overthrow of the Directory and establishment of his Consulate in 1799—the final destruction of the French Republic and the ideals on which it was founded by the forces of Energy perverted and leagued with Urizenic power:

> No more remain'd of Orc but the Serpent round the tree of Mystery.
> The form of Orc was gone; he rear'd his serpent bulk among
> The stars of Urizen in Power, rending the form of life
> Into a formless indefinite & strewing her on the Abyss
> Like clouds upon a winter sky, broken with winds & thunders.
> (*V/FZ, VIIb,* 214–18)

It is the process Camus described in *The Rebel:* "the metaphysical demand for unity" which every revolution poses at its start proves impossible to fulfill, and so "a substitute universe" is constructed. Then inevitably "rebellion, cut off from its real roots, unfaithful to man in having surrendered to history, contemplates the subjection of the entire universe."† Orc is now a dragon of endless war, a serpent coiling around the Tree of Religious Mystery (symbolizing, as Morton Paley has suggested, Napoleon's re-establishment of the Catholic Church in France in 1800), a "King of wrath & fury" bejewelled like Napoleon at his coronation in 1804, who will ultimately burn himself out in the fires of his own wrath and be consumed in the Last Judgment.††

The fate of Orc thus shows the transformation of the idea of Energy, as it took historical form in the events of 1789 and after, running through all the now-too-familiar mutations of force calling up counter-force, triumphant violence hardening into regressive power. But in rejecting Orc, Blake did not reject the eternal principle of energy or emotion. In *Vala,* Orc is shown to be merely a debased temporal form of Luvah, one of the four eternal principles of the human spirit. Luvah stands for all the emotions: not only in their highest form as Love, supremely manifest as Jesus, but also—here the pun on *lava* enters—the passions in their eruptive and disruptive forms, in which they pour forth like fire and harden into hate, the final debasement which Blake names Satan. The long-drawn-out psychic conflict which *Vala* recounts— the "war among the members" of the Eternal Man Albion—begins with the revolt of Luvah asserting his supremacy over the other Zoas, upsetting the balance of the four-fold humanity; and the total war that follows shows the fate of society ruled by mere

† *The Rebel,* pp. 224, 145–46 (quoted by Morton D. Paley, *Energy and the Imagination,* p. 115).

†† A graphic proof of these changes is found in the transformation of the heroic youthful nude of "The Dance of Albion" into the grinning serpent-scaled demon of "Satan Smiting Job with Sore Boils" (*Illustrations of the Book of Job,* pl. 6), in which Satan, holding a vial of poison, bestrides the Job of suffering humanity in the same pose as Albion "giving himself for the Nations." The subject of this engraving is repeated in a tempera painting variously dated from c. 1799 to 1826 (Figgis, *Paintings of William Blake,* pl. 61): perhaps as an illustration of "the terrible smitings of Luvah" in *Vala* (V/FZ, III, 79–82). Morton Paley, who has anticipated me in making this comparison, also notes that Satan has no genitals—the ultimate symbol of the transformation of repressed sex into hostile violence. An intermediate stage between "The Dance of Albion" and "Satan Smiting Job" might also be noted: the figure of "Fire" in pl. 5 of *The Gates of Paradise* (1793) is shown in the same pose as the other two figures but brandishing a spear and a shield.

self-assertive passion. Only the self-annihilating Love exemplified by Christ, the continual sacrifice of self for others, points the way back to the original unity from which mankind has fallen, or forward to that Jerusalem which Blake has vowed never to cease struggling to build "in England's green and pleasant land."

For building the good society was the task of Blake's lifetime. Years before the outbreak of the French Revolution and after the downfall of Napoleon he was concerned with the revolutionary theme, and in this longer perspective the rise and fall of Orc appears as an interlude or even an aberration. His first volume of *Poetical Sketches* contains several dramatic fragments assailing war as mere senseless suffering inflicted on the people by their rulers in the dubious name of Ambition and Industry and Commerce. The ballad "Gwin King of Norway," an allegory of 1775, prophesies the overthrow of a tyrant king by a citizen army: yet even this victory is won at the cost of thousands slain and the land devastated. *Tiriel,* Blake's first prophetic poem, shows the abuse of royal power by a mad king who is recognizable as George III as well as Lear and Oedipus; and *Visions of the Daughters of Albion* suggests that the women of England are enslaved sexually, economically, and spiritually as much as the Negroes in the West Indian colonies whose recent revolts had been savagely crushed. In the *Songs of Innocence,* along with children playing in country fields, happy in the protective love of parents, we are shown children sold as chimney sweeps at the age of five or six, orphans led in regiments to church by beadles armed with switches, and little black boys rejected by English children because of the color of their skins. In the concluding poem of *Innocence* Blake voiced the faith that these injustices will disappear like shadows with the "opening morn" of 1789. Three or four years later he has moved from Innocence to Experience. In "London" his savage indignation is unrelieved by any hope that childlike faith or adolescent energy can redeem the sufferings of men: all are chartered, branded, manacled, blackened, bloodied, blighted by a curse which even if it is man-made—the product of human institutions—seems ineradicable. For a brief time Blake apparently

219

believed that violent social change like that taking place in France in 1792 and 1793 would bring about the new age. A four-line redaction of "London" written in his Notebook shortly afterward gives this revolutionary prescription:

> Remove away that black'ning church,
> Remove away that marriage hearse,
> Remove away that man of blood,†
> You'll quite remove the ancient curse.

But the "mind-forg'd manacles" were not so easily stuck off, as Blake later acknowledged with the ingrowing of Orc's chain of repression. As the 1790's wore on, it became all too clear that mere violent action would accomplish nothing if it left men's minds unchanged.

The beginning of this realization can be seen in "The Tyger." This poem, drafted in the autumn of 1792, voices Blake's response to three crucial events of that time††—the victory of the revolutionary troops at Valmy, the proclamation of the French Republic, and the September Massacres; and the perennial ambiguity of the poem seems inherent in its genesis. The savagery of the massacres—at least as they were reported in England—raised a crucial question: were the forces of revolution simply "a great beast," a tiger or a lion, or could they be viewed as "the just man [raging] in the wilds / Where lions roam"? That is, was there some intelligence working in them, humanizing them, forging some purpose through them? The question is essential to the poem if its real subject is understood to be not the tiger but his creator. In image after image Blake focuses on the "immortal hand or eye," the mighty shoulder, the art and strength of a superhuman blacksmith who fetches the molten iron from the furnace, steeps it in the well, twists it and rolls it and hammers the beast into shape and symmetry on the anvil. If no such creative principle is at

† Blake first wrote "place of blood," suggested by the "palace walls" of "London," but immediately changed "place" to "man." Erdman suggests the reading "palace of blood"; but "man of blood," as John Holloway points out, was seditious enough, with its echo of "Thou man of blood"—*i.e.*, King David—from 2 Samuel 16:7.

†† Erdman's gloss of "When the stars threw down their spears" by the defeat of the First Coalition at Valmy is generally accepted as indicating the date.

work, then the wrath of the tiger expresses no ulterior judgment, and the sufferings of "London" are all there is, inexplicable and ineluctable. It is this intentionality that Blake is seeking through the insistent questionings of the poem: on the historical level, perhaps some political leadership to "frame" and direct the fearful energies of revolution; on the metaphysical level, some ultimate intelligibility in history.

At this crisis of his times, Blake urgently needed to posit some shaping principle in the events unfolding in London and Paris. And it is significant that he already describes it in the image of a divine blacksmith, at least a year before he will emerge as the figure of Los in *The Book of Urizen*. In that poem Los will create the prototypes of Blake's mythological universe in three prototypical acts of creation—hammering the inert matter of Urizen into form, giving birth Adam-like to his female counterpart Enitharmon from his own divided substance, and begetting the uncontrollable future in Orc. By these acts Los brings a substantial and meaningful world into being: he is a creative surrogate for his own creator, stamping his work with a designing hand. If this is what Los himself signifies, then his seeming slothfulness and fallibility in *Europe* and *Vala* have a meaning: he is, after all, a fallen Eternal, and the world he has made is flawed from the start. His first act in *Urizen,* after his creation is complete, is to baptize Orc "in springs of sorrow," then bind him to the rock with "the Chain of Jealousy," in a tragic repudiation of his own energies. The way is prepared for the long misadventures of *Vala*. This suggests a negative answer to the question of "The Tyger," "Did he who made the Lamb make thee?"—unless we recall Blake's axiom that "All deities reside within the human breast." Los is certainly no Christian God, no Jehovah discharging his wrath through the Tyger as his instrument. Though Los will later undergo a spiritual regeneration and take on some of the attributes of Christ, through most of *Vala* he is a figure of mankind as such, erring but striving. When in "The Tyger" he dares to aspire on wings and seize the fire, Los is a Daedalean or Promethean rebel against divine order and teacher of divine arts to men.

221

At best he is the symbol of the human imagination shaping its world and giving meaning to experience; and this activity will at last create the Humanity which man must "learn to adore." Los's final meaning, then, is the difficult lesson that man makes himself, and must continually remake himself.

But two or three years after Valmy it must have seemed that man was unmaking himself. In 1795, while recounting the rise and fall of Fuzon in *The Book of Ahania,* Blake wrote *The Song of Los* as the conclusion to his cycle of historical prophecies. It is as pessimistic as all Blake's work of that dark year. In "Africa," a brief conspectus of man's intellectual history from Adam to the present, Los views the rise of religion—really the death of the Gods—as a long decline from man's original spiritual vigor. The seven great religions of the world (Hindu, Hebrew, Greek, Christian, Mohammedan, Nordic, and "Natural") have been instruments for the progressive enfeeblement of men's minds. In "Asia," Los sees history coming to an end in the dark night at the close of the 18th century, with famine and pestilence and fire and oppression, and the promise of apocalpyse sounds faint. The material universe whose creation was depicted in *Urizen* as a gigantic mistake was cut off from Eternity from the start, unredeemable unless the Eternal Prophet could somehow illuminate it with a purpose beyond history. To reshape history and give it a new meaning was to keep Los "unwearied labouring and weeping" at his anvil through a long time of trouble.

For the work of imaginatively recreating the world went on, even as the Orcan eruption of revolutionary energy cooled and hardened into the Urizenic "stony laws" of the Napoleonic order. Beginning with *Vala,* Los emerges as the hero of Blake's long epic and the representative of all men who try to understand why the times have failed them while refusing to give up their vision of a better time. This is an immensely sobered and deepened return to the heroic Innocence of those children, orphans and chimney sweeps and little black boys, whose love and faith survive in an unjust and loveless world. In a few lines written in his notebook sometime around 1810 Blake uttered this imperative:

> The Angel that presided o'er my birth
> Said, "Little creature, form'd of Joy & Mirth,
> Go love without the help of any Thing on Earth."

Blake now sees the possibility of revolutionary change in men's lives depending on a profound change in men's minds, which in turn depends on a deeper change in men's hearts. In the final revision of *Vala* as *The Four Zoas,* in passages added around 1804 or after, it is the cataclysmic event of Jesus' self-sacrifice that works this change. But this was no easy solution for Blake, but the outcome of a long crisis of religious belief. Wisdom is not bought for a song, but "with the price / Of all that a man hath, his house, his wife, his children." This is the bleak message of "The Grey Monk," which Blake drafted shortly after his arraignment for sedition in Chichester in August 1803.† In the figure of the pacifist Monk tortured by Charlemagne for "condemning Glorious War," we may glimpse Blake himself, tormented by the sight of the sufferings his outspokenness has caused to those he loves. Because of his writings, the Monk's brother died in prison and his wife and children are starving, while her father and brother have risen in fruitless rebellion. But "God commanded this hand to write," and he must continue to speak the bitter truth: armed revolt is useless, for the hand of vengeance which crushes the tyrant will become a tyrant in his stead. The only way out of the nightmare of history is to persuade the tyrant to relent.

> "But vain the Sword & vain the Bow,
> They never can work War's overthrow.
> The Hermit's Prayer & the Widow's tear
> Alone can free the World from Fear.
>
> For a Tear is an Intellectual Thing,
> And a Sigh is the Sword of an Angel King,
> And the bitter groan of the Martyr's woe
> Is an Arrow from the Almightie's Bow."

This is the "mental fight" to which Blake dedicated himself in the opening lyric of *Milton;* but in doing so he did not lose sight of the physical sufferings of the people of England under the burden of twenty-two years of war with France. Press gangs, workhouses,

† The title reflects the fact that the Gothic courtroom at Chichester was once a Grey Friars church, as Erdman points out.

hangings, enforced prostitution, rising infant mortality, famine, mutiny, the spread of the factory system and the rise of agricultural prices benefiting the rich and robbing the poor: Blake watched them all and recorded their horrors in a steady indictment throughout *Vala* and *Jerusalem*. But the worst horror is the death of the soul in the industrial war-machine of England:

> And all the Arts of Life they chang'd into the Arts of Death in Albion, . . .
> And intricate wheels invented, [tyrannic] wheel without wheel,
> To perplex youth in their outgoings & to bind to labours in Albion
> Of day & night the myriads of eternity: that they may grind
> And polish brass & iron hour after hour, laborious task,
> Kept ignorant of its use: that they might spend the days of wisdom
> In sorrowful drudgery to obtain a scanty pittance of bread,
> In ignorance to view a small portion & think that All,
> And call it Demonstration, blind to all the simple rules of life.
>
> (*Jerusalem*, 65:16–28)

The interlocking wheels of industrial machinery have become the visible symbol of the mindless and heartless order of modern society:

> . . . cruel Works
> Of many Wheels I view, wheel without wheel, with cogs tyrannic
> Moving by compulsion each other.
> (*Jerusalem:* 15:17–19)

And by a brilliant inversion of the image, Blake's new hero becomes the counter-revolutionary, Jesus who "strove against the current of the wheel." In *The Everlasting Gospel* Jesus is still the revolutionary exemplar of *The Marriage of Heaven and Hell,* whose "natural" virtue was to break the Ten Commandments, to act "from impulse not from rules." But he has become more than this: a force working upward against the "natural" downward momentum of history. Blake first hinted at this saving possibility in several of his designs for Young's *Night Thoughts,* where, as Foster Damon pointed out, the eternal cycle of Nature or History, symbolized by the snake with its tail in its mouth, is counterpointed by an ascending line of Humanity, figured as a man or woman reaching upward. Around 1804 Blake embodied this visual metaphor in a new schematization of history mitigating the pessimism of *The Song of Los.* The Seven Eyes of God—a term derived from several biblical references, all suggesting religious vision—represent the stages of man's spiritual evolution, each eye typifying a new and higher conception of divinity. Each new

224

vision is an attempt to counteract the inertia of history embodied in Satan or the Selfhood—the innate egotism of the human being, the murderous impulse toward domination—by some act of regulation or release working up from primitive vindictive punishment (Molech) through legalistic righteousness (Jehovah) to the freedom of understanding and forgiveness embodied in Jesus. This advance can be read as a growing tension rather than as an ascent, a sharpening conflict between truth and the forms of error which Blake symbolizes in the twenty-seven churches, the successors to the seven false religions of *The Song of Los*. But error now appears not as imposed from without by religious or social institutions but as arising from the selfhood within each man, to be overcome only by an act of individual self-annihilation such as Jesus'. Blake has evidently become convinced that the nature of society or politics is such that men in groups invariably act out of selfhood: at present, regeneration is possible only in the "Minute Particulars" of one man doing good to another. We can only hope ("England! awake! awake! awake!") that the end of history will bring the shadowy "Eighth Eye" to realization in a new collective humanity, a society founded on the annihilation of individual self-interest which will at last release mankind from the endless cycles of historical error. Till that day the revolution will be enacted not as a prophetic event occurring within some more or less foreseeable future, but as a Last Judgment or renunciation of error within the individual spirit, occurring in the apocalyptic dimension of the eternal present. So Blake's final image of liberation is a moving imperative of amnesty and release:

> Go therefore, cast out devils in Christ's name,
> Heal thou the sick of spiritual disease,
> Pity the evil, for thou art not sent
> To smite with terror & with punishments
> Those that are sick, like to the Pharisees
> Crucifying & encompassing sea & land
> For proselytes to tyranny & wrath;
> But to the Publicans & Harlots go,
> Teach them True Happiness, but let no curse
> Go forth out of thy mouth to blight their peace;
> For Hell is open'd to Heaven: thine eyes beheld
> The dungeons burst & the Prisoners set free.
> (*Jerusalem* 77:24–35)

What commands our admiration to the end in Blake is his ability to maintain the tension between good and evil, the possible and the longed-for, the clear-eyed view of history and the vision of eternity. He was continually reaching toward more inclusive unities of experience—"organization" is one of his most characteristic terms, and "all," on the evidence of the Concordance, was his most frequent word—that would not exclude any aspect of the psyche, any individual or group within the larger whole. The one thing he could not admit within his system was the Negation— that principle of Urizen at his worst, that denies the right of its contrary to exist; yet even this must be left free to destroy itself. The fate of Orc in history was to become such a negation. Yet the fact that Orc and Urizen first appeared as the principles of Energy and Reason in *The Marriage of Heaven and Hell,* dialectically opposed yet necessary to each other as those contraries without which there is no progression, implies that their struggle was first conceived as a "mental fight," a creative antagonism, and not the kind in which one side eliminates the other: and Blake fought to keep this dialectic alive. So Orc in his original identity appears as the spirit of youthful protest, the saving diabolical nay-saying spirit which discovers in all the antithetical beliefs and outlawed forms of life those truths which any society neglects or rejects to its peril. And Urizen in his original form as "the bound or outward circumference of Energy," like the "firm and determinate outline" that was Blake's cardinal principle in art, is the unfallen Prince of Light who at the end of *Vala,* after admitting the error of his negations, restores order among the Zoas and leads the constructive work of the harvest of nations. Yet in his attempt to eliminate Orc, Urizen becomes a deadly affirmation of mere order, the kind of valueless, causeless, and purposeless logic that can turn society into a technological juggernaut and the earth into a desert; while Orc, in purposing merely to break free of his chains, can only rape, burn, destroy all that oppose him, and finally wind himself like a python around the symbol of power he has displaced.

It is the possibility of a meaningful activity forging these two contraries into a productive symmetry that Los holds out, harnessing power and mind in a humane synthesis, building the

226

eternal city in which fallen man will be recreated. In Blake's final view of heaven at the end of *Jerusalem,* his old antagonists Bacon and Newton and Locke appear along with Milton and Shakespeare and Chaucer, to wage life-giving wars "with intellectual spears, and long winged arrows of thought."

> Mutual in one another's love and wrath all renewing
> We live as One Man; for contracting our infinite senses
> We behold multitude, or expanding, we behold as one,
> As One Man all the Universal Family, and that One Man
> We call Jesus the Christ; and he in us, and we in him
> Live in perfect harmony in Eden, the land of life,
> Giving, receiving, and forgiving each other's trespasses.
> (*Jerusalem* 38:16–22)

It is a Utopia predicated on change, a heaven pulsing with life, contracting and expanding, allowing for love and wrath, individuality and unity, "going forth and returning," "giving, receiving, and forgiving each other's trespasses." If we ask what in the end this has to do with the problems of England in the dark years after Waterloo, the answer may be nothing—or everything. As Bronowski has suggested, the puzzles of Blake's world had grown too hard and bitter for any immediate solutions. Looking back today, we can see how the struggle for political liberty that erupted in 1789 called forth in the counter-response of the industrial and agricultural revolutions more economic and political enslavement than before. The problems themselves were not to be analyzed for another half century or more, by the dialectic of Marx patterned on that of Hegel which, as Bronowski pointed out, Blake so strikingly anticipates. It was Blake's great achievement to see more clearly than anyone else in England the human terms of the problem: how the "Minute Particulars" of Albion were being "degraded and murdered" by unidentifiable forces which like brickmakers cast men's souls into a mold and bake them in bricks to build the pyramids of society. Against this deadening unity Blake never ceased to fight: like Camus' rebel, to the end he "obstinately confronts a world condemned to death and the fatal obscurity of the human condition with his demand for life and absolute clarity." Such an effort keeps a man and a society alive; this is what it is to "keep the Divine Vision in time of trouble."

Shakespeare and "the revolution of the times"

HARRY LEVIN

It is Henry IV, in his insomniac monologue on the burdens of the kingship ("Uneasy lies the head that wears a crown"), who longs to "read the book of fate" and thereby to learn how "the revolution of the times" works out its endless round of permutation, erosion, and levelling (*2 Henry IV*, III.i.31.45–6). Henry IV is not our favorite among Shakespeare's kings. We may well prefer his son; and, significantly, most of us prefer the latter in his role as Prince Hal, before he parted from Falstaff to become King Henry V, Shakespeare's nationalist hero whom some of the critics have regarded as a prig and a jingo. All those sovereigns fascinated Shakespeare even as they continue to fascinate us—not less so the very worst of them, Richard III, whose dramatized rule was notably less responsible or legitimate than that of Henry IV. We should also note in passing that it is still another usurper, Claudius, King of Denmark, who voices so ardent a fervor for the divine right of kings: "There's such divinity doth hedge a king . . ." (*Hamlet*, IV.v.123). Rulers are at best ambivalent figures to

228

Shakespeare, as they are to themselves in their moments of soliloquy. We sympathize with Henry IV so long as he is the injured Bolingbroke, but our sympathies shift to Richard II when Henry ascends the throne and turns into a cold-blooded politician, while Richard becomes a victim in his turn.

Henry's desire to read the book of fate is characteristic of this ambivalence, for he concludes his speculation by predicting that any reader so privileged "would shut the book, and sit him down and die (2 Henry IV, III.i.56)." Well, either we are made of sterner stuff, or we have been hardened through recent years by watching the revolution of the times every evening in our living rooms. From where we sit, there is even a kind of romantic escape in the glimpse of a defunct heroism that we get from contemplating conflicts which are settled by alarums and excursions rather than by mass bombing or international hijacking. Truly, we have witnessed more than our share, as Macbeth did, of "Bloody instructions, which being taught, return/To plague th'inventor (I.vii.9)." Yet, stripped of their knightly armor, their heraldic trappings, and their patriotic rhetoric, Shakespeare's monarchs act out a sorry record of turbulence and treachery, of arrogant wrongs and smoldering revenges all too often fated to reach their grim *dénouement* at the Tower of London. It is rather cold comfort for us to be noting the precedents they set. But, since the spacious mirror he sets before us has already reflected so many topical problems of the eventful interval between his time and ours, we should not be surprised to see it now flashing back images which are more recognizable than reassuring.

"The times are wild," we hear at the outset of the Second Part of *Henry IV* (I.i.9). The somber king will prophesy "rotten times," though the ebullient Pistol will herald the "golden times" promised by the enthronement of Henry V (IV.iv.60; V.iii.94). The new regime will usher in a triumphant interlude, from a nationalistic point of view; but that triumph will be brief; and Shakespeare sustains it only by cutting off the play at Henry's betrothal, just two years before his premature death. The melancholy trilogy that covers his son's reign does indeed treat of "heavy times."

"O bloody times!" the king himself cries out, when on the battlefield he encounters a son who has slain his father. Then, in a parallel casualty of war, a father who has slain his son appears, exclaiming: "O pity, God, this miserable age (*3 Henry VI*, II.v.63, 73, 88)." When the royal uncle, Humphrey, Duke of Gloucester, warns the king, "Ah, gracious lord, these days are dangerous," Humphrey is already doomed to death; but so, before too long, is Henry VI (*2 Henry VI*, III.i.142). The backdrop for the major sequence of Shakespeare's dramatic histories is civil war at home—the War of the Roses between the houses of York and Lancaster—and imperial war abroad—the Hundred Years' War between England and France. The Yorkist tyrant that emerged from the struggle, Richard III, selfishly thinks of the age as his "golden time," but publicly professes it "this troublous time"; and it was, of course, a reign of terror (*3 Henry VI*, III.ii. 127; II.i.159).

Golden ages are by definition either Edens or Utopias, taking place either long ago or not yet. During the stormy moment we tend to look backward or forward toward some vista of tranquillity. As the Archbishop of York complains, in the Second Part of *Henry IV*, "Past and to come seems best, things present worst (I.iii.108)." Shakespeare's extended historical pageant, with all its assassinations and executions, has recently been summed up by Jan Kott as a "succession of kings climbing and pushing one another off the grand staircase of history." These plays are described as representing a "naked struggle for power," in which the only values involved are "hate, lust, and violence." Mr. Kott, a Polish dramatic critic who has lately been promulgating his interpretations in this country, seems to have derived his inspiration not so much from a knowledge of Elizabethan drama as from the so-called Poor Theater of Jerzy Grotowski, Antonin Artaud's Theater of Cruelty, and the Theater of Beckett, Ionesco, and the Absurd. Mr. Kott has been writing in justified revulsion from a political situation which he has seen doubly overridden by the Nazis and the Soviets. Consequently, he discerns no meaning whatsoever in history. Like some of the most disaffected among us, he can descry no alternative to violence in life, and he attempts to draw Shakespeare into his anarchistic camp. But, if I were permitted the Shakespearean license of a pun, I would add that "camp" is the *mot juste.*

Thus, a few years ago the Royal Shakespeare Company revived *Titus Andronicus*—that early experiment which most of us are content to regard as a gory reduction to melodramatic absurdity, so crude that some devoted critics have sought to exonerate Shakespeare from its authorship. When this grotesque revival came to play in Poland, Mr. Kott hailed it as a naturalistic slice of life, telling things precisely the way they were. Not long thereafter, the British director Peter Brook returned the compliment with a production of *King Lear,* stressing its similarity—which no one before Mr. Kott had ever thought of—to Samuel Beckett's *Endgame.* Now, updating Shakespeare has been a continual and an inevitable process in the living theater. Jonathan Miller directed a London production of *The Tempest* last year, in which both Caliban and Ariel were exploited Africans and Prospero was a colonial despot. Given the widespread assumption that the successful director is a man who can compose the wildest variations on the themes with which Shakespeare provides him, there would seem to be no limits to the display of such ingenuity. We might well expect an up-to-date version of *The Taming of the Shrew* to be restaged as a parable of Women's Liberation. Yet after nearly four centuries of garbling, piracy, adaptation, emendation, and bowdlerization, readers of today have closer access to Shakespeare's text than perhaps they ever had before.

Naturally, they are bound to read it in the variable context of their lives—our lives. Mr. Kott introduces his book by declaring:

Shakespeare is like the world or life itself. Every historical period finds in him what it is looking for and what it wants to see. A reader or spectator in the mid-twentieth century interprets *Richard III* through his own experience. He cannot do otherwise. And that is why he is not terrified—or rather, not amazed—at Shakespeare's cruelty. He views the struggle for power and mutual slaughter of the characters far more calmly than did many generations of spectators and critics in the nineteenth century. More calmly, or, at any rate, more rationally.

One might conceivably question those last two adverbs. Calmness and rationality are not among the attributes of Mr. Kott's approach. But it is their conspicuous absence that has keyed his voice to the irrational frenzies of our epoch. The appealing title of his provocative study is *Shakespeare Our Contemporary*. The endeavor of scholars and commentators or of teachers and students, moving in the opposite direction, is to make ourselves contemporaries of Shakespeare. Ben Jonson, who first put a classical stamp upon his immediate contemporary through a much quoted eulogy, declared that Shakespeare "was not of an age, but for all time." All time, however, comprises a succession of different ages, and we count a dozen generations from Shakespeare's to our own, each of which has had its own modes of apprehending him. To be contemporary, after all, simply means being temporary together. Some of our younger contemporaries may not remember that the passing instant has always been *now* until it has passed. On the other hand, nowness—like newness— is subject to wear and tear and change and decay. The rock-and-roll production of *Twelfth Night* that played off Broadway only yesterday will some day seem as dated as Dryden's and Purcell's operatic improvements on *The Tempest* during the Restoration. Mr. Kott and Mr. Brook—like ourselves—will pass along in the procession, and Shakespeare will remain to be reinterpreted by future generations.

And yet "there is a history in all men's lives," as the Earl of Warwick tells the moribund Henry IV (2 Henry IV, III.i.80). Jonson also hailed Shakespeare as the "Soul of the Age." Timely as well as timeless, he was not without his own consciousness of the everchanging *Zeitgeist*. He even anticipated the German term that modern historians use, when the Bastard speaks in *King John* of "the spirit of the time (IV.ii.176)." To be sure, the pedants have accused him of anachronisms, such as citing Aristotle in the midst of the Trojan War. But though he may not have distinguished very clearly between Achaean and Alexandrian Greeks, contrary to what some critics would maintain, he recognized the distance and the difference between the Romans and the Elizabethans. The single authentic sketch that we possess of

232

his drama in Elizabethan production depicts the cast of *Titus Andronicus* in something like Roman dress. What is more to the point, his ancients and moderns differ sharply in their ethical outlook. The pagan suicides of Brutus and Cleopatra, judged by the Stoic creed, are noble ends; whereas Hamlet is precluded from, and Ophelia is attainted by, such a death, because of the Christian canon against self-slaughter. Shakespeare, then, was working between two temporal dimensions: the legendary and the contemporaneous, the old unhappy far-off times about which he wrote and the epoch in which he wrote—a time-conscious epoch, highly conscious of the portentous transition it was making from the Elizabethan to the Jacobean era, through the *fin du siècle* of the sixteenth into the dawn of the seventeenth century.

This diachronic attitude toward history, the sense of a vital interrelationship between past and present, comes out most expressly in the mature historical plays. For example, the choric allusion to the troops of the Earl of Essex returning from Ireland in *Henry V* carries an almost journalistic vibration of topicality. When the Lord Chief Justice alludes to "the unquiet time" in the Second Part of *Henry IV,* Shakespeare is actually quoting a chapter heading from one of his sources, the chronicle of Edward Hall (I.ii.143). As a propagandist for the house of Tudor, Hall's grand design had been to trace its claims and fortunes from the dynasty of Lancaster, which he presented in a eulogistic light. Does it follow that Shakespeare was a sycophant of the Tudors? He was presumably a loyal and discreet Englishman at a time when monarchy was popular, and his plays are not without their flattering salutes to royalty. Yet he indirectly got into serious trouble when his company revived *Richard II* at the height of the Essex conspiracy. The earl, whom he had gone out of his way to salute through the Chorus of *Henry V,* was the hope of many to supplant the aging queen. To reenact the spectacle of Richard stepping down from his throne and giving up his crown, it was felt, would fan the flames of revolt. The deposition scene could not be printed in the earlier quartos of the play.

This revival was linked with an all-too-timely book, focusing upon the dethronement of Richard and suggestively dedicated to Essex by its seditious author, John Hayward. When the Star Chamber censured Shakespeare's actors, Queen Elizabeth is reported to have angrily asked: "Know ye not that I am Richard?" At the present distance, it is hard to detect much resemblance between the two rulers or their respective situations and political styles. Later poets would hark back wistfully toward what Tennyson designated "the spacious times of Queen Elizabeth"; and it is true that the Elizabethans enshrined their Virgin Queen in all the aura of courtly compliment; yet her greatest literary glorifier, Spenser, even while addressing her directly, expressly states that hers is not a golden but a stony age. His poetic monument to her, *The Faerie Queene,* was left hardly more than half-finished; the Seventh Book, with which it tapers off, was to have celebrated the virtue of constancy; it is significant that the surviving two cantos are wholly preoccupied with the antithetical characteristic, namely mutability. Here we are not very far from the fragmented vision of Donne's *Anniversaries.* A strong authoritarian emphasis upon stability, as we gather from those who talk so loudly about law and order today, can indeed express deep basic emotions of anxiety and insecurity.

Twentieth-century scholars who have reconstructed a picture of the Elizabethan world view, such as Hardin Craig, Theodore Spencer, and E.M.W. Tillyard, emphasize its elements of tradition, hierarchy, and fixity. But here their Elizabethan witnesses may have been protesting overmuch out of a distrust of innovation, alienation, and disruption. *Terra firma* had its abysses for them, as it would have for Pascal, as it has for us. Hence, like Hamlet in Queen Gertrude's closet, they display two contrasting pictures of the human condition. Naturally the new subjects of Elizabeth had their trepidations when they beheld a young girl crowned as a ruler, after a period of dynastic and religious turmoil when Protestants and Catholics had successively been burned at the stake and royal claimants beheaded in the Tower. Fortunately, she proved to be long-lived and strong-willed. She presided over England for forty-five crucial years—years which saw its emergence from the status of an island off the coast of Europe to a world power, having wrested the hegemony of the seas from Spain. This was predestined to be accompanied by magnificent fanfares in literature and the arts. But it also caused accelerating tensions, particularly in her later years, when the question of a successor was so much in the air. Then the succession itself, which brought in the Stuarts, and with them a mounting series of economic and social crises, scarcely succeeded in staving off by much more than a generation the formidable revolution ahead.

Meanwhile, at the turn of the century, while Shakespeare was transposing his interests from history and comedy to tragedy, there seems to have been a more general crisis of belief. Scientific skepticism had something to do with this creative unrest at the intellectual level—that New Philosophy which, as Donne served notice, was calling all in doubt. So Shakespeare, in the little metaphysical poem addressed by Hamlet to Ophelia, could echo the heretical observations of his exact contemporary, Galileo, with a single monosyllabic line: "Doubt that the sun doth move (II.ii.117)." So Yeats's anguished cry for lost authority, "the center cannot hold," has its prophetic counterpart in Donne's lament for "all coherence gone." That could not be the prevalent mood for long, yet the undertone was heard and voiced by more serious spirits. Behind the gorgeous pageantry and the official mythology looms an apparition of chaos. The image of man in his ideal dignity is loftily sketched by Hamlet, even while he is denouncing man's bestial corruptibility: "How like an angel in apprehension; how like a god (II.ii.302–3)!" Perfection of brain and body is attuned to the commonweal, the body politic; nature is in harmony with the supernatural, which is providential and benign. (I am following Shakespeare by indulging in musical metaphors.) The universe is designed to revolve so harmoniously that its reverberations constitute the music of the spheres, and man is so much at the center of things that his acts have planetary significance—or, conversely, astrological determination.

A deviance from these ideals is the basis of tragedy. Richard III foresees his villainous destiny in his own deformity; his twisted body is "like to a chaos (III.ii.161)." An old conception shared by Shakespeare held that the artist was a demiurge, a second creator after God, who by his artistic creation imposed cosmic form upon chaotic matter. Romeo's first inkling of tragic disillusionment evokes the exclamation: "Misshapen chaos of well-seeming forms (I.i.177)." Similarly but much more explicitly, Othello's protestation makes it clear that everything is staked on his relation with Desdemona (III.iii.90–2):

> **Perdition catch my soul**
> **But I do love thee! and when I love thee not,**
> **Chaos is come again.**

The Moorish hero in the service of Venice has just brought about, as the Herald announced, "the mere perdition"—the total loss, and here the usage is literal—"of the Turkish fleet (II.ii.3)." Othello soon will be warning Desdemona that the loss of his talismanic handkerchief would entail terrible consequences (III.iv.67–8):

> **To lose't or give't away were such perdition**
> **As nothing else could match.**

It would prefigure nothing less than the lost world of their love, and so it turns out. Victimized by Iago's plot, he victimizes her and finds himself facing the ultimate perdition, loss of soul. Seldom can a word that would be forbidden by the Victorians have been bandied so roundly back and forth across the stage. "Damned Iago" is "a damnèd slave," a "damnèd villain" who has told "an odious damnèd lie (V.i.62; ii.244, 316, 181)." But it is Othello who damns himself "beneath all depth in hell (V.ii.138)." He has sworn a premonitory oath in the tense scene where Iago opens up the abyss: "Death and damnation, O (III.iii.396)!" Chaos, in fulfillment, has come again.

It is easy to understand why a rage for order seizes upon Shakespeare's characters when they are confronted by menacing circumstances.

> **All form is formless, order orderless,**
> **Save what is opposite to England's love,**

236

says the papal legate Pandulph in *King John* (III.i.253–4). Since he is plotting with the King of France against England, his argument must be taken with some degree of ironic reservation. More regularly, it is England's well-being which is threatened by decomposition. When the Earl of Northumberland receives the bad news about the death of his son Hotspur, he calls for universal dissolution. "Let order die!" he exclaims (*2 Henry IV*, I.i.154–6),

> And let this world no longer be a stage
> To feed contention in a lingering act.

Pursuing a familiar train of Shakespearean imagery, he envisions the whole of life as a drama which now has come to its dark and murderous catastrophe. The routing of the Lancastrians by the Yorkists in the Second Part of *Henry VI* prompts the loyal young Clifford to voice the same sort of reaction. "Shame and confusion!" he cries (V.ii.31–3),

> All is on the rout.
> Fear frames disorder, and disorder wounds
> Where it should guard.

Then, when he discovers the body of his father slain in battle, he utters his apocalyptic apostrophe (40–2):

> O, let the vile world end
> And the premisèd flames of the last day
> Knit heaven and earth together.

The atmosphere in tragedy is normally heavy with doom, but in Shakespeare the very language reechoes that word. An individual doom signifies a judgment, such as a sentence of death or exile, often arbitrarily handed down, as in the case of *King Lear*. But inevitably the individual tends to associate his personal fate with the last judgment of mankind. Condemned to die on All Souls' Day in *Richard III*, the Duke of Buckingham responds: "Why, then All Souls' Day is my body's doomsday (V.i.12)." Romeo enlarges the malediction, seeing his banishment from the presence of Juliet as—worse than death—a *dies irae*. "What less than doomsday is the Prince's doom (III.iii.9)?" After the parley before the Battle of Shrewsbury, in which he will be killed,

Hotspur closes upon a gallant note of foreboding: "Doomsday is near. Die all, die merrily (*1 Henry IV*, IV.i.134)."

Hamlet is likewise ready to recognize the imminence of the world's end; but for him the recognition comes as part of a sardonic interchange, when Rosencrantz tells him the news "that the world's grown honest," and he rejoins: "Then is doomsday near (II.ii.234–6)." A graver portent of impending fatality is Horatio's introductory description of the omens that preceded the death of Julius Caesar, when the moon was "sick almost to doomsday with eclipse (I.i.120)." Dreams, ghosts, and other portents admonish the tragic protagonist that he is standing at the verge of a cataclysm. When Macduff proclaims the murder of Duncan, he exhorts the sleepers in Glamis Castle to rise up as from their graves (*Macbeth,* II.iii.73–4):

> **Up, up and see**
> **The great doom's image.**

In much the same emblematic vein, when the blinded Gloucester is reunited with Lear, he hails the mad old man as a prefiguration of the final disaster (IV.vi.133–4):

> **O ruined piece of nature! this great world**
> **Shall so wear out to naught.**

Just as Shakespearean tragedy may be said to reenact the Fall of Man, so it may be said to anticipate the Day of Judgment. Thence its unremitting quest for justice—not legal justice, which is constantly being challenged, nor poetic justice, which too neatly balances sufferings with rewards and villainies with punishments, but the problematic sanction of a higher morality, a tragic ethos, an insight into the *rerum natura*. Where Shakespeare's histories deal with "time misordered (*2 Henry IV,* IV. ii.33)," largely upon the plane of politics, his tragedies and comedies have their divergent ways of dealing with disorder. Gloucester may have been right in his superstitious warning: "Machinations, hollowness, treachery, and all ruinous disorders follow us disquietly to our graves (*King Lear,* I.ii.110–12)."

Moralizing over the fall of Richard II, his gardener puns and attributes it to his "disordered spring (III.iv.48)." Richard, in his last soliloquy, uses a phrase which curiously rhymes, when he compares his kingly negligence to the "disordered string" of an instrument (V.v.46). The word *disorder* does not seem to have been used by Shakespeare for disease, although the latter figuratively comes to stand for the former, as students of his imagery have shown. In comedy, disorder is misrule in the sense of prankishness, confusion, or revelry, as with those disorders of Sir Toby Belch which Malvolio vainly seeks to curb in *Twelfth Night* (II.ii.89). Ultimately these must be set straight. Bachelors must get married; deceivers must be exposed; and poor old Falstaff, who by his own confession lives "out of all order," must be dropped by his erstwhile companion now destined to rule (*2 Henry IV*, III.iii.17). Approaching our terminology from the more positive side, we observe that the word *order* is employed more frequently in *Measure for Measure* than in any other Shakespearean play—and rather more equivocally, as is hinted by the self-balancing title. The drastic measure of the law-and-order governor, Angelo, against those citizens who live out of all order elicits countermeasures which prove him to be a hypocrite and a reprobate. Municipal corruption is weighted against civic reform, permissiveness against repressiveness.

All drama oscillates between order and disorder, as the defeated French do at Agincourt, the Constable of France embracing the cause of disorder, the Duke of Bourbon cursing: "The devil take order now (*Henry V*, IV.v.18, 23)!" Shakespeare's ideas of *order* can be glossed as a command at the very simplest (to give or take orders), then as a compact like the "threefold order ta'en" by the enemies of Henry IV (III.i.71), still again as a protocol like Lady Macbeth's "Stand not upon the order of your going (III.iv.119)," and not least as a vocation (taking orders, holy or chivalric). More broadly, actions may be scaled to a moral order, incidents be framed within a world-order. Every drama must terminate, in effect, with the kind of resolution that Augustus Caesar formulates in the tag-line of *Antony and Cleopatra* (V.ii.363–4):

> Come, Dolabella, see
> High order in this great solemnity.

Furthermore, Shakespeare not infrequently moralizes the scene with a set speech or homily or *exemplum,* placed in the mouth of an elderly character such as the gardener in *Richard II.* His instructions to his assistant constitute a little allegory and act out, as in a morality play, the deathbed forebodings of John of Gaunt— his fears for "this blessed plot, this earth, this realm, this England (II.i.50)." In each case, the ideal of commonweal is held up as a model in order to stress its current violation. The king's garden— and gardens were a most congenial analogy for the man from Stratford—"the whole land" was "full of weeds (III.iv.43–4)." Why, then, "should we . . . /Keep law and form and due proportion (40–1)?" Under a more fortunate dispensation, when Henry V would be attaining "the world's best garden," France, the Archbishop of Canterbury spells out a sociological lesson with a fable of the honeybees (I.ii.188–9),

> Creatures that by a rule in nature teach
> The act of order to a peopled kingdom.

The passage that is invariably cited, when Shakespeare's conceptions of order are discussed, consists of some sixty lines from the longer speech delivered by Ulysses to the Greek council of war in *Troilus and Cressida:* "The specialty of rule hath been neglected (I.iii.78)." Now this is neither an everlasting gospel nor an eternal verity; nor does the speaker represent Shakespeare himself, any more than do his other personages. This is a diagnosis, which leads to a strategy. Ulysses is not really a *raisonneur* like those neutral moralists of Molière; he is the wily strategist of the Greeks; and they, we should recall, were much less sympathetic to Western Europe than to the Trojans from whom it claimed descent. Against the contextual background, the eloquence dwindles into semi-scandalous questions of personality, notoriously the unheroic mockeries of Achilles, before it is interrupted by the challenging mission of Aeneas. The other purple passage of Ulysses, the argument with which he works on the vanity of Achilles, whom Shakespeare presents as an effeminate brute, is

240

devoted to the topic of opportunity and the spirit of opportunism, "emulation" or competitiveness. The line of thought that is amplified and illustrated by Ulysses' oratorical exposition had been propounded by Sir Thomas Elyot, the authoritation apologist for the ruling house, in his book of *The Governor*. "Take away order from all things, what should then remain?" Elyot rhetorically inquires, and his answer to his inquiry begins: "Certes nothing finally, except some men would imagine eftsoons chaos . . ."

Ulysses takes a more affirmative tone when he appeals to the heavens, and instances the well-regulated movement of the sun and the planets around the earth according to the old Ptolemaic astronomy—which, a generation before Shakespeare's birth, had been all but discredited by the more open and less anthropocentric system of Copernicus. For the Trojan War, as for the Middle Ages, it could still exemplify a pattern of office and custom, hierarchies and priorities, functioning together "in all line of order (83)." This is what the more orthodox commentators have stressed. But we have already noted that Hamlet, as a man of the Renaissance, registered some doubt about the traditional world view; and the central part of Ulysses' picture dwells upon its negative aspect, not the ideal but the *status quo*. It is a harrowing evocation of plagues and portents and the ensuing disintegration of nature when the cosmic machinery grinds to a halt. "O, when degree is shaked, / Which is the ladder of all high designs," the sequel is earthshaking (101–3). Thereupon institutions fall apart and anarchy prevails. And it is here that Shakespeare takes up Elyot's point (109–11):

Take but degree away, untune that string,
And hark what discord follows. Each thing meets
In mere oppugnancy.

Notice that, as the usual Shakespearean harmonics give way to cacophony, the discordant images are orchestrated to a strained and cracking diction. If there were no bounds, if everything were utterly unbounded (111–13),

The bounded waters
Should lift their bosoms higher than the shores
And make a sop of all this solid globe.

This solid globe! One cannot imagine Shakespeare writing that line without hinting at some cross-reference from the world to the stage in his habitual fashion, and from the Trojan War to that artistic microcosm known as the Globe Playhouse. The climax of the conjuration is a view of life conceived as a lawless struggle for naked power, *homo homini lupus*, and emblematized by the figure of a son who strikes his father dead. Shakespeare had displayed an early tableau of parricide in the Third Part of *Henry VI*, and would go on to dramatize its motivation in depth with *King Lear*. *Troilus and Cressida* has been unfavorably compared with Chaucer's *Troilus and Criseyde*, possibly because Chaucer sympathized more with the lovers. Though their love perforce is bittersweet, he brought out much of its sweetness, whereas Shakespeare gave equal stress to the war, and thereby clouded the drama with bitterness. Everyone is exacerbated in the mutual suspicion of the disunited allies and the protracted stalemate of the two superpowers. The attitude that finds its scurrilous vent in the cynical curses of Thersites makes the play as powerful a disavowal of war as the *agitprop* of Bertolt Brecht.

Another famous attempt to reaffirm the conservative norms of society is the fable of the Belly and the Members, as told by Menenius Agrippa in *Coriolanus*. Here again the story had been previously recounted by the archconservative Elyot; but, though Menenius goes even further in his patrician bias than Ulysses, Shakespeare utilizes dialogue rather than monologue and allows the heckling plebs to lodge a strong counterargument. Under any thoughtful scrutiny, the identification of the Senate with the stomach is as questionable in logic as it is in physiology. The quick-witted First Citizen, whom Menenius does not altogether refute by branding as "the great toe of this assembly," has a case to make for the leg, the arm, the head, the heart, the eye—in short, for the other social estates (I.i.150). If the citizens are incited by the demagoguery of the tribunes, they have a genuine grievance in the "dearth." Probably their protests reflect a concern for the famines and riots that had broken out in the Midlands shortly before Shakespeare wrote his play. The antidemocratic tirades of Coriolanus himself have made him the most controversial among Shakespeare's heroes. The ideological conflict between him and the populace becomes so strongly polarized that, on various occasions, it has inflamed its audiences. As a student in Paris during the nineteen-thirties, I myself witnessed a performance at the Comédie Française which prompted rioting and contributed to a general strike and the fall of a government.

One of the reasons why Shakespeare turned from the English histories to his Roman tragedies, I suspect, was that the setting of a model republic in the distant past accorded him freer scope for dramatizing politics than did the thornier issues he encountered closer to home. There, too, he could shift his focus from kingship to citizenship. He could balance, as he does in *Julius Caesar*, democracy against dictatorship, the rabble-rousing Mark Antony against the liberal Brutus. The latter, brought reluctantly to engage in an act of violence, brings down upon his head and that of Rome the retributive forces of counter-violence. In his troubled hesitation he likens his mind to a country undergoing a revolt (II.i.67–9):

> the state of man,
> Like to a little kingdom, suffers then
> The nature of an insurrection.

The term *revolution,* for Shakespeare, retained its mechanical connotation and its medieval application, the cycle of Fortune's wheel. *Revolt* was the catchword; and Shakespearean dramaturgy abounds in what King Lear terms "images of revolt," some of which I have been trying to relate and elucidate (II.iv.86). If it celebrates rebellious barons on the battlefield, it can also envisage disgruntled mobs fighting in the streets. Because of such an episode, which may have been written by Shakespeare himself, the collaborative play of *Sir Thomas More* was banned. Nonetheless Shakespeare's treatment of Jack Cade's rebellion forms a serio-comic underplot to the Second Part of *Henry VI* and the author virtually appends his signature when he shows the rebel run to earth in a Kentish garden rather than a London street. Even on Prospero's enchanted island, the threat of revolution is raised by Caliban and the two drunken clowns.

Nor should we forget, amid the many counterclaims to our

attention in *Hamlet,* that climactic scene where the mob breaks into the palace, revolting against the regime of Claudius. Something is rotten, we know; the state is disjoint and out of frame; the time is out of joint, and Hamlet has been born to set it right, to set his father's house in order. Can he be considered to have fulfilled that resolve? In seeking to redress the regicide, he has embarked upon a course of incident and accident which results in his death and seven more deaths, and which leaves the state of Denmark under the rule of its hereditary enemy. Tragedy always culminates when the survivor takes over, with an appeal for the restoration of order — or, at least, for the reestablishment of continuity. Inevitably, its final couplets try to modulate its funeral eulogies with brave words about carrying on and with whatever silver linings can be dimly discerned among the still lowering clouds. All this can place the tragic events in perspective, but it cannot palliate them for us, insofar as we have truly felt them. I see very little point in pretending, through some Hegelian exercise in cosmic optimism, that tragedy is other than pessimistic. Scotland has been turned into a chaos by Macbeth. Deliberately he curses: ". . . let the frame of things disjoint (III.i.16)." When Macduff reenters with his severed head and announces that "the time is free (V.viii.55)," we rejoice with Malcolm and the rest. But the line of future kings that stretches out is not to end so happily with the Stuarts as Shakespeare implies. History can outdo even tragedy in its reversals.

Tragedy does not pretend to encompass the totality of experience, in any case, and Shakespeare had an especially poignant feeling for its intermixtures with comedy, not to mention his feelings for the happier spheres of the purely comic or the lyrically romantic. The ills that flesh is heir to — he knew well — have their compensations, and he might have ruefully smiled at this sentence from a recent editorial commentary in *The New York Times:* "It is a Shakespearean irony that new prospects for peace exist precisely because all industrial societies, Communist and capitalist, are in the process of tearing themselves apart." Shakespeare's name is justly invoked in that immediate and momentous connection, since he had so comprehensive an over-view, so keen a sense of the long run. Life itself was so much larger than people, he realized, that their best intentions were more likely than not to go astray. He was also fully aware that destruction was the underlying precondition of renewal, and that any person who understood this had found his identity even while losing it, had earned—like Enobarbus—"a place i' th' story (*Antony and Cleopatra,* III.xiii.46)." Heretofore most Americans have had no difficulty in dwelling, with William Dean Howells, upon the smiling aspects of life. Shakespeare becomes increasingly meaningful as, at his profoundest, he habituates us to learning the worst; as he initiates us into the *mysterium iniquitatis,* the mystery of evil; as he offers us, through the tragic catharsis, a retrospect of life and a foretaste of death; as he heartens us, by our momentary survival, to take an ethical stance against over-whelming odds.

Notes on prophecy and apocalypse in a time of anarchy and revolution: a trying out

TONY STONEBURNER

1. It appears that the contemporary reviewer, be he journalist or scholar-critic, cannot write about current literary works without employing the words *apocalypse* and *apocalyptic*. Our poetry, fiction, drama, and their mutations express both in subject and in idiom a world in which human production clutters more and more thickly, and weighs more and more heavily upon mankind until catastrophic devastation incinerates or otherwise wipes it out. The reviewer has had to repeat the words so regularly that their recurrence seems automatic and glib.

The purpose of the present notes is to suggest that a fuller historical and literary grasp of the biblical genre called apocalypse (or apocalyptic) and prophecy—its major predecessor—might so inform our use of these words that our resorting to them would become the less frequent as it became the more precise—and all this refinement not for the sake of fussy antiquarianism or exacting pedantry but for the sake of illuminating what we read in a time of deception and repression (and of their proposed correlatives, anarchism and revolution).

Apocalypse has been fashionable not only with journalists but also with scholar-critics. Two of the most instructive of these, Northrop Frye and Frank Kermode, have made the term familiar even as they have forced it to suffer deformation. For Frye, apocalypse is part of his over-all scheme. His idiosyncratic use furnishes a correction to the popular one: if it signifies a human and cosmic finish that is nothing but negativities (hell and damnation within the historical horizon), his signifies heaven and beatitude. Frye treats the apocalyptic and the demonic as though they were polar opposites (rather than treating the apocalyptic as the synthesis or interaction of intensest positivities and negativities in which the former have the ultimate victory, as biblical scholars do). He properly makes clear that the final meaning of apocalypse is hope but he improperly hides that its penultimate meaning approximates despair, for the negativities almost overwhelm. Hoodwinking darkness almost snuffs out the light. Evil almost overwhelms good. Indeed, within the mundane realm evil rules, except for a few hold-outs in their marginal enclaves or underground. Martyrdom is the normal measure of their faithfulness. But that is the next-to-last word of apocalypse, not the last. The utility of his reducing the word to half its meaning is that it gives a rectifying emphasis to the half usually forgotten in ordinary use.

For Kermode, apocalypse is a far-fetched and witty example of what the imagination creates in defense against and conquest of the overwhelming character of undifferentiated experience, which must be simplified and ordered if we are to take it in and respond to it but which must not be so streamlined and tame that it does not remind us, as we read it, of expectation-disappointing and surprising experience itself. Kermode considers apocalypse as a fiction with its arbitrary and artificial accentuating and contouring by "temporizing," in order to supply us with an example of a fiction to which we are not already adjusted and in which we are not already at home, like the novel or the short story. To make his point about anticipation of the plot and pleasure in a twist on the part of the reader, he concentrates less on a description of apocalypse in itself (the literary expression of a community) and more on the rearrangements it requires when its calendar and clock are out of date, but groups desire to regard it as having authority concerning the schedule of the culminating events of history and perhaps the universe (the literary expression of a community borrowed, and therefore altered in meaning, by another community: McLuhan has made us sensitive to a double process which applies here—a new medium uses the medium which it replaces as its content and in so doing alters its meaning). Kermode concentrates on the aspect of (communally-displaced) apocalypse which Marxists might call the facet of necessary illusion (let us synchronize our waterproof watches so that our face hands, second, minute, hour, will gesture identical dial-readings at the end of all things). He asks, What do persons do when the end is tardy? But he does not ask what the promise of the end was designed to enable the readers of the work (or auditors at a communal gathering) to do. The promise enables them to do something specific in a difficult situation. Kermode is interested in the more general, epistemological act which the promise enables them to do: to space time and establish distance within it. In the self-understanding of persons who belong to an apocalyptic community, what oppresses is not epistemological or psychological but institutional and what threatens is not chaos of sensation or imagery but arrest, imprisonment, death externally and apostasy internally. The promise enables the reader or auditor of the work to be faithful to what is most important to him in the present. If the apocalyptic promise of the end foreshortens the future it does so to sponsor and support faithfulness in the present. The importance of the work for the members of its original community was NOW. But Kermode stresses THEN, a secondary beat. His cunning and erudite account of apocalypse is provocative for a theory about fiction. But it is out of focus or misleading as a description of apocalypse.

248

The words *prophecy* and *prophetic* have undergone a similar, if less dramatic, mutilation in the linguistic usage of journalists and scholar-critics. The same failure to grasp the genre, or a decision to formulate it with an emphasis that disregards historical study but that assists the favorite personal system or theory, dogs *prophecy* and *prophetic* as it dogs *apocalypse* and *apocalyptic*.

My purpose is to promote exchange of knowledge. If journalists and scholar-critics suffer too great a degree of ignorance about the recent work of biblical interpreters, so do biblical interpreters suffer too great a degree of ignorance about the recent work of scholar-critics. Specialization makes us dyslexic. We scramble our letters anagrammatically and arrange new meanings or nonsense or their combination. We misread. Biblical scholarship, for example, remained trapped in speculation that continued to look in the wrong direction much longer than necessary as it attempted to understand oral composition—a crucial item for interpreting many literary characteristics of the Old Testament and the New Testament—because it remained ignorant of the exploration of the field by Lord and others. Likewise literary students do not draw on the resources of generic distinctions made by biblical scholarship for their interpretation of literary works that bear one or another direct relation to revolution. As a result, or so I assume as I assemble these notes, our reading is less penetrating and less subtle.[1]

2. Upheaval disturbs established institutions. In response, they bring their weight to bear. They want things to settle down. If they alter their position, it is only to remain in control.

The imagination plays a role in relation to the upheaval in its rise and fall. It creates the literature which makes persons conscious of the lack of freedom and justice not as a slogan but as a concrete human experience. It creates the literature of protest and resistance, summoning readers to undermine and replace the intolerable *status quo*. The imagination creates mutations of literature, like demonstrations and happenings, graffiti and post-

249

ers, in which life tries to assimilate aesthetic intensity to the public sphere by swallowing up aesthetic distance and tries to enact the metaphors of literature in the public sphere as on a stage or within the frame of a painting. It creates the immediate record of the upheaval. Finally, in the aftermath (whether lip-smacking or wound-licking) of the upheaval, the imagination, recovering aesthetic distance, transmutes the immediate record of participation into a mediate figuration of experience.

3. The imagination of revolution derives in part from the imagination of *prophecy* and the imagination of *apocalypse,* or so I am assuming for the purpose of these notes. The first says that the attitudes and actions of persons are decisive for the destiny of peoples. The second says that the very structures of society are pliant and susceptible to total alteration; the new can replace the old, at least at the moment in which God changes and exchanges them utterly. The imagination of revolution combines the first (decisive human action) and the second (docility and ductility of institutions at the moment of transformation). Human action will totally alter the structure of society and dialectically produce the radically new. From the nadir of social estrangement and exploitation to the zenith of human fulfillment and harmony, freedom and justice and peace, is no distance at all. Persons would not undertake a revolution if they did not imagine that their effort would make a considerable difference and that social reality is plastic to drastic change. Only nihilists, assuming that cosmos is a rigid cage of incarceration and society is a sadistic prison-keeper and that the structures of neither are in their control or under their influence, defy what is not responsive to them and act to destroy as much of it as they can as they themselves are destroyed (in mercy-suicide).

A careful reading of *prophecy* and *apocalypse* prepares us for a careful reading of literary works that bear one or another direct relation to revolution.

4. Prophecy and *apocalypse* as we know them in the Bible and

250

related documents are two religious-literary genres. Their broadest spiritual and ethical presuppositions are identical. Martin Buber writes, "Common to both is faith in the one Lord of the past, present, and future history of all existing being; both views are certain of His will to grant salvation to His creation."[2] Although the prophecy which we know in the Bible has non-Yahwehist precedents in other cultures and although apocalypse has non-Jewish successors, both are the product of the Hebraic religious genius. Both prophecy and apocalypse protest things as they are in the name of God. Their condemnation of the *status quo* and vision of social and cosmic renovation invite a theological-ideological and literary-critical comparison of prophecy and apocalypse with the linguistic expression of drop-out anarchism and knock-down, blow-up revolution.

5. Having briefly stated the commonalities, we turn to the contrasts. Spatially, geographically, prophecy and apocalypse are one in origin but temporally, chronologically, they are two. Both are products of the Near East, prophecy in the period of the monarchy (from Saul to Zedekiah, half a millennium) and apocalypse in the period of late Hellenism.

Both are an imagination of the religion whose foundational and normative event is divine liberation from Egyptian slavery as it interacts with the circumstances of the time. Each occurs in a specific political-social situation. Prophecy belongs to independent nationhood and monarchy, to the Judaic and Israelite kingdoms. Apocalypse belongs to subservient incorporation in thickening empire, to the expansionist Seleucidian and Roman tyrannies. Prophecy addresses persons who have responsibility for the formulation and implementation of policy and maintenance. It assumes that those who are in control are capable of undertaking major adjustments in the structure of classes and the operation of institutions, are capable of reform, are capable of actual alteration and rearrangement. Prophecy is political. It speaks to rulers, officials, priests, professional prophets, and the people as a whole, for it is they who exercise power, who decide and enact policy.

251

Prophecy announces their guilt for the past, but it also invites them to *turn* in the present.

Apocalypse addresses persons who lack economic-political-social importance and suffer alienation from the institutions that channel power. It assumes the possibility of (passive) resistance (unto martyrdom). It addresses members of a religious community which has been reduced to a sect by political impotence and persecution at their refusal to surrender its particularity and submit to religious conformity as part of governmental policy to consolidate dominance. The members of the sect experience alienation both from the official institutions of the oppressor—which like all totalitarian states cannot tolerate differences—and from the official institutions of fellow believers who impress them as compromisers and apostates (the community of the Dead Sea Scrolls, in some sense such a sect, has a double foe: an external military empire and an internal contaminated sacerdotal, sacrificial cult of the Temple in Jerusalem). Apocalypse says to their impotent purity, *stand* (even unto death).

6. Prophecy and apocalypse are also two distinct kinds of composition. Prophecy is originally oral poetic composition. It is organized according to the outline of a royal message. The core of its content is verdict and sentence rendered by God as judge in his heavenly court on the behavior of persons who often managed not to be brought to justice in a human court.

As far as we know, no pre-exilic prophet reduced his own prophecy to writing and what precipitated its original transcription is as much a mystery as the recording of Homeric epic in writing. Those who preserved and arranged the words-from-God, and recorded them before or after they arranged them, were probably assistants or disciples of the prophet. "The writing prophets" as the appellation for the prophets under whose names the midwifing editors collected words-from-God is a misnomer.

Apocalypse is from the start written (predominantly) prose composition. It consists of a sequence of episodes. It contains historical allusion and literary quotation. It is pseudonymous for a variety of reasons, including the desire to borrow spiritual authority from the wise men of an earlier period under whose name the work appears, to lend verismilitude to the account of the past, pre-dating it as an account of the future, to keep secret the actual authorship from the agents of a police state.

Except for God-talk, there is little that is mythological in prophecy. It draws its images and figures of speech from the world of men, from the ranges of secular life, like a basket of summer fruit and a plumbline. It is full of word-play. Apocalypse is crowded with mythological beings and reshuffled ancient or archetypal religious symbols which offer notations for psychological depth and for a transcendent realm. The language is often stiff and stilted, liturgically turgid or proclamatorily clamorous. If prophecy is ordinary language intensified by figure and trope, apocalypse is special language, elevated and rarefied by archaism, and circumlocution and formula. If prophecy is down-to-earth, apocalypse is up-in-the-air, surrealistic, weird.

The content of apocalypse is usually double. It has narratives about exemplary persons who prefer death to disloyalty to God or impurity of life (think of the stories at the beginning of the Book of Daniel or the summarizing prediction about the two witnesses in Revelation 11); they demonstrate that men can rise to religious heroism even in the most oppressive periods, and challenge the members of the community to whom the work speaks to demonstrate the same heroism. It also has a schedule of events. It appears to be a forecast from the past of things to come, and the accuracy of the litany-like forecast seems uncanny. So far, it seems to be right on the mark. I say "seems" because its claim of composition in the past is a fiction. Indeed, it may be the case that apocalypse is the first crude effort of the human imagination to write historical fiction. Of course, the composition that pretends to be a composition of the past with a prediction of its future (but the past of those for whom it was published) is actually the composition of the present of those for whom it was published. No wonder its fictional prediction seems so accurate. It is a forecast written with hindsight, with two bold exceptions. Most of the

253

schedule of events is limited to history masked as prediction, but the schedule also designates the present of the author and his public, usually as a period of severest and most violent trial for members of the sect, and, in their view, an axial moment for human destiny, and designates the immediate future (so that *now* subtly becomes *soon* and *soon now* without any elongation) as the crucial moment in which history enjoys such drastic transformation that it loses its character as conflict and strife, and institutions with their impersonality and indirectness give way to immediacy and spontaneity of relationships (think of the chapters at the end of Revelation). The aim of the heraldic and emblematic calendar is to show persons about to give up to the totalitarian state as it crowds and crushes them, that they can stand for what they believe. If they will only hold out *now,* relief and vindication will be theirs *soon.* Better to be true and die than to be false and survive, for to die for being true is to participate proleptically in the triumph of the Truth about to emerge and to survive by being false is to be brought up short, to speak mildly, by that triumph.

Again the point is that the *present* is the focus of apocalypse. Of course it rehearses the past as a sequence of worsening epochs in order to acknowledge that the present is the absolute hell-pit of history. Things have to keep getting worse in history and things could not be any worse. Evil is maximal and all but total. At the same time apocalypse projects the future as the in-pouring of the completely new replacement for the previous epochs and their exploitive and tyrannical arrangements. Apocalypse more nearly answers the practical and existential question *How can I be true to my convictions, now?* than the speculative question, *When will eternity subsume history?,* or the psychological-epistemological question, *Why does mind impose "start" and "finish" on the continuity of ceaseless flux?*

I would suggest that the reason that apocalypse after apocalypse has to be written (sometimes by no more than revising or recasting a previous one) is not so much that the half of it that is calendar or schedule proved wrong. (Of course the specific future as it became the present did not dramatically change the flow of

254

history. It was conspicuously continuous with the past.) Apocalypse is less to help folk synchronize their watches for the culmination of history and more to help them set themselves to endure persecution and death with integrity (not *Will it be on time?* but *Will I be true?*). Certainly there is a tonic element of encouragement in the promise of imminent incursion of the new and an intoxicating element of vindication. I do not want to deny that these futuristic elements operate; they contribute to the character of the genre. But the answer to the urgent question is NOW (stand by your convictions) rather than SOON (God will perform total renovation). The *I will* of God is important to the fiction of apocalypse to the degree in which it braces or enables the reader of the work to stand at the moment. The fulcrum is *soon* but the lever is *now*. The imminent future as total alteration gives faithful people purchase on the slippery present, which would otherwise offer them no foothold for maintaining their position.

7. When educated persons mention prophecy, they are usually referring to the books of the Old Testament which carry the names of persons who spoke words-from-God. They have in mind especially Amos, Hosea, Isaiah, Micha, Jeremiah, Ezekiel, and the other and anonymous prophet(s) of the exile. That we know the names of almost all of them indicates that prophecy, in contrast to pseudonymous apocalypse, is the work of a known person in a public place, a known person who takes the risks of delivering a message whose content is unwanted (he puts his life on the line and yet as he understands them the words are not his own but the words-of-God; the words are the words-of-God and yet the very process of truth-telling intricates his life and words and works in the words-of-God: medium becomes message).

If in the past scholars misnamed these figures the "writing prophets," they also more appropriately called them the "high prophets" to stress their ethical Yahwehism, in contrast to the cultural religion of prophets of court and cult who tended to be yes-men to the establishment which supported them, and to stress, in contrast to the collective and choral character of the existence and action of prophets of court and cult, their individual vocation and mission with a correlate individual theme and idiom in the message which they delivered (so that, for example, scholars call Amos the prophet of a righteous God who requires human justice and Hosea the prophet of a merciful God who requires human forgiveness and Isaiah the prophet of a holy God who requires human humility and faith; and so that scholars differentiate the sheepherding imagery of Amos from the agricultural imagery of Hosea or the urban imagery of Isaiah and Jeremiah).

8. Prophecy seems to be the creation of the interaction between the other religions of the region and Yahwehism. It is an institution which the two Kingdoms probably borrowed from their neighbors. There are many questions from psychological and sociological viewpoints about the transplantation and development of the institution. In what sense is high prophecy continuous with the earliest manifestations of the institution outside and inside the Kingdoms?

Prophecy seems to have been an ecstatic group activity. The ecstacy seems to have been induced and sustained by chant, dance, instrumental music of a repetitious kind, and, upon occasion, ritual undressing and self-mutilation, and, yet again, miming a message or presenting it with emblematic objects. The group seems to have been organized, perhaps footloose, perhaps regulated by itinerary, perhaps established at a single center of worship, in at least some instances attached to the court and under royal patronage. Perhaps the group supervised and performed cultic acts. Probably it offered a service similar to that of an oracle, supplying answers to questions put to it, especially by rulers in the role of generals about to wage war. And no doubt the tendency was to reply to the king with what he was eager to hear: Do what you want; God favors it.

Is high prophecy ecstatic or sober? If it is ecstatic, is the being-beside-oneself induced by monotonous mechanical means? Is it occasional? Is high prophecy a large organized group activity, a small voluntaristic group activity, or a solitary activity? Is it professional or amateur (Amos said, "I am no prophet, nor a prophet's son; but I am a herdsman and a dresser of sycamore trees, and the LORD took me from following the flock, and the LORD said to me, 'Go, prophesy to my people Israel.'"—Amos 7:14b—15 RSV)? Is it cultic or profane, religious or secular? If it is both, which component receives the greater emphasis? Is it beneficiary of royal sponsorship or is it self-supporting or is it avocational? High prophecy strikes us as a mutation of the popular form of prophecy found both outside the two Kingdoms and inside the courts of the two Kingdoms. But the evidence puzzles. The pieces do not fit together.

In spite of our ignorance concerning the institutional and vocational implications of prophecy, *two things seem clear about its verbal expression.* High prophecy continues to employ, in a more and more elaborate presentation, the "message form" which belongs to it from its earliest historical appearance. And it continues to utilize, with greater and greater emphasis until it becomes the identifying characteristic, the "trial scene."

The message form is common to the ancient Near East over a long period. It emerges to facilitate long-distance royal communication as city-states expand into empire. The command or inquiry of the ruler can go forth without his personal presence, yet with his royal authority. *Thus says so and so* commissions the messenger at the place where it originates and authenticates the message at the place where he delivers it. There is nothing specifically or specially religious about the form. Kings no doubt used it long before priests did and before prophets did. It is essentially an oral form (yet it was the determining force for the epistolary form that arose in that same land-mass upon the invention of writing).

The message form occurs within the earliest extant evidence of an extra-Hebraic analogue to, or anticipation of, prophecy, the letters from Mari. From the beginning to the end of prophecy, the message form was fundamental. Indeed, when the message form started to disintegrate, prophecy began to disappear, giving way to, among other things, apocalypse.

257

To use the language of Claus Westermann, upon whose analysis in *Basic Forms of Prophetic Speech* I am dependent, the message form consists of the "messenger formula" *Thus says so and so* (at the moment of messenger-commissioning but, with a metamorphosis of tense, *Thus said so and so* at the moment of message-delivery) or *Behold;* a report on an occurrence (in a perfect tense); a command or summons (in an imperative mood). Sometimes a conditional promise of benefit reinforces the command or summons (*if you do it, you will get such and such*). If the message form occurs within a narrative there is usually a report of the sending of the messenger with designation of the addressee or recipient and of the place where he is to be found; and the commissioning of the messenger, with messenger formula, and two-part message (the part in the imperative mood joined perhaps with a conditional promise). The messenger formula resembles a signature on a letter, or a seal on it or its container, or a signalling by quotation marks that one is using the language of another or a signalling the source of a statement by asterisk of number for annotation.

Because it originates as an oral mode, the message form tends to promote brevity and clarity of expression. It probably belongs to the history of every form that it undergoes elaboration and expansion to the point of collapse or mutation. Prophecy moves toward chaos and elephantiasis. No doubt the introduction of writing into the process of oral communication—as means of composition, as means of transmission, as means of storage after delivery—intensifies the process of exploring the limits to complication and to enlargement before incoherence prevails.

Prophecy is not homily or oration and to the extent that it comes to approximate their low-or-high-keyed length it abandons itself.

Prophecy, by its very nature, seems to have elected to express itself through the message form. The God (YHWH) who at this period does not speak directly to His people sends the prophet as messenger to them. The messenger formula is usually *Thus says the Lord.*

What is the message? In the letters from Mari the message

protests the failure of the king to sponsor cultic acts or to consult the god of the cult. The vested interest of the cult personnel is conspicuous.

In the prophecy of Yahwehism, by contrast, the self-interest of the messenger seems the furthest thing from his mind. He risks his own interest. He sometimes suffers ridicule, persecution, mobbing, imprisonment, death in consequence of delivering the message (the Book Jeremiah gives a vivid, visceral, if not continuous, account of the various negativities which Jeremiah experienced from youth to old age as a result of his message-delivering vocation). What is the message which he transmits? It is an uninvited and unwelcome message (in contrast to an answer received from an oracle in response to an inquiry). It is a message of judgment, in both a technical juridical sense and a theological sense. It is a message from a judge, from YHWH as judge. The message declares guilt and announces the sentence, the punishment which future historical events will unfold.

The two Kingdoms had a judicial-legal system in which a person could seek justice according to the law. But certain persons seemed exempt from the exacting process because of their rank or special office: the king, the officials of the court, the priests of the established religion, the professional prophets of the court and of other shrines, and the people as a whole. No one indicted or tried any of these in the usual run of things. If they broke the law, their violation tended to pass unchallenged and uncharged.

But Yahwehism was the project of ordering a people by the keeping of the covenant, including its evolving body of law, between God and His people. None was to break it, to be unfaithful to YHWH or unjust to a member of His people. Certainly the leaders in "church and state" were not to be exceptions.

In the credibility-gap between the holding of all responsible by Yahwehism and the failing to call everyone to account by the two Kingdoms, prophecy arose with its mythical or fictional courtroom scene. The two-part message included the charge or indictment and the proclamation of judgment or sentencing. The first part, the accusation, corresponds to the report part of the message

259

form (the part in a perfect tense): *So and so has done such and such.* What it reports is common knowledge. The infraction of the religious-political-ethical law is flagrant. The prophet does not have inside information (either the secrets of God—it is no secret that God condemns such behavior—or secrets of the court). He needs no leaks for his knowledge. Therefore he can speak briefly. The accused, the addressee, knows what the prophet is talking about; other persons present know too. The culprit may elude the judgment of human trial but he does not escape the judgment of divine trial. The accusing and announcing of sentence against the wrongdoer make up the content of the message form in the prophecy of Yahwehism. The personal experience of the messengers became more and more an aspect of the message itself (the marital experience of Hosea an enactment or parable of the divine message; the celibate experience of Jeremiah a model of the Suffering Servant of the anonymous prophet of the exile and of the figure of Job in that earth-and-heaven-shaking poem.)[3] Perhaps mention should also be made that the more general address of the later prophetic message may reflect the more general address of the message form as used by imperial governments in an attempt to speak to the people, past rulers of nations who resisted their expansion or rebelled against being puppet-governments, a form of psychological warfare and propaganda, to demoralize them and undermine support for resistance (see 2 Kings 18:13–20 or the Book of Isaiah 36:1–8,21–22).

The message of judgment is the core of prophecy. The books associated with high prophecy, however, surround such messages with narratives, prayers, and promises of benefits, as well as editorial items. But judgment is the differentiating characteristic. The narratives are related to the historical compositions in other parts of the Old Testament, the prayers to the psalms and other liturgical poetry, the promises of benefits, especially in their picturing of the fulfillment of creation, to apocalypse with its cosmological scope.

Prophecy itself, particularly high prophecy, is delivery of the message of divine judgment by a human being, and, as its essence concentrates with the passage of time, judgment on more and more persons, from the king, at an early period, through the secondary leadership of the nation to the whole people, in the final phase of prophecy. The circle on the water surface spreads from the dropped pebble.

The promises of benefits which seem to belong particularly to professional court-attached prophecy resemble the answers of an oracle. They are the asked-for (sychophantic) answers to king-put questions. But the announcements of judgment came like a person from Porlock or any other cause of *coitus interruptus* (Ahab calls Elijah "You troubler of Israel"—1 Kings 18:17 RSV —and, at a later encounter when he is about to enjoy the gains of wrongdoing, he asks Elijah, "Have you found me O my enemy?" —1 Kings 21:20 RSV).

Why did prophecy become a part of the religion of Yahwehism? and why did high prophecy—so disconcerting—emerge from ordinary prophecy, so parasitic on, and supportive of, the establishment?

9. The irony (and perhaps the deepest meaning) of the trial scene as the predominant content of the message form in higher prophecy is that an institution (borrowed from neighboring pagan societies, in all likelihood, and borrowed probably as merely one more trapping of monarchy when the tribes found that the tribal confederacy did not enable them to maintain themselves in their country against their rivals with central governments and conscription and taxation, and therefore as far from Yahwehism as possible to begin with) became the powerful agent for keeping the traditional faith. The divine King had a means of expressing his tension with the human king and his people when the desire of the human king did not conform to the will of the divine King— and the means was initially alien to Yahwehism. It is as though God used the farthest-out and strangest thing to accomplish the closest intention.

10. Hannah Arendt, in *On Revolution,* suggests that revolution

261

erupts only when people can imagine the possibility of improving the conditions of a whole society or of mankind, the possibility of rearranging things so that there do not have to be the poor. If we borrow her notion of revolution we can assume with her that the French Revolution was the first all-out revolution. Prior civil wars were fought for another purpose—to determine what small or large group within a society would have ascendency and dominance.

Yet justice was the issue in the upheaval that divided the Kingdom asunder into Judah and Israel, at least as far as prophecy was involved. A government that introduced class distinctions and conscription and taxation disregarded the covenant and was careless of justice. Prophecy prepared for, and contributed to, the split which occurred in the name of faithfulness to YHWH, just as later, in the northern Kingdom, it prepared for, and contributed to, the replacement of a dynasty with no devotion to righteous YHWH by a dynasty faithful to Him. In both cases, prophecy was deeply involved with the more-than-political, almost-revolutionary events.

These two instances in which prophecy had a role in conspiracy and overthrow remind us—as exceptions—that prophecy was essentially *verbal, vocal,* a call to action and not an action. Prophecy was speech in conventional forms with vigorous language, vivid imagery, strong figures, and profound tropes. But the action was not the responsibility of the prophet, the action was the responsibility of the persons who could reorder society, from the king through his bureaucracy to the whole people. Reordering of society toward conformity with the covenant was the essential possibility for prophecy. The word of judgment was to call folk to *turn.* Even when it named direst doom as punishment for radical disregard of God, it was a call. Although the condemnation sounded final, it included an implicit conditional clause: *Doom comes if you do not alter your present ways.* Reform can restore the conditions commanded by the covenant. There do not have to be the poor. Reform is enough. Revolution is unnecessary. Coup d'état or palace revolt makes possible action by those responsible for the order of society which will result in conformity to the conditions commanded by the covenant.

(Apocalypse thinks that institutions are so corrupt and self-interested that they can neither elect nor enact reform and that people who submit to their closed society cannot alter it significantly, and that people who belong to a sect loyal to a transhistorical God are politically impotent: there is no human possibility for the improvement of society; only a divine interruption and culmination of history can establish a life of freedom, justice, and peace. Prophecy addresses sinners and asks them to stop doing what they are and to start doing what is right; apocalypse addresses saints and asks them to stick to it. Prophecy is political; apocalypse is miraculously and mathematically cataclysmic. Prophecy invites people to save themselves in cooperation with God. Apocalypse sees no hope on the horizon; only from over and beyond it can come our salvation. Yet prophecy recognizes that people may elect not to cooperate with God. People may elect their own doom. Worse than that, Judaism later discovered, history is ambiguous and ironic. Election of righteousness does not, in history, guarantee freedom, justice, peace—or prosperity. There is a deeper despair than that people carelessly let doom occur—there is the despair of those who trust the promise only to discover that history cannot produce the goods: the Book of Job. If history promotes despair, then faith must leap beyond history, and it must leave nothing decisive to human beings. The possibility of salvation must be altogether a divine possibility. Hope cannot be for the present world; it must be for the pristine world that takes the place of the present world.)

11. As Martin Buber says in the essay already quoted, the prophetic message addresses *the center of surprise.* The word of the god speaks to human freedom. A message of doom is not irrevocable. If there is a human turning, a divine turning will answer it. Reality is dialogical in its farthest-reaching social and historical dimensions. The prophet does not announce the inevitable. Nor does he curse the people.

263

12. Apocalypse expresses hope that will not disappoint. Between the present ulcerous and ugly moment and the fulfillment of that hope in the future establishment of good, an absolute catastrophe occurs to the present order of things. There is doom for evil order and disorder. But, good riddance of bad rubbish, it is nothing to lament, merely something to endure. So apocalypse says *stand* and says *hope:* the end of all things is cheering and good news, for just beyond their annihilation is a pristine and prismatic world, gracious and lovely and prompt to appear for all who by their integrity within a society, like an iron maiden (the whore of Babylon), have apprehended that newness by wholehearted anticipation.

13. When educated persons mention apocalypse, they are usually referring to books of the Bible, including the Apocrypha, such as Daniel, Second Esdras, Revelation, and to a number of extra-scriptural works.

14. Apocalypse often has astrological and astronomical details, dreams, enigmatic language, heraldic beasts and monsters, numerological patterns, and vestigial mythological beings; it usually has a pairing, or opposing, of good beings with bad, in which the bad are often a grotesque, obscene, and ugly parody of the good.

15. An example of antithetical parody is the anti-Christ, in Revelation, a demonic or monstrous version of the Messiah, opposed to the Anointed One and of an opposite spirit and yet using similar methods, as if evil, in opposing good, condemns itself to imitate good but externally, grossly, and unattractively.

16. In prophecy the messenger appears in person (or, as several incidents in the Book of Jeremiah suggest, takes responsibility for the message which he delivers). The already generally endangered author of apocalypse does not make a public appearance as the author of his work, does not put his life so close to his words that they are indistinguishably one in his personal and vocational action (as they become in the message-transmission of the prophet). Authorship is probably always more distancing than a personal appearance and direct address. Pseudonymous authorship is no doubt even more distancing. Apocalypse is very literary.

17. If prophecy is addressed to wrongdoers with power to pivot policy in another direction (at right angles, even to 180 degrees), apocalypse is addressed to the righteous without power, who suffer all but can alter nothing in their world.

18. Is Marxism, at least when popularly understood as a rigorous articulation of a sharply-jointed iron dialectic, prophetic or apocalyptic? To the extent that it is the protest of righteous indignation against injustice and the call for human cooperation with social tendencies already operative in history to reorder institutions for the service of all persons and the enhancement of their humanity, it is prophetic. To the extent that it is phasal and irresistible (a Marxist like Garaudy would deny that it has that character), indeed has a timetable in which necessity, nexus of interacting cosmic and social forces, keeps its appointments, and therefore has an invincible ground of hope that perfection will become actual, and to the extent that reform is seen as treatment of symptom rather than disease (the reinforcing and prolongation of, to speak mildly, useless institutions rather than their disappearance, withering, drying up, blowing away), it is apocalyptic.

19. One could test the utility of these notes on prophecy and apocalypse by bringing them self-consciously to a reading of such works as Blake's prophecies, Russian poetry since 1917, Brecht's plays, Latin American poety by Marxists, recent volumes by Denise Levertov, and other works that bear some relation to revolution, and discovering if the sense of the two biblical genres had made one more discerning and penetrating, and if it had enabled one to grasp more (a greater scope) and to make subtler distinctions (a greater refinement). Although works of this kind are perhaps the ultimate test of the utility of knowledge of prophecy and apocalypse, they also seem the too obvious place of trying out that knowledge and too neatly tailor-made for it. One wants a place not self-evident. Therefore I have decided to make the life and work of David Jones the place of trying out. Religiously a Roman Catholic convert, and literarily a modernist, David Jones would ordinarily be seen as a traditionalist, not a revolutionary. Critics frequently write about him in this way.

If knowledge of prophecy and apocalypse makes us more discriminating readers of his works, it is likely that it will make us more discriminating readers of works conspicuously related to revolution.

David Jones served in World War I with Royal Welsh Fusiliers. He experienced the heat of battle in France, where he was wounded in a leg in 1916 and almost died from trench fever in 1918. During convalescence in Ireland, he experienced the chill of "occupying" a country.

The war was the decisive experience in the life of David Jones. Ironically, its destruction was crucial for his formation, its chaos foundational to his being. He incorporated its half-apocalypse of all-hell-broke-loose into his life. It is as though an accident became an essence. War seized one stronghold of his imagination and controlled how he thought. War that had previously been one thing among many became a major one among a few, all of which overlap (craftsmanship, the sea, Wales).

The war was also the occasion of his discovery of Roman Catholicism not only as an institution at the core of Western civilization but also as the faith at the core of his own life. It initially manifested its ingathering power to him in the liturgy. He stumbled on a celebration of the Mass in a barn behind the trenches. Perpetually cold, he was hunting for firewood. The farm building seemed to promise what he was after. For some reason, before entering, he put his eye to a hole in the wall. The interior was plain but not empty and dark, as he expected; the altar was improvised, if I remember the story correctly, from tin food-containers. The candlelight surprised him. The worshippers, many fellow soldiers known to David Jones, surprised him even more. The concerted and unific action surprised him most of all and moved him deeply.

David Jones does most things slowly (or at a pace which respects the nature of the result). The Catholic faith irradiated his imagination, yet he took his time in submitting to the Roman obedience. The wartime eucharist probably occurred in 1917, but David Jones did not become a Roman Catholic officially until 1921.

At the same time, he was feeling strongly the inadequacy of conventional art school education in spite of the fact that both at Camberwell before the war and at Westminster after it, he received instruction that delivered him from false and vulgar models, introduced him to post-impressionism, and responded to him with encouragement, sympathy, and understanding. He was feeling more and more the need to have a firm grounding in the craft or science of his art before doing any further groping for a style to express his own vision.

Upon the recommendation of Fr. John O'Connor (who received David Jones into the Roman Catholic Church; who also received G. K. Chesterton and, earlier, furnished him with the model for Fr. Brown, the fictional detective; who translated Maritain's *Art and Scholasticism* and Claudel's *The Satin Slipper*), and with the permission of the headmaster of his art school, David Jones went to Ditchling Common, Sussex, to join a community of Catholic craftsmen. An apprenticeship to carpentry was abortive (although, as a man who turns all things to use, including failure and losses, he eventually had numerous indirect benefits from the experience, from his rendering of shipbuilding in *The Chester Play of the Deluge* to the almost Homeric catalogue of woods recited by Eb Bradshaw in *The Anathemata*[4]), but an apprenticeship to engraving had direct benefit, offering him his first medium of artistic and imaginative mastery (especially in *The Book of Jonah, The Chester Play of the Deluge, The Rime of the Ancient Mariner*) and gave him minimal supporting employment for a decade. Equally fruitful was the liturgical and theolog-

267

ical life of the community. Most fruitful of all was his friendship with Eric Gill, (an unintentional) founder of the community, a fine and solid craftsman, a convert to Catholicism, and a Christian anarchist (bearded, gowned Gill had thoughts on clothes, sexuality, family, community, and war which seem to anticipate ones popular now in the counterculture and the New Left; he once even had in mind doing that presently fashionable thing, getting a farm in upper New England).

Gill influenced the thought of David Jones a great deal but the younger man also had his own experiences, insights, and learning. He tested what Gill said—and accepted it, qualified it, refused it. They had an ongoing debate, especially about the nature of art. Theoretically, Gill wanted to reduce art to the craft of making. David Jones wanted to insist upon the dimension of the gratuitous. Gill wanted to reduce the gratuitous to the flourish of the artist as he concludes a piece made either to order or according to convention. David Jones wanted to insist that the gratuitous include preeminently the symbolization by which selves and societies orient and order their lives. No doubt they also debated the liturgy and war. Gill—with Fr. O'Connor—was an early advocate of Mass-in-the-round and helped to plan two edifices for worship built on that principle. David Jones, a longtime admirer of the baroque Mass, knew that change of any element in the service meant at least dislocation, if not downright debacle. Indeed, in the wake of Vatican II, with the Englishing of the Mass and those consequent dislodgings of other elements, David Jones has had to suffer deprivation of a most loved thing.

During World War I, Gill, a man with wife and children and engaged in carving the Stations of the Cross for skyscraping Westminster Cathedral, London, did not enter military service till on toward the end. His experience in the army was brief, interrupted by illness, limited to England, and otherwise superficial (biggest loss, his beard; biggest gain, training in truck driving). World War I changed the life of David Jones. It barely touched that of Gill.

As Gill explored farther and farther the social implications

268

of Catholicism and his interpretation of art as craft, and came more and more to denounce in talks and publications industrialism and capitalism which deprived human beings of the source of a good life, he saw war as closely intricated in the other two evils, and became a vigorous pacifist. As the rise of fascism and the lethargy of other nations during the '30's brought the world toward international conflict, he devoted more and more energies to advocacy of the pacifist position and the organization of a peace movement, even till the very dark eve and fire dawn of World War II. Its outbreak was cause of heartbreak for Gill, and discouragement to the brink of despair.

For Eric Gill, World War II was the conclusive evidence that the West was not Christian, and refused to be Christian; was not just, and refused to be just. It had had a choice and had preferred suicidal fratricide. For David Jones, World War II was the conclusive evidence that the West was in a final civilizational phase, and on the verge of ruinous collapse. Therefore it had a different range of meanings for him. Perhaps, in one aspect, the war was a bracing challenge for David Jones. A whole nation—and he with it—put on the disciplines without which there was no hope of defense of the islands, no hope of defeat of the enemy. As a man interested in questions of strategy, tactics, logistics, the war also had an aesthetic-intellectual interest. It was a matter of life-and-death; at the same time, it was fascinating.

Equally important to the contrast between responses to the war by Gill and by David Jones were the latter's convictions that man is always a soldier and that every civilization comes to an end. What account of history could omit or underemphasize either matter? Within history there is the Mass in which the transhistorical God who experienced intrahistorical existence in the Incarnation makes available the benefits of that history-redeeming event (Annunciation-to-Ascension), ever the same and ever anew for the faithful daily at a thousand altars. Everyone has to experience the destiny of his epoch, the condition of his times. There is no escaping the circumstances of the cultural phase in which one finds his life. They will determine the material and mental forms which compose his world. His survey of other worlds does not offer him a loophole or escape hatch. He must suffer the destiny of his age. The only "out" (and it is likewise an "in") is the Mass. God makes Himself present to persons in every period and within its condition. Or, put another way, the Church has a life that outlasts cultures, a continuity that carries from the old one to the new one. Although it too reflects the circumstances of its phase and finds expression through the same set of material and mental forms to which the rest of the culture is limited, what it expresses is permanent. Christians are not completely encapsulated in their cultural period. God gathers his people to Himself from out the ages. If man is always at war, and especially so at the end of a civilization, God has not abandoned him, straitened as he is. World War II did not surprise David Jones—it was what was to be expected. It did not enforce despair—every point in history is equidistant from Eternity.

Eric Gill wanted to make a cell of good living, in a germinal and growth-eager sense, against the tendency of the times: David Jones saw our epoch as one in which Christians would find themselves more and more worshippers in the catacombs. Gill was prophetic and announced both what should and what should not be done. David Jones was explanatory about why things had to be as they were. Gill invited his contemporaries to act—to prevent the war, to stop the spread of industrialism and capitalism, to counteract. David Jones felt the futility in every effort to counteract. Put up with it—and live in the Mass.

The contrast stands out in the first two of the final three paragraphs of his essay "Eric Gill as Sculptor," written soon after the death of Gill early in World War II.

Mr. Gill once said to me something of this sort, as far as I can remember: "What I achieved as a sculptor is of no consequence—I can be only a beginning—it will take generations, but if only the beginnings of a reasonable, decent, holy traditon of working might be effected—that is the thing." I quote this because I think it is of historical documentary importance. It expressed his hope—I think myself it was a forlorn hope, and I think he thought so too. Before there can be again a "sculpture" flowering, in the sense he meant, on the buildings that modern men inhabit, and determined in its form by the character of those buildings, which in turn must express the nature of the gods of the builders, many things must be accomplished, much must happen. Those happenings can only be of an apocalyptic nature, however long drawn out.

270

The astonishing thing is that within certain bounds, and in spite of all deficiencies, he achieved what he did achieve—the relative success is the surprise, not the obvious limitations.
(Epoch and Artist, p. 295)

Where Gill spoke of modest and uncertain beginnings, David Jones saw a horrendous and certain end.

Is there something apocalyptical about David Jones? He himself uses the word "apocalyptic" in this passage.

He once told me that he is more interested in beginnings and endings than in middles. Traditionally the subject of first and last things is eschatology, and apocalypse is one kind of doctrine of the last things. His focus and scope apparently include apocalypse. Is it central, marginal, or transmuted?

20. The poetry of David Jones sees the end of many things, not rubbish but lovely and precious things, ancient and fine and rare, made with care and kept with care, whose loss one suffers with regret and grief and a plumbing of the depth of their irretrievability. For him, each culture carries the doom of death inherent in organic being.

21. Eric Gill was a person with a prophetic manner, in that he urged persons to turn, emphasizing the desirability of their doing so by projecting the disastrous consequences of their pursuing their present course. That has not been the manner of David Jones, who has been enough of a Spenglerian to think that a society has, of necessity, to go through its phases toward decline and death. Members of the society are the victims of its coarsening process. Victims can counteract it, at most, by refusing to say *yes* to the disintegrative forces of its process, by inward loyalty to other, finer phases than their own (but outwardly they can only resign themselves to it; they cannot resist it effectively, for every action directed against the disintegrative force only contributes to it). Victims cannot extricate themselves from their phase, but they can, if they are Christians, participate in the transcendence of the phase and the foretaste of eternity through the Mass. Their phase is not the final word on their lives; eternity is. Eternity-anticipating eucharistic bread can be daily bread.

271

One suffers his phase yet can draw on resources beyond it for a triumph over it in spirit. David Jones says neither *turn* and alter all nor *stand* (even unto death) in the hope of vindication and fulfillment. He says resign outwardly and lay hold of whatever you can to keep and fulfill yourself inwardly.

22. We see that David Jones is much concerned with "endings" when we consider his modernist poems in prose and verse, *In Parenthesis* (1937), *The Anathemata* (1952) and the work-in-progress many parts of which appear in the David Jones special issue of *Agenda,* Spring–Summer 1967; two parts of which have had separate publication as small books, *The Fatigue,* 1965, and *The Tribune's Visitation,* 1967— so reads the title page, but it actually came out in 1969. Each of them focuses on an end-time: *In Parenthesis,* on the end of ancient warfare in World War I and its replacement by mass, mechanized, and total warfare, as a small unit of soldiers "register" that end; *The Anathemata,* on the (possible) end of the West, as a worshipper at Mass in Britain during World War II meditates the continuities dynamic in the West and registers the threat that they may snap, but not without the comfort of the permanent character of the Mass; the work-in-progress, both on the end of minority cultures as the Roman Empire swallows them and on the end of non-Christian antetypal anticipations and approximations of the Christian myth from Incarnation to Atonement as 'the thing itself' replaces its adumbration.

23. Although I wish to concentrate on the poems by David Jones which accumulate toward the completion of his loose-knit and polyphonic work-in-progress, first let us look briefly at *In Parenthesis.* Its setting is World War I, in which (capitalistic, industrialized, nationalistic, imperialistic) Europe attempted self-murder. War lost any human scale that it may have had in the past. The soldiers of the small unit which the poem follows move toward disablement or death. The poem shows that, even in the midst of impersonalism and dehumanization, soldiers can find pleasures of a domestic kind and of an aesthetic kind, companionship with fellow soldiers, and solidarity with fellow victims of the system of international warfare, including the enemy. In its framing devices, *In Parenthesis* makes clear that man has always been *homo furens* (David Jones quotes the Spenglerian definition—"Man is a weapon-using carnivore"—as accurate, in *Epoch and Artist*, p. 85), at least in Western Europe. Some critics have taken his theme of the combatant as a permanent manifestation of man to mean that *In Parenthesis* is a conservative poem, disclosing war-making, terrible as it is, as belonging inextricably to human nature. But such an interpretation ignores a double emphasis in Dai's Boast, the centerpiece of the poem, in which the speaker declares, by means of allusion to Arthurian motifs, that arrogant ambition condemns young men to death ("The Bear of the Island: he broke it in his huge pride, and/ overreach of his imperium./ The Island Dragon./ The Bull of Battle/ (this is the third woeful uncovering)") and that such terrible events, and worse, are released by a failure to ask why such things are happening ("You ought to ask: Why,/ what is this,/ what's the meaning of this./ Because you don't ask,/ although the spearshaft/ drips,/ there's neither steading—not a roof-tree").

David Jones includes two inevitabilities in the poem, a large one, the civilizational phase of Europe, and a small one, the Battle of the Somme. The lesser fatalism functions as the epitome of the greater. Pathos of an ironic ignorance underlines both. Over and over the poem discloses that persons involved, whatever their rank and whether from battlefront or headquarters or back home, do not know what they are doing or having others do. The general ignorance, so lethargic and lethal, is the reason that the question, so desperately called for in Dai's Boast, is the one hope of breaking the links in the inexorable chain of events. Probably only in this single passage in all his writing, the crucial one for *In Parenthesis*, does David Jones approach the prophetic mode, implying that what is does not have to be, implying that human freedom can actualize alternatives. The conservative, traditional elements only make clearer the cry for deliverance from periodic world war. (*The Anathemata* acknowledges that the end of the West, terrible to contemplate, is possible. The West is deeper into its disintegration. But the whole poem is so permeated by the epoch-outlasting and history-transcending Mass that it comes to be a profound consolation not only for superficial losses but also for tragic devastation.)

As the intuition of *The Anathemata* is not identical with that of *In Parenthesis,* so the intuition of the work-in-progress is not identical with that of *The Anathemata.*

The center of the work-in-progress as a whole is the crucifixion of Jesus. It anchors the poems in time and place, round about Jerusalem and round about 30 A.D. That center, in the conviction of David Jones, is the axis or hinge of history. All things turn on it. Without it there is no ultimate meaning to things. It makes all the difference, in both individual and communal existence, for if it be love that permeates being in all its permutations, then what would otherwise be pathos or tragedy can be fulfillment and triumph.

Yet the discerning of love at work in the crucifixion of Jesus is neither self-evident to sensation nor the necessary implication of the data of that execution for logic. Faith knows it, but faith is closer to dream and imagination and liturgy and art, inasmuch as it is a symbol-oriented and symbol-engaging activity.

Though the crucifixion is at the center of the work-in-progress, it is the literal subject of only one poem, "The Fatigue." In the others it is the secret center, present only by allusion and analogy (such as references to the death of gods) and by context. In "The Fatigue" that dying receives explicit meditation, in a representation more nearly ikonic and liturgical than photographic and naturalistic; but even in "The Fatigue" the irony of not knowing what they are doing, of accidental relation to the crucial event of history, on the part of the soldiers who carry out the killing as an extra duty, and on the part of the bureaucratic operation which determines which soldiers get stuck with the dirty work, receives as much attention, and more, than the crucifixion itself: as though the whole poem were a triptych and the narrow atonement-celebrating central panel flanked by two wider ironic ones.

In "The Hunt" the passion and dying of the crucifixion receive allegorical representation as a heroic action. Jesus in dying was more victor than victim. He knew what he was doing. He laid down his life in pursuit of a purpose, initiating the process that included his dying, a labor in which he travailed to accomplish no small thing (to employ litotes), the redirection of human destiny in both its historical and eternal dimensions. David Jones lauds that *agon* in "The Hunt," under the figure of Arthur chasing the boar, as recounted in the medieval Welsh prose tale "Culhwch and Olwen" from *The Mabinogion.* Such a combination of biblical and Celtic elements no doubt sounds arbitrary until one remembers that many scholars think that the historical Arthur (or at least the legendary one), no king but a leader of the defense of Britain against invading Saxons at the collapse of sub-Roman Britain, gathered to his perhaps historical story Celtic mythological narratives. Then if one remembers that the Arthur of larger proportions than history carried out a raid on the sea-protected otherworld, and that the Church came to present the triumphant action of Jesus on the cross under the mythological narrative of the harrowing of hell, and finally if one remembers that David Jones will always incorporate things Celtic and Welsh (and indeed, in the work-in-progress, develops the minority culture of the Celtic tribal community as the dramatic contrast to the Roman Empire), then one acknowledges that although there is something astonishingly farfetched, there is also something appropriate in linking otherworld-raiding Arthur and hell-harrowing Jesus.

In "The Wall" the passion and dying of the crucifixion are present only indirectly:[5]

> ... All should turn out to see how those appointed to die take the Roman medicine. They crane their civvy necks half out their civvy suits to bait the maimed king in his tinctured vesture, the dying *tegernos* of the wasted *landa* well webbed in our marbled parlour, bitched and bewildered and far from his dappled patria far side the misted Fretum
>
> You can think a thing or two on *that* parade ...
>
> now all can face the dying god the dying Gaul without regret.

But you and me, comrade, the Darlings of Ares, who've helped
a lot of Gauls and gods to die, we shall continue to march and
to bear in our bodies the marks of the Marcher—by whatever
name they call him . . .

The poem concerns the relation of the center to the circumference, both politically and epistemologically. It is as though "The Wall" were variations on a theme from *The Iliad:* "Tell me now you muses who have your homes on Olympus, for you are divine and you are at hand and know all things—but we hear but a dull rumor and know nothing." Rome is at the center of empire. Those there are in the know. Jerusalem is on the edge of empire. Those there don't know what they are doing. Yet empire depends upon their doing it, upon their guarding the circumference. Virtue inheres in the performance of military duty in an expanding empire, or so used to think the speaker of the poem—a Roman soldier, as is also frequently the case in other parts of the work-in-progress—but now dull rumor drones that brave obedience is no longer the central virtue (but only a peripheral border-watching one). Gold-getting and thing-having now constitute the central virtue. The social core of empire already has the softness that will surrender itself to hard attackers and raiders. It does not know what it is doing. Virtue does inhere in the ignorant ones on the wall who obey orders, for they maximize and actualize possibilities within their limits.

There is a yet greater irony in "The Wall." Although the soldiers on the wall in Jerusalem stand at the circumference of the old order to which they belong, far from Rome, they also stand at the center of the new order which is inaugurated by the passion and dying of Jesus. Centrality withdraws itself from an old locality and reestablishes itself in a new. Rome will become secondary; Constantinople will take its place in matters of empire and Jerusalem in matters of ultimate concern. Later, Rome will regain centrality, but a centrality satellite to the centrality of Jerusalem, and only when it has given up its imperial claims and its opposition to the death of Jesus as the crucial event of history and has become a servant to that event. "The Wall" reverberates with historical irony.

276

There is only a hint of endings in "The Wall." Although there is no explicit consideration of the end of Rome, there is, in the second passage quoted above, explicit reference to the end of minority cultures, both their mythologies and their human members, as empire engulfs them. To exist in such minority cultures is to experience an end that is the opposite of apocalypse, to experience the worsening not of the institutions which control and inform existence but the worsening of external pressures on those institutions, to experience the end not of evils but of goods, to experience not hope but despair. What replaces the minority cultures is Roman civilization with its uniformities, impersonalism, and exploitation. In apocalypse, perfection follows on catastrophe. In the recitation of the end of minority cultures (his examples are usually Celtic), David Jones indicates that regulated, systematic catastrophe follows spontaneous, cataclysmic catastrophe when empire defeats one, first, and then, even more terrible, includes one. Assimilation into its gross being is the final degradation.

We have now reached the heart of the work-in-progress, a triad of poems, "The Dream of Private Clitus" and "The Tutelar of the Place" and "The Tribune's Visitation."

Two of these, "The Dream of Private Clitus" and "The Tribune's Visitation," like "The Fatigue" and "The Wall," contain, or are, the talk of soldiers, in colloquy, soliloquy, and interior monologue, in Jerusalem at the dying of Jesus. The other of them, "The Tutelar of the Place," is also to be thought of as a speech or an interior monologue by one of the soldiers.

"The Dream of Private Clitus" has three preoccupations: the relation of center to circumference (again); the beneficent earth-goddess as the Roman center; dream as a model for extra-factual or symbolic modes of knowing. In the first of these preoccupations, the speaker of the poem asserts the opposite truth to the truth of the soldier on the wall in the poem of that name. The soldier on the wall says that he has almost no communion or even communication with the center. He continues to receive orders from it but he no longer receives symbols of common purpose. His orders seem out of touch with his situation and at odds with the central intentions of empire. The soldier of the dream (a dream which he had twenty years before, beyond the walls in retreat after the battle of Teuteburger Wald, Prussia) outlandishly reports communion with the center from even beyond the circumference, communion with Tellus Mater, the earth mother, at that center, by a dream of her. The goddess makes gestic promise of gathering him to her lap. In the midst of war, he participates in her peace. Here is a wide-reaching and deep-tucking patriotism (or "matriotism"), not to be confused with propaganda and public relations, as at least one passage makes clear.

> And homing eagles winged above those windy arches and this,
> some of them reckoned, an auspicious sign and Lugo said: See,
> the Roman bird. But I said: Lugo, don't talk wet. Don't talk
> like a civvy who's arranged another war.

And not to be confused with gold-getting and thing-having as a motive of empire.

In the second of these preoccupations, the speaker of the poem, the soldier of the dream, asserts the same truth as the speaker of "The Tutelar of the Place," even though each of them says it with an awareness of the other as the enemy. We will attempt to formulate their common truth when we come to the other poem.

In the third of these preoccupations, the speaker of the poem asserts the validity of knowing by extra-factual symbols and therefore the validity of liturgy, myth, and poetry (as representative of all the arts) against the denial of memory, piety, and poetry by the speaker of "The Tribune's Visitation," and in so doing describes many characteristics, under the image of dream, of the modernist poem, with its dream-like discontinuities and metamorphoses. The poem presents two items, one toward the beginning, the other toward the end, that indicate the power and the impotence of the imagination. Its strength in projecting what-will-come occurs when the soldier of the dream looks up into the far-reaching branches of the trees from the floor of the woods and sees gothic arches and imagines them as an architectural form optional to the only ones that he knows, Roman arches. Its weakness in projecting what-will-come occurs when the speaker of the poem consciously sets himself the task of picturing a post-Roman world but cannot accomplish it. The imagination is not an instrument of technological reason; it cannot be manipulated by consciousness. Yet recalling meditatively and playfully the northern forests, Clitus foresees gothic arches which will become key signatures of the post-Roman world.

Empire is governmental anticipation of industrial technology in that it aims at the uniformity which produces interchangeability. Pierre Teilhard de Chardin says that union differentiates (think of a marriage). Uniformity, however, renders all alike. Empire opposes individuation and difference. That is why incorporation in it is the final degradation. It transubstantiates us to a lowest common denominator. It revamps us from core to surface and leaves us puppets or zombies. Whatever we are, we are not ourselves, for those uniquenesses that distinguish us have been removed.

"The Tutelar of the Place" has a single overwhelming preoccupation. How can we preserve the differences which make us what we are in the face of a civilization that demands uniformity? If the totalitarian government of that civilization is not altogether efficient, we can live in gaps left by its mistakes and its insensitivities to certain ranges of reality. We can, perhaps, conform outwardly but retreat into inwardness and dreaming. If we cannot, it is better to die than stagger and grunt as in the parodying of life by a monster of Frankenstein.

A member of the Roman Empire, off base, facing outward, and in retreat, cannot imagine the end of his society in "The Dream of Private Clitus," but a member of a Celtic tribe, at home yet already being incorporated in swallowing and assimilating empire, has to imagine the end of his society.

Here we move very close to what would popularly be called apocalyptic in the poetry of David Jones. Empire, as heavy imposition and estranging, oppressive exploitation, that takes all energy but returns only mundane rewards (and they minor), that does not let a person be himself or call his soul his own, ingests a tribal society. Its members desire relief, escape, snatches of respite—or death, for it is a parody of both life and death to contribute being to, and draw being from, that devouring, insatiable, and inhuman organism. There is no integrity of personal or communal being within it. Yet there is no mythological-theological hope that death is entrance into freedom and justice and peace or that standing and staying pure even at the most devastating moment establishes the guarantee of vindication both for individual existence and for the universe itself. And there is no call to revolutionary action. Tribal societies have no military defense against empire and its war-making machines. David Jones registers the negatives of empire in their full specific gravity. He shares the revulsion from "what is" (in a final civilizational phase) with apocalyptic and revolutionary communities. But he does not share their different hopes. He practices resignation, a heroic, if debilitating, stance.

Divinity transcends space-time. Categories of place and period would seem inappropriate for deities—and in all likelihood are when the transcendent Triune God or Whoever or Whatever communes Self with Self. But for human beings locked in them there is no knowing anything except through space-time categories, including what does not fit those categories. Yet, so "The Tutelar of the Place" affirms from the perspective of Celtic tribal culture (and so "The Dream of Private Clitus" echoes, from the viewpoint of Roman imperial civilization), divinity does not disdain to commune with those who use what-they-have to draw on resources of power and purpose beyond-what-they-have (does not disdain and may even take the initiative in introducing itself by means of confusion of categories: Revelation; Incarnation).

What differentiates us is the core of our being, and it is from, and with, that individuating core that we commune with divinity. To lose our special characteristics, the result of evolutionary, historical, and individual development, is to lose both self and the language of knowing and loving divinity. To be a member of a culture assimilated into the functioning of an empire is to lose relation with the only deities that one knows and loves.

What dominant societies do to minority cultures is devastating.

What dominant societies do to themselves, to judge by the final poem in the work-in-progress, "The Tribune's Visitation," is even more devastating. Such societies usually have had early beginnings as tribal cultures and been nourished by locality and the stories of that place. But eventually they outgrow their origins. "The Tribune's Visitation" imagines what happens when expansion performs deracination. They repudiate the past and the means of knowing it, memory and poetry and song, assuming that nostalgia incapacitates persons from carrying out the tasks of empire. Experience of pluralism no doubt makes one skeptical: if there are so many places, each with its set of stories of gods and heroes, it is unlikely that any of them is true, including ours, even though we are successful in conquest. Psychoanalysis suggests that fixation on early experiences is the source of neurosis. Forget the past. Have done with it and other illusions, other resortings to extra-factual symbols. Face the present. Face the future. They may look empty and bleak. But they are all we have except for our mission to enforce the uniformity of empire everywhere. So speaks the tribune, in a fierce welding of grimness and exaltation, in an effort to confront the human and cosmic situation with differences eradicated.

If in "The Tutelar of the Place" David Jones imagines things getting worse and worse for "primitive" man and his annihilation by dominant societies, in "The Tribune's Visitation" he imagines the birth of superman, a human being putting under and behind him his imagination-and-symbol-nourished humanity and pushing out into a reality limited to factual knowledge and technocratic management. In "The Tutelar of the Place" dream is alternative to death; in "The Tribune's Visitation" life is identical to death. David Jones can imagine horrible endings, but in the work-in-progress, at least to date, he has not created an image of the overcoming or replacement of the worst by the best. His poetry is only half-apocalyptic, having the first half but lacking the second, the image of fulfillment and perfection looming and leaning us-wards out of the threatening, otherwise undifferentiated future.

24. If the poems of David Jones, in spite of their focusing on endings, are not revolutionary, they are also neither prophetic nor apocalyptic, but are, within the horizon of history, fatalistic about civilizational worsening, and are, beyond that mundane horizon, affirmations of human fulfillment. If history is loss, eternity makes the loss good. That faith comforts and consoles bereavement at loss. Human doing and making, supremely so in the Mass (and David Jones is sensitive to these in great detail), hint the eternal ingathering and transfiguration of human action and suffering. That meaning enriches and energizes the enduring of the negativities which make existence agonistic in the midst of ordinary doing and making, yet it does not charge existence to challenge or change the basic situation.

25. It is our hope in the gathering of these fragments that knowledge of prophecy and apocalypse illuminates the poetry of David Jones in such a way that configurations of meaning, present but previously unnoticed, or, if noticed, undeciphered, now come clear. Perhaps if that knowledge sheds light in one place, it will shed it in another.

Notes

1. My aim is modest. I am not a contributor to biblical scholarship or summarizing expert in the subject. My knowledge of the field is secondary and fragmentary. But perhaps even a partial and inexpert report will lead others to investigate the field on their own and invite the specialist to speak with all his know-how and know-what from one humanistic discipline to another.

2. Martin Buber, "Prophecy, Apocalypse, and the Historical Hour," *On the Bible: Eighteen Studies,* ed. Nahum N. Glatzer, p. 174.

3. A poem, by the way, that Dr. Cross of Harvard suggests in "New Directions in the Study of Apocalyptic" (*Journal for Theology and the Church,* VI, 157–165) stands at the collapse of prophecy with its confidence that history is the two-edged sword of divine justice and the coming into being of apocalypse with its appeal to psychic depths and cosmic heights and whatever other symbols of transhistorical being it can muster to face the nonsense, to speak mildly, of history, or the insanity or madness, to speak wildly, of it, or the nightmare, to speak with the craftiness of a Joycean mask, of it, and to hope for the overturning of its dehumanizing process.

4. See "Redriff," *TriQuarterly* 21, pp. 9–12.

5. See *TriQuarterly* 21, pp. 1–5.

Milton's sonnet "On the late massacre in Piemont": a note on the vulnerability of persons in a revolutionary situation

ALLEN GROSSMAN

Si non vales, non valeo.

1

Milton's most famous sonnet, when seen in its historical situation, compels us to discuss the nature of poetry in relation to history, and particularly those moments in history when important social changes are taking place. The trial and judicial killing of a king in 1649 was a unique event in the political life of Europe, and created unique legal problems such as the question of the competence of the court to try the person upon whom its authority was based. The hierarchical civility in which the social value of persons was previously identified had been destroyed at its root in response, as it were, to the Baptist's revolutionary slogan, in *Matthew* 3:10, "And now also the ax is laid to the root of the trees." The killing of the king and the establishment of the Commonwealth was, like revolutionary acts in general, an initia-

---

Useful material about this sonnet can be found in E.A.J. Honigmann, *Milton's Sonnets* (New York: St. Martin's Press, 1966). I am indebted to Professor Honigmann.

tive in the interest of new and more desirable relationships among men. What I shall point to in Milton's sonnet is the clear sense that the effort to establish the new dispensation, the *novus ordo,* entailed a corresponding devaluation of personal identity such as to suggest that the means of revolution and its ends are in conflict one with the other.

Further, I wish to propose that most of Milton's poetry is, like this particular poem, an effort to restore meaning to experience which his very deep, indeed inveterate imagination of revolution, as reflected for instance in the early "On the Morning of Christ's Nativity," tended to place outside previous categories of meaning; but for which his imagination of revolution or for that matter reformation provided in the end no sufficient categories of intelligibility. Marvell's image of the author of *Paradise Lost* destroying the world to avenge his sight seems to me a substantially true statement about Milton's motive as a poet. Milton's sense of history (and consequently of moral *experience*) is always in advance of his sense of the intelligibility of that experience, and his poetry is an attempt to restore the sightedness which the ability to understand experience confers. Milton's poetry is part of the unfinished history of the secularization process which by destroying old servitudes created new freedom, without, it seems, at the same time creating viable conditions for the practice of that freedom.

If politics has as its goal the reduction of violence, and religion the conservation of value, then the Waldensian massacre was a case of politics and religion at the breaking point. Milton's poem comes at the end of a long series of political addresses written by Milton on behalf of Cromwell's government, aimed at redress for, or at least influence over, an ongoing atrocity committed in enforcement of a territorial settlement by Carlo Emmanuele II, Duke of Savoy and Prince of Piedmont, against the Vaudois (or Valdenses, an ancient Protestant sect excommunicated by the Church in 1215), some of whom lived in certain valleys of the Pellice and Agrogna rivers, tributaries of the Po. On April 24, 1655, a plan to root out these heretics completely was put in action by the Marquis of Pianezza, commanding a force of Piedmontese,

French and Irish. That this attempt at genocide was a matter of religious concern as well as political—if the two are separable in this period—was apparent from the shocked response of the Protestant English nation as news reports of which Milton's poem makes use made their way back out of the desolate valleys of the Italian Alps.

First of all, God's providence with respect to his elect (his "seed") was called in question; secondly, God's ability to avenge visibly assaults on those under his care was being tested before the audience of a nation whose leader got his early education from Dr. Beard, author of *The Theater of God's Judgement Displayed;* thirdly, the ability of the Lord Protector of the international Protestant community to protect was called in question. The purpose of the revolution was to establish a new premise of relationship within the Protestant community (as in the biblical phrase "we are all members of one another"); correlatively, each member of the extended body of the Protestant community became in a new way vulnerable and in a new way obligated by reason of his participation in the new autonomy of the communal person. Genocidal atrocity turns sectarian religious identity into a fatal stigma unless some redeeming meaning can be attached to the lethal consequences of belonging to the persecuted party. The purpose of Milton's poem seems to be to summon meaning from God as the origin of meaning to redress an imbalance between experience on the one hand and value on the other.

The text of *On the late Massacre in Piemont* follows:

> Avenge O Lord thy slaughter'd Saints, whose bones
> Lie scatter'd on the Alpine mountains cold,
> Ev'n them who kept thy truth so pure of old
> When all our Fathers worship't Stocks and Stones,
> Forget not: in thy book record their groanes
> Who were thy Sheep and in their antient Fold
> Slayn by the bloody *Piemontese* that roll'd
> Mother with Infant down the Rocks. Their moans
> The Vales redoubl'd to the Hills, and they
> To Heav'n. Their martyr'd blood and ashes sow
> O're all th'*Italian* fields where still doth sway
> The triple Tyrant: that from these may grow
> A hunderd-fold, who having learnt thy way
> Early may fly the *Babylonian* wo.

God is summoned (a gesture which if it is not redundant must be evidence of its own futility) to transform meaningless death (slaughter) into meaningful death (martyrdom). The pastoral landscape appropriate to the world of sheep and shepherds has been transformed (and this emphasis is already contained in contemporary accounts prior to Milton's poem) into that desolate unfulfilling realm, that world from which meaning has been withdrawn, with which we are familiar from Sidney's double sestina in the *Arcadia* or Blake's mythology of the fallen Tharmas. That the violence which the Waldensians suffered was genocidal in character is emphasized by the stress, also derived from contemporary accounts, on the destruction of women and children. The racial immortality of this community is threatened; and this community is the acknowledged parent of the Protestant community in Europe. Morland in his *History of the Evangelical Churches of the Valleys of the Piemont* reports that Cromwell was "often heard to say that it lay as near or rather nearer his heart than if it had concerned his nearest and dearest Relations in the World." Echo in English pastoralism is the sign of a fulfilling universe, but in this poem about ultimate scarcity the succoring vales are filled with cries which they amplify toward heaven or God upon whom in direct, unmediated relationship the Independent Protestant must depend. The poetic speaker commands that God turn slaughter into martyrdom by "sowing" (that is, turning into instruction, for "the seed is the word of God," *Luke* 8:11) the "blood and ashes" of the Waldensians who, not in their own persons but in this indirect manner, will create consciousness of oppression in Catholic Italians.

The divine rememberer is commanded to conserve, in the face of the inability of the human community to identify the slain and to compensate their incomparable pain, the memory of his primitive servants. The asymmetry between conspicuous merit and atrocious destiny, between value and experience, has been further exacerbated by the assault upon the generative persons in the community, mother and infant, so that collective immortality, the life of the community, is threatened; this as a consequence of the religious self-identification of its individuals. By turning passive suffering into intelligible sacrifice the Lord will promulgate sufficient knowledge so that captives of tyrannical religion in still unconverted Italy (which Cromwell had vowed to liberate) may become conscious of their subjection and turn away in a revolutionary gesture from the destruction which the inevitable historical process directed by God has in store for that nation. In the transformation of pain into consciousness the individuality of the martyrs is lost but their consequence, "redoubled" like their groans, has become a hundredfold. Violence has been turned into consciousness of oppression, which in turn rescues a part of the human community from the counter-violence of God, masked in the typological shadow of the "*Babylonian* wo." The grammatical hiatus, the withheld substantive ("hunderd-fold, who") in the last line but one, calls attention to the sacrifice of individuality which creates an unconcealed pathos in the conclusion of the poem, not unrelated to the peculiar posture of the speaker who in the face of the unredeemed event commands God to act, as he has not yet done, in a way consistent with the rationality of his nature. The bond between the speaker of the poem and the Waldenses is that of spiritual filiation. The speaker derives assurance of his religious identity from the ancient faith of the Waldensian saints, as from a spiritual by contrast to a natural family ("*our* Fathers"), whose slaughter consequently threatens the roots of his spiritual being. *They* have borne the cost of *his* identity, and their vulnerability portends the extinction of his party "root and branch."

We may imagine (with Masson) the circulation of Milton's sonnet in Cromwell's government at the time when all but the last of an extensive series of diplomatic remonstrances over the Piedmont massacre had been composed and dispatched. Milton had written on Cromwell's behalf to the Duke of Savoy, to the heads of state of Transylvania, Sweden, the United Provinces, the Swiss cantons, Denmark, to the Cardinal Mazarin, and others in part to assert the hegemony of Cromwell as the Protestant power in Europe, in part because not to do so would be a breach of communal solidarity with the Protestant kinship. But the Piedmont massacre shared the singular character of all atrocity; it was an occasion demanding redress in excess of anybody's (even a Lord Protector's) ability to effect redress. The details of the Piedmont event were unusually arresting to the England of the day. The newsletters (*The Perfect Diurnal, The Weekly Post, The Faithful Scout, Mercurius Politicus*) recounted week after week the ingenuities of torment (impalement, evisceration, cannibalism) inflicted on the Waldenses who were the most deserving because the most ancient of God's Protestants.

As in the case of some modern atrocities, the event seemed perverse evidence of human creativity, not only in the extraordinary ingenuity (a kind of inspiration) with which millennial strategies of barbarism were explored and executed (and later illustrated, like important experiments in science, by Morland in his *History*) but also in the sentiment which pervades the event of enormous, almost superhuman labor accomplished. The discrediting of the immortality of the other is a great labor which from the time of the early martyrs of the Roman amphitheaters possessed that quasi-theatrical character conserved in a title such as *The Theater of God's Judgement*. This aspect of atrocious event (its discontinuity with ordinary experience, its traditionality, and its quasi-aesthetic character) renders all the more difficult the discrimination of the personhood of the victim, and all the more exigent the restoration of one's own mastery over the fascination of the spectacle by the devising of a response. The problem is additionally complicated by two considerations at least: in the first place no civil society can deliberately respond to an atrocity in kind, and in the second place (as the Christian knows better perhaps than any other religionist) no man's pain is equivalent to anyone else's, in which case response in kind is merely random reprisal. The Christian God was himself a victim of an atrocious death (we are reminded of Herbert's Christ of "The Sacrifice": "Never was grief like mine") which because, despite the irreducible singularity of all pain, a perpetual claim upon every man's capacity for feeling, an obligation to imitate the Passion, by its nature inimitable.

288

The Piedmont massacre was an occasion not merely for the practice of the science of the justice of God, but also for the justification of man's will to be real over against the fact of the isolation of the psychic locus of pain, and therefore the person in pain, from all access of participation. Pain (or its unverifiable and undeniable evidences in others) disintegrates community by centering personhood upon its psychic incommunicability. In addition, the vulnerability of one part of a community is equivalent to the vulnerability of the whole ("We are all members of one another"). The Piedmont atrocity involved the tampering with the genetic continuity of the people as is clearly indicated from the emphasis in contemporary accounts on the rape and evisceration of women and the cannibalism of children. Since the Low Church depends centrally on the holiness of individual interiority and the redemptive character of sectarian distinctness, pain may be seen as a socially disintegrative parody of inner light, and genocide as the annihilation rather than the creation of the self in communal identification. Under these circumstances participation in a community with characterizing marks results not in the immortality which communities confer upon the individual but, by a radical irony, in that oblivion from which the community was designed to rescue the singular person. These considerations are some part of the situation which lies inferentially in the background of Milton's sonnet.

Eschatology (reliance on final, post-historical remedies) is the contrary of politics, and indeed Milton's poem exhibits no allusion to that reliance on the eschatological justification of the individual (the perfecting in the flames) which characterizes primitive Christian attitudes towards martyrdom. By contrast to other sonnets of Milton which are meditations on the meaning of names in a fame culture there is also a total absence of singular identity in the report of the Waldensian event. Milton's poem exhibits these persons as they were known to their executioners, as anonymous members (unidentifiable amputated limbs, as it were) of a fatally identified community. Martyrdom is traditionally an adjunct of the epistemologies of faith. Only the will to die is sufficient to assure a community of the non-duplicitous character of man's

289

hopefulness. As Professor Boime reminds us, men must, traditionally, die in order to be trusted. But victimage and martyrdom are not identical and Milton wishes to deal with victimage in terms of martyrdom, a chancy and in itself potentially duplicitous gesture toward meaning.

Above all, Milton's poem-opening (the strong conjunction of the imperative and vocative, "Avenge O Lord") is a command to God that he behave in a manner consistent with his predicates, that he give meaning to an event which threatened the whole of life with meaninglessness. The prayer gesture commands the continuity of moral reality by a volition of the human will as exhibited in language. The God addressed is the God of history, vengeance being the abhorrent but rational evidence of a compensating intelligence in history.

And when he had opened the fifth seal, I saw under the altar the souls of them that were slain for the word of God, and for the testimony which they held: And they cried with a loud voice saying, How long, O Lord, holy and true, dost thou not judge and avenge our blood on them that dwell on earth. (*Rev.* vi: 9–10).

The speaker in Milton's poem declares that vengeance (the application of meaning to experience, central meaning to central experience) has not occurred. An abyss has opened up between fact and value which threatens to discredit retrospectively the revolutionary initiative. Milton's speaker, driven to the boundaries of the autonomy of the will, both moral and political, demands that the book of history be opened at the fifth seal, that victimage become martyrdom and that martyrdom exhibit its epistemological, its inherently gnostic essence.

The poem, like the journalistic accounts on which much of its language is based, contains iconic representation of dehumanized speech, "their moans," the hidden soul of harmony untuned. The incorporation of prayer in poetry, which is the effect of Milton's sonnet, repeats the motive of the will toward the reconstitution of the threatened continuities of vital relationship, speech being the culture of human intercourse with God. The sealing of man from God by the dehumanization of speech or the destruction of its agent, the poet, was already a subject of Milton's imagination in "Lycidas" and is the awesome eventuality aversion to which compels the *Areopagitica*. We may recall that a characterizing mark of Milton's shorter poems is the pastoral *topos* of the resonant, compensated responsiveness of mind and world, the *echo*. Plenitude of sanctioned experience is affirmed when as in Spenser, "The woods shall to me answer and my echo ring." In the poem before us human utterance is not confirmed but rather distorted, amplified, and expelled by the landscape. As in Sidney's double sestina, the subject of which is the disappearance of the central symbol (origin of meaning) from experience, the Italian vales have become barren mountains and are filled with cries instead of music. This more than infernal landscape of existential degradation is the true Miltonic Hell. The "vale" is the generative fold in which English poetry displays man's life as justified under the figure of audible speech and within the ordered set of stations discriminated by the diurnal cycle from the hour before dawn to the hour after sunset. In the world of this poem the ample vale has been transformed into a strait place, a place of anguish; tortured outcries (the true voice of feeling) are redoubled without becoming intelligible, forced up out of the human universe by the impossibility of social response, toward God whose equally unresponsive hiddenness is the occasion of the poem. Milton's sonnet incorporates a prayer-form which itself incorporates the wordless outcry of total violation. Prayer supervenes when the secular will has reached the boundary of its autonomy. Poem incorporates prayer when religion also reaches the limits of its singular authenticity. At the bottom of this poem is a wordless cry (voice separated from meaning) upon the interpretation of which, through God to the human community, the speaker in the poem must by the logic of his situation stake his authority both as a poet and as a religious man.

There is in Milton a constant competition between the immortality which the poet facilitates by means of his privileged access to the collective continuity of the human community across time, and the alternative immortality ("eternity") of which God is agent as the perfect rememberer. Milton's central subject in

"Lycidas," for example, is the supersession of an art-mediated fame culture by a God-mediated culture of redemption, and such in effect is the subject also of the early "Ode on the Morning of Christ's Nativity." The Piedmont sonnet represents the point of crisis of the successor culture in the interest of which the feudal hierarchies of king and episcopacy were overthrown. The Waldensian massacre is the test as to whether the revolution effected an instauration of the value of existence or an irreparable devaluation leading to hopeless vulnerability in the extended body of the Protestant community. Milton is the poet of a crisis in the intelligibility of experience, which experience in the form of history (*The Theater of God's Judgement*) must resolve, if resolution there is to be. Milton's major poems are placed at flawed moments in the nexus of value and experience (of which the creation itself is always potentially one, as indeed it has become in *Paradise Lost*) when consciousness is ready for new explanations. In the absence of divine manifestation the moral person is thrown back on his secular resources for the sustaining of value, and speaks as a poet—the agent of memory in history—to the God who is the agent of memory beyond history. This poem-in-little and *Paradise Lost* in its vastness are evidence of the exhaustion of the human will in the labor of value, the poet come to the end of his authority.

The elegiac *topos, ubi sunt?* ("Where were ye, nymphs, when the remorseless deep?") corresponds to the situation of the speaker in our sonnet. The pains of the laboring mother in the "Nativity Ode" (the predecessor of the mother of Orpheus in "Lycidas" and the mother slaughtered with her children in sonnet 18) are rendered meaningful by the birth, from the marriage of divinity and history, of the miraculous child. "Lycidas" deals in terms of individual life with the same moment which, as a crisis of collective life, is the subject of the "Ode." In the "Ode" the pains of the suffering mother are expressed as the shrieks of the dying gods of the older dispensation. In this way an intact hypothesis about the meaning of history makes possible the principal business of religion, the transforming of pain into value or, more specifically in the case of the "Ode," an absolute disseveration of the dying part from the substantial *ego*. In the Piedmont sonnet this has become impossible. In "Lycidas" the intervention of redemptive transformation ("Weep no more, woeful shepherd, weep no more. . . .") against all hope and without explanation solved the problem of the loss of intelligibility through the transformation of its agent. But in the poem before us the Providential Solution has itself become a "false surmise." "Vengeance" in this poem could not be a form of counter-knowledge to empirical knowledge about history, since the Revolution, like all revolutions, has given itself as a hostage to history. Sonnet 18, like most religious poems in this period, is an appeal from a fame culture which has failed toward a transcendental rememberer (God as the successor form of Mnemosyne) who, however, does not, as in "Lycidas", remember, is absent as the hand which wipes the tears forever from their eyes. The gnostic component of martyrdom has been lost or is un-manifest, and the body of the new community of the revolution cannot amputate the being in pain, for that being is itself.

Milton as a theocratic revolutionary was the apologist of an anti-episcopal church in which individual identity was to be sustained by a direct relationship to God, and in which the sect or community of men was totally present in all of its parts as in a brotherhood. Feudal ecclesiastical hierarchies substantiate identity and mediate authority from above so that the community has a symbolic identity that transcends and at critical moments supersedes its parts. The revolutionary (the regicide) has the task of authenticating identity from below in the mysterious and yet to be defined totality of the new fraternity. Indeed, the revolutionary looks into the abyss between realms of value where value has lost one set of symbols and has not yet acquired another. Further, the fragility of the new regime of value once established may be shattered at any moment, for it is the hostage of its all too falsifiable hypotheses, as Cromwell with his obsession with the simplicities of military success knew very well. Beyond the military trial of God's preference lies the much more risky and unexplored enterprise of building Jerusalem. The Piedmont massacre was an occasion when the abyss was once again opened. A fast day was decreed by the same government which had sanctioned the atrocities of Wexford and Drogheda (which Tory historians such as Maurice Ashley still justify), a subscription for the Waldensians was taken in the whole of England, diplomatic letters were dispatched, documents gathered, a history written, and this sonnet which summons the Author of being to avenge, remember, and make efficacious as meaningful event the pain of the victims.

Milton's imagination of revolution as the supersession of one ground of value by another preceded (as the "Ode" and "Lycidas" make apparent) the historical revolution in which he took part. Milton was throughout his career the apologist of the vast shifts in meaning which are the condition of the coming to pass of new value and which at the same time imperil all value: the Fall of Man, the birth of Christ, the Cromwellian revolution are central and cognate instances with the difference that the last-named gave truth as a hostage to history as an inescapable present. Defense, apology, justification are Milton's characteristic gestures. "Lycidas," for example, works in the personalistic elegiac *topoi* with the fundamental predicament of the death of meaning, of which the metaphor is the morally inexplicable bodily disappearance of the archetypal singer-priest whose culture is discredited by its proved inability to conserve its central practitioner. Milton is always the apologist, never the philosopher. Freedom depends on the moral autonomy of the reasoning individual, but reason in Milton is bound up in the intensely personal gesture of the gigantic rhetorician who, by mingling his will with his discourse, summons a meaningful state of affairs rather than defines its conditions. Milton's prose functions as a preemption of reality rather than a description of it, and in this reflects the limits also of the kind of poetry which he practices. His thematic gigantism in poetry and hypotactic comprehensiveness in prose suggest that for Milton psychic totalism is manipulated as an argument against cosmic nihilism. Milton's early life and education were in effect a gathering of authority toward the crisis which the proem of *Paradise Lost* seeks to master. The limits of his poetic style which Eliot saw very clearly and the limits of his rational apologetic are seen in the effort, which Marvell intuited in him, to exchange

294

mind (as language) for world, rather than submit to the evidences of final complexity in historical experience.

2

Milton's sonnet, which is our subject, is an occasional poem, the occasion being the absence of any compensating event by which the Waldensian atrocity could be rendered consistent with a Providential view of history. Either history is evidence of the congruence of God's rationality and man's or it is not. If it is not, then there is nothing more to be said, since tragedy is not a possible alternative interpretation of history within the Miltonic frame, for it does not conserve the central value of the marriage of mind and world. There can be only one aesthetic (comedy) in *The Theater of God's Judgement*. Overshadowed by a possible cognitive dysfunction between God and man (which would make idiocy of all speaking) the speaker in the poem turns to prayer of the spontaneous or ejaculatory sort (as defined in, for example, Taylor's *Holy Living*). Such prayer depends on the prior readiness of the praying person, and explores the heart as given, since there is no time for the heuristic self-recollection of the meditative tradition, Milton's sonnet is therefore a prayer-like poem which, like all prayers (and all lyric poems, the characterizing mark of which is always the solitude of the speaker), is a strategy toward solving the problems which arise when the speaking person recognizes the final one-sidedness of cognitive experience. Prayers and poems also resemble one another in that they come at the end of a sequence of verbal strategies of another sort, as Milton's sonnet comes at the end of a sequence of diplomatic documents seeking political redress for the Waldensians. The exhaustion of social means, the abandonment of the historical fraternity which cannot protect though ruled by a Protector, and also of the languages of society which are imperfectly defended against duplicity, lead to the assertion (a kind of palinodial despair) of a prior filiation (God) toward whom language is directed in another way, since the Christian God, unlike the social other, knows the heart of the speaker directly (we might say intuitively).

Milton's prayer-like poem, unlike earlier such poems on the

295

ejaculatory model which are frequent in the canon of English poetry in the period (e.g., Donne's "Batter my heart. . . .") is only indirectly on behalf of the speaker. Milton is singular in his acknowledgment of history as part of the self. The massive grammatical tropes (imperative, vocative) which mark all prayers of petition are administered on behalf of a separated limb of the brotherhood of true Christians. The revolution broke down the sacramental narcissism which governed the earlier tradition of English religious poetry, which had as its subject the redemptive predicament of the Christian individual. The supra-national fraternity of God's children has become the body on behalf of whose pain the speaker in the poem petitions God as the origin of the meaning of experience.

In the earlier poetry there is a scarcity of pain, the capacity to feel one's humanity as God experienced it, and a superabundance of meaning which shames and accuses the laboring soul (see, for example, Donne's "Good Friday, Riding Westward"). In this poem of Milton there is a superabundance of pain and a waning of existential certitude. The Miltonic-Cromwellian revolution having tampered, in the interest of the perfection of relationship, with the canons of civility (regicide, divorce), having destroyed the king's Englishmen and invented God's Englishmen, is consequently dependent directly at every moment, as Cromwell declared himself to be, on the rationality of Providence. The sense of what Horace called the unweepable (*illacrimabilis* is the term Horace in *Carmina* 4,9, applies to those who lack representation, lack a bard) nature of those who, like the victims of atrocity, have no just or compensating images of themselves, overwhelms the heart when the social world (the world in which men are visible to one another) is disrupted, or when new (hitherto unrepresented politically and artistically) classes of persons claim a moral stake. (See, for example, John Philip's translation of Las Casas' *The Tears of the Indians, Being an Historical and True Account of the Cruel Massacre and Slaughter of Above Twenty Millions of Innocent People,* which was dedicated to the Protector in 1656.) Milton's speaker is pitched toward prayer by the mimetic desola-

296

tion of persons who represent the annihilated self (as in "Lycidas,"
"He must not float upon his watery bier / Unwept. . . .") which is
a possible destiny deeply understood by all men, and not the least
by Milton. God is the recognizer (redeemer, rememberer) of the
inward self-recognition of all persons. The Puritan independent,
like the Jew, seeks affiliation with and justification before that
God, rather than in lesser human communities, and is therefore
dependent for self-recognition on the complex epistemologies of
the transcendental Deity, and ironically also on the historical
world to which he has given himself as God's hostage.

Christopher Hill touches on Milton's subject when he says:

Things were always going wrong, but it was the duty of the godly to make them go right, to
snatch impossible victory to the greater glory of God. It was *in defeat* that Milton set about
justifying the ways of God to man. Both the sense of sin, and the feeling of justification,
came, ultimately, from readiness to break with the tradition, to obey the internal voice of God
even when it revealed new tasks, suggested untraditional courses of action. (*God's Englishman*,
p. 243.)

As I have indicated, Milton's poems both before and after the
Commonwealth take as their subject the rational continuity of
value and experience expressed as the relationship between God
and man. Both the human individual and the human community
are intact when that relationship is expressible in intelligible
speech. When it is not, man lies scattered as on the Alpine mountains cold. The forces in Milton's work early and late pitted
against the survival of the human image ("the blind fury"), and
the forces which conserve that image, are in a relationship of
critical tension, uncertain combat. Everywhere the birth and
continued visibility of the human image is threatened, the diurnal
cycle invoked both as a promise and as a peril to "the human face
divine", since only through divine intervention is the hour before
dawn turned into providential day. The continuity of the human
image in the culture of fame is a contingency of the continuity of
the human community. Milton's poetic subject up to *Paradise
Lost* is in general the inadequacy of historical communities to
remember and thereby conserve the human image, and the
consequent necessity of turning away from society in the apostro-
phic or palinodial gesture toward a new grounding of the human

image in its remote and absolute origin, God. Politically this means regicide, and psychologically a turning away from secondary relationships, from self-realization in the social world, toward symbolic versions of primary relationship, that is to say religion. Hence *Paradise Lost* is an attempt to reconstruct the human community from its origins in the primordial parental world of the generic first parents, against whom disobedience becomes once again the fundamental prohibited act. The Waldensian sonnet lies in a mid-region between stages of this process, and is in effect an example of the historical predicament without which the apologetic substance of *Paradise Lost* would be unintelligible. That the rejection of the social origin of the substantiating symbols of human identity ("What could the Muse herself, that Orpheus bore?") in favor of a prior transcendental account of symbolic origin (the Uranian muse) in effect pits the existential desire for intelligible existence directly against the evidence of historical experience is a paradox. It is this paradox which links Miltonic religious independence with secular states of mind. In Milton's sonnet 18 "vengeance" would be a justification of the human will toward a human version of existence, and the sonnet finds that will at the outermost limits of its autonomy. The palinodial turning away from a tyrannic society in which only parodic versions of the human form are possible, toward a new version of community which has no historical form, links the *Babylonian* wo with apocalyptic (anti-historical and anti-natural) aspects of the romantic imagination. The resolution of the conflict of the "sense of sin" and the "feeling of justification", of actual personal and political situations and the desire for perfect personal rectitude and social authenticity, is incomplete in Milton. The "gathered churches" of Cromwell's new model cavalry, which descended on its enemies screaming psalms, is as final an image of the aberration of the attempt to actualize integral transcendentally substantiated human communities in history as is the awesome and terrible balance in Milton's style between the world-destroying and the world-actualizing powers of the word.

298

In the epic tradition of the West, in the *Iliad* and *Aeneid,* the "true" God sends down real weapons in the service of his favored warrior. By contrast to Blake, who interiorized the struggle, Milton is a non-visionary, mythographic poet for whom God's presence in history will be manifested in some real and visible order of the human community or not at all. There is in Milton no sentiment such as the Blakean "mental fight," which seems in fact to have been derived as an imaginal response to the failure of the historical Commonwealth. The critical and defining predicaments of value seem in Milton to move from inward and symbolic to outward and historic. For example, the relationship between Milton's representation of the Waldensian massacre and the Miltonic theme of the world's threat to discourse and therefore to the continuity of the human image through representation in the historical community can be seen in the *Areopagitica* (1644):

> We should be wary therefore what persecution we raise against the living labours of public men, how we spill that season'd life of man preserv'd and stor'd up in Books: since we see a kind of homicide may be thus committed, sometimes a martyrdome, and if it extend to the whole impression, a kind of massacre, whereof the execution ends not in the slaying of an elemental life, but strikes at the ethereall and fifth essence, the breath of reason itself, slaies an immortality rather than a life.

The Waldensian massacre was just that "slaying of an elemental life" which threatened the "breath of reason itself." For Milton an oppressive society is a continuous assault on the human image, and immortality itself, so long as it is contingent upon the right order of society, is vulnerable. In the Piedmontese atrocity Milton's metaphor of the books reverses itself. The slaying of "an immortality rather than a life" becomes genocide, and the vulnerability of immortality becomes unendurable but not unimaginable. In Morland's *History* the depiction of the assault on the generativity of "The ancient Stock and seed of the Primitive and Purer Church" extends to the disemboweling of praying women and the hanging of men by the genitals. The immortality of a community in history, as it admits of no boundaries in historical time, admits also of no boundaries in social space. Religious wars are conflicts over competing and mutually exclusive claims to occupy the same real

299

existential universe which in Western civilization is represented by the negation of mortality. The price of communal authenticity which is the condition of individual immortality is the destruction of meaningless social mediations. The result is the vulnerability (except for God) of men who are all members of one another, and who by reason of their redemptive claims and affiliations occupy too much space in the world, as did the Waldensians in the valleys of the Pellice and Agrogna rivers.

The English revolution conceived as a theological event was in fact a counter-revolution in the interest of the transcendental tyrant against his ministers, the king and the episcopacy. When history is placed thus directly under the hegemony of the prior tyrant, historical event becomes *prima facie* a test of the efficacy of Providence. Milton's polemical career including *Paradise Lost* is in effect an argument with the human community on behalf of the intelligibility of experience conceived as a direct exchange of recognition between the sect and its divine master. The initiative of *Paradise Lost* to justify the ways, not of man to God, but of God to man confirms our sense that God has failed his test (history being the unendurable and perverted theophany), and that poetry must intervene as the instrument of the human will toward meaning *per impossibile*. In young Milton's confident "On the Morning of Christ's Nativity" the birth of the divine surrogate of the self, the child God, compensates history for the agony of revolution. The aging revolutionary by contrast finds that the successor culture no longer sustains the cost of its establishment, which was detected first in the moans of the dying gods of antiquity but later in the cries of the slaughtered mother and infant, the divine primal group, in the transmogrified pastoral landscape of the Italian Alps. Milton, by contrast to his immediate predecessors in the religious subject, is not merely a lay poet but a secular poet. The function of poetry, in Milton and after, is not to register the *agon* of man in response to the demands of God, but to reconstitute the "false surmise" of a sacramental universe. The pervasive theme of temptation in Milton incorporates the conflict between experience and value. The Miltonic sentiment of this conflict bears

300

out Marvell's fears:

> That he would ruine (for I saw him strong)
> The sacred Truths to Fable and old Song,
> (So *Sampson* groaped the Temples Posts in spight)
> The World o'rewhelming to revenge his Sight.

The bourgeois revolution was the occasion of a trial of God. The Waldensian massacre was an episode in that crisis of the relationship between value and experience which the revolution precipitated. The bourgeoisification of literature (not to mention the still to be anticipated proletarianization) was and still is an incomplete task. The mimetic privilege (the privilege of image) which is the secular correlative of divine remembering has by no means been accorded to all the members of any society. In our time the recognition of the human other as real, and by his very existence a prior value to all more abstract values, is the major social crisis to which poetry speaks. The Waldensians are the image, such as it is, of the self driven beyond recognition and therefore outside of existence. Milton's prayer-like poem is in effect a secular version of the prayer which brings man before God, in his inner form as language, for acknowledgment. Poetry and prayer represent the will of man toward self-identification in the fundamental value of the person manifested in the ambiguous medium of language at the boundary and breaking point of the autonomy of the instrumental will whose forms are religion and politics. In post-revolutionary cultures the function of poetry is the reconstitution of human identity, so far as poetry can reach, in the face of the perhaps impossible deficit created by "liberation."

301

Hermann Hesse: apostle of the apolitical "revolution"

KRYSTYNA DEVERT

Twenty-five years ago Hermann Hesse was awarded the Nobel Prize for literature for his last major work, *Magister Ludi,* published in 1943. His popularity in Europe, and also in South America where his works were widely translated, had been based primarily on the success of *Demian,* published in 1919, fifty-two years ago. These dates are of interest because of the current popularity of Hesse's novels with members of a generation removed from the author by the culture of a separate continent, several wars, decades of technological progress, and a discontinuity of intellectual sources.

Hesse called his books "autobiographies of the•soul," and, indeed, the striking aspect of his work is its continuity of theme, through novels, poems and essays. It is a search which Stephen Koch has considered "adolescent," while Thomas Mann saw them as 'prophetic of the future," calling the novels "great works of longing." What is the future that Hesse had prophesied? What was he longing for, and why do so many now seem to share his longing?

Hermann Hesse was born in 1877 in Calw, Germany. His father was a missionary and he too was to have followed a religious calling. Yet by the age of fourteen he was already feeling oppressed by the future decreed for him, out of tune with the ideas which were to guide him, and he ran away from the seminary at Maulbronn. An intervention by a famous theologian on behalf of Hesse's father induced such guilt feelings in the adolescent Hesse that he attempted suicide. The resultant estrangement from his family was never healed or forgotten: *Peter Camenzind* (1904), *Under the Wheel* (1906), and *Rosshalde* (1914) all show the concern with a conflict produced by the assertion of one's own beliefs in the search for the self against the pain and disruption this causes to others. In the first two novels the conflict is resolved by a passive acceptance of the traditional life which the protagonist, filled with expectations of success, had once so willfully left behind.

The expectation which constantly frustrates Hesse in his early novels is that of finding order through knowledge, of making an intellectual pattern out of chaotic interaction of the self and outer reality. This expectation he finds difficult to abandon in spite of its frustration:

Indeed it did not escape me that school and school science were an inadequate patchwork, but I was biding my time. Beyond these preparations and fumblings there lay, I assumed, a realm of pure intellect and an un-ambiguous, dead-certain science of the truth. Once I reached this realm, I would discover the meaning of the dark confusion of history, the wars of the nations, and the fearful questions that bother each and every soul.

That vision of the "realm of pure intellect" haunted Hesse until it found full expression in the construction of Castalia in *Magister Ludi,* but much earlier, even, Hesse understood that in the process another part of his existence was being repressed and denied:

For I often dream of myself laying naked on some shore as an animal, generally a seal, conscious of such intense feeling of well being that, on waking, the recovery of my human dignity fills me not with pride or joy but with regret.

When Hesse first tries to capture these sensual moments in words, his intellectual standards intervene:

303

> Then, suddenly I realized how far removed my still born pipe dreams were from real, genuine, austere art. I burned my poems and stories.

While the soul longs for ecstasy, the intellect demands an austere order, a learned cumulative attainment of worth. For a while it appears to Hesse, still under the influence of his earlier religious upbringing, that suffering might be the medium through which experience might be processed and digested so as to fuel the spirit. Peter Camenzind fashions a fulfillment out of his defeat and disappointment. He is estranged from his father, his one close friend dies in a swimming accident, his great loves are swathed in such romantic haze that they can never be consummated and neither can his ambition to be a great poet. But it seems that he was wrong to pursue happiness and success; about to declare his love for a woman he admires he finds out that she loves another; when he questions her about that love she answers:

> Love isn't there to make us happy. I believe it exists to show us how much we can endure.

For Peter this is an important revelation.

> I began to understand that suffering and disappointment and melancholy are there not to vex us, or cheapen us, or deprive us of our dignity but to mature us and transfigure us.

He finally finds peace caring for a deformed cripple, Boppi. Boppi's experience of life is most limited; he has no choice of loves, of professions or adventures. His only decisions are what to make of the little that life has offered him.

Boppi "under the stress of horrible agonies and deprivations, had learned to accept being weak and commit himself into God's hands without being ashamed." When Boppi dies, Peter returns to his village home no longer striving, but with a newly learned acceptance and tranquility.

In *Under the Wheel* (1906), the theme of ennobling suffering is less central but still apparent. Hermann Heilner, a sensitive and poetic boy, rebels against the oppression of the school and runs away. His best friend Hans, incapable of such total rebellion, is finally destroyed by it. Filled with longings he cannot make coherent with the life imposed on him, Hans dies by drowning after a drunken spree. Hesse comments on the escaped Hermann's later fate:

After many further brilliant escapades and misfortunes the passionate boy finally came into the strict discipline that a life of suffering can impose and although he did not become a hero, he at least turned into a man.

Hesse's later struggle is mirrored in *Rosshalde* (1914). The painter Varaguth is held in a sterile, unsatisfying life because of his love for his small son. He tries to renew himself in his art, but feels that his creativity is drying up at its very source—himself. Encouraged by a close friend (a relationship which foreshadows that of Demian and Sinclair) and finally freed by his son's death, he leaves for India (where Hesse had traveled a few years before) to find himself and to shake off the guilt and suffering which had been stifling his life.

Rosshalde heralds the new understanding about the self, which in the pivotal novel *Demian* (1919) explodes into the full-bodied self-assurance that comes of a fresh and sudden insight, illuminating all, changing everything. *Demian* represents Hesse's leap into existentialism.

So convinced was Hesse that this was indeed the turning point of his development, as well as the turning point of the intellectual history of Europe, that he published the book under a pseudonym, concerned lest his already well-known name detract from the newness of the ideas. In the fifteen years which had elapsed between the publication of *Peter Camenzind* and of *Demian*, the terms of the search had indeed changed for Hesse:

I have been and still am a seeker, but I have ceased to question stars and books; I have begun to listen to the teachings my blood whispers to me.

No longer concerned with unfulfilled artistic ambitions fallen short of prescribed standards of excellence, no longer determined that an intellectual order should re-establish the lost innocence of freshly perceived experience, Hesse now focuses inward:

I did not exist to write poems, to preach or to paint . . . neither I nor anyone. All that was incidental . . . An enlightened man had but one duty—to seek the way to himself, to search for inner certainty, to grope his way forward, no matter where it led.

The strength and credibility of his new insights came from their being forged under a storm of personal calamities: a father's death, a son's illness, his first wife's mental breakdown, and his

305

own psychic collapse, as well as the profound ideological shock of World War I. The intellectual crisis in Europe for which Hesse spoke was the crisis of the established intellectual order which had served Western thought from its Greek origins.

In Sight of Chaos (1920), a series of essays written at the same time as *Demian,* outlines Hesse's immediate intellectual sources. It includes two essays on Dostoevsky, which became a vehicle for Hesse to express his ideas about the course of European civilization. He foresaw an advent of the "Russian Man," a Karamazovian ideal, a "departure from all established ethics and morality in favor of an attempt to understand everything, to accept everything." "European Man," on the other hand, unwilling to face a reality which more and more forced a relativization of moral decisions, had codified his behavior into a rigid set of rules which, with the sanction of God, relieved man from having to make free choices. Not quite ready for an existentialism which acknowledged no deity, Hesse nevertheless now stood at the threshold of an existential position and longed for a God which did not depend on "this wretched faith in sacred opposites," a God which went beyond good and evil or encompassed both. The Karamazovs searched their subconscious for the impulses European culture had so carefully attempted to repress, and in their act of self-recognition came to full maturity. To recognize one's inner impulses is to recognize and accept conflict and chaos as a pre-condition of a spiritual reevaluation. If man is to be reborn, he must first destroy all the conceptual categories which have served him till then.

In the new notions of relativity which were challenging the classical theories of matter, space, and time, and their Aristotelian origins, in the new inner determinism of psychoanalytic theory, Hesse saw an overthrow of the existing order—a revolution. But revolution not of political upheaval but of internalized change.

"It is possible," he writes, "that the whole 'decline of Europe' will take place only inwardly, only in the souls of a generation, only in the reinterpretation of worn out symbols, only in the transvaluation of spiritual values."

This is the revolution that Sinclair lives in *Demian,* the Nietzschean revolution of rejecting all values so as to assess for the first time what "value" they really have, based on Nietzsche's principle "that every man is a unique wonder," that he must find the way to himself though the price be loneliness and alienation from the "herd," and that the herd will try hard to convince him that "all loneliness is guilt."

When Sinclair reproaches himself for so brutally separating from his mentor, Pistorius, when he feels ready to go beyond the latter's teaching, he justifies it saying:

Each man had only one genuine vocation—to find the way to himself. He might end up as a poet or madman, as prophet or criminal—that was not his affair, ultimately it was of no concern. His task was to discover his own destiny—not an arbitrary one—and to live it out wholly and resolutely within himself. Everything else was a would-be existence, an attempt at evasion, a flight back to the ideals of the masses, conformity and fear of one's own inwardness.

Following Nietzsche, Hesse expects a new order based on a change in the very substance of man. Yet neither had a program for that change. If the change was to come through a violence born of existential despair, Hesse thought he saw that hopeful violence in the first World War, as Demian observes:

Deep down, underneath, something was taking shape. Something akin to a new humanity . . . The most primitive, even the wildest feelings were not directed at the enemy; their bloody task was merely an irradiation of the soul, of the soul divided within itself, which filled them with the lust to rage and kill, annihilate and die so that they might be born anew.

The task of Hesse's new man is not to create the new order but to recreate himself so as to be ready for it when it comes. This readiness means a complete self-knowledge, he must accept the potential validity of all ideas, the potential actualization of all deeds. For if a truly new man is to emerge, he must choose himself out of a full range of his potential, his choice must be made in full psychological and physical freedom, unhampered by past notions of "good" and "evil," of acceptable and unacceptable. Precisely because the new order is unknown, precisely because there is no program, there can be no predetermined choices. The evolving man must be able to "think of crime, to dream of it, to be acquainted with its very possibility," and yet to find his own basis for moral behavior.

307

All his subsequent work is an attempt to illuminate, work out, and understand, the consequences of that existentialism. What is fascinating about Hesse is that his personal turmoil so closely mirrors the philosophical gropings of his age, and we must be grateful that he gives us so much of himself in his work, for it is that blending of thought and experience which ultimately instructs us best. The young seminarian rejected the religious values of his family and school, and his determined search for values which would be congruent with his inner stirring led to a disruption of all of his relationships, including the relationship to himself—a psychic breakdown. And so Hesse begins the painful recreation of himself, the integration of the conflicting inner forces.

Until then, the concept of man's nature implicit in all classical philosophy had been fixed as a creation of God with a permanent and essential existence in his consciousness quite apart and prior to any individual actualization. Dostoevsky had understood in the possibility of the non-existence of God, the acceptance of every aspect of human thought and behavior. Nietzsche had asserted as a historical fact that God was dead. Hesse found in both these men the intellectual support for his own growth. These, too, were the roots of Sartre's atheistic existentialism. For if God does not exist, but man does, then the essence of man, or the concept of human nature is *only* that which man conceives himself to be, *after* the fact of his existence. "Man is nothing else but that which he makes of himself," says Sartre. "That is the first principle of existentialism." The existential man has no recourse to any higher consciousness, he has no one to share the burden of his responsibility. This is Kierkegaard's "dizziness of freedom," man responsible to himself and for himself, defining his very nature, yet isolated from all other men by his newly discovered sub-consciousness which makes him, in Hesse's words, "able to interpret himself to himself alone."

There are two aspects of the existential stance which are important to examine in the context of Hesse's later work and their divergent consequences for our present condition. One is the old philosophical chestnut of mind-body dualism in existential

308

terms—for Hesse the relationship between an inner and an outer reality; for Sartre an ontological dualism, the "for-itself" (*pour soi*) and 'in-itself' (*en-soi*)—roughly, consciousness and experience. Both men were rooted in Cartesian philosophy, and Hegelian dialectics assume the priority of the "inner reality," though with somewhat different consequences.

Sartre, a political activist, employs this priority of consciousness to impress upon men the burden of responsibility which their existential freedom places upon their shoulders: for if man is the sole being whose existence comes prior to his definition, and if in fact it is he who defines all of reality, then he is not only responsible for himself, but for that reality as well. Every act he performs, every decision he makes defines him and not only describes his essence but prescribes the essence of all men and commits all men to his action. Thus every human act implies a (moral) choice, and given existential freedom, "it is impossible not to choose." To assume fully the existential responsibility, we must choose freely from a full range of possibilities for action, and the preservation of that freedom for oneself and for others becomes a new basic principle of existential morality. All actions must be taken in the name of freedom.

Ivan Karamazov's exclamation that "Everything is permitted" is "not an outburst of relief or joy," says Camus, "but rather a bitter acknowledgment of fact." Hesse, on the other hand, alone and in exile, envied by Thomas Mann for his "political detachment from all German politics," understands his existential free-dom to release him from that responsibility. He asserts that each man is responsible only for his own definition; it is all he can be expected to understand, and his ultimate obligation is to "do his thing." In another of the essays, *Zarathustra's Return*, written in Nietzsche's style, Hesse asserts that the welfare of one's country could best be served if each individual attended to his own psychic cure and growth. For any external conflict, says Hesse, is a conflict within ourselves. "What isn't part of ourselves does not disturb us." Whereas in Hesse's earlier works the pro-tagonists were caught in a conflict between an inner need and the demands and pressures of the world they lived in and wanted to succeed in, a conflict which produced guilt and suffering, and which eventually destroyed them—in *Demian* Hesse justifies a concern with the inner reality alone. Sinclair is instructed "that there is no reality apart from that which we have within us." It is in the realm of that inner reality only that Hesse is willing to play out his existentialism.

Just like young Hesse, many of us have experienced a disillusionment with the prevailing values, a frustration in our search for an intellectual order to replace or justify these values, guilt over the failure to fulfill our own (and others') expectations, as well as fear of loneliness which threatens to come with full self-realization. We too have been influenced by psychoanalytic theory (Hesse was in treatment with a pupil of Jung) and our attention has been turned inward to ourselves, suggesting perhaps that we are the source of our own discomfort, that our suffering has only a subjective necessity, and that there is a possibility of a rebirth or a recreation of a new self which would not be vulnerable to such impingements on its freedom.

Hesse understood that nothing less than his survival was at stake. His personal and political world was crashing around him; to take a stance in relation to it might have been too demanding and frustrating a responsibility; to reject such responsibility might create an even more crushing guilt. One possible solution was to assert that the world was irrelevant, to deny it an existence separate from that of the self. *Consider the dilemma:* If that outer reality was indeed a creation of prior consciousness, then to alter the course of that consciousness was to alter the reality; but if the world of experience had an unalterable validity of its own, then it simply could not be contended with and the only outcome of coming in conflict with it would be destruction of the individual.

This was the situation in which Hesse found himself at the conclusion of World War I, and this is where many of us find ourselves today. Two, three, four wars later. The events of the intervening fifty years have made our personal realities fully as terrifying as Hesse's. We have exhausted all institutional sources of spiritual strength—church, state, even family. We have attempted to change the flow of our lives, to change history, only to find ourselves crushed "under the wheel" of a historical force and direction which has seemed alien to and unaffected by any inner reality. Philosophically, we have been misled into accepting a dualism of reason and passion, and have agreed to distrust passion and to allow ourselves to be ruled by reason. For a time we have believed that once possessing adequate "information" we could make decisions without a need for moral choices; or again, not trusting ourselves to make moral choices, we sought to discover some higher order where such choices had already been designated by a superior moral consciousness (God) or a superior intellect (computer). Ours was only to understand these decisions and carry them out with this authority.

We, too, had been misled by the Cartesian *Cogito ergo sum,* accepting the assumption that, if our existence presupposes consciousness, both follow the same laws, obey the same logic. And so, heady with the control we could exercise over our ideas (this applies, of course, only to the Western tradition), we have attempted to construct a cumulative intellectual history on the supposition that we were thus, in fact, controlling our destiny. But an intellectual history gave us no control over the evolution of our experience. *And it was experience we really wished to control, not ideas.* The notion that a causal relationship exists between the two has always been philosophically seductive. Every time we describe our experience, philosophize about it, draw conclusions from it, we protect ourselves from the full realization of the sense of its immutability. A most successful psychoanalysis can only change the patient's future behavior, but it does not change the events of his childhood nor the fact of its trauma, nor the effects of childhood trauma for anyone else.

From Augustine to the positivists we have found our minds and our vocabularies inadequate to the task, yet the belief had persisted that with some clearer understanding, better tools, or in some yet to be discovered realm, we could create new modes of experience. So far the outer reality has stood fast under the ideo-

311

logical onslaughts. Separated by hundreds of years of political science, historical analysis, social philosophy, and scientific theory, the tortured prisoner in a Greek jail feels the same agonizing pain and doubt that tore through the heretic questioned by the Inquisition. The violence perpetrated by American imperialism varies in only minor technological ways from the destruction of the Roman conquerors. And likewise, no new revelations about the inadequacy of language, no Wittgensteinian hair-tearing over the presumed impossibility of verbal communication, diminishes the lover's pleasure when he hears that his love is returned. Each man's experience becomes a new totality, still alienated from that hard-to-modify reality.

Hesse's writings after *Demian* represent a continuing search for a way of unifying that outer and inner world. What begins as an attempt to express their interrelationships, ends with the construction of Castalia in *Magister Ludi* (*The Glass Bead Game*), a total world of inner reality, a realm where the contradictions are finally resolved, and the reality is a reality of intellect alone. Castalia is that "beautiful world" of "beautiful people," where the needs of one's own individuality are the same as the needs of the order. It is that "alternative life style" we have all been searching for. The metaphor that best serves to express that kind of unity is that of music—Hesse uses it both in his work and personal life; here intellectual categories have direct translation into a sensual modality. The intricacy of the experience faithfully represents the schema of the ideas, yet neither can be properly said to *cause* the other. Life in Castalia is a perfectly-composed, perfectly-performed symphony.

The final defection of Knecht (the Magister Ludi) from Castalia has been variously interpreted. Did Hesse consider that Knecht must reenter the world because he now had something valuable to contribute—he was to become a teacher; or did the Magister find Castalia wanting? Knecht himself feels a compulsion to move on as expressed by an early poem of his, which he finds, entitled *Transcend!* It seems that even in Castalia one begins to feel limited. In any case, the interdependence of Castalia and the outer world had to be admitted in spite of the isolation, and Knecht feels something akin to a hunger for that rude outer reality. He needs it to renew himself. He begins to see an existence in Castalia as parasitic.

In the novels leading up to *Magister Ludi,* Hesse's characters had treated experience as raw material for their inner growth, making the self a more or less sophisticated consumer of experience, at first allowing indigestible globs of it to be forced upon them to their own detriment, later learning to pick and choose only those experiences which directly contributed to their desired growth. The logical extreme of this view is to willfully create experience best suited for the evolution of the self into a proper inhabitant of the spiritual realm. Such is the progression from *Steppenwolf* to *Magister Ludi.* The real and the imagined begin to lose distinction because they serve the same purpose, the education of the self, and that is their only relevant reality.

In one of the stories appended to *Magister Ludi,* presumably the posthumous stories of Knecht, an Indian boy, Dama, is in the service of a yoga but cannot be fully accepted as a disciple since he is ambivalent about his spiritual commitment and tempted by images of the world of action and pleasure which he would have to abandon. While fetching a jug of water from the river, a metaphor Hesse uses frequently for the relentless forces of life, he experiences a vivid hallucination of an entire lifetime of adventures. When it is over, he is stunned by the sudden understanding of what it would be like to be caught helplessly in that current of life with no assurance that his most urgent desires would ever be fulfilled. "He no longer wanted anything but to check this endlessly turning wheel, to stop this endless spectacle, to extinguish it all." That is why we hurl ourselves against that reality, looking for death, looking for peace. "He had been properly awakened," says Hesse, "having breathed a mouthful of reality." The boy now gladly accepts his apprenticeship.

It is difficult to get away from that river of life. It is "everywhere at the same time . . , and for the river there is only the present." Siddhartha tries to commit suicide in the river before he becomes a disciple of Vesudeva, the ferryman. There are drownings in two other novels, and when Knecht leaves Castalia and engages himself once more with the present, he too drowns even before he has had a chance to teach his first lesson. So even after the experience of Castalia, an engagement with reality still leads to destruction.

At the start of World War I, Sinclair was busily making himself ready for the new order that was to emerge from the violence. In 1919 he predicted, "the new is beginning and for those who cling to the old the new will be horrible." "What will you do?" Demian challenges Sinclair.

What indeed? The new was horrible for all. By 1943, the year that Hesse published *Magister Ludi,* all of Europe was at war again. Sartre was fighting in the Resistance and six million Jews were on the way to their death. Hesse had spent the intervening years in self-imposed exile in a small Swiss town, rationing to himself those destructive "mouthfuls of reality." Did he still believe that "what is not a part of ourselves does not disturb us"? When Knecht leaves Castalia, weary of his disengagement with reality, is it too late for him? Too late for us? Does he drown because he is not used to the world? And at what price do we get used to it?

We find ourselves again at a time when the pressures for an existential responsibility seem more than any one of us can bear. We do not long any more for our lost innocence, for few of us believe that we have ever had it. We long for a future; not to create that time of peace, but to be able to partake of it. We are less prepared to make the revolution than to act as if we had already made it. It comes from an exhaustion of the spirit which Hesse exemplified, and the temptation to withdraw from that painful confrontation with reality, by means even as drastic as drugs and insanity, is almost irresistible. Even our new spiritual language reflects escape: what pleases us or gives us sustenance is "far out" or "out of sight," and an inner experience is called a 'trip'. Though there appears no resting place in sight, we still cling to the hope that somewhere, out beyond our reach, is a realm of these

314

experiences, a realm we must prepare ourselves to inhabit. We have tried to sustain ourselves with a longing for a "free space," some yet unconquered or undiscovered frontier of social structures across whose boundaries we will be propelled by a new awareness.

This is the essence of the panacea of an apolitical revolution. It may be a neurosis. A numbing delusion. What we are promised, or promise ourselves, is not a revolution, but a post-revolutionary utopia. A concentrated effort by which, if we close our eyes and cleanse ourselves of bad thoughts, a better world will magically appear. Implicit in such thinking is an assumption of causality, unexplained and unjustified, between a change of consciousness and the development of a new society. Implied, too, is a time sequence, as if these two events occurred in separate contexts.

The notion persists. Marcuse in *An Essay on Liberation* (1969) claims: "Beyond these limits [the limits of established societies] there is also the space, both physical and mental, for building a realm of freedom which is not that of the present." This is to be preceded by a "liberation," a "historical break with the past and the present." For both Hesse and Marcuse this is a form of Hegelian idealism without its dialectical ramifications. It is precisely the agony of the existential position that we cannot break with the present, that we are trapped in the flow of the experience in its inner and outer totality, chained to its turns as Sisyphus to his stone, never able to separate the demands of the task from the forces of gravity. There is neither that moment of freedom to stand away and make a decision, nor the sequence that separates the necessity from the act. The essence of a critique of the "revolution of consciousness" is that *there are no political thoughts, only political acts:* acts which affect others as well as ourselves. And that we are denied the comfort of their separation, denied a consciousness that would fall into the "free zone" of idealism, the gap between the essential man and his perhaps accidental environment, and finally that we cannot assign priorities, causal or existential, to the inner or outer reality.

Merleau-Ponty, the late French philosopher, in his phenomenological criticism of Sartre, sees in the dualism of consciousness and

315

experience an illness, a giving in to the frustration of political impotence. Such dualism would condemn us to thoughts we cannot act upon, to ideas that lodge themselves like indigestible bones in our throats calling forth nausea. For Merleau-Ponty existence can refer only to an *involved consciousness,* an inner reality in constant dialectic with its environment. He sees a breakdown of that dialectic as a neurotic malfunction.

If there is no duality of existence, there can also be no duality of practice. It is, therefore, that *simultaneous* change of both circumstances and the self that is properly revolutionary practice. It is important, too, that in understanding the existential dialectic we do not view the synthesis of the inner and outer forces as a stepping stone, a partial achievement in a cumulative road to some final, total achievement. For that final goal, be it freedom for Sartre; a reality which mirrors the most enlightened intellectual evolution for Hesse; or Marcuse's "ideal society"—it is never to be *achieved.* That is the precondition of its power to motivate. It must remain as elusive as immortality. And our existence must be judged by how we choose to *approach* it and not where we arrive.

The strength of our existential stance, the measure of our courage, is the depth of our longing and discontent. Our only power is the courage to continue asking those awkward questions about the purpose of our existence. Any attempt at a final satisfaction of that quest stifles the revolutionary impulse, imposes a static illusion on what can properly be only a continuing process and ultimately ends in disabling disillusionment.

Is that unity of purpose ever to be known, the fulfillment, personal or social, ever to be achieved? Yes and no. No as a final goal; yes, as an accident of being. Why is it that in bed with the right partner or engrossed in a delightful book, we are not likely to question our existence?

Perhaps moments like these are the only possible moments of fulfillment, when all that we are and all that we could be, and every aspect of our relevant circumstance, converges into a harmonious totality. Moments that peak the existential continuum, but have no order in time, cannot be anticipated, cannot be willfully achieved. We mistrust them because we have been taught that such unity is something we must strive to eventually achieve, or else that it is a paradise we have once had and lost. And so we set ourselves the impossible, heartbreaking, and alienating task of shaping a perfected future out of the existential chaos. It is difficult perhaps to ever accept an alternate notion—that the chaos of our daily experience could co-exist in time and space with the perfection of our inner selves. And that the glimpse of the possibility of a unified totality is in fact a recurrent accident of that chaos. It is as if our true self were a jewel lost in the sea and while the returning tide may toss it briefly onto the sand, each appearance anticipated, yet each a surprise, it remains irrevocably and permanently lost. Its brief appearance serves only to remind us that what we are looking for is possible, and to bind us to the search.

On Solzhenitsyn

RAYMOND WILLIAMS

We are used to thinking about two kinds of relationship between literature and revolution. There is the work of writers who precede a social revolution, who directly or indirectly expose the values of a society that needs radical change, and who sometimes succeed in articulating the consciousness that will surpass it. These writers are of many kinds, from the lonely, often isolated figures who offer new visions or definitions of humanity, to the more engaged, more negotiable and negotiating critics of society, whose reference to political change can often be taken as direct. From a Blake, that is to say, through a Dickens and a Hardy to a Wells. Characteristically, in belonging to a pre-revolutionary period, they can be seen in some historical perspective. We understand Turgenev and Tolstoy and Chekhov better because we have 1905 and 1917 as points of projection and of actuality beyond their work. We are indeed sometimes in danger, just because this is so, of subordinating them to history: seeing not works but phases, limited approximations to a more lately revealed truth. And this is especially so if we adopt unconscious evolutionary assumptions, that we ourselves (who are often not history) have arrived at some higher and ratifying point, from which we can look back in detachment at the struggle to create and to define.

Some retrospect is similarly available in the second familiar relationship: that of literature created in and by a revolution: the works of a disturbed and heroic, a transforming and liberating time. And here again there is considerable variation. There are the seized moments of absolute change: Blok's vision of Christ at the head of a Red Army detachment; Pasternak's recreation of the moment when it seemed that the gods had come down to change the whole world; Yeats's "all changed, changed utterly, a terrible beauty is born." Or the more recent:

Los poetas cubanos ya no sueñan ni siquiera en la noche . . .

unas manos los cogen por los hombros,
los voltean, los ponen
frente a frente a otras caras
(hundidas en pantanos, ardiendo en el napalm)
y el mundo encima de sus bocas fluye
y esta obligado el ojo a ver, a ver, a ver
(Heberto Padilla).

But then there are also these moments lengthened into history: not only the breakthrough but also the civil war; not only the liberation but the blockade, the waiting, the tension, the fatigue. By Russian writers, especially, we have been given these narratives: some monumental and in the end academic; others— say Sholokhov and Pasternak, for all their deep differences— engaged and alive in the revolutionary history. Writers and readers elsewhere can look back to these times, experiencing revolution through the power of a novel or a poem; sometimes experiencing it as a substitute, while their own actuality closes in.

But there is a third relationship between literature and revolution: not necessarily the most difficult but perhaps the most difficult to admit. A new society is created by a real revolution, and then, in the modalities of history, it lasts; it lasts fifty years; acquires its own developing and difficult history. Within that society, if literature is to live, the moment must come when the experiences of liberation and transition are not enough

319

to write about. And what should happen then? For in the name of the revolution one kind of literature, one version of reality, has come to be consecrated. It has also come to be formalized. The writer who questions it, who goes on to his own new work, is writing how? *Against* the revolution? *Against* the revolutionary society?

It is how it will often be seen: from inside the society and, more bitterly, from outside. It is bad enough when such a writer is misunderstood, is even slandered, by his own contemporaries and countrymen. In writing his works he has joined, they say, the "evil breathers," the slanderers of revolutionary society, the enemies of the revolutionary state. It is worse when it has to be added that there are indeed such people, and that they are highly organized. A writer of this kind is exposed, almost at once, to a virtually unbearable tension. Slandered and then stopped in his own country, even directly repressed, he is simultaneously, and in ironic proportion, flattered, publicized, promoted by people and organizations who are indeed, and without equivocation, enemies of his society. But then one kind of writer, to whom all this happens, can collapse the tension; can move quickly to one of its poles. He may emigrate, physically or spiritually. And indeed if he is not, in any sense, a revolutionary writer, if in his ideas and values he truly belongs with his society's enemies, there is little real tension, though there may be plenty of difficulty and hardship. But the man who stays, and more important the writer who stays, is under extraordinary pressure. He does not belong with his colleagues who are slandering him nor with most of the people outside who are flattering him. If he is one kind of writer, a radical visionary, his social situation may correspond with his literary situation, though it will still not be easy to bear. But if he is a writer of another kind—a realist novelist, overwhelmingly concerned with contemporary actuality, and with the actuality of his own people and society who are officially rejecting him, the tension and the challenge are obviously very great.

Alexander Solzhenitsyn is the outstanding example of such a writer in our time. Certainly in Soviet official terms, he is a dissenter. But he is in some important ways different, on all the evidence we have, from the group of dissenters with whom he is often identified. Some of these (and I do not hold it against them, I simply record it) are writers who would be reactionary in any society. That they have behind them and around them the experience of what happened to the Russian Revolution, of the long deformity of Stalinism, of the stagnation after Stalin, is documentary but not essential to any adequate reading of them. What they arrive at, what they value, how they see other people, is very familiar to us, not only in our reactionary but in much of our orthodox literature. We have to respect their difficulties but then leave their friends, for there are more than enough, to welcome them.

Solzhenitsyn, so far as I can see, is of a different kind. He is a very Russian writer, but then so are some of the others. He is also, more centrally, a realist and a humanist, and in his interests, his values and his methods is in some very important ways an identifiably Soviet writer: a definition that for all the difficulties still has some meaning. In trying to see what this meaning is, we may be able to understand him better, and to understand some of the unique difficulties of his situation.

Of course it would also be possible to indicate a different analysis. It would be possible to say that through the difficulties of its historical development the Soviet Union, half a century after its revolution, has many points in common with bourgeois societies after their revolutions, so that a writer like Solzhenitsyn is in effect a critical realist: paradoxically a critical realist, in the middle of an officially socialist society. I do not say that this may not prove in the end to be right. There are many things we still cannot know about him and his work. Yet I distrust any such category which would exclude the reality of the Russian Revolution. Its consequent history can certainly not be evaded: not while we are reading Solzhenitsyn. But neither can its original history: its new relations between men. Deep in Solzhenitsyn's work, so far as I can read it, are values which belong to the experience of that revolution, just as so much of his material, so many of his insights, belong to the experience of the revolutionary society which built prisons and labor camps on an almost unrealizable scale. This is all very different, it seems clear to me, from the modes of the nineteenth century critical realists. Solzhenityn's methods, too, belong to a society that has seen, even if it has then also been blinded to, the realities of a popular literature. Yet I leave the possibility in suspense. If it is not already true it may become true, given the extent of the pressures.

Meanwhile, however, there needs to be a different emphasis. Let us look at it first in terms of ideas: though first by reason of accessibility rather than by any estimate of final importance. From what ideas, to what ideas, is Solzhenitsyn's creative experience directed?

"Don't ever make this mistake. Don't ever blame socialism for the sufferings and the cruel years you've lived through".

That is the voice of Shulubin in *Cancer Ward*. It comes in the tenth chapter, *Idols of the Market-Place,* of what is published in English as the second part of the novel. Shulubin is talking to Kostoglotov, the bitter, enduring, visionary man who is the pivotal character and at least in that sense Solzhenitsyn's own mode. Shulubin says it to him; Kostoglotov does not altogether accept it: that reservation is necessary and important. But still the whole discussion is of great directive importance. These are two men in extreme pain: victims of cancer, victims also of state repression. This is how Shulubin is seen:

Perched on his thighs he was so twisted that he seemed to be bent backwards and forwards at the same time, his arms stretched out and his interlocked fingers clasped between his knees. Sitting there, head bowed, on the lonely beach in the sharp lights and shadows, he looked like a monument to uncertainty.

It is in that essential context that the ideas are introduced. Shulubin is suffering more than even Kostoglotov, but then he has also done more, has been a time-server, even a book-burner. His physical state is now so terrible that he will "lose the company of human beings." And it is this man who can say:

The man with the hardest life is the man who walks out of his house every day and bangs his head against the top of the door because it's too low.

Kostoglotov, by comparison, seems to have only his own pain. He didn't even burn books; he had none to read, in his camp. So:

Don't ever blame socialism for the suffering and the cruel years you've lived through. However you think about it, history has rejected capitalism once and for all ... Capitalism was doomed ethically before it was doomed economically, a long time ago.

What values, then, will men live by?

I should say that for Russia in particular, with our repentances, confessions and revolts, our Dostoevsky, Tolstoy and Kropotkin, there's only one true socialism, and that's ethical socialism.

Kostoglotov puts the familiar materialist objection:

Where is the material basis? ... There has to be an economy ... That comes before everything else.

Shulubin then introduces three names: Solovyov, Kropotkin, Mikhaylovski. From a distance these seem, at first, an unusual mixture. Solovyov (1853–1900) was an idealist philosopher: teaching the spirituality of all being and the possibility of universal brotherhood. Kropotkin, of course, was a scientific anarchist and prophet of mutual aid, guild socialism, the overcoming of the division of labor. Mikhaylovski (1842–1904) was a Populist leader, an idealizer of the peasant commune, and in the end a skeptical radical. They can be said to have much in common, as they are cited by Shulubin: a new society is created from known and reasoned values; it is not the consequence of economic developments, and it is an ethical rather than a political surpassing of material historical developments. All, in this sense, are opponents of Marxism. They are also (and the distinction needs stressing) obvious opponents of a discernible Soviet ideology of productivity and plenty leading to happiness. As Shulubin puts it:

When we have enough loaves of white bread to crush them under our heels, when we have enough milk to choke us, we still won't be in the least happy. But if we share things we don't have enough of, we can be happy today.

Or again:

One should never direct people towards happiness, because happiness too is an idol of the market-place. One should direct them towards mutual affection. A beast gnawing at its prey can be happy too, but only human beings can feel affection for each other, and this is the highest achievement they can aspire to.

This is hardly a political program. Indeed, as Shulubin puts it, "no one should have the effrontery to try to plan happiness in advance." But it is clearly and identifiably a social position: one of the original and still one of the most powerful critiques of bourgeois society and of capitalism; a widespread element, today, in the socialist and radical movements of the developed industrial societies. And the question I put (knowing the strength of the Marxist critique) is not first whether it is enough as the basis for a revolutionary movement, but what happens to a revolutionary movement or system which in developing beyond it, in understanding more of the process of historical change, has overlooked or discarded or come down to paying lip-service to its central and continuing human emphasis. It is not, in any case, a position from which one can "come over" to capitalism, since capitalism is still the most absolute form of the disease it identifies. As a position from which a version of socialism can be criticized—a version in which there are socialist institutions of production but in which these are given priority over all other actual and potential socialist relationships—it has some obvious value. But this is to limit it to direct politics. The question we have really to ask is about its value to a writer: its usefulness, and limits, to a writer like Solzhenitsyn.

And what we have then to say is that Solzhenitsyn is not only Shulubin. I believe that Solzhenitsyn, if he had to generalize his beliefs, would make a summary very close to that which he puts in the mouth of this character. But as a novelist he sees this same man as a "monument to uncertainty": these are intimations of value, within a process of suffering. And it is important to remember the fact of the dialogue with Kostoglotov:

"Oh no, I want happiness, you'd better leave me with happiness," Oleg insisted vigorously. "Just give me happiness for the few months I have before I die. Otherwise to hell with the whole . . ."

In the camps, in a kind of absolute scarcity, he and his friends thought there was a lot of good in private enterprise; it made things available, and they had nothing. This harder, more skeptical response is not a denial of the ethical argument, but it is its accompaniment. Through the detailed development of both responses, Solzhenitsyn shows something more than a debate;

he shows a historical process: a widespread demoralization; a glimpse of alternative values; the stress of actual relationships, from and towards both positions. The humanist writer is undoubtedly there, but so is the realist. The two modes of vision, the two processes, are continually active.

Solzhenitsyn's meanings, that is to say, can be seen more clearly in the substance of his fiction than in his arranged formal discussions. None of the discussions ever goes far enough to stand on its own, except as a general indication. The goodwill of the indication is obvious; so also, as in many related cases, may be its naivete. I will admit that there are times when I wonder if Solzhenitsyn is more than a documentary writer, who through an exceptional personal history has come into contact with material of such exceptional and yet general importance that he has only to recount it, and to add a few general ethical reflections, to be hailed in the West (as with that material would in any case be almost certain) as a writer of genius. This is in any case a question that has to be put, if we are to retain any critical integrity. In a fair amount of *One Day in the Life of Ivan Denisovich,* and again in much of *Cancer Ward,* some impression of this kind almost inevitably builds up. The characteristic method of loosely linked sketches can be related, of course, to the habit learned in the labor camps where there were no materials for writing and so incidents and anecdotes were memorized and habitually retold. But then this relation leads us back into the material, rather than out of it. It would be dishonest to suppose that by one kind of standard in fiction—the kind that in East or West gets abstracted as "construction"—Solzhenitsyn's novels could not be shown to be loose, incomplete, suggestive, without sustained depth or context. Here and there, of course, this has been done. And any contrary position requires more than some act of affirmation. It requires detailed demonstration. What I want now to put forward is what seems to me to be the critical case, on two counts. I want to relate the "documentary method," and especially the technique of linked sketches, to a position in experience which is in the end

325

social and political, and which cuts across most of our received definitions of art and of formal social criticism. I want then to go on to argue that in *The First Circle,* which I think is very clearly his most important novel so far, there is a creative development of a very original kind which established him as by any standard a major writer.

The "documentary" question first. There has been a profound tension, through this century, between the demands of received form and the demands of any extending social consciousness. In the West we know mainly the related tension: between received form and the fluidity of subjective experience. Most of our important and original writers have been remaking the novel towards that kind of subjective fidelity, and from within the exploration new forms have crystallized: Lawrence's *Women in Love* was, in English, the outstanding transitional work. The shift was made, one might say, from what had been, essentially, a liberal social history to what is now, essentially, a liberal psychology. Form, which had been the balancing of a group and an environment, became internal and symbolic. Criticism followed. Few Western readers of *Cancer Ward* can resist asking themselves whether the disease is a symbol of the Soviet body politic: the growth cells becoming malignant. Or the prison camp: the human condition: the universe of the concentration camp. With effort, certainly, any of this can be sustained. But it is radically irrelevant. Cancer won't work as a symbol of a specific social disorder, when it is described as Solzhenitsyn describes it: a general and terrible human fact. Again, in real prisons there is more to do, as again Solzhenitsyn shows, than to project a victimization as an abstract condition. The familiar starting points of modern bourgeois art are then in a real sense not only irrelevant but damaging to Solzhenitsyn. Once the sympathy created by what has happened to him, in the camps and in his subsequent persecution as a writer, has been, even momentarily, set aside, it is clear that *by these criteria* he is not a major writer. We are looking in the wrong place for the wrong thing, quite as much as his official Soviet critics.

Certainly the liberal social history, as the basis for form, had to be gone beyond. But the particular direction in which, in our historical circumstances, this went left a whole area of human experience untouched. The concept of the group, in any active sense—and beyond it the concept of the sustained existence of others over and above any parts they may happen to play in our individual existence—was by now out of reach. Serious exploration, it came to be thought, cut away inwards, towards the crisis of a sensibility or towards its projection as an abstract, unhistorical condition. The recognition of others, let alone the searching out of others, became in itself problematic: a function, primarily, of the isolated sensibility or condition. And it is, then, very interesting that the description "documentary" had to be coined for those writers and other artists whose imagination was intrinsically of an extending kind. Orwell went through this crisis as a writer, thinking he had failed when he was writing not "art"— the received and temporary definition—but "rapportage" and "pamphlets." It was in this work, however, and not in the attempts at "art," that he became a significant writer. He found the liberating forms almost against his will; against the will of the assumptions by which he continued to be governed. Now the irony is, with Solzhenitsyn, that he inherited a different set of assumptions: those of Soviet revolutionary and popular art. The writer must go out to the people, see what is really happening, record everyday struggles and crises. There was never anything at all wrong with this emphasis (though to make it exclusive, especially in a transitional period, leads quite directly to bullying). What was wrong was what happened next: that if you saw what was happening you contradicted, violently, the official version of what was happening. Soviet fiction got a bad name, in the West, for two very different reasons, which need to be sharply distinguished. There was the hack fiction, some of it very professional, which was at best selective reporting and at worst deliberate manipulation. But there was also the popular fiction which, by what it was trying to do, outraged (it is still so; it is so with some of our own radical writers) the social and artistic assumptions of late bourgeois art. Not only by what it did but by what it was trying to do: the description of people at work, the emphasis on ordinary experience. The bourgeois jokes about tractor-fiction are very significant. That is a world of work and of working people which has to be declared "not art," which has to be dismissed as "propaganda" or at best "documentary," because the admission of its emphasis would, very thoroughly, challenge and eventually break up the bourgeois novel. And then just as this point might be seen, the other part of the process occurred. Much of the fiction began to betray itself in its own terms, becoming not what was happening but what in the official picture, with just a blemish here and there, was supposed to be happening.

Dudintsev, in *Not by Bread Alone,* was at a limit of this process: setting ordinary values, of work and loyalty, against the muddle and corruption of the system which was supposed to embody them. That, if you like, is critical realism. But the contradictions were much deeper than that, and at their center were the camps. Solzhenitsyn, as I see it, had behind him, when he came to write about the camps or about the exiles in hospital, all the real strengths of revolutionary popular fiction, but now with this deep irony: that they were recording, at a significant center, the character of the post-revolutionary regime. Or not quite, at this stage, the character of the system. The writer comes across people, rather than discovers them. There is this abnormal isolation: the dominating environment of the camp or the hospital. There is a central figure who defines one kind of value: a hard-strained, unsentimental, truth-telling survival. That figure is then the tendency of the narrative: its governing stance. But form, beyond that, is deeply extending and in one important way casual. People are met and known, lost sight of, moved on from, seen again but without highlight, crowded out, as all are, by the no less significant reality of others. It may have happened, at first, without conscious planning: this form was, after all, a real experience. But this concept of, as it were, the negative group, which is yet sharply human, individualized, needing absolute attention, is the organizing principle of *Ivan Denisovich* and

328

Cancer Ward. To have constructed them differently would have been—it is what bourgeois form now is—to exclude. A documentary fiction, a fiction of sketches and encounters, tales passed from mouth to mouth, interrupted yet always urgent histories, is in this radical sense a fidelity: a basis for humanism and for realism, neither self-centered nor exclusive, holding to that reality of the human person—that socialist reality—that we are indeed individuals and suffer (as bourgeois art can record) but also that we are many individuals, and that the man next to us who irritates or comforts us is also a center and has beyond him innumerable centers: all subjects, all objects; a recognition that forbids any formal emphasis which would reserve centrality or significance, by some principle of selection, to the more human among humans.

Thus *Cancer Ward* begins with the arrival of a minor administrator, Rusanov, who has a large tumor on his neck and is put in the cancer wing. We see the place through his eyes: an observation of others who are suffering, in this old, overcrowded hospital. He is without sympathy and sees people in ugly ways. The intrinsic suffering and the ugliness of exposure are seen through a mind which is in part shocked by the terrible physical thing that has happened to him, in part accustomed to a distaste and contempt for others, an habitual but now disturbed consciousness of his own privileged position, which we would know as a class feeling and which is in fact a familiar viewpoint in Western fiction of this kind. It then moves to his neighbor, Kostoglotov, a political prisoner now in perpetual exile, who has been brought in almost dead but who is responding to radiation treatment. This other mind, which becomes dominant in the novel, is in a different way bitter: seeing as much of suffering and exposure, with that inevitable observation which comes from being shut up with it; politically skeptical at a depth which takes over from ordinary politics and becomes a whole crisis of belief; but also, with his returning energy, capable of seeing what Rusanov never sees—the humanity of the others, the endless and selfless work of the doctors and nurses, the goodness of ordinary life and experience as against the obsession with social position and material success of

329

Rusanov. These contrasted viewpoints, and the suffering that is seen through them, are the basic success of the novel. Then towards the end of the first part, though also more briefly elsewhere, the novel moves to see the same scene through yet other eyes, in what is really, in its brief development, a series of sketches, and it ends with an obviously staged discussion of sincerity in literature: the tension between telling the uncomfortable truth of the present and the doctrine of imagining, within this, the seeds of a different life.

It is thus a difficult novel to read, let alone to judge. What we see with Kostoglotov, or with the nurse Zoya, or the doctors Dontsova and Gangart, is of course painful, in so much suffering, death, humiliation of the body, but life flows in this, deeply involved and felt. To see with Rusanov is sickening, and it is only relatively late that the novel succeeds in defining his distorted consciousness: not only the self-pity, the contempt for others, but these as the weakness which have made him that kind of administrator: a cold, frightened, self-interested manipulator of others, in the name of a system. And by that time, in fact, we have also got what connects but is sickening in his consciousness: the naked ugliness of others who are suffering and who disturb one's own suffering.

It is untidy of course, It has the awkwardness of any radically new emphasis. The wrought works of an older sensibility make it look unfinished, tentative. People ask not only where is the familiar form—the continuity of attention—but where is the new consciousness? Where, say, is the socialist consciousness of this revolution that builds prison camps? Almost a child can do it; read, rehearse and repeat the theoretical explanations. Beside them, certainly, the gestures to "ethical socialism" can seem velleities. But this is cutting deeper back. For cannot theory of an advanced kind coexist with the most absolute, willed and unwilled, failures of human recognition, of the kind that here, sentimentally and unsentimentally, is the first of all values? The touch in the dark of a corridor of a cancer hospital; the feel of sun on the hands and on other hands; the pity that must be more than pity for a disease not only seen but shared. And to put it in terms of ideas, if Solzhenitsyn believes that this kind of close, absolute human recognition was more present in the "ethical socialism" of the nineteenth century than in the "Marxism" which for sound economic and political reasons seemed to surpass it, I for one think he is right, though I doubt whether we could recover the recognition by going back on the historical insights; we would have to go on from them, and that is where many of us, in very different societies, now are and move.

It is a dangerous passage. Human recognition, as an idea, has a version that betrays as well as a version that saves. It can shrink to recognition of people like ourselves; ourselves multiplied; a bourgeois humanism. Or, perhaps even more dangerously, to a recognition of absolute others: poor devils of others in camps and hospitals; men not like us, victims of our enemy; men whose suffering is to be pitied and exploited—the exploitation in the pity—as we hold them at arm's length and see not them but, in our terms, a system. In getting beyond pity—in his roughness, irritation, anger, laughter—Solzhenitsyn is honest, emotionally, in an exceptional degree. He stays with his people and with what is happening to them because in a deep way he is one of them: not an observer or a mirror, but a man in this collective: a surviving individual in this surviving, decimated group. It is the survival of the people, under so heavy an experience, that comes through as a value in the surviving, articulate, bitter and compassionate man.

Except that *The First Circle* is different. Its experience and organization are different. Unless I misread it, a much harder idea than a realist humanism is there as its form. The design is there in the title; that is why I think I have read it correctly, though there is always room for doubt. For the method at first seems the same: linked sketches of people, seen, lost sight of, reappearing, disappearing. All that is continuous is the common and dominating environment: the special prison for intellectuals. I have said already, about the earlier work, that the collective is in a sense a negative group: they relate, often positively, but within fixed

331

lines, not of their own choosing, that are the limits of their freedom. Yet the idea of the negative group, once established as the general situation, is left in the background; the immediate recognitions are more important.

In *The First Circle,* very differently, the idea is central. The linked sketches are not illustrative of casual, involuntary meetings and discontinuities within a dominating environment. The very absence of real links—voluntary, positive, aiming at continuity— is now the defining quality of a system. It is not so much the negative group, in that earlier sense, as a kind of seriality: all the links arbitrary and in a more profound way negative; the seriality, the lack of real connections, including the imprisoning as well as the imprisoned, the dominators as well as the dominated. The thread of narrative is connected to just this idea. What is being done, centrally, is work on the human voice, work on the very medium of recognition and discovery. Ostensibly this is to serve state security: to allow scrambled messages, that limited betrayal —the service of official secrecy—which is still only the tip of the iceberg. For the really dangerous and dreadful discovery is a means of recognizing individual human voices, in quite new and specific ways: recognition of anonymous telephone voices. Not just the passive state secrecy but the active state investigation. The most positive value of all, this absolute value of recognition, is now so transvalued that it is the means of men's betraying each other, betraying others they have never even known or seen. It is easy to talk, abstractly, about the perversion of a system. This, concretely, is a systematic perversion of terrifying depth. Knowledge, kindness, loyalty, self-interest, fear, ambition: all feed, in this serial system, into mutual and collective betrayal. The ethical contrasts, though not at all renounced, are back in a different world. Ethical criticism, we say easily, when we are telling the story of our intellectual development, developed, and had to develop, into social criticism. It is a much harder process than we ordinarily imagine. It is not a surpassing of ethical values; that leads straight to the terror. It is a perception of ethics as relationships over so wide a range, from the temporary affair to the state institution, that most of our ordinary points of reference dissolve.

That the connections in *The First Circle* are arbitrary, at first only a restless shifting from this person to that, is in the end the meaning: a series of arbitrary connections which compose an objectively arbitrary reality. The work on the voice has a central irony, as we have noted: that detecting, understanding, scrambling voices is being done by men who need to speak in their own voices, to describe their common condition. But then, the irony goes deeper, into the construction of the novel itself. For what happens in it, in its essential form, is also a kind of scrambling, in which a human society (that connected community which is the ordinary form of the realist novel, and which had even survived, through the emphasis on recognitions, in *Ivan Denisovich* and *Cancer Ward*) is fragmented into pieces of sound which can be understood only when they are put together again in a particular way: when the series is surpassed and the real connections made clear. Yet these connections are themselves negative. Characteristically the novel ends with a misreading, by an observer, of a conventional sign. The vans used to convey prisoners around Moscow are painted to look like bulk food trucks, with MEAT in four languages on their sides. As the prisoners are being driven away to the distant camps, a foreign correspondent sees their van and makes a note:

... clean, well-designed and hygienic. One must admit that the city's food supplies are remarkably well organised.

This is the kind of false decoding—a false decoding of signals both true and false which can no longer, within the system, be distinguished—in which all the characters are involved, and which is then the characteristic form of social relationship. In a more profound sense than that in which we ordinarily use it this is a system of alienation, at the very roots of meaning.

What is false must be corrected; must be replaced by truth. That is one characteristic form of dissent, of critical dissent, and in part, certainly, it is Solzhenitsyn's role. But there is a more radical dissent: not the correction of a system, but the finding of human values beyond it. Inside that van something of this kind happens:

> The prospects that awaited them were the taiga and the tundra, the Cold Pole at Oi-Myakoi and the copper mines of Jezkazgan, kicking and shoving, starvation rations, soggy bread, hospital, death. No fate on earth could possibly be worse. Yet they were at peace within themselves. They were as fearless as men are who have lost everything they ever had — a fearlessness hard to attain but enduring once it is reached.

It is the kind of fearlessness which Solzhenitsyn himself has so consistently displayed. But in the van it is different:

> Half-listening to the noise of the engine the prisoners said nothing.

The end of this work on the human voice is this kind of silence; a fearless silence; a coming out on the other side of suffering. It is, then, not critical realism; nor is it, in its silent waiting, a revolutionary realism. Clearly it could go quite another way: "at peace *within themselves.*" We do not yet know. It is a moment of silence, after so many false messages, after the ending of ordinary hope and of all conventional reassurances.

"For a country to have a great writer is like having another government." This is said by one of the characters in *The First Circle,* and the idea is in the great tradition of Russian realism: literature as another source of information and values; another center of decision and truth. Historically, such realism has preceded a change; it is not the change in itself. Hanging on in his own country, where he can no longer be published; reaching back for this kind of conviction and commitment; finding and exemplifying a courage that may endure because it has known and faced terror: this is where Solzhenitsyn now is.

III
POPULAR CULTURE

Sixteen notes on television and the movement

TODD GITLIN

Though these notes are disconnected in form, and may seem flatly self-contradictory in places, I beg indulgence. I wish to call attention to the argument that unites them in sequence.

Notes 1–6 describe the power and mission of commercial television. (This essentially frightening analysis is as far as most critics go.) Notes 7–12 shift gears, attempting to show the dialectical motion of television's effects: its capacity to produce and nurture effects opposite to the ones it intends. The radical movement of the sixties is seen as, in part, a reflection of television's contradictory effects. The ending might be happy if one ended there, but dialectical development does not cease at will. Notes 13–15 continue to follow the dialectic, suggesting that the parent phenomenon (media) never relinquished control of the child (movement), but maintained power by insinuating itself into the core of the child's behavior. The movement is still crippled partly because it sees itself as a television image, not as a social reality. But thankfully the dialectic does not stop here, and this society will continue to reproduce its opposition. Finally, in Note 16, I suggest rudimentary considerations for liberated media.

1

The development of mass broadcasting media was inseparable from the history of capitalist war-making and consumption-making enterprises. Imperialism and consumerism were the parents of invention. Mass broadcasting developed hand in hand with the electronics industry, both being central to production in advanced capitalist society.

From the time of Marconi's first radio patent in 1897, his most avid supporters in England and America were military men. When he arrived in the United States in 1899, according to liberal historian Eric Barnouw (*A Tower in Babel,* Vol. I of his *History of Broadcasting in the United States*):

It was, in various ways, the perfect moment to approach the United States armed forces on the subject of wireless . . . The city was preparing a spectacular welcome not for him but for the hero of Manila Bay, Admiral George Dewey . . . It was an hour bursting with manifest destiny. The American republic had suddenly turned empire, with overseas possessions . . . Such a nation would also, like the British Empire, have to think about communication . . . In fact, to inform Washington of his victory and subsequent actions at Manila, Admiral Dewey had had to send dispatch boats to Hong Kong, whence the news was telegraphed westward, going over British-controlled cables . . . Somehow it didn't fit with the new world posture. At this juncture Guglielmo Marconi arrived in America . . . As the new century dawned, the equipping of ships with wireless proceeded at a rapid and quickening pace . . .

One of the first experimenters with wireless transmission was Pittsburgh professor Reginald Fessenden. Backed by two financiers, Fessenden sent out signals that were picked up, on New Year's Eve, 1906, by the banana boats of the United Fruit Company. "United Fruit was already experimenting with wireless, by which perishable cargoes could be directed to profitable markets, and scattered plantations could be coordinated." United Fruit bought Fessenden's equipment and became a Caribbean radio "pioneer." Inventor Lee De Forest saw the handwriting on the wall; one of his publicity brochures envisioned the Pacific becoming "an American lake" through the magic of radio.

When World War I came, several giant corporations—AT&T, General Electric, Westinghouse—claimed large chunks of the new enterprise. "By the end of the war period they controlled all principal patents, which put them in position to dominate later developments." After the war, the Navy wanted to control the new gadgetry, but other government elements wanted to put radio "in the hands of some one commercial concern and let the government keep out of it." Moreover, the government insisted that American business be in a position to preempt British-held Marconi interests. Some fast maneuvering by General Electric, approved by President Woodrow Wilson, resulted in the formation of the Radio Corporation of America, RCA, as the American receptacle for radio patents. GE, AT&T, and American Marconi transferred their relevant assets to RCA in exchange for stock. Provision was even made for a government representative with "the right of discussion and presentation in the board of the Government's views and interests concerning matters coming before the board." Meanwhile, a Westinghouse vice-president conceived of the idea of a mass market for radio receivers. On the basis of Westinghouse work, this corporation also bought into RCA, as did United Fruit.

As radio voice transmission began, the RCA combine moved, with government protection, to dissolve the threat of mass amateur broadcasting. AT&T began to experiment with commercial messages on its New York City station. By the end of 1924, coast-to-coast hookups were common, again with the economic purpose primary: "AT&T would thus without delay be able to offer sponsors a group of stations as a package." It wasn't much more of a step to the full-blown network. RCA put together the National Broadcasting Corporation, sharing ownership with GE and Westinghouse.

From the beginning, oligopolistic media were linked with oligopolistic commodity production; advertising agencies, new on the scene, performed the marriage. The National Biscuit Corporation became the first million-dollar advertising account when several hundred local cracker factories were combined for the sake of a common trademark in national advertising. Meanwhile, commodity production came to require regular marketing of new goods; mass media had to become the pipelines. And as corporations came to understand their need for instant

337

access to a national market, the networks became more powerful —especially RCA's NBC, with the parent company's patents on vacuum tubes and other radio hardware. As radio yielded to television, oligopoly strengthened its hand.

2

The mass media in capitalism are private properties before all else. Their prime self-conscious function is profit-making. Their structure is corporate structure par excellence. The executives shift from corporation to corporation and in and out of government like any of the corporate elite. This is rudimentary, but it is the beginning—though by no means the end—of any analysis. The political function of the media is yoked inseparably to the economic. The commercial is the message, and the message is a commercial.

That a radio or TV station is a business, not a public service, is made clear by the language of a law passed in 1952. In ruling on a proposed change of hands, Congress declared that the Federal Communications Commission "may not consider whether the public interest, convenience and necessity might be served by the transfer, assignment or disposal to a person, other than the proposed licensee." Here again law follows reality.

The product is not a simple commodity, or the sum of all commodities, but is in the first place consumption itself—the creation and reproduction of a privatized, moderated, consuming "man." The product is also ideology, "culture," "ideas," "information." Thus the economic decisions amount to political-ideological decisions. The television networks ask: How can we carve out a larger share of a given market (youth, old people, blacks, suburbanites), or create new markets? This is their basic and primitive catechism, surrounded but not buried by all the trappings, litanies, textual exegeses, casuistry, and downright rationalization characteristic of any religious mystification. Fundamental is the market question, first posed as economics, then camouflaged as value-neutral technique ("What do the people want to watch?"), emerging finally as ideology. The commercial

338

is the purpose, the essence; the program is the package. But as with physical commodities, more and more attention has to be paid to the package to maintain sales.

That the objective of the TV industry is to manufacture the consumer as well as to sell the specific product is perhaps clearest where women are the targets. "In a free enterprise economy," a leading motivational analyst told Betty Friedan (*The Feminine Mystique*), "we have to develop the need for new products. And to do that we have to liberate women to desire these new products. We help them rediscover that homemaking is more creative than to compete with men. This can be manipulated." This analyst admitted he could just as well advise women to compete with men in the mainstream economy, but pointed out that his advertising clients would not look favorably on such a message.

The dynamic of relations between sponsor (investor) and program (package), at least before 1960, could not be clearer than in Fred Friendly's account of CBS (*Due to Circumstances Beyond Our Control*). Friendly, who quit as president of CBS in 1966, started out in CBS with Edward R. Murrow, producing *See It Now,* the documentary which thrilled liberals in 1954 by attacking Senator Joseph McCarthy.

See It Now . . . saw the light of day primarily because of a sponsor, the Aluminum Company of America. After the antimonopoly decision of the federal courts, Alcoa had decided to embark on an advertising campaign designed more to improve its institutional image than its sales, and the idea of a Murrow television program interested the company. They bought it without a pilot program . . . In 1953, *See It Now* enjoyed something close to autonomy. Our mandate came from William S. Paley [chairman of the board of CBS, and World War II deputy chief of psychological warfare for the Allies] and Irving W. Wilson, the president of Alcoa. Actually, *See It Now* had been created and given a place in the nighttime schedule and Alcoa was willing to pay for it.

Friendly and Murrow produced a show, controversial for those years, defending a lieutenant the Air Force was trying to fire on grounds of presumed Communist family connections. In fact the connections were nonexistent, making the case ideal for civil-liberties liberals. After the show was broadcast,

The advertising manager of Alcoa called to say they were proud to have been a part of the broadcast . . . After praising the broadcast, Mr. Wilson said it was still his company's position that they would make the aluminum and that we would produce the programs; at the same time,

339

he hoped that *See It Now* would not now devote itself to "civil-liberty broadcasts" to the exclusion of all else.

The president of CBS, then and now, was Frank Stanton, originally a market expert. Friendly writes that Stanton was a busy man: "He was absent from his office only to attend a meeting of the RAND Corporation, the Rockefeller Foundation or the Business Council [Stanton was a member of all three boards of directors], or to fly to London to consult with Henry Moore on a statue for Lincoln Center, of which he is a trustee, or to fly to Vietnam on a government information mission." Stanton was disturbed about the McCarthy broadcast: "there was certainly no suggestion that McCarthy was justified, but [Stanton] believed that such controversy and widespread doubts were harmful to the company's business relationships."

During the 1954–55 season, Friendly continues,

we also did a two-part report on cigarettes and lung cancer, and both CBS and Alcoa felt the pressures of the tobacco industry, which buys both air time and aluminum foil. The attitude at CBS was, "Why does Murrow have to save the world every week?" . . . The pressure on Alcoa also mounted. Aluminum salesmen had difficulty explaining to irate customers why their company felt it necessary to sponsor programs against McCarthy and for Oppenheimer, against cigarettes and for "socialized medicine"—which is what some doctors thought our program on the Salk vaccine advocated. *In addition, Alcoa's market was changing. The short supply of aluminum caused by the Korean War was ending; increased competition demanded more of a hard sell. The job that* See It Now *had been purchased to achieve had been done; for many the name Alcoa had become a symbol of enlightened corporate leadership.*

Then NBC put *The $64,000 Question* opposite *See It Now.*

Alcoa had been paying some $50,000 for *See It Now* at 10:30 p.m.; now Revlon was paying $80,000 for the quiz and would be paying more than that a year later. Our time slot was now infinitely more valuable than it had been a month before.

Paley and Stanton took *See It Now* from its weekly slot, made it monthly and irregular. "For all of *See It Now*'s abrasive quality," Friendly recalls, "I don't believe that there was any determined plot on the part of Bill Paley to whittle Murrow's influence and independence. I believe that the decision to change to irregular programming was primarily a business calculation to create more financial yield from the time period. That others in the company hoped that the weekly headaches would be eased to monthly ones was strictly their dividend."

340

The profit decision, predating the political decision, generated it as a "dividend." And the object of CBS' "headaches" was no flaming revolutionary, but the kind of liberal who once took the managers to task for preferring to broadcast salable entertainment rather than a public-service warning that Russia was pulling ahead of the United States in missiles: Edward R. Murrow, who ended up as Kennedy's director of the U.S. Information Agency. The span of permissible dissent, even while it lasts, is narrow indeed.

In the early days of television, as this case history tends to confirm, program control was left ultimately to the individual advertiser. But around 1960, according to Barnouw (Vol. III, *The Image Empire*), the networks began to assert ultimate authority over programs, and advertisers began to trust them to do so. In other words, the networks achieved control by acting in the interests of advertisers *as a whole,* i.e., capitalism as a system. From the broadcaster's point of view, the new procedure was more rational. The three networks were now sure enough of their rationalizing role that they could stand majestically as adjusters and managers of the entire communications pyramid, much as the state oversees production as a whole although it must sometimes step on one corporate toe or another.

3

Advanced capitalism cannot do without mass media. The system of giant corporations (advertisers *as a class*) must manage consumer demand and instigate needs for new products, lest profit, investment and production stagnate.

The medium exists to process individuals whom the processors regard from afar as a mass; capitalism has reduced them to that level. Everywhere but at the acme of the social pyramid, people are treated as interchangeable parts. The medium heightens the processing of these powerless individuals into a formless mass of integrated, consuming Americans as variously and gaily packaged as the Standard Brands themselves. Not being allowed to participate in the core of the society, the bulk of the mass reduces to

341

passive spectators precisely those which advanced capitalism needs. The stupefaction of leisure continues and enlarges the stupefaction of labor. And the message to consume is built into both commercial and program in the form of well-appointed "middle-class" life-styles, language, concepts, problems, etc.

Television does not invent the consumer demand, which is created by the totality of the manufactured environment, experiences, and needs, but *focuses* it so that the consumer may be allowed to alleviate the tension between his needs and his suffocated experience—all to the profit of the corporation. This tension-reduction is the aim of programming which strives to *compensate* the viewer for what is fragmented, belittling, and confusing in his own socially shaped and limited life. The environment that generates alienation then intervenes with pro football and moon-shots—vicarious and boiled-down adventure—in order to ameliorate the estrangement between man and work, man and man, man and total society.

These compensations—including commodities—capitalize on the existence of needs which are not fulfilled by life in capitalist society; and some of these needs, however distorted by mass media, are real: love, sex, security, fun, etc. As the West German Marxist and poet Hans Magnus Enzensberger argues, "The attractive power of mass consumption is based not [not only, I would say—T.G.] on the dictates of false needs, but on the falsification and exploitation of quite real and legitimate ones without which the parasitic process of advertising would be redundant. A socialist movement ought not to denounce these needs, but take them seriously, investigate them and make them politically productive." (*New Left Review,* 64, Nov.–Dec. 1970) The sports-car that objectifies and exploits sexual drives is keeping back a full consciousness of the objectification of sex in this society, and is therefore a fetter; but sex itself is a genuine need. Enzensberger is right to add that the damning of the presumably integrated working class for selling out its true needs flows from the prejudices of the middle class, just as Ellen Willis has pointed out that "consumerism" can be a charge thrown at women by radical men anxious to preserve their own privilege. (Willis, "On Consumerism," *Socialist Revolution*, III.)

But in the process of warping need and individuality, the compensations only heighten the level of alienation. The system delivers the goods but the goods do not make for a good life. Alienation spirals out of control and feeds neurosis and psychosis. Leisure as escape from alienating labor becomes alienated leisure, supplied with commodities (including television itself) to fulfill needs that are themselves either unfulfillable or alien to the individual. There can be no consciousness of true needs until people recover them in the process of emancipating themselves. Then they will not need a television to see their images.

The dependency of giant corporations on mass communications was enshrined in law in a 1961 National Labor Relations Board ruling. According to Harry J. Skornia, a communications professor (*Television and Society*), the NLRB "ruled that a broadcast station's services can be considered a product in the meaning of labor law. In this sense, the broadcaster is not in the public service; he is an indispensable part of the production process. As the Board reasoned, the station, 'by adding its labor in the form of capital, enterprise and service to the automobiles which it advertises for the . . . distributor, becomes one of the producers of the automobiles.' By adding such labor in the form of advertising in order to make the automobile salable, the radio station 'becomes a very important producer.' " This is especially marked in the case of corporations which regularly market new goods, like cars, appliances, soaps, shaving equipment, etc. Without instant access to the market (which they create), these corporations would stagnate.

By 1967, liberal economics, letting some of its blinders down, noticed that "sales and advertising have an organic role in the system." (John Kenneth Galbraith, *The New Industrial State*.) Beginning in the 1920's, with the consolidation of the capitalist political economy, Keynesian measures (mostly war) took care of overall demand; advertising took care of specific consumer demand. Advertising changed from product display and information to the manufacture of needs ("motivation"). In 1890, total expenditures in the United States were $360 million; in 1920, $2.9 billion; in 1940, with the Depression, down to $2.1 billion; in 1950, $5.7 billion; in 1966, $16.5 billion. After newspapers (linked in chains, wire-services, syndicated columns), the largest medium of advertising is television ($2.8 billion in 1966). Of this total, about half is concentrated in *network* sponsorship. Again Galbraith: "The industrial [corporate capitalist—T.G.] system is profoundly dependent on commercial television and could not exist in its present form without it."

Central to the strategy of overripe capitalism is that people be rendered passive, be rendered consumers; that television, in the language of (presumably male) admen, "penetrate" the household and pin down its watchers like so many butterflies on the collector's board. "The general effect of sales effort," writes Galbraith, "is to shift the locus of decision in the purchase of goods from the consumer where it is beyond *control* to the firm where it is subject to *control*"—except that it is not the individual firm that moves into control but the state and the total economy. Of all the mass media, television is most effective at removing life-choice control from the individual to the company, and from the individual to the corporate economy in general. The Director of Marketing Services of S. C. Johnson & Son (Johnson's Wax), in a 1966 speech to a university-sponsored, *TV Guide*-financed seminar for television executives and admen, pinpointed the medium's qualities: "Television is an attractive medium because it is a mass medium in quality and frequency . . . The medium is extremely well-suited to low-interest products because it is an intrusive medium. Products can be injected where they are not wanted—which doesn't sound very moral but which is a fact of life with television . . . Television is the medium which depends least on consumer cooperation to develop a rich response to symbolic stimulation . . ."

Having manufactured and activated (pacified) the mass consumer, television manufactures his taste for new techniques, model changes, planned obsolescence—essential functions in advanced capitalism. "Television stimulates with its great selling force," the corporate salesman says; "it stimulates obsolescence, so we are in a product rat race because of television." In turn, this built-in, mind-choking cycle keeps capitalist television a *mass* medium that cannot for long tolerate programs which do not "appeal" to the acculturated mass: "At substantially increased costs it is going to be difficult to introduce these new products unless they are of a market-shaking dimension. Thus, the stimulus of television will in effect entrench the present products where they are now. As television becomes more fractionated in its audience appeal, it becomes less valuable as a mass medium . . ." (August Priemer in Stanley T. Donner, ed., *The Meaning of Commercial Television.*)

Of course the "fractionated" audience would be an array of publics, each with its own art and information matrix. But as long as the media must constantly re-invent the mass for the sake of sales, C. Wright Mills's vision of a nation of interdependent but self-motivating publics is literally utopian.

4

Whether deceptively labeled as "entertainment," "news," "culture," "education," or "public affairs," TV programs aim to narrow and flatten consciousness—to tailor everyman's world view to the consumer mentality, to placate political discontent, to manage what cannot be placated, to render social pathologies personal, to level class-consciousness.

Mainstream sociologists Paul Lazarsfeld and Robert K. Merton have noted that the mass media's power derives "not only from what is said, but more significantly from what is not said. For these media not only continue to affirm the status quo but, in the same measure, they fail to raise essential questions about the structure of society." Given the centralization of media control, it could not be otherwise. The advertisers are surely buying something for their investment.

This is not the place for a complete catalogue of media methods, but a representative sampling can be suggested. The networks sublimate popular yearnings, unsatisfied in alienated daily life, into fantasy (fast-moving, devil-may-care heroes, images of

345

beauty, upward mobility, etc.). They isolate disaffection and organized opposition into compartments called "deviance," and make *them* (us) the social problems to be solved. They shoehorn latent discontents into jokes (like Dick Cavett's monologues on a decomposing New York City), making powerlessness easier to live with, helping individuals find solace in smugness ("I at least [wink] see my puniness—and I can laugh at it"). They make social issues private, individual: husband versus wife, parent versus child, cop versus robber. Women's liberation is flattened into bra-burning and man-hating, while otherwise sex roles are stereotyped to conform with sexist imagery. Problems are presented as singular and isolated, and solutions are quick and easy, requiring no social change. The networks fragment news and entertainment into easily visible and digestible bits, assiduously avoiding integrated, socially comprehensible views of the world. They offer images of strong fathers (Dan Blocker in *Bonanza,* Captain Kirk in *Star Trek,* the paternal cop in *Mod Squad*) to rectify youthful unrest, whereas in the first flush of mass affluence in the fifties it was necessary to loosen Father's grip, with the genial, permissive, ultimately wise image of Ozzie Nelson and of Robert Young in *Father Knows Best.* They conjure up myths of the inevitability of progress for minorities, smooth their rough edges, digest them into acceptable or, at least, comical roles; cultural attributes (Lincoln's natural hair in *Mod Squad,* the Beverly Hillbillies' twang) are permissible outside a political context.

Television ignores production workers as creators of value (the only exceptions that come to mind are *The Honeymooners* and *Life of Riley*—even Archie Bunker in *All in the Family* is apparently a foreman); the heroes instead are managers, nondescript suburban types, cops, assimilated minorities, housewives who cope, and patriotic crooks and teams of crooks. If this bias is so deeply embedded in the networks' and ad agencies' modes of operation as to be unconscious, it sometimes rises to the level of consciousness. Eric Barnouw cites a 1954 letter from an advertising agency to playwright Elmer Rice, explaining why his *Street Scene,* with its "lower class social level," would be unsuitable for telecasting:

346

We know of no advertiser or advertising agency of any importance in this country who would knowingly allow the products which he is trying to advertise to the public to become associated with the squalor . . . and general "down" character . . . of *Street Scene* . . .

On the contrary it is the general policy of advertisers to glamorize their products, the people who buy them, and the whole American social and economic scene . . . The American consuming public as presented by the advertising industry today is middle class, not lower class; happy in general, not miserable and frustrated . . . *(The Image Empire)*

Television, however hip to the "contemporary scene," deforms it into a cornucopia of what Herbert Gold called "happy problems."

Again, the television program serves as a partial and alienating compensation for what is lost in the process of experiencing capitalist society. The more penetrating minds in broadcasting know it. Dr. Ernest Dichter, the motivational analyst made notorious by Vance Packard in *The Hidden Persuaders,* saw in the western series "a defense against frustrations of modern society." Barnouw writes: "Most people felt a great hopelessness, he wrote, about the world's problems. But in westerns 'the good people are rewarded and the bad people are punished. There are no loose ends left . . . The orderly completion of a western gives the viewer a feeling of security that life itself cannot offer.' *In Dichter's view the western seemed to serve the same emotional needs as consumer goods,* and their alliance was presumably logical." (*The Image Empire,* citing *Broadcasting,* Sept. 2, 1957. My italics.)

Overall, television reduces potentially recalcitrant, unintegrated, authentic experience to predictable formulas, which by their pervasiveness and reliability foster the illusion there is nothing new, authentic, or revolutionary under the sun: or, if there is, it is esoteric, Camp. How much this reduction is specific to commercial/bureaucratic structures is indicated in a 1954 article by T. W. Adorno: ". . . the technology of television production makes stereotype almost inevitable. The short time available for the preparation of scripts and the vast material continuously to be produced call for certain formulas." These formulas are ideological shorthand: "The more stereotypes become reified and rigid in the present setup of cultural industry, the less people are likely to change [the media's] preconceived ideas with the progress of their experience." *"In the present setup":* surely we can imagine another system of programming, capitalizing on the wealth of

347

talent trained and untrained, which would not require such stereo-typy; but to gain access to the liberated media there would have to exist a popular movement capable of expropriating the present tycoons.

The late-night talk shows may illustrate the subtlety of television's workings. Fifty years of film-making have elevated the movie star-celebrity to high status in the society. The viewer would forget himself in identifying with the golden idols. But in the process the stars became so much larger than life they could no longer serve as points of identification. Thus the function of the talk show is to *reduce* the star or hero in stature, to show that the star is "just like you"; without script or director, he doesn't always know what to say or how to move. The mechanism of identification is restored to its alienated compensatory status, and the viewer gains back a little of what he lost living in the margins of the victimizing culture.

All these methods of flattening consciousness work day-to-day without the need for explicit censorship, though censorship is the method of last resort. The 1964 series *East Side/West Side,* which had star George C. Scott progress from Concerned Social Worker to Concerned Congressional Aide, was dumped just as Scott was about to conclude that new social forces had to be organized. (They would be liberal, of course, but even liberal movements, operating beyond hope of private solutions, were tabu.) More recently, there is the case of the Smothers brothers— but by strictly market standards the Smothers brothers were already a bad risk—and of TV writers protesting against network refusal to show interracial couples.

News is most regularly censored, since unrehearsed reality is more intractable, rough-edged, than pre-packaged, pre-screened "entertainment," even when the officials try to smooth the edges with carefully modulated news voices; but even there, explicit censorship is usually unnecessary, given the networks' prior definitions of "news" and their choices of reporters. Underneath all "news," all "entertainment" runs the message of the mainstream: everything is solid; the world is given; there are problems

348

but see! we have recognized them and are solving them one at a time. Sevareid will soothe, Howard K. Smith will scowl, Brinkley will wink us past the rough places. The exceptions (occasional documentaries; network coverage of the Michigan Avenue police trauma) are dressing for the one-way window.

These flattening effects are not peculiar to the mass media. Viewed systematically, all production of consumer products in a post-scarcity capitalist economy is tailored, beyond the sale of any particular product, to the manufacture of insatiable consumer appetites—the manufacture of consumers "them"selves. All corporations develop a self-serving ideology to convince their consumers that the company "gives the people what they want." The mass media distinguish themselves by their *pervasiveness*. The average TV viewer watches four hours a day.

5

The impact of American television programming is worldwide, and is a sizable obstacle to the development of national and revolutionary cultures, especially in the Third World.

The most comprehensive study of the mechanics of worldwide diffusion, "cultural imperialism," is Herbert Schiller's well-documented book, *Mass Communications and American Empire* (Augustus M. Kelley, 1969). Schiller summarizes his argument this way:

Mass communications are now a pillar of the emergent imperial society. Messages "made in America" radiate across the globe and serve as the ganglia of national power and expansionism. The ideological images of "have-not" states are increasingly in the custody of American informational media. National authority over attitude creation and opinion formation has weakened and is being relinquished to powerful external forces. The facilities and hardware of international information control are being grasped by a highly centralized communications complex, resident in the United States.

What is being pressed upon the residents of Rio de Janeiro favelas and Tunisian villages is the gospel of consumerism. The more canny planners in the American government well understand the power of broadcasting to inculcate habits and self-images appropriate to the globalization of capitalism. If the villagers are starving now, the giant corporations are already looking to the

349

other side of the climb toward subsistence, and distributing etiquette books—in the form of television programs and films—instructing the natives on proper behavior in the farthest reaches of the American empire. Messages are also beamed toward the rising middle classes of the Third World, offering them models for emulation. An intra-governmental committee reported in 1966 that "telecommunications has progressed from being an essential support to our international activities to being also an instrument of foreign policy." (Cited in Schiller.) Schiller, editor of the *Quarterly Review of Economics and Business,* understands why new revolutions want to erect electronic walls around their frontiers, to stop the dumping of American trash on their populations. But the American ruling class needs to keep beaming those messages into the Third World, not simply because they derive a sizable portion of their sales and prospects for sales from that source, but also because in the "battle for men's minds" the Americans want to hold the machine guns. The corporate elite too have their image of "the new man."

6

To a great extent, the consciousness of men and women under advanced industrial capitalism is formed (limited) by their relationship to the means of *communication.* The major means of communication are education and the mass media. The most powerful of the media is television.

Over 95% of American households own television receivers. The automobile stands for personal mobility, the TV set for "personal" (impersonal) link-up with "what's happening." The car redefined physical space, the TV redefined citizenship. So much is commonplace from McLuhan. But McLuhan trips off to the myth of a "global village," a tuned-in community of syncopated sensation. There was a time we might have said he simply didn't notice that the terms of the "community" were rigged from the broadcasting centers, that the "community" was rather a shopping center of split-up, split-off greed-nodes. "Clearly the manipulators of [advertising and market research] controls are

350

irresponsible and will probably so continue as long as the flow of merchandise and profits remains unchecked"—McLuhan, 1947! Twenty years later, the ad buster has become adviser to the admen, high priest to the new church of consumption.

McLuhan's speculations on the scintillating "coolness" of TV lost their magic in the face of some obvious characteristics of the medium. First of all its convenience: "entertainment," diversion is no farther away than the other side of the living room. Second, its show of immediacy, its technical capacity to summon the illusion of connection with faraway persons, places, things, all this makes it—and by extension its messages—far more compelling than the other easily accessible media: radio, newspapers, and mass magazines. The habitual watcher seems literally *entranced,* hypnotized, made passive. If the viewer is already dazed by the conditions of his work and the sheer weight of the alienating environment, TV deepens the narcosis.

7

While it flattens consciousness, TV also backfires.

Are we no more than "the darkening crosshatch where the media intersect"? (William Gass) Marcuse envisaged us that way in 1964 deprived by corporate technology, and specifically by media, of the very ability to envision an alternative. But then a movement erupted throughout the West, an opposition with an opposed consciousness.

In 1969, Marcuse published *An Essay on Liberation* to square his one-dimensional analysis with the revealed fact of another dimension. But his attempt at synthesis finally failed because the one-dimensional thesis itself was not dialectical, did not show how one-dimensional forms could generate at least the seeds of their negations. For one thing, he missed the ambiguity of television's effects.

Television is a medium of reinforcement, simplification, instantaneity, and symbol manipulation. Each of these processes heightened sensitivities which fed the movement.

REINFORCEMENT: Television, in one of its faces, is a lens

351

which heightens what it treats and diminishes what it ignores. What it writes, it writes large. Partly this is technically inherent: because the screen is small, there is no room for clutter, detail, refinement, ambiguity. Partly it is because of the way time is compartmentalized (time is money, whether or not the station is commercial): there is no *time* for anything but the most simplified complexity. The medium therefore lends itself to propagandistic representations of reality, whether in the guise of "news" or "entertainment." To some extent it trains the viewer to exaggerate any existing trend which TV "treats," and to demand clear, simple images. In a time of social peace, like the fifties, television reinforces peace. In a time of social dissidence, like the sixties, television amplifies dissidence.

SIMPLIFICATION: Certainly there is a very intense impatience over social reform. I think this impatience is caused—at least in part—by television, which makes all social problems seem more urgent and intense.

Furthermore, television doesn't teach us how democracy works. It is too much governed by show business! Its commercials proclaim instant solutions for upset stomach, neuralgia, or bad breath, and its news reporting sums up even complex events in half-hour programs with a neat wrap-up at the end. The boring details of the democratic process, such as hearings before city council, endless facts about taxation or school budgets—these you seldom learn on television.

Today, we are dealing with a whole generation of youngsters who know about 'democracy' as a slogan. But they don't know a lot about its actual operational requirements—the patience, the tedium, the long debates and compromises needed to arrive at democratic decisions.

Therefore, I have an unverifiable feeling that maybe one of our problems is that we have created within the younger generation, largely through television, a whole bunch of young people who are impatient with the democratic process because they don't understand it. They think that violent and immediate 'confrontation,' which has all the advantages of television drama, is the way to solve social problems.

The speaker: S.I. Hayakawa, in *U.S. News & World Report,* February 24, 1969. He is on to something. Translate "democracy" to "going through sealed-off channels, crawling through unresponsive bureaucracies"; translate "compromises" to "surrenders of human initiative," and you have another tribute to the ambiguity of television's effect. Not that TV is alone among media, only that its pervasiveness and commercial requirements (cost, mostly) exaggerate the simplification effect shared also by radio and the press. *TV's simplification and channeling of desire resemble the effect of commodities themselves:* the creation of a need followed by an instant solution, which is not a solution. The French Situationists are right to see commodities themselves as spectacles. (Guy DuBord, *Society of the Spectacle*.)

INSTANTANEITY: Blacks meet police dogs and fire hoses in Birmingham; students seize Columbia buildings; that night, millions watch; a new possibility, a new symbol, enters the general consciousness, energizing those who are ready to reclaim their lives or at least to take action. Time shrinks along with space. That quantitative shrinking becomes qualitative, partly because the event is more vivid than older media could make it (that might be true of each successive wave of new media), partly because the illusion of being *present* at the event makes it more easily reproducible. One unhealthy result is the two-three-many movement syndrome, the simple imitation of the media version of an event— a visible sequence ripped from its real circumstances. Events in one place have always modeled events in another (the Russian Revolution sparked others as soon as the word spread), but TV's acceleration of time enlivens the models.

SYMBOL MANIPULATION: Ripping an event from its surroundings, its formative reality, also makes symbols stand out in bolder relief. The sit-in, the draft-card burning and turn-in, the slogan "Black Power" were all disseminated to previously uninvolved publics, were all made electrifying, partly because of television.

All these effects, working under the surface of one-dimensionality, have helped push the first TV generations into radical politics. The effect continues, though the results (see Note 15) are many-sided.

8

Commercial television splits the consciousness, of young people above all. Invading the disintegrating family, it becomes a major school of socialization, though vastly different lessons are learned by young people who experience affluence and those who do not.

On the one hand, television promises salvation (love, beauty, mobility, happiness) through consumption and bourgeois manners; it turns jingles into household ditties. On the other hand, television and the society as a whole fail to make up for the failure of commodity production to produce the advertised results. The consequences of disappointment: for relatively affluent whites, a certain cynicism, "cool," underneath the glittering surface of administered happiness; for manual workers, frustration when industrial discipline collides with the expectations of consuming leisure; for ethnic minorities, frustration because the goods dangled in the living room are inaccessible.

For those who have the wherewithal to consume, consumption becomes a necessary but finally empty *behavior,* a kind of sleepwalking; a stance, not the ground of a new identity. Not surprisingly, the first television generation—the generation that reached high school in the late fifties, the generation that made Woolworth boycotts, freedom rides, peace marches, and the Mississippi Summer of 1964—first experienced American hypocrisy (the betrayal of liberalism *by its own lights*) in advertising. Disgust for advertising, as mirrored in *Mad Magazine,* was central to the first post-McCarthy breakout: the Beat consciousness. Not long afterward, Kennedy's Federal Communications Commission head, Newton Minow, was calling television a "vast wasteland." Official liberalism, which always lags behind new social forces, joined the sixties.

Young manual workers, as Jim Jacobs (*Leviathan,* March 1969) has pointed out, grow up in a culture that deprecates or ignores manual work, only to face a work-reality that demands more and more industrial discipline. Television lies and the ruling class is losing its ability to cover up the lie. Jacobs feels this is one central impulse behind the new militancy among rank-and-file production workers, especially the young.

Blacks have goods thrust in their faces, but not the money to buy; therefore ghetto revolts were, in one of their aspects, commodity riots, looting, "getting what [TV says] is ours." When the post-scarcity economy defines leisure goods as one's birthright, one will act accordingly.

Mass media themselves, though, cannot deepen these tensions

into a revolution against the idea of property accumulation itself. One-dimensionality finally swallows part of its negation. Kids learn that some commercials and programs (authorities) lie, that the entire world of television programs is a lie, but at the same time they learn to tune out on authority while going through the motions of acceptance: they learn how to live with lies.

Whether the cool-acceptance or the cool-skepticism triumphs, whether skepticism turns to disgust or even directly to revolt, depends on the magnetic power of a movement to define an alternative—not just a life-style, which is too easily absorbed, but a workable method of political engagement. TV helps form the revolutionaries—persons who have been led to develop new needs that cannot be met under capitalism—but the revolutionaries are then left to their own devices, and must somehow overcome the institutions of their own birth. Finally, only a totally opposed consciousness can counter the culture's total assault.

9

Television may incidentally inspire a negative, radical consciousness; it is also conspicuously counter-insurgent.

As a popular movement arises, television moves to manage and contain it; the more insistent the Left, the more consciously will television move against it, by direct opposition or by selective incorporation. (This counter-insurgency meets both market and ideological criteria.) By the late sixties, news and documentary shots were playing up black capitalism and the "silent majority" of students. (Now that a majority of students support anti-war protests, no more is heard of this "silent majority.") After the invasion of Cambodia, news shows played up those students who went to work within the system for "peace Congressmen"— as an alternative to violent insurgency. Night-time programming discovers the virtue of casting blacks in bourgeois roles, as an indispensable but low-status technician (*Mission: Impossible*), even as co-star (Bill Cosby in *I Spy*) and star (Diahann Carroll as *Julia*): the first two promote anti-communist integration, the other the idea that well-fed, well-groomed blacks make good neighbors.

355

"Black power," a vague concept from the beginning, is incorporated and made mundane; the amplified symbol is broadcast through static. *Star Trek* conveys the magic of welfare imperialism made cosmic, as the Starship *Enterprise* cruises from planet to planet discovering that Utopias, however well-intentioned, are evil, and vanquishing them with good old earthly knowhow. *Mod Squad* refurbishes the police image. *Room 222* acknowledges that problems exist in high school, but argues that sensitive teachers will solve them one by one. The two young lawyer shows teach the viewer his problem can be solved in the courtroom. Similarly, between 1964 and 1966 networks introduced a plethora of spy shows, of which *Mission: Impossible* was the most durable. At a time when the first news was leaking out about "the invisible government" (Wise's and Ross's book of the same name was published in 1964, focusing the furor over the Bay of Pigs), the spy shows justified assassination, cloak-and-dagger technology, and intervention in other countries' affairs. According to Eric Barnouw (*The Image Empire*), *Mission: Impossible* told its writers: "The villains are so black [sic] and so clever that the intricate means used to defeat them are necessary."

10

Counter-insurgency at its most farsighted sometimes requires that social adjustments be made. The networks, acting in behalf of advertisers as a whole—and therefore the stability of the society as a whole—attempt to channel consciousness into the mode of liberal reform. They may even create an issue and seem to disrupt the status quo—but only because the status quo is itself shifting. The attempt is to reach a new, more reliable center of gravity.

It is only superficially paradoxical that one of the society's most conservative institutions periodically assumes the role of mover and shaker. Along an earthquake fault, small movements of the earth are required to avert a major shift. There are actually two quite central functions here: (1) distant early warning to the elite, and (2) preemptive mobilization of the mass. The monopoly of ideology can be held only if it remains sensitive to, and even anticipates, potentially disruptive social stress. But this sensitivity requires a reform mentality, which is, of course, what upsets Vice-President Agnew. At least an important segment of the networks must finally take the side of adjustment—change which they, along with other reform forces, aim to control.

A case in point is CBS's 1971 documentary, *The Selling of the Pentagon,* about the military propaganda machine. A more powerful piece of muckraking I have not seen on television: with Pentagon lies revealed to be lies, no wonder Agnew, Secretary of Defense Laird, and House Armed Services Committee Chairman Hebert rose in scathing and curiously helpless indignation. Yet CBS felt so strongly about the show that they rebroadcast it, and, still more brazen, punctuated it with CBS News President Salant's devastating rebuttal of the right-wing charges. CBS had something very strong at stake: what? Pursuit of the truth? But why this truth, and why in 1971? And what led the producer to include in the show not just revelations of the Pentagon's deceits but the rare self-critical revelation that CBS's own demigod, Walter Cronkite, had himself narrated pro-war films for the Pentagon? Why admit to the taint, even if only to purge it?

One may believe that a courageous documentary team decided on their own to expose the Pentagon, and somehow bulled their way past resistance from their superiors; or one must conclude that the superiors themselves—including ex-RAND Corporation Chairman and CBS President Stanton—thought the Pentagon had to be opposed in 1971. Striking as it is, the second hypothesis seems infinitely more plausible, more in accord with what we know about the rules of hierarchical institutions when something important is at stake; the more important, the more centralized the chain of command. But then what was at stake?

The clue lies in the fact that one wing of the ruling class (the wing not holding power) has concluded that the war is a catastrophe—it is polarizing the country, inspiring total opposition, and vitiating needed reform. This enlightened managerial section of the ruling class badly needs to (1) find a scapegoat for America's pursuit of a disastrous war, and (2) channel anti-war disgust away from capitalism/imperialism as a system. No doubt *The Selling of the Pentagon* exculpated Stanton himself, in his own estimation. But CBS sought more than absolution—consciously or not, they sought to focus critical attention on the Pentagon *as an isolated institution* and thereby away from the corporate system as a whole. Perforce they would channel rising anti-military sentiment, even encourage it, even risk losing control of it (cooptation is a tricky business), and, as a byproduct, try to teach anti-militarists to look to the benevolent network, and to reformers in general, for assurance that the "problem" is being managed. The message once more is that everything, after all, can be handled at some elite conference table; no popular intervention, no mass movement, is required, except perhaps as the legions of a new reformer champion. After the unmistakable force of the broadcast is dissipated, however vivid the discovery of the evil, what is left is politics as usual.

11

The rule of "covering the action" is at odds with the media's interest in flattening consciousness. The media then portray the event but obscure its meaning.

Of course, in potentially inflammatory situations, the networks adjust the rule, as in their decision to play down or eliminate coverage of ghetto and campus revolts. They more often spread consciousness that something halfway recognizable is going on in the world. For all their mystification of cause and effect, the networks helped turn the population against the Indo-Chinese war—not actively against it, but at least bored with it or soured on it. Without offering any analysis of the origins and stakes of the war, the news shows' prolonged daily coverage, with steadily climbing body-counts and repetitious battle scenes in slogging geographical obscurity, beamed the unmistakable message that the war was unwinnable. That the newsmen lacked enthusiasm for the war—by comparison with coverage of World War II at least—was visibly obvious, and more than balanced out the simple-minded militarist deceit of the occasional war documentaries and the nostalgia for World War II in the many war programs. Television thus reminded viewers that the war was going nowhere, and that it was ugly; the population became weary of the war much faster than if there had been no television coverage. But of course no one can grasp the political nature of the war through television; one will never know what created the war in the first place, or hear the word "imperialism," or be reminded that the United States government has more of a stake than "freedom" or "democracy" in Southeast Asia; and the awesome facts of bombing raids, the destruction of villages, refugee camps, etc., are fragmented and denatured by their juxtaposition to Excedrin and lipstick commercials. The other side of war-weariness is general stupefaction.

12 ·

TV news coverage also polarizes attitudes.

Television of the 1968 Chicago police riot deepened the commitment of the Left, but whetted the thirst of the law-and-order Right. Television amplifies symbols, but cannot (at least in any given short run) change the way people will receive them. Those inclined to favor the police come to favor them all the more (71 % of Gallup's sample), and inversely.

But the broadcasting ideologues move quickly to keep polarization from getting out of hand. Cronkite apologized to Daley; CBS News ordered its previously fair-minded reporters to invent and play up a "silent majority" of moderate students whose "involvement" they hoped would void SDS's base. . .

13

TV debases all experience. As Priemer of S.C. Johnson & Son says, "This is the medium which in effect *packages an experience* and brings the consumer into it. Television provides him with a response which he would otherwise have to contribute in a major part *out of himself.*"

The gleeful strategist thereby acknowledges, implicitly, that there must be a standard of *authenticity* which television violates,

359

some notion of a person's experience in relations with others and with events which he forms from *within* those relations (I experience this room not as the image of it you offer me, but as it feels to me). In practice, as we all know, authenticity and the "within-ness" of experience are extremely hard to define— bombarded as we are by the prevailing culture and socialization— except by intuition, as if from some pit of our being where the culture has not penetrated. But there is such a thing, we are sure of it, and it is this authenticity which all commercial mass media— that is, all mass media under capitalism—*must* violate; otherwise the goods might not get sold and the system might lose its reason for being. The risk is too great to chance.

Political experience is no exception to the debasement. Nothing is real unless it appears on TV. Demonstrators still surge to their separate homes from a campus uprising to catch the 6:00 news and assure themselves that something "really happened." Since the demonstration has almost always failed to achieve its purpose, ending the war or whatever, the only lasting "reality" it can have is what leaks through the television screen. This anticlimactic upshot is not the movement's fault, but inheres in the political situation within which the movement has found itself. If the event is not "covered," or is patently distorted, radicals will be angry at the networks, but underneath the anger is a sense of diminishment, a sense that the community of brothers and sisters, the demands, the billyclubs pounding, might not "really" have happened at all.

When experience becomes a commodity, the only remedy is to demolish the media and to create the movement as an alternative source of values, network of relations, and standard for authenticity. This Long March has barely been begun.

14

An intensity of direct political experience tends to break TV's hold on the consciousness.

First, living an event from the inside and then seeing the news distortion breaks one's confidence in television's coverage of that event, and then, by extension, may break any association between "coverage" and truth *in general*. An example: The striking Richmond, California, oil workers, having been beaten by police early in 1969, were now inclined to disbelieve the media's hostile account of the student strike at San Francisco State. And second, collective political experience establishes a new threshold for the sense of solidarity, and makes TV less "involving" by comparison.

15

But the media transform the movement as they transform all reality: they package it and retail it as a titillation or as a lightning-rod for the Americans' rage and bewilderment. Their capacity to flash the picture of a face or a symbol instantly around the world heightens the identification of politics with personality and symbol. Such identification backfires on radical politics, which becomes deformed to suit the needs of the media rather than the needs of communication to an outlying audience.

Politics becomes identified with certain public personae, particularly the ones who know how to condense their politics to media images or resounding slogans—Stokely Carmichael, the Yippie handful, and others. Then these individuals come to be received as leaders, though they cannot be held accountable to any definite group. So the media end up defining the national leaders; thereby they define the nature of revolutionary politics. The now-mediated personalities are tempted to temper their politics to the demands of television coverage—either to moderate them or to reduce them to simple formulas and symbols most easily disseminated through media. Tempted, and without firm resistance from a movement for which they pretend to speak, they almost always fall.

Likewise, there is a temptation to design projects or events for their mediability—the 1965 National Teach-In with its placid politics and acceptance of the matrix of debate, the 1965 Selma March, some aspects of the 1968 Chicago demonstrations ("the whole world is watching"). There are sometimes impressive

361

reasons to run the risk of being defined by the media, but such events are prone to reduce politics to those symbols most easily amplified. The Weathermen are children of television, for example, and the media are glad to transmit the symbols of their actions to identify radical politics with bombing. The network, with their quick reaction times and flexibility, have the advantage in amplifying symbols before the symbols can be altered, leaving the movement dependent on mass media (and on underground media enamored of the same symbols) for pointers of recognition. This unhappy parasitism teaches the young to emulate the most mediated forms of politics, the most violent, the least explained: it amplifies the symbols in its own bourgeois terms, distracting attention from the *causes* of bombing. Thus do the media exact revenge on the first turned-on generation. The very action which television stimulates and magnifies becomes deformed in the course of its infancy—it becomes routine, unthought, a spasm response to the latest atrocity. The movement loses the initiative to the media, and between the theatrical episodes it withdraws to its hibernation nooks and waits for the next crisis, the next "offensive." What began as exciting theater, helping the actors to define their political identity, degenerates into containable rage and narcissism. Here radical politics remains until it can separate itself from mediated images and come up with actions which are real and instructive to the participants and at the same time actually mobilize the best thoughts and energies of viewers—rather than leaving them mystified, or, if activated, activated into blind repetition of an event regardless of political circumstance.

Steady outreach beyond the youth ghettos, precisely the kind of organizing that is most necessary if a fragmented and bewildered movement is to become a popular upwelling, is also the least photogenic. Spectacular events should arise, if at all, as the fruition of steady work, not as a substitute for it. (It has become traditional for organizers of spectacular events to call them preludes to organizing campaigns, but this is ritualistic rhetoric. The events themselves almost always leave the participants either let down, reconfirmed in old patterns, or anxious to repeat the spectacle.)

It is no accident that, as I write, the two most lively and growing movements—women's and GIs'—are the least accommodating to the demands of mass media.

16

A revolutionary movement must aim to transform mass media by liberating communications technology for popular use. Nationalization of the technology by itself does not solve the problem of access—who is to have it, and under what conditions. One-way communication must disappear, and the producer-consumer relation be changed to a relationship among communicators. This requires a transformation of production (for subsistence, joy, human relationships) which would drown out the clamor of partial compensations.

The mass media in capitalist society are primary centers of capitalist enterprise, primary pipelines for capitalist values, primary weapons of social control. Thus the reconstitution of America requires expropriation of the mass media, which in turn requires the organization of publics who would then be capable of *using* the technology. Simply transferring control to the state, along English or French or Eastern European lines, would accomplish nothing except the creation of a new object of alienation. The stabilization function of the mass media in capitalism does not need commercials. Likewise, the rise of nonprofit "educational" television satisfies scarcely any of the need for unalienated, direct communication and betokens not the abolition of classes but rather a division in the present ruling class. Educational television represents the effort of its more enlightened wing to convey a more complex and civilized version of the world to an educated public. But if educational television's political criteria are looser than the commercial networks', they are nowhere near loose enough. Their main function seems to be channeling higher culture and liberal politics to people who claim high culture as a birthright. There is another function too: *New York Times* television writer Jack Gould once pointed out that educational television is "a lightning rod to draw away minority complaints against the practices and productions of commercial broadcasters." As things stand now, educational television and an occasional network muckraking documentary are like the last meal on Death Row.

Nor can an upsurge of popular pressure reform the present television system into a true medium of communication, as liberal FCC Commissioner Nicholas Johnson advises. External pressure can criticize this show and applaud that one, but it cannot transform the one-way direction of flow or the calcification of image into object. Since the days when President Hoover consulted with the broadcasting magnates before enunciating communications policy, government institutions including the FCC have shown themselves fundamentally and necessarily beholden to the men in power. This should occasion no surprise; it is the pattern, and, indeed, the rationalizing purpose of government regulation in general. Johnson's call for consumer activism does not challenge the networks' right to dominate the airwaves and does not assert the public's right to control, not just influence. Without contesting for power, the citizenry can only place a Band-aid over the hole in the dike.

But the purpose of insurgency is not power for its own sake, and in this regard media are no different from any other seat of power. As Enzensberger writes, "A socialist perspective which does not go beyond attacking existing property relationships is limited. The expropriation of Springer [the West German media baron] is a desirable goal but it would be good to know to whom the media should be handed over. The Party? To judge by all experience of that solution, it is not a possible alternative. It is perhaps no accident that the Left has not yet produced an analysis of the pattern of manipulation in countries with socialist regimes." Power must be contested in order to be dispersed, not hoarded. "The question," as Enzensberger adds, "is not whether the media are manipulated, but who manipulates them. A revolutionary plan should not require the manipulators to disappear; on the contrary, it must make everyone a manipulator."

And indeed the mass media are suited to this visionary proposal, for they are "egalitarian in structure" (Enzensberger). That is, the technology permits the multiplication of centers of power and initiative. A liberated society would at the very least abolish the national networks and make phone and broadcast facilities free, two-three-many-way and accessible to all individuals, groups, and communities. (National hookups for extraordinary occasions would be possible, but as organized publics become accustomed to their own initiative they would lose the need for national audiences.) Some of the technology exists (conference calls) and the rest, including feedback devices, is within striking distance. Of course such a Utopia would not be practicable without publics organized to make such demands on the technology: publics organized, indeed, in the process of making the revolution. One can easily imagine techniques for apportioning television time, which, though now limited artificially—consider all the unused UHF channels and the fact that the Pentagon controls about half the possible wavelengths—is still slim in proportion to the number of publics that could demand free time. For example, any group that could mobilize a given number of petitions in its behalf might have the right to a certain amount of television or radio time; the more adherents to the group, the more time. Even minorities unable to muster the requisite number of petitions could be allowed some time. (According to FCC Commissioner Johnson, such a petition plan already operates in Holland.) The cost of television cassettes could be reduced and, contrary to present corporate plans, the cassettes could be made interchangeable brand to brand. A steady traffic in home-produced cassettes would throw open the technology to all. A system in which communication replaces mediation would be complex, but business already does much of it for itself (closed circuit and cable television, WATS lines, teletypes) and what we need is an enormous expansion in scale and access. But since mass media are organic to advanced capitalism, which monopolizes the communications resources, no real public communications system is possible short of revolution.

More, the revolution necessary for equal access to technology would itself require the liberated technology. Consider this image of production in a revolutionary society: workers share control of industry with communities and publics. (Workers would not operate the factory strictly on their own, since industry has consequences—like pollution—which affect people other than the workers in any particular factory or industry.) Cynics have cited the inclusion of outside forces as an argument against workers' control, on the assumption that public opinion can only be mobilized by representative democracy, whereupon we are back to the present system. But two-way technology offers the possibility of debate among rival positions, followed by a directly democratic vote employing television feedback devices and computers. The technology does not prohibit this development; rather, it brings it within the realm of technical possibility. Here is another case in which capitalist property relations (owning the right to public airwaves) impede the forces of production (the technology *and* skilled workers) and must be overthrown in order to liberate them.

The impulse arises to chant "Smash the TV sets, smash them all"—how we chortled when Robert Gover's Kitty did just that in *The Hundred Dollar Misunderstanding!* So estranged have we been from TV in practice that we tend toward an easy Luddite attitude, assuming that the technology itself is pernicious. But the technology in itself has the capacity to help us realize our humanity by compensating for physical distance, even if we use it, like the telephone, only to discover its limitations. Politically, open communications could constitute an obstacle to the pyramiding of power that characterizes all previous civilizations, since power requires, among other things, a monopoly of information at the top. Therefore we do not propose Luddism as a response to mass media, but rather a decentralization of power through the use of technology. The alternative, indeed, is a calcified, centralized communications apparatus which, like Eastern Europe's, cannot even trust the citizens with that marvel of two-way communications, the duplicating machine (Enzensberger).

The new comics and American culture

PAUL BUHLE

> The end of the history of culture manifests itself on two
> opposite sides: the project of its transcendence in total
> history, and the organization of its preservation as a dead
> object in spectacular contemplation. One of these move-
> ments has tied its fate to social critique, the other to the
> defense of class power. (Guy Debord, Society of the
> Spectacle)

Art in the twentieth century, as the Frankfort school theorists
have noted, has lost its aura and become a mere extension of
production.[1] "High Culture" withdraws from the masses to
preserve itself, but by the very act of withdrawal undercuts its
own ability to express universal values and becomes increasingly
incomprehensible.[2] At best, the older forms of Art are removed
to a pedestal, and are backward-looking to a time of flowering
bourgeois culture in Europe when they could be both meaningful
and relatively popular. At worst, they are transmuted via the
cinema and other forms into a kind of pacification for the modern
intelligentsia: one steps into an expensive theater to watch a
profitable "Art" movie, certain that such activity provides relief
from the fetishized relations during working hours at the factory or
the university. In fact, as the Situationists put it, Culture becomes

367

a prestige commodity which sells itself and others, a striking example of manipulation through mass false consciousness.[3]

One could say, pessimistically, that mass culture has destroyed the basis of all Art, high and low. Walter Benjamin suggested that Guillaume Apollinaire's vision of War as the supreme Art was a logical outcome of Art-for-Art's-Sake. Mankind's "self-alienation has reached such a degree that it can experience its own destruction as an aesthetic pleasure of the first order." This pleasure is felt by viewers of *Fellini's Satyricon* (or films of a similar genre).[4] Meanwhile, the more utilitarian art such as poster-making becomes more and more for the hucksterism that Culture has been made: undisguised trash ladled out in ever-greater quantities for the population. Theodor Adorno commented in the late 1940's that even the ideologies of repression seemed unimportant, as the totalitarian force of absolute reification threatened to absorb Culture entirely.[5]

Yet simultaneously with this cultural decline, social conditions have become increasingly prepared for a mass overcoming of the limitations hitherto imposed upon Art. Born of the division of mental and manual labor, Art faces the potentiality of a society in which this division is at last transcended. The abolition of scarcity and the beginning of "true human history" (as Marx called Socialism) imply that all facets of life including each cultural artifact may both "function" and serve deeper desires. Within technological developments, as Jeremy Shapiro observes, the "dream becomes translatable," the unconscious mind is rearranged and combined with the formerly "outside" world in a new fashion. The capacity of Art, to "synthesize the universal and the particular, form and content, in a manner that was impossible in other realms of experience," becomes a capacity of all life. Thus the promise of mass participation in the highest social forms, now offered as a vulgar apology for the quality of life within advanced capitalism, may under transformed circumstances be redeemed. The much-discussed "one-dimensionality" of men and women today may be seen as a mere educational period in human history.[6]

368

Nowhere more than in American culture do these threats and promises of mass society seem observable and salient. From colonial days, American life has offered an alternative to the dichotomy of "inwardness" (the development of the human spirit) and historical activity (the development of the world's resources). Americans have stubbornly refused to accept an inorganic view of life, in which one may either think or do; rather, they have insisted that, by acting, the individual gains a new interiority, one which is informed by the struggles of life. Less restricted in nearly all aspects than European society, American social forces have spawned rich forms of mass culture such as the cinema, jazz music, and comic strips, and such nakedly philistinistic trash as modern advertising. The ongoing "struggle between the powers of light and darkness," temporally represented in America by the forces for social transformation and those leaning toward barbarism, has been in recent decades accelerated to a furious pace.[7] Cultural rejuvenation presents itself in hundreds of ways from the revolt of the young to the more general effort to reconcile Americans with their remaining natural resources; and meanwhile cultural decadence continues to make inroads through the deadening of the senses in urban environments, the repressive desublimation of "skin shows" in nightclubs and through movies, and the transformation of politics itself to a game of transparent "images" designed to soothe rather than persuade. Perhaps nowhere in the West will the outcome of this struggle become apparent earlier than in America. And we may find that the most apparently pedestrian forms, such as comic strips, can provide us with significant clues.

Comic strips first appeared around the turn of the century, in an era where a reconciliation of mass culture and the developed Arts seemed altogether possible. Concurrent with the rise of jazz and the silent cinema, "yellow journalism" newspapers carried several of the most extraordinary comics ever published. "Little Nemo," by Windsor MacKay, was a continuing story, drawn in luridly beautiful art-nouveau patterns, of a child's marvelous dream adventures. Although each strip was ended

369

by a call from Nemo's mother, over the years the child gained increasing control of his dreams.[8] Around the same time "Krazy Kat" appeared, drawn by George Herriman, a study of social relations through the lives of three desert characters: a mouse of indefinable sex, a "kat" in love with her/him, and a "kop" who invariably arrested the mouse for heaving a brick at the kat. Herriman's characters spoke in an accent which strongly suggested both Dickens and Yiddish, and in a way that broke down logical word structure. (For instance, when Ignatz the mouse remarks that "The bird is on the wing," Krazy answers that "From rissant obserwation I should say the wing is on the bird.")[9] These two strips were joined by the wildly nihilistic "Katzenjammer Kids" (about whom "the Captain" once said, "For them kids reality iss nix!") and a number of other strips, the best of which were at once popular and artistically innovative works. Together they suggested, perhaps, a strand of the contemporary thread that John Reed claimed to have found linking Cubism to the Industrial Workers of the World.[10]

In much the same way that the liberating aspects of ragtime were subverted through stylized jazz (e.g., Paul Whiteman) and the social drama and comedy of the Chaplin films, for instance, were replaced by shallow romance and "family humor" in later years, the comics were gradually, unevenly, stripped of their lunatic qualities. Despite their physical enlargement in the 1920's, their quality stagnated. In the 1930's sheer draftsmanship improved, as in the Tarzan strips of Burne Hogarth and Hal Foster, but imagination dwindled. In political terms, the graphic realism from the jungles of the Phantom to the urban setting of the various crimebuster detectives hid a literary fantasy: that America was all right except for the intrusion of outlaws, later Japs and Nazis, and still later Reds. During wartime the comics further degenerated into regimentation. Underground comics entrepreneur Don Schenker remembers his disappointment when the always-racist Terry joined the military and Dick Tracy realized that funny-looking people were criminals.[11]

During the late 1940's there was something of a revival. Will

THE SPIRIT

WILL EISNER

THE TWO-FISTED SPIRIT, SO MUCH FEARED BY THE EVIL UNDERWORLD, IS NONE OTHER THAN DENNY COLT, WHOM THE POLICE BELIEVE DEAD.

BURIED BY MISTAKE IN WILDWOOD, THE SPIRIT USES THE VERY GRAVE HE AROSE FROM AS A HEADQUARTERS FOR HIS WAR AGAINST CRIME....

Hidden underground in desolate, forgotten Wildwood Cemetery, is the Spirit's secret hideaway ----

Here, under the seemingly bleak surface is a complete home and laboratory from which many criminals have been traced and sent to justice ... only Ebony, the Spirit's faithful little friend, shares these secret vaults with the great crimefighter ---

OH, EBONY, I .... HEY!! WHERE ARE YOU?

Two weeks ago, the Spirit and Ebony rescued a young woman from a crashed plane ... she was badly hurt, so they rushed her to a hospital ... BUT, on their way, they were halted by ANOTHER girl, who, at pistol point, took the injured girl into her car and drove off ---

The next day, the papers announced the news that Gloria Fillum missed the fatal plane, but that a girl friend had used her ticket instead ..... one look at Gloria's picture, and the Spirit left at once for Hollywood ....

YES, I MIGHT AS WELL FACE IT!! THE SPIRIT IS AFTER ME... BUT WHY SHOULD I WORRY... TO ALL THE WORLD I'M GLORIA FILLUM... AND ALL THE LUXURY THAT GOES WITH THE NAME IS--- MINE!!

Eisner's "The Spirit" was an extremely innovative, well-drawn strip filled with personal irony. Walt Kelly's "Pogo" displayed far more true brilliance of caricature and dialogue before the strip's overt politicization. Even the work of Al Capp, which in its maturity became the worst sort of parody, provided some interesting American archetypes through "Mammy" Yokum and her kin. Later, Charles Schulz and a very few others offered minor relief to the tedium of such strips as "Juliet Jones" and "Judge Parker." Jules Feiffer developed a self-consciousness of middle class neuroses for a limited, mostly middle-class, adult readership. Yet altogether, the comics of the late 1960's were far inferior to their counterparts a half-century earlier. "Mary Worth," "Kerry Drake," "Apartment 3-G," and most others lack even the rudiments of a good comic strip: they are crudely drawn, weak-plotted, and almost completely humorless.

During the final years of the Depression, the first widespread numbers of comic *books* appeared. These were the bastard children of cartoon animation and the older newspaper comics, expertly designed for an audience of children. As Jules Feiffer recalls, there was in the first days of the books a real madness among the artists, a frenzy-producing sense that a *new art form* was being invented, as indeed it was.[12]

In part, the kids' comic books posed a means for children to learn in a world where real-life adults were excluded. The main characters of the most popular variety, super-heroes, were direct emanations from the fantasies of American children and children-grown-up. The heroes (and a few heroines) shared the brutality and racism of their counterparts on the radio, the newspaper strips, and the "bloody pulp" magazines, but their values were not wholly those emerging in post-war, state-regulated capitalism. At the very least the super-heroes were indifferent to making money, suspicious of the authority which police and the armed forces in the real world demand, and, in the best comics, brilliantly ironic about the irrelevance of their own powers to solve social and personal problems.

On the other hand, the comic books were scarcely resistant to the worst values of the larger society. In many strips near the end of the war, the super-hero received a commendation from F.D.R. or J. Edgar Hoover. The flag was waved relentlessly because the books were so unrelievedly mediocre. One incident reveals the generally unutilized power of the strips for social manipulation. "Wonder Woman" was begun and promoted to put forth the heroic role of the American woman during wartime. In 1943, All American Comics hired tennis champion and leader of women's physical culture Alice Marble, and William Moulton Marston, inventor of the lie-detector machine and a notable author on women's specialized qualities as a civilizing influence upon society, to create a female leviathan. These authors equipped Wonder Woman not only with great physical powers but also with a mythology, in which the gods had decreed that whenever men could dupe this genuine Amazon with pretended love, she would lose her strength and become as weak as *every other woman.*[13] Yet even Wonder Woman, so carefully designed for social impact, was drawn artlessly. Feiffer notes that after the first breathless years of comic books, the artists themselves settled down, became average middle-class Americans less interested in experimentation with the comic form than in the regular salary checks which hack work produced. The few exceptionally well-drawn figures (e.g., Captain Marvel, a partial-parody on Superman, ultimately destroyed in an oligopolistic copyright battle with the latter) were no more popular than the worst drawn. A generation later the super-hero comics made a comeback through the Marvel and DC companies' lines. In the last several years, the comic titans have been humanized psychologically and to a lesser extent physically. And while they have grown more vulnerable, they have also absorbed a smattering of populistic politics (patronization of blacks and hippies, implied attacks on repressive symbols such as Judge Julius Hoffman, etc.)[14] Still, the major paths of innovation in comics lie elsewhere.

The most significant innovations in the postwar years occurred in the "Funny Animal" comics, above all in the Duck Family series. The comedy of animal-people fits a classic archetype for literary humor: tremendously active, emprical-minded but modestly dignified creatures living out adventures, usually freer in their options than ordinary humans.[15] Their animal and human roles were merged to exaggerate characteristics, for example in the shy Mickey Mouse, the noisy and irritating Donald Duck, or the dog Pluto who somehow retains his submission as a pet even outside ordinary "human" society. Carl Barks, who drew many of the Duck adventures, has been the most inventive and painstaking artist in all comics, both in storyline and artwork. Indeed, Barks' creations may be properly considered the most nearly complete crystallizations of comic art yet produced. During Barks' most fruitful period of the early and middle 1950's, he drew a series of tales involving Donald, the Nephews, Scrooge McDuck, and Gyro Gearloose with an exquisite care for details and above all a sensitivity about the nature of Americans. His characters reflected a sort of transplanted Dickensianism in their portraiture: Donald Duck, the short-tempered, easily angered but well-meaning uncle, too lazy and individualistic to hold onto a regular job; Scrooge, the hard-hearted American Capitalist who is solely devoted to the increase of cash in his vault; the nephews Huey, Looie, and Dewey, with their infallible Junior Woodchuck book crammed with all conceivable mechanical details; and Gyro, a haywire Henry Ford.[16]

Around the same time the wildly destructive Bugs Bunny, with his ruthless attacks on the small property-owning conservatism of Elmer Fudd, further developed the ambiguity inherent in the "Funny Animal" motif. Sometimes Elmer would chase him with a shotgun (as an ordinary, carrot-robbing rabbit), sometimes Elmer would have to run against him for mayor or otherwise compete with him on a human level. Meanwhile Little Lulu appeared, brilliantly playing upon the tensions between small boys and girls, and between all children and the adult world. In a typical story, Lulu would be obliged to submit to Tubby's boylike insistence upon getting his own way (either because he made too much trouble otherwise, or because Lulu's mother enforced politeness toward boys), but would triumph through some shrewdness. Parents were almost invariably middle-aged and dull-witted. Like the Duck family, Bugs and Lulu have survived the advent of television. But their circulation (and by implication, importance to children) dropped off seriously in the late fifties and early sixties, and the quality of the caricatures often did as well. The finest stories are now found mostly among the items "Reprinted by Popular Request," both in the case of Barks and that of Marjorie Henderson Buell, artist of Little Lulu.[17]

In the boom years of the comics during the late 1940's and early 1950's, a far smaller but equally important development had been taking place. William M. Gaines, heir to a minor comic book company, created a line of "EC" comics which carried out the boldest satire of American society at the time, and largely inspired the shock which resulted in the Comics Code Authority. One of the most famous figures in comic strip history, Harvey Kurtzman, had written a satirical post-war comic, "Hey Look," which despite its crude drawing was a breakthrough in intent. During the late forties he emerged as a major editor of EC, perhaps the most exacting editor ever to direct a comic series. In the EC science fiction comics, retained by Gaines despite their financial losses, Kurtzman researched his subject heavily and wrote only three or four stories per month.[18] The result was a scrupulously careful drawing style and a story line unsurpassed in action comics, as in "Judgment Day," a science fiction strip concerning orange robots who treat blue robots as inferiors. In the strip finale, the Galactic Republic inspector refuses citizenship to the planet, and the Earthman from the Republic takes off his helmet—to reveal that he is a Negro. In EC war comics, published during the Korean conflict, an unvarnished, unpatriotic view of war was offered, revealing what joyless lives are led by the average servicemen.[19] EC's satire comics, *Mad* and *Panic,* were brilliant attacks upon the banal and self-destructive elements of American life. For instance, in a satire on Barks' Donald Duck, a character is dragged out of the panel for refusing to wear white gloves (as the totalitarian "Walt Dizzy" had commanded); or Joe McCarthy is rendered a huckster in a satire on a television show, "What's My Shine?" Artists

375

Wallace Wood, Jack Davis, Bill Elder, Al Feldstein, and Basil Wolverton brought a wealth of detail and intricate plotting unsurpassed except by Barks himself.[20]

However, along with the boom of the comics a fear of their power had grown among censorship-minded citizens, especially those Catholic lay activists who sought to impose bans on improper forms of popular culture. In 1954, the would-be suppressionists were given their Bible, written by New York psychologist Frederic Wertham and titled *Seduction of the Innocent,* a supposed documentation of crime-provoking comics. At last, Congressional investigations developed and Gaines was brought to court over his horror series, a money-maker for EC which helped finance its less prosperous but more aesthetic lines. In time, the Comics Code was created, a self-censoring agency. Although ostensibly voluntary, the code operated so that books without the seal of approval were driven off the stands by political goon-squads composed primarily of PTA groups. The results of this repression were twofold: first, as with all regulating agencies, the Comics Code Authority wiped out most of the small competitors; second, literary censorship, turned political, and EC comics which revealed any doubts about the correctness of patriotism and the American Way were refused. (In the story mentioned above, "Judgment Day," the Code Authority insisted that the human spaceman be made a Caucasian. Gaines refused and closed out the Incredible Science Fiction line with that number.) The Comics Code demonstrably did not halt the rise of juvenile delinquency.[21]

Gaines ultimately dropped his comics for *Mad,* which was transformed into a magazine, and from savage satire to family-comedy-humor which middle-class American teens could enjoy without threat of insight. McLuhan called the transformed *Mad* a "TV vestibule," an extension of the media.[22] Kurtzman left *Mad* after a disagreement with Gaines, and spent much of the following decade attempting to recreate an adequate vehicle for his satirical talents. *Humbug* and *Help!* lasted several years each, but neither they nor a one-shot magazine *Trump* succeeded financially. In the mid-sixties Kurtzman abandoned his ambition and joined the staff of *Playboy* for which he wrote (and his former artist, Bill Elder, drew) "Little Annie Fanny," a harmless titillator. Yet Kurtzman had made his impact upon both artists and a vague but real following of readers who—to judge from personal testimony—regarded themselves as an Embattled Minority within a very repressed and repressive society.[23]

The Undergrounds

Certain artists who began drawing "underground" strips for comics and newspapers in the middle and late sixties shared few attitudes with their overground contemporaries. Although influenced by the best work within the tradition, especially that of Windsor MacKay, Carl Barks, Wally Wood, and Basil Wolverton, the young artists carried into their efforts a different and more independent attitude. Many of the earliest undergrounders drew for college humor magazines, which had been the major dissident voices on the campuses from the late forties to the early sixties. While repetitively irreverent and "daring," the magazines had sometimes published short stories and drawings of real value and, more important, had brought together varieties of outgroups whose very existence refused to the rah-rah fraternity-sorority pace-setters the full awe of the campus. Other artists drew and wrote for, or published, "fanzines," hectographed or mimeographed publications of extremely limited circulation (anywhere from 50 to 500) which had sprung up originally among science fiction fans in the late thirties with the growing accessibility of mimeograph machines.[24] By the late fifties, hundreds of adolescents put together their own fanzines, sometimes exclusively science fiction oriented but often as broad as the editor's interests, from comics to politics.

Only with the growth of the underground newspapers, however, did the artists find a medium which could furnish a substantial ready audience for their work. Implied in the creation and rapid spread of the underground press in 1966–68 was the creation of a new community, actually many fairly similar communities of culturally alienated people, almost all of whom were young. *Mad*

377

may have appealed to a self-repressed tradition of cultural alienation in the 1950's but its editors and artists hardly knew who or what its audience was, and comics-collectors like fanzine readers and publishers were usually mere eccentrics rather than any sort of social rebels. In the 1960's, however, all of America recognized the archetypal long-haired, dope-smoking, sexually freer units of young people who gathered in college towns and big cities and increasingly avowed their own distinct identity. The youths began to see in their papers, roughly, what ethnic groups had seen in their own specialized sheets at the turn of the century: a sense of identity which the mass press could not provide. Rather naturally, the youths began to look for comic strips which reflected their needs and sense of humor rather than those of Juliet Jones and Brenda Starr.

By the mid-1960's, several immediate predecessors to the underground comic books had already appeared. Joel Beck, an artist for the University of California satire magazine *The Pelican,* drew a small, crudely-printed book, *Lenny of Laredo;* Jack Jackson, of the *Texas Ranger* humor magazine (which, like several of the best of its type, was banned from the campus) at the University of Texas, put together *God Nose* with the help of Gilbert Shelton and others; also in Austin, Foolbert Sturgeon published his own *Adventures of Jesus.* All shared a satirical tone which was barely a step removed from collegiate humor and *Mad* magazine, and their circulations were extremely limited. The breakthrough to a mass audience came in 1966 and after, with the publication of Gilbert Shelton's drawings in *The Rag* (Austin's underground paper, significantly one of the first hippie-political, community sheets, located in an early center for widespread bohemian life-styles), the appearance of several strips in New York's *East Village Other,* and the distribution of a few underground papers heavily devoted to comics, such as *Yarrowstalks* from Philadelphia. In 1967–68, the few papers turned into hundreds, and as loose reprinting practices immediately developed the better artists were given exposure across the country.

378

In early 1968 two little-magazine publishers in Berkeley, Don Donahue and Charles Plymell, were so fascinated by Robert Crumb's drawings in *Yarrowstalks* that they sought him out to draw a comic book.[25] In February, ZAP # 1 appeared. ZAP was taken up by Don Schenker, the owner of a poster business in Berkeley. While publishing ZAP # 2 and # 3 over 1968, Schenker also initiated *Yellow Dog,* the first all-comics sheet (published in tabloid form its first dozen issues, and in comic book form thereafter).

Schenker did no editing (i.e., requesting artists to rewrite or change their work). On principle, his notion was that the comics artist was the "cartographer" of the hip community in development, the archetypal figure "who is sickest of the madness" of the outside society and "rather than die, found in desperation a doctoring talent" in himself.[26] In the next several years Schenker played a vital role in the comics' development: promoter, distributor, non-editor, he had encouraged the artists to go their own way at their own rates of development.

The results were immediate. First with a trickle—perhaps fifteen comic paper numbers and books appeared in the year from early 1968 to early 1969—and then with growing numbers the comics began to circulate in head shops and a few newsstands around the country. By mid-1970 their circulation was extended to a sales of 40,000 of the best books, and a readership which far exceeded nominal sales since any one book would be frequently circulated among several hands within the community.

To those adult Americans who are on fringes of the hip community but do not regularly read underground newspapers or comics, only one artist is likely to be familiar. Robert Crumb most thoroughly of all the artists comprehends, portrays, and embodies the dilemmas of the middle class. As a child he drew comics with his brothers and sisters. Even before puberty, he was "publishing" an amateur comic called FUNNY FRIENDS, in reality a composition notebook which was handed around to neighborhood pals. In the late fifties, he and a brother published FOO, a fanzine imitation of EC Comics which after a few issues went bankrupt.

380

Crumb later claimed that he was more influenced by the enemas administered by his mother than by anything else, but more probably the metropolitan environment of the several cities where he grew up made a lasting impression upon him. As his brother-in-law, Marty Pahls, reflected, Crumb was shaped by "the whole tradition of Americana, from open trolley-cars and minstrel shows down through the 1920's vocal crooners and hack-cartoon styles through the jive of the Forties and the pimple-rock teen-ageism of the Fifties, to the truss ads in the back of tabloid newspapers and the little old Polish ladies on the back of the Euclid Avenue bus" in Cleveland.[27]

In 1962, Crumb was hired by the American Greeting Card Corporation in Cleveland, and promoted to the Highbrow Cards division (from which several of his unsigned cards are still available). In 1964 he married and went to Europe, and during his two-year stay contributed several strips to Harvey Kurtzman's *Help!* magazine including sketchbook commentaries on Bulgaria, and on Harlem.[28] In 1966 Crumb returned to America, living first in Manhattan, then Cleveland, and finally San Francisco's Haight-Ashbury. Since that time he has traveled around a good deal, settling finally in a farm in rural California, with his wife, a goat, and some chickens. He makes one grand tour a year for about two months, meeting friends and new people, collecting old 78 records for his jukebox, and gathering ideas in his sketchbook for his work the rest of the year.[29]

The transformation of Crumb's style from the mid-1960's has been very substantial, as can be grasped from a study of his first commercially-published books (in fact, the first of any underground artist), *Head Comics* and *Fritz the Cat*. Early Fritz strips are clearly in the college humor tradition, with a purposefully "sexy" quality and a surprise ending. Over several years Crumb added greatly to the complexity of the Fritz strips, drawing some in the *Fritz* book which are the comic equivalent of novel length. In "Fritz Bugs Out" (1965) and "Fritz the No-Good" (1968), Crumb derives a familiar campus character who drops out to go through a series of adventures from smoking dope to becoming a half-hearted revolutionary terrorist. At times in these strips,

Crumb's drawing reached its most intense level through his careful, detailed sketchwork and his improvisation of comic equivalent-to-cinema camera shots (most nearly perfected in comics by Carl Barks). Yet the central characters, and above all Fritz, remained one-dimensional, the stories revealing merely action rather than character development.

Crumb is far better known for his more sketchy but characterful drawings, in which he reveals a powerful cultural critique of American life. In the first several pages of *Head Comics* we learn that Crumb is "one of the world's last great medieval thinkers" (at least a half-ironic self-assessment), concerned with offering the reader perceptions about "Life Among the Constipated" in middle America. His story of "Whiteman" ("The story of a civilization in crisis") reveals that American as worst beset by his own self-delusions and repressions. Several rhyming sequences, includ-

ing "Stoned." ("He She It Stoned/Epileptic Fit Stoned/Phoney Baloney Own Stoned/Call Em On the Phone Stoned") and "Hey Boparee Bop" (including the verses "Surrender to the Void, Cloid/But I'm Looking for My Lost Cross, Boss/Ferget this Apple Sauce, Hoss. . . .") typically provide an entertaining narrative which leads inexorably to a description of the repressive Protestant values turning Americans' energies in upon themselves.

Crumb is perhaps best known for the characters created during his Haight Street days and maintained fitfully since. "Mr. Natural" is a guru based, according to one story, on a real spiritualist that Crumb's friends visited or, according to another, on an acid-vision Crumb himself had. In any case, Natural illustrates and elaborates the clearest perceptions of the Youth community: on the one hand he insists upon a rigor of life which puts aside television, rock music, and in short all of the mess of metropolitan living; and on the other hand shows that he is no dreamy mystic but rather practical-minded about eating, making love, and destroying the illusions which separate hippies from meeting the problems of the outside world. Natural's alter-ego is Flakey Foont, an average, sexually repressed middle-class American male who partakes in all the apparatus of Youth Culture (drugs, language, etc.) without, however, being able to liberate himself. Lost in the labyrinths of modern civilization, Flakey remains horny, takes too many baths, and constantly tries, unconvincingly, to show Mr. Natural that his spiritual advice is no longer needed. It is generally believed that the character-source for Flakey is Crumb himself, and in fact Foont does bear a resemblance to an earlier caricature, "Edgar Crump," who is more transparently autobiographical.

Comic readers have often been surprised at Crumb's utilization of violence and sex. He has sought to use both in order to reduce the distance between real life and the strips, without, however, diminishing the caricaturist, or "larger than life," aspect of comics. Often an internal joke is played by his utilization of comic-like forms for realistic purposes, as in an early strip, "Those Cute Little Bearsie-Wearsies," which depicted two teddy-bears seriously discussing their homosexuality. In one of his most startling strips, "Neato-Keeno Time" (starring "Pam Goodvibes" and "Pete, the Teenage Prick," two typical high school figures), the hero stabs his girlfriend to death with a fork, rapes her, and later uses the fork for dinner. Crumb's best-known ploy, however, has been pornography. With the encouragement of S. Clay Wilson, and the printing aid of Don Donahue, Crumb collaborated in the creation of *Snatch Comix* in 1968.[30] Snatch and its successors were clear satires on the old "Eight Papers," or "Tijuana Bibles," which circulated the country via traveling salesmen and truck drivers from the 1930's to the 1950's. Here, Crumb claimed to give the public what it wanted: titillation, carried to such an extreme, however, that the product was a self-lampoon, the ultimate commentary on the ludicrous and pathological implications of Americans' sexual fantasies. Ironically, the major legal action against underground comics came with one of Crumb's less blatant sexual satires: in ZAP # 4, he pictured incest without guilt, a joyful father-daughter and mother-son set of relationships (including oral-genital sex) which led the happy parents to conclude that youth is "the Hope of the Future"—indeed, a perverse future for American life.[31]

Recently, Crumb seems to have passed through his pornography period and turned to other tasks. In several full books and many strips, Crumb has taken up the problems of city life in greater detail. One comic about Detroit in particular, *Motor City,* suggests that the machines are taking over, wiping out the "fleshopoids" whom they despise. Another, properly called *Despair,* reflects upon the overwhelming nature of the problems in America and counsels no hope as the only "salvation" to the constant hostilities, sexual fantasizing, and fruitless searches for meaning that Crumb sees around him in big cities. Other comics extend the characters Crumb has created. Mr. Natural is surveyed more fully in a comic entirely of his own, including a hand-lettered prose commentary on Natural's suspected origins, as analyzed by Crumb. (In fact, the study greatly increases Natural's Americanism: snake oil salesman, prophet, wanderer, he is many things to America's past half-century.) "Honeybunch Kaminsky," first pictured in

"Snatch" as "Jailbait of the Month," is carried through an extensive narrative, "She's Leaving Home": here, the struggle for self-fulfillment of a sixteen-year-old runaway focuses around non-understanding parents, brutal police, a love-making but exploiting boyfriend, and finally the Women's Liberation Movement. "Bobo Bolinski" ("Just a Nutty Little Nobody from Newark, NJ"), an industrial worker, stumbles from one problem to another. And "Projunior," an avowed revolutionary (and sometimes lover of Honeybunch) goes through the paces of struggling with his own rhetoric for relevance.

Crumb's most obvious blind spot has been his use of female stereotypes, not so much in a cruel fashion but rather as cardboard figures off which to bounce the existential-sexual dilemmas

of males. In *Big Ass Comics,* women became the ultimate castrators, female vultures who, however, would do anything for a good stiff prick. In *Motor City* # 1, Lenore Goldberg, Crumb's caricature of a militant women's activist, was treated with insight but without empathy. As a result, criticism was showered on Crumb from a variety of sources. According to rumor, Crumb was hard-hit by the criticism that his drawing had aided in the repression of women by seemingly picturing their problems as sexual hang-ups, so hard hit in fact that he abandoned drawing for several months. A partial response was offered in *Motor City* # 2, where the same Lenore Goldberg is pictured experiencing

The Origins of MR. NATURAL

THIS TINY BATTERED PHOTOGRAPH MAY BE THE FIRST ONE EVER TAKEN OF MR. NATURAL, BUT THE EXPERTS HAVE DIFFERENT OPINIONS. BACK OF PHOTO IS INSCRIBED WITH THE NAME "FRED" BUT IS NOT MR. NATURAL'S HANDWRITING.

EARLIST KNOWN PHOTOGRAPH THAT IS DEFINITELY THE VENERABLE ONE IS THIS PORTRAIT SIGNED "F. NATURAL, WESSINGTON SPRINGS, S.D., 1908" HANDWRITING EXPERTS HAVE VERIFIED THE SIGNATURE, AND AN OLD-TIMER STILL LIVING IN ALCESTER, SOUTH DAKOTA, RECALLS A MAN NAMED FRED NATURAL WHO JOBBED AROUND THAT AREA IN THOSE DAYS. HE REMEMBERS HIM AS A "NICE QUIET FELLOW".

MANY OF YOU Mr. Natural fans have asked that we run an article on the man's past life and early background. Certainly a life history on Mr. Natural is a fascinating idea, and so, with a certain amount of skepticism, we set about investigating. Our doubts were confirmed as we ran into one blind alley after another, and finally were forced to abandon trying to fill in several large gaps in his past. Whole decades, in fact, are entirely missing. A frustrating experience for the conscientious historian and Mr. Natural enthusiast.

His childhood is completely clouded in obscurity. His birthplace and birthdate are entirely unknown. No records have been found, and no relatives, and, of course, no one has been able to squeeze an ounce of information out of the Old Man Himself (except, according to him, that his father is still alive and well, but he won't tell us where.) All knowledge of his life has been gathered without his help or support, and the whole

project leaves him "cold", as he puts it.

The 1908 photograph is the earliest proof we have of his existence. The photo was sent to us by Mrs. Ada Cooper, a Mr. Natural fan who found the old picture in a trunk full of her mother's belongings. Mrs. Cooper says she can never remember her mother, now deceased, ever mentioning that she knew Mr. Natural.

As for his age at the time the photograph was taken, he appears to have been between thirty-five and forty, which would make him close to one-hundred years old today!!

Not a clue exists as to his whereabouts between 1908 and 1921, the year our wild young wiseman moved to Chicago, where he stayed up to 1929. Here we lose track of the elusive sage for another seven years. But we managed to hunt down several people who knew him in "that toddlin' town" in the twenties, and so have gathered a fairly complete picture of Mr. Natural's adventures through that lurid decade.

In the fall of 1921 Mr. Natural got a job in a drugstore as an errand runner on the near north side. (Some believe the drugstore was a front for a speak-easy and that it was Natch's job to deliver

387

adventures that end somewhat unhappily but realistically: trapped by a police agent's trick, Lenore splits for Canada and begins to rebuild a primitive, communal life for herself. Crumb's latest book, *Home Grown Funnies,* however, returns to stereotyping through the guise of the "Earth Mother" mythos. The heroine of a lengthy story is a Yetti or "Abominable Snowwoman" who gains power over a typically repressed American male caught accidentally in nature. For Crumb, women remain larger than life.

The enduring theme in Crumb's mature work is the utterly destructive nature of a modern American culture. The civilization of the cities is for him a dying civilization, with no apparent reserves to extricate itself. Crumb offers a "return to nature" as a panacea, but apparently only half-seriously, for he knows that the centers of power to destroy or transform the society remain within the cities. He has no solution to modern dilemmas. He may, as in a recent satire for *Slow Death Funnies,* vaguely urge the Flakey Foonts all over America to do something about the

crisis. But, in any case, Crumb's power is not in his exhortation, nor in his political wisdom per se. His vision of American life is one-dimensional, lacking any real sensitivity to the values of the older ethnic (mostly working-class) and black cultures or the vibrancy contained in the women's self-development. Crumb is a destroyer of illusions, a pathologist of America's fantasy of Progress; as such, he is a supreme realist who provides humor to force down the message about that which is sordid and

WONDER WART-HOG'S
Believe It or LEAVE It!
ZAP
YOU DON'T KNOW HOW GOOD YOU GOT IT HERE IN AMERICA, BUB.
FOR EXAMPLE:
SOME UNFORTUNATE NATIONS ARE CONTROLLED BY SECRET TOTALITARIAN NEO-FASCISTS, MASQUERADING THEIR PHILOSOPHY WITH SUCH MISLEADING WORDS AS "CHRISTIAN," "DEMOCRATIC," ETC.
DER HONOR GUARD ISS FORMED, YOUR MOST EXALTED AND BELOVED EXCELLENCY!
AT EASE, OBERLIEUTENANT.
IN SOME FOREIGN COUNTRIES GOVERNMENT SPIES "TAP" PRIVATE TELEPHONES AND OPEN PEOPLE'S MAIL WITHOUT EVEN ASKING THEIR PERMISSION!
CONTINUED

unendurable for whole human beings. He reinforces the seriousness of his intent, finally, by a perpetual attempt to destroy illusions about himself. In *Despair Comics,* he mocked "panty-waist"
artists who elevated their work, reminding the reader that Art
was "only lines on paper." Elsewhere, he intimates that the
readers are not so unlike him—they are potentially talented but
frustrated, unable to see their ways clear to constructive action.
Indeed, the power of Crumb's humor rests upon his dialectical
relationship with the reader: he is Edgar Crump (or Flakey
Foont) and simultaneously a voice of explanation and exhortation. His dilemmas are ours. His fears and desires, which manifest
themselves as the height of wry humor, are ours also.[32]

Only one other artist combines a similar level of skill with a
more-or-less constant productivity. Gilbert Shelton may be considered the over-30 dean of the comics, and unlike Crumb, who
seems to act only through drawing, Shelton has brought together
a publishing firm and generally kept things going among artists.

Shelton's work goes back to the very early 1960's, when he was
a graduate student in history at the University of Texas. He began
drawing strips and cartoons for local college humor magazines,
typically intellectualized and political in a liberal-radical way.
Shelton's first great innovation was "Wonder Wart-Hog," a
super-hero satire right out of the old Superman tradition. The
alter-ego of WWH, Philbert Desenex, worked at the *Muthalode
Morning Mungpie,* and with the help of the 900-pound wart-hog
dealt with super-villains, race riots, and other calamities. Although
the strip was at times obvious, Shelton even by then revealed
his subtle sensibilities, rare among the heavy-handed college
humorists. Moreover, his stories were fully developed *as stories,*
a rarity outside mainstream comic art. Shelton was certainly
the only underground comic artist to attempt to reach a mass-
circulation audience in the mid-1960's. The producers of *CAR-
toons* and other hot-rod humor magazines brought out two issues
of *Wonder Wart-Hog Magazine,* drawn by Shelton and Tony
Bell. Its 150,000 copy run fell flat over the indifference of vendors
to place the magazine on their stands. Shelton also drew for

Help! and later for the Austin RAG. In this last medium he contrived a new group of heroes which proved to have enormous popularity: the Fabulous Furry Freak Brothers.

In the Freak Brothers, the Youth Community had representative figures to conjure with: they spent most of their time smoking dope, searching for it, philosophizing about it (Freewheelin' Frank's famous adage runs: "*Dope* will get you through times of no *money* better than money will get you through times of no *dope!*"), and evading narks and cops. Even Crumb's Mr. Natural (a guru-type existing in big cities) and Flakey Foont (the semi-straight whose caricature hit too close to home) were not the universal, identifiable figures that the Freak Brothers were. And by drawing them more consistently, and publishing them more regularly in the underground press, Shelton made them available to more freaks and proto-freaks than any other underground comic characters.

In 1968, Shelton published his own comic in Texas, suitably titled *Feds 'n Heads*. The cover brandished a cop telling a hippie that "*We* don't *allow* no hippies here in Gruntville!" and inside were stories about peyote, a novelty page (with items like "Exploding Joint," "Hidden Cushion Police Siren," and "Little Book of Unsolveable Puzzles for Speed Freaks") and, significantly, Wonder Wart-Hog heading for San Francisco. In the fall of that year, Gilbert headed there himself, to join the rapidly developing center for underground comics artists. In January of 1969,

391

LIFE of the PARTY

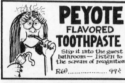

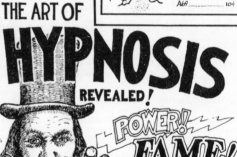
392

393

Radical America Komiks appeared, the first overtly political comic published by the new artists. Shelton drew most of the material and recruited the other strips. Most notable were a satire on the overground comics star "Seargent Fury," called by Shelton "Sergeant Death" and turned into a bumbling super-patriot who has to call in Wonder Wart-Hog to save him from the Chinese Reds; and a Furry Freaks strip, which, like the Sergeant Death strip, showed Shelton's vastly improved drawing style and his superb sense of timing. Shelton's use of angles (at points rivaling Barks in unique perspective if not in detail), his development of characters to human proportions, and his ability to portray dope highs all point to his remarkable creativity.

Shelton, like Crumb and the other underground comics artists, has indicated his own indifference to "Art" in the traditional sense. He claims to have little interest in his drawing except to make a very marginal living and to help artists get published. With the money from *RA Komiks* Shelton helped to create Rip-Off Press, which has produced several of the best comics. Shelton thinks of himself as a philosophical anarchist, yet he is clearly one of the most political of artists, as his recent book, *Hydrogen Bomb Funnies,* indicates. He claims to have little real interest even in his characters, compared with overground artists: Wonder Wart-Hog's personality underwent several changes according to Shelton's whim, and in his last (perhaps final) strip, the Hog raped Lois Lamebrain with his snout. Yet, despite his stated intention of merely providing "entertainment," Shelton has already achieved more: he created his own form of Americana, or rather reflected it from bits and pieces of old and new folklore. Although he lacks Crumb's incredibly sharp cultural perceptions based upon a view of the totality of American life, Shelton has done an enormous amount to provide a bridge between the older comics tradition and the underground comics. He is above all a story-teller, with an empathy for his characters which is rarely apparent in under- or overground comics. According to Mike Barrier, perhaps the most lucid critic of Funny Animal comics, "No other underground cartoonist has gotten so good so fast as Shelton, and no other is so interesting to watch." Certainly, few other artists of the genre were so long in the preparation for that burst of development.[33]

The closest counterparts to Shelton's background and capability for actually producing comic books are Jay Lynch and Skip Williamson, two Chicago artists. In the early sixties Lynch and Williamson, both several years younger than Shelton, began cartooning together, trying unsuccessfully to get their work accepted by *Playboy*. Both sent in cartoons to *Help!*, which were accepted, did work for *The Realist* and a variety of other magazines and papers. In 1967 they created *The Chicago Mirror*, a postcollege satire-and-humor magazine which reflected some Chicago political and cultural developments, including the drugs that Lynch took. After three issues and the encouragement which Crumb's *ZAP!* provided, Lynch and Williamson converted their magazine into *Bijou Funnies*, the second regular comic book series to appear in the underground.[34]

Much of *Bijou* reflects Williamson's and Lynch's own work. Williamson created a sort of thirties hipster, Snappy Sammy Snoot, who found himself overtaken by Youth Culture on the one hand and the hostility of the cops on the other. Williamson also has done several of the most famous political strips of the last several years, such as "Class War Comics," and he and Lynch combined to produce the second, and most important, political comic book hitherto, *Conspiracy Capers,* directed at raising money for the Conspiracy Seven. Better known, however, is Lynch's creation, "Nard 'n Pat," which has appeared in virtually all the underground comic books and papers. A satire on forties overground characters, the two heroes are buddies, with an ambiguity toward Pat's status: is he human because he balls human women, or is he a cat because Nard pays for his food and shelter? Within this ambiguity, Lynch relates essentially a long series of gags. Although the characters in one sense have not developed as far as, say, Mr. Natural, and the drawing has not become as sharp or innovative as Shelton's, Lynch especially has continued to grow and elaborate themes through "Nard 'n Pat." And,

perhaps because Williamson and Lynch are more sophisticated politically than nearly any other comics artists, they can provide in-jokes for the Left as few other underground artists can. One of Williamson's strips, reprinted in the short-lived Weatherman newspaper *Fire This Time,* suggested to the reader that "When yer smashin' the state, kids . . . don't forget to keep a smile on yer lips an' a song in yer heart!" In a Lynch strip, similarly, Pat as a budding porn novelist was reprimanded by Nard, who suggested he write "nice stuff." Pat replied: "Come the revolution there'll be no more Nice Stuff!"

A very different underground comic milieu existed on the East Coast, around the short-lived comics tabloid *Gothic Blimp.* Nearly all the *Blimp* artists seemed to share a sense of the violence and social conflict of daily life in Manhattan. The most respected artistically is George Metzger, whose machine-like warriors are drawn with the closest attention to details, in an unending series of destructive battles and other encounters. The story here, and even the caricature of what we ordinarily think of as comic strips, has become lost; what remains is a grotesque world, perhaps of an unending World War III, with no human winners.

Very similar in motif is the work of two other artists whose work appeared in *Blimp*, Vaughan Bode and Spain Rodriques. Bode's work very closely reflects the science fiction fanzine drawing that he has done. Like most other artists, Bode drew from the time of his childhood, finally began publishing around his college years, and when the opportunity arose, founded *Blimp* to offer space to the work of artists whom he might not like or even understand but who seemed in the process of self-development. His own work includes elaborate portfolios of weapons and brutalized attitudes in the final war of mankind, which is begun by humans but finished by machines directed by computers ("Big Mama," one is called). The machines, which fly, talk, think, and even wear "Peace" signs occasionally, are clearly the most degraded form of Man's heritage.[35]

Similarly, Spain Rodriques treats the strip as if it were merely a medium, with little inherent necessary form. His "Trashman" is an extension of the worst social tendencies of the present, without a rebirth of class struggle per se. In his anti-utopian future of America, the rich grow ever more decadent and indifferent to ecological wastage. Their barbarian pursuits include cannibalism for festive occasions. The heroes are Trashman (recruited by the "Sixth International," a terrorist revolutionary organization) and his cohorts, who live in more-or-less Youth Culture "free areas," and who, though technologically over-powered, make forays to defend and extend their territory. In a typical episode which encapsulizes the fantasies of many youthful revolutionaries, Trashman and his followers break into an opulent dining hall and spray the ruling class with machine-gun fire.

Rodriques' drawing is strong and complex, although occasionally repetitive. He manages an internal joke once in a while, like the introduction of R. Crumb as one of the killing-and-fucking heroes. But his story-line is no match. Rather, his con-

ceptions are alienated, humorless, empty even of the hopeless empathy that Bode gives his characters.

Kim Deitch, another of *Blimp's* main artists, is also curiously non-comic in tradition. He came to New York in 1966 as a painter, and only gradually became interested in traditional, and then underground, comics. His stories are heavily plotted, with surrealistic characters such as "Uncle Ed, King of 'Em All," an aging pudgy husband who is in reality (i.e., in disguise) the greatest fucker in America, Deitch, along with several other former *Blimp* principals, has been recently drawing for *Insect Fear*.[36] These "Tales from the Behavioral Sink" tell repeatedly and gruesomely of Americans who deserve a horrible death and receive it. Gigantic bugs and other creatures leap out of the closet as if repressed fears were at last coming true. The most natural artist for *Insect Fear* was also a *Blimp* artist, and in fact once the most influential figure among the artists: S. Clay Wilson.

Wilson is from small-town America, a refugee from Kansas living in San Francisco. According to his old friends, he has been drawing the same kind of subjects since he was an adolescent: motorcyclists, demons, perverted pirates, dykes, and heterosexual sluts, all of whom display the characteristics that middle-class America finds abhorrent, from Sade-like infliction of pain to exaggerated and revolting physical features to open homosexuality. According to Crumb, Wilson opened the way for future comics by rejecting all the mores of good taste and internal censorship. Wilson's drawings tend by their very nature to be repetitious, occasionally even boring. Nevertheless, his importance is beyond question, particularly because he initiated the influential smut comics (*Snatch, Jiz, Cunt* and *King Bee*).[37]

Another reason for Wilson's popularity is the tenacity of the EC ethos, the underground super-popularity of the old EC comics unavailable except as now-rare originals and over-priced reprints. One minor comic line, published by Gary Arlington's San Francisco Comic Company, envisions its fundamental inspiration in the old EC horror comics. As the inside cover of *SKULL* # 1 ("100% Horrid!") comics explained:

HI KIDS! EVER WONDER WHAT HAPPENED TO THOSE GREAT OLD **HORROR** COMIX THAT USED TO SCARE THE SHIT OUT OF YA WAY BACK IN THE 50'S? REMEMBER? WELL, THEY ALL DISAPPEARED, AN' IT WASN'T **BLACK MAGIC** WHAT DONE 'EM IN, EITHER! THOSE COMIX ARE **GONE!** UNTIL **NOW**, THAT IS! THINGS BEIN' AS THEY ARE THESE DAYS, A FEW OF US OL' CHARACTERS DECIDED IT WAS TIME TO REVIVE TH' **HORROR** COMIX ... IN KEEP-IN' WITH TH' TIMES, Y'UNDERSTAND! ... SO HERE GOES ~ SKULL COMIX GONNA LAY IT ON YER SKULL ... BUT YA BETTER BUY THIS **FAST** (OR BETTER YET, **STEAL IT**)- 'CAUSE YA NEVER KNOW WHEN THEY'LL HAVE AN-OTHER GREAT COMIC BOOK CLEANUP!

Yet the drawings are no more than half-imitations of the old strips. Despite the nostalgia, there is no real effort to recreate the EC line. The artists clearly recognized that there were things in America of 1970 much more terrifying than the supernatural.

Of the other various minor comics publishing companies around the United States, only the Krupp Comic Works in Milwaukee is obviously a stable, growing center for new publications. The leading artist and entrepeneur at Krupp is Denis Kitchen, who is an active member of the Socialist Labor Party, a small educational organization which has continued to agitate for a government of workers' councils since the turn of the century. Kitchen's political attitudes play a curious role in his own drawings and publishing. At times, Kitchen seems acutely aware of the nature of day-to-day life in an ordinary industrial city (in this case, Milwaukee) and the ongoing conflicts between Youth Culturalists and the working class. At other times, Kitchen and his fellow artists at Krupp appear strangely unaware of their comics' negative political content—especially those which manage weak jokes at the expense of "Women's Lib."

The most important production by Kitchen is *Teenage Horizons of Shangri-la,* a comic devoted to high school life. Contributors include Dan Clyne, a seventeen-year-old from Chicago who describes adolescent problems with worms; Jay Lynch, whose nostalgic commentary on the 1950's depicts a principal singing to himself "Duke Duke Duke Duke of Earl Duke Duke. . . ." and Kitchen whose "I Was a Teenage Hippie" works on several different levels—on parents, teenage confessions, and the hip community. While *Horizons* lacks any single powerful strip, its focus and consequent insight are impressive. Recently, Kitchen's company published the first three-dimensional comic book in fifteen years, with a center spread of Milwaukee blowing up toward the reader (from a bird's eye view) on nine different levels. Here again, the execution is weak, but the conception strong.

The development of comics has produced a good deal of dross. The Print Mint especially, but also Krupp and the other smaller companies, have been so anxious to publish that much of the recent material appears mediocre, especially compared with the small but fine production of the first ten or so underground comic books. Unfortunately, several of the visually finest artists have drawn very little. Andy Martin, whose work appeared only in early issues of *Yellow Dog,* is a George Grosz-like satirist of American political life. With utmost care for detail Martin developed his character: "Professor Anatole Murayev," "Dr. Caligari, Famous Gynecologist," and "Hop-Frog, the Lunatic Crippled Genius Dwarf." Similarly detailed is the style of Robert Williams, formerly a paid cartoonist for Ed "Big Daddy" Roth's motorcycle magazines in Los Angeles. Williams' strips are rich with detail, as in his only book, *Coochy Cooty Men's Comics.* His vision of America is dark, and somewhat similar to that of Crumb. (In one well-known strip, Williams depicted the pelvis as a "tremendous horror, a shit seething demon, that turns man's mind into lecherous cesspools, and holds mankind bound to reality, refusing man His place as a magic deity.") Yet his drawings so completely fill the page that the literal meaning is only partially important, and in any case is detectable only after detailed examination.

Several other artists whose work appeared frequently in *ZAP* and other Bay Area comics are so little in the comics tradition that their work deserves mention. Victor Moscosco and Rick Griffin are described by Don Schenker as "purely visual . . . a-literate," with spoken lines left out entirely (as in Moscoso) or used as part of the geometry (as in Griffin). Both draw material to be looked at rather than read. Clearly, Griffin—like several other artists—comes out of the Disney tradition, which he bends and transmogrifies to his own effect; yet much of his work parallels that of Moscoso, whose influences stem directly from Dali, Klee, and Magritte. Both seem heavily influenced by acid. Also drug-oriented is the work of the primitivist Buckwheat Florida, Jr., which Schenker calls "doodles raised to certain power . . . open and naive." Florida's solo comic book, *Suds,* has a string of unfinished stories, developing around the page in no particular

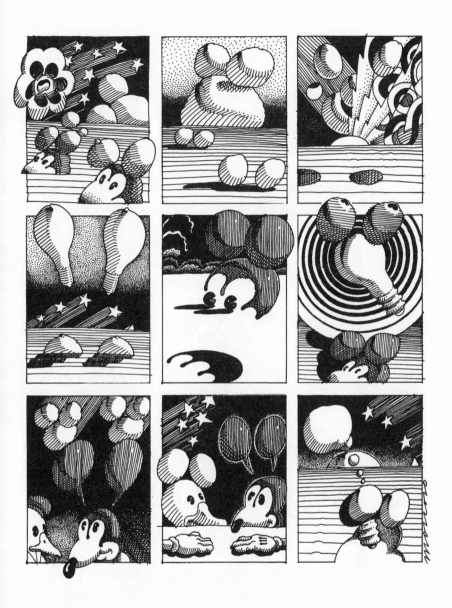

403

404

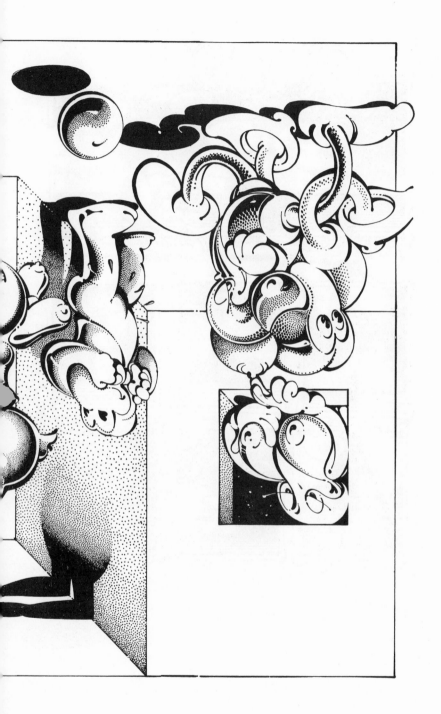

407

order with absolutely no relationship to talent or stylistic concerns. At best, his work is honest, transparently autobiographical social commentary on speed-brained activities and fantasies.

More recently, there have been several quasi-political comic books which reflect, in varying degrees, the influences of political radicalism, establishment repression, and ecological waste upon the artists. Gilbert Shelton's *Hydrogen Bomb Comics* is roughly similar to *Radical America Komiks,* an amalgam of work by the more overtly politically-conscious artists. *High Flyin' Funnies & Stories* presents the first book publication of Bill Crawford's work, known throughout the underground press for the lead character, "Rufus the Radical Reptile." In spirit, Crawford is perhaps more directly attached to the Left movement than any other artist, and his work conveys the frustrations and ironies of recent political practice. More grim in its political intent is *Slow Death Funnies,* an anti-utopian depiction of ecological stagnation and (if unchecked) total self-destruction. Dave Sheridan, Gary Grimshaw, Jack Jaxon, Kim Deitch, and Gilbert Shelton collaborate in driving home a heavy message that there is no alternative to the total assault on the polluters and the powers-that-be who gain from environmental desecration. Finally, an All Women's Liberation comic book had been produced by *It Ain't Me Babe,* drawn by former *Blimp* artist Trina and five other women. The general theme of this comic is mythos, powerfully plotted but less powerfully drawn. Intended for women rather than a general audience, *It Ain't Me Babe* is able to bring off internal jokes, and is rarely (much more rarely than other politically oriented comics, in fact) heavy-handed. Rather, it stresses the endless backtracking and countless pitfalls that face women's struggle, and the contradictions that even fighters must endure.

NOTES

1. The following interpretation of the transformation of Culture is principally derived from these sources: Theodor Adorno, "Cultural Criticism and Society," in *Prisms* (London: Neville Spearman, 1967); Herbert Marcuse, "The Affirmative Character of Culture," in *Negations* (Boston: Beacon Press, 1968); Walter Benjamin, "Art in the Age of Mechanical Reproduction," in *Illuminations* (New York: Schocken, 1969); Jeremy J. Shapiro, "One Dimensionality: The Universal Semiotic of Technological Experience,"

in Paul Breines, ed., *Critical Interruptions* (New York: Herder & Herder, 1970); David Gross, "Toward a Radical Theory of Culture," *Radical America* II (November–December, 1968); and Guy Debord, "Negation and Consumption Within Culture," in *Society of the Spectacle,* published as *Radical America* IV (June–July, 1970).

2. Adorno, *op. cit.,* p. 23; Benjamin, *op. cit.,* page 224.

3. Gross, *op. cit.,* pp. 6–8.

4. Benjamin, "Epilogue" to *op. cit.,* pp. 241–42.

5. Adorno, *op. cit.,* p. 34.

6. Shapiro, *op. cit.,* especially pp. 152–64. One should note, however, that with the exception of Guy Debord and Walter Benjamin, the above theorists derive their revolutionary hopes from the accumulation of "negative experience" by certain segments of the population rather than from proletarian upheaval in the classic sense. Shapiro distinguishes himself from Adorno and Marcuse by asserting a certain optimism toward the results of technology. Benjamin, before his tragic death in 1940, was of all those influenced by the Frankfort School most attached to the revolutionary Left. Debord, along with others attached to or influenced by the Situationist International, has learned from the Frankfort theorists without absorbing their pessimism.

7. Robert C. Pollack, "Dream and Nightmare: The Future as Revolution," in Michael Novak, ed., *American Philosophy and the Future* (New York: Scribner, 1968), offers valuable insights into the exceptional characteristics of American culture.

8. Some of MacKay's strips, including a few of "Little Nemo" and others—especially the brilliant "Nightmare of a Welch-Rarebit Eater" and his portfolio "City of Tomorrow" —have been reprinted in *Captain George's Whizzbang,* a nostalgia-tabloid which frequently republishes old comic material (published by Memory Lane Publications, 594 Markham St., Toronto, Canada).

9. An excellent appreciation of Herriman's work is offered in a chapter of Gilbert Seldes' *The Seven Lively Arts* (New York: A. S. Barnes, 1927). One volume of some Herriman strips was collected as *Krazy Kat* (New York: Holt, 1946), and reprinted in 1969. Another volume has recently been published: *George Herriman's Krazy Kat* (New York: Madison Square Press, 1969). For an erudite analysis of these volumes, see an essay by Bill Blackbeard, "From a Corner Table at Rough-House's," in *Riverside Quarterly* (40 University Sta., Regina, Sask., Canada), Vol. IV, # 4. Blackbeard is proprietor of the Academy of Comic Art in San Francisco, but an infrequent writer on the subject.

10. One of the extremely rare revolutionary critics of comics is the American surrealist Franklin Rosemont. In paying his appreciation to Herriman, MacKay, and others, he noted especially his feeling toward the Funny Animal comics, saying: "For me, a single Bugs Bunny comic book of the early 1950s . . . will always be worth more—in terms of freedom and human dignity—than all the novels of Proust, Sartre, Faulkner, Hemingway . . . Such a judgment, which will probably strike some as excessive, possesses at least the virtue of complete seriousness." From "The Seismograph of Subversion," *Radical America* IV (January, 1970).

11. Don Schenker, "Snatch Zap! Underground Comic," *Californian Weekly Magazine* (of *Daily Californian,* Berkeley), Feb. 18, 1969.

12. Jules Feiffer, *The Comic Book Heroes* (New York: Dial, 1965), especially pp. 50–53.

13. Mary Beard, *Women as a Force in History* (Second Edition; New York: Collier, 1962), pp. 54–55; Steranko, *History of the Comics* (published by Supergraphics: 501 Spruce St., Reading, Pa. 19602), Volume I.

14. See, for instance, *Batman,* November, 1970; *Flash,* December, 1970; or virtually any number of *Spicerman. Rolling Stone* has recently taken cognizance of overground comic developments: see Tim Ferris, "Spider-Man Meets Pusher-Man," *Rolling Stone* # 79 (April 1, 1971).

15. See for example the description of Odysseus in Alex Preminger, ed., *Encyclopedia of Poetry and Poetics* (Princeton: Princeton University Press, 1965), p. 143.

16. The finest discussion of Barks was offered by Mike Barrier, "The Lord of Quackrly Hall," *Funnyworld* #8. Barrier has also produced a serialized bibliography of Barks' comics in *Funnyworld* (Box 5229, Brady Sta., Little Rock, Ark. 72205). See also an interview with Barks in *Comic Art* #7 (c/o D. & M. Thompson, 8786 Hendricks Rd., Mentor, Ohio 44060).

17. See, for instance, "Walt Disney's Christmas Parade," December, 1970, for an extraordinarily fine Barks story from 1951, running the entire length of the comic. Although Barks did not sign strips, the discerning reader can determine which are his.

18. "Bill Gaines," in *Squa Tront*, an extraordinarily fine fanzine devoted to EC comics (published by Jerry Weist, 1849 S. 127th St. East, Wichita, Ks. 67207).

19. "The Container of Rainy Days," *Rainy Days* #27, published by D. & M. Thompson (see address for *Comic Art* above).

20. An entire number of *Graphic Story Magazine* has been devoted to Basil Wolverton, #12 (c/o Bill Spicer, 4878 Grenada St., Los Angeles, Calif. 90042).

21. "Bill Gaines," in *Squa Tront, op. cit.;* and an exceptionally fine comment, "Graphic Story World," by Richard Kyle, in *Graphic Story Magazine,* #11.

22. Marshall McLuhan, *Understanding Media* (New York, 1964), Ch. 17.

23. This attitude has been expressed by different writers, but with particular emphasis by Jacob Brackman, "The International Comix Conspiracy," in *Playboy,* December, 1970; also note Robert Warshow, "Paul, the Horror Comics, and Dr. Wertham," printed in *Mass Culture,* Bernard Rosenberg and D. M. White, eds. (New York, 1957), which relates a father's attitude toward his son in an "EC Fan Addict Club."

24. The best treatment of fanzines is a history of science fiction fanzines to 1950, Harry Warner, Jr., *All Our Yesterdays* (Chicago: Advent, 1970).

25. Don Donahue, "A Much Wilder Suck Than You Think!" *Organ* (Box 4520, Berkeley, Calif. 94704), September, 1970.

26. Schenker, *op. cit.*

27. Quoted by Michael Barrier in "Crumbum," *Funnyworld* #8.

28. See for instance *Help!* January, 1965, with Crumb's Harlem sketches, a Fritz the Cat strip, one of Gilbert Shelton's "Wonder Wart-Hog" strips and cartoons by Skip Williamson and Jay Lynch.

29. Dave Schreiner, "Robert Crumb Encounters Wisconsin," The *Bugle-American* (PO Box 1725, Madison, Wis. 53701), Sept. 25–Oct. 1, 1970. This newspaper, in part edited by Denis Kitchen, carries a substantial group of regular underground comic strips and sporadic reviews of comics over and underground.

30. Gerard van der Leun, "The Unreal History of Snatch Comix," *Organ,* September, 1970, an exceptionally perceptive article.

31. The apparent reason for the bust of *Zap* #4 was its open distribution. Unlike *Snatch, Jiz,* etc., which were sold generally under the counter and were frequently unavailable outside California, *Zap* was openly offered for sale in head shops and book stores around the country.

32. There has in recent months been considerable speculation about Crumb's drawing style, specifically in *Despair Comics* and *Home Grown Funnies.* His drawings appear subtly changed and somewhat more crude, leading some to suggest that Crumb's latest material is being drawn by someone else. In all probability, however, the shift represents Crumb's efforts to avoid stereotyping of his work by presenting a sort of parody of his own style. *Despair* and *Home Grown* remain close enough in art, but especially in theme, to Crumb's previous work to suggest a kind of generalized fumbling at social analysis beyond the limits of Crumb's current, essentially negative, level. Whether Crumb can transcend his own limits remains, however, to be seen.

410

33. Michael Barrier, "Notes on the Underground," *Funny World,* # 12.

34. A narrative document from Jay Lynch, describing his past and his intent, was included in one of the first public commentaries on underground comics: Bob Abel, "Comix of the Underground," *Cavalier,* April, 1969.

35. Regrettably, some of Bode's weakest drawing has been reprinted in book form as *Deadbone Erotica* (New York: Bantam, 1971). Drawn originally for *Cavalier,* this Bode series features only two major character-types: "Lizards" and "Broads," both under-developed as characters.

36. There has been another product from the *Blimp* Group: *Swift Comics,* also offered in paperback book form (New York: Bantam, 1971), including long narrative stories by Kim Deitch, Art Spiegelman, Allan Shenker, and Trina. These are plotted as if mediocrity were the publisher's criterion.

37. It is interesting to note that both Wilson and Crumb greatly admire an artist even less respected generally than Wilson: Rory Hayes, an utter primitivist whose artwork is simplistic, crude, and violent. For Crumb, Hayes possesses the "most pure" attitude of any artist, because he "doesn't know how to be artistic or how to be clever." Quoted by Gerald van der Leun, "The Unreal History," *op. cit.*

The author wishes to express particular gratitude to the following: Mari Jo Buhle and Dave Wagner for insight into Crumb and the Funny Animal comics, respectively; Michael Barrier and Denis Kitchen for invaluable aid and advice in many aspects of comics; and Gilbert Shelton, for his many kindnesses.

Paul Buhle was founder, and is editor, of *Radical America,* which under the editorship of Gilbert Shelton issued one number of *Radical America Komiks* in 1969.

May, 1971

411

U.S. iconography and the Yippie media termites

HUGH FOX

Maybe it begins with comic books, TV, Pop and Op art, the contemporary ease of reproducing and modifying all varieties of sight/sound images. It certainly has something to do with movie myth. I think of Myra Breckenridge's "lectures" on U.S. film— the film becomes reality. Myron takes film-values as viable and exemplary and becomes Myra, the Super Star. Harlow, Dietrich, Marilyn Monroe ... faces and figures thirty feet high. And Zorro, Clark Gable, John Wayne, King Kong. Fed on this myth which pretends to be everyday reality (and really does spill over very visibly in life in southern California), real everyday reality becomes muddy and insipid. The nervous system fed on movie myth becomes used to constant tension, climax, a kind of continuous electronic orgasm. The temptation is to become the Marx Brothers, Dietrich, or King Kong. Books didn't move, the Count of Monte Cristo as book didn't hit all the senses; the reader had to re-create the Count inside his head. But when Dracula

412

drinks technicolor blood and you can hear him slurping, the print–mind-creation step is eliminated and in its stead the mechanism is BECOME A SUPERSTAR. I remember my mother telling me: "You're a good-looking boy, you could really make it big in Hollywood or on TV." Repeat this "image" a million-million times and you have All American Super Star Spillover Reality.

Abbie Hoffman and Jerry Rubin are Super Stars. Their image precedes their reality. Their "whatness" is all image. They function in terms of their image and are not hitched up to or coupled with any *other* function than the re-impacting and re-stocking of their image-power. Whatever is kinky and krazy-kat is blown-up and inflated; the real person—like Marilyn Monroe just before she committed suicide, like the Judy Garland who posed for the "What Does a Legend Wear?" fur coat ads—is replaced by the highly energized pure image, the IKON in front of which the mind does automatic homage. We Americans are, after all, "the faithful" in a faithless century looking for new altars and new symbolic gods. Their "books," *Revolution for the Hell of It* (Hoffman), *Woodstock Nation* (Hoffman), and *Do It!* (Rubin) aren't Count of Monte Cristo type books, print that has to be "translated" into images, but turned-on "media books," half-book, half-"screen," the extension of type into total-image. Rubin calls *Do It!* "Scenarios of the Revolution," and *Woodstock Nation* is "A Talk-Rock Album."

There is hardly a page in any of these three books that is "straight." Everything is McLuhanish (Quentin Fiore-ish), designed to create a discontinuous, fragmented visual grenade. You can't get "bored"; the thought-presentation line breaks up, jumps, turns into a fist, and gives it to you in the eye. The March on the Pentagon is broken into *Charge!* (picture of Indians in full war regalia), *Siege!* (picture of a Roman (?) orgy) and *Victory!* (picture of a clenched fist). You talk about pigs, pigs oink all over the page; you talk about Reagan and there he is, hands up in the air, being held up by a Japanese-American kid in a cowboy outfit. Cartoons, comics, big type, little . . . all mix together to

413

form a simplified, essentially visual collage. Eldridge Cleaver eating watermelon, Mayor Daley looking like Genghis Khan, a cartoon of Nixon as a green-eyed dragon, a drawing of a tearful flower child wearing a crown of thorns, her blue hair spread out across two pages. Lots of room. Lots of super-type ZAPS and BOOMS! And when our Super Stars descend into mere words the style becomes terse, short, telegraphic. We're listening to the Evening TV News reported by a turned-on Karl Marx who's just been reading the works of the latter-day Tom Wolfe:

> The Stock Exchange official looks worried. He says to us, "You can't see the Stock Exchange."
> We're aghast. "Why not?" we ask.
> "Because you're hippies and you've come to demonstrate."
> "Hippies?" Abbie shouts, outraged at the very suggestion. "We're Jews and we've come to see the stock market."
>
> Vision: *the next day's headlines:*
> NEW YORK STOCK MARKET BARS JEWS.
> We've thrown the official a verbal karate punch. He relents.
> (Jerry Rubin, *Do It!* p. 117)

In a sense the vision of the headline precedes and directs everything else. The scenario works backwards from the climax (Kong on the Empire State being shot by planes) and builds "reality" around the ultimate effect. Everything is stated categorically, no theories, maybes, mights. It all comes out with the impact of Kirk Douglas slugging away in *Champion:*

> Puritanism leads us to Vietnam. Sexuality insecurity results in a supermasculinity trip called imperialism.
> (*Do It!* p. 111)

> The money-economy is immoral, based totally on power and manipulation . . .
> (*Do It!*, p. 122)

> The Law-and-Order apes and this senile dinosaur we call a government have flipped out. Preventive detention, the no-knock clause in the new drug laws, appointment of Burger and Haynsworth to the Supreme Court, and the extensive use of wire-tapping by the Justice Department are all part of a wave of repression.
> (*Woodstock Nation,* p. 75)

There's even one point in *Woodstock Nation* where the page becomes a strip of movie-film: OUTLINE, YIPPIE! MOVIE, and especially here the grafting of movie and non-movie, everyday and

414

Hollywood-myth reality comes clear. Who are the typical Yippie personalities? Billy the Kid, Marilyn Monroe, Franz Kafka. How is the Grand Central Station demonstration (1966) to be "inflated"? "Sequence ends with shot of Klan riding in from 'Birth of a Nation.'"

"The Marx Brothers are our leaders as they run through restaurants cutting off people's ties," says Yippie leader Jerry Rubin in *Do It!* Ties are part of our "reality-reference" system. You don't take them off, but cut them off. "Snip" is the sound of revolution.

We are surrounded by an elaborate symbol system which exists as a self-contained, all-inclusive reality. It is a total control system extending to the way we dress, how we talk, where we live, everything we do. Our sanity is intimately bound up with our keeping within the limitations of this system.

The Yippie is the first electronic existentialist. Both iconoclastic and an icon-manipulator, he is cellularly aware of the conversion of the U.S. into an icon-manipulation state, but at the same time uses the same techniques to create his own mass-media mythology. He tears down his parents' and grandparents' past and replaces it with a series of anti-tradition symbols which consciously are used to both cancel out and replace that past.

Once you realize that, in Artaud's words, "everything in the destination of an object, in the meaning or the use of a natural form, is a matter of convention" *(The Theater and Its Double)* then you suddenly slip in between things and their conventional meanings and find yourself able to disrupt the conventional, expected Thing-Meaning relationship, which in turn automatically disrupts the whole social-civil order which is essentially based on this relationship.

Police, judges, cops, firemen, old ladies with canes as objects of pity/respect are all kept in their functional order because of the ontological order that is already determined precisely by their definition. Or put it this way: as long as the White Man is the Massah, the Black Man bows, but the minute the Massah becomes "jes plain folks" like us, BANG!!! Black is ugly as long as black is defined as ugly; define it as beautiful and it becomes beautiful. DEFINITIONS AND CATEGORIES PRECEDE AND DEFINE OUR MOST INTIMATE PERSONAL VISIONS.

To the Yippies everything is "scenario," surface, projection. The U.S. system of stars and stripes, eagles, judges, cops, "The Law" is a manipulated symbol-system—unreality projected on the retina of the public's eye. Behind this symbol-system, though, the "reality" is very different. Ahistorical, the Yippies seldom look back to the "good old days" when the U.S. patriotic symbol bag represented what it said it represented; instead they tune in on the Now and are convinced that now the U.S. system represents repression, control, a hierarchical goal system aimed joylessly at "making it," a straight-laced, linear culture afraid of spontaneity, irregularity, anything unprogrammed or unexpected. To Jerry Rubin the confrontation between the Yippies and the Army during the march on the Pentagon explicitly defined the differences between the "straight" and the "Yip": "It was the psychedelic vs. the linear, free vs. fixed, spontaneous vs. uptight."

The Yippie is a supremely alienated outsider who needs "straight" society to serve as an audience for his alienation antics. He sees presidents being sold like cigarettes and can't buy the image that is fashioned by the Overlords for public consumption. He resists being "the public," but is totally public in projecting the war between his nervous system and official government nervous-system control on the same screen that is used by the controllers.

Hollywood-type mythologizing can either "control" (contain) or explode reality off the screen. Film has an inherent tendency to present "the real and unreal within one undifferentiated unity" (Morin, *Le cinema ou l'homme imaginaire,* p. 162) but the pre-Acid, pre-Pot world kept a line between the "screen" and "off-the-screen." The Pot-Acid mentality erases all kinds of lines and one of them is the line between the imaginary and the real. You're driving along the San Diego Freeway in L.A. on a Saturday afternoon. It's been six months since you last dropped acid, and all of a sudden the sky begins to explode and break apart. You "know" it's not happening—or is it . . .?

Jean-Jacques Lebel calls vicarious, excitement-stimulating media the "containment industry." You're supposed to go to films and watch TV and, by vicariously living through TV and film reality, fulfill your wishes, leave the theater or the set and be "released." Containment is supposed to mean catharsis—even purgation. And it can work for a straight, linear mind.

The linear mind is as straight as printed lines on a page. It is abstract, can separate and splinter the senses, isolate sight from sound from touch from the kinesthetic sense. The linear mind is used to being fragmented, is uncomfortable when called upon to be original . . . spontaneous. It is much more at home following instead of originating, duplicating instead of creating. It understands commandments, codes, laws, and regulations. Ask it to explain Thoreau's statement in Walden, "I cease to exist and begin to be," and it panics. The linear mind flees from any kind of total, totally-sense-involved experience. Its greatest horror is to have to face "being" in the raw, unprocessed and unpackaged. This is the central problem underlying Heidegger's *Zeit und Sein* and McLuhan's *Verbi-Voco-Visual Explorations*. The American Mind of the thirties and forties was "straight," work-oriented, Depression-haunted, convention-confined. It was all tied up in a classical bourgeois straitjacket. Then under the radiation-influence of affluence (forgetting the specter of the Crash), and the thorough conversion of non-media-attached-Mind to total media-attachment, vicarious containment gradually became literal imitation and fantasy became the blueprint for fact. The glorious Bluebird of Happiness World was there on the screen and you didn't have to sweat it all that much to just joggle along (surviving!) . . . You had time and money to start converting your everyday reality cells into pure myth. The Super Star system, after all, didn't glorify the bourgeoisie. The idols weren't just clean-cut Puritan-*ethos* types. Dietrich in *Kismet,* the Marx Brothers in *Duck Soup* or *A Day at the Races*, Gary Cooper in *Fountainhead* (the Super-Ego against the Masses) . . . or *The Graduate* graduating violently away from Mrs. Robinson and her whole hold-the-line, preserve-the-appearances world. In the history of the films we move from gangsters to superwomen (and, to a lesser degree, Superman) hero-outlaws and (more recently) anarchists, "individuals," Elliott Gould in *Getting Straight* actually saying he didn't pass his M.A. exam because *he didn't like it*. We move from manipulation by a system-code to expression of an Emersonian-Thoreau-ian I WANT, THEREFORE I AM. Movie-myth becomes merely the first layer, the raw material for a new mythology in which we write our own scenarios, are our own stars.

First the bourgeois world is jettisoned, the outsider emerges "free from property hang-ups, free from success fixations, free from positions, titles, names, hierarchies, responsibilities, schedules, rules, routines, regular habits," as Jerry Rubin puts it—and then once restraint of dull, tarnished old bourgeois tradition disappears (only hats off to bourgeois affluence!!), then media myth can take over. A star is born. We can become our fantasies, live out our movie dreams off the screen. Becoming modified we have returned to the pre-written world where our total psychic reality merges with and mythologizes our total environment. McLuhan in *Counterblast*:

> We begin again to structure the primordial feelings and emotions from which 3000 years of literacy divorced us. We begin again to live a myth.

Mediafication began at the turn of the century (*The Great Train Robbery*—1903), but didn't become "total" until the fifties and sixties. Now the film-TV-Hifi "envelope" is complete. Reality outside this electronic "envelope" has all but disappeared. Rubin and Hoffman hardly function outside their own image-receptor world. Then add "dope" and the mind itself becomes an automatic myth-image maker. Like Hoffman at Woodstock:

> Things were becoming very unclear and when I saw a guy throw a spear at me like in the movie "Bwana Devil" and I even saw the red-and-green tint that you saw when your 3 D glasses fell off, when I saw that, and when I ducked no less, I knew I was on some real powerful shit. I knew I had taken some weird acid . . . the trouble was I couldn't figure out whether it was the red or the green or the blue† or the no sleep or the 300,000 people, or the shaky bridge, or that African spear thrower.

This "dope"-electronic-envelope combination isolates the already-mediafied individual from non-mind reality, and MIND

---

† Various "colors" of acid were circulating at Woodstock, some reported to be poison.

(with all its historical, collective unconscious content) takes over. The whole distaff, magic-thinking, hocus-pocus, super- and preternatural repertoire of psychic tricks becomes everyday routine. "Abnormal" states become "normal," taboo becomes dogma, make-believe becomes belief. As Abbie Hoffman puts it in *Revolution for the Hell of It*:

We are cannibals, cowboys, Indians, witches, warlocks. Weird-looking freaks that crawl out of the cracks in America's nightmare. Very visible and, as everyone knows, straight from the white middle-class suburban life.

The Yippie Generation was supposed to soak up North American media violence, live out their nightmares vicariously, and stay "contained" within visible and controllable channels: have your Bunny, your Hifi, your Mustang, Tornado, Hurricane, your X-rated movies with all that juicy flesh-visibility, your vicarious TV wildness, your liquor (but not your Pot), bowl, swim, speed, fly. Soak it up, live it vicariously—AS DEFINED. Only the media already had given American youth electronic nervous systems in the fifties, and Pot and Acid gave all reality the unreal exaggeration of a mythic dream. Heads became TV movie studios; Egos and Ids became directors and movie heroes; psychic content became scenarios and shot-sequences. Was the African spear thrower really out there? Was perception perception of the "out there" at all, or a replay of *Bwana Devil . . . or* the creation of a new very personal head-movie production?

We are supposed to grow up and out of "fantasy" when we enter the responsible work-*ethos* world.

Only the Yippies haven't grown up. "We want to be heroes, like those in the history books," complains Jerry Rubin. "We missed the First American-Revolution. We missed World War II. We missed the Chinese and Cuban Revolutions. Are we supposed to spend our futures grinning and watching TV all the time?" The Yippies are eternal juveniles who refuse to read the controlled-media road signs. Their heads are TV sets, their imaginations TV screens, their nervous systems electrical information circuits gone wild. "We create reality wherever we go by living our fantasies." (Jerry Rubin)

During the trial of the Chicago 8, at one point Bobby Seale attacks one of the most sacred keystone symbols in the U.S. national icon-system: "You have George Washington and Benjamin Franklin sitting in a picture behind you, and they was slave owners. That's what they were. They owned slaves." Judge Hoffman, the perfect example of the conventional image-custodian (and protector and manipulator of courtroom procedures, rules, traditions) is deeply disturbed by this attack on the symbols that serve as the basis for his whole psychic order and equilibrium: "I didn't think I would ever live to sit on a bench or be in a courtroom where George Washington was assailed by a defendant in a criminal case and a judge was criticized for having his portrait on the wall." Take one small procedural detail like standing up in court when the judge gets on the bench. Hoffman, the archetype of the Straight World, bothered time and time again, goes so far as to read into the record, "Let the record show again the defendants have not risen."

What separates Judge Hoffman from Abbie Hoffman is the fact that while the judge accepts the symbol-world around him as absolute reality, Abbie Hoffman is an electronic relativist. Making films, watching (or even more, performing on) TV, being soaked in film, recorded- and tape-reality programs the psyche to a kind of image-making alignment whereby the mind merges with the image-making machine, becomes a camera, recorder, projector. All reality becomes "hot," "instantaneous information," and image-activation becomes instinctive, "natural." Totally divorced from sequential, abstract print-culture, the Yippie mind functions in an active, turned-on Now. "Don't rely on words . . . rely on doing . . . Move fast . . .," says Abbie Hoffman in *Revolution for the Hell of It*. And then he goes out and writes when he does write, "Don't let things get stopped or 'static,' keep them moving—'books' they aren't 'books' but images interlaced with words."

Genet's massive examination of the dependence of civil order on clothes ("uniforms" in the larger sense)—symbology in *The Balcony*—plays like everyday life in western society. The bishop is a bishop because he has on bishop's clothes, the cop's uniform defines and underlies his "reality," the white-shirted tie-wearing businessman's function is essentially linked with his function-defining clothes. Try to be a secretary in a large company without wearing stockings. Just go barelegged and get ready for the "supervisor"—or your fellow secretaries—to descend on you. Wear overalls instead of a mini-skirt. Tied to the myth of "objective reality," the straight world tries to eliminate subjectivity, asymmetry, disconformity, caprice, by fitting everything into an easily definable and identifiable visual hierarchy, a hierarchy that becomes a prime target for Yippie debunking: "The yippies try to liberate people by getting everybody to change their clothes. As a transitional stage towards Communism, the yippies demand that everybody change his job and his clothes every few months . . ." (Jerry Rubin)

Moving down toward the core-elements of U.S. symbology, the Yippies attack money, the sacredness of the court system (this was the meaning of the trial of the Chicago 8), the procedures for electing presidents, the ivory tower isolation of the military. They went into the Stock Exchange in New York and started throwing money down from the visitor's gallery. The media turned it into a monumental event because the media feed on high hysteria and pandemonium. Rhythms have to break, expand, overflow. The moment the screen gets dull it's dead. The Yippies' techniques ("Turn every event into historic and mythic significance," as Rubin puts it) are media-techniques. They are perverse, anti-world PR men trying to flood the communication channels with the same kind of bazazz that monumentalizes entertainers, products and the rest of the "news." This year air-space isn't as easy to come by as last, and Hoffman is touring campuses, re-programming himself—temporarily—to live performances again. But once he becomes news enough, ZAP! back on the screen.

Being "hot," though, action-involved, totally post-Gutenberg— not like *Meet the Press,* Gutenberg sequentialness unsuccessfully transposed into a post-Gutenberg world—the Yippies on TV

421

become what Abbie Hoffman refers to as the "figure" (active element) thrown up against the "ground" (passive element) of the programming surrounding commercials or "hot" news like Yippie events.

The Yippie "hot" anti-event during the democratic convention in Chicago was the nomination and election of Pigasus, the Pig, as President of the U.S. Although the surface of the whole nomination-election process had lost much of the credibility of any inner meaning, it was another of the sacrosanct ceremonies of U.S. society. By programming the news media with an anti-event simultaneous with the "real"-event, the whole sacred aura of the "real"-event was merged and confused with its anti-event double. In a sense this anti-event approach set the tone for the whole Nixon administration. Cops become "pigs" (another basic-image attack) and pigs (pigasuses) are nominated for the presidency.

The Yippie attack on the Pentagon was another myth-making, symbol-confusing anti-event, matching magic against weaponry, and phoney, invented aphrodisiacs (LACE) against logic. The idea was to surround the Pentagon and by exorcising it cause it to lift ten feet off the ground. The exorcism went like this:

We Freemen, of all colors of the spectrum, in the name of God, Ra, Jehovah, Anubis, Osiris, Tlaloc, Quetzalcoatl, Thoth, Ptah, Allah, Krishna, Chango, Chimeke, Chukwu, Olisa-Bulu-Uwa, Imales, Orisasu, Odudua, Kali, Shiva-Shakra, Great Spirit, Dionysus, Yahweh, Thor, Bacchus, Isis, Jesus Christ, Maitreya, Buddha, Rama do exorcise and cast out the EVIL which has walled and captured the pentacle of power and perverted its use to the need of the total machine and its child the hydrogen bomb . . . etc.

Seen from the point of view of the traditional, "straight" protester, the whole Fug-Yippie show was—as Robert Lowell put it— "damn repetitious," but in terms of guerrilla theater it was easily as effective as Jerry Rubin's appearing in front of the House Un-American Activities Committee dressed in the Spirit of '76 uniform. The point was not merely to neatly, nicely, and politely protest a war and bring it all to the level of a suburban tennis match, but to concretize and "illustrate" the evil symbolized by the Pentagon itself. Ed Sanders of the Fugs, stealing some of

Jerry Rubin's and Abbie Hoffman's fire, in a beautiful upstaging of the Yippies, went on ceremonially ousting Pentagon money and Pentagon generals, secretaries, soldiers, bureaucracy itself . . . The media-machine was stoked with the neatly-adapted mumbo jumbo of a sorcery-oriented world that dredged up Hollywoodish witchcraft that mocked itself as well as the Pentagon's "evil" it pretended it was exorcising.

The Yippies are apocalyptical, messianic, prophetic. They are all passengers on the celestial railroad on the way to the City of God. They believe in paradise now, the end of money, work, the profit incentive. As Abbie Hoffman puts it in *Revolution for the Hell of It*: "Work is competition. Work was linked to productivity to serve the Industrial Revolution. We must separate the two. We must abolish work and all the drudgery it represents."

In the reality-turned-scenario world of the Yippies there is a great need for "material," plot, background, "flavor," and like the Great Beat Self-Mythologizer, Jack Kerouac, the Yippies use anything out of their individual and collective past in order to cast themselves in the roles of prophets and wizards. Rubin and Hoffman ("Yippies are Jewish hippies"—Rubin) are particularly good at milking their "Jewishness" for super-mystic prophetic-guru effects. They don't have to play Hindu or Navaho Indian medicine man . . . Instead they plug into their Judaic prophetic heritage and become Old Testament prophets in a post-Christian world.

In a tenth century letter from "Saadia" to the "Children of Israel" we find:

Children of Israel! Know that man's soul will not find rest in this world, even if it finds the Kingdoms of the whole world, because it knows that the world-to-come belongs to it . . .

Children of Israel! Do not push away the faith in God from your eyes, and keep in your minds the fear of God . . .

Children of Israel! All nations gathered silver and gold in their treasuries, but as for you, your silver and gold is the Torah and the Midrash . . .

Children of Israel! Know that you eat in order to live, but that you do not live in order to eat . . .

Saadia's letter is a classic summing up of the essence of Jewish

423

tradition: the elevation of faith and spirituality above secularism and materialism, a disbelief in this world, an anticipation of the "world-to-come," a respect for sacred learning (the Torah and Midrash) combined with a disdain for wealth.

Hoffman and Rubin like to think of themselves as wild-haired freaks (free-ks) and madmen, C-R-A-Z-Y. They claim that they are TV-maddened weirdos on endless kicks-trip, trying to duplicate Marx Brothers' and TV excitement in everyday life. They claim that for them the world is just Artaud-, McLuhan- and Warhol-inspired theatrics, that the overview view from their perch above image-manipulated America enables them to disbelieve in appearance and debunk the whole phoney system as media-fraud.

OK on one level—if we accept them as totally secularized, media-transformed electronic ecstatics, with the contemporary put-on scene flowing through them. But then in *Revolution for the Hell of It* Hoffman writes:

I once wanted to start a newspaper called the New York *Liar*. It would be the most honest paper in the country. I would sit in a dark closet and write all the news. The paper would be printed with lemon juice, which is invisible until you heat it with an iron, hence involving the reader. I would write about events without ever leaving the closets. We all see things through a closet darkly.

We see God through a glass—darkly. We see the world around us (and inside us) through a closet—darkly. Hoffman's deepest wish is to reject totally "outside information." He wants to shut out the outside and write like Jeremiah, the chosen *nabi* (announcer), not about actualities or possibilities, but prophecies, in the dark, waiting for an inner, mystic illumination. Hoffman is an exact representation of the picture of the prophet that Buber gives in *Pointing the Way:*

The prophet speaks the word that it is his task to speak; he is borne by this task, proceeding from a divine purpose and pointing to a divine goal. The spirit moves him; not only his organs of speech but the whole man is taken up into the service of the spirit. The body and life of the man become a part of this service and by this a symbol of the message.

Hoffman's whole concentration on acting crazy, letting go,

losing control is a traditional part of the Hebrew prophet's allowing his own "selfness" kinky, schmaltzy parody to be submerged under the imperativeness of the message that is "flowing" through him. And, as Buber points out, the prophet's commitment is total, not merely intellectual, but a total life-style, ontological commitment. When Hoffman de-emphasizes the importance of McLuhan he does so on the grounds that McLuhan is "merely academic." The Yippies, in contrast, are action- (total commitment) oriented: "What we seek are new living styles. We don't want to talk about them."

In 1946 anti-government (establishment) resistance in the U.S. was still cloudily theoretical enough for Paul Goodman—in *Drawing the Line*—to discuss at length the differences between a "technology of surplus" and a "technology of scarcity," and how, in a society of surplus, the worker can be controlled by having too much and hearing too much of the wrong (or "right"—depending on the point of view) kind of information. He is even allowed a certain amount of dissent in order to give him a feeling of "freedom." The ideas are valid and still relevant today, but the whole approach is disengaged from any sense of immediacy or urgency. It is lukewarm, low-key, drawn-out, low-pressured. By 1960 C. Wright Mills, in a "Letter to the New Left" (*New Left Review*, Sept.–Oct., 1960), was announcing, "That Age of Complacency is ending . . . We are beginning to move again." Rejecting the classic Marxist concentration on the working class as *the* pivot point of change, Mills, looking abroad, sees the intelligentsia (students, the young) as the probable force of future social change. But the view is still toward the future, the pressure not immediate but anticipated.

The Port Huron statement of the SDS in 1962 is a much more prickly, paranoid, "hot" document. Generalized theory shifts to specific U.S. problems: racism, the Cold War, the Bomb, the split between the U.S. government and the people, the loneliness, estrangement, and alienation of the individual in contemporary industrial society. There is a special focus on the beginnings of

425

student radicalism contrasted with the mass apathy of the majority of students and campuses.

Between 1962 and 1969 two major forces were at work in American youth. The very visible, vocal, extroverted force was that of the Hippies—energized, colorful, psychedelic Beats who believed that an alternative counterculture could be created in the very midst of "Moloch-country." Hooked on the idea of the "technology of surplus," they believed that their Hinduized, orientalist, mind-blowing, sense-expanding ecstaticism could exist as a kind of "overflow" of U.S. industrial energy. They were to be the "aesthetic component" of the military-industrial complex and live unmolested in a world of *satori*, sutras, mantras, electronic and chemical tripping out.

Simultaneous with this Beat-derived mysticism, however, the activist, militant, hard-headed, guerrilla-enamored radicals, inspired by Fidel Castro and Che Guevara, tuned in on U.S. as an imperialist world-power (not as protective Big Daddy), were preparing for a genuine social revolution. As the 1969 "Weathermen" statement of SDS puts it (in *New Left Notes,* June 18, 1969): "The goal is the destruction of U.S. imperialism and the achievement of a classless world: world communism." Amusingly enough, in the "Weathermen" statement C. Wright Mills' "Letter to the New Left" is echoed, almost parodied as the young are identified with the working class: "Most young people in the U.S. are part of the working class." Classic Marxism keeps hanging on. To a great extent inspired by Mao, Che, the Black Panthers, and the "Third World," these new deadly serious activists wholeheartedly accept the "outsider's" view of U.S. society. Their psychic observation tower is located in Cuba, Red China, North Vietnam, the jungles of Guatemala. The specific purpose of SDS is to "relate each particular issue to the revolution." The result: setting up the "Establishment" as ploys for insurgent action . . . as in the People's Park incident in Berkeley in 1969.

The Yippies are a kind of comic-relief SDS deviationists. SDS

426

is serious, hung-up, almost solemn. Revolution is business for them. But the Yippies are burlesque comic revolutionaries confronting the whole hard, solemn U.S. scene with the weaponry of disbelieving zaniness, irony, ballyhoo. They are theatrical guerrillas investing in their theater the "idea of extreme action, pushed beyond all limits . . . the agitation of tremendous masses, convulsed and hurled against each other . . ." that is called for by Artaud in his *The Theater and Its Double.*

"The Yippie idea of fun is overthrowing the government" (Jerry Rubin), though, and the Yippie "program," which includes the abolition of all money, work, censorship, drug laws, prison sentences for blacks, all laws related to crimes without victims, which wants to break down U.S. society into "various tribal groups" and wants everything (clothing, housing, education, transportation, food) free, is essentially the same as the SDS Weathermen statement: "The goal is the destruction of U.S. imperialism and the achievement of a classless world: world communism." The Yippies are anti-logical, dadaistic, psychedelic, mind-blown revolutionaries who, following Castro's rule-of-thumb principle that "action is one of the most efficient instruments for bringing about the triumph of ideas among the masses," move everything into action-images, icons, the information symbolology of hitting the mind hard with hard-sell visibility— like action commercials on TV.

The U.S. Military-Industrial Beast has been under attack for a long time now. During World War II the enemy was well defined; the Beast itself was younger, leaner, more active. Since 1945 the Beast has gotten flabby and the attacks against it are not quick and decisive but continuous, debilitating, and from a vast number of separate sources perhaps ultimately but certainly not proximately related. Cuba, Vietnam, the Middle East, Latin America . . . the perimeters of the Beast's very fibers and tissues are overextended and overstretched, and the blood-loss at these perimeters weakens and drains the whole organism.

Now with the Yippies the attack centers on the Beast's own

427

internal survival systems. The Beast maintains its own internal equilibrium through genetic coding (education), metabolic regulation (court system), an anti-toxin, anti-disease system (police), a peripheral nervous system that records the world around it (informers, police spies), and a central nervous system (newspapers, TV, movies, etc.) that brings the information into the brain (the policy-makers). Through its brain the Beast knows what it is, where it is going, what it must do to survive, and once the brain and central and peripheral nervous systems are destroyed the whole rest of the organism begins to die.

Rubin in *Do It!* writes:

> Crime in the streets is news; law and order is not. A revolution is news; the status quo ain't.
> The media does not *report* "news," it *creates* it. An event *happens* when it goes on TV and becomes myth.
> The media is not "neutral." The presence of a camera transforms a demonstration, turning us into heroes . . .
> Television keeps us escalating our tactics . . .

By plugging into the media the Yippies have effectively interfered with the Beast's own grasp of its identity. When the police in Chicago started clubbing the news reporters who had come to "record" the Yippies' demonstrations in 1968, it was the surfacing of an inter-organ "war" within the physiological structure of the Beast itself. The nature of media is such, however, that it automatically absorbs and exploits whatever is "new." The Yippies, raised and programmed by the Beast, attack their own past.

They attack the Beast's future by entering and disrupting the schools. They botch up the Beast's metabolism by clotting up and trying to neutralize the courts . . . but more effectively than anything else they blur and confuse "information," program into the Beast's amoral, production/consumption brain all sorts of confusing notions about morality and good and evil. SDS leader Tom Hayden, testifying before the National Commission on the Causes and Prevention of Violence stated, "The truth is that we all live under a system that requires violence because it is based on the exploitation of man by man ... against this backdrop, the 'violence of the Left' is minor. Our total violence over the last five years has not reached that of a single B-52 raid in Vietnam."

The danger of the New Left is not in its present violence, but in its awakening in the Beast a moral sense. For the Beast a moral sense would be a fatal disease ... which the Beast senses and fights against so violently. Julius Lester in his *Revolutionary Notes* sees the Yippies precisely as a consciousness-stimulating force which has politicized "thousands who could not be politicized through facts, figures, or theories."

When this disease of politicization first began to spread and the Beast became increasingly aware of its own beastliness, it first hated itself, then the hate turned to self-acceptance. Now acceptance has become defiance and the Beast's whole organic structure is relegated to one function—the survival and triumph of bestiality ... at any cost.

IV
CRITICAL CONSCIOUSNESS

Ideology and literature:
American Renaissance
and F.O. Matthiessen
GEORGE ABBOTT WHITE

for Louis K. Hyde, Jr.

For a long time I anguished over the stance of this essay. Should I adopt the distance, the cool disinterestedness of the professional critic and "open" the text of Matthiessen's masterwork, demonstrate the tense balance between vast design and numerous shrewd insights that gave American literature its classical period and critical coherence and American Studies its model and imperative? R.W.B. Lewis once remarked that Matthiessen invented the American Romantic Movement; Roy Harvey Pearce suggested his achievement in characterizing criticism, after his death in 1950, as Post-Matthiessenian; an entire generation of critics, including Harry Levin, Perry Miller, Henry Nash Smith, C.L. Barber, Leo Marx, Joseph H. Summers, J.C. Levenson, G. Robert Stange, and Lewis, have testified in writing and conversation to his massive influence as a teacher, colleague, friend. And more than one has reminisced about the personal impact of *American Renaissance*[1]. Should I resurrect interest in the book, attend to Matthiessen's neglect by assembling a telephone book of footnotes, the tortured roadmap through professional journals in his defense?

Or, focusing on this most important work of Matthiessen's varied career, assuming old and young are well aware of its centrality, should I relate the story of its origins, gestation, the shapes it took to finished product? Certainly people would also be interested in chatty literary facts: That this slight Yale graduate ('23) only began to read American literature while completing a B. Litt. at Oxford (on Oliver Goldsmith); that his original thesis topic at Harvard in the late Twenties on Walt Whitman was rejected because there was "too much already written" on the poet; that his 678-page magnum opus was initiated by a letter in the early Thirties from friend and publisher W. W. Norton asking for a "small" book on American literature, and that that request over a decade expanded, intensified and became more inclusive, exploded into nothing less than a major assessment of American "art" and "expression" having its center in the mid-Nineteenth century with Emerson, Thoreau, Hawthorne, Melville, and Whitman, but ranging retrospectively for rich "links" to Shakespeare, Donne, Herbert, and Milton, prospectively to James, Mann, Eliot, and Hemingway, including considerations of oratory and opera, clipper ship building and Greek Revival architecture, the open-air painting of Millet, Mount, and Eakins; that his 1006-page typescript was painfully, and regretfully, rejected by Norton as far too long and too expensive to publish (even though one house reader remarked in a memo: "It certainly represents ten years of solid work . . . a Gibraltar of the period and a milestone for future scholarly reference."), by Houghton Mifflin ("too detailed, too exhaustive for the general reader . . ." needing "a lot of combing out and simplification . . ." because "it is a scholar's book . . . you, in brief, know too much on the subject."), and finally accepted by Oxford University Press (New York) in the late autumn of 1940, *in toto,* on the condition that Matthiessen provide a subsidy of $1000 (almost a third of the cost of

431

publication, which Oxford was only too glad to repay as the book rapidly caught on). As interesting too Matthiessen's determination to get things right, even in type, even if "author's corrections" came to $348.04; his search for the title appropriate for a book that would endure ("I have written," he would say to his publisher in rejecting *'Life and Letters'* as a subtitle, "not just for this year, but to last."), from *Man in the Open Air,* to *From Emerson to Whitman,* to *Literature for Democracy,* to *American Masterwork,* to *The Great Age in American Literature,* to Harry Levin's apt suggestion made only six months before actual publication[2]—all resulting in the "big book" he wanted, 2 pounds $9\frac{1}{2}$ ounces, containing some 300,000 words, "each of which," *Time* magazine was acute enough to note in a two-page review, "was put there with evident care."

But would all this be merely avoiding something at once more necessary and more difficult?

Historian William Freehling has recently written that as conflict in our society increases, either overtly in the prisons of Attica, or covertly, quietly, with teenagers shooting heroin in suburban high school bathrooms, older explanations of division become either obsolete—as was the case with Beard's struggle between rich and poor, or impossible to respect—as with the "consensus" historians in the past few years. What explanations remain after these first possibilities? Freehling speculates:

A second possibility, which now promises to be the latest form of orthodoxy, is to construct psychological explanations for American history. The new psychological historians tend to accept a consensus view of American society. They find an understanding of political controversy; not in divisive social reality but rather in paranoid misperceptions of a reality hardly divided at all. The psychological historian's work depends on the important truth that what men perceive at the time, not what historians later know to be true, governs the historical process. Their work has been encouraged by the relatively recent acceptance in this country of intellectual history, with its emphasis upon ideas, beliefs, and persuasions. More important, the new psychological historians have arrived at a time when Freudian explanations are all the rage.[3]

Beyond historical explanations, this new *emphasis* is being utilized not only by historians, cultural or otherwise, but by biographers and literary critics. For literature, what began in the Fifties with the exciting examination of Stephen Crane by John Berryman, continued, on a very high level, with Aileen Ward on Keats, Leon Edel on James, Justin Kaplan on Twain, and most recently, John Unterecker on Hart Crane. These are the peaks, however, rising from a dull, expansive plane. Grasping at the psychological, English departments retooled for a new "scholarly" production where microscopes were rapidly turned into cold steel chisels. Judgments grew diffuse, other-worldly, oddly forgiving. With all motives suspect, all action explained pathologically, the effect was also increasingly reductive (most blatantly the case in psychology with Bruno Bettelheim's academic credentials and scholarship explaining away rather than explaining youthful protest). In a review of *The Progressive Historians* (1968), Robert Sklar approached the political consequences of such methodology:

The fact of the matter is that young scholars have attacked [Richard] Hofstadter's view of history not because he is in some way identified with a consensus school of history but because of the overt political views he has expressed in his historical works. Hofstadter has been a leading exponent not of a consensus view of history but an elitest view of history. His influential historical works have concentrated on finding fault with the motives, style, and perspective of political movements for social change and social justice, stressing such factors as anti-intellectualism, status consciousness, and anti-Semitism to the neglect of specific political proposals and concrete social circumstances.[4]

The method, the atmosphere, is here however, and no historian, no biographer, no critic, can afford to ignore it, if only in rebuttal. To write of Matthiessen at this time and not deal, in some way, with the psychological life would be the height of irresponsibility. And what a wealth of contradictions: The youngest of four (and the only one without red hair), born on the West Coast of a quiet, well-bred New England mother and an irresponsible, two-fisted industrialist father, broken family, raised with the mother in the Midwest and East, schooled in New York at Hackley, then Yale where he was, among other things, the crusading Managing Editor of the *Yale Daily News* as well as the leader of a Bible study group, off to Oxford as a Rhodes Scholar, and back to America, at Harvard, for his PhD. Teaching at Yale, then Harvard, at elite Eliot House, this young scholar who had done his thesis on Elizabethan translation rapidly turned for subject to America, writing first about a regionalist, Sarah Orne Jewett, a cosmopolitan, T.S. Eliot—before *American Renaissance*—and then

James, the James Family, and Dreiser after. At home in Boston's fashionable Louisburg Square, he summered in a small town in Maine—Kittery—where he would drink with welders from the nearby Navy Yard and with visiting poets from England; vacationed in Santa Fe, where he worked with the progressive Senator, Bronson Cutting, writing on Yeats for *The Southern Review* one day and on miner's strikes in Gallup for *The New Republic* the next (where, on more than one occasion, he narrowly avoided a beating by anti-union goons). Throughout the Thirties, this student of Lowes and Babbitt and friend of T.S. Eliot filled a week, for example, by helping to organize a meeting of the Harvard Teacher's Union (which he would later serve as president, from 1940–1944), writing an article on Elizabethan drama, teaching a Whitman poem or a Shakespeare play, tutoring on the "Economics" of Henry James, raising money for the Loyalists, discussing the Puritans, worshipping at Christ Church in Cambridge, or, more likely, the "higher" Church of the Advent on the back of Beacon Hill. The man who wore Brooks Brothers suits (out of somewhat embarrassed convenience), whose friends included Washington lawyers, New York brokers, United States Senators, who found "the best China tea obtainable in Boston, and . . . served [it] in a quietly exquisite early American ware," was also the man who denounced the Truman Doctrine, who would later tirelessly campaign the North End tenements for Henry Wallace (and give a seconding speech at the Progressive Party convention in Philadelphia in 1948), and will $5000 to the socialist magazine, *Monthly Review*. And at the center of his life was his life-long homosexuality and more than twenty-year relationship with the American painter, Russell Cheney. The tensions, the tendernesses, the loyalty of that relationship alone could prompt a study that would give us, perhaps, new understandings of love itself.

Close, very close, though not close enough. One stance remains and perhaps this is the place to make clear my own interest, or need, and what I conceived to be the larger needs of my generation in pursuing the "meaning" of Matthiessen after my discovery of him in the mid-Sixties at the University of Michigan.

A discussion of ideology and its end/irrelevance/counter-revolutionary quality began in the mid-Fifties. In addition to a rather disingenuous avoidance of ends and instrumental concentration on means, this discussion on the part of older intellectuals was freighted with the baggage of the Thirties and Forties, some of which Noam Chomsky finally unpacked when he wrote:

When we consider the responsibility of intellectuals, our basic concern must be their role in the creation and analysis of ideology. And in fact [Irving] Kristol's contrast between the unreasoning ideological types and the responsible experts is formulated in terms that immediately bring to mind Daniel Bell's interesting essay on 'the end of ideology,' an essay which is as important for what it leaves unsaid as for its actual content. Bell presents and discusses the Marxist analysis of ideology as a mask for class interest, in particular, quoting Marx's well-known description of the belief of the bourgeoisie that 'the conditions of its emancipation are the conditions by which alone modern society can be saved and the class struggle avoided.' He then argues that the age of ideology is ended, supplanted, at least in the West, by a general agreement that each issue must be settled on its own individual terms, within the framework of a welfare state in which, presumably, experts in the conduct of public affairs will have a prominent role. Bell is quite careful, however, to characterize the precise sense of 'ideology' in which 'ideologies are exhausted.' He is referring only to ideology as 'the conversion of ideas into social levers,' to ideology as 'a set of beliefs, infused with passion . . . [which] . . . seeks to transform the whole of a way of life.' The crucial words are 'transform' and 'convert into social levers.' Intellectuals in the West, he argues, have lost interest in converting ideas into social levers for the radical transformation of society. Now that we have achieved the pluralistic society of the welfare state, they see no further need for a radical transformation of society; we may tinker with our way of life here and there, but it would be wrong to try to modify it in any significant way. With this consensus of intellectuals, ideology is dead.

There are several striking facts about Bell's essay. First, he does not point out the extent to which this consensus of the intellectuals is self-serving. He does not relate his observation that by and large, intellectuals have lost interest in 'transforming the whole way of life' to the fact that they play an increasingly prominent role in running the welfare state; he does not relate their general satisfaction with the welfare state to the fact that, as he observes elsewhere, 'America has become an affluent society,' offering 'place . . . and prestige . . . to the onetime radicals.' Secondly, he offers no serious argument to show that intellectuals are somehow 'right' or 'objectively justified' in reaching the consensus to which he alludes, with its rejection of the notion that society should be transformed. Indeed, although Bell is fairly sharp about the empty rhetoric of the 'New Left,' he seems to have a quite utopian faith that technical experts will be able to come to grips with the few problems that still remain; for example, the very fact that labor is treated as a commodity and the problems of 'alienation.'[5]

At this distance, the notion that America was an "affluent society" with a "few" problems to be solved by "experts" seems nothing less than a cruel joke. In 1960, it encouraged, by reaction, a substantial reformulation of social and political questions by young intellectuals, many of whom were to join the Student Non-Violent Co-Ordinating Committee (SNCC) and head South or find Students for a Democratic Society (SDS) and remain in the

435

North. They were good students (countless studies have shown them to have been highly-integrated, idealistic, and intelligent); they studied hard. They read all the assigned texts for class, but schooled themselves, each other, on what was unassigned, beyond the acceptable academic parameters—William Appleman Williams, Paul Goodman, Herbert Marcuse, and especially, C. Wright Mills; men who denied that ideology was only what you called Communism or a pejorative label for any systematic thought that was prophetic, visionary, and *textual*, emotional, committed, and *structural*.

By the mid-Sixties, everyone, everything seemed in motion. Campuses were a blur of one rally after another, a succession of Teach-Ins; students were being arrested North and South by the thousands; and many of the most imaginative young thinkers and writers I knew were turning to "organizing"—mobilizing either poor black/white communities in the North, or the rapidly-expanding antiwar movement on campuses beyond Ann Arbor. More than a few white middleclass students were actively searching for ideology, for coherent explanations of what was happening and what they should be doing. As Paul Potter, the fourth president of SDS, wrote:

Most of us have a very abstract idea of what ideology is and we combine that with a deep anti-ideological bias that we have inherited from the society. The two of course are related. The abstract sense is that ideology is a musty, 19th century sort of thing that is European in origin, until the 20th century when it finally caught hold in the underdeveloped world. Our sense of ideology is that they are rigid, closed religions in character and sectarian by effect, that is, they make false separations among people.

All of this supports our anti-ideological bias—until of course we reach a point of political frustration where suddenly the idea of a rigid (well-worked-out), closed (self-confident), religious (authoritative), sectarian (distinguishing Us once and for all from Them) system becomes appealing.

And where was I?

In the words of the Welsh artist/poet, David Jones, I was "in parenthesis," in a hiatus with half a dozen imperatives pulling me toward a shrouded future. What I thought most important, what I wanted most to do, was to study and teach literature, though how could I justify that to my community and myself when the most anyone could do was react decently to each day's crisis?

About this time a friend, a graduate student in his mid-thirties who was my intellectual and spiritual mentor, gave a sermon on April Fool's Day entitled "April Fools," in which he disclosed and joined the lives of four who had died in April: Bruce Klunder, Dietrich Bonhoeffer, Teilard de Chardin, and Matthiessen. All were, in Tillich's phrase, "on the boundary," all were "fools" in the world's eyes because when Life called, they had responded with their whole beings, for others. He quoted I Corinthians (17–35), the irony of God's having made foolish the "wisdom" of the wise, and encouraged his audience to think of the four as they would think of the Apostles; men sentenced to death who were "foolish" for Christ's sake. After giving a revealing sketch of each man's life, their uniqueness as well as what they shared with the others, he asked us to consider: "Does love call us to norms other than rationality and prudence?"

Afterward, moved, I asked my friend if he had ever met the Harvard critic, Matthiessen. He had not met Matty, in fact, he had seen him only once, at a distance, in the late Forties in Gambier, Ohio, at the Kenyon School of Letters. But he told me that his study of *American Renaissance* had been a personal encounter; a major maturing event in his life.

The reader familiar with American colleges and universities in the last twenty years will appreciate my own sense of great excitement mingled with disappointment. Why had this man's achievement and his history been withheld? I vaguely remembered that works *had* been cited, though with no special emphasis, and as I learned from others, if one questioned, always the embarrassing silences, and then the qualifications, the tactful withdrawals—"he was a difficult man," "he was too involved in politics," "he committed suicide, didn't he?" It was obvious that this withholding was not crudely organized, calculated, only congruent with the reigning (unspoken) academic norms about what was proper, and not unrelated, in literature, to another kind of ideology that went under the rubric, the New Criticism.

437

The New Criticism firmly denied a political component to literature or literary studies, and by the Sixties had secured a deathgrip upon literary response. "Political." The *word* was impossible; to speak then of the *value* of a work that involved judging the insight, experience, decisions, and the commitments that it embodied was out of the question. Such a stand seemed quite wrong to those who agreed with Cleanth Brooks that "poems are not substitute philosophy," or had been convinced by Wellek and Warren that literature occupied "a special ontological status" in which ideas were important to the final product only as brute stone was important to the monument. Such theorists thought of ideas as scaffoldings, important to the builder, perhaps, but torn away when the structure was up; or they thought of ideas as a kind of concrete material, passive and feminine, in which essential form was disposed and housed, made visible.

The manifold dangers of this attitude have, by now, been thoroughly catalogued; but George Steiner in his essay, "The Retreat from the Word," and elsewhere throughout *Language and Silence* (1967), says it most convincingly when he speaks of the "submission of successively larger areas of knowledge to the modes and proceedings of mathematics" (read the New Criticism's pretension to the status of technology; to scientific positivism, exactitude, and the predictive—all of which, finally, are under severe and searching reformulation by scientists themselves) while sacrificing history, values, and ethics on an altar of narrow, narcissistic aestheticism. To those about me for whom literature was an examination of human experience, a way of speaking with significant clarity of man's situation in context; a living mirror, a judge, a projection of possibility, this was more than unsatisfying, it was intolerable. With Emerson we knew that words meant qualities and things, that even taken as the most formal and pure of human actions, art neither becomes itself indifferent nor urges indifference in its witnesses. From what little I knew of Matty, he seemed an essential, viable link with the past. His *praxis* had been to illuminate his own present through simultaneous com-

438

parative judgment with past and future, while deeply involved in that present. The crucial thing for me, for us, was that his life could illuminate large missing areas of historical experience. Naturally Matty, and *American Renaissance,* represented a threat to the academic orthodoxies.

(This is not to say that the silence about Matty was only political. Research has led me to believe that it had very real, very justifiable social and personal components, which could be considered political only in the most abstract sense. *History and Literature* at Harvard College in the Thirties and Forties was a committee and a field of concentration, Matty was both the chairman and the senior tutor. Many of America's major critics were taught or taught as fellows in that program under the joint tutelage of Perry Miller and Matty. The late law professor Harold Solomon recalled it as " . . . the most exciting field. They took only 50 people and everyone was expected to go for honors. It was *demanding:* enormous reading, a general qualifying exam, individual and group tutorials." Their concern for history and literature was intense, and very competitive: all wanted to please. This dynamic in itself set them off from the rest of the College. Certainly there were other factors: Many of them were involved politically, as Communists, Trotskyites, liberals, pacifists. They published magazines, wrote editorials, organized rallies; they were movers and shakers on the campus and from the outside, they were easily viewed as a closed and elite circle. Lesser circles in the Academy have been known to generate extreme resentment even paranoia among those "left out." Yet it is important to understand that as resentments can build themselves into structures and methodologies, those structures and methodologies have other than merely personal bases; their construction does not take place in a social vacuum.)

I don't think I will ever forget eagerly purchasing Charles Feidelson's *Symbolism and American Literature* (1952)[6] around the time I discovered Matty only to find, in the Introduction, these words:

The first large-scale attempt to define the literary quality of American writing at its best was Matthiessen's *American Renaissance*, which is 'primarily concerned with *what* these books were as works of art,' with 'the writer's use of their own tools, their diction and rhetoric, and . . . what they could make of them.' Yet even in this magnificent work, which reorients the entire subject, the sociological and political bent of studies in American literature makes itself felt indirectly. Despite Matthiessen's emphasis on literary form, his concern with the 'artist's use of language' as 'the most sensitive index to cultural history' tends to lead him away from specifically aesthetic problems. This 'one common denominator' which he finds among the five writers treated in his book is not, in the final analysis, a common approach to the art of writing but a common theme –'their devotion to the possibilities of democracy.'

Feidelson continues:

It is more likely that the *really vital* [my italics] common denominator is precisely their attitude toward their medium—that their distinctive quality is a devotion to the possibilities of symbolism.

And there it is. Feidelson's comment is instructive not only because it is characteristic of a way of doing literature and a period of time, but because it is, in itself, a judgment that is ideological. It is not value-neutral, it is not objective, it is not non-political. This is inescapable. Notice his definition of literary "quality." It immediately excludes any criteria beyond the aesthetic. This is fine if you are talking about "aesthetic" quality, but it becomes a purposeful ideological construction when you conflate "literary" to mean "aesthetic." *American Renaissance* is thus acceptable, worthwhile, when it falls into the hopper of aesthetics. To miss the bin is to be faulted, nothing less—when "the sociological and political bent of studies in American literature makes itself felt," even "indirectly"! This is another level of silence about Matty and *American Renaissance* and one I have taken upon myself to address in this particular essay precisely because no one else has thought it either important or possible to elucidate. Even those who have recently, finally, written about him, have avoided ideological concerns because, I think, they still operate within the narrower conceptions of what is permissible, and that to consider other criteria, to broaden and humanize the definition of art, would necessarily denigrate or demean the status of Matty's criticism.

Of course it would. And that is exactly the point, for the issue that Feidelson illustrates is more than cloudy; hidden by language and conventions that cannot easily be challenged. *American Renaissance* cannot be discussed or evaluated not because it is a "bad" book (which would at least make explicit the criteria of badness) but because to raise those *kinds* of questions would be in poor taste. Such poor taste was obliquely the subject several years ago when Richard Poirier spoke in Boston. With Norman Mailer and *Armies of the Night* (1968) as his text, he asked whether or not, besides obscene language, there weren't other items contemporary criticism was unwilling to examine, whether or not we had "a criticism that only looks at what it has been asked to look at"? Frederick Crews was more specific when he wrote, "I do believe that our literary studies generally do have an ideological cast, less in what they say than in what they refuse to consider." (PMLA, May 1970, # 3) Very well. What was refused? Negotiating between the name-calling of "repressive tolerance" and "scholarly neutrality," the social and political conditions that gave rise to the war in Vietnam, Crews carefully noted the larger conceptions operative in American society by raising the following questions: Who consumes literature? Who encourages literary production? What are the values of those people/institutions? From this followed questions on class, status, violence; ignored questions about justice and injustice, power, control; absent questions which, if answered in a fuller context, would finally explain why our criticism is obsessed with coherence and order, why it supports, in fact, blind routine, obedience, authority.

To speak about literature ideologically then, would simply be to reintroduce the world; to raise old questions about the nature and purpose of literature and literary criticism, to ask, among other things, for a criticism in Leo Marx's words, "alert to lapses of moral vision." Some of these questions, some of that morality and value can be found in examining *American Renaissance*: the influences upon the work, the work itself, the faults it embodies because of its ideology. To do so is not only to plumb Matty's work ideologically, it is to plumb the contradictions of his life, their part in his achievement and his tragedy: How to make judgments both within and without History; how to make meaningful connections, join those things which are different yet necessary; how to achieve unity of being so that one *does* what one *says, is* what what one *believes*.

II

A way to proceed would be to examine *all* the influences upon Matty—critical, religious, social, personal, and otherwise—ideologically. Although this has been done to some small extent with his critical background by Richard Ruland in his very useful *The Rediscovery of American Literature* (1967), especially the lengthy, well-conceived chapter on Matty, and recently by Giles Gunn ("Criticism as Repossession and Responsibility: F. O. Matthiessen and the Ideal Critic," *American Quarterly,* December 1970), such an examination, albeit fascinating and worthwhile, would clearly be beyond the scope of this essay.

We could, however, in the distant past, recall the social concerns of Taine, and Sainte-Beuve's desire to relate works-to-life. Pause longer to remember that Arnold (with his enormous influence upon Eliot) was one of the poets most read at Yale during Matty's undergraduate years, and, as he opens one of his last and most important essay/lectures, "The Responsibilities of the Critic" (Hopwood Award Lecture, Ann Arbor, 1949), pointedly mentioned by Matty as his "first critical enthusiasm"; an enthusiasm whose reflective quality was to become a part of him throughout his life. Arnold's poetry to those about Matty assumed the necessary but unwelcome status of the mid-nineteenth century Dissenters—divisive, profoundly melancholy, even "romantic." The poetry was far more. For the man for whom History was a matter of stewardship and a burden (bringing everything but heart), the diligent school inspector who saw education as the only mode of metamorphosis, poetry was a means of secular salvation. The poems were not read as "dreams," as Douglas Bush would have us believe; dreams yearning to "a primitive mythological world of simple joy and harmony." While it is true they demonstrated the extreme divisiveness of man's "inner life"—the instinctual desire for emotional gratification, the intellectual or spiritual

442

desire for symbolic or enduring states, they also revealed Arnold as the master of the elegiac, one whose poetry could "repossess" and celebrate what was forgotten or lost. His poems had the virtue (among many) of seeing man in human scale, and, as in "Dover Beach," often dramatically oscillated between Greek and Christian images to create new human and humane metaphors. The split between the poetry and prose may have been what Matty acknowledged to be Eliot's point of departure from Arnold (besides his asking art to assume the role of religion), Arnold's attention to poetry's *spirit* rather than poetry's *form*. But for Matty poet and critic joined in the "high seriousness" of their calling: to criticize life, to enhance it, to make men do more than merely endure. Matty more than appreciated Arnold with his "elegant yet reserved, cool yet able to glow into warmth, careful never to flare into heat" style.[7] Beyond style, he was moved by Arnold's indictment of the middle class and its indulgent Philistinism, the abuses of the ruling classes, and any literature that was not "useful" in a larger social sense. He incorporated Arnold's "moral strenuousness" into his classroom and his relationships and his "reserved idealism" into his daily life. "Awareness," "wholeness," "unity of being," are Matty's words (and desires) as Arnold's and as Arnold in his later years would concern himself with the crucial problem of the proper relationship between the individual and the State, so Matty in his "Method and Scope" preface to *American Renaissance* would name as one of his major themes "the relation of the individual to society."

Remember too that Matty, in the Thirties, praised the earlier of Paul Elmer More's *Shelburne Essays,* while rejecting More's support of a natural aristocracy, his zeal to defend property (" . . . the rights of property are more important than the right to life."), and his tolerance for the *status quo* (his unreconstructed conservativism encouraged him to publicly defend strike-breakers). Matty was the student of More's fellow New Humanist ("ethical conservative," in Ruland's phrase), Irving Babbitt. In this context, Ruland contends that Matty learned more about literature from the "Right" than the "Left," but if he did—assuming that

443

we have agreed on the definition of "learned,"—then it was a highly-selective learning, by opposition as much as by acceptance. In *From the Heart of Europe* (1948) (his highly-revised journal of teaching at the first Salzburg Seminar in 1947 and in the fall, at Charles University in Prague; a book which Austin Warren has called "as much a spiritual autobiography as a political document") he remembered:

By far the most living experience in my graduate study at Harvard came through the lectures of Irving Babbitt with whose neo-humanistic attack upon the modern world I disagreed at nearly every point.

Matty could not agree with an attitude that neatly divided the world or literature into corrupt Europeans and innocent Americans, nor one that supported, with few reservations, unbridled capitalism. In a review of two books in 1942, one about Babbitt and one by him, Matty would praise both the integrity and intensity of Babbitt's teaching and sympathize with his sorry treatment at Harvard, respecting his "insistence on the complete moral responsibility of the individual." He would also be grateful for Babbitt's exposure of the weaknesses of Romanticism, "the falseness of any anti-social aesthetic," the "disasters of being either sheltered academics or shallow liberals." Yet it was necessary to challenge Babbitt's "atomic individualism" and to recognize that "much of Babbitt's political thinking was reactionary."

In an essay on Eliot published shortly after his death in 1965, Stephen Spender recalled the Twenties as a time when undergraduates and graduates alike worried about what was "real" and how, if at all, to live real lives. The imaginative writings of "D. H. Lawrence and the vague intimations of psychoanalysis [encouraged us] to think that we might discover our real instinctual selves in sex." That was England, Oxford and Cambridge. In America, in New England, the psychological primitivism of Lawrence had an energy (especially in *Studies in Classic American Literature* (1923)) that greatly moved Matty. He knew, in the writings of Eliot and others, that the rational in Christianity, and indeed, in much of Western thought, had deep, often irrational and pagan roots, and that criticism needed to tap those

444

roots. But while "phallic consciousness" strove for better relations between the sexes, between men, it all too often resulted in brutal exploitation in the name of some desperate retreat from constricting, middle class society. Matty could understand the need of the artist in modern industrial society to set himself apart, but exploitation, even in the name of art, could not be excused. With the Agrarians,[8] Lawrence shared a hatred for machines and the industrial society that destroyed "organic" ties of man to land, man to man, yet the passion of that hatred, Matty was well aware, easily turned into hatred for contemporary industrial society; contempt for the taste of the public into contempt for the public itself. Lawrence, like Yeats, could both praise the "folk" for their vitality (and, one suspects, their fixity and their images) while at the same time making racist, anti-Semitic, aristocratic statements, denouncing the "mob" whenever it organized and moved to challenge inequity. Like Yeats too, he was obsessed with authority and rule based on the natural superiority of individuals and his fiction increasingly moved towards states of violence, blood, and blood-sacrifice. He translated those ideas himself to their social equivalents ("For the mass of people knowledge *must* be symbolical, mystical, dynamic. This means you must have a higher, responsible, conscious class: and in the varying degrees the lower classes," and "the secret is to commit into the hands of the sacred few the responsibility which now lies like torture on the mass . . . " and "men have got to choose their leaders and obey them to the death. And it must be a system of culminating aristocracy, society tapering like a pyramid to the supreme leader."); equivalents that were inherently close to a fascist conception of society. When Lawrence could write, "There is poetry of this immediate present, instant poetry, as well as the poetry of the infinite past and the infinite future. The seething poetry of the incarnate Now is supreme," however, the Matty who was also moved, personally and critically, by "Tradition and the Individual Talent" (1917), could hardly support this, except in the intense positivistic sense that I.A. Richards trained the mind to read poetry.

445

Matty had acknowledged Richards along with Eliot in his "Responsibilities" lecture, saying that "the talents and principles of [them has] been the most pervasive force upon the criticism of the past quarter-century." Their method "was a criticism that aimed to give the closest possible attention to the text at hand, to both the structure and texture of the language,"—its effect was "considerable," and "their work has thereby become instrumental in the revolt against concentrating exclusively on the past." Indeed, according to C. L. Barber, it had an immediate effect upon Matty after Richards' visit to Harvard in 1929 and before Eliot's in 1932:

Eight English Poets [which Matty taught in the early Thirties] . . . was inspired by I. A. Richards . . . It was a very seminal course. It was not chronological. We read eight poets in depth with close analysis. It was the new criticism before New Criticism was advertised . . . we would read and talk about poetry without a systematic line of argument. A typical comment by Matty would be: ' . . . now to round into another approach.' He would use the key passage.

But there was a connection. As Barber remembers:

Yet there was the old world behind Matty's innovation too. He was thorough and systematic in the old ways—a strict sequence backed up with bibliography. That was the base you never saw. He took over Lowes' Shakespeare course one year. I remember seeing after his death a great box of handwritten cards for the 16th century . . . the point is that he had worked all that background out.

Richards was a "challenge" to Matty's own evolving critical method, and Richards' influence would be apparent in the close analyses of Eliot's poetry (*The Achievement of T. S. Eliot* (1935)), which, although "obvious" to the British (TLS), did more than any other book to introduce Eliot to the American academy. That method would also reveal itself in the "key passages" in *American Renaissance,* but by 1945, in reviewing Karl Shapiro's *Essay on Rime* (1945), Matty would write: "In denying I. A. Richards' claim that 'poetry can save us,' in affirming that all great art must have its tap-root in adequately human moral values, Shapiro would seem to have established a solider 'hope for poetry . . .'" In "Responsibilities," he would question the value of Richards' method even more closely in saying, "we have come to the unnatural point where textual analysis seems to be an end in itself," condemning the irresponsible reductionism that would turn literature into "a puzzle to be solved."

446

It is obvious that methodologically, as well as ideologically (by contrast, by argument, dissent, and even by acceptance and contradiction, as is most the case with Eliot, to be discussed below), Matty learned a great deal from the Right. Another equally-fruitful path, in spite of its being a *via negativa,* would be to follow Matty's praise (and principally and more often his censure) of those critics closest to him politically—progressives, socialists, Marxists, Marxians—keeping in mind that one is often harshest and most demanding of those one cares about most, especially when that caring is not an abstract exercise, but a way of enhancing "the possibilities of life in America."

By far the most important was Vernon Louis Parrington's three-volume *Main Currents of American Thought* (1927, 1930) that moved in great sweeps from Calvinist gloom through Romantic optimism to modern pessimism. In *The Progressive Historian,* Hofstadter said, "It is hard to re-create the excitement generated by *Main Currents* in the years between 1927 and the mid-1940's." Howard Mumford Jones remembered some:

... who can forget the tingling sense of discovery ... All other histories of literature were compelled to pale their intellectual fires. We were free of Anglo-philism, of colonialism, of apology at last ... Here was a useable past, adult, reasonable, coherent.

And Trilling, in his famous essay, "Reality in America" (1940, 1950), could attribute to Parrington, "an influence on our conception of American culture which is not equalled by that of any other writer in the last two decades." In print, and in letters to his editor at Oxford at the time of *American Renaissance,* Matty agreed. "What I have tried to do," he wrote, "is take off where Parrington stopped, and do for the evaluation of our literature what he did for our liberal thought."

The question was the content of that influence. A democratic idealist like Turner and Beard, Parrington revived and celebrated the traditions he valued most—of early dissent, of Jeffersonian and Jacksonian democracy, and of secular enlightenment. But like Turner and Beard, he did not merely "stop"—his writing was an embodiment, not a halt—and Trilling's critique in 1940 ("Parrington, Mr. Smith and Reality," later "Reality in America"), while directed in part against the Stalinists who had played fast and loose with Parrington's lexicon and Parrington's past (and later, in 1946, 1950, directed against those naive liberals and fellow-travellers who, in lauding Dreiser, had badly confused "the Right, the Good, and the Correct"), still had Parrington's tome squarely in the sights, and when the trigger was pulled, the result, according to Hofstadter, was "devastating." No one could deny Parrington's efforts: utter faithfulness in going beyond the narrow, conventional, snobbish, genteel work before him (although Trilling rather deflatingly let us know just how little, intellectually, that work amounted to), laboring 16 years under terrible conditions (Hofstadter noted the frequency of the word 'bitter' in Parrington's painful letters), sitting on publishers' doorsteps for 10, but this earned few points from Trilling whose stern verdict was that Parrington's mind was "too predictable to be consistently interesting."[9] *Key here is to note that in spite of the political motive behind Trilling, his critique was very much the kind of critique Matty would make, but did not (at least not in print).*

Trilling had no problem whatsoever in putting his finger on Parrington's non-trivial errors (and by indirection on those glowing Marxists who would inflate and misuse him). Parrington's "method"—a rather humdrum economic determinism (which even the Marxists pronounced as a "not subtle enough" materialism)—Trilling witheringly judged as "not much more than the demonstration that most writers stick to their own social class." From the first word it was all very deliberate, Trilling was after larger game: nothing less than ideologues and an entire culture. He quickly demonstrated that Parrington failed to apply his souped-up determinism equally (the villains undergo analysis, the heroes are pronounced healthy and run free) and, with a little close reading, isolated passages that made it embarrassingly obvious that Parrington shifted the meanings of his two crucial words—'romanticism' and 'realism'—as often as he shifted the camera to new actors. Still, not *the* problem, for Trilling insisted—almost ideologically we might say—that Parrington's errors of ambiguity were not matters of skill, not "lapses of taste." If a

448

writer's being a "romantic" was but a venial sin in Parrington's cosmology, not being an honest intellectual evoked blistering damnation in Trilling's—especially when ideas were so blatantly the handmaidens of ideology. We see that Parrington's problem was not only one of mind, "a limited sense of what constitutes a difficulty . . . ," or aesthetics, a bafflement before a work of art that was "complex, personal and not literal," it was first, that he made an ideological cookie-cutter and then applied it to "reality" in a way that pre-judged reality (in his case, a liberal-progressive cookie-cutter, though one that had radical, and as he admitted later, Marxian, edges); second, those individuals like Hawthorne, Poe, and Henry James ("never a realist," wrote Parrington, "a self-deceived romantic"), who were skeptical of certain aspects of America, who practiced their art in a somewhat "abstract" way, who, in short, had *ideas* about rather than presenting the experience itself, didn't fit the mold, were not only relegated to second-class citizenship in the republic of American history, but were shamed, scorned, and made to carry the taint of not being quite "manly" enough; third, that avoiding the "complexity" of "reality" (e.g., admitting motives other than rigidly economic, explaining how ideas *developed* rather than merely recurred, allowing that those he disagreed with had affective spirits too), by conflating the meaning of democracy to exclude complexity as a possibility, in the "service" of "the broadest possible democracy," was hardly a service and beyond encouraging Philistinism, was very likely an adumbrating danger.

Elevated to a much-praised dictum, those attitudes fostered public censorship and personal blindness, a stifling of criticism about means and ends, and finally, worst, established a false dichotomy between mind and experience—that the latter is always to be preferred by true democrats who are "feeling" men and the former is always to be regarded as more than a little suspect. Speaking of Parrington's critique of Hawthorne, that he was "forever dealing in shadows," Trilling reminded us that "shadows" are quite as real as anything in the galaxy, but that the real task for a critic was to get behind the metaphor and see what

449

truth it bespoke, what reality it was trying to explain. To avoid this, even in the name of the best of causes, was moral tunnel vision, and so

Parrington still [1950] stands at the center of American thought about American culture because, as I say, he expresses the chronic American belief that there exists an opposition between *reality* and *mind* and that one must enlist oneself in the party of reality.

The distortions Parrington embodied were not isolated. If he provided the general framework for discussion, it was Van Wyck Brooks who, much earlier and then much later, provided specific and other, literary evaluations. A man wears many faces, but Matty recognized only two with Brooks: the early Brooks of *The Wine of the Puritans* (1909) and especially *America's Coming of Age* (1915), and the later Brooks of *The Flowering of New England* (1936) and *The Times of Melville and Whitman* (1947). Close to radical Randolph Bourne, Brooks had distinguished between "highbrow" and "lowbrow" cultures in America and the need for their integration—a curative act the arts, functioning as a social force, would perform. This Brooks was an awakener, earnest, vigorously "concerned with ideas" and "critical discriminations" and even though he was read by "hundreds instead of thousands," this Brooks made "stringent demands for a culture adequate to our needs," which was "the strongest influence [along with Lewis Mumford's] on my own first work." The other Brooks seemed worse than a pale stranger to the first, smiling a foolish smile while letting his friends down by abandoning his principles. Bernard DeVoto had said that Brooks' earlier opinions had *depressed* the writers of the Twenties and naturally Matty had argued that it had *challenged* them, but the disagreement was impossible to broach to Brooks. The recent collection of letters between Brooks and Mumford painfully records the reason, a shattering mental collapse—from 1925 until the early Thirties— which Hilton Kramer, in a review, says was brought on "by the unresolved conflicts inherent in the severely critical attitude Brooks brought to his early books on American culture." Brooks' striking disengagement was more than a disappointment to Matty, but Kramer identifies it as an ingredient central to Brooks' cau-

450

tious mental rehabilitation in the Thirties; a rehabilitation "predicated on an absolute refusal ever again to face the worst" about American culture, or to face his own need "to think about himself as a patrician, a yea-saying idealist."

Brooks had argued with conviction for a "usable past" and by the time his *Flowering of New England* appeared, Matty, already a year into the actual writing of *American Renaissance,* had taken this earlier notion for his guide. Thus, his review of the book in 1936, gives us a sense of his immediate felt needs as he delineated how far the later Brooks had fallen away.

There were several glaring absences: true historical context and causality (Matty suggested that Brooks consult Becker and Beard); a respect for the aesthetic integrity of works themselves; a feeling for the complexity of moral values, indeed, values themselves; a sense of the "brooding darkness" of life, or tragic skepticism. During this period it was not as though Brooks was himself wholly oblivious to the political crises about him (in this year, 1936, he ran for the Connecticut legislature on the Socialist ticket), yet in spite of the fact that his actual involvement was seen by him as more of a "sop" to his conscience; conscience, connected to ideas in his book had a strange, disembodied quality, not unrelated to his more demanding psychic economy and by projection, to what *he* conceived his times needing. In anticipation of Perry Miller's book (1939) however, Matty questioned those ideas, and needs by taking issue with Brooks' statement that his subject was "the New England mind," and gave as an example of Brooks' actual avoidance or weak treatment of ideas, Brooks' portrait of Webster composing the Bunker Hill oration while wading up a stream trout-fishing—there is an allusion to Burke, and then the "sublime," "but beyond that," wrote Matty, "there is hardly anything about the orations themselves, and none of Parrington's analysis of Webster's leading ideas, either in their relation to their conditioning by Boston Federalism, or in their derivation from Montesquieu and Harrington."

Brooks' biographical-descriptive method, which was highly-individualistic and pressed into the service of his regression to

451

simple harmony, appropriated the writer's words in a way that "blurred distinctions," slipped into "discursiveness and paraphrasing." The reader, as a result, had no specific *feel* for either writing or writer, only a diffuse tone or taste, not unlike tepid pablum. Although Brooks included models of valuable "cultural salvage" in his attention to the homely details of New England life and especially, Horatio Greenough's lectures on "functional aesthetics," there is no examination of the works to reveal—what is crucial to Matty—"the principle of life inherent in them." While Thoreau receives scattered references on fifty pages, there is "literally no analysis of *The Week* or of *Walden* as works of art," so that Thoreau is "diluted" to a voice indistinguishable from Bronson Alcott's.

The early Brooks may have directed this method with the same dangerous subjectivism as the later, but at least he recognized differences, ideas, and wrestled with them, and the end was critical in a social sense. By *The Flowering of New England,* his needs had changed and he could continue to state the same dismal attitudes he shared with Parrington about Henry James, calling James' moral concerns with the quality of life in America "furtive apology," contrasting them unfavorably with the confidence he celebrated in other, "healthier" writers. Here, Brooks' method denies a moral complexity that grows from a literal complexity in style and technique—Matty notes that the earlier Brooks had "stringent dissatisfaction with the deficiencies of our civilization," while the later affirms indiscriminately and naturally can easily avoid the choice of Hawthorne as the focal point for his work; Hawthorne, with "his rare understanding of the problem of evil." Indeed, it is with Hawthorne and James (a connection Matty would develop in *American Renaissance*) and Brooks' critical avoidance of their engagement with evil and tragedy, that Matty makes clear his major disagreement. The image of our past that Brooks was, in effect, disseminating to thousands, was a sentimental one where life, to use Quentin Anderson's apt metaphor, was seen as a jam closet and the critic's function merely the rather menial task of sorting and labeling the jars. Absent is the "clash and struggle" of another reality—the demanding, intractable, morally confusing one Brooks' subjects actually experienced; a reality literally refined, by Brooks, into one shimmering, pleasant Brattle Street where all is brick walk and neat frame, charming conversation, calm agreement. Matty must interrupt it all and point Brooks to Ware's *The Industrial Worker:* 1840–1860 (1936) to demonstrate that his picture of farms and farmers for example, is a fantasy, that the common man was not without severe conflicts too.[10]

Like the present, the Thirties were a period in which Marxist thought was treated seriously. People recognized crises and realized they had to act—reality needed to be explained and conclusions had to be drawn. If you were a reader, literary circles, as Alfred Kazin vividly described them in *Starting Out in the Thirties* (1965), were dense with Marxist language, if you were a writer, you needed to know Marxism as the necessary philosophic and political vocabulary, and if you were a professor, especially at an Eastern school, like Matty, many of your students were likely either to be Marxists, familar with the ideology, or with the causes.

Where conflict was wanting in Brooks' world by studied intent, for critics like V. F. Calverton and Granville Hicks it was a central fact of existence. Their Marxism was more than a vague consideration of the social and political background of literature: History was an objective sequence, a dialectic of conflict, a struggle between two classes in complete contradiction. For them, the economic material base determined the social structure as a whole as well as the psychology of the people within it. This was, as Matty wrote in many places, an inadequacy for him—materialism was incapable of explaining enough reality. But rather than judge *a priori* in his criticism, he always dealt first with how much was explained and how well.

Calverton's *The Liberation of American Literature* (1932), (reviewed just after Matty had joined the Socialist Party for a brief time), was, unfortunately, a clumsy oscillation between terse brilliant observations and jargon-filled simplifications that went

453

boringly on. For the man who would be writing a book in which the organic theory of Coleridge was central to every writer studied, Calverton's tissue-paper thin theses that "were develop[ed] and then compel[led] to interlock with the mechanical rigidity of an intricate system of cog-wheels" must have been as disconcerting to read as Matty's last work on Dreiser was to write. Glib, Calverton did give

a forceful description of the gradual disintegration of our nineteenth-century middle-class individualism as measured by the change in our writers from the confident optimism of 'Self-Reliance' and 'Song of the Road' to the widespread disillusion and despair of the present . . . ,

and his informing sense of Turner's thesis and "remarks on the society that [had] formed Eugene O'Neill and Robinson Jeffers was 'penetrating.'" But all this was simply thrown away when set in such an insular framework. Many of Calverton's distinctions were badly confused (as Matty demonstrated in a fashion similar to Trilling on Parrington), ill-conceived, or annoyingly inaccurate; Calverton didn't seem to have *read* what he wrote about. Finally, Marxism, even Calverton's variety, was not the only lens that explained that

the movement of our culture has been from the center outwards, that our most powerful individuals have again and again been dangerously isolated from or opposed to society as a whole, and that the construction of a society in which both the individual and the group can have some measure of full development is the gravest problem with which we are faced.

And

The service of the Marxian critic could lie not in the constant repetition of the catchwords, bourgeois and proletariat, but in some at least tentative definition of the meaning of these terms in relation to American society; not in emotional proclamations of an unexamined faith, but in coming to grips with the problem of what the virtues and defects of a proletarian culture in America might really be.

Hicks' *The Great Tradition: An Interpretation of American Literature Since the Civil War* (1934) stood in marked contrast, evoking sympathy (for he was trying to do for the late nineteenth and early twentieth century what Matty was preparing to do for the mid-nineteenth century) and admiration in his description of the boundaries of Marxist methodology. The quality of Hicks' achievement was indicated by favorable comparison in Matty's review with Parrington's last, unfinished work, *The Development of Critical Realism* (1930). Unlike Calverton, Hicks had "read widely" and "reflected penetratingly" and had applied his test of the value of an author—"the extent to which the author's work reveals the actual economic forces at work in the life of his time"— with discernment "as exacting with Jack London and Upton Sinclair as [it] is with Adams or Hay." His conclusion was another "challenge" to Matty—his view that the great tradition of our literature was "in the voice of protest against abuses and revolution to transform them."

Marxism, with its man-centered commitment, forced Matty to state both his conception of art and artist and their role in society. For Hicks, "literature is inevitably a form of action," which Matty saw as "one of the great services of Marxian criticism, that it has brought to the fore the principle that 'art not only expresses something, but it also does something.'" Matty's response was that art acted upon life by giving it "release and fulfillment." It was on the basis of this role that he objected to Hicks' deliberate exclusion of Mark Twain, Henry James, and Emily Dickinson. Hicks assumed that "literature does not speak to man directly unless it grows out of and deals with his own immediate material occupations." If Matty questioned the adequacy of the material, then the meaning of "protest" and what art "does" were at once broader and more subtle than Marxist criticism—at least then, in Hicks' hands—would acknowledge.[11] With humor, one hardly needed Freud to see the purposefully-ironic value of its play in the world, say, of *Huck Finn*. And if Marxism was a mythology of human future, a vision of human possibility rich in moral demand, then Hicks had to deal more fully with James than his sensitive attention to (and dismissal of) James' skill ("an elaborate technical game"), and objection to the world James created as too remote, in a class sense. Matty anticipated contemporary theologians in arguing that "reality" is created by a dialectic between the economic and material and the moral and transcendent and that it is an insult to common sense as well as a deprivation of the spirit to impose insular judgment, ignoring the "permanent attributes of humanity beyond the confines of any given milieu." The society in which James moved *was* limited, but James, Matty

455

said, had created a world from it; the world of necessary fulfillment and its relationship to "common" reality was not so simple as one-to-one. A great artist creates a "heightened reality" in such a world even if that reality, upon first glance, seems nothing but a glitter of surfaces. Beneath the poems of Emily Dickinson lay a "tragic intensity," and taking as his text Eliot's *Ash Wednesday,* Matty pointed to nuances, deeper moral nuances, crucial to a truly humane consciousness. ("[Hicks] is unaware that the richness of that series of poems depends on the very precision with which Eliot suggests the almost impalpable alterations of the mind between skepticism and belief.") To ignore the immediacy and complexity of experience poetry registers upon *consciousness*[12] was to allow Marxism to impose artificial (as opposed to organic) self-denial and stark historical purpose that instituted, both to society and the individual's ultimate loss, a limited range of private regard. While in the short run this may have its "immediate" unidimensional political usefulness, in any longer sense, it is disastrous. "Consequently," wrote Matty, "it is necessary to preserve by wise evaluation far more elements . . . than Hicks stresses for the tradition of *realization* in American literature exists not in contradiction to but in counterbalance of the tradition of *revolt* Hicks would repossess."

Reviewing Newton Arvin's *Whitman* (1938) and Edmund Wilson's *The Triple Thinkers* (1938) afforded Matty the opportunity to continue to question and affirm what he considered a "usable past" both in conception and technique; affirmations that would make their way into his own growing manuscript. Much earlier, he had praised Arvin's somber study of Hawthorne (1930) for revealing Hawthorne's exposure of the "easy optimism of his time." Arvin also saw that Hawthorne's preoccupation with guilt had its social as well as personal sources, that the most powerful evocations were those of guilt emerging from extreme separation: man isolated from man, man isolated from society. His study of Whitman as socialist was, by contrast, ebullient, though detailed and searching.

Matty could appreciate the problems involved in sorting

456

through the maze of Whitman's contradictions, for although deep into his own interrelated writing on Hawthorne and Melville (and close to a breakdown, intense, though brief), Whitman would be the subject of the succeeding chapters. The poet who admired William Leggett, the adherent of leftwing Jacksonianism, Matty knew, was "inevitably different from the admirer of Grant and Carnegie . . . who [became] enthusiastic about free trade [but looked] hopefully to internationalism . . . who radical[ly] affirm[ed] humanity . . . " but was at times "by no means clear on abolition or unprejudiced about the Negro . . . who, in the period of great plunder, [could] still keep his Jacksonian distrust of inequality, but was nevertheless excited by the spectacle of the triumphant march of industry." Fortunately, Arvin was "aware of the necessity at every juncture of distinguishing between Whitman's superficial complacencies and the deeper loyalty to his instincts, but," Matty wrote anticipating his own emphases, "the pages which deal with Whitman's religion seem to be the one occasion where his own firm materialism cause him to describe a kind of scientific poet who could not possibly have produced 'Song of Myself.'" Demurs aside, one could praise Arvin for his qualifications and the careful, "restrained eloquence" which saw Whitman embracing so much of the vital, common life, not as a romantic gesture, but "because he was himself quite literally one of the people," who could say unaffectedly, "I have imagined a life which should be that of the average man in average circumstances, and still grand, heroic," though Matty had two further strictures: Arvin believed Whitman to have "a special claim on a socialist audience, 'to be the real "ancestor" of our own generation and of the future,' because he voice[d] the 'healthy, forward-moving, progressive life of his times.'" He also held that Whitman's optimism was "an intrinsically more creative attitude" than "the repudiation of it by men like Poe and Melville." This was a softness, a cheer-leading repossession that echoed Brooks, and Matty took serious issue, quoting Yeats' remark about Emerson and Whitman seeming "superficial" because they lacked a "Vision of Evil," and concluded his review saying,

Is the availability of a poet to be made to correspond to the degree in which his opinions chime in with our hopes? Is not rather the function of the artist to bring to concentrated expression every major phase of human experience, its doubts and anguish and tortured defeat as well as its cheerful confidence? Indeed, is not one measure of the great artist his refusal to yield us any innocent simplification, his presentation of an account of life as intricate in its harsh tragic matching of good and evil, as complex in its necessities of constant struggle as the life that we ourselves know? Will any less dense past correspond to our usages as mature human beings?

In the Eliot book, Matty had thanked Wilson for his work on Eliot and a more general "stimulus and challenge." If Richards had forced Matty to weigh every word, then Wilson's sense of "fundamental decency" (Delmore Schwartz's phrase) related word to world. Wilson's judgments had the firmness of Eliot's morality, most vividly expressed in the novel, *I Thought of Daisy* (1929): What good is literature, questions Wilson's young narrator, if it emerges from broken, incomplete lives? With *Axel's Castle* (1929), Wilson, in Matty's words, had felt with "Proust and Joyce we had completed a cycle . . . that they had given full expression to an epoch of decay in which the individual was isolated from fruitful cooperation with society." Isolation may have contributed to the craftsmanship of those who exploited symbolism, it may also, Wilson suggested, have produced a sensibility that retreated from History only to cultivate the power of language. Wilson roundly criticized Valéry for his reactionary condemnation of Anatole France, Proust was reproached for snobbery. In Matty's review of *The Triple Thinkers,* ten essays which ranged from Pushkin to Shaw, Wilson's earlier historical concern with isolation gained substance by engagement with Marxist theory and history, but Wilson's essays suggested an exhaustion in the encounter. "The dominating accents in which he now writes," noted Matty, somewhat sadly, "do not voice hope but are those of a disturbed and disillusioned radical."

Wilson's route was instructive. The Thirties had seen him writing movingly of social protest in reporting events like "The Lawrence Strike" and "William Z. Foster Before the Fish Committee," and in "The Case of the Author," in *The American Jitters* (1932), Wilson had had the honesty to apply Marxism to himself in an entirely open way:

458

It began to dawn on me that the best people were usually satisfied with a very thin grade of culture, that when you tried to go into the adventures of creation or the exploration of the causes of things they didn't follow or approve of you . . . I have tried at one time or another all the attitudes with which thoughtful Americans have attempted to reconcile themselves to the broker's world . . . they were all ways of compromising with the broker.

He also had had the honesty, after studying Marxism and visiting Russia, to question Marxism itself,[13] though the result seemed to be a Marxist theory irredeemably tainted, even poisoned, by a Stalinist practice.

Passing over analyses of authors like A. E. Housman and Flaubert, Matty used Wilson's essay on an American, John Jay Chapman, with its "fully rounded quality" and "dense interweaving of quotation and comment" to probe in a highly-compressed and allusive way, inadequate repossession and the subtle relationship of form to content. Quoting, with approval, Wilson's observation that Chapman's role "was to take the Thoreauvian intransigence into society instead of solitude," that his method was to turn to his own native experience ("he wrote from the center of his instincts"), Matty agreed that the quality that made Chapman "much our best writer on literature of his generation" was a demanding moralism. But although "Wilson cites many passages from Chapman's letters and essays to show the truculent integrity of his protest against the commercial standardization of his day," the quality of the moralism on which he bases Chapman's claim to present attention is flawed by the very technical expression Wilson takes for granted. Chapman's work, according to Matty, lacks "wholeness of design and execution," which reveals itself ideationally in his essays on Shakespeare and Dante—"a series of impressionistic fragments" that merely voice "emotion" and "hardly wrestle centrally with the works under concern." Attention to form is ideological; attention to form is seen as attention to clarity and depth of thought and that, in turn, as attention to the "weight" of morality. As a parallel, Matty introduces Wilson's "deft recording of the aloof pale coolness of [Paul Elmer] More's personality as he encountered it on a Princeton weekend." A matter both of method (Wilson's emphasis upon cue and intuition and casualness with More's *works*) and ideological avoidance, for in spite of More's politics, Matty notes that he, and Babbitt, "perceived the vagueness of the Emersonian strain, insisted on more severe obligations to society with a centralized grasp that makes much of Chapman's intransigence seem merely willful."

So it is clear that the moral calculus must conclude not initiate analysis. It is not, Matty cautions, simply a matter of comparing Chapman's "generosity" with "the drastic narrowness of Babbitt's social sympathies," but realizing that an unsympathetic and *shallow* reading of More's *The Skeptical Approach to Religion* can only result in a sympathetic but equally-shallow and thus, over-valued estimate of Chapman's later religious writings that verges on "religiosity." Marginally concerned with craftsmanship, Wilson, unlike Eliot and quite like Brooks, courts indulgence with personality (an annoying error in *To the Finland Station* where ideas are sometimes reduced to personal anecdote and, as Brooks, the "human side" of Marx and Lenin is sentimentally pumped) to the end that his repossession lacks discriminations that are ultimately useful while inflating to an unearned (though unconscious) optimism. In retrenching to "personal honesty, courage and integrity" as criteria, Wilson returns to the Emersonian tradition, though avoiding for the most part, close parallel with Brooks, especially the personal as all-important, all-explanatory; Brooks' cheerful individualism that Matty felt bound to counter. So much so, that one of the Norton readers of *American Renaissance* concluded one illuminating house memo with:

Matty must eliminate the body-blows at Van Wyck Brooks. It is not necessary to pack such devastating punches and after all, not only is Brooks the reviewer's darling of the moment, but he has made an enormous contribution to the market we will perforce have to go after.

III

To the reader in 1941 *without* an ideological orientation, *American Renaissance* must have seemed a maddening array of authors, works, and themes; a vaguely-chronological linkage of sixty-four quite separate essays.

He is told at the book's beginning that "Dewey . . . found [Emerson] . . . the philosopher of democracy," (4)[14] but that

460

Emerson's radical contradictoriness, illustrated in such essays as "Wealth," and "Power," "working on temperaments less unworldly than their author's, have provided a vicious reinforcement to the most ruthless elements in our economic life." (4) The new consciousness of which Emerson was a part reversed the older relationship of individual to State, believing that the nation existed for the individual. "Emerson's growth was fostered not merely by the renascence of idealistic philosophy, but likewise by his eager apprehension of the possibilities of American democracy." (13) Yet, while "he often enjoyed most the ride through the North End, because, seeing men and women engaged there in hard work, or in the unrestrained attitudes of common life, he quickened to the sense of being near the very source of art—as he did not at the formality on Tremont Street," (27) "it is no long step from his indiscriminate glorification of power to the predatory career of Henry Ford, who still declares Emerson's *Essays* to be his favorite reading." (368)

He later learns that Thoreau's "contribution to our social thought lies in his thoroughgoing criticism of the narrow materialism of his day . . . He objected to the division of labor since it divided the worker, not merely from the work, but reduced him from a man to an operative, and enriched the few at the expense of the many." (78) "The social standards that Thoreau knew and protested against were those dominated by New England mercantilism . . . he insisted that it was essential to re-examine the terms under which . . . absorption [of the individual into society] was being made, to see whether the individual was not being ruthlessly sacrificed to the dictates of mean-spirited commercialism." (78–79) The carefully-crafted *Walden* was a new reality set against a mass of iron materialism in which men were cast into machines. Thoreau's "revolt was bound up with a determination to do all he could to prevent the dignity of common labor from being degraded by the idle tastes of the rich." (173) And, "as a critic of society he had the *advantage* [my italics] of being close to its primary levels. The son of a man who had failed as a small merchant and had then set up as a pencil-maker, sign-painter, and jack-of-all-

461

trades, Thoreau came about as close to the status of a proletarian writer as was possible in his simple environment." (78)

One next finds that "What terrified Hawthorne most about the isolated individual was the cold inability to respond to ordinary life." (28) Like the other four writers, Hawthorne was sensitive to common speech and ideas; three of his four novels were on contemporary themes which incorporated his "fond shyness for common existence and 'for vagrants of all sorts.'" (239) He had "hoped to make his art a bridge between man and society." (239) More specifically, Maule's Well, the spring in the Pyncheon Garden in *The House of the Seven Gables,* one is told, "was originally wrested from a poorer family," (260) and a later, long chapter—"Hawthorne's Politics, with the Economic Structure of *The Seven Gables"*—strongly counters More's earlier remark that Hawthorne was "singularly lacking in the political sense" and "indifferent on the slave question." (316) With alternating portraits of the "decayed gentility" of Hepzibah Pyncheon and the "plebeian capabilities" of her niece Phoebe, "Hawthorne deliberately etched a contrast between the Pyncheon family and rising democracy." (324) "Hawthorne had observed in one of his early sketches . . . the influence of wealth and the sway of class" (325) and in *The House of the Seven Gables* his examination of Colonel Pyncheon and his cruel powers raised "objections to the incumbrance of property [that] often ran close to Thoreau's." (326) Writing a decade after that novel, about his European experiences, Hawthorne ended "his chapter on English poverty with a deepened awareness of what he had slurred over in his novel, and with at least a faint perception of the need for collectivism: 'Is, or is not, the system wrong,'" he wrote, "'that gives one married pair so immense a superfluity of luxurious home, and shuts out a million others from any home whatever? One day or another, safe as they deem themselves, and safe as the hereditary temper of the people really tends to make them, the gentlemen of England will be compelled to face this question.'" (336–337)

Hawthorne and Melville stood in marked opposition to the Transcendental optimism of Emerson, Thoreau, and Whitman, as they deeply questioned the extent to which man could be free. It was not, however, a purely *individual* question to Melville who "saw through the evils of imperialist expansion." (382) And "the latent economic factor in tragedy remained part of Melville's vision at every subsequent stage of his writing," (400) whose sketches "Poor Man's Pudding and Rich Man's Crumbs," and especially "The Tartarus of Maids," went further into detailed accounts of poverty. "In the day when the magazines had been giving idealized versions of the lot of the Lowell factory-girls," Matty wrote, "he tried to picture the actual conditions in a New England paper mill where 'machinery—that vaunted slave of humanity—stood menially served by human beings.'" (400–401) Ships were both more powerful extensions of industrial society as well as more vivid social microcosms: ". . . he studied 'the Social State in a Man-of-War,' and found that its cog-wheels of author-itarian discipline kept 'systematically grinding up in one common hopper all that might minister to the moral well-being of the crew! . . .' His own assumptions of democratic justice come out in the unanswered question, 'who put this great gulf between the American captain and the American sailor?' He believed that an incurable antagonism must result where two classes, the officers and the men, are in perpetual conflict, and where the smaller of the two groups is backed up by all the controls of power." (403) Of course Ahab in *Moby Dick* represented, symbolically, the ascen-dency of one group in which power, concentrated in an individual and buttressed by technology, could sway all: "There was none who could stand up against him . . . morally enfeebled, also, by the incompetance of mere unaided virtue or right-mindedness in Starbuck, the invulnerable jollity of indifference and recklessness in Stubb, and the pervading mediocrity in Flask." (447) "The Cap-tain's career is prophetic," Matty stressed, "of many others in the history of the later nineteenth-century America. Man's confidence in his own unaided resources had seldom been carried farther . . . The strong-willed individuals who seized the land and gutted the forests and built the railroads were no longer troubled with Ahab's obsessive sense of evil," however, "they tended to be as dead to enjoyment as he, as blind to everything but their one pursuit, as unmoved by fear or sympathy, as confident in assuming an identification of their wills with immutable plan or manifest destiny, as liable to regard other men as merely arms and legs for the fulfillment of their purposes, and, finally, as arid and exhausted in their burnt-out souls." (459) Melville wrote of these, but not without cost—"Dollars damn me," he said in despair, "what I feel most moved to write, that is banned,—it will not pay. Yet, altogether, write the *other* way I cannot. So the product is a final hash, and all my books are botches." (400)

Whitman, in his later lonely years could generalize Melville's felt contradiction, Matty highlighting his "frank avowal that the workers alone could overthrow this predatory domination [of the robber barons]," (360) "that the critical issue was the struggle for adequate distribution of wealth, since 'beneath the whole political world, what most presses and perplexes today, sending vastest results affecting the future, is not the abstract question of democracy, but of social and economic organization, the treatment of working-people by employers, and all that goes along with it— not only the wages-payment part, but a certain spirit and principle, to vivify anew these relations.'" (589)

All these judgments on History, social systems, institutions, and individuals, and hundreds of other judgments about "common" experience and "common" materials; individualism and community; idealism and materialism; cultural maturity and a usable past—were not without elaborate justification that constituted an ideology. Now what bound these writers together may well—in some limited sense—have been Feidelson's "devotion to the possibilities of symbolism," but as Henry Nash Smith wrote shortly after Matty's death in 1950, "The symbolic method could lend itself to widely divergent readings of the nature of the universe and of man." Matty did not assume that art was prior to experience or to man himself; he made no abstract division between form and content, the artistic vehicle and the ethical matrix in which it had its being.

Of course one obviously had to "know" the work on its own

464

terms in order to be able to "use" it, but there was a necessary reciprocity between work and world—hence, in order to explicate a varied symbolic ground, Matty was compelled to plumb metaphysics and ethics. *His determining values—for "great art"— were quite clear: tragedy articulated the highest values in the aesthetic realm, democracy in the political realm, and each were joined and interrelated by a shared Christian ground.* To speak of Emerson meant not only speaking of Thoreau—whose retreat to Nature was but a "progress report" on Emerson's Transcendentalism—or their common interest in "The Metaphysical Strain" as found in Herbert, Browne, and Milton, but also of the effect of Coleridge's theories of art and the sculptor Horatio Greenough's espousal of democracy, organic form, and functionalism. Emerson's Transcendentalism was as much a way of knowing as a way of being, a way of ordering society as ordering one's psyche—the parameters were nothing less than total, though emphasis (whether Calvinistic residue or Hinduistic incorporation) depended upon the particular author. Matty's sum of the "best" parts went something like this: Since the universe is of a piece, since men are organically related to a finite Nature and each other (as well as to an infinite Spirit), a functional relationship of equals predicates democracy; and the innate inability of man— in Time—to achieve the perfection which he can intuit/imagine— beyond Time—predicates tragedy. Reality then is *both* real and ideal, abstract (or symbolic) and concrete (and literal), and the course of man's existence a fruitful dialectic between these poles. Art is man's hope as well as the expression of man's physical and spiritual needs, the degree to which that art embodies those relationships—of individual to world to cosmos to transcendent—and their necessary, and painful, contradictions is the degree to which it is useful, true, and beautiful.

Naturally Emerson's thought and his art did not always agree, nor did Thoreau's or Whitman's, but even Hawthorne and Melville could agree with the organic principle as received from Coleridge and could accede to Emerson's three propositions,[15] Melville's Ahab exclaiming, "O Nature, and O soul of man! how

465

far beyond all utterance are your linked analogies! not the smallest atom stirs or lives on matter, but has its cunning duplicate in mind." Their readings of the nature of the universe and man diverged radically—Emerson could, unlike Thoreau, ignore the ugly and brutal aspects of nature, though both held an optimism, with Whitman, that identified evil with *external* restraint. In 1841, for example, Emerson could lecture that "the terrors of sin had lost their force," worse, " 'that grief can teach me nothing.' " (181) Hawthorne and Melville, as Matty repeatedly emphasized, were separated from these three in particular and Transcendentalism in general, by a recognition of evil that was societal *and* individual. Grief, an understanding of tragedy, "taught" them everything. Hawthorne, however, was limited by a mind and art that confined itself "to moral and psychological observation." His Calvinist inheritance was an interpreting grid that *delimited,* according to Matty, fully tragic exploration. "Melville could be neither so cool nor restrained." (435) "Hawthorne could conceive evil in the world, but not an evil world." (334) Melville's value, on the other hand, lay not only in the fact that his imagination was "unchecked by formal education," that his was "a far more passionate temperament," (435) that his experience of the world was greater, that he had suffered more and more deeply, but, that to Matty, his sense of *spiritual reality* had a tenuous but nonetheless more direct connection with the religious *dogma* of his Presbyterian forebears. Thus, the white whale could express relentless primitive energy, kin to the demonic, elemental drives in Ahab's heart (and the Faustian intelligence unleashed, or rather, lashed by/to an Idea), Moby Dick and Ahab, as well as the crew, could participate in evil—their evil as much a function of their very existence as of their cruel relationships with one another, as Ahab's indifference to, or frontal assault upon, the Absolute, *with genuine, felt sense, of something infinite and precious, essential, judging, and redeeming, on the very edge of being lost or already cast into the nameless Abyss,* the result being: "Hawthorne was concerned with depicting the good and evil within man's heart. Melville [was] not so concerned with individual sin

466

as with titanic uncontrollable forces which seemed to dwarf man altogether." (441) Melville's tragic questioning, in short, could purge and reaffirm radical humanity and radical human values with the subtlety of Eliot testing belief in *Ash Wednesday,* the power of Shakespeare shaking the foundations of society and cosmos in *King Lear.*

No accident then, that after numerous references, an exposition of tragedy that is solidly societal occurs a third of the way into *American Renaissance* less as a corrective to the marvelously-developed discussion of organic form than as an overarching supplement:

[The author of tragedy] must have a coherent grasp of social forces, or, at least, of man as a social being . . . the hero of tragedy is never merely an individual, he is man in action, in conflict with other individuals in a definite social order. (179)

And while " . . . the impulse from Emerson was the most pervasive and far-reaching . . . that Whitman's extension of Emerson's values carried far down into the period after the Civil War," (587) it is the tragic sensibility—"the experienced realization that man is radically imperfect . . . yet still capable of apprehending perfection, and being transformed by that vision" (180) that is seen as ultimately most "useful" (in Matty's rich and complex sense of utility), and most in need of repossession.

The "Method and Scope" preface to *American Renaissance* concluded with a long quote from Louis Sullivan on the usefulness of scholarship and societal demands upon the scholar:

". . . his works must so reflect his scholarship as to prove that it has drawn him towards his people, not away from them . . . that his scholarship has been applied for the good and the enlightenment of all the people, not for the pampering of a class . . . that he is a citizen, not a lackey, a true exponent of democracy . . . In a democracy there can be but one fundamental test of citizenship, namely: Are you using such gifts as you possess for or against the people?"

In a letter to his editor at Oxford, Philip Vaudrin, just after publication, he wrote:

Now [Alfred] Kazin's review in the Herald-Tribune gives a chance to call attention to the democratic strain of the book, about which I am most concerned.

And later, to Robert E. Spiller:

I want to thank you for your criticism in *The Saturday Review.* You could hardly have evaluated my book in terms that would have gratified me more. I was delighted that you singled out the democratic strain, which no other reviewer so far has given the weight which seems to me to attach to it.

467

The "democratic strain" was most explicit in the section of *American Renaissance* on Greenough that placed in relief his praise of the capabilities of the common man (in social, in political, affairs), the notion that a social system should be built upon the "sacredness" of the individual, yet see him in a decentralized community of equals ("We have no great families," Greenough said in conversation, "we have colossal men." 147), that men should not be separated from one another by political power or elevated function ("[Greenough] had used as an example of false division any religion that isolates the priestly function from ordinary life." 147), naturally "demanding social and economic equality as the only right foundation for art," (148) "that the artist must find his impulse and completion in the community." (152) Greenough's encompassing democracy saw "man in his full revolutionary and democratic splendor as the base and measure of society," was aware of divisions within ("[his] welcoming acceptance of passion and belligerence . . . " 151), and denied "all attempts, whether in the social structure or in art, to divide man's wholeness so to disperse and drain his vitality. The unity for which he fought was always 'the subordination of the parts to the whole, of the whole to the function . . . '" (151)

While Emerson and Thoreau could praise "The Metaphysicals" for their "completeness," their "organic wholeness" (Matty relating this to Eliot's concept of "unified sensibility"—the whole man, affective and intellectual creating in unison), while Thoreau and Whitman could condemn a society so structured that it coldly divided man from man, and Hawthorne value the native and be sensitive to transfiguring religious dimensions, it remained for Melville to effect the most complete realization of Matty's determining values. "His fervent belief in democracy," wrote Matty, "was the origin of his sense of tragic loss at the distortion or destruction of the unique value of a human being . . . His continued assertion of the nobility, not of nobles but of man, was couched in religious terms from *Redburn* to *Billy Budd*. [16] But the terms were equally democratic." (442–443) Man could fall away from the organic bond either through carelessness or a sinful

Faustian will to power. His redemption from a "wolfish world," in Melville's words, and corresponding isolation, came through "sympathy with another human being" that was clearly religious, though not without irony, as Matty demonstrated in *Moby Dick*, showing that "the sense of Christian brotherhood [was discovered] through companionship with a tattooed pagan . . ." (444) Perhaps Matty's most powerful identification of this achievement came two-thirds into the book:

Melville's hopes for American democracy, his dread of its lack of human warmth, his apprehension of the actual privations and defeats of the common man, and his depth of compassion for courageous struggle unite in giving fervor to the declaration of his purpose in *Moby Dick* . . . It comes in "Knights and Squires," where, summing up his motley cast of characters, he is conscious that he may seem to be endowing ordinary whalemen with too heroic gifts:

"But this august divinity I treat of, is not the dignity of kings and robes, but that abounding dignity which has no robed investiture. Thou shalt see it shining in the arm that wields a pick or drives a spike; that democratic dignity which, on all hands, radiates without end from God; Himself! The great God absolute! The centre and circumference of all democracy! His omnipresence, our divine equality.

"If, then, to meanest mariners, and renegades and castaways, I shall hereafter ascribe high qualities, though dark; weave round them tragic graces; if even the most mournful, perchance the most abased among them all, shall at times lift himself to the exalted mounts; if I shall touch that workman's arm with some ethereal light; if I shall spread a rainbow over his disastrous set of sun; then against all mortal critics bear me out in it, thou just Spirit of Equality, which has spread one royal mantle of humanity over all my kind! Bear me out in it, thou great democratic God! who didst not refuse to the swart convict Bunyan, the pale, poetic pearl: Thou who didst clothe with doubly hammered leaves of finest gold, the stumped and paupered arm of old Cervantes; Thou who didst pick up Andrew Jackson from the pebbles; who didst hurl him upon a war-horse; who didst thunder him higher than a throne! Thou who, in all Thy mighty, earthly marchings, ever cullest Thy selected champions from the kingly commons; bear me out in it, O God!"

. . . Through such symbolical figures Melville discloses what wealth of suffering humanity he believed to be pitted in the dynamic struggle against evil. By this full-voiced affirmation of democratic dignity, even of divine equality, he reveals also with such assurance he felt that a great theme could be created from the common stuff of American life.(444–445)[17]

From this apogee of realization, the relationship of other themes woven through *American Renaissance* becomes evident. The positive value attributed to the unity of "The Metaphysicals" was as much a result of the *nature* (and ideological context) of the language they used as the way in which they used it. Where the Renaissance Court had been the source of *all* value and the artist its servant, custodian of memory and celebrator of a client aristocracy (like Jonson), the emergence of verse written by priests (and believers) gave language a new base and imperative. Private and personal—as well as public—concerns were translated to a symbolic, specifically Christian universe; religious belief authenticated as it declared *all* themes sublime, *all* subjects relevant and worthy.[18] while introducing a coherent language truly social: Herbert in his "low" style had a lexicon open to the multitudes and Milton, in spite of manifold classical allusion, could elaborate a theme even the humblest could appreciate. In responding to these writers, as Matty demonstrated, our Americans could reach beyond elitist eighteenth century modalities, gain a liberating vitality, as they drew upon the experiences about them.

It was not only a matter of Thoreau, for example, exploiting all the senses (as opposed to Emerson's singular occularity), but "from the beginning of his career [asserting] . . . the social foundations of language: 'what men say is so sifted and obliged to approve itself as answering to a common want,'" wrote Thoreau, "'that nothing absolutely frivolous obtains currency . . . the analogies of words are never whimsical and meaningless, but stand for real likenesses. Only the ethics of mankind, and not of any particular man, give point and vigor to our speech.'" (86–87) Emerson was the leader in restoring to "the common man . . . all the rights of art and culture, which always tend to be perverted to mere sectarian and class uses," (4) and insisting that "daily surroundings" were the "stuff" of poetry. Emerson's theory led to Thoreau's practice, his keen interest in "farmer's lingo," "rural slang," and the speech of daily life; the "native strain" in Hawthorne; and, of course, Whitman's sympathy for "common life" and endless catalogues of subjects "near at hand." Greenough had praised "the beauty of objects that had sprung out of an adaptation of structure to the needs of common life—the New England farmhouse, the trotting wagon, the clipper ship." (145) No surprise then, that the painters Matty used as analogues to Whitman's images ("Whitman's Landscapes") participated in this economy by painting those structures and implements and conveyances, their builders and their users. Mount, in "Long Island Farmhouses," had a realistic "accuracy of vision," Millet, in Whitman's words, gained "his unique majesty of expression" in "portraying people as heroic as they were," (603) and Eakins "shared Whitman's feeling of solidarity with ordinary people." (606)[19] The realistic portrayal of common subjects at common activities (eel-spearing, boat-racing, playing baseball, doctors demonstrating anatomy) was direct and functional, concrete, vivid, and unsentimental, though often (as with Thoreau, Melville, and Whitman) deeply offensive to prevailing genteel tastes. The unpretentious result, however, was a record and celebration of "democratic character," and the pictoral embodiment of nothing less that "the heroic possibilities of the common man."

The validity of such subjects and language released new energies, though not without accompanying hazard. As Raymond Williams observed in *Culture and Society* (1958), two of the main components of "culture" that emerged from the Romantic movement were the autonomy and high calling of the artist (recalling Trilling's characterization of Keats as a "hero") and the idea that art itself was a superior truth. Just as the painter could lose the viewer and himself in the object, so the writer, in his focus upon the self (without the Metaphysical's redeeming belief that established the response of a larger community), courted the disasters of individualism: isolation of the artist and alienation of the self. Literature became not so much an emotional fulfillment as a substitute for emotion, a mode of psychic salvation. Though Coleridge had introduced a valuable critical lexicon that allowed Emerson to wage the Transcendentalist "revolution . . . against the formulas of eighteenth-century rationalism in the name of the fuller resources of man. Coleridge [stressing] . . . what was to become one of Emerson's recurrent themes 'the *all in each* of human nature,'—how a single man contains within himself, through his intuition, the whole range of experience," (7)—Coleridge's Christian skepticism of such introspection, unrestrained, was lost. "To his [Emerson's] cheerful temperament," wrote Matty, "the turning of the individual upon his own inner life was a matter not for resignation but exuberance." (8)

471

The results of such "exuberance" however, were another matter. Matty's fear, amply illustrated, was not one of the community establishing a bland, an anesthetized hegemony over the individual, but rather one of the individual realizing such hegemony over the community, generalizing his own worst impulses. ("Predatory," "reckless," "rapacious," are recurrent adjectives he uses to characterize this extreme individualism rationalized and actuated within industrial capitalism.) On a societal level, "the individual as his own Messiah," coupled with Emerson's attraction for force and power, meant division of the community, denigration of the common man, destruction of belief, and with that, destruction of egalitarian ethics and the possibility of transcendence: The Emersonian will, with Ahab as the archetypal figure (proud, tyrannizing, objectifying man become God) could sweep all to doom. On the individual level, the precious artist or inhuman intellectual could result in simple incoherence and monstrosity (not unlike Poe, or our contemporary speed-freaks), or the withering isolation of an Ethan Brand, unconnected to any tradition, any human being.

"What saved Emerson [however] from the extremes of rugged Emersonianism was the presence not merely of egoism but also of a universal breadth in his doctrine that all souls are equal. What stirred him most deeply was not man's separateness from man, but his capacity to share directly in the divine super-abundance." (8) Emerson was interested in "consciousness, not with self-consciousness," "he always felt a repugnance to self-centered introversion," (8–9) What were Emerson's lecture-tours across America, one might ask, but democratic contact with the masses, as Whitman's more direct "talking to society." And where Emerson, and Thoreau could seem cool, it was Whitman who did full justice to all three elements in the classic French articulation of "democratic faith." As Matty would write years later in *From the Heart of Europe*:

Liberty and equality can remain intellectual abstractions if they are not permeated with the warmth of fraternity ... Whitman knew ... as Emerson did not, that the deepest freedom

472

does not come from isolation. It comes instead through taking part in the common life, mingling in its hopes and failures, and helping to reach a more adequate realization of its aims, not
for one alone, but for the community. Something like this was what Whitman had in mind
when he said that his 'great word,' the one that loved him most, was 'solidarity.' (90)

The apparent dichotomies between feeling and thought, the
individual and society, had parallels in each writer's questioning
of reality: What *was* its nature, material or ideal? The agreement
with Emerson's principles, as we saw earlier, was one of emphasis.
His ground was Plato—his "representative man" who could
"bridge the gap between the two poles of thought . . . reconcile
fact and abstraction, the many and the one, society and
solitude." (3) Emerson's practice, however, was marred by an
excessive idealism that created veiled hierarchies between himself
and his readers; the works lacked the directness, the concentration
of the other writers, avoided too much raw experience, with the
result that "this formula [a poetics that established an ideal world
"better" than the world of common experience] encouraged him
to ignore experience whenever it was in harsh or ugly conflict with
his optimism . . . 'Details are melancholy; the plan is seemly and
noble.'" (52) The other writers followed less the "plan," allowing
pattern to emerge, organically, from their materials—Thoreau's
anger at objectified "things" did not keep him from sinking into
reality (rather than rising above it like Emerson), dealing with both
inner and outer experience; Melville could rhapsodize on the
ethereal qualities of the abstract, glassy sea, yet remember the
dark solid fins beneath its surface; and Whitman's move "from
transcendentalism back to a kind of materialism" was finally
through encounter with concrete people and concrete events and
his growing understanding of *public need,* rather than by abstract
reason.

The most useful, achieved works to Matty were works that
critically participated in both realms of being—a crippling paradox
to most, though understood and lived by those who accepted the
paradox of God made man, wine made blood, the Incarnation
and Resurrection. An interesting sidelight on this was the "problem" of George Ripley, the founder of Brook Farm. According to

473

Arthur Kinoy, who wrote his senior thesis[20] under Matty that Spring of 1941, Matty had wanted to include a chapter on Ripley in *American Renaissance* because "Ripley went further," recalled Kinoy, "with social thought. He was the religious man who found his way beyond Utopian Socialism into materialism. Matty hadn't thought through Ripley, he was fascinated by the pendulum between idealism and materialism." Studying Kinoy's thesis and taking seriously his remembrance that "to a great extent, what Matty was thinking, I wrote," one sees the figures and ideas that gave *American Renaissance* its historical solidity. Kinoy carefully noted the societal changes that preceded the creative "moment" of the 1850s, specifically, the Depression of 1837 and the fact that in the years that followed, all the shocks E. P. Thompson chronicled in *The Making of the English Working Class* (1963), manifested themselves in America with nothing less than "the destruction of the social mores of two centuries." (71) Ripley left the ministry to go into the streets because a Christianity faced with an "economic system [that] seemed to mock the inherent divinity of every human soul," wrote Kinoy, "laugh at the brotherhood of man, make a sham out of the concept of the individual as free agent," (84) logically and faithfully became a Christianity whose aim it was to remake society since "it [capitalist industrialist society] stood in the way of salvation." (94) In addition, the liberal/conservative argument within the powerful Unitarian Church was more than Ripley and Orestes Brownson airily arguing against Andrews Norton's charge that German literature (and German idealism) were "inappropriate." Liberals embracing the new idealism also meant intellectual independence from English empiricism and English ways: incorporating democracy and internationalist thought as opposed to elitist sectarianism and the maintenance of a theological aristocracy. Where Norton felt Transcendentalism as a marching movement, a "conspiracy to overthrow Christianity," Ripley's "sharpest criticism of Norton was the charge that his point of view implied an aristocratic concept of culture. He accused Norton of taking Christianity from the masses and placing it in the hands of a learned minority."[21]

Ripley's anger over a theological cabal, a Christianity that refused to soil its hands, a 12-hour day, 6-day week, had its justification in what he had repossessed of intuitive theories of cognition from Emerson, Coleridge, the German philosophers, as much as in his repossession of Scripture (what Matty would call the "imperative" of the Second Commandment). Anger over injustice was transformed into action to correct injustice; it represented the faithful "use" of feeling scholarship for the mass of men and women, not a select group ("Open our doors!" Ripley had preached to his congregation.). And as much as it drew upon native materials and native conditions, it gained its fulfillment, its rich, tragic maturity, from a continuity with what had gone past. As Christ was Emerson's most "representative" man, so the lonely and unemployed formed Ripley's strongest friendships; where Parrington in *Main Currents* sought after heroes for our democracy and elevated them beyond imitation, Matty in *American Renaissance* found the heroic in the common, available under our bootsoles. Where the favored subjects of Parrington were without divisive pain, those in *American Renaissance* scarcely seemed to avoid it. Where the Progressive historians—Turner, Beard, and Parrington—pointed to a great country that had somehow gone shamefully wrong, the ideology inherent in Matty's reading of our past could affirm "still undiminished resources" and possibility, though with restraint and a deep sense of humility and limitation.

IV

The classic pejorative definition of ideology is found in Karl Mannheim's *Ideology and Utopia* (1929):

The concept 'ideology' reflects the one discovery which emerged from political conflict, namely, that ruling groups can in their thinking become so intensively interest-bound to a situation that they are simply no longer able to see certain facts which would undermine their sense of domination.

Understood as a masking for self-interest, the most obvious occasions in *American Renaissance* serve to introduce us both to "errors" ideology can produce and the contradictions in Matty's ideology. The past the book so energetically repossesses is gener-

475

ally delineated as non-trivial, almost, as Henry Nash Smith has said in conversation, unrelievedly so. From the athletic, masculine frontispiece—a daguerreotype of Donald McKay, poor Nova Scotia boy become builder of the mightiest clipper ships—to the recurring analyses of tragedy that beg a coherent social order, the epoch Emerson to Whitman embodied is depicted as "full," "adult," "mature,"—with a textural center in Edgar's phrase, "Ripeness is all." Indeed, the phrase, a favorite with Eliot as well as Matty, opens the book and reappears, significantly, twice more. The contexts shift, but there is a woven intent: initially, paired with a passage from *Representative Men,* "ripeness" connotes a historical moment immense with "perceptive powers" and "adult health"; again, in praising Melville's achievement of cultural and artistic independence ("reading the *Mosses,* Melville had been stirred for the first time by the sense of living at a moment of ripeness for American life and art . . . " "he had pushed off from the safe shores of his narratives of experience and had made his first excited trial of his own creative depths in *Mardi* [1849]. He had recently scored, in his copy of *Lear,* Edgar's profound affirmation, "Ripeness is all." (187); finally, in suggesting how Hawthorne's "way of conceiving a rounded character" demonstrated a democratic and Christian strain that expressed itself with "tragic power" that embraced "the tragic attitude." (349)

That the intent is Matty's attempt to enhance a past and not Shakespeare's meaning is evident in examining J. V. Cunningham's essay, "Ripeness is All." Tracing the phrase through Shakespeare's plays, placing it in context in *Lear,* Cunningham shows its meaning to be neither special insight nor maturity but the mechanical, biological, process of growing old. Having prevented Gloucester, in an earlier scene, from committing suicide, "that act," says Cunningham, "which consummates the sin of despair," Gloucester having accepted his situation "in the spirit of Christian resignation," then relapsed. Edgar's words were meant to "stiffen his resolution," to remind him of the unrelieved continuum of experience, "that the fruit will fall in its time," *and* (with emphasis on passive acceptance of Christian Providence and not

476

Stoic endurance) that "man dies when God is ready." Cunningham concludes: "The difference in meaning is unmistakable: ours looks towards life and his [Shakespeare's] towards death . . . "

The omission of Poe, brought to my attention by Charles Newman (undoubtedly remembering Poe's inclusion in Feidelson's treatment of symbolism), presents a more ambiguous though willful case. In a footnote to the "Method and Scope" preface, Matty explained that the reason was "more fundamental than that Poe's work fell mainly in the decade of 1835–45" and not within the organizing center of *American Renaissance, 1850–1855.* When he continued, writing that Poe failed to share "the main assumptions about literature that were held by any of my group," (xii) Matty was speaking (unconsciously) of ideological exclusion: The relationship between Poe's work and his values. Although the fact that Poe was "bitterly hostile to democracy might serve as a revelatory contrast," Matty is not about to make it, and the work is implicitly faulted.[22] One could write a book, Matty suggested, about the "effect of his narrow but intense theories of poetry and the short story," but *American Renaissance* is concerned with substance and not only with influence. We are to understand, quietly, that Poe's beliefs, his ideology, resulted in an inadequate art—"No group of his poems seems as enduring as 'Drum-Taps,'" is Matty's comparison, and "his stories, less harrowing on the nerves than they were, seem relatively factitious when contrasted with the moral depth of Hawthorne and Melville." (xii) Points of tangency are, however, noted. *American Renaissance* does contain references to Poe as critic: his concern for craft, for concentration of expression, for a nationalistic defense of American literature in the face of English condescension. Yet craft is clearly not enough. One has the sense of an ethical adolescence about Poe, that even his obsession with death was more giddy fascination than mature, useful, *understanding.*

And if Poe is left out, what can one make of Hawthorne's inclusion, at least in the sense of "democrat"? Matty argued that Hawthorne's work repossessed not so much the grim Calvinist actuality of sin as the consequences of that sin *in society,* that his democracy was partly the use of "common speech," but also the democracy of shared suffering. The argument also seems to be that Hawthorne's sense of the past was radical and dynamic rather than conservative and static because he accepted tradition but (unlike Eliot, for example) rather than seeing people, events, and ideas (or, in Eliot's case, authors and works) of the past as having a simultaneous existence in which their relationship was spatial, he saw them historically, developing in a linear fashion. Sin was not a cyclical reality, or an eternal recurrence then, but a choice each generation—as in "My Kinsman, Major Molineux" —made.

Although Matty stresses the socially-centripetal function of Hawthorne's stories, he is less than convincing in explaining his author's "inordinate detachment." Perhaps Hawthorne *did* feel isolated and misunderstood, but this, as Ruland has ably pointed out,

draws from Matthiessen his customary denunciation for the society which must ostracize its artists and thinkers. The blame is New England's, not Hawthorne's . . .

Well, we must ask, was Hawthorne's rather un-democratic mistreatment of Melville also New England's fault? And what are we to make of Matty's praise of *The Blithedale Romance?* The Brook Farmers may have participated in "one phase of the contemporary myth, in the quest for Utopia," (652) but Hawthorne's response was distorting as history and fairly simple-minded as art. Matty wrote of Hawthorne that, "However inadequately worked out some of his social criticism may be, there is no questioning the acuity with which he saw the weaknesses of Brook Farm. He could not help feeling that its spirit was essentially that of a picnic, of an escape to a woodland paradise." (652) But those of us familiar with the complexity and seriousness of contemporary communes might question on the one hand the "democrat" who simply could not share manual labor (c.f., *Autobiography of Brook Farm,* 1958), or the collective that did not confront his daydreaming individualism while it was attempting "inner rebirth," and on the other, the fiction that had as its principle message that the regeneration of society was impossible without the prior regeneration of the individuals comprising it. Even Saint Augustine would balk at that.

Ruland also praises the "treatment of the book [*The House of the Seven Gables*] in commercial, industrial, and class terms,—complete with reference to Engels," but aims a justified broadside at the passage quoted earlier on English poverty, saying, "His effort to bring Hawthorne into the fold [of socialism] is the baldest instance of thesis-riding in his otherwise honest book." Yet what Ruland bypasses seems to me to be even worse. Matty's "subtle investigation of the novelist's paradoxical conservativism and membership in the Democratic Party," is not subtle, it is unreal. When Matty writes, "the most significant thing about Hawthorne's politics for his interpretation of human destiny is not that he was a skeptical conservative in a setting of Emersonian liberals and Garrison radicals; it lies rather in the paradox that he was also a Democrat. . ." (318) we have a blatant mis-reading of history or ideological distortion. Pierce's Democratic Party was certainly not the "party of the common people." By the time of Hawthorne's support, and campaign biography (and post in Liverpool, second in importance to London), it was an old, tainted, established party with the rhetoric of Jackson but with actions considerably less than the laudatory term, "Jacksonian."

In our time we have seen repeated drives for the extension of democracy from political to cultural realms, and protestations of "elitism" directed especially at literary critics. This was sensed, even in the forties. Spiller tells us that Matty, speaking on the state of American poetry prior to 1948 in Philadelphia, "warned against the 'serious cleavage' it revealed 'between what we have learned to call mass civilization and minority culture,'"[23] and how that same cleavage tended to divide our critics into two camps, aestheticians and sociologists. William Empson recalled Matty being asked a half-serious question about the "literary quality" of "Li'l Abner" one evening at the Kenyon School of Letters in the summer of 1948, and, according to Empson, "going on for over an hour with great seriousness about Al Capp, and comics, and what they could tell us about American society." And although not specified, in *Form and Fable in American Fiction* (1961), Daniel G. Hoffman wrote that "in literary criticism, F. O. Matthiessen showed in *American Renaissance* how valuable is an awareness of the essential connection between popular culture and literary traditions." Yet reading both the beginning and end of *American Renaissance* reveals a contradiction.

At the beginning Matty writes that Hawthorne and Melville were scarcely "popular" authors, that no single book of Emerson's sold more than a few thousand, that Thoreau kept seven hundred unsold *Waldens* and that Whitman "gave away more copies [of *Leaves of Grass*] than were bought." Matty was aware that Longfellow was, during this period, selling hundreds of thousands, that there existed an audience to snap up "the ceaseless flux of Mrs. E. D. E. N. Southworth's sixty novels"; and he quoted Hawthorne's famous letter to Ticknor in 1855 ("America is now wholly given over to a damned mob of scribbling women, and I should have no chance of success while the public taste is occupied with their trash—and should be ashamed of myself if I did succeed.") only to make his own premises clear: "Such material still offers a fertile field for the sociologist and for the historian of our taste. But I agree with Thoreau: 'Read the best books first, or you may not have a chance to read them at all.'" And to quote Ezra Pound, "The history of an art is the history of masterwork, not of failures or mediocrity."

The conclusion of Hawthorne's letter ("What is the mystery of these innumerable editions of *The Lamplighter,* and other books neither better nor worse?—worse they could not be, and better they need not be, when they sell by the hundred thousand.") raises a question as interesting (and important) as Pound's elitist definition of history. Indeed, *What is the mystery?* Why did Americans quite literally *consume* Maria Cummin's *The Lamplighter* (1854) then, and all those other tear-drenched "novels" of dead babies and lost loves in the decade before the Civil War? Or why do they consume *The Valley of the Dolls* or *Love Story* now? (One could also question the assumption of certain novels and their consumption in American colleges, but that is another essay.) Implicit

480

in *American Renaissance* is the understanding that one reads one kind because they are "critical" and avoids the other because they give "mass taste" unmediated. Yet what this means for a democracy (or the direction of novelists and poets) is as unclear as what a glance at the sixteen-page index means for cultural maturity.

In a work demonstrating organic relationships, innumerable reference to the line of English poets, from Chaucer thru Spenser thru Shakespeare thru Milton thru Pope, with concentration on "Metaphysicals" such as Donne, Herbert, Crashaw, Vaughan, and Marvell, and "Romantics" such as Wordsworth, Coleridge, Keats, Shelley, and Byron, is understandable. Less understandable, for a literature attempting to assay its own experience and generate forms adequate (and congruent) to the expression of that experience—escape, in fact, from demeaning, debilitating judgments by English and Continental critics—are references to Cervantes, Valery, Proust, Schiller, Kafka; a half dozen to Pascal, Flaubert, and Tolstoy; a dozen or more to Dante, Goethe, Baudelaire, and Mann. The point of course is that following one relationship necessitates energizing an entire "infrastructure"; speaking of the "Metaphysicals" and "Romantics." one must speak of the "Moderns"—and admit, once and for all, the internationality of literature. The effect is curious, even contradictory: Certain American authors are excluded from discussion or slighted simply because they cannot stand up against the Continental competition, and you are tempted to agree with Philip Rahv's judgment that the references inflated the Americans, and that Matty's judgment oscillated between pre-and post-inflation, never completely settling on one or the other. Another aspect or question is whether the references really explain or whether, as Ruland says of Matty's countless citations of Shakespeare, and Shakespeare's "echoes," they "come closer to being tedious and unreadable than any others in his huge book." If the latter is so, *what* are they? Could they be ideological shoring?

All this brings us closer to the central contradictions of belief

481

and truth, tragic skepticism and the "paralysis of the will" (to borrow Truman Nelson's phrase), Christian tragedy, and Eliot,— but there is one more base worth touching as a prelude, Quentin Anderson's, in his latest book, *The Imperial Self* (1971). His contention, as the *New York Times* put it in a sub-head, is *Emerson, Whitman and James as prefigures of creeping apocalypse,* or as Leo Marx began in a review of the book in the Times' Sunday *Book Review* (25 April 1971), "Is the anarchic temper of modern art and literature a menace to society?" Marx says later, of this "visionary strain,"

What distinguishes writers of this persuasion . . . is their effort to encompass all of reality within their own imperial consciousness. In their work society is not a hostile or repressive force, as it is for their alienated European contemporaries, it is simply irrelevant.

Anderson's argument, as it relates to Matty, is both frontal and insidious. Frontally, Matty, along with critics like Feidelson [!] was in part responsible first, for the reclamation and praise of figures like Emerson, Whitman, and James, the celebration of modern literature in general, and "consciousness" ("hypertrophy of the self," says Anderson) in particular, and second, that their very methodology effected a withdrawal from History and an ontological reorganization of reality (what Anderson elsewhere has called "that bleak existential wind [that] began to blow from Emerson forty years before Nietzsche"):

The effect of the New Criticism has been to cut art off from the messiness of lives and the incoherence of history . . . The end of criticism as it was practiced in the quarterlies during the 1940s and 1950s seeked to assure us that our writers were, like the other great ones, secure in *achieved form* [my italics]. F. O. Matthiessen's *American Renaissance* was an admirable accomplishment in this kind. (35)

The insidious argument is Marcuse's *Eros and Civilization* (1955) stood on its head, or unrepressed sexuality generalized to produce social chaos. Anderson shows Emerson's avoiding the responsibility or authority of the Father, Whitman dissolving the Father, in fact, "otherness," in "Crossing Brooklyn Ferry," and James calling into being the "androgynous divine man." These authors, and their works, so it goes, have destroyed the Father, the nuclear family, genital prominence, hierarchy—they are the ultimate subversives, and they have done their job well. And Matty with his homosexuality, stands in the shadows as a repudiation of "mature" adult heterosexuality in addition to his laurel of faded social ideals. And as corrosive to societal order as the rest.

Surely this study of Matty's ideology demonstrates a felt sense that literature matters, that it "affects" society, though whether one can place the entire responsibility for what Anderson sees as the *disintegration* of our society is questionable. Whether or not Matty is guilty as a "New Critic," is more questionable. Whether he is also "guilty" is even more questionable. Earlier, and throughout, we have seen his awareness of what Anderson calls "inner imperialism" in Emerson. His rather extended discussion of Whitman's psychic economy (536–540) made very clear that the element that kept Whitman's ego from sailing off into the cosmos, or him parading as a poet-Messiah was his "Quaker strain." ("Whitman's mystic abandon was held in check by a . . . concrete humanitarianism." 539) If anything, the problem of "society and solitude" seems, ideologically, tipped in favor of just that social, historical concern Anderson feels is utterly lost. And as far as the homosexuality, it was Freud's notion that the homosexual is either the least or *most* engaged in society. Surely a reading of *Democratic Vistas* or "Drum Taps" would demonstrate the humane and constructive direction Whitman took, and critics other than Matty have amply discussed the powerful ethical questions James' novels plumb.

Of course much of Anderson's argument is oblique to Matty's ideology by its very reductionist nature and the number of questions it noisily begs: Has our society disintegrated, or is the clamour Anderson hears on the steps of his own Hamilton Hall but an echo of the righteous selfhood Emerson demonstrated when he publicly declared he would not obey the Fugitive Slave Law, "By God!"? Anderson's concern about the "death of the family" would hardly move a woman with three young children and an ugly husband, who has just returned from a "consciousness-raising" group of women, nor his fear for the dissolution of sexual identity for a man, or woman, locked into an aggressive, domineering role by a society that needs (or

483

excessively rewards) their warped talents. It *was* important for reality to be perceived, shaped, to Matty. Although the world, in a Catholic sense, surely existed, the function of the artist was to record it as well as interpret it. But to suggest, as Anderson does, that like Arnold nothing was "real" unless it was embedded in artifice is to misconstrue the ikon of his whole life. People were clearly more important than art, but his ideology never presumed to separate one from the other. The real problem that Anderson does not face in his inclusion of Matty with Feidelson, is where has he been these past decades? It is also to ask just how central religious and/or ethical belief actually is to social coherence (assuming that coherences does not simply encase inequity), whether radical individualism was a necessary response on the part of people like Emerson to a feeling, ethical, humane, vacuum created by the excessive and elitist rationalism of the Enlightenment and the social retrenchment of institutions like the Church in the face of the State. His cultural history would be more useful, and his ideological judgments more sound, if he explained History less exclusively in terms of "modes of consciousness" and looked to social and economic conditions beyond his study.

In perhaps the longest review of *American Renaissance,* Granville Hicks in 1941 raised central questions about the book's ideology when he suggested that Matty had listened too much to Eliot (and Eliot's "sterile formalism") and too little to Greenough. What he called "an essential lack of clarity [could] . . . be traced to specific confusions and evasions." Hicks wanted to know, since Matty had stated that "the transcendentalist theory of art is a theory of knowledge and religion as well," whether or not it was *true.* Five writers, he noted, achieved "a high level of literary achievement." But was this because of, or in spite of, their philosophical premises?

Hicks' questions ignored the rather simple congruence of language with reality and the fact that religion, at least the Christian faith, not only followed this congruence theologically, but also helped—as Eliot's criticism—to create context, criteria, and reception, for the creation and appreciation of literature that emerged *within* that context. The values and *Weltanschauung* believed by Matty were not wholly accepted or believed by Hicks (or at this point in time, by a good many others), but in recreating context (which we do when we encounter a work, whether it is Job or Shakespeare), we tend to enter into a kind of sympathy that either alters, translates, or abolishes prior criteria for judgment. Or we judge the work "stupid," "uninteresting," or "inadequate," and move on.

Hicks pushed his questions, both intellectually and personally, when he quoted Matty on "the empirical truth behind the Calvinist symbols." Eliot had said where he lived in the early Thirties when he wrote, in "Thoughts After Lambeth":

The world is trying the experiment of attempting to form a civilized but non-Christian mentality. The experiment will fail; but we must be very patient in awaiting its collapse; meanwhile redeeming the time: so that the Faith may be preserved alive through the dark ages before us; to renew and rebuild civilization, and save the world from suicide.

Was Matty's stress upon Hawthorne's understanding of evil any less arrogant; was it an aesthetic or a religious judgment? Which held? And was the correlation Perry Miller delineated between Puritan theology and modern psychological observations merely Matty's "deliberate concession to the pragmatists"? Eliot, Matty had written, "came to believe that the choice lay between further disintegration of the sort Hawthorne already foresaw, and a return to dogma upon which to base more adequate values than James." Which way would it go? Hicks wanted to know whether this too was true, in an empirical sense. And if it was, then it should be stated, and proved.

By 1935 Eliot was writing in "Literature and Belief":

Literary criticism should be completed by criticism from a definite ethical and theological standpoint . . . The 'greatness' of literature cannot be determined solely by literary standards.

Which of course was a return to the moral tradition of Arnold and a radical reorientation of the "formalism" Eliot was thought to support. Hicks' position was that Eliot had made clear which criteria were valid for him (and, in his own totalistic way, for society). Where was Matty? "Matthiessen," he wrote, "consistently seems to be availing himself of the support of religious attitudes." Yet he made, to Hicks' mind, no admission of this, nor did he seem

485

conscious of the implications of his application of Original Sin, in a social context. Matty's belief, to Hicks, was not his "own business," not if people took literature seriously. He felt that it resulted in an "underestimation" of Emerson, to name but one of the five. Hicks' main point was that Matty's belief, utilized as an aesthetic criteria (which was not admitted and thus, could not be attacked, openly), denigrated Emerson for his "optimism"; an emphasis upon "man's goodness" that to Hicks' mind was responsible for "many achievements, some of which seem all the more valuable as the danger of our losing them grows. Democracy, to which Matthiessen is deeply devoted," he continued pointedly, "developed out of a growing confidence in human capacities, and though that confidence may need to be curbed, to destroy it altogether is to destroy democracy too."

Naturally the issue was far more complex than Hicks presented it, and his conception of the "origins" of democracy was by no means agreed upon. But by overstating his case—making the pulls upon Matty's loyalties appear more diametric than they actually were—he spoke more truth than he knew. This has been developed more fully most recently by Frederick Curtis Stern in his thorough discussion of Matty and tragedy in his dissertation ("The Lost Cause: F.O. Matthiessen, Christian Socialist as Critic," 1970). While Hicks argued the aesthetic distortion Matty's ideology presented, and the very real social distortion that resulted when it was applied with as much intelligence and learning as Matty contained (especially antagonized by what he regarded as Eliot's lofty "assertions" and the political effects of Eliot's tragic skepticism), Stern pushed further, carefully following Matty's changing conceptions of tragedy, their contradictions and inadequacies. Where one could grant that at least one of Hicks' objections to Matty's ideology could be "resolved" by a "generous" reading of Christian theology (as *was* the case with Matty), Stern's final judgments were somewhat more difficult to counter, given the strength of Matty's loyalties.

The popular or adolescent notion that tragedy was "gloomy" presented little problem for Stern as he quoted Matty's discussion in *The Achievement of T. S. Eliot* (1935), but even then, wrote Stern, "how does one reconcile sources for a view of life and letters as contradictory as Christianity, socialism, and 'the tragic,'" especially when it is extended, as we have seen, to a broad social context, as in *American Renaissance?* Stern's firm conclusion was that at least one element of Matty's ideology delimited "aesthetic" realization, his Christianity. Noting discussions of Eliot's *Murder in the Cathedral* by Francis Fergusson and Louis L. Martz, Stern singled out their sense that Christianity, like Enclosure in nineteenth century England, both provided a haven and made *a priori* judgments about the nature of reality and human possibility. Furthermore, "the problem," wrote Stern, "is larger than that of Christian tragedy, but really involves any tragic protagonist whose destiny is directed by a pre-determining, salvation-promising force, and whose response to that destiny is equally directed by the same force" (including Marxism). "In effect, we know who wins. 'True tragedy,' quoting Susan Sontag on Leon Abel's *Metatheatre,* 'says there are disasters which are not fully merited, that there is ultimate injustice in the world.'" Of course there are Marxists who argue that tragedy is "optimistic" because it affirms man's capacity to endure and his will to prevail over History; like the Existentialists they know man will *struggle,* even in the face of overwhelming forces, which, though not "winning," is a kind of victory. And there are Christians besides Auden (with his neat distinctions between Greek and Christian tragedy, the one of "necessity" and thus unavoidable, the other of "possibility" and thus quite avoidable) who point out that Christian tragedy under the "tougher" Greek rules is possible in two instances: for the sinner who lives outside all-encompassing Grace, for the man, like Nietzsche, who rejects Grace.

Although Stern's judgment that *The Scarlet Letter* is distorted to achieve a tragic "reading," or that *Moby Dick* is forced into second place behind *Billy Budd,* the "purer" Christian form, incorrectly, have their moments, the real contradictions for Matty, one senses, likely lay elsewhere—in his own role as teacher and critic. Not doing God's wishes—"being humble before God"—

may be seen as "stupid" as Stern suggested, or painfully unavoidable, borrowing Niebuhr's more forceful conception of Original Sin, but no matter how the rules are laid down, or argued, it is the constant *living out* of contradictory positions that is the hardest; the knowledge that someone might judge one's perception as "reduced" tragedy, or the establishment of "another standard," or "insufficiently dogmatic," was Matty's own special trial, which even Eliot, at his suicide, pronounced "inadequate."

How then to speak of Eliot in whom the contradictions of Matty's life have the intensity of a great solar mirror; how to explain the cold passion of leathery belief, the willful ecstasy of the empty automatic genuflexion, the gray purgatorial pall where it is always late afternoon and the old man sits, slightly bent, in the garden with vest and watchchain, the eyes barely focusing, the head barely nodding. Eliot, for whom Matty had the diligent sophomore's awe of the *knowing* tutor; Eliot, who erected barriers so skillfully no one could scale them and blew bridges so carefully that no one—even when they knew—would admit to being the wiser; Eliot, who in the recent deluge of articles and reviews about his *Waste Land* was unfailingly mentioned as a banker one always expected to foreclose, yet as "retiring" and incredibly "shy" (whom Conrad Aiken could remember in 1922 "turn[ing] on me with that icy fury of which he alone was capable"); Eliot, who put as much personality, shards of skin, old scars, nightmares, into his poems as any poet in history and still carried off the pose of "impersonal" with perfection.

Clearly no place to begin a discussion which at some later date will have an entire book to give it resonance, or when an old friend, an ex-president of SDS, writes saying:

Your letter arrived, starting with your contretemps with [Christopher] Ricks, when I was just discovering Eliot, having begun a long, let's even say epic with a small bow, poem & then being told it was coming to resemble The Waste Land in structure; since then I've been reading the reverend with great admiration, it/took me this long before I could admire his mastery, & now it strikes me that hardly any American-English poetry has gone beyond him, that in any case he must be absorbed in order to be transcended . . .

But let us say it as well as we can. Very slowly, how could Matty, as a radical democrat, as a socialist, have the regard (even fear) for

Eliot that he did. Eliot, let us say it plainly, with his *very bad politics?*

The simplest explanation, though it explains little, was that Eliot, early on, was very, very "useful" to Matty. St. Louis and Harvard and then embracing England, and the Tradition. For a young man wrung through the wringer of the flux of America, and then to experience, encounter (no other way to describe the brutality of *The Waste Land:* maw, vortex, abyss; passion, power, frustration, passivity), a voice that began to put the pieces in place, to, as Austin Warren said of Robert Lowell, grind one's ancestors into paint. Eliot was immensely useful before Matty's morality gained political direction and the contradictions became unmanageable. In *The Achievement,* Matty, shaking off vague traces of sentimentality in his book on *Sarah Orne Jewett* (1929), could isolate the high value Eliot placed on "character," note that it was revealed in intense "moral and spiritual struggle" and not in "bewildering minutes" of passion. Then, Eliot's attack upon "Progress" fitted Matty's growing fears of the dangers of individualism, which, translated to the political realm, meant the dangers of willful leaders.

Matty could warn against the "direct reading" of a poet's life from his works and take a certain pleasure in the fact that he received Eliot neither as a "modern prophet of disillusionment" nor a religious writer who stressed the "emptiness of life without belief." Ignored was the anti-semitism, in conversations about Eliot House, in asides in the lectures—*After Strange Gods*—he gave at the University of Virginia (the dangers of those "free-thinking jews" to "held" values); an anti-semitism observable at first glance, as John Harrison reads it in his closet-rattling book, *The Reactionaries* (1966). Ignored too the elitism that would withhold the meaning of that "red rock" until the Apocalypse; an elitism that would assure those who "knew," "Evil is rare, bad is common. Evil cannot be perceived but by a very few." Matty would also, in a long note in *The Achievement,* avoid difficult strategic questions about tragedy in the modern world; questions John Strachey raised in *The Coming Struggle for Power* (1933). Strachey was not "against" tragic writers, only the use of tragic skepticism as a justification of the *status quo*—"[he] objects," wrote Matty, "to what he conceives to be an inferiority in the work of present tragic writers owing to the fact that they confuse the unavoidable tragedies of human existence with the entirely avoidable tragedies of the decaying capitalistic system." (126) At that point, Matty's disingenuous tack was to deny vision to those attacked: " . . . the assumption that the tragic writer can stand outside his age abstractly conceiving a new basis for life, and at the same time create a vision of life as he has known it seems to me inhuman; indeed, it seems purely verbalistic." (126) Fine words, which later in the note he bends to sway the argument to a defense of "propaganda," but cleverly distinguishes between "propaganda" and "art." Eliot was ideologically necessary, to the point that later in the book, while Matty mentions that *The Criterion*, the magazine Eliot edited for years, was "increasingly taken up with contemporary politics," he also provides an awkward cover for Eliot in saying, "I am not here concerned with the direct applicability of Eliot's political ideas [e.g., about Charles Maurras and the Action Francaise]; indeed, he frequently confesses himself an amateur in such matters . . . " (143) Indeed. One would never know it from the authority with which Eliot wrote the Commentary for *The Criterion* or, as Harrison emphasizes throughout his book, the fact that Eliot was *not* an ignorant man, especially when he committed himself to print; that he, as Yeats, Pound, Lawrence, Lewis, saw himself as a leader and when he spoke, expected listeners.

One finds no fewer than 97 entries for Eliot and his works in *American Renaissance*. Though Eliot's applicability in terms of tragedy, socially, had been broadened, there were a number of concepts that continued to be "useful" in building the book: Eliot stressed craft and consciousness over "inspiration"; insisted that poetry presented the *real* and prose the *ideal;* naturally channeled individualism into corporate structures and checked passion before it ran its course, perhaps destroying others; heightened the dramatic; repossessed the "Metaphysicals";

490

embodied corruption, sin, evil, and, of course, tragedy. As we have seen, these all had enormous value in Matty's development of a *schema* for the book which could be chronological, but also thematic. Eliot was the sounding board and the pruning shear, the measuring stick and the sturdy prop. Yet for all his "usefulness" it is evident, on ideological grounds *within* the context of Matty's developing ideology, that reconcilation with Eliot was impossible. Even within *American Renaissance*, one sees the strains. How could one reconcile Eliot's royalism with the Transcendentalists' democracy, his "knowledge," purposefully distancing (for whatever reasons), theirs the image of open and palpable egalitarianism. Realization was painfully coming home to Matty. One could only play with Eliot's "reaction against the centrifugal individualism which characterized the America into which he was born" *(The Achievement*, 144), so long. Then one was forced to ask what exactly were his ideas and where his commitments lay. Poems may well be written with words, but wasn't it Emerson who said words mean things?

In Matty's preface to the 1947 edition of *The Achievement* he could begin with,

My own views of the poet [since the first edition, twelve years ago] have inevitably undergone some change, but though I now see limitations of which I was not conscious in my first absorption in Eliot's earlier work, I am even more impressed by the contemplative depth in his subsequent production.

and then draw the line:

My growing divergence from his view of life is that I believe that it is possible to accept the 'radical imperfection' of man, and yet to be a political radical as well, to be aware that no human society can be perfect, and yet to hold that the proposition that 'all men are created equal' demands dynamic adherence from a Christian no less than from a democrat.

A short time later, Eliot published his *Notes towards the Definition of Culture* (1948), in which, as Raymond Williams noted, his conservatism became much more evident, and strident. In his introduction he wrote:

What I try to say is this: here are what I believe to be essential conditions for the growth and for the survival of culture.

And then followed it with some very strong words:

If they conflict with any passionate faith of the reader—if, for instance, he finds it shocking that culture and equalitarianism should conflict, if it seems monstrous to him that anyone

491

should have 'advantages of birth'—I do not ask him to change his faith, I merely ask him to stop paying lip-service to culture.

One hardly needs to point to the diction—"passionate faith," "shocking," "monstrous," "lip-service"—to sense Eliot's feelings about altering class lines in England, or the national educational system. That spring of 1948, after the excitement of the first Salzburg Seminar and the Cold War tensions and pressures of lecturing at Charles University in Prague that fall, Matty could try to make even clearer where he was, ideologically:

> . . .I have been influenced by the same Protestant revival that has been voiced most forcefully in America by Reinhold Niebuhr. That is to say I have rejected the nineteenth-century belief in every man as his own Messiah, along with other aberrations of the century's individualism; and I have accepted the doctrine of original sin, in the sense that man is fallible and limited, no matter what his social system, and is capable of finding completion only through humility before the love of God.

> Such doctrines have often been pronounced meaningless by my radical friends; and I, in turn, have felt a shallowness in their psychology whenever they have talked as though man was perfectible, with evil wholly external to his nature, and caused only by the frustrations of the capitalist system. Shakespeare and Melville are witness enough that man is both good and evil.

> But I would differ from most orthodox Christians today, and particularly from the tradition represented by T. S. Eliot, in that, whatever the imperfections of man, the second of the two great commandments, to love thy neighbor as thyself, seems to me an imperative to social action. Evil is not merely external, but external evils are many, and some social systems are far more productive of them than others. Thus my philosophical position is of the simplest. It is as a Christian that I find my strongest propulsion to being a socialist.

The contradiction, Matty's tragedy, was that although he could *say* such things and make them appear clear and resolved, they were not. To the end of his life, only two years after this statement, he was plagued not only by the mounting strains of the Cold War, at home and in Europe; by threatened investigations in Massachusetts and red-baiting at Harvard; by I-told-you-so soldiers, home from killing who wanted only the security of "abstract" thought and a PhD at the end of the line on the G.I. Bill; by his colleagues at Harvard and in the academic community at large;—but by himself; his inability to believe in the "rightness" of his own work; unbelievably, its integrity, its honesty, its soundness of perception and judgment. And as his great friend Louis Hyde has said, "He was without Russell," who had died in 1945 at the age of sixty-three.

Perhaps the dominant tone in all of this is that of judgment;

492

judgment on the direction and substance of what was closest and most important to Matty: his work. Judgment for him plainly had its center, for all his disagreements, with none other than T. S. Eliot. Why Eliot had this "hold" on Matty, even up to the last month of his life where he was arguing with Eliot's publisher (and Eliot himself) for the inclusion of a greater number of Eliot's poems for the *Oxford Book of Modern Verse* (1950) he was editing, may never be certain. But there are several thoughts worth thinking out loud in connection with Matty's ideology.

His convictions were held, as we have seen, very deeply, and as a fuller study will show, formed early. As Austin Warren has said so well, Matty's "*Weltanschauung* was more than *merely* an intellectual construct." He was a most passionate human being, arguing strongly about ideas, building long and deep friendships with all varieties of people, sensitive to their life's contours as well as his own.

It was Eliot himself who introduced or really validated the practice of extra-literary criteria entering into what had been "aesthetic" judgments. He tried, as did Matty, to explain these judgments in terms of a fairly generalized morality; a coherent ethical system. It was all very calm, very unruffled. But beneath the system—certainly a part though not all of that system— existed another system: the machinery of personality. It was that system that was constantly denied, by both men. A reader from another completely different poetic tradition with fresh perceptions and a relatively untrained eye and ear experiencing Eliot's poetry and then listening to either the disclaimers about its "content" or its "meaning" would be forced to conclude that either the critics couldn't read or the words had no specific meanings or perhaps no meanings at all. Someone might patiently explain to him that the words really didn't "mean" what they were supposed to mean, that they functioned exclusively as symbols. At any rate, our visitor might run into I. A. Richards and if the both of them read *The Waste Land* together, our visitor might find himself immediately agreeing with Richards about "the pervasive concern with sex" within the poem. But Matty for example would immediately move to another level, especially if he were forced to be specific about images or symbols of sexuality, something Delmore Schwartz in "T. S. Eliot as International Hero" (1945) did not avoid. Schwartz, in running through Eliot's poems from "Prufrock" to "The Hollow Men," noted the generalized intertwining of frustrated, perverse, impotent sexuality and its counterpart, symbolically, in religious belief. But he also followed, very concretely, the meanings of the images, not simply what their meanings might be on another level. From his reading of the poems, one can draw, as perhaps our visitor, a picture of sexual encounter that characterizes a most basic experience, a most common experience, a shared experience, as the most disgusting possible event in which two human beings could participate. People are mocked, cheated, seduced, brutalized; sexuality is always sordid, violent, and/or unsatisfying; men are generally in constant anxiety over performance and either betrayed or exploiters; women preen, possip, then seduce or are seduced, or are used, symbolically, as the "great whore" of History. The "act" of lovemaking, whether it is in the boathouse of nobility or a divan in a cheap flat is inevitably a farce or peep-show. Marriage, the most sacred of events, is portrayed as tawdry and ludicrous. So much for what's there.

In her very useful discussion of tragedy in *Religion and Literature* (1971) Helen Gardner looks at Christian tragedy, Christianity, and notes the "severity" with which it regards "the flesh" and "sins of the flesh." Today these notions as perhaps many others—from political to social realms—appear to have lost all their denotative force. But for Matty, and for Eliot—for their community—this was most assuredly not the case. In his "Memoir" (1966) of his friend, the late Herbert Read remarked:

> ... Eliot was as controlled as the best of us ... Perhaps too controlled for general converse. From the beginning there was a withholding of emotion, a refusal to reveal the inner man. I always felt that I was in the presence of a remorseful man, of one who had some secret sorrow or guilt. What I took for remorse may not have had its origins in personal experience; a feeling of guilt may be caused by a realization of 'the all-consuming power of original sin.' This Eliot, like Kierkegaard, certainly possessed.

What lay back of Eliot's tortured guilt, his grotesque poetic

494

repetoire of sex? Was it merely an "intellectual construct"? Or was the Eliot who could write a seething, heartbreaking poem like *The Waste Land*, turn on an old friend with "fury," a man of passion like Matty too? It does not matter at this point whether or not the speculations of Robert Sencourt's *T. S. Eliot: A Memoir* (1971) are accurate, though one wonders why Richard Ellmann, who, in his review in the *New York Review of Books* (18 November 1971) so skillfully narrated Eliot's *blitzkrieg*-like marriage to his first wife, should be so utterly hostile to Sencourt's rumours of *Eliot's* homosexuality, whether it was in his youth or when. The rumours certainly have been circulating long enough and certainly at this point in history should not demean Eliot, rather, in the same sense that Matty's silent containment of guilt and suffering in a Christian context gain meaning, and understanding, and sympathy, so too would Eliot's; Eliot who had poetry, at least, to displace his pain. The main point is that *whatever* amalgam of experience Eliot's guilt contained, it radiated an authority that was in some deep sense, determining for Matty.

V

Matty's ideology, forged from religious and labor experiences across America and Europe, case-hardened in the painful fire necessary to give it expression and made supple by the encounter with a real world (the Hawthorne and Melville sections were composed in the summer and fall of 1938 while travelling through Germany and Russia), made resilient yet enriched, opened, by cooperative criticism given in friendship (*American Renaissance* was read, nearly section by section, to dozens of scholars and writers—young and old—who visited Kittery and Boston), was not the ideology of a man who had not died to the world—who did not know its terrors and its joys. As he rejected the retrenched cynicism of the Academy so he rejected the blithe reformer *outside*, ignorant of the possible and the day-to-day limitations about ordinary people.

It was an ideology capable of many tasks. *American Renaissance* was, in a most radiant way, one of those tasks, fulfilling a massive responsibility to what many saw as one community. But Matty lived in many worlds—and one world—and had many responsibilities—and one responsibility. There are those who disdained the implications of his ideology in other spheres, or worse, denied that the organic principle he so seriously and strenuously acknowledged and embraced had *any* validity, even for him. For them, his ideology was a "mistake," his manifold actions those of a "dilettante." The facts speak otherwise. In late 1939, while Matty was at work on the chapters on Whitman, Charles Olson could write about the pains of creative scholarship (Olson had done yeoman service in making available to Matty his own scholarship on Melville's annotations of Shakespeare) and in the next sentence add, "I almost phoned you one day two weeks ago to draw on your union knowledge when a strike I've interested myself in here [Gloucester, Massachusetts] threatened to break out . . . "

It was an ideology with roots in poems and chalices and ordinary men and women, but it was also an ideology in touch with Matty's own deepest experiences whose reason for being lay in service to others. As Paul Sweezy, editor of the Monthly Review, recently wrote me:

> . . . it is ridiculous to say that Matty's socialism was emotional and without any base. But I don't think he had tried to think through an independent assessment of U. S. capitalism and its tendencies. He more or less accepted the analysis of those he respected and were in general political agreement with him. I well remember his reaction to the copy of my *Theory of Capitalist Development* (published about the same time as *Am Ren*) [a year later] . . . He read it at once and with great care, and his evaluation was generous to a fault . . . there is no doubt whatever about the depth of his knowledge of U.S. labor history. He knew a lot more than I did.

And comparing the different roads to socialism and what it meant, once there, was Alfred Kazin, writing to Matty about a misunderstanding over the singing of "The Internationale" at Salzburg:

> But for you the song is something else—perhaps because you never learned the words as a child, and so have never had the experience of hearing its hymnal parodied by the 'believers.' For you Socialism is a personal ache, a moral choice of solidarity with another class; it is also a reflection of your spiritual loneliness in the present system. Simply (and how long it has taken me to say it this cleanly!), for you, Socialism is a matter of good faith—I could not sit down with Ella Winter, or Fierlinger, or Harry Bridges, for five minutes without getting into

a battle. That is the thing I have had to understand about you; that is what the stale ex-Commies of PR [*Partisan Review*] can never understand. They assume, as I have so often tended to assume, that anyone who supports the Soviets in any way must be a scoundrel; for they have been knocked out of all generosity and faith by the furious internecine struggles within the radical movement. It would take a book—and am writing only part of it in "A Walker in the City"—even to begin to explain the bitterness which people who have grown up in that movement feel toward the Communists. But I am ashamed that I, who am opposed both to Communism and "anti-Communism," should have been trapped by that bitterness in responding to your book [*From the Heart of Europe*].

Critic, scholar, teacher, Matty touched all manner of people and as in *American Renaissance* sought to bring them together not without identity, not without differences, but on the basis of what Kazin called "good faith." In this respect, perhaps the most apt closing remarks are those of Jean-Paul Sartre in memory of Maurice Merleau-Ponty, the French phenomenologist:

In many archaic religions, there are holy persons who exercise the function of *lieur* [literally, binder or trusser]. Everything must be attached and tied by them. Merleau-Ponty played their part politically. Born of union, he refused to break it and his function was to bind. The ambiguity of his heuristic Marxism, of which he said, at the same time, that it couldn't suffice that we had nothing else, was, I think, that it made possible meetings and discussions which will be continuous. Thus he did, for his part, make the history of this post-war period as much as it can be made by an intellectual. But, inversely, History made him while being made by him. Refusing to ratify the ruptures, hanging on with each hand to continents which were moving apart, he finally found, but without illusions, his old idea of catholicity. On both sides of the barricade, there are only men. Thus the human invention is born everywhere . . . It sufficed that the *lieur* used all his strength to keep the two terms of the contradiction together, to delay the explosion for as long as he could. The creations, daughters of chance and reason, will bear witness that the reign of man is possible. I can't decide whether this idea was late or early in October 1950. One thing only is certain. It was not on time. The entire world was being shattered.

Notes

1. The sheer density of the book limited, I think, its accessibility, and its sales, though steady, were nowhere near as spectacular as those of Beard or Parrington, totalling but 30,000 in thirty years. Paperback sales suggest a new, more receptive audience is now present, that the book need no longer depend for its influence upon an understanding few; selling half as many in three years.

2. Some critics have regarded the title as misleading, but Matthiessen thought it more than a convenient handle for publicity purposes. In a letter to Oxford in the early part of 1941, he answered a query:

The one strict objection: that what I am dealing with was more a birth than a re-birth, I can cover by a few additional sentences in the preface. They all, except Hawthorne, thought of themselves as belonging to an age of reaffirmation of the great timeless values; Melville specifically likened the period to that of the Elizabethans; and at several points in the text I have referred to their achievement as a Renaissance. There is no other word to convey an era of creative ripeness.

3. "Paranoia and American History," *New York Review of Books,* 23 September 1971.

497

4. "Historians: Simple-Minded and Complex," *The Nation,* 18 November 1968. The issue Sklar can only briefly pursue is crucial to the historical consciousness of the Forties and Fifties, indeed, the entire Cold War period. For a refutation of Hofstadter's generation's identification of McCarthyism with the earlier Mid-western Populist-Progressive reform movements, see Michael Paul Rogin's *The Intellectuals and McCarthy: The Radical Specter* (1967), and in particular, for elite initiation, manipulation, and direction of phenomenea such as McCarthyism, see Ronald Steel's review of Dean Acheson's *Present at the Creation,* "Commissar Acheson," *New York Review of Books,* 12 February 1970.

5. "The Responsibility of Intellectuals," *American Power and the New Mandarins,* (1967, 1969), pp. 343–394. The literature on ideology, as Norman Birnbaum has noted elsewhere, is very large. For a fuller discussion in this particular context, see *The End of Ideology Debate,* Edited with an Introduction by Chaim I. Waxman (1968, 1969); "The Concept of Ideology," by George Lichtheim, in *The Concept of Ideology and Other Essays* (1967, 1969), pp. 3–46; and "The Revival of Political Controversy in the Sixties," by Christopher Lasch, in *The Agony of the American Left* (1969), pp. 169–212, especially pp. 171–179.

6. In *The Imperial Self* (1971), Quentin Anderson has said of this work: "This seems to me one of the ablest minds ever to deal with American literature. But it is almost impossible to read now . . . because of its isolation of artist and works in a realm of art so claustral. Almost every issue of importance is refracted into this oddly insular world. But there are no persons with imaginative or emotional commitments in the context it creates; there is no history save that of the inwardly determined symbolizing process itself. The book is now a rather scary exhibition of the costs of denying history." p. 260n.

7. The words are Lionel Trilling's in his remarkable *Matthew Arnold* (1940). See especially Chapters 2, 7, 8.

8. Matty was to become very close to several of the Agrarians, though not without reservations, especially in the case of Davidson, to their racism. John L. Stewart's critique of the social and political thought of the Agrarians is caustic, though set in a very full context in *The Burden of Time* (1965). See also Allen Guttman, *The Conservative Tradition in America* (1967), pp. 148–157. The Matty who loved his Kittery 18th century boat-builder's cottage and rowing on a pleasant Atlantic was sensitive to the pastoral elements in the agrarian vision and could agree with the dangers they saw in industrialism even as he was not against the process itself; he was as aware of what was happening to the rural South in the 20th century as he was aware of the price paid by English farmers in the 19th for industrialization of that nation. Although, with Emerson, machines and their power could impress him, he also had a keen sense, both in his time and for the future, of the problems technology would pose, especially a technology devoid of humane control. In an article written in 1943, "The Humanities in War Time," Matty said: " . . . the most perceptive scientists now grant, as they did not do in the era dominated by simple mechanistic views of progress, that there are limitations to their kind of knowledge, that there are modes of truth which the arts and philosophy and religion alone can articulate . . . It is the role of the student of the humanities to recognize those limitations and to raise questions of value. A magnificent concrete instance of just such discrimination is furnished by one of the great achievements of modern painting, Rivera's frescoes in Detroit. Their main subject is the building of the Ford car, as a modern man the painter was fascinated with studying every technical aspect of that process. But as a humanist he was also concerned with scrutinizing the ends to which our industrial age was moving, and in two companion panels he contrasted beneficent science, finding its expression in the hospital laboratory, with malevolent science, producing poison gas."

9. Hofstadter's critique is much milder, though patronizing (as he is to Turner and

Beard). It is almost as if it were only a matter of technique, style,—"the nobility of his [Parrington's] conception became an obstacle: his plan required him to read so extensively that penetrating inquiry was possible at only a few points . . . to write with such rigid compression . . . not a single writer could get extended discussion." Incredible, not naive, incredible. Hofstadter is perfectly well aware that small points total large conclusions; he does not want to talk about why people, and above all, historians, "bought" progressive history in such quantities for so long.

10. Malcolm Cowley in his Introduction to Brooks' autobiography, brushed aside such concerns as "the discordant voices [of] some of those in the political left where one heard complaints that Brooks was no longer a leader and a prophet . . . " but in 1947 Lewis Mumford could be more insistent: "By closing your eyes," he wrote to Brooks, "to what has actually been going on around you, by refusing so amiably to take sides, you have left out the bitter tragic element in the lives of Thoreau, Melville, Whitman, and have ranged yourself with the proper 'gentlemanly men,' who felt that these people were barbarous, hysterical or mad, because they made inconvenient issues over matters that gentlemanly men were careful never to take a position on."

11. One recalls Ralph Ellison's angry reply, asked if he regarded *Invisible Man* (1952) as "purely a literary work as opposed to one in the tradition of social protest?" "Now, mind," cautioned Ellison, "I recognize no dichotomy between art and protest. Doestoevski's *Notes from the Underground* is, among other things, a protest against the limitations of nineteenth-century rationalism; *Don Quixote, Man's Fate, Oedipus Rex, The Trial*—all these embody protest, even against the limitations of human life itself. If social protest is antithetical to art, what then shall we make of Goya, Dickens, and Twain?" *Paris Review Interviews, Second Series* (1963).

12. Matty's insistence on the value of consciousness anticipated present positions. The relationship between change in consciousness and change in social structure was not seen as so central, or possible, in the Thirties; the formulations of Georg Lukacs did not have currency—the extreme of which can be seen in the writings of Sartre. See also Marx's essay in this collection.

13. *To the Finland Station* (1940), Wilson's study of the revolutionary tradition in Europe and the rise of socialism, was sensitive to people acting in history *as people,* as well as "historical figures." His conclusion likely impressed Matty with its respect for "the technique of analyzing political phenomena in social-economic terms," but also with its questioning of certain "ideals and ideas"; its attack upon authoritarianism and autocracy in Russia; its hatred of "class privilege" and "exploitation" and its insistence upon socialist *ethics.* In connection with the latter, Wilson had written: "The taking-over by the state of the means of production and the dictatorship in the interests of the proletariat can by themselves only guarantee the happiness of the dictators themselves."

14. All page references to the Second Impression (1941).

15. 1. Words are signs of natural facts. 2. Particular natural facts are symbols of particular spiritual facts. 3. Nature is the symbol of spirit.

16. Just how honestly explicit Matty could be in defending the integrity of *each* value was seen in June of 1941 at a dinner given by the Harvard Student Union and the Teacher's Union in honor of the publication of *American Renaissance:* "I feel that I am among friends," Joseph H. Summers recalls Matty saying, "and I do not want there to be any misunderstandings. Some of you are Marxists. I am not a Marxist. I have been influenced by Marx as has anyone who has seriously thought about political matters in the last fifty years. But Marx was more often successful in coining effective slogans for immediate political action than in arriving at statements of philosophical truth. If any of you really believe that religion is only 'the opiate of the people,' you cannot hope to understand the five figures I have tried to write about in *American Renaissance."*

17. Arthur Kinoy, one of Matty's two tutees in the Spring of 1941, recently reminded me that this passage was crucial to Matty ("He loved it. He would read and re-read it.") and speaking of *Moby Dick* itself, remarked, "He raised all of us on it."

18. The most incisive yet adumbrating exposition of this process is Erich Auerbach's "*Sermo Humilis,* Excursus: Gloria Passionis," *Literary Language and Its Public in Late Latin Antiquity and the Middle Ages* (1958, 1965), esp. pp. 35–36, 65–66.

19. This section of *American Renaissance,* in fact, Matty's entire sensitivity to visual representation and the artist as craftsman, owes much to his friend, the artist Russell Cheney.

20. "'Arise and Depart, For this is not your Rest,'" A Study of the resignation of George Ripley from the Ministry of the Unitarian Church on Purchase Street, in Boston, in the year 1841, Bowdoin Prize Essay, Harvard University (1941). All page references to the Bowdoin essay.

21. Charles Crowe, *George Ripley: Transcendentalist and Utopian Socialist* (1967), p. 114.

22. Ruland flatly states: "The central reason why Matthiessen found it difficult to write anything deeper than the biographical chapter in the *Literary History of the United States* (1948), was that he found most of Poe's work beneath criticism."

23. This gap was to be bridged by historians and writers alike and the method was to be a focus upon what contemporary historian Jesse Lemisch has called, "history from the bottom up." Matty's text was Thoreau's essay on Carlyle (1847): "Balancing Thoreau's belief that history must be written as though it happened to the writer," Matty wrote, "was his equally strong conviction that if so written it would not be the history of reigns but of peoples." (632) He noted that "on the basis of such a theory Parker held Prescott's dramatic pageants to amount to no more than a rhetorical *tours de force,* the product of a superficial aristocrat. In Parker's solid if somewhat naive objections we come to the democratic core of New England transcendentalism. For Parker believed that an American historian must write in the interest of mankind . . . He must be occupied with the growth of institutions, not with glamorous spectacles." (633)

Acknowledgments

For permission to reprint material thanks are due to Louis K. Hyde, Jr.; Donald Gallup, Benicke Library, Yale University; Whitney Blake, Yale University Press; Sheldon Meyer, Oxford University Press; George Brockway, W.W. Norton & Company; Houghton Mifflin; C.L. Barber; Barbara Probst Solomon; Arthur Kinoy; Robert E. Spiller; William Empson; Todd Gitlin; Alfred Kazin; Charles Boer, "The Charles Olson Estate"; and Paul M. Sweezy. For research grants that enabled me to gather information I am grateful to the Louis M. Rabinowitz Foundation, Inc., and the Department of English and American Literature, Brandeis University. Finally, for a community in which this work meant something I thank the Rev. Harvey H. Gutherie and Irwin Freedman.

500

The politics of the imagination: the problem of consciousness
SOL YURICK

> *"What if the machinery were reversed? What if the*
> *habits, problems, secrets and unconscious motivations of*
> *the wealthy and powerful were daily scrutinized by a*
> *thousand systematic researchers, were hourly pried into,*
> *analyzed and cross-referenced, tabulated and published in*
> *a hundred inexpensive mass circulation journals. . ."*
> *(Martin Nicolas, Remarks at the American Sociological*
> *Association Convention, 1968)*

Literature, revolution, politics: in the days of the Cold War they used to say writing well was *truth,* the best politics of all. We were taught, in the fifties, to eschew the obviously political; the province of Literature stood above mundane temporal considerations. Protest novels came close to being the eldest literary sin of all. Proletarian fiction was a bust. Socialist Realism was simplistic propaganda. Joyce, Eliot, Pound, Stevens, Hemingway triumphed; Ginsberg was resisted but won slowly.

Art and revolution: incompatible? One is an act of creation and reconstruction done over a relatively long range of time; the other is done in the hard world . . . people begin to sabotage, run and shoot. But Lenin tells us "(when) . . . the revolution is made, at the moment of its climax and exertion of all human capabilities . . . the *class conciousness,* the will, the passion and the fantasy of tens of millions . . . are urged on by the very acutest class struggle." Odd word that, "fantasy." Strange word for a hard-headed revolutionary; what's it mean? Is fantasy a *scientific* way of comprehending the world? What kind of fantasy is the "proletarian" revolutionary kind in opposition to?

I received help in writing *The Bag* which, at least in some parts, was a group effort. Partly because of this I was able to "predict" the Columbia uprising and the role of computer technology in reordering the world. In turn I helped my helpers to write *Who Rules Columbia?* Enlightening experience: that chasing down and expressing of one of the concealed dimensions of the world: behind the Auchincloss world, benign-looking Grayson Kirk, elite schools in their timeless ivy, cultural studies, the community of intellectuals, existed a parallel world which hinted at secrecy, collusion, conspiracy, profit-making, rent-gouging, racism, world-destiny/shaping priorities . . . But we had arguments, my collaborators and I. It wasn't enough to merely talk about interlocking directorates, but psychology, personal as well as institutional. We had to talk about the ironic dichotomy, the dissonance between overt greed and what one got taught in school courses; we had to talk about the ideological/expansive nature of that university in terms of knowledge proliferation and a growth corps of serviceable people and what is or is not useful about having an education that included Camus' *The Stranger,* or *The Divine Comedy,* or Daniel Boorstin's counter/Parrington-Beard history, or Paul Samuelson's *Economics.* It wasn't enough to merely say that education serves the ruling class, which is true enough, but to talk about how.

Grayson Kirk on the Board of Directors of Consolidated Edison (which provides the energy to feed) and IBM (draining work energy from the ghetto and other, oil worlds): IBM and data-processing, which is a *conversion* of information/reality, a transubstantiation/compression of fact into bits: all-world outlooks (and history) at Columbia processed into useful comprehension by IBM hardware: IBM educational systems for IBM world markets and IBM on-line and random-access memory banks (and what is worthy of being included in those banks and what is not/discarded . . . W. W. Rostow yes, Marx no). A world as growth

502

tapping into an endless energy source on sale for everyone: against the endless energy source drawn out of people themselves rendered unmemoried, or memoried by sale . . . Real-time memory for sale which had to include *Mont-Saint-Michel and Chartres*, for example, but not the slum-lord policies of Bobby Kennedy.

In a sense *conscious* literary/political education began for me when I was writing *The Bag*. I found it impossible to say things simply: I found it impossible to be timeless. Everything interfused with everything else. I began by wanting to write a novel about the way Welfare worked. In trying to solve certain practical problems, the book grew and new problems were raised, which at the same time interacted with what was happening in the world outside at that time. Michael Harrington had called for a new Dickens to chronicle the plight of the poor, that invisible nation, and to some extent I saw myself in that tradition . . . but what I was discovering was that Dickens had been soft, reformist, unwilling to face certain realities; that the robber barons of the nineteenth century had gone underground and had appeared again transformed, in a variety of unlikely places; the art of robbery had become indeed sophisticated and subtle.

The violent, the aberrant, were *not* representations of some skewed end of a Gaussian curve but were the everyday normal and, in their small unwilling ways, contributors to the Gross National Product. They were *not* the presentations of a romantic/competitive imagination in conflict with other literary individualistic imaginations who were new-product-driven into one-upmanship and outlandishness, but were normal. Poverty programs were *not* supposed to succeed but had another aim entirely, both for the poor and for those who were hired to ameliorate their condition. That new classes were being generated and manipulated to ultimately stave off revolution became obvious; the Movement was doomed to failure in this phase of history. The problem of consciousness, the way in which we view reality rose up through the paradigm of case history, essay-writing: my experiences in trying to write a constantly rejected article on Welfare for *Commentary* made me understand the political basis of rejection—too

503

much passion; a violation of the canons of sociological/scientific objectivity and detachment—and Norman Podhoretz as character in action appeared in the book, demonstrating that editing had an ongoing covert political dimension. Writing books, magazine articles, psychological history, case-history became, if one did not have an analysis, a compartmentalized, jargonized, *political* way of viewing the world where the politics disappeared into social science. Stylistic demands were also implicitly political. And more, novel writing and the demands of success, or even survival, had an implicit political and economic dimension.

At the time I was reading Fanon's *Wretched of the Earth*. Fanon condemns Western culture and talks about its contribution to colonialism as a mode of conquest, a way of separating an elite from a colonized people and using them as the Mother Country's agents. At first I was outraged. A Black whimsy. A miraculous birth of a Black past, which, aside from the demands for justice and economic self-determination, did not compare with a culture which stood above history and was a-racial, a-cultural, the final (so far) development in an evolutionary process. Culture was for *all* men. If only *they* could learn to incorporate and love our culture, which was an apolitical gift from the Gods, we could love and incorporate their culture too . . . culture which existed in one dimension. But since I tried to express these feelings with some degree of honesty, dramatically, culture fractured, split into multiple realms, and the utmost act of imagination was to preceive what was happening in another *political* space which is *geographically* in the same place. For if space is defined by coordinates, what if those definition points are political and economic? How would a character who lived in another realm feel and act? More, I had to write such a character as if I meant it, give him his dignity and due *against my own inclinations:* caricature, satire was easier.

Possibly the major breakthrough came for me when the revelations of CIA investment in the field of Culture itself, that timeless arcanum, was announced: the Congress for Cultural Freedom was in some sense bought and there were some very high literary and philosophical types who were involved. At the same time Movement friends were demonstrating to me that Defense and Intelligence communities were funding studies in every social science possible; obviously there was a need, a use, a payoff. What was an expert in Arabic Aristotelianism doing working for the Department of Defense? A question was raised: was this a feature of our time and no other? Was there a Golden Age Athenian equivalent for the Institute for Defense Analysis? What did it mean that Marlowe worked for Queen Elizabeth I's intelligence service? Did the Congress for Cultural Freedom have historical analogies and if so, were there historical continuities?

These days fiction writers have a choice of going into the social sciences and using those methodologies, or of taking extensive flights of whimsy, head-biography, and thus seem to be opening new fields of inner space. For ideologists and hapless novelist/poets, this constitutes the New Frontier, where one could reap a vast harvest of intellectual goodies for a new mass market of intellectually trained university consumers who dig irony, fantasy, the antique leap . . . the last refuge of the Romantic with whom Cartesian isolation has caught up . . . though in the long run, it turns out, as it has before in American history, that power-elites have long ago speculated in this inscape, buying off vast tracts of psychological dimension. Real space belongs to the military and detachments of money interpenetrate pockets of resistance.

The Left, the Movement, revolutionary, anarchist youth, dropouts, freaks and heads proposed the primacy of the self and the personal vision . . . a direct mediation with reality, much in the same way that early Protestants dealt directly with God, very much in the American Holy Roller tradition, and partly this was a development arising from the false consciousness of freedom and the bewildering options of the paperback revolution. There seemed something wrong to me (not morally) with the concept of the writer merely writing out of his own experience without having in some sense tested out and lived the life of his subjects, which is to say having tried to live a different class and economic life.

And while I was writing, revisionist social scientists and

505

historians began to challenge establishment social science and in a very important sense these people were my collaborators too.

I began to ask myself questions about my culture, my education, and began to come up with interesting answers . . .

At this point I'm writing a Marxist detective novel. But merely writing a fiction, what could at best be a *roman à clef,* which implies audience passivity, proscenium, would no longer do. The fiction has not only to intersect with reality, with the public world, but has in some sense to challenge that politically possessed reality.

A Marxist detective novel—what's that? In part I'm still learning. Certainly if bourgeois detective and police work provides accumulative-protective property and property-relations-defending-justice, then the Marxist detective would work for distributive justice, disaccumulative justice . . . defending the claims of a robbed class reappropriating.

A case that fascinates me is Truman Capote's *In Cold Blood;* a Mansonite, Starkweatherian kind of case . . . one that, within the context of bourgeois society, seems to defy solution.

What bothered me most of all was the public's and critics' reaction to the book. The book was hailed ecstatically as a new breakthrough when in fact it was part of a rather banal genre which could only be called why-did-they-kill; Sunday supplement stuff. Capote talked about his fabulous *memory* . . . but then, he had all the records . . . or did he? Apparently he paid a number of interviewees never to tell their version of the story, which meant that he controlled the memory of these two men on a national level: their public memory. Heisenberg: what happens in cases like this was, it seems to me, that the interviewer's ability to reshape the consciousness of the person interviewed to fit useful, dramatic patterns was operative. Hadn't I done this myself as case-historian and dispenser of money for the Department of Welfare? The questions and the cues inform the interrogated of the desired answers, more or less. One of the killers had, according to Capote, a recurrent dream about an avenging parrot. There was something familiar about that dream. Dream of the killer or a plagiarism from Flaubert's "A Simple Heart"? (and why did Chaucer feel compulsions to rewrite Boccaccio?) Historians dug into the past to write about similar sensational cases when, in fact, it seemed to me that this crime was rather common . . . certainly it happened every day and night in the slums. There were certain ambiguous feelings on Capote's part about the head of the murdered family, Herbert Clutter, a sense of contempt, and yet the dictates of the genre demanded that Clutter be a good guy. And the wife, Bonnie Clutter, seemed too much out of Tennessee Williams . . . I couldn't understand this involvement, this excitement, and why rational critics had presumably lost their heads . . . It wasn't even that well written, in fact it was obvious, in spite of Capote's claims, that he had written it fast and sloppily. Other facts began to appear: Capote presented only one of the two men, Perry Smith, as his killer (and identified strongly with that killer) and in so doing perceived the Clutters of the world as his enemy . . .which they were—when in fact the two men had participated. Why lie? Artistic compression? After all, Capote had called it a non-fiction *novel,* a nice turn of phrase. And what about Clutter himself? There were hints about his *social role* which indicated that he was no ordinary moderately wealthy farmer but had held a high agricultural position in the Dulles-Eisenhower administration . . . and, given the history of American agriculture, the only successful farmers were . . . what? Successful, competitive, surviving fittest, or, from a Marxist position something else? Was his murder due merely to a random throw of the dice, a blind God-finger pinpointing a modern version of Job? And as I began to investigate it, I learned certain things about Clutter, his national, institutional, class and personal past, things no one talked about at all . . . and the character, the *psychology* of Clutter and his killers, began to change . . .

But most of all the question of why considerable masses could be moved by this book troubled me. What in their consciousness under what circumstances could evoke a desired reaction?

Then, after a suitable time had passed, after the nation had its meed of titillation at the awful murder, when its terrified dreams had subsided, Capote gave a big party at the Plaza in New York. He invited four hundred people; the new Ward McAllister of the new Liberal Elite. When I saw the guest list, when I read about the party, my immediate instinctive reaction was, "What are they celebrating?" A man and his family had been killed. Two men had been executed. The balance had been restored; the torn fabric rewoven. Capote made a lot of money. Marx on the productivity of crime: ". . . He (the criminal) produces not only compendia on Criminal Law, not only penal codes . . . but also art, belles lettres, novels, and even tragedies . . . The Criminal breaks the monotony and everyday security of bourgeois life. In this way he keeps it from stagnation and gives rise to that uneasy tension and agility without which even the spur of competition would get blunted. Thus he gives a stimulus to productive forces . . . "

The grand party Capote threw represented several things; a celebration of the restoration of the *liberal* version of the torn fabric of society; a celebration of a rite of harvest, where the produce was not only mere money, but the recapture of a whole apparatus of symbols and symbolic forms, a re-formist re-definition of reality which re-stores what has almost slipped loose and at the same time worked to combat the eye/toothers and their crude outlooks which will not suffer killer *or* Capotes. For a moment, a glimpse of American history had been afforded, an American history that twenty-five years of Cold War history and culture had been trying to wipe out.

In searching for the real criminals it was not only necessary to understand completely, from a Marxist point of view, all of American History and Culture, but its economics, its real politics, its ruling ideology, and the contribution of all these inputs to the maintenance of a proper consciousness, a consciousness which was stronger than the police, than the military, than the repressive hardware itself . . . that to perceive the real killers and the real killings in this rather banal case took a wrench of consciousness which began to approach madness. For to see Marxist reality against the painful pressure of a bourgeois world is to approach madness in the sense that it is painful and panic-producing since we are the products of this culture and it hurts to *sustain* an alternate vision—no, a vision which is in active opposition to what people take for granted; madness in the sense that the majority of people led by one set of consciousness-determiners could define this opposition vision as mad . . .

Some of the problems confronting us were these:

1) A new theory of psychology and character which is at variance with received psychology and its practice since Freud . . . in fact a new definition of what constitutes the unconscious. In short, Freud and Marx are incompatible; to perceive in the free movements of free individuals social interconnections whose strategic rigidities are hidden has priority.

2) A reexamination of all our approved literary artifacts and the way they have been generated, established, or interpreted into impotence, treasured, not only by the bourgeois culture, but by many Marxists . . .

3) A study of the social sciences and their relation to culture and class; since the social sciences have appropriated the realm of the novel and disguised the ideology in "testable" quantification . . . the literary-in-non-fiction confronting the non-fiction-in-literature and fantasy.

4) A study of the *real* history of man . . . what really happened in the concrete world.

5) What became necessary was to ask some questions:

   a) Is a new theory of conspiracy, a more sophisticated and elegant theory necessary? Marxists have after all been too respectable.

   b) If, as Marx proposes, man produces his own consciousness, *who possesses the means of production?* After all, what real liberties for expression have writers been permitted through the ages?

   c) Mao asks, "Where do correct thoughts come from?" Let us ask the same question.

   d) Jung asserts the collective unconscious. We ask who collected that unconscious; what contents and forms have been left out of that unconscious?

6) How could one usefully view the ongoing universe and, more

especially in the case of literature, how could one record it, record its deliberately obscured inner reality, write its real history? In short, the question of strategy of discourse arose now.

We were told by the McLuhanites that linearality was dead but the global village is going to be wired by CBS, RCA, IBM, General Dynamics, Litton Industries... Non-linearality was already the mode of fiction and poetry from at least as far back as Sterne... more, it was the mode of history presentation... for the modern parataxical vision is possible, no even necessary, because there are hidden levels of cultural consensus and agreement which provide the organic links and ideological direction uniting inputs of random data... Non-linearality in the hands of the establishment (especially if it is dependent upon a heavily-invested-in technology) which needs computer-histories to run it could only imply a hidden politicized realm of being... an acceptance of the bourgeois world with at best a small guerrilla war between the right wing and the liberal cultures. In short, the new culture is still bourgeois and is more than ever capable of manipulation. Non-linearality in the hands of the Left relies on an outmoded means of re-production and romantic, individualistic, free-association brownian motion which, because of its lack of coherence, is capable of being engulfed by a rationalizing, centralizing system. The alternate culture is at this time being economically coopted and ideologically defeated because it depends upon a whole realm of acceptance which the world resists, or turns to profit.

Simultaneity in the modern bourgeois fiction world is oddball coincidence at best, free-play of the mildly insurgent imagination.

Einstein tells us that coincidence depends upon the position of the viewer... when light or news from two events reaches him at a certain time... Simultaneity is relative. *But simultaneity also depends upon a political climate which provides the lenses with which to view the ongoing world.* And Heisenberg and Bridgman already admit that the observer and his instruments, as well as their paradigms to apprehend the universe, determine in some sense what can be seen and is acted upon, changing the reality of those under-observation events. Of course they don't speak about the *class* and *social* views of the observers...

510

7) If there is a climate of belief, an orchestration of faith, can we say that in some meaningful sense, since it supports an ongoing capitalist bourgeois system, there is such a notion as a Central Bank of Symbolic Forms (rather than a *Spiritus Mundi*)? That this bank contains not only dominant symbols, and formal relations, modes of transaction with symbols, and that these symbols act as symbols of domination?

Get in touch with your feelings, the new breed exhorts us; that was supposed to be the first step toward making the revolution. But what if those very *feelings* represented, as Marx asserts, the policeman in the mind? I don't care what acid freaks thought they saw and felt, they were still relating to, painting their feelings in terms of, traditional dominant symbol systems. There was a class content to their visions which depended to a large extent on class-determined tracked-access to education. What we react to instinctively (and there is, I propose, a difference between bourgeois instinct and Marxist instinct), interposing our lust/hunger for freedom which may in the long run be a petit-bourgeois freedom: the small shopkeeper, the home industry manufacturer setting up in business with an emotional-content loan from the Central Bank of Symbolic Forms, while resenting the struggle against the mass consciousness industries which are putting him out of business with their glut of mind-deadening schlock; but proud of being a member of a saved elite which keeps those special products for itself and its sub-class. The petit-liberal (and I distinguish this kind from the corporate liberal who has the long range vision—or as it's taught to him by the ideologues of the Congress for Cultural Freedom—and sees the necessity of paying the social overhead to keep sound-money policies ongoing) intellectual's desire for a mode of consciousness which simply isn't there, represents a reformist request for a little equality please, or, at best, even a share in the wielding of power.

We spent a lot of college time reading and analyzing T. S. Eliot. The analysis was also a way of involvement and through involvement came belief and from belief came another way of viewing the world.

The parataxic vision according to Joyce, Eliot, and Pound is still operative and anyway, without those three, the methodology of acid rock groups, the new media, is impossible: they've done their damage.

Eliot thought that his poetry could be understood by factory workers.

I once saw a street fight where one heroic and half-mad suicidal street kid was being beaten up by a gang. He called on his friends to help him—his friends who were all dead: dead of overdoses, dead in Vietnam, dead of police and prison poisoning. The ghosts didn't concretely materialize but had material reality in the heads of the attacking gang, and they fled in terror. Odysseus going down to Hades to seek advice from the shades of his dead companions. Where indeed did those correct thoughts come from?

Eliot, damn it, is right. Stalin and Mao on literature are dead wrong.

Dickens was contemporaneous with Marx. And let's not have any illusions about Dickens being *subversive,* as so many radicals do: he was a petit-liberal to the core, a reformer whose politics of sentimentality dictated that a change of ruling-class heart would solve everything . . . all those happy endings. Dickens served as one of those information conduits by which the Grand Liberals could apprehend the social threats from beneath, find ways to adjust to ongoing and disruptive realities, pay their social overhead.

Dickens, in *Bleak House,* has a character, Krook, who has obtained important documents as a part of his business in garbage; these documents hold a key to a mystery of the past. Krook and the documents burn up through spontaneous combustion. What did Dickens mean by that? Sheer joy of writing crazy scenes? The bizarre and titillating incident? Possibly. Yet he insists on the scientific validity of event. This event implies coincidence, conceit, miracle, the upsetting of the usual order within a bourgeois framework. Is it possible that outrageous coincidence (which social science admits as rare exceptions) in the bourgeois world is not coincidence from a Marxist world view? *Certain* wild concomitances, certain wonders, strange meetings, brought together by what seems to be the sheer whim of the author, may in fact be dreary linearality in a Marxist world?

Or is the spontaneous combustion a metaphor, a uniting of disparates into a symbol hinting at conspiracy; also a way of obfuscating reality, a conclusion-retardant, deferred gratification?

What's conspiracy, or conversely, what's not conspiracy, depends upon a social point of view, a class view: a set of different world assumptions provides a different political lens with which to see into and through a bourgeois veil of mystification. The socialist vision reveals where the bourgeois mode conceals. Obfuscation is a politics. Dickens weaves things together outrageously . . . he bends reality to achieve certain unlikely ends which persuade us of . . . what? A trip through disaster . . . but the end is assured, happy.

Parataxis. Short takes. Resnais-ism in action. Forcing for the initiate the cultivation of the discipline of memory which provides a hidden dimension of inter-connectivity beneath the parameters, dictated by class interests which in our society hide class. For the uninitiate, memory is discouraged. Memory is relegated to reference books where even indices are politically generated. Paradigmatic schemes assist or force us into definitions of events and objects. Lévi-Strauss talks about memory systems which perceive reality in primitive groupings which seem to imply prodigious abilities to remember. A change in the economy takes place and an infusion of library technology creates instant amnesia and high dependency. A metaphor: the basic material of the genes as material-shaping information: a predetermined program . . . social genetics, the invasion of an alien, in-forming program-virus which reshapes ideas and remembrances. . . . Life for different groupings arranged in terms of power-wielding is a struggle against disease of the mind and body.

Who controls memory controls history.

(Truman Capote—who controlled the history of the killed and the killers—whose memory was in turn shaped.)

Who controls history also controls the dissemination of a-history, national memory-lack, a form of disarming ideology. And history, as fed through the educational system, is the national act of forgetting.

Certainly almost all modern cultural artists, writers, scientists, social scientists are born out of the middle classes. Rarely are they of the ruling elite. Therefore in some sense they are always the servants of the ruling classes, depending upon an ongoing economic system to survive. They constitute an infra-structure with a certain self-interest not always in perfect gear with the interests of the ruling elites: they have their own visions and their inner conflicts as they try to advance the claims/visions of their social groupings, proclaiming that they are, because of their sensibility, insight, humanity, training, the fittest to rule (and if not rule, advise) . . . philosopher kings, poet rulers, cultural priests . . . But certainly for the last twenty-five years they have fought bitterly about everything but politics wherein a broad Cold War consensus reigned. To be sure there were intense personal, egotistical, reputational conflicts, but these differences can in practice always be adjudicated, resolved by an infusion of money and a minority share in the wielding of power.

Oedipus is usually interpreted as a ritual reenactment of certain eternal components, certain universal elements common to all man. The protagonist should be a middling man, the man with a tragic flaw, an obsessional sort of man, a compulsive kind of man, *a specialized type whose speciality is out of whack in a time of crisis,* when the right skills have turned wrong because of a new development in history (this is me, not Aristotle) . . . neurotragic at a time of national breakdown.

Did the Athenians have the advanced and very modern sense to manipulate their culture consciously? Was there an Athenian Congress for Cultural Freedom which rewarded politically correct plays? We don't know: concrete history has (been) faded and only the eternal verities remain, the tragic flaw, the neurosis, the compulsion . . . But expediency, murder, high passion, rape, brutality, debasement, sadism, incest, excess in every form . . . are these merely dramatic aberrations, flaws? Isn't self-advancement through sex, an identifying of national with class and personal passions, a commonplace in the realms of power? Doesn't the drive for power mean that a man becomes his specialization, his mode of advancement, his useful flaw? Even then?

Freud's modification: stages of development common to all man, stages discarded upon reaching adulthood . . . an abstraction of a situation more common to rulers (and, oddly, among the lower order), an ongoing way of life, a progressive's view of history made case history. Freud's view is ultimately a middle class one . . . a view which pleads for rationality, for reason theoretically, but in practice leads to something else . . . a diminution of dangerous passions among the therapized and an ignoring of them among the powerful. From a position of non-power he assumes guilt will strike one down for terrible deeds committed in fantasy or otherwise. Is this really the way it really works, without people being trained? But guilt—for politicians understand dialectical materialism in action instinctively and can abstract the pragmatic from an intellectual theory for their own uses—is what the power figure feels in a different way, and only in a certain historic and political context. Sophocles, Aristotle, Freud: the ideologue's viewpoint is hidden in their theories.

It is necessary for the rationalized world of today to either theatricalize reality—put behind a proscenium of one sort or another, where it is safe, edifying, draining (which is to say cathartic)—or to internalize, to wish away from the real world, brutality, murder, childbeating, sodomy, motherfucking and fatherstabbing and create the attendant guilts: acts which are all commonplace when one fights for survival or power or space? It is only the middle class intellectual who insists that these acts are internal: when they spill over, the perpetrator must suffer guilt. That is, he does if he has an audience . . . of millions if the media elect to elevate the case into national drama: of one, if the sufferer goes to a shrink. (I wondered: did the killers of that Kansas family *feel* those things, suffer remorse according to Capote's vision— though there are contradictions there —or did they learn the proper categories, the expedient categories of expression?) There's a strategy to such a view, a politics of suffering in public . . . But ultimately *Oedipus* and *The Oresteia* came to this: they were forms of national history, a discrediting of a dangerous past, a warning to the elites of Athens that modern society

515

could not be run along the lines of the brutal past. Much as liberals and corporate apologists say that we have advanced up the evolutionary scale from the robber-barons of the nineteenth century (Kolko: *The Triumph of Conservatism*—the Morgan-Gary meetings where gilded-age industrialists and financiers sought to compromise trust lusts, to rationalize and compromise their murderously competitive drives . . . Field of the Cloth of Gold . . .). Those plays were ideological and concealed reality for the Athenian spectators. A new mode of empire building required new social relations, a burying of blood feuds for national purposes. Royal children are not, after all, raised by their parents directly and are not only strangers to them but impediments to power: rulers don't think of their parents in the same way that middle class people do.

If fathers and mothers are relative strangers to their children then why does the mysterious link of blood persist . . . other than being a fertile power-perpetuating mystique which becomes dysfunctional (in the neurotic or psychotic sense) upon the point of *discovery,* exposure, which is *then* termed abberration, sin, drama? . . . But what is the dramatic, the tragic hero, in his non-dysfunctional personal/social phase like? Is there a mechanism of trading off ruling-class dysfunction onto other strata of society?

The rich, the powerful are plagued by anxieties of a different order: possibly they have different psychologies, which is to say that their motivational substratum is different and not the same as for other classes, groupings. Is *Oedipus* or *The Oresteia,* seen from the point of view of the Athenian hegemony, which occurs later in time, a retroactive validating of the ongoing regime? Athens mediates these conflicts: Pericles presides and the furies are rationalized/transformed into the Eumenides (or the Constitution of the United States, if one prefers) and revenge goes underground while the threat of anarchy from the rulers themselves is adjusted. Is it possible that one of the prime motives for writing these plays is to legitimate the Athenian imperial drive; a form of national memory? Are they in some sense *propaganda* plays? Are they paeans to the new rational age of Athenian

516

civilization? The new age demands a different outlook. (One thinks of all the ex-socialist and leftist novelists, those men of goodwill and concern of the thirties who turned, in the Cold War Period—the American Century—to a celebration of American Life in their works . . . an American Life which in fact existed for a very small class of people. Bellow writes *Augie March* while the Communist Party is being squelched and the Rosenbergs are being participated in the national enfertilizing. Trilling writes *The Middle of the Journey,* one of whose protagonists is Whittaker Chambers, the Dostoevskian turncoat, as a warning to those who had, in their innocence, flirted with the notion that the Soviet Union represented the wave of the future.) And is there an implicit comment in these Greek plays about the Less Developed Countries, a comparison of their primitive, brutal underdevelopment, their lack of culture and proper business ways, countries which can only be brought to the point of culture and civilization by an infusion of Athenian culture?

Tragedy is a useful fiction which promises eventual retribution. But in real life there is no such thing as retribution, and tragedy is after all not the divine restoration of the torn fabric, but the story of the loser. Tragedy for the grand bourgeoisie, for the elite class, for the royal striver is an incompleted deal, an empire not put together. What will Truman's retribution be? J. Robert Oppenheimer, a reader of the classics, who, after the first atomblast, likened himself unto Shiva, was brought in to see Truman, wringing his hands and moaning that he had blood on his soul, having degenerated from flame-creating Shiva/Prometheus into a suppliant: Truman said to keep that fool away. "*I* dropped it, not him."

Tragedy is an integral part of a university education. Then the hundred great books find their way into everyday life in a thousand metamorphosed ways: one reads them in the newspapers and in the comic books and sees them in the movies and in TV commercials . . .

The proscenium bothers me, that division of labor, that cutting off of audience from the players. But the theater goes another way these days; theater's in the streets now. Have we all been moved to the other side of the proscenium? The theater's empty except for a few people lost in the darkness, sitting in the diamond circle while the stage is crowded beyond bearing . . . all social relations are theatrical now, all except on the bottom and the top . . . The catharsis now is achieved in new forms; we all participate as actors.

Catharsis, a theatrical notion, a desired effect brought with great success into our time, a little political notion of great value . . . for it leaves real and possible counterproductive passions in the theater . . . or on the shrink's couch, or in the encounter group, or in the dropped-out-of-the-production-process hallucination (definitely not the fantasy Lenin was talking about), or in the slurping of macrobiotic foods, or in the transcendental meditation, or Zen, or even neo-Hegelian-Marxist orgasmic dis-concrete juggling of the dialectic without the rumbling stomach and the running sores on the flesh . . . without the outrage . . . I act out, therefore I am.

Unresolved emotions can be dangerous in society . . . especially if they can't be given a unified social content, if they are undirected. The human condition as defined by Aristotle and Freud (or if you prefer, Talcott Parsons or Milton Friedman, or Jacques Ellul, or W. W. Rostow, or Zbigniew Brzezinski, or Herman Kahn . . . and if you don't know these names, learn them; they have affected you more than Spenser, or Kerouac, or Brautigan) is as immutable as scientific theories of child development; and Athens is a universal timeless place-name after all, interpenetrating everyday life, conquering it, bending it, bemusing it. And hasn't America concerned itself obsessively with Athenian and Roman notions? The problem, which this coming age may yet totally solve, is to deal effectively with timeless human passion in a short-term way; surplus passion and energy that hasn't gone into fueling the state and the economy becomes dangerous till a rationalized, quantifiable, and profitable way can be constructed to exploit it. And after all aren't there ways of quantifying and converting passions into useful forms already ... the psychodetecting tests?

Implicit in the notions of a Freud, the theory and the *practice* (which is in reality against the theory) are useful fictions to assist in the rise of a subclass of intellectuals in its claims against the older, irrational, overtly murderous robber barons; a kind of defused-revolutionary infra-structure using a guerrilla tool which, however, was turned into an economic and political tool in a variety of forms; a vast cooling apparatus which converts concrete political and economic passions into neurosis, turns anxieties into currency and reshapes energies and contributes to the growth of political economy.

Stolen labor time, commodified, monified, metamorphosed, and quantified, drains the poor of time. Time energy sucked upward permits the bourgeoisie to reconvert time/commodity and flesh out *their* past history ... set a foundation of tradition to validate their present. Sucked-up time-energy fuels the accelerating capitalist drives into escape velocity.

Devoid of time, the lower orders lose their history, and slowly their institutions, their rituals, their eternal static worlds collapse, and like so many obelisks and steles their selected mores are looted into books where they stand as desocialized and interpreted monuments.

A metaphor, a unity of parameters, presupposes that things, events, can be compared, united and those united items make assumptions of the space between (dependent upon culture and tradition), violating space and time, making a quantum leap from one realm of being into another without going through intervening space. For instance, to talk about *tragedy* in relation to the *Pentagon Papers* and the Vietnam involvement is to fictionalize intent into tragic flaws (and blind destiny) of the principle actors in that event, to conceal economics ... to implicitly compare them to middle class intellectuals ... A coincidence in fiction does the same thing in time and the Central Bank of Symbolic Forms validates the transaction (or does not accept it),

519

where it becomes acceptable, not challenging. Where such connections are challenging, heightened rules of evidence and validation are invoked . . . *bourgeois*-scientific laws . . . sociology and establishment political science and economics disprove coincidence . . .

About the ruling stratum, the intellectuals, the social scientists are mute for all their massive social science. The ruling strata do not undergo the same kind of therapy so beloved of the middle groupings and are not written about fictionally with any reality . . . not yet. Possibly they have a different psychology . . . What does this mean for the creation and production of literature (as well as its interpretation)? What is the consciousness of writers whose social background is relatively narrow? Do they really speak for all man for all time?

The *Bible,* the Old Testament in particular, is still the current handbook of the capitalist class. Paradise Lost, expropriated after settlement and development, was redistributed. For the poor there was nothing, or unremitting toil. For the middle classes there was management or paradise achievable as the end product of psychotherapy. The Old Testament teaches us important lessons on the growth of political endogenetic class-perpetuating economy through discipline and accumulation containing the notion of sex/procreation as a productive process promising possession of the world. This notion in W. W. Rostow's *Stages of Economic Development* becomes the mysterious autonomous *élan vital* of compound interest, where for Marx it represents a stolen surplus value, both modern societal dynamic-under-capitalism, and conscious act . . . *credit,* Marx tells us (and Melville confirms) is *Protestant.* The New Testment with its guide to teleological gratification is the handbook of the lower strata.

Both testaments were used adroitly by the bourgeoisie in its fight to ascend. The Old Testament with its emphasis on destiny and economic growth enabled the bourgeoisie to fight its way upward and seize power. After the Reformation the Old Testament was advanced as a handbook again, especially in America. When the bourgeoisie had made it they could begin to reinstitute the

New Testament, which was used to assure that the challenging lower levels did not spill over into their space time . . .

In the Middle Ages the Great Chain of Being was invented to symbolize the notion of place, of class, of stratum, or degree from the microcosmic to the godly macrocosm. It operated as an implicit mystique which in fact chains all people in place. When open-ended time-destiny was introduced by the Reformation, the shattering of the static orders took place. History, therefore, began. The chain became stages of history; progressive development. The Great Chain of Being became unlinked from its divine upper mooring, and no matter how high man climbs, a new link appears. The revisionist Great Chain is converted later into scientific notions of progress, evolution, myth hidden away, converted into hard observation, theoretical notions, data, empiricism which perceived that brutal competition, possessive individualism on all levels, was the working out of man's progressive and transcendent destiny . . . and science was able to rationalize the contradictions and competition. A theory of origins and development was applied to social development which had implications for the way one handled all diverse cultures which were fitted together serially.

Why anyway are we hung up on the hunger for simplification and prime causes? Can multiple scientific theories exist dialectically? Why the insistence on scientific elegance? Is it a case of aesthetic-hunger as an intrinsic human hunger or is it a socially transmitted *Angst?* The need to rationalize the world may be a proprietary lust to simplify the universe to that it can be dealt with from some centrally controlled nexus. Anyway, the major question is, who funds that lust and what conditions limit the search for elegance? Mathematics and logics may be a form of the three dramatic unities another way. One thinks of the *Folk Motif Index* with its conveniently numbered and quantified motifs so that one can analyze any folk tale, legend, myth, story, novel (or social science analysis for that matter) in numbers.

Of course corporations, whose deliberations and production goals shape our destinies and feelings, have two sets of account books. There is a set available for public inspection, only when legal forces press the corporations to the wall: and even then there are gentlemanly accommodations between government and corporation lawyers. And anyway who's an accountant to decipher the messages? (Krook, an illiterate, cannot read the documents that have come into his possession.) The secret set of books, the coded languages, the sets available to those who rule these corporations incorporate many secrets. (The true frozen deliberations are secreted from the lower echelons themselves . . . total loyalty is bought, in rare cases, by a gradual ascent of the ladder of compromise and fidelity and cemented by marriages.) There's a multiple, ongoing deception and covertness involved here: the real books convert and commodify passion, history, destiny, superstition, elite genetics, ritual, mythology, inherited symbolology, totemism, magic, into numbers (the Central Bank of Symbolic Forms), which is to say that a great and terrible and insatiable ruling class hunger is institutionalized: memories of great past feasts (the eating of Thyestes' children, the gobbling up of the Caledonian boar, the munching of the manna), creation myths, growth myths, division of labor (the magical helpers) myths, death and perpetual life myths, personal lusts all preserved and chronicled in profit and loss columns.

Krook in *Bleak House* is mockingly called the Lord Chancellor and represents the hidden and revelatory set of books . . . the manifest accumulatory lust personified in an old-fashioned way—as Marx talks about capital personified in *The Capital*—but then Krook is old-fashioned . . . the covert dimension of capitalism and capitalism's representative, its demoniac force, is hidden away from Dickens because he dare not present the real Lord Chancellor. And yet there's the uneasy beginning of an apprehension there . . . the process of chancery— of what looks to Dickens as mad, irrational, confused, but is a systematic intentional and expansive delayed settling of estates in *Bleak House*—shows the evanescence of accumulated static treasures, a process that Dickens would persuade us a change of heart, reform, will ameliorate.

And one wonders if in some way the killers of the Clutter family came for a settling of accounts . . . a revenge for past thefts wherein the historical (1959) unrelationship between killer and killed is joined in the past in a history that has been wiped out of national consciousness, but not unconsciousness, not the fantasy . . . a remembrance of Indian wars, cowboy exploitation, the gradual corporate agglomeration of farm lands, the destruction of the small farmer which creates a great population shift to the cities whose attendant disruptions and poverties are to cause me such trouble in *The Bag*. Is this a motivating factor that operates in the *unconsciousness* of the killers? Are we to look for motivations, *psychology,* in the Morrill Act and in grants to railroads . . . Is *this* the fantasy Lenin talks about?

Another reality reintrudes. What about that spontaneous combustion in *Bleak House* which eliminates Krook and his papers, destroys the usurer (and we should remember the Marxist analysis of usury and capitalism as modes of accumulating surplus)? Fire: a burning off of the mortal dross leaving the immaterial spirit, the immortal past: a concealing of evidence: a symbol of revolution: a gift from Prometheus . . . In the long run the injustice of the legal system is not to be abolished by paralegal means, by help from the wrong class but, through attrition and the wills of good men, will be mitigated, be assured; of the political and economic system that has given rise to this state of things, Dickens testifieth not. Odd for a man living the same time as Marx; odd for a man writing when the British empire was reaching its zenith; odd for a man writing when the industrialization of industry was proceeding in brutal forced marches (in fact in *Bleak House* Dickens praises the industrialist as the model of rationality); odd when the books of Marx and Dickens are full of testimony of the horrors of industrial life. The fear of poverty runs like a miasma through Dickens' works, but the notion of Capitalism as a system is alien to him. Are we to blame him for this?

And yet that combustion, the laughable and irreverent burning of the documents, the act of it, the suddenness of it, the irrational interjection of it, provides a glimpse of reality seen another way.

But think of the unities-breaking contempt for versimilitude, this fortuitous intrusion, this revolutionary act, the simplistic sweeping aside of style and plot-prolongation, this resolution contemptuous of the rules of fiction, this violation of Aristotle, this chance happening which makes commentary on the long and suffering and enlightening way around. But the economy of novels-production requires suspense, prolongation, sudden appearances, the convergence of characters, coincidence, mystery which couldn't be shattered (and the legal system, no matter what its grotesqueries) which forces Dickens into obfuscations as foggy as his enveloping law-metaphor, the mystery of its unfolding which forces Dickens to distort himself and the evidence of his senses to reach for idealistic moral lessons and sentimentality and the happy ending no matter what the vicissitudes: but reality implies the unhappy ending always.

(And one thinks of the residue of sentimentality, the demands of the ancient patterns of justice, which force Capote into the directions he takes ... directions so abhorrent to him that he must deny his alienating success-disciplines by giving a satyr-play party at the Plaza.)

Krook really is a caricature—laughable, a grotesque, a creature out of some ridiculous other world. Much like the pawnbroker Raskolnikov killed. Modern criticism with its psychoanalytic orientation persuades us that Dickens generated his distortions out of some infantile fantasy ... hypostasized his *personal* monsters: a psychic emanation, a fantasy really. Laughable: people aren't like that: maybe a few aberrants who don't belong in the main stream of literature. We are to be persuaded that Dickens drew heavily from that timeless storehouse of magical figures which paralleled his insecurities. We chuckle at Dickens' caricature. Social science has obviated that strategy by confining the caricatures to madhouses or handbooks on pathology ... or to fantastical literature ... and as for coincidence, quite out of the realm of scientific verisimilitude ... a degeneration of miracles in a rational age ... but why, that's a temporal fiction that has to journey through another dimension to closely juxtapose unjuxtaposable people and events.

We remind ourselves constantly that for all the brilliance of his language he offends the realistic sensibility with his baggage of tricks. Or is that what we've been taught to believe? (Mafia connections with the board of trustees of the University of Columbia? Unbelievable. Krook-like tricks? Incredible.) And perhaps part of what saves him is his marvelous use of language. And the grotesque, the caricature, is forevermore relegated to the realm of fiction, but the greater fiction, the norm, is the province of the social sciences.

But what if the grotesque manifestations from Dickens' unconscious are shaped by *real* terrors? For what does it do to one's world view to live in terror based on a realistic appraisal of the world? What the fuck is unreal, psychological, about the fear of starvation and failure? What is unreal about parents who cannot protect their children (as Dickens' couldn't protect him) because the world provides no protection? Thus, possibly fantasy presentations are dissonant retranslations (because there is never enough information and it's too terrifying to look at things straight) of real events, prefiguring of events, of real power figures whose identity is not revealed. For Dickens' own life exemplifies the removal of maternal supports—*not* psychic wounds inflicted by neglectful parents, but parents made neglectful by an insupportable system. This is the world Marx talks about, the world of the enclosures and the factory, the world of the destruction of the petit bourgeois . . .

In science, while making small concessions to the strategy of the observer and experimenter, no social analysis is given. Kuhn, in *The Structure of Scientific Revolutions,* discusses the tenacious social and psychological *investment* scientists give to their theories, but relegates it mostly to psychology and resistance to change. About investments in the ongoing socio-economic and political world orders nothing is given. Scientists, when new world theories emerge, frequently break down, or put another way: what's the relation of Cold War policy to the rise of psychotherapeutic theory and *practice?*

All forms of recorded observation are *ex post facto* and imply a mode of seeing things, an interest in vision. Since the vastness of

525

the sensual world doesn't permit a total rendering of inter-relations, we apprehend the world by choosing strategic parameters to describe and stand for the totality of interactions and social relations. No matter how astute the reportage, no matter how naturalistic and piling-up-of-detail the novel contains, no matter how assiduous the collection of data, basic assumptions, hidden ideologies dictate not only what items are seen to be significant, but what are the permissible modes of interaction and connection . . . as well as what is unreasonable.

Science has hidden its mythologies best of all. What is a logic, in modern terms, is a useful abstraction (which set into concrete practice has concrete social effects) which orders the world and affects the lives of people in concrete ways . . . but may upon examination reveal the last secret hiding places of metaphysics and religion.

Faust breaks the static mode, accumulates experience, loots the ancient world of its mythic energy-treasures, and grows from personal experience-sampling to reinvest those experiences in public works . . . making the transitions symbolically from the feudal world to the bourgeois world. And in the bourgeois world, though we would contemplate it forever, no project is eternal. Thus, while Faust, the person, the individual, wants to halt and contemplate something generated out of himself and the forces of the past, an inversion has taken place and the experiential dynamic of the bourgeois world now in effect *samples the man as experience* and Faust the initiator no longer exists and the process of eternal restlessness has been instituted. (Marx views the world of the bourgeois as an inverted world where the everyday conceals the monstrous common perversion: Proust at the end of his *Bildungsroman* finds the world totally inverted: the fools, the greedy, the social climbers, the inverts, have risen to the top of the social pile.) Sexual relations are transmogrified into the sexual organic productive process ("The eternal feminine draws us upward") from the one to one sexual relations of humans . . . the Old Testament re-productivity into the means of production . . . In short, Faust changed the *relations of production* which were in contradiction, lagging behind the new means. Faust then is elevated into entrepreneur. Think of Rimbaud who, after the poetic and wandering years, became a businessman.

Faust is meaningless without Job, as is *Moby Dick*. The adulations of the Kafka-esque vision, so pushed and taught in the Cold War period, which wryly praises the irrational, not to say the irascible, God of the Hebrews, counsels the acceptance of an absurdist view of the world, most fitting and proper for the powerless. But so many of the literary Cold Warriors who would persuade us that they were Joseph K., or K., were in fact so many Herr Klamms.

Our myths of the hardy pioneer farmer tell us that he moved where he wanted to because of his restless heroic spirit, his very Americanness. But we never conceive that the farmer, the pioneer, was driven westward by a variety of controlled social and economic forces not dictated by himself. Wasn't Clutter, just out of an agricultural land grant college (established by that Morrill Act) a county agent; and wasn't the county agent system in the past funded by railroads and Rockefellers who endowed the General Education Board, those same Rockefellers who take such an interest in the education of students at Columbia, at Cornell, at Chicago, etc.? Really: are we to believe that a pair of ignorant jailbirds had this history at their fingertips as they lingered in the prison at Lansing, Kansas (Lansing, the name of John Foster Dulles's grandfather who was Wilson's Secretary of State; Lansing who so bitterly hated the Russian Revolution)? Was Lansing also *a state of mind* in which the killers were imprisoned?

And because of its very style, because of the missing dimension, mystery draws the reader to and into the events of Job, *In Cold Blood, Bleak House, Faust*—involves him, directs him to interpret and reinterpret (looking for the failure of perception in himself), looking for rationality behind the irrational drama, analyzing according to the rules not quite stated, but learned. Mystery is an energy-suck which shapes the inquisitive energies, the rationalization-hunger: mystery, obfuscation, obscurity are a strategy-breeding investment of time and commitment whose direction

527

is determined by the rules of the game.

Alvin Gouldner in *The Coming Crisis of Western Sociology* makes some telling points about the strategy of theoretical obscurity which could easily be applied to the works of Joyce, Pound, Eliot, or, for that matter, to any of the canon of works taught, and the way in which they were taught in the university. The New Critical approach provided the practical paradigm for teaching all works of literature and was an outgrowth of the strategies of their composition and the politics of reputation-achievement. The very *lacunae* in these works hinted at a coherent conceptual scheme which was discoverable by a sort of mathematical proof which was already shaped by a collection, a bank of existing reference points with distinct rules of value-comparison and interchange; an accretion of tradition. Where the mathematics did not exist, it was invented.

Works like *The Cantos, The Wasteland, Ulysses, The Castle* cultivated a discoverable but endless mystery to the initiate who, briefed by the author, helped create a caste of priests who spread the word through the university and the high literary magazines . . . which engendered a movement, an industry, devoted to these works. The movement generated not only an economic mode of literary life as criticism, but created ways of dealing with reality in the mass media. Eliot is the father of the fast cut of the television commercial: he is the father of the modern bourgeois movie. This technique was reinforced by the growth of the therapeutic movement. Pursuit of the mystery took precedence over the pursuit of the mundane and obvious truth. The grimly realistic, the political, the concrete social relations, the whole sensual dimension of a book like *Ulysses* was destroyed by Joyce's very titling of the book and the way in which he trained his intellectual salesmen; the sales-methodology annunciated that symbol and analogue and allusive shadow were realer than concrete. The game was too fascinating to forgo.

Man tries to shape his environment materially and philosophically. Shaping environments requires concrete actions, agreement

528

about the proper climate necessary and how to achieve that climate. The notion about a progressive continuity, a unity to history, is not a new one, but the notion of spreading that idea of progress with its current optimisms, its brutalities of modernization all over the world, while attempted before, was never attempted in such a religio (where the religious component was hidden)-material way with such an extensive, fluid, subtle, powerful apparatus as America had, and was in a unique position to use, after the Second World War.

And possibly the very almost-success of this vast attempt was insured because it masked its operations under the guise of freedom and permitted a whole range of contending tendencies to coexist . . . everything but the socialist. Intellectuals who had lived through the mind-narrowing Stalinist debacle of the thirties now had available funds, encouragement to give range to their ideas: phenomenologists and existentialists and poets no longer had to go hungry. Experts in recondite fields could now find havens for their esoteric pursuits which found employment in universities, in the media, in think tanks, in defense and intelligence-funded studies. They were paid not only to explore their specialties, but to develop schools of thought with followers while at the same time they fragmented a continuous reality, a whole vision of the world; the notion of man-expressing-social-class-forces was turned into free-romantic-ironic-tragic-existentialist-hero man. The collaborational interaction of man and spheres of knowledge was obscured, an illusion especially attractive to novelists and poets.

Now if one accepts the notion of the accumulation and conversion of surplus labor in the realm of the material, one must accept it in the realm of the idea, the emotion, the psychic energy . . . that this accumulation in the realm of energy and commodified time, the particulars of a stage of time quantified can be converted, metamorphosed into a kind of *currency* and, given the expansive nature of capitalism, permits the reinvestment of that currency which goes into the further reshaping of the environment, of all of history, past, present, and future, and the atmosphere of that history in every phase of interpretation, scientific, economic, historical, sociological, anthropological, literary, philosophical, etc., into a contiguous and developing system . . . which tended to destroy, devalue other systems which were at serious variance; not only the socialist, but other, older systems which resisted incorporation into the general hegemonic scheme . . . systems which raised messy and unresolved questions about the nature of things.

(Some points of resistance: If ancient mariners of the Pacific Ocean could sense and navigate the world with organic sensing devices and a few sticks with astonishing precision, what did that imply for a civilization that had a heavy investment in an expensive technology which itself had to be subject to the capitalist laws of obsolescence?

If it were indeed possible to manipulate the self, the body into health through societally-supported-amplified mind magic—and which requires certain non-industrial conditions of existence (transcendence; non-mechanical; non-prosthetic)—what did that imply for a profit-oriented medicine?

If it were possible to apprehend dreams, fantasies in a *political* way, what did that imply for a heavily-invested-in psychological science?

If carbon-dating is invalid—as it now seems to be—what does that say about the *need* for dating, the need for an ideologically contiguous developmental progressive history which validates the present regime?

If there is an inexplicable plethora of unrelated languages, what does that imply for the need to first find some common—controlable—universal source for language?)

Symbolic currency: The Central Bank establishes a certain *directed* validity to the hoard of symbols, rituals, fantasies, presentations, metaphors, archetypes, ideas, intellectual concepts: credits (gives faith-currency to, reflects investment), defines, values, commodifies ideas: more, it establishes the way these are to be linked together and the manner in which they are to be used, the transactional mode (or plot . . . which is to say cause-effect, historical transactions, interconnections, seriality) which expresses reality. These modes of operation mask the transactional exchange and interest-bearing relations, which further validate and reinforce bourgeois relations. And, like so many workers, enables intellectuals to forge the very ideational chains which bind them to a process which increases the need to turn over ideas and philosophical systems into more and more evanescent fashions, heightens anxieties in a world which seems more and more to have no solid base, where eventually all abiding values disappear, encourages cynicism about any values, turns intellectuals into entrepreneurs with a little loan from the Central Bank, heightening their investment in the ongoing state of things, social relations, and psychological processes. One could compile a list of approved symbolic transactions and currency within the banking rules.

All of which means that, certainly since the Second World War during the period of expanded growth of the universities, a concrete means, an apparatus, a structure, a productive system for the diffusion of ideology had to be established on a level never before done . . . the elite university with its socializing functions (which had to some extent socialized the offspring of the robber barons) proliferated and a massive operation was mounted to convert into currency the dead, accreted, dormant cultures of the world. At the same time the operation ensured that the division of intellectual labor would obscure a larger synthetic view of the world by heightening specialization and narrowing outlook . . . which the peculiar nature of cultural analysis and thesis production ensured. And while a proliferation of specialties offered themselves to the student—proving that freedom within the system existed— the notion of a contribution to the growth of the body of knowledge was one of the factors to spur on the student . . . that, of course, and the need to escape the possibility of being a laborer . . . and coupled to the fact that one's material success was bound up in the system. Question: if all these specialties contributed to the

531

growth of knowledge, where did the Grand Synthesis take place? Competitive relations kept narrowing the field of specialization. One proved things, one generally did not disprove them. The verifiable was encouraged. The political seemed leached out, for politics was "ideology," but masked politics persisted in a thousand ways . . . Cold War politics.

There are certain approved ways of expressing the world and transcribing it. There is an ahistorical mystique ascribed to the symbol-currency which shadows the real, a timelessness which transcends history, certainly the messy claims of proletarians and Marxists. The symbols are codified; passion becomes currency; currency relations shape passions into approved expressions and into approved inner feelings; quantification doesn't have to be written out in numbers only; the crippled hero, for instance, the anti-hero, is a symbolic number expressed another way, breeding irony, detachment, impotence. One explores oneself and, filled with the currency of the Central Bank, assigns changeless cosmic meaning to what one finds there, distorts and legitimates the personal and feeds it back, with a certain increment of subjective energy, converted energy, into the system. One asks also, then, what is *not* permissible currency? We remember the dangers of the love relationship, for instance, in *1984*.

But, Marx says, "By thus acting on the external world and changing it, he at the same time changes his own nature. He develops his slumbering [Lenin's fantasy?] powers and compels them to act in obedience to his sway." But in order to do that one must become aware of the symbolic bank and also of the directors, the many branch managers of that bank. When you deny the reality of a ruling class and a supportive ideological establishment, nothing's left but psychotherapy or the New Criticism, or the novel of personal and whimsical experience.

With the aid of a fast-burgeoning therapeutic establishment which had the same engaging literary practices and priorities, the translation of the real into the dramatic/literary became a fact and tended to help break up static, outmoded counter-productive relations. Thus, Orwell's model, with its picture of the one-to-one love was gradually being fulfilled, and this throws light on the question Job's wife asked and the reason she was shunted off off the stage so quickly.

Symbols became symbols of domination which evoked the proper, useful response to themselves, the apolitical response, the isolative, non-organizing response. Where the cop hit you over the head with a club, the shrink used transference. The whole deadly notion of transference, when the transfer-object validated the ongoing state of things, was of a political-economic act which reinforced what was already hailed in the Romantic tradition, the lonely asocial hero.

If there is an inner political/metaphysical coherence, a logic to Eliot, or Joyce, the search in the cloudy *lacunae* evoked involvement and that very involvement was converted to commitment, allegiance, as one struggled to understand the material being worked over, and which became a way of viewing life itself. It is the method I stress here, not the content, the social content, which was avoided. A system of theatrical infinite regress was set up and one could amuse oneself with the symbols forever. Caught in a terrible contradiction, the intellectual, in a parallel manner, acted out the closet drama of therapy which reinforced this infinite regress. It was a productive commitment in terms of money and emotional involvement, a draining of energy increment which was poured into sustaining a reality which was further and further divorced from what really happened in the world (which is not to say that the bizarre didn't happen in the world, but it was defined as aberration, not as a commonplace): looking for inward and true meaning became a lifetime task, a costly task whose subsidization involved one in the productive process. But remember this: the powerful don't dare involve themselves in these forms of soul-searching.

Similarly, in the literary world, the university apparatus, having set up its mode of abstracting all into a kind of currency, provided a market which forced one to play with this new true reality as seen through the eyes of this new poet. Criticism became more important than the production of literature as the apprehension of reality was ceded more and more to the social sciences which were supposedly concrete, but were in fact ideological fictions. The very notion of modern systems-analysis involves the style of the short story well done, tightly written. Games theory, which excludes reality . . . And it was these very deadly games which became a contradiction in capitalism, preventing it from adjusting as swiftly to threats as it once did; in fact bred the revolutionary forces which now must be stamped out: but the contradiction was that the intelligence was needed by the bourgeoisie and the intelligence was in the hands of a middle class that waged a class-interested subliminal warfare and wanted reform (having been taught that reform is possible) and entrée into the corridors of power . . . which some of them got . . .

All of which begins to answer Antonio Gramsci's question: how does the ruling class maintain its hegemony? Surely more than a gun is needed. Ongoing life requires ancient mystiques to validate just accepting a Ford, Coca-Cola, Gleem. Revolutionaries have ignored this aspect too much. Demonstrations, activism resistance, *these* one could involve oneself with, while many reserved whole areas as having nothing to do with change and accepted the idea that there are realms that are timeless, outside history, spaces one could go back to after the revolution came. Taking a building was easier than taking one's head . . . for the immutable was a non-political turf you could always escape to. *We* weren't going to make the crude mistakes of the Stalinists with their dreadful socialist realism, never thinking that it was precisely the failure to deal with 100,000 years of ideology, consciousness and class war, a distrust of *those* fantasies which had driven the Stalinists into their position. Read Stalin on linguistics to see what I mean: he denies language as an instrument of production.

Understand, there is a political economy of the production of imagination, What is to be the novelist-aiding-a-revolution-to-be-born's idea of plot, of character, of motivation, of consciousness, of the subconscious?

Now it becomes possible to ask, is there a revolutionary unconscious dimension to the acts of the killers, and did the Clutter family

534

deserve to be killed? (Never mind how right or good those politics were.) Was there in fact a whole dimension of *ideological* plunder that was looted when the killing took place? Can we in fact talk about social relations as a form of property? And if so, how was that property restored? And in order to understand my *left-instinctive* reaction, what completely hidden dimension of sub-ruling-class-suppressed consciousness must my Marxist detective have?

And how, now, must the Marxist critic reappraise the past collective body of culture and what counter-notions must he introduce and what suppressed body of works must he discover and understand; how to reexpropriate the stolen past?

The conspiracy theory of history? Three men in a little room making plots? The instantaneous response of a system to those plots? We're Marxists, aren't we? History and its stages, relations of production and all that, mass waves of masses, social forces and the emergence of classes, and the large sweep of social events and the gradual realtering of social reality—what it's all about, isn't it? Economic change: material base. Right? But maybe, because we wanted to validate our attacks on capitalism, we had recourse to the most respectable sources of information and used them to point out the contradictions . . . and the very use of that respectable material denuded our attack of its ferocity. We have forgotten Marx's pungent language. *And we have forgotten that conspiracy is a social force too.*

What's a conspiracy then? A plot is a story—a systems manager's limitation of reality which effects certain changes, a manipulation. In a book it's a fiction: in life it's a practical fiction.

A plot is something else: a covert action against . . .

The Civil War ended unresolved, after all: the South has never forgotten or forgiven the Northeast. That old economic struggle has had uneasy accommodations and renewals of fights.

There are those who reject the conspiracy theory of JFK's assassination. We have been trained to adore heroes and fetishize the random event. But . . . after all, defense spending began to move south and west after that assassination . . .

The South invokes the demon Wall Street and Eastern Bankers

too. Can we forget the virulent nativist element, the anti-ethnic, anti-Catholic sentiment of Protestant America? Johnson had a lust for power; that was undeniable. The right wing of the CIA had reasons to be angry at Kennedy for a certain lack of militancy against Cuba, and the South has always been vitally interested in Cuba, an interest which reflects itself, for instance, in the fight over Bloody Kansas.

All this is unreasonable: too many factors; the mind cannot accept this meld of interests and coincidences. Yet, when one reads C. Vann Woodward on plot and conspiracy in *Reunion and Reaction,* one finds a conspiracy/conflict which ranged from Washington/Philadelphia to San Diego, which involved railroads, racism, a stolen presidential election, a compromise with Northern and Southern Whigs, cajoling, intimidation, and bribing of congressmen and electors, land grants, labor unrest . . . Yet, on the other hand, if one reads Grodinsky's *Transcontinental Railroad Strategy* one finds nothing of this at all, though he writes about the same people and the same times. (In passing we note that frozen whaling-money accumulations are loosened from their sleep to be reinvested in railroads . . .) And does this book constitute an element of an ideological counter-plot to make history respectable . . . ? Are plot, conspiracy, murder, assassination the province of Balkan states and Byzantine empires only?

The great railroad duels of the latter half of the 19th century brought on depression, panic, hunger, despair, goads to the divine expansionist policy . . . and the gradual degradation of a working class. And are the psyches of the now living slum dwellers in some way shaped by those days?

Conspiracies remain hidden. They are translated into immutable facts of nature, the drift of events, exceptional experiences.

The same could be said for the little dialogue between Mephistopheles and God in *Faust.* Not only is Faust not consulted, but the masses are not even evident, nor is the Mobility to be seen anywhere in the terrain of the *Divine Comedy.*

We are obsessed with the whimsy of a Minderbinder in *Catch-22.* But we must never think of the international bankers who, during the Second World War, met every few months or so above the mundane and terrestrial struggles going on beneath the Magic Mountain all over the world . . . bankers of *all* belligerents meeting in Switzerland to adjust monetary difficulties, regulating the destinies of all nations, whose interest, certainly, required a stability while this regrettable, albeit productive, old-fashioned display of primitive blood was raging below them on the European plain. Can we ever forget the debates and discussions on Mt. Olympus and meanwhile, at that very moment, in another space, which did not know of the Olympian space, on the windy plains of Troy?

Or, one thinks of the separate peace, which is to say ongoing commercial intercourse, which was negotiated between Standard Oil and Nazi Germany, while Mailer, in *The Naked and the Dead* perceives another space, a space with individuals, characters, heroes who have a different psychology, but again one wonders if a psychological analysis from a social point of view demonstrates more the resolution of different individual struggles, reflecting concrete struggles of vast power forces, and where the residue of individualism is minor indeed . . . And yet Mailer peeked into the tents of power where his general foretold the organization, the Spartanization of the world, but spent the rest of his career fleeing that vision.

Why talk and propose an absurdist Minderbinder (though the name is exquisitely apt) implying by style a hilarious levity—that Minderbinder is at best a laughable aberration? Minderbinder is the ruling classes at work. And therefore *that* humor is not only inaccurate but misleading. The capitalist as a grubby little man? Ridiculous.

Conspiracy is a unanimity of hidden strategies implemented, a concert of actions designed to achieve certain practical effects. Obviously power among conspirators of power is implemented and powerlessness is not. Conspirators of the right class possess the means of changing national priorities and personal psychologies.

Economic coercion has consequences for psychology. For

537

instance the Homestead Act is perceived to open up land for the landless: a version of the safety valve. Is it thinkable that the Homestead Act is a method of opening up and settling and developing land for a coalescing ruling elite who control money and power in the East, a method of providing a labor force to prepare land for the later agri-businesses? Was this an act of conspiratorial foresight? We are expected to think that adventurous spirits ventured forth rather than that they were moved by economic agrarian failures in the East, as well as propaganda. Because of legal loopholes, the big land corporations had already *hired* farmers to hold the land for them. We never consider the variety of structures employed later on to remove the small farmer, the overseers, the county agents, the credit structure, the ability to manipulate markets and railroad rates . . . *or that the murdered man, Clutter, had been a county agent in his youth,* and that one of the killers was the son of poor Kansas dirt farmers, for whom the doors of opportunity had been closed before he was born . . . another space to him. And in the realm of ideological psychology, neither killers nor the killed understand their roles and motivations.

What is the meaning of the Fourteenth Amendment when it is written by a railroad lawyer? Conspiracy, then, is not mere unanimity, but may also involve conflict of interest which is resolved by temporary truces.

But if nation- and world-changing conspiracies which have effects on character, personality go on, what are we to say about character and plot and the role of the literature producer? Poets, novelists have seen themselves in the forefront of consciousness when the fact of the matter is that they have muddled in the rear.

When the bourgeoisie emerged, its ostensible style was more sober. No more of the ostentatious panoply of the feudal upper classes who were more primitive and gaudy in their approach. In short, the Puritan Ethic.

The Puritan Ethic was a myth reinforced by powerful symbols. Weber, who proposed the notion, took ideology and sobriety and destiny and steady accumulation and rationalization proposed by the apologists of the bourgeoisie for fact. In point of fact, research reveals that they were ostentatious and gaudy too, and spent money at a great rate, gratifying themselves: certainly the second generation did. Gratification and a sense of constant deprivation required the speeding up, the increasing of the velocity of the mode of accumulation, a changing of the mode of production, a constant and restless heightening of the process.

Among the bourgeoisie, however . . . well, what is it that takes place among them?

Can we forget now the revelations of the sex lives of the Victorians? . . . and we remember that it is the "uptight" upper classes that practiced every conceivable "sin" known . . .

The idea was and is publicly promulgated in a thousand different ways and reappears in a thousand guises. The popular notion that mental health is the province of the poor and breakdown is the province of the elite is still among us. And the sobriety of executives, their hard-working qualities are trumpeted in books and magazines. And yet, I've been able to find out from talking to psychiatrists that the elites are healthier, live longer, don't need long-term shrinks, that they indulge their tastes in ways that only alternate culture revolutionaries dream about . . . that almost every large financial transaction is celebrated with orgies, and that, for example, the transactions of businessmen and diplomats with the Trujillo regime are not only recorded in books but accounted for in photographs. What is it that they haven't done and tried? It's just kept a secret, and conservation of indulgent sexual energies for the rich implies spending of sexual energies not loosened for the lower orders. Sexual behavior has a class content and is a kind of secret property in the form of sexual surplus value sucked up to the top . . .

What madness of secreted ostentation goes on. What lusts are not indulged and how many business transactions are not sanctified with orgiastic fertility rites? But, if there are celebratory rites which are kept secret, what about the public sacrifices, the myths which provide the models for public behavior?

What would total exposure do to explode the myths? If you

539

need a destiny-contributing work-force whose energies and labors are necessary, can you reveal to them that you worship the Golden Calf and somehow remain sober and productive at the same time? The Old Testament Jews reject graven images. Graven images arrest action, take away from the notion of process and turnover and labor, hypostasize the ruler; the lack of graven images is a tactic of secrecy and a lack of focus.

And what secrecies reside as legend, myth, fantasy, fear, anxiety; what dreams of conquest lie buried in the hearts and mind of the ruling elites?

What stories and legends do they tell one another, what strategies do they confer on their young within the family, within the class, within the university, from generation to generation? Do they still talk about the great Promethean revolts of 1789, 1848, 1871, 1917 when God's immutable order was overturned?

How then is the revolutionary vision, the socialist vision, the glimpse of the unborn world, to provide the dimension from which writers draw their strength? What is a revolutionary literature that goes beyond mere stylistic play? Possibly our notions of the components of a novel, a poem, a play must be entirely different.

Social dimensions abut and touch but remain discrete from one another. The introduction of the invisible and suppressed worlds, political worlds, into the consensus universe creates dissonances which reach into and shatter the accepting consciousness. The non-revolutionary novelist accepts a world and opts for unrecognizable styles and formalistic uses which affirm his shopkeeper's individuality . . . drawing credit in the form of ideological currency from the Central Bank. At best he attacks the dreariness of mass culture, proposes a superior model, but wants to change nothing: bemused by the weary insupportability of life, he becomes arrogant, absurd, obscure, ironic, tragic—in short, a hero who proposes reforms available only to a few.

Thus: crudely one conceives of disparate realms: the Marxist sphere and the bourgeois space. If bourgeois accumulation includes stolen labor-time energy which fills bourgeois history and culture and provides the way of viewing events, people, continuity, what then does the Marxist realm contain? Marx, in *Capital* proposes the organicity of the capitalist system where historic stages of production go on serially and simultaneously, but which is obscured by the ideological function of bourgeois thought . . . laid out serially . . . Accepted historic events, celebrated characters who live for us all, both real and fictional, who attract us because of reinforced emotive content, mythic content, symbols of domination implanted in one's head from the earliest date, have the ability to create force-lines of vision and emotion, perception, understanding, space and cause-effect shaping which mobilize the attention of man-in-bourgeois society. Thus, to break the lines, the patterns, the relations, the forcing system, one departs from one event/character/social-force cluster into another dimension, a Marxist dimension, and reemerges with an entirely different mode of connections into bourgeois dimensions, creating linkages which look like astonishing coincidences, which did not exist before and which are in struggle with the assumptions of the usual reign . . .

Only when the author perceives that even the inside of his sacrosanct head is policed by a ruling hegemony and his work is obliquely censored by a ruling economy, when he decides to adopt another politics, then he begins to see things another way— plot, character itself. One reads Pynchon for this struggle, and Cortàzar's *Hopscotch*. Tragedy is after all what happened to unsuccessful rulers and representative men: what has this to do with him and what really happens in life.

Plot: it assumes a certain logic which already accepts an ongoing reality. One thing follows another. Faulkner, Joyce, Sterne: for all the experimentation there is an implicit and simplistic time-scheme . . . brute reality reveals that these visions are games . . . flounderings which are absolutely necessary . . . as experiments . . . the turning to mystery, a detective story on the page rather than in real life. But what if the solutions to mysteries proposed by the author could only be resolved in the public, the political world?

Everyday received reality in the context of another political

541

view of the world becomes dreamlike, surreal, grotesque . . . a world of Krooks and Ahabs and Grayson Kirks and Rockefellers and McCarthys and Jobs. Yet, given the overbearing weight, the historic and current support of the most simple of statements, the transmission, the writing down of the alternate world of resistance must go into the unconscious dimension of the reader and jar loose the moorings of world constructs . . . we are still condemned to write in two languages: logic confronting logic, myth struggling against myth, fact against fact . . .

But, in beginning to understand this and trying to communicate it, the author finds a world of incredible and brutal reversals . . .

Yet, sometimes, the writer breaks through. *Moby Dick*. Not an abstract vision, not an allegory but a world in which the concrete productive modes of men are shown and how they change consciousness when there is a change, a qualitative change in the mode of production . . . the day-to-day things one does on the assembly line, as it were, an excursion into the dimension of grand imperial theory in which the destiny of America itself is laid down. To put the novel, as the critics did, into a timeless symbolic and archetypal realm beyond the concrete expansionist working reality of America and its sense of capitalist/manifest/grand-religious mission accepts the hidden strategy of depoliticizing it. And yet everything points to Melville's politics: the ship of state, ironically named after the Pequod Indians whom the Puritans wiped out, the concrete corporate venture assembled with the capital of small investors (as the Pilgrims and the Puritans were corporations first and religious freedom seekers second . . . funded by entrepreneurs in land development schemes) whose profit-and-loss considerations were given an additional and vital impetus by its religious (and racist) dimension (the three harpooners; the crew of all nations) with its captain, Ahab-Dulles, the director of the ship of the State Department gone mad, seeking the final confrontation with the ultimate of all raw materials in the Asian sea. For weren't there manifest-destiny mongers who spouted the idea of reaching the far Pacific shore on which the destinies of mankind, represented by Americans, would be resolved? The white whale, the ultimate symbol of the accelerative material-consuming process. Concrete workday realities are worked out which chronicle the dreary accretion but which is absolute disaster to apply to some symbolic hyper-sum of all. For whale-catching in itself postulates one stage of the productive process in one manner of velocity and the catching of the white whale means that the velocity reaches (since there's some godlike principle in it) infinity, Rostow's take-off point, the escape from Earth and earthly consideration, fueled by the assembled labor of the centuries, for the whale's infinite mass, which means acceleration into a dimension where time works differently and proposes the take-off point of the bourgeoisie, a space ship fueled by the histories and energies and fantastical powers of masses finally tamed.

The Reformation, if it taught anything, taught the primacy of one's own conscience, which is to say that one mediated with God directly, unencumbered by the levels of approval of the hierarchical Church . . . which continued to exist, but were masked.

Which contributed to a fantastic release of energy which had gone into maintaining the old social relations, an energy which could be converted into an accumulation of capital. The progress-arresting icons and old logics were smashed and the frozen perceptual and worship-energies were freed. Clean churches unencumbered by kitsch and golden calfism. The forces needed to bind social relations were in time to be channeled into the factories, and new binding forces were generated to keep the whole thing from flying apart.

There was a danger of anarchy here. A new feudal-hierarchical strategy, a new classicism was required, one that permitted energy and capital accumulation at a great rate, which is to say an absence of classical and traditional restraints, which would at the same time keep those restraints, but somehow hidden, for the overt presence of rulers and hierarchy was a contradiction. Religious and hierarchical and moral relations were translated into economic relations. But mere economic relations were certainly not enough: there was a danger here of the center falling

543

apart, since the divinity of the economic mission was not yet established. Debates must have gone on as to how this was to be done.

Such debates could generate a *Paradise Lost*. Which reconstituted symbolically the notion of hierarchy and could account for free will (a constipated free will, to be sure) and the roots of the anarchical sinfulness of man and a warning about rebellion outside of the terms of free will laid down. The devil, as productive force, as force behind the divine drama, comes more into his own. The decay of the old institutional forms permitted the rise of a new ruling class, the bourgeoisie, and a subtle ideology which proposed on the one hand freedom, democracy, free choice, but covertly proposed the new classicism which was contained within economic relations. *The Index* . . . censorship was always a provocation to revolution, so there had to be an invisible *Index*.

Romanticism postulated the next challenge, advancing the claims of dissenters, who inverse-Promethean-like, armed themselves with the old-institutional devalued capital, the energies of the Jesus-blessed poor and the simple, and readvanced the long-deferred claims of the Christianity of Christ before they were thermidorianized by the new bureaucrat, Paul.

Eventually a compromise was reached. Stratification, degree, hierarchy went underground and ideological science was advanced to resolve the contradictions of the world. One could apparently be free on the bottom, where freedom meant murderous competitive free enterprise where the fittest survive, while the top more and more controlled the environment and directed what functional populations would survive by controlling the material and spiritual means of production, economics, politics, law, culture . . . When you could materially indulge yourself, the philosophy "everything is permitted," as Dostoevsky put it, could be implemented. If every fantasy can be gratified it's no longer fantasy. But when you are taught this freedom and indulgence without the power to gratify, "everything is permitted" becomes the realm of mini-relations, a realm which, one is to be persuaded, is the higher reality. This is the realm of the powerless.

544

Underground control and stratification of the emotions themselves led to a casting into the realm of the aberrant those who didn't fit the ruling class's notions of *The Dictionary of Occupational Titles*. Dickens' caricatures, his grotesques, then, are nothing more than overspecialized creatures out of their age and out of their occupations, the detritus of the enclosure acts, but certainly not psychotics (and one reads Foucault's *Madness and Civilization* on this) for the resistance point of view. That the overspecialized man, a lawyer, an assembly-line worker, is a grotesque and a function-distort is never considered, for who asks how men in their professions distort their potentially boundless humanity to get where they are. Think of this: *is a man bound to an assembly-line a compulsive, an anal compulsive, who is acting out someone else's compulsiveness . . . and if not, why not?*

Still, the streets are full of these unclassifiable, irrelevant people and they grow in numbers every day and constitute a threat made to the ruling order by the potential way they have of perceiving the world that rules them . . . and acting on it. How would one deal with this?

The formula of this dialectical contradiction which separates again along class lines is contained in *The Brothers Karamazov:* everything is permitted to The Grand Inquisitor. There are other ways of expressing things mathematically than mere quantification, and mathematics anyway is a closed system. Everything permitted on the top means Ahab, whose actions have consequences for people's personal psyches. Everything permitted without power means grotesquerie, psychology, free speech without tangible material changes, the theater of the absurd, the theatricalizing of everyday life roles, fragmentation not only of person from person, but intra-temporal-person . . . But one pays for acting out one's fantasies in limited space and with limited resources; they have to be amortized and that energy outpour comes from some sphere of the world and even their energy loss can be translated into commodity.

Bleak House is about inheritance: the court process of chancery which is a legal mechanism for expropriating frozen resources through an extended court process which involves heirs not only in the legal process, but emotionally too, training them in greed and madness, breaking them in the process and destroying outmoded social relations, remnants of a romanticized feudal stage . . . It is one of the many dynamics for freeing frozen, slowly expanding pools of money. Dickens views it as an irrational process and takes a reformist view of it.

Dickens is revolted by Krook, whom he ironically terms the Lord Chancellor of what appears to be a reversed and mock-court apparatus, who has in his possession illegally gotten letters and documents, discarded as junk—which threatens the continuity of the system as well as of the action, threatens an ideological plot-resolution which couldn't end the way Dickens wanted it to end; the happy ending, the sentimental ending is Dickens' stock in trade. Those who have suffered incredible things resign themselves and live happily ever after. Some die, but that's to spice up things. Which, though there is protest, is a validation of the ongoing world which Dickens does not dare look into too deeply. At best it's an ironic plea for reformation before the true revelation and its powers are given to the grotesques, the caricatures, the underworld where the accepted world is inverted and thus revealed, the plot scrambled, and the unsmooth upsticking parameters of reality demand another approach to plot, character, the very notion of protagonist.

The law is irrational, confused, and its procedures are irrational, wanting reform. But it is never considered that a ruling class gone underground rules in part by the very flexible obfuscations of the law. Dickens' description of fog in the first chapter is taken to be a metaphor for the law whereas in actuality it is a metaphor for ideology itself which obscures Dickens' vision. In Dickens all suffer under the law; in life the rich do not suffer by law.

Krook is a lord, not of misrule, but paralaw, the real concrete ongoing day-to-day behavior of law. The Lord Chancellor, ironically, barely appears. Krook mediates the invert world and the ongoing acceptance world.

Krook cannot read in a world which proceeds by vast quantities of written material, implying that *he* cannot proceed along the acceptable logical pathways which only petit liberals and rationalists believe in.

Krook and his actions provide a kind of lens in which ongoing sensual reality, which is always brutal, can be revealed: he stands for a node in which a variety of social processes coalesce, conflict, fuse in swirling uneasy alliance, a manifestation of dissonances, a person with a character as well as the expression of force-lines.

Krook, triumphant, denies the prevalence of sentimentality which obscures the world: restores again and again the ongoing world.

Krook, in Dickens' hands, is a warning to the elite to reform themselves.

Krook is the spirit of usury, an outmoded form of accretion.

Krook alive, Krook triumphant, is a danger: he is also a revelation of the system in its ongoing phase. Krook must be eliminated by "supernatural" means, anti-scientific means (the aberrant, unpredictable—though scientifically explicable—event), spontaneous combustion at that very moment when the documents are about to fall into the wrong hands. It's not that spontaneous combustion doesn't occur: it's the timing that makes it miraculous. And in this conspiratorial (an unwilling conspiracy between Dickens and the ruling elite, a conspiracy which brings a sigh of relief to all, a conspiracy which will later bring tears to everyone's eyes . . . tears of joy . . . a bad compromise) event, a denial of a bourgeois science to save bourgeois science, is revealed the possibility of a science freed of ideological presumptions which reveals at last truth, messy fantasies concealed in the interstices of quantification, lines of tradition-force which unite the steps from one point of logic to the next, totemism hiding in mathematics, logic, a magical means of manipulating the universe in abstract philosophical/ideological schemes, rituals embodied in symbolic logic, worshipful (but frequently revised) celebrations of the ongoing order and the goodness of God tucked away in sociological systems. An ancient burning away of the mortal dress, which is to say those aspects which are now outmoded, diseased, contradictory and dissonant to the ongoing system in its new phase.

Science looks for rationality and in this, certainly in all forms of bourgeois social science, the mystique of order, rationality, degree, perfectly accountable relationship, elegance, hierarchy demand an accounting of all phenomena from one nuclear beginning; and in demanding that, the tendency to account for all loose ends, all deviancy, becomes a political procrustean apparatus for leveling the disturbance which can only be accounted for by a revolutionary system of apprehension. This science, this order-hunger embodies the Christian vision. In short, a science with a built-in tendency toward totalitarian accountability which is slowly beginning to fulfill itself in these days. Observation from a political position and analysis which denies the brutal contradictions is the first step to conversion, and conversion's an act of murder.

To have misdefined what the killers of the Clutter family did, to have the killers kill off their own consciousness was a process of conversion, and in a sense, literally, Capote played the part of an Inquisitor . . . What is it that the Marxist detective does? Recognizing the execution of the killers, Perry Smith and Dick Hickock to be a crime, a restoration of an ongoing criminal system, he recognizes the death of the Clutters to be an execution, a revolutionary court judgment, and goes back to find where the real crime took place in order to make Smith and Hickock aware of the political motives of their act . . . an awareness that would have saved them from execution . . .

The Krooks of the world, the crooks, the criminals, the underside, the unaccountable, the reversal world postulate a diffused (but frequently cooptable) revolution which is controllable . . . Fire is the metaphor for Krook, explosive fire. It's a potentially murderous underclass seeking the analysis in order to seek its due for the dehumanization visited upon it in the past, implying a reversal of the usual and covert Christian hierarchical order, and a monetary drain on the system, threatening to upset things by having access to mysterious documents, cynically parodying the rich and powerful, a living parallel to the criminal behavior of the rich, which protects itself from fire. The assassins are not so much the illiterate and unproducing-of-ideology upper strata as the intellectuals sprung from the middle classes who produce the ideology and the literate producers.

The conflict of Krook and the ruling men produces a metaphorical stress-lens which reveals monsters. No man becomes rich without thievery and no rich enterprise exists except by employing illegal means where it cannot get its thievery read into law.

The fact of the matter is that for Dickens, Krook *was* a psychic emanation, a dream figure. But since he couldn't perceive the demoniac forces of capitalism, Krook became to him its manifestation and it is, for Dickens, psychic forces like these that are exemplary of the system, not the individual.

Bleak House, then: a pernicious, an evasive mystery story.

Capital, a healing mystery story, which finds the criminality in process and accessories during and after the fact.

We are led to believe that the secret documents have been burned up, destroyed once and for all, but they are recovered after all. But first the content of those letters, the putative content, is exposed dramatically. The letters, then, the secret documents, the burned-edge will, reveal a revised history. Dickens looks about him and discovers concrete reality but revises it. Marx sits in the British Museum and revises ideology and brings out the systematic nature of the imperial lusts of the British. The system absorbs the money, the anguishes, provides a few happy endings, and goes on. Marx perceives that there are no happy endings. In some sense, the burned yet restored documents are those Dickens never dared to write.

The accepted detective story finds the criminal, focuses on the individual, and restores the theft. The accepted detective restores property and reinforces the ignorance of the criminal.

Lord Dedlock is punished, presumably for his trespasses, but his slums live on, while the burgeoning rational industrialist is counterpoised against Dedlock (an old means of accumulation as against a new one) and found to be sane, rational, brusque, a kindly, disciplined businessman. Of the final disposition of the slums nothing is mentioned: of the starving laborers, nothing is mentioned. Of the continuing theft of labor and time and the systematic alienation of people into caricatures nothing is mentioned.

The burned documents, rescued from the fire, must be perused in another space entirely, a resistance space that coexists with bourgeois space . . . it's only there that they make sense.

As for Krook burned off from his person . . . why he, as force, enters and fuels the ongoing system.

There have not been any happy endings.

Not yet.

You understand I'm groping here. This is a description of a progress, a kind of evaluation and self-criticism. Also missing is the rest of it; this is part of what turned out to be a short book and will be a longer book.

More: there is no WE to this, not yet . . . no proper climate of belief supported not only by readings and discussions, but actions. The form is even wrong, but a step. There exists a whole technology for information exchange and that will appear in the book itself. What's missing is a complete analysis of how information, literature, and popular culture are disseminated . . . the concrete modes of doing so, especially featuring a sociology of the publishing industry. What's also needed is an inflected kind of language, but one that is inflected with political, economic, historic modifiers . . . but that's building. This is necessary to create a melded form which heals the rents in the division of knowledge, specializations. As for a formal aesthetics, I can't talk about that at all. I found that different aesthetic needs developed out of the needs of each of my three books as well as the one I'm working on now.

What's also missing is the erosion of the overriding sense of individual competition, without the visible cannibalism . . . some new form which acknowledges the group and the individual. We should be able to use one another's ideas and information exchange as a basis for this. The Movement has not been singularly successful in this: the old individual forms, the old competitions have continued to exist.

And as for the notion of group action, this means also that people of different disciplines must be able to work together . . . social scientists and creative writers, poets and mathematicians. And always, there must exist the sense that our consciousness is in conflict not only with the conciousness of the ongoing society, but with the consciousness of those masses who are worked upon through all the media.

Finally: this paper has been written to create responses and what I can only call comradely struggle . . . which means responses and counter-responses.

I thought to include a bibliography, but that will appear in the book itself. I have some notions of a dialectical bibliography and have to work those out more clearly. And as for bibliography, that is always modified by conversations, arguments, struggle, and testings against reality.

Susan Sontag's "New Left" pastoral: notes on revolutionary pastoralism in America

LEO MARX

On another occasion, he [Lenin] and Gorky were listening to Beethoven's Appassionata: *"I know nothing [Lenin said] that is greater than the* Appassionata: *I'd like to listen to it every day. It is marvelous superhuman music, I always think with pride—perhaps it is naive of me— what marvelous things human beings can do!" Then screwing up his eyes and smiling, he added, rather sadly: "But I can't listen to music too often. It affects your nerves, makes you want to say stupid nice things and stroke the heads of people who could create such beauty while living in this vile hell. And now you mustn't stroke anyone's head—you might get your hand bitten off. You have to hit them on the head, use force against anyone. Hm, hm, our duty is infernally hard."*

1

A puzzling feature of recent American radicalism has been the promiscuous mingling of pastoral and revolutionary motives. According to received definitions the two are irreconcilable. The psychic root of pastoralism is the seemingly universal impulse, in the face of society's increasing complexity and oppressiveness, to withdraw to a simpler environment "closer to nature." For most men in most times and places, needless to say, the pastoral retreat has not been a live option. There seldom has been any place for them to go, and even if there had been, they lacked the means of getting there and starting a new life. In the West in the modern era, the notable exception was the colonization and continuing resettlement of the American continent. This recurrent "event" no doubt accounts for the peculiarly strong hold of the pastoral ethos upon the native imagination. Still, the fact remains that most of the pleasure derived from the pastoral ideal has been a vicarious pleasure mediated by the work of artists and writers. The concern of pastoralism, moreover, has been to change the individual consciousness, not the structure of society. It has been an aesthetic ethos for the privileged, not a political program for the masses.

Since the emergence of the New Left, however, this distinction has been obscured. One of the first rallying cries of the protest against the Vietnam war—*Make love not war!*—is a nice example. To older radicals it seemed a curiously apolitical slogan. But to initiates familiar with the esoteric pastoral idiom it was another invitation to retreat from a brutal society and be like shepherds: simple and caring and poor, and contemptuous of The World. *Make love not war!* is a variant of a call the disaffected young have been hearing through every medium of the counterculture, and during the sixties, as we all know, many heeded the call. They became hippies, flower people, psychedelic tripsters, transcendental meditators, organic food cultists, ecology activists, rural communards, etc. To sympathizers like Charles Reich they all had enlisted in the ranks of a "revolution": "There is a revolution coming," he writes. "It will not be like revolutions of the past. It will originate with the individual and with culture, and it will change the political structure only as its final act. It will not require violence . . ." How appropriate that he prefigures this unique revolution as a *greening* of America!

In view of what has been happening to our society, the strength and ubiquity of these pastoral impulses is understandable enough. What remains puzzling, however, is the effortless way they have been combined with seemingly disparate revolutionary impulses— not all of them by any means as bland and dreamy as the Reichian greening. Many of those who responded to the pastoral invitation thought of themselves, and were thought of by others, as political revolutionaries in the Marxist tradition. Often they joined, or lent support to, SDS, Progressive Labor, Black Panthers, Weathermen, Trotskyists, Maoists, and old-fashioned Communists. Anyone who has marched for civil rights or peace knows something about the easy fellowship that is possible between what might be called the pastoral and political groups within the movement. Many adherents of the counterculture move back and forth between the two. Yet the reasons for skepticism are compelling. It is not easy to imagine how an aesthetic ethos of disengagement and renunciation could be lastingly incorporated in an authentic revolutionary movement—one that aims to transform the system of wealth and power.

Respected authorities on pastoralism and revolution support this skeptical view. The most influential study of the pastoral mode written in this century, William Empson's *Some Versions of Pastoral* (1935), begins with an attack on the very concept of "proletarian literature," the reigning doctrine of revolutionary writing in the thirties. Empson argues that it is a bogus concept. It pretends to be written by, for, and about the people, but it is neither by nor for them, and in most cases it is not really about them either. Which is to say that it is not about the industrial working class. On inspection the hero "worker" often proves to be the courtier-shepherd in disguise, an unbelievably self-contained, sensitive, contemplative man who has few material needs or worldly ambitions. Your typical proletarian novel, says Empson, is an example of covert pastoral. Whether or not he is correct about that need not concern us here. What does matter is the presupposition (which he treats as axiomatic) that pastoralism—so far as it has political significance—tends to be counterrevolutionary. One of its chief functions, he says, is to assuage the anxiety and guilt of the dominant classes by figuring a "beautiful relation between the rich and the poor." (Who writes and reads "proletarian" novels anyway? Surely not the proletariat.) By masking an upper class sensibility in the garb of a shepherd or a working man the pastoralist tells us that differences between the classes don't matter. It would be ironic, but not inconceivable, if today's Ivy League radicals in blue denim were performing a similar service for the Establishment. In any case, the political effect of pastoralism, as Empson describes it, is to reinforce illusions of class harmony.

If Empson is correct, the revolutionary pretensions of contemporary pastoralists are just that—specious. And it is striking, it must be admitted, how often the spirit of the old pastoral, with its patrician, quietistic bias, makes itself felt in Mitchell Goodman's fascinating compendium of New Left writing, *The Movement Toward a New America, The Beginning of a Long Revolution* (Knopf, N.Y., 1970). For example, Goodman includes an excerpt from Gary Snyder's *Earth House Hold* in which Snyder explains why "Tribe" is the proper name for the radical counterculture. Like gypsies or American Indians, he says, the disaffected young believe that "man's natural being is to be trusted and followed." The signal by which they recognize each other all over the world is "a bright and tender look, calmness and gentleness, freshness and ease of manner." They belong to a Great Subculture which has had many earlier outcroppings in history, though fewer in the West than the East; it has always been inherently subversive of any society based on hierarchy and specialization, and now that our urban industrial system is proving to be obsolete, the Tribe is prepared to lead mankind into its next great phase: the exploration of consciousness itself. For Snyder, like Virgil or Spenser or Frost, the withdrawal to a rural or wild setting is primarily a means of arriving at the pastoralist's true destination: a Platonic landscape of the mind.†

† Let me here acknowledge a large debt to Richard Cody's fine study, *The Landscape of the Mind: Pastoralism and Platonic Theory in Tasso's 'Aminta' and Shakespeare's Early Comedies,* Oxford, 1969.

What chiefly interests him is the creation of an environment favorable to the contemplative life. If there is something of an anomaly about the idea it is partly because it appears in a volume dedicated to the prospect of a left-wing revolution. Just how anomalous that combination is becomes evident when Snyder describes the kind of man he regards as an ideal recruit for his Tribe:

... a man of wide international reputation, much learning and leisure—luxurious product of our long and sophisticated history—[who] may with good reason wish to live simply, with few tools and minimal clothes, close to nature.

Perhaps we should not be surprised to discover that this lordly figure, an embodiment of the orthodox aesthetic theology of Renaissance pastoralism, survives in America in 1970. No doubt Snyder could produce a few real-life examples. But the question remains: how can his withdrawal from society conceivably help to effect a revolution?

Empson's notion that the pastoral ethos is in a profound sense counterrevolutionary would be supported, I think, by most modern authorities on political revolution. It is not difficult to guess what Lenin, for one, would say about the pastoralism of today's American radicals. As the anecdote cited at the outset suggests, he was highly sensitive to the conflict between aesthetic pleasure and political commitment.† One of the chief lessons of history for him, as for any Marxist, is that power seldom if ever has been relinquished without the application of counterpower. To make a revolution, therefore, it is imperative to win the support of a majority of the working class. And that in turn requires the existence of a well-organized, ideologically sound, disciplined, combative vanguard party.

But of course one of the distinguishing marks of the New Left has been a deliberate repudiation of party organization and ideological rigor as prerequisites for revolution. As if obeying the old pastoral injunction to reject the aspiring mind, the new radicals have adopted a lifestyle which features gentle, other-

† Gorky's story about Lenin's response to Beethoven's work is retold by Edmund Wilson in *To the Finland Station*, New York, 1940, p. 386.

worldly virtues: openness, spontaneity, tolerance, eroticism, nonviolence. *Make love not war!* Surely Lenin would regard this slogan as symptomatic of the kind of anarchic, all-or-nothing romanticism which actually undermines the serious work of a revolutionary party. Those whose sympathies are engaged by the New Left might find it disconcerting to reread Lenin's *"Left-Wing" Communism, An Infantile Disorder* (1920) with the recent history of American radicalism in view:

The petty bourgeois, "driven to frenzy" by the horrors of capitalism, is a social phenomenon which, like anarchism, is characteristic of all capitalist countries. The instability of such revolutionariness, its barrenness, its liability to become swiftly transformed into submission, apathy, fantasy, and even "frenzied" infatuation with one or another bourgeois "fad"— all this is a matter of common knowledge.

From a Leninist viewpoint the pastoralism of today's radical movement is a typical petty bourgeois fantasy, a self-serving, aesthetic response to the ugliness and horror of the Vietnam era. Its appeal therefore is restricted to the white affluent middle class. Although it pretends to offer an alternative to the military-industrial empire, this ethos of disengagement actually may be relied upon to leave the institutional structure of society intact. So far from being a revolutionary program, indeed, it is a symptom of a widespread "infantile disorder."

In the light of all this, how much sense does it make to speak about "revolutionary pastoralism"? If we cling to received definitions like those advanced by Empson or Lenin, we obviously must conclude that there can be no such thing. The term is self-contradictory, an oxymoron in a class with, say, "violent pacifism." The very emergence of the concept might be said to indicate the confusion of aesthetic and political motives at the core of contemporary radical behavior. On the other hand, there are good reasons for thinking that the definitions themselves may in some measure be obsolete. The fact is that a large and steadily increasing number of people are committed to some version of the pastoral ethos as a means of revolutionizing American society. Not only do they believe in it but, what is more important, many are trying to live by it. Who can predict the long term

557

political consequences of their withdrawal from the dominant culture? After all, there is no precedent—certainly not Russia in Lenin's time—for the development of a revolutionary situation in an advanced industrial society like our own, with an immense, morally confused yet materially sated middle class. The technical possibility of economic sufficiency for the entire population makes an incalculable difference. If there was one fact of collective life which always had made pastoralism seem politically fanciful, unrealistic—a mere utopian dream—it was the seemingly unalterable fact of economic scarcity. Circumvent that barrier and it becomes reasonable, at least, to imagine a revolutionary vanguard activated by those extraeconomic (moral and aesthetic) motives which dominate the pastoral ethos.

Notice, also, that certain New Left intellectuals have begun the job—almost without intending it—of reconciling this classic aesthetic philosophy with the more practical, militant, and egalitarian strain of revolutionary thought inherited from Marx and Lenin. Although the term rarely is invoked, pastoralism is a major theme in most discussions of "cultural revolution." I have already mentioned Mitchell Goodman's collection and Charles Reich's *The Greening of America* (1970). Perhaps most significant here is Herbert Marcuse's *An Essay on Liberation* (1969), for he argues (as an avowed Marxist) that an *aesthetic ethos* may well provide "the common denominator of the aesthetic and the political," the possible form of a free society. For Marcuse even the psychedelic withdrawal, which he sees as creating "artificial paradises within the society from which it withdrew," may contain a kernel of the revolutionary form he seeks to define.

But in my view no recent work has brought this subject into clearer focus than Susan Sontag's brief essay (it appeared originally as a magazine article), *Trip to Hanoi* (1968). This is not to say that Sontag answers the question I have been discussing, "Can pastoralism be a revolutionary ethos?" In a literal sense, after all, the question is unanswerable right now. The only way to confirm the revolutionary potential of this or any other ethos is, finally, in the event. Besides, *Trip to Hanoi* does not deal expressly with this question. It is not a book *about* pastoralism so much as it is an effort to resolve the conflict between aesthetic and political motives as that conflict is experienced by a writer directly confronting the appalling consequences of our global politics. What concerns Sontag is how to live in good conscience if one is an artist, a radical, and a highly rewarded citizen of the American empire. She answers the question in the time-honored manner of the American writer, as an account of her temporary disengagement from this complex society, and of an exemplary journey—a brief encounter with another, simpler, more virtuous way of life. The result—somewhat inadvertent to be sure—is a pastoral, or rather a political meditation in the pastoral mode. Although *Trip to Hanoi* does not answer my question, it does more than any piece of writing I know to sharpen the issues, and to explain why we are now witnessing the appearance in America of that strange new form of political behavior, revolutionary pastoralism.

2

When Susan Sontag accepted the invitation to visit North Vietnam in the spring of 1968 it was "with a pretty firm idea" of not writing about her experience. At the time she could not imagine what her subject would be. Although a committed opponent of the American invasion, she doubted that she could add anything worthwhile to the already eloquent opposition to the war. Nor did she have any illusions about contributing to the immense store of knowledge about the situation in Vietnam. For that she had few qualifications and several handicaps. She was not an Asian specialist; she did not know the language; she would only be in North Vietnam for two weeks, and during that time she and her two companions almost certainly would see little other than what their guides wanted them to see. These were all good reasons for her reluctance to write about her experience, but being an unregenerate writer she succeeded in overcoming that reluctance. She gives the reasons to her readers nonetheless, presumably so that they can defend themselves against her fallibility.

Before the trip, moreover, she had another, less obvious reason, at once psychological and literary, for thinking that she would keep silent. She confesses to having had a block against expressing her political views in print. Before going to Vietnam, she explains, "[I] had been largely unable to incorporate into either novels or essays my evolving radical political convictions and sense of moral dilemma at being a citizen of the American empire." In part that is because she had been introduced to radical politics during the Stalinist era. Her later disillusionment with the "philistine fraud" of the American Communist Party had made it difficult for her, as it had for other radicals of her generation, to tolerate the standard jargon of the Left. Even such respectable words as "capitalism" and "imperialism" had given her trouble until the late sixties. By sharing all of these qualms with her readers early on, Sontag manages to invest *Trip to Hanoi* with that peculiar literary self-consciousness so characteristic of writing in the pastoral mode. In effect she makes her literary problems themselves—her inhibitions, her difficulties in shaping her responses, her dubious authority and credibility as an observer—one of her overt themes. As a result, the reader is invited to question everything. Why did she abandon such compelling scruples against publication? What was there about the Vietnam experience which freed her from the inhibiting results of her disenchanting political childhood? Why should we credit her judgments? Having been warned against her unreliable observations, why should we believe what she tells us about the Vietnamese and their country?

Much of the bite can be taken out of these questions when we recognize that the chief subject of this odd book is not Vietnam. *Trip to Hanoi* is primarily an account of an interior journey. It describes what happens inside the mind of an American writer who briefly undergoes that extreme political, psychic, and moral stress we Americans call "Vietnam." The word refers not only to a place on the map—a country, a culture, a people—but to a conflict within the American consciousness. From the official government viewpoint North Vietnam is the Enemy, whereas for radicals like Sontag it had come to be the ideal Other. At least that is how she had felt while she was still in the United States. Once she gets to North Vietnam, however, she is compelled to recognize how much of warring America she has internalized. The conflict also is in herself. Hence the structure of *Trip to Hanoi* is largely determined by two sharp turns of feeling which separate the book into three parts. The first section records Sontag's initial "culture shock," her dismay at coming up against a seemingly impassable barrier between herself and the real, living embodiments of the ideal Other. To convey the immediacy of this reaction she relies on the journal form, a selection of notes she had made during the first five days of her visit. This is a time of disappointment, exasperation, confusion and gloom. She suffers from a kind of sophisticated homesickness. But about the fifth day, just when she is ready to give up on the Vietnamese— give up hope of understanding and liking them—the first turn occurs:

And then, suddenly, my experiences started changing. The psychic cramp with which I was afflicted in the early part of my stay began to ease and the Vietnamese as real people, and North Vietnam as a real place, came into view.

At this point, beginning the central section of the book, Sontag abandons the journal. Now we get a discursive, essayistic tribute to the moral beauty of the Vietnamese. It is in fact such an extravagant, uncritical apostrophe to the grace and simplicity and virtue of these embattled people that the reader's credulity is likely to be strained—especially since Sontag seems to have forgotten all of her own strictures against trusting her impressions.

But then, just when a normally skeptical reader might be ready to give up on *her*, she confronts what she calls her "crisis of credulity." In effect she says, "If you are having trouble accepting what I have written, I confess that I was having trouble believing the evidence of my senses." This second turn is for me one of the more illuminating passages in recent American writing. It marks the point of impact between our sophisticated, skeptical Western culture, grounded in notions of human imperfection or original sin, and certain brutally simple facts of contemporary political life:

The moment one begins to be affected by the moral beauty of the Vietnamese, not to mention their physical grace, a derisive inner voice starts calling it phony sentimentality. Understandably, one fears succumbing to that cut-rate sympathy for places like Vietnam which, lacking any real historical or psychological understanding, becomes another instance of the ideology of primitivism. The revolutionary politics of many people in capitalist countries is only a new guise for the old conservative culture-criticism: posing against overcomplex, hypocritical, devitalized urban society choking on affluence the idea of a simple people living the simple life in a decentralized, uncoercive, passionate society with modest material means. As eighteenth-century *philosophes* pictured such a pastoral ideal in the Pacific Islands or among the American Indians, and German romantic poets supposed it to have existed in ancient Greece, late twentieth century intellectuals in New York and Paris are likely to locate it in the exotic revolutionary societies of the Third World. If some of what I've written evokes the very cliché of the Western left-wing intellectual idealizing an agrarian revolution that I was so set on not being, I must reply . . .

I break off the excerpt at this point in order to direct attention to the range and significance of the issues Sontag has raised and must resolve in completing that crucial sentence. But first let me emphasize what may seem to be a merely formal, literary aspect of the dilemma. She is writing a report about her experience in North Vietnam when she evidently realizes, part way through, that she has fallen into a stock literary attitude. Or is it *merely* a literary attitude? That is a large part of the dilemma, and one that American writers have been up against for at least two centuries. In any case, it is not only an attitude she has assumed, but an entire conventional mode—a more or less complete way of organizing pieces of writing. Just how conventional it is may not be immediately apparent, for in a sense the topicality of her subject is a disguise. But the truth is that she is writing a pastoral, yes another pastoral fable of a well-established American design. At the risk of oversimplifying and schematizing a supple mode, let me describe an ideal type or model of the design. It is a blend of traditional pastoralism and the nineteenth century travel romance, a distinctive American mode exemplified in such classic works as Melville's *Typee* and *Moby Dick,* Thoreau's *Walden,* Mark Twain's *Huckleberry Finn,* Hemingway's *In Our Time,* Faulkner's *Go Down, Moses,* and many others.

3

The design is formed by a symbolic landscape, a narrative structure, and a coordinated series of mental states. A central figure, often a first person narrator, takes us through the tripartite scheme. We first meet him in a relatively complex environment,†

† The distinction between the complex and the simple in the pastoral mode is a sociological, not an ecological, distinction. The key to complexity is differentiation of function,

dominated by organized social institutions he perceives as oppressive, alienating, antihuman. It is a technologically-oriented culture which tends to perfect the means of life and neglect the ends. He suffers from a dissociation of his inner and outer experience. The first stage of the action therefore is a retreat in the direction of nature—nature as represented by a sector of the landscape, either rural or wild, marked by fewer signs of human intervention. The retreat is an escape, to be sure, but it is also a quest.

The second and central stage, accordingly, may be described as an exploration of this new setting in search of an alternative to the repressive culture. The protagonist's aim is a recovery of innocence, nothing less than a simpler, happier, more harmonious way of life. At some point, as if to confirm the wisdom of the initial retreat, he enjoys an interlude of ecstatic fulfillment. Anxiety and guilt are supplanted by a sense of belonging and virtue. Often this idyllic moment, which has distinct erotic and religious overtones, involves an encounter with a person of non-Western origin—an American Indian or a black or an Oriental. But of course the fulfillment of the pastoral impulse proves to be ephemeral. Certain other standard episodes heighten the sense of transience. There is the "interrupted idyll," when a machine (or some token of advanced technological society) suddenly bursts into the relative peace and quiet of this simple world, thereby reminding the central figure of the implacable advance of history and of his own place in it—or, more subtly, its place in him. Often, too, there is a chastening, even frightening encounter with the idealized or natural other, reminding the protagonist that Nature and the simpler way of life close to nature can be wild, foreign, threatening, and that he severs his cultural bonds only at the risk of a total loss of self. In short, the

or the division of labor, and this does not necessarily entail intellectual or emotional complexity. According to this criterion, the United States is a complex society, Vietnam is a simple one, regardless of the inner complexities of Vietnamese culture. Interestingly enough, this distinction between the complex and the simple is the exact reverse of the ecological distinction. A Brazilian rain forest is an infinitely more complex, hence more stable, environment than Manhattan Island, where most biological niches are unfilled and there are few organisms besides humanoids and microbes. But "closeness to nature" in literary pastorals refers to simpler ways of life, and only indirectly to the ecosystem.

retreat makes possible some consciousness-expanding moments, but no basis for a lasting alternative to the repressive culture from which it emanated.

The third and final stage of the action, therefore, entails some kind of return. But the conclusions of these pastoral fables tend to be obscure and often deliberately equivocal. It is not clear just what the retreat has accomplished. The most optimistic version hints at the possibility of some new way of life, a best-of-both-worlds compromise between art and nature figured by a "middle landscape." This is a domain which was once thought by dreamers like Jefferson to lie somewhere between over-civilized Europe, with its excess of sophistication and suffering, and the underdeveloped terrain of the American west—threatening, barbaric, mindless, impulse-ridden. But of course the Jeffersonian dream of realizing the pastoral hope in a political order was not fulfilled, and our writers reverted to (so far as they ever had departed from) the usual literary way out. The only possible locus of a resolution, they seem to say, is in consciousness and, more specifically, in works of art. In the aesthetic closure, and only there, can we enjoy the pleasure of having it both ways.†

4

Coming back now to Sontag's *Trip to Hanoi*, the two sharp turns of feeling already mentioned provide the transitions between the initial retreat, the exploration of a culture "closer to nature," and the return to the complex world. At first Sontag withdraws, in the usual westward direction, from a technologically advanced society (it is now militarized and murderously aggressive) to the relatively simple world of its peasant victims. She is sympathetic with the Vietnamese, of course, but she finds that these admirable people are mentally much *too* "simple," *too* "close to nature," for her taste. They seem to live in a two-dimensional

---

† This is a telescoped version of an argument I have set forth in detail in *The Machine in the Garden: Technology and the Pastoral Ideal in America* (New York, 1964), and in "Pastoral Ideals and City Troubles," Smithsonian Annual II, *The Fitness of Man's Environment* (New York, 1968).

world, a kind of "ethical fairy tale," endlessly repeating the same simplistic, Manichean account of their melancholy history. Their repetitive, sloganized, resolutely unironic discourse strikes her as a kind of pathetic "baby talk." Her feeling of superiority makes her anxious and guilty, but as an intellectual she is particularly sensitive to verbal crudity. For example, they refer to Americans as "imperialists" and "henchman" and "cruel thugs."

Although . . . the quaintness of phrase makes me smile, that is just what they [the Americans] are—from the vantage point of helpless peasants being napalmed by swooping diving metal birds. Still . . . such language does make me uncomfortable. Whether because I am laggard or maybe just dissociated, I both assent to the unreserved moral judgment and shy away from it, too. I believe they are right. At the same time, nothing here can make me forget that events are much more complicated than the Vietnamese represent them. But exactly what complexities would I have them acknowledge? Isn't it enough that their struggle is, objectively, just? Can they afford subtleties when they need to mobilize every bit of energy to continue standing up to the American Goliath?

Sontag's ambivalent response to the rudimentary vocabulary of the Vietnamese is only one aspect of a larger, all-encompassing ambivalence. It derives in part from the monotonous single-mindedness of this beleaguered socialist society. Granted that these people are virtuous, even noble, what is there here to occupy the mind of a Western intellectual? "Of course I *could* live in Vietnam, or in an ethical society like this one," she tells herself, reassuringly, about the third day, "—but not without the loss of a big part of myself." There is something a bit comic about Sontag and her two American companions in Hanoi, all deeply alienated from the American cause, talking nostalgically about San Francisco rock groups and *The New York Review of Books.* It is comedy not unfamiliar to writers of pastoral:

Corin: And how like you this shepherd's life, Master Touchstone?
Touchstone: Truly shepherd, in respect of itself, it is a good life; but in respect that it is a
            shepherd's life, it is naught . . . Now, in respect it is in the fields, it pleaseth
            me well; but in respect it is not in the court, it is tedious. As it is a spare life,
            look you, it fits my humour well; but as there is no more plenty in it, it goes
            much against my stomach.†

The serious point is that Vietnamese society may be morally superior to American society (Sontag has no doubt about that),

† *As You Like It,* III, ii.

but from the standpoint of intellectual, psychological, or aesthetic variety and range of interest, it strikes her as manifestly inferior. But, again, this is a familiar bind of the artist, intellectual, or "complex" man, disclosed by pastoral: he looks at the rustic, worker, or "simple" man with what Empson calls a "double attitude." "I am better in one way," he says to himself, "but not so good in another." So with Sontag: ". . . while my consciousness does include theirs, or could, theirs could never include mine. They may be nobler, more heroic, more generous than I am, but I have more on my mind than they do—probably just what precludes my ever being that virtuous." The dilemma is painful. Hasn't she—haven't all American intellectuals—been morally disabled by what might be called the "high stimulant" quotient of our culture? She finds in herself the condescension of someone from a "big" rich culture visiting a "little" poor one. "My consciousness . . . is a creature with many organs accustomed to being fed by a stream of cultural goods, and infected by irony." Moral seriousness, as she conceives it, entails irony, an awareness of contradiction and paradox—the complexity which has been ironed out of Vietnamese discourse. "Part of me," she confesses, "can't help regarding them as children—beautiful, patient, heroic, martyred, stubborn children." Discovering this double attitude in herself generates much of the disappointment and depression of her first few days in Hanoi. At the time the conflict seemed too deep ever to be resolved, and perhaps it was: "the gluttonous habits of my consciousness prevent me from being at home with what I most admire, and—for all my raging against America—firmly unite me with what I condemn."

She appears to have reached an impasse in her effort to have a satisfactory contact with the Vietnamese when, suddenly, her experience begins to change. This is the first turn. The anxiety-arousing retreat is over. Now the Vietnamese as "real people" and Vietnam as a "real place" come into view. She notes the callowness and stinginess of the first responses she had recorded in her journal. She drops the journal form for a straight discursive style. What follows in the middle section of the book corresponds to the "exploration of nature," the search for an alternative way of life, in the paradigm of American pastorals. In this case the result is a kind of idyll, if only on the plane of the intellect. All the traits which she had found baffling now prove to be understandable and attractive. Even the simple language and the slogans acquire a remarkable resonance and grace.

Take the saying of Ho, repeated to us so often: "Nothing is more precious than independence and liberty." Not until I'd heard the quote many many times did I actually consider it. But when I did, I thought, yes, it really does say a great deal. One could indeed, as the Vietnamese have, live spiritually from that simple sentence for a long time. The Vietnamese regard Ho not as a thinker but as a man of action; his words are for use.

In Vietnam, a society animated by revolutionary will, language serves a different function. Because they don't suffer the isolation of the private self, or the discrepancy between private and public experience (a condition which nurtures irony), language is for the Vietnamese an instrumentality. It is not for them as it is for Western literary intellectuals a medium of consolation or of aesthetic pleasure or of resolving inner conflicts. In North Vietnam words, talk, literature are ancillary to collective action. Once that is understood the words take on new meaning, new beauty.

Virtually all of Vietnamese behavior now appears to Sontag in a similarly flattering light. She is impressed by the astonishing calm of the people, their lack of hate, their magnanimity toward America and Americans, their habitual emotional tact, their almost universal capacity for heroic renunciation. Somehow they manage to combine the martial spirit with a civil life which "places great value on gentleness and the demands of the heart." They really believe, she decides, in the goodness of man, and in the possibility of achieving something like the pastoral ideal.

It was my impression that the Vietnamese, as a culture, genuinely believe that life is simple. They also believe, incredible as it may seem considering their present situation, that life is full of joy. Joy is to be discerned behind what is already so remarkable: the ease and total lack of self-pity with which people worked a backbreaking number of hours, or daily faced the possibility of their own death and the death of those they love. The phenomena of existential agony, of alienation, just don't appear among the Vietnamese—probably in part because they lack our kind of "ego," and our endowment of free-floating guilt.

These are great, possibly exaggerated claims, but as the last statement indicates, they are not based merely on impressions.

567

Sontag has consulted the experts, and much of her analysis turns upon the distinction between a culture founded on shame, like Vietnam, and a culture energized by explosive charges of guilt, like our own.

And yet, even if one grants the logic or plausibility of her argument, it is hard to believe. It is hard for an American these days to believe that people can be so lacking in rancor or personal ambition. It is hard to believe they can be so self-effacing, so controlled, so committed to a common cause, or, in a word, so virtuous. Sontag relies upon the deep reserves of mistrust in us as she builds up to the second turn. She talks about the virtues of the Vietnamese with shameless certitude and enthusiasm until, as I have said, our credulity is near exhaustion. But then she discloses a similar failing in herself, and we get the remarkable passage, already quoted at length, in which she reports how a derisive inner voice accuses Susan Sontag, the writer, of sentimentality and related literary offenses.

This passage is reminiscent of the "interrupted idyll" which recurs in American pastorals. What threatens to obliterate the vision of harmony in this case is not a machine, of course, it is merely a "voice" representing the magisterial Western idea of a self-contained literary culture. That idea comports with the high degree of specialization in our technological system. The "voice" tells Sontag that the way of life she has been describing was invented by Theocritus and Virgil; it is a mode, a body of conventions, a cliché called "the pastoral ideal." It belongs to literature, not to life. Or does it? Has she been forcing her account of Vietnamese culture into this ancient literary mold? Or is it possible that what she has seen in Vietnam might serve to validate the germ of another truth about human possibilities which had always been there, buried, invisible, or hedged about by irony? This is the crux we reached earlier with her statement: "If some of what I have written evokes the very cliché of the Western left-wing intellectual idealizing an agrarian revolution that I was so set on not being, I must reply . . ." The sentence ends: "that a cliché is a cliché, truth is truth, and direct experience is—

well—something one repudiates at one's peril." She continues: "In the end I can only avow that, armed with these very self-suspicions, I found, through direct experience, North Vietnam to be a place which, in many respects, *deserves* to be idealized."

There it is. Although she immediately qualifies this statement, acknowledging certain "crimes committed by the present government" of North Vietnam, she never retracts it. She is compelled by her "direct experience" to put down that skeptical inner voice, and to *believe* that the Vietnamese are more or less as she has described them. The moment is an extraordinary one because writers working in the pastoral mode generally have managed to avoid this ultimate crux. Is there any basis in reality for crediting such an extravagant display of the human capacity for virtue? For most writers the issue never has arisen. They have been protected by the well-known "artificiality" of the mode—its obtrusive and often idiotic conventionality has precluded any need for moral seriousness. When they have pressed beyond the limits of its equivocal conventions, moreover, they invariably have taken the ironic way out. Literary pastoral is a treasure-store of devices for having it both ways, even with respect to the nature of human nature. A characteristic solution is to use words, as Frost would put it, which say one thing and mean another. The choice is thereby passed on to the reader. In this case, Sontag might have described what appeared to her to be the ideal character of the Vietnamese, but in language contrived to cast doubt on her judgment, and to disclose the deceptive conventionality of her account. By invoking the criterion of "direct [i.e., not merely literary] experience," however, she aims to neutralize the cliché and so, in effect, to validate the hope which pastoral invests in the retreat from the world of power and sophistication.

What makes this passage all the more striking to anyone familiar with Sontag's earlier work is the evident turnabout in her ideas about the relation between art and reality. To my mind, at least, she had hitherto been a critic distinguished by a far greater interest in bold aesthetic effects than in the sense of life they presumably were intended to convey. The essays with which she had established her reputation as, in the words of a *New York Times* reviewer, "the most controversial critic writing in America today," had seemed to court notoriety by extreme statements of currently fashionable, brittle, and resolutely apolitical notions about art as a kind of highly specialized, cerebral enterprise comparable to symbolic logic in its virtually nonhuman abstraction from the concerns of the common life. I am thinking especially of "Against Interpretation," "On Style," and that much discussed, virtuoso exhibit of pseudo-academic chic, "Notes on 'Camp'." Only the year before her visit to Hanoi, moreover, Sontag had discussed the pastoral mode, in the clever Empsonian manner, as a merely formal resource, a venerable body of conventions like those used in pornography. Her chief point about the pastoral in that essay ("The Pornographic Imagination") is that it "depicts relations between people that are certainly reductive, vapid, and unconvincing." Of course that is true about a great deal of pastoral literature, but it could not be further from the discoveries she makes in *Trip to Hanoi*. In this book, at least, she seems to abandon her frigid aestheticism, as many literary people have done under the pressure of our current civil crisis. My point about the pivotal statement on "direct experience" is that there she seems to endorse the incipient moral seriousness of the pastoral convention. So far from depicting a vapid and unconvincing idea of human relations, it now seems to embody an ethos one might conceivably live by in America today. What strikes us as idealized in her account of Vietnam, she now claims, is not merely an expression of a stock literary attitude imported from the West; it has a basis in political reality, in the actual substance of the contrast between the Vietnamese and American ways of life.

But what is to be done with this new knowledge? Earlier she had invoked "the old severe rule: if you can't put your life where your head (heart) is, then what you think (feel) is a fraud." How can she possibly put her life where her head presently is? How can she cast her lot with these admirable people and their noble revolutionary cause? By "cast her lot" I don't mean to imply that she ever seriously considers remaining in Indochina. Of course she comes home on schedule. But the question that informs the closing pages of this book, as it does the "return" in all American pastorals, is: how will this withdrawal have changed her life? How might it, if we take it seriously enough, change ours?

5

It is hard to respond decisively to the conclusion of *Trip to Hanoi*. The ending, like the journal extracts at the beginning, is colored by a deep ambivalence. Indeed, the strongest appeal of the book is precisely its lucid expression of the dilemma confronting countless Americans these days, particularly members of the professional middle class who are morally alienated from a society which so abundantly favors them. The issue, in the end, is what sort of re-entry Sontag contrives.

I came back from Hanoi considerably chastened. Life here looks both uglier and more promising. To describe what is promising, it's perhaps imprudent to invoke the promiscuous ideal of revolution. Still, it would be a mistake to underestimate the amount of diffuse yearning for radical change pulsing through this society. Increasing numbers of people do realize that we must have a more generous, more humane way of being with each other; and great, probably convulsive, social changes are needed to create these psychic changes.

Imprudent or not, the conclusion of Sontag's pastoral essay manifestly rides on the ideal of "revolution." But just what does this ever-so-tentative avowal of revolutionary purpose mean? If "great, possibly convulsive social changes" are a necessary precondition of the psychic change she wants, then would not the pastoral ethos of disengagement and a "return to nature" be irrelevant at best and an "infantile" diversion at worst? The way she describes the causal relationship harks back to her orthodox Marxist past. On the other hand, her goal—"a more generous, more humane way of being with each other"—catches the tone and spirit of the pastoralism which pervades the counterculture nowadays.

True to her conflicting feelings, Sontag provides abundant evidence for the harsh skeptic who would reject this ideal of revolution, either on political or literary grounds, as a neat bit of self-serving evasiveness.

Politically speaking, her Vietnam experience would seem to be of little or no help to an American who is drawn to the prospect of revolution. In spite of the boldness with which she affirms the ideal aspect of North Vietnam and its citizens, she admits that a Southeast Asian peasant society struggling for national independence hardly can provide a model for American radicals. How can we emulate the behavior of the Vietnamese? An even more troubling question is whether highly favored, white, middle class intellectuals like Sontag could ever adapt to some hypothetical equivalent of that morally superior society. Early in the book she had raised the question herself:

Of course I *could* live in Vietnam, or an ethical society like this one—but not without the loss of a big part of myself. Though I believe incorporation into such a society will greatly improve the lives of most people in the world (and therefore support the advent of such societies), I imagine it will in many ways impoverish mine. I live in an unethical society that coarsens the sensibilities and thwarts the capacities for goodness of most people but makes available for minority consumption an astonishing array of intellectual and aesthetic pleasure.

What this means is that the intelligentsia of Europe and the United States may be too privileged, may have too much to lose, ever to commit itself wholeheartedly to an authentic revolutionary cause. True, some will adopt radical opinions; like Sontag, they will "support the advent of such societies" (how abstract and remote she makes it sound!), but are they likely to summon much passion or will for a cause that almost certainly would, if successful, deprive them of so many pleasures? Whatever their opinions, whatever kind of society they "support the advent of," the truth is that most such indulged intellectuals are likely to find themselves aligned, in a crisis, with those who would preserve the system they enjoy. In those dismal first days in Vietnam Sontag acknowledged as much about herself. It was her "mental appetitiveness" and her lust for intellectual and aesthetic variety which seemed to disqualify her from entering into the spirit of the place. She might have added the seductive prerogative that an advanced bourgeois society bestows upon artists and intellectuals by supplying them with astonishingly specialized roles. One obvious reason for her ambivalence, and her relatively accommodating re-entry, is her desire to be "Susan Sontag"—critic, novelist, moviemaker, radical. Perhaps this is not so much a matter of fame or of vulgar notoriety as it is of the opportunity for an individual to acquire a unique combination of talents. In the light of the commonplace notion that advanced industrial technology is a threat to individualism, this may seem something of a paradox. North Vietnam is a much smaller country, with a far less demanding and intricate technology, but it is unlikely to produce anyone as individualized as Sontag. She is a distinctive product of a culture which exalts the individual performance of the most highly specialized skills. Of all the ways in which our society rewards its intellectuals, perhaps none is more effective as a solvent of the radical will.

From a literary viewpoint, also, the conclusion of *Trip to Hanoi* might be described as an easy, conventional compromise. It seems to follow an old familiar pattern for resolving the pastoral opposition between complex and simple ways of life. Sontag returns to the corrupt world of power and wealth, and to all of the possibilities for pleasure she had found missing in the rarefied moral environment of North Vietnam. At the same time, by invoking the ideal of revolution, she testifies to the spiritual change wrought in her by the retreat. A skeptical Empsonian critic also would observe, no doubt, that this vague political affirmation may help to assuage her guilt. It is like the rustic's posture Frost adopts, and so cagily satirizes, at the end of "New Hampshire," when the farmer-poet is challenged by a New York sophisticate:

> Well, if I had to choose one or the other
> I choose to be a plain New Hampshire farmer
> With an income in cash of say a thousand
> (From say a publisher in New York City).

One might conclude that *Trip to Hanoi* merely illustrates, once again, how well the pastoral mode can serve the writer who wants nothing less than the best of both worlds.

My own sense of the matter, however, is somewhat different. It would be a mistake, I believe, to dismiss Sontag's measured claim, at the end, that she came back from Vietnam with a fresh conception of what a revolutionary commitment might entail for privileged Americans like herself.

Soon after leaving Indochina she is in Paris hearing from French acquaintances about their recent experience in the abortive May revolution. What strikes her is the fact that they are still possessed by the new feelings they had discovered when, for a few weeks, "vast numbers of ordinarily suspicious, cynical urban people, workers and students, behaved with unprecedented generosity and warmth and spontaneity toward each other." In Paris they had known a change of heart like the one she had undergone in Vietnam. At first she too had been cynical and suspicious, unable to credit the self-effacing solidarity and simplicity of the Vietnamese. But then, with the suddenness of a conversion, she had begun to enjoy a brief but exhilarating reprieve from the inhibitions on love and trust enforced by our competitive, individualistic culture. Later she again was compelled to overcome the same inhibitions, although now they took the form of literary scruples—scruples about invoking what our literary culture would assume to be the mere pastoral cliché "of the Western left-wing intellectual idealizing an agrarian revolution." But this time she breaks free, allowing herself to move beyond the limits we habitually set on our trust in human motives. One consequence of this psychic liberation, it seems, was to free her from the block she formerly had had against writing about her political convictions. It is as if she suddenly had regained confidence in the compatibility of her aesthetic and political aspirations. In Vietnam, as in Paris, the "revolution" had made possible a notable widening of the boundaries of human sympathy.

In many ways, then, *Trip to Hanoi* exemplifies the recent, though as yet imperfect, assimilation of American pastoralism to the politics of protest and radical aspiration. An inchoate thrust toward such a politics has been latent in the writing of native pastoralists since Thoreau's time. The retreat in the direction of nature has always had for its aim an amplified conception of human nature. By disengaging from the dominant bourgeois-Protestant culture with its constricting norms of work and success, sexual identity and family life, pastoralists then and now have been seeking alternatives to the shallow personality type encouraged and rewarded in our society. It is worth recalling, moreover, that in the classic American fables of the nineteenth century the "exploration of nature" usually involved an inspiriting contact with representatives of non-Western culture. Today's young radicals, in their refusal to pursue routine careers, gain the chance to imagine, and sometimes to enact, a simpler, less specialized, more spontaneous and affectionate way of life. What makes today's pastoralism different, however, is the degree to which it is informed by a heightened political awareness. In the present state of American society, the old-fashioned return, with its emphasis upon private accommodation and aesthetic consolation, no longer seems adequate or even possible. To be sure, only a visionary capable of denying the realities of political power would dream that such a creed of renunciation and its privileged adherents could, in and of themselves, transform the basic structure of this complex and powerful society.

The contribution of the new pastoralists to revolutionary politics, therefore, is for the time being chiefly exemplary. By enlarging the scope of feeling they exemplify all of those affective possibilities now foreclosed by the corporate state. They herald the emergence of a politics responsive, in ways that were inconceivable in the era of scarcity, to aesthetic motives. If such a program is compatible with a revolutionary ideology, it is because, first, it prefigures the transformation of the dominant culture and, second, because it provides a model for the transformation of human nature—of man himself—which has always been the ultimate concern of both pastoralism and left radicalism. Whether the pastoral ethos ever can be made to appeal to a larger, less privileged segment of the population, is of course unpredictable. One of the chief claims I would make for Sontag's New Left version of pastoral is, indeed, the vividness with which she discloses the limitations of the ethos at its center. That disclosure is not theoretical or abstract; it is evoked directly by her candid account of the inner resistance with which she herself met the prospect of a more ethical, egalitarian society. We are thereby compelled to recognize what rare qualities of mind and will, a capacity for virtual self-transcendence, are required of those favored Americans who would presume, under present circumstances, to call themselves revolutionaries.

Some green thoughts on a green theme

JOHN SEELYE

*Sirs: . . . For years, your readers have been told about the
terrible social and economic costs of packing too many
Americans into sprawling cities: the rising crime rate,
stumbling mass transportation, smog, ghettos, polluted
water, crowded schools. The other side of the coin—
people leaving the farms and small communities—is less
dramatic but still a part of the gradually diminishing
quality of our national life.*

*This tragedy besetting America has been under
way for decades and is a product of many factors, among
them the population shifts induced by federal government
activities and our free enterprise system's aversion to
controls and government planning.*

*The quality of life in America need not continue
to slide downward in both our congested and unpopulated
areas. But it will if we do not get some strong national
leadership to show us how to pull up our socks.*

William L. Guy
Governor
State of North Dakota
Bismarck, N.D.

The idea of the Garden is universal, and it is universally a Good
Idea, associated with prelapsarian happiness, with a Golden

Age, an Arcadia, an Eden, but it is also an idea whose meaning is defined by contrast: the happiness of Eden is threatened from within by the Devil, and ends with expulsion into the harsh world outside, expulsion from the beginning predetermined by the Divine Scheme, the Garden henceforth to be the nostalgic subject of regret and recrimination. The Garden is the type and symbol of the Womb, which is likewise haunted by necessity: nine months' stay and no longer—or death. Birth or Death, and Birth but the first outward push towards eventual Death. *Et in Arcadia ego.* The Garden therefore is a deep and a sacramental idea. It is also a political idea, perhaps for America *the* political idea, but America is not so much the end as a phase of a process, one more heave of the universal womb.

At once sacramental and political, the idea of the Garden is also an important literary force, responsible for several "versions" (in Empson's phrase) "of pastoral," versions which (as Empson demonstrates) betray a political impulse. "Pastoral," as a literary idea, has its origins in the idylls of the Greeks, which in turn presumably developed from some dim, preliterary, sacramental source and, by way of Theocritus, inspired the mannered bucolics of Virgil—the *Eclogues*—and accounted likewise for the lyric intensity of his *Georgics,* which are a poetic rendering of the materials of Cato's (and Varro's) *De Re Rustica.* Since it was Virgil who

This ramble covers much of the same pastoral territory claimed by the scholarly imperatives of Henry Nash Smith's *Virgin Land: The American West as Symbol and Myth* (1950, 1970), Leo Marx's *The Machine in the Garden: Technology and the Pastoral Ideal in America* (1964), Edwin Fussell's *Frontier: American Literature and the American West* (1965), and Leslie Fiedler's *The Return of the Vanishing American* (1968). I should like to declare a special indebtedness to Fussell's study, and cite as well two recent essays by (respectively) Marx and Smith with which I take issue here: "Pastoral Ideals and City Troubles," in *The Journal of General Education,* XX (1969), and elsewhere; and "Consciousness and Social Order: The Theme of Transcendence in the Leatherstocking Tales," *Western American Literature,* V (1970).

Reference within is also made to D. H. Lawrence, *Studies in Classic American Literature* (1923); William Empson, *Some Versions of Pastoral* (1935); Bruno Snell, *The Discovery of the Mind,* trans. T. G. Rosenmeyer (1953); Peter Thorslev, *The Byronic Hero: Types and Prototypes* (1962); and George A. Starr, *Defoe and Spiritual Autobiography* (1965). Ethel Seybold's *Thoreau: The Quest and the Classics* (1951) provided ample testimony for established the Arcadian convention adopted or adapted by later English Renaissance writers, and since his pastoral mode was nothing if not political, whether implicitly, as in the *Eclogues,* or explicitly, as in the *Georgics,* let us start with Virgil.

Virgil's *Eclogues* occupy, perhaps define, what Bruno Snell has called a "spiritual" and what Leo Marx calls a "middle landscape," a world of the pastoral imagination, a purely literary world borrowed from the Greek original, and bearing only a marginal relationship to the Italian countryside of Virgil's day. But it is a world which, however much "spiritual," cannot escape the necessities of political involvement. In the very first eclogue, we are presented with the paradigm of the Displaced Shepherd, Meliboeus, whose exile is an allusion to the redistribution of farmlands by Augustus to his returning veterans. Those shepherds who are allowed to keep their lands, like Tityrus (Virgil), do so with a great sense of gratitude to the "young god" in Rome, the Emperor who has abjured them to leave off their erotic pastimes and poetry and return to their neglected fields and flocks.

Though a number of the succeeding eclogues are devoted to the erotic burden of the traditional Greek model—for the most part the theme of unrequited love—they all must be read in light of the first, "expulsion" poem. In the fifth eclogue, the theme is the death and deification of Daphnis, an allegorical reference to the martyrdom of Julius Caesar, and, most important, the fourth, or "messianic" eclogue, prophesies a return to the Golden Age under the rule of Augustus, an event heralded by the birth of a mysterious child. Though the language is literary and the situations traditional, the peace of Virgil's Augustan garden is again and

Thoreau's classical influences, but my treatment of Thoreau is chiefly indebted to Sherman Paul's *The Shores of America: Thoreau's Inward Exploration* (1958). Though we stress different themes, his exegeses, particularly of *The Maine Woods,* have allowed me to be sparing in that regard.

The epigraph is taken from *Life* ("Letters to the Editors"), July 30, 1971, and the Sunday *New York Times,* mentioned within, is for July 25, 1971.

Perhaps I should add that the section on Thoreau is from a study-in-progress on "The River in American Literature," and that certain other aspects of this essay have appeared in different form as *The Kid* (1972).

again interrupted by events which reflect or are caused by the affairs of the outside world, disruptions which provide the *Eclogues* with their chief tension, a unity of disparities. The pastoral world, though a spiritual landscape, a world of art, cannot escape the temporal imperatives of Rome or the source of those imperatives, cosmic revolution. The poet may celebrate the green world of Arcadia, but he also must celebrate the golden rule of Augustus, which permits the pastoral peace to continue.

What is implicit in the *Eclogues* is explicit in the *Georgics,* supposedly commissioned by Maecenas, the Roman patron of literature who encouraged poets to serve the interests of the State—that is to say, the efforts of Augustus to return the Empire to tranquillity after an age of civil wars. Where the *Eclogues* are concerned with the world of imagination and poetry, the *Georgics* describe the very real world of the Italian countryside, providing a rich blend of folkways and myths reflecting the order of Nature— the cycles and signs which every farmer must heed—which likewise is reflected in the order of the State. The Sun and Augustus are at the center of cosmos and microcosmos respectively. Though the *Georgics* is basically a poeticized handbook of agrarian practices, including detailed description of farm management and such technical aspects as plow construction and beekeeping, it is also a celebration of the land and rural values, most particularly the concept of work. The *Georgics* themselves are a sort of enforced labor, which Virgil turns to in each book with a sigh of resignation, only occasionally allowing himself a digressive flight of the imagination.

The philosophical (and mythic) center of the *Georgics* is found in the last book, for the orderly kingdom of the bees, described at length, is a symbol of the ideal state among men, a state of temporal felicity which depends, as the story of Aristaeus implies, on maintaining good relationships with the gods through sacrifice and devotion. The story of Aristaeus, his descent into the watery kingdom (never far from the pastoral scene) and his

579

struggle to wrest an answer from Proteus, is, moreover, a sort of mini-epic, a symbolic preparation for Virgil's most ambitious undertaking, the *Aeneid*, a celebration of Empire and Augustus. But the *Aeneid* is in many ways an intensification and heightening through narrative and drama of the themes found in the *Georgics* and *Eclogues:* taken together they represent the ideal, triune achievement of the classical poet, the "pastoral," the "didactic," and "epic," each containing elements of the other, and the epic in turn containing elements of the dramatic genres, comedy and tragedy. All three have an increasingly intense political emphasis, as if reflecting the consciousness of the poet that to dwell in Arcadia is not only difficult but undesirable—"inglorious ease" is the way Virgil puts it at the close of the *Georgics* (Loeb translation). Those who live in a spiritual landscape do so at the expense of others, whether exiles, like Meliboeus, or soldiers, like Pollio, who risk death and deprivation so that shepherds may dally in the shade, or leaders like Augustus, who struggle to unify the Empire and keep it from division.

Though the classical divisions separate pastoral from didactic, if the essential quality of "pastoral" is the idealization of rural life, then both the *Eclogues* and *Georgics* are versions of pastoral, the one "spiritual" and imaginary, the other utilitarian and "realistic," but both indicative of the political implications of the green world. In Virgil's case, pastoral politics are decidedly establishmentarian, of the nostalgic or reactionary kind. The *Georgics*, in particular, establish rural morality and pursuits as the basis for a sound nationalism, a time-honored precept for orderly (i.e., repressive) governments, from Moses to Mao. Getting the people back to work on the land is the ground rule of *Realpolitik*, cities being the places where immorality and intellect (and counter-revolutions) are fostered. Virgil is throughout a poet of Empire and Emperors, whose pastoral mode is a blending of nostalgia for an earlier, simpler Golden Age, the promise of a political messiah who will return the world to peace and prosperity, and an emphasis on the rural, agrarian life as a moral and economic basis for a healthy State. If the pastoral realm is the middle landscape, life there is an idealized existence, a pattern perfectly in harmony with the forces of nature, all vibrating to the echo idea of national well-being and orderliness. Land, and life on the land, is after all *the* imperial imperative.

It is also the Jeffersonian imperative, and the Jeffersonian vision for America, though dear to the hearts of academic liberals, is nothing if not Virgilian pastoral, half-dream, half-dung. Somewhat democratized by Enlightenment ideas of natural rights, Jefferson's concept of freedom is based on a primitive land-capitalism, and his concept of government is elitist—autocratic. Though modified by Rousseauistic concepts of individualism, Jefferson's pastoralism was clearly an inheritance of the neo-Augustanism of the 18th-century English, which was in turn a reaction against the Civil War of the previous era. The natural ideal for the English Augustans was the Park, nature manicured and refined, with the concomitant pastoral ideal of repose in a rustic retreat. Much of this, interestingly enough, emerged from the enforced leisure, the rustication of Pope and his Tory friends, early on a sort of exile band, kept in the country by the reigning Whig ascendancy and forced to make a virtue of necessity. The result, however, was a conventionalized complaint, the groaning of the Augustan man in power (the Virgilian moan) that all he really wants is to remain secluded in his home in the country, reading, writing, etc., etc., which Jefferson so often uttered and which his Liberal posterity so often takes seriously.

The sources of Jeffersonian agrarianism are manifold, but like his beloved Palladian architecture, it bears a clear, neoclassical mark. Jefferson, sitting atop his Monticello, his "little mountain," like Washington on nearby Mount Vernon (which has both military and pastoral associations), is the Olympian intellectual-political leader as his predecessor was the Olympian military-political founder of his country, both going halvers with the Augustan image. The kind of agrarian autocracy (or squirearchy) that Jefferson envisioned, moreover, depended on America's

581

producing raw materials for Europe's dark, Satanic Mills, thus keeping all the squalor, filth, and intolerable deprivation where it belonged—somewhere else—like the slave system, itself an essential hypocrisy, a luxurious means of maintaining America's political independence and spiritual and intellectual freedom. Jefferson's equivalent today is the suburbanite who relies on zoning and other "sensible" regulations to keep the squalor somewhere else. "I've got mine" is very deep in the pastoral consciousness of America: Tityrus is with us always, for the Middle Landscape is nothing if not Middle Class, the Spiritual Landscape its counterpart, a sort of licensed grove, academic or otherwise.

As Edwin Fussell demonstrates, the Jeffersonian Landscape was most clearly blocked out by an immigrant Frenchman, Hector St. John de Crèvecoeur, whose *Letters from an American Farmer* provides a clear diagram of American pastoral on the Virgilian plan. The domain of Crèvecoeur's Farmer is the middle area between the Eastern seaboard and the Western wilderness. Unlike the industrious, virtuous, mercantile Easterner or the luxurious, vicious, slave-exploiting Southerner, the dweller in the Middle Landscape has only land for his wealth, and must depend on his own labor, but ownership of that land grants him a delightful blend of tranquillity and freedom—a perfect state of pastoral (georgic) independence, with manual labor as an ethical norm, the family as the chief social and economic unit, and plenty of time for more spiritual activities like pursuing bees and writing essays. Like the Virgilian model, the Farmer derives his virtue from contact with the land, and as in the Fourth Georgic, bees are put forth as a social ideal, a miniature commonwealth, for the Farmer is a loyal subject of the English monarch.

The political and economic landscape of Crèvecoeur's America is singularly like that of Virgil's Italy, but there is one great exception: the Frontier. The nearest thing to the American idea of the Frontier for Virgil would have been the northern limits of the Roman Empire, fronting the Britons, the Gauls, and the Germanic tribes, but Virgil does not regard this as a dynamic,

582

ever-moving zone. He shrinks in civilized distaste from the idea of the barbarians as from the hardships of the soldiers stationed on the border. That line is regarded as a fixed zone, a sort of Roman Wall protecting the well-being of the farmer-citizen. There is, that is to say, no accommodation in Virgilian pastoral for wildness. All is either spiritual and Arcadian or domesticated and georgic. Nature may threaten, but she can be placated by observing the correct rituals and making the proper sacrifices, and the farmer who keeps his yearly rounds in harmony with natural cycles will prosper. The Virgilian Middle Landscape is one of balance and fixed proportion.

The Farmer's world is similarly balanced and cyclical, but the planetary movement of the Middle Landscape has as its antithesis the lateral, linear movement of the frontier zone to the West. The Farmer regards the Frontier with 18th-century eyes, which saw raw Nature as the type and symbol of chaos, associating it with all things bad, including political turmoil and rebellion. The Farmer therefore regards the Frontier as a borderland of anarchy, where civilized men are quickly reduced to semi-barbaric hunters, the ease of the backwoods life tempting from the normal (Virgilian) labors of agriculture, and where Indians, the inhabitants of the wilderness beyond, quickly degenerate, taking on the worst vices of civilization. Though a bad place, the frontier is a necessary evil, and the lazy backwoods hunter of today prepares the way with ax and gun for the more industrious, agrarian settlers who will follow him tomorrow. The frontier, clearly, is part of a larger, benevolent design, and wildness is an undesirable element, but one capable of being converted to tame, rolling farmland. Crèvecoeur's diagram, then, provides us with an ideal scheme of the benevolent pastoral statism that exists at the outbreak of the Revolution, and on which Jefferson posited his agrarian utopia, where wildness is accommodated by being domesticated.

But all this is changed in the last chapter of the Letters, when the outbreak of revolution forces the Loyalist Farmer to flee westward, leaping the frontier zone and heading into the wilderness with his family. Though he hopes that other settlers will follow him, the Farmer has nonetheless become part of the farthest frontier, and the nice pastoral decorums of his Middle Landscape existence are shattered for evermore. Once Tityrus, he is now Meliboeus, the exile. This retreat to the farther landscape is, as Leo Marx has shown us, a mythical component of American experience and literature, but it is one which has no equivalent in the Virgilian pastoral mode. Virgil, like Tityrus, stays behind to extol the State, while Meliboeus is heard of no more. In the westward flight of Crèvecoeur's Farmer, we witness a complex shift of values and sympathies that anticipates a new phase of pastoral thought and action, not so new perhaps as renewed, which opposes romantic rebellion and restlessness to neoclassic balance and harmony: wild, as opposed to mild pastoral, set in the Farther, not the Middle Landscape.

At heart a Middle Landscaper, a man of deep loyalties to the system and the State, the Farmer is made a rebel in spite of himself. In fact, he is a neutral, who objects to being victimized by marauding Indians in the pay of the King, but who does not wish to join his neighbors in self-defense, which will be surely interpreted as revolt. He finds himself in the middle indeed, and solves his dilemma by escaping it, but in seeking some sort of haven in the wilderness he becomes a virtual outlaw and anarchist. It is this Farther Landscape, this Wild Pastoral, which is endemic to the American pastoral experience, and which is the source of our native radicalism as well. It may be opposed to the values and meaning of the Middle Landscape, for its sources are anything but Virgilian.

Wildness as a positive concept is positively romantic, but like so many romantic concepts, it is strongly rooted in a remote, mythic antiquity. We may trace elements to primitive Christianity, but other aspects include the inheritance of those northern barbarians whom the civilized Virgil regarded with such distaste. Let us start, however, by opposing Christian pastoralism to the Virgilian variety, for the Man of Peace comes down to us with distinctly radical if not revolutionary implications. Though Christian pastoralism shares with the Virgilian mode both the concept of the shepherd as an ideal man and the idea of a messianic leader—aspects in the first part a heritage of the Old Testament, agrarian traditions, but which, because of the Roman contingency, may have an iconographic and mythic debt to the classical (pagan) tradition as well—beyond the images there is a radical difference in emphasis. Christian pastoralism, like Virgil's, may have held out an ideal of simplicity and purity to a world troubled by political turmoil, but it was not an ideal which found universal favor with the wealthy, ruling classes—Virgil's audience.

Though they use similar symbols, Christian and Virgilian pastoralism are virtually antithetical concepts. Despite the apprehensions of the Roman colonials who put Christ to death, Christian pastoralism was not a nationalist movement, nor was Christ a sort of Jewish Zapata or Guevara. Christian pastoralism did not look to the temporal establishment of a new Golden Age, but to a New Jerusalem, a kingdom beyond this one, where Edenic bliss would be gained by all who were willing to renounce their claims to earthly prosperity. Revolutionary Pastoralism, if we may call it that, is posited on a salvational, mystical, transcendental notion of a future, not a present state. It is not only evangelical, therefore, but evolutionary. By contrast, Reactionary Pastoralism is strongly tied to ideas of a temporal state, and hence to ideas of permanence, order, status quo, which it promises to effect by a moral and political retrenchment, made desirable through the appeal of nostalgia. Reactionary Pastoralism may be somewhat mystical in its concepts of harmony, with the ideas of home, soil, race, nationality, and hero-leader being held in a sort of transcendental union, but such transcendence never questions the supremacy of the State, the infallibility of the Leader, and the duty of the Citizen to obey any and all mandates. Christian Pastoralism, by contrast, ennobles and elevates the individual over any temporal authority, bearing as it does on the uniqueness of every soul, which will find perfect union not on earth but with God the Father beyond—in the Farther Landscape. Both kinds

585

of pastoralism look to messiah figures, but where Christ is a self-effacing, self-sacrificing teacher, elevated by martyrdom to a sacramental agent of personal salvation for every man, Augustus is a symbol of Empire, all-pervasive, all-powerful, a God on earth beyond whom there is no appeal, but who at most can only render a temporal, Middle-Landscape felicity.

Where the Virgilian Middle Landscape is an elitist haven of earthly happiness, the Christian (transmundane) Farther Landscape holds out hope of eternal joy to the lowliest. The lowly are cherished, not because their labors are useful to the State, but because they are the antithesis of the State, whose symbols are power and wealth. What is Caesar's has his image on it, but what Christ seeks has nothing engraved upon it, nor can it be stored in treasuries or granaries. It is best found in that *other* Farther Landscape, the desert places of the world, whether the howling wilderness of John the Baptist or the deserted Garden of Gethsemane. These are the places of the spirit, where one may find oneself and one's God in solitude, and where one finds a spirituality transcending the frustrated desire for beautiful shepherd boys. Unlike the Virgilian Arcadian Landscape, this Farther Landscape is less pleasurable than penitential, and gives way to the anchorite's cell of the Middle Ages.

In the Middle Ages also the idea of the Farther Landscape merges with the pagan matter of the Arthurian legends, emerging as the perilous quest for the Grail, the archetype of that retreat which Leo Marx detects in so much American literature. For it is also the original of the many questing journeys endemic to the Romance and to its lateral descendents, the Picaresque novel and the *Bildungsroman*. Elitist, surely, and extrapolated from feudal notions of caste, the knightly element of the Romance tradition was, as Henry Nash Smith has shown us, to provide a native American (and purportedly democratic) literature with one of its greatest dilemmas. In Spenser's *Faerie Queene*—where the classical (humanist) tradition is neatly blended with the Christian—the problem is apparently solved through the symbolic rise of Saint George (a name meaning "Farmer," from the same root as "georgic") from humble rustic to national savior, thus bridging the matter of class. But, as in the Virgilian pastoral tradition, the nominal salvational emphasis is but part of the larger tribute to a secular leader, Queen Elizabeth, and the overall purpose of the poem is to portray the ideal secular citizen; the Gentleman, another elitist model which haunted a purportedly egalitarian America, largely through the nearly legendary (for the 19th-century American) figure of Sir Philip Sidney, himself the author of *the* Elizabethan pastoral, *Arcadia,* like *The Faerie Queene* a blend of classical and romantic elements, in effect establishing the setting for Shakespeare's fantastic romantic (salvational) comedies.

Throughout the various versions of Elizabethan pastoral, there is a constant (Christian) stress on the contrast between the simple life of the countryside and the corrupt, vicious life in the town and court, a theme entirely missing from the Virgilian model, in which the town (Rome) and the court (Caesar) are looked to for order and harmony. Thus Spenser's Colin Clout is no fantastic, Virgilian shepherd, but a recognizable English countryman, a rough, honest contrast to the decaying manners of the cosmopolitan center, and the prototype of the "good man" so essential to the English satiric mode. He has his equivalent in Royall Tyler's *The Contrast,* the "good American," the inhabitant of the Middle Landscape who is held up against the "bad American," the effete snob who has taken on European airs, a contrast which was to become, as we have already seen, part of Jefferson's foreign and domestic policy. This type springs ultimately from the emphasis on the Worthy Lowly in Christian pastoralism, and appears both in Langland's and Chaucer's Plowmen. Those rural, medieval exemplars of agrarian goodness are closely tied to the well-being of the State, forming a link between the farmers of Virgil's *Georgics* and those of Jefferson's ideal commonwealth by introducing the common man, not the king, as the keystone of society. *Piers Plowman,* in particular, emerging as it did from the Lollard controversy of the 14th century—with its stress on a strict imitation of Christ's simplicity—at once renewed the egalitarian intimations of primitive Christianity and, by using it as a gauge for political reform, laid the basis for 19th-century agrarian populism.

But all of these exemplars of rural goodness (including the populists, who, as the last hold-out of Jeffersonian agrarianism were basically land-capitalists fighting against the centralization of power by the railroads and banks) are inhabitants of the Middle Landscape, and are reforming rather than truly revolutionary elements. Revolution in the modern sense of the word is a Romantic idea, made possible by Rousseauistic concepts of the individual and the State, but in the medieval legends of Robin Hood there are already suggestions of the radical implication of the Farther Landscape, for the Outlaw in Green inhabits a version of Wild Pastoral, lurking in Sherwood Forest with Maid Marian and his Merry Men. Though legendarily of gentle birth (the romance imperative), Robin Hood, like all outlaws, forswears his rights and privileges, and identifies himself with the cause of the lowly, rendering unto the meek their rightful inheritance here and now, one of his chief lieutenants a renegade cleric. The figure of Robin Hood is a powerful mythic blend, undoubtedly sharing with the militant, masculine, powerful Christ of medieval poetry resemblances to such a pagan god of the woods as Odin, and having a certain underground quality, too, in league with those other wearers of the green, the faery folk, in particular Robin Goodfellow —Puck. It is in the figure of Robin Hood that Christ turns outlaw, ultimately merging with such charismatic latter-day saints as Zapata and Guevara, rendering the radical implication of the Farther Landscape by applying salvational attitudes to this, not to some other domain, and implementing it by guerrilla warfare. The wildwood becomes a *rude* Arcadia, dominated by a hunting not a shepherd culture, a haven and an asylum for the oppressed and disenfranchised. If, in primitive Christianity, the wilderness is the penitential dwelling place of prophets and seers, in the legends of Robin Hood it becomes a jolly sort of green gaol, the only haven for good men when corrupt men are in power, and a place from which to sortie forth and punish the degenerate establishment.

The green element is the faery element, connoting change (growth), misrule, revolution, and it is an important aspect of Shakespeare's plays, where good things happen outside, in the country and the wildwood, and bad things happen inside, in the castle or the town. Whether it is Lear's heath, the Forest of Arden (a coincidental anagram for Ar[cadia-E]den), or Prospero's Island, the natural world is a place of redemption, realization, relaxation, or recreation, one which is often associated with exiled Right during the reign of tyrannical Wrong. Lear is but the strongest example: there is also the Duke of *As You Like It* and Prospero and Timon of Athens, the Duke in particular being colored Robin Hood green. But in Shakespeare's benign world of melodramatic oppositions, evil takes care of itself: it is the role of good chiefly to wait out its turn (or return). Those, like Lear and Timon, who rage, go mad, and die.

For Leo Marx, Shakespeare's paradigm of the New World is Prospero's island, an Arcadian utopia wrested from a savage, hag-ridden wilderness by the power of white magic—that is to say, by the civilizing power of knowledge, symbolized by Prospero's books. This is, again, the Virgilian version of pastoral, in which the salvational power flows from the East, in which, as for Crèvecoeur, wildness is regarded as something unholy, bestial, pagan, fit only for conversion into an orderly garden. Marx points out that the tidings from the New World tended to represent America as either an Arcadian, Edenic Garden or a Howling Wilderness, and that *The Tempest* tries to accommodate both visions by emphasizing the conversion of Wilderness to Garden. But Marx, who is interested in the Garden aspect of the New World, seems to ignore the tendency of the Arcadian news to come out of Virginia and points south, the Desert news to come out of New England. This dichotomy is as much a matter of climate as it is of ideology and propaganda, but certainly we can see the cultural and economic reasons behind a Cavalier Arcadia and a Puritan Desert. The Puritans *needed* a Wilderness, to be voices in, just as they needed (in the worst way) satanic Indians, and it is they, not the establishmentarian-pastoralist

Cavaliers (whose heir was the Middle-Landscape architect himself, Thomas Jefferson), who self-consciously inhabited the Farther Landscape, establishing in the American consciousness for good and all the compound image of adversity and virtue which was to become the dominant popular idea of the Frontier. Though hardly a version of Robin Hood, the Puritans were outcasts, were fugitives, at once a Chosen People and Prophet-Saints, pariahs and seers who cherished the image of the New World as Desert, a place of trial and hardship in preparation for a world beyond, but a world mirrored in its secular equivalent by the governance of divinely elected Saints.

The Tempest has nothing to do with this vision of the New World. Notably, the hard work has all been done before the play begins. The castaway parable which may be read as a symbolic representation of those many tidings which came from New England during the late 17th and early 18th centuries was not written until a hundred years later, and is Dissenter Defoe's *Robinson Crusoe*. Despite Defoe's nationality, the thematic content and seminal influence of *Robinson Crusoe* is such that for all intents and purposes it could be read as the first American as well as the first English novel, a fork as it were in that interesting, bipartisan genesis. Like Crèvecoeur's *Letters,* Defoe's *Robinson Crusoe* provides us with an ideal diagram of the imperial imperative, the process by which the Farther becomes the Middle Landscape. In a sense it takes up (though fifty years earlier) where the Farmer's narrative leaves off, on the Frontier, and modifies Crèvecoeur's conception of the Wilderness by making of it not merely an asylum but actually a salvational, a transforming territory.

Regeneration takes place on two levels. On the metaphysical level, Robinson Crusoe is a parable of spiritual (psychological) salvation, as George Starr has demonstrated, a fictional, high-adventure version of spiritual autobiography. Crusoe, having disobeyed his Father by running away to sea, becomes, in his own words, a "Jonah," and after a series of light taps of warning from Providence, is marooned on a desert island, where, in his own words, he becomes another "Adam." Providence supplies him with a Bible and a shipload of supplies, and in time revelation, and still later, companionship and rescue. As Crusoe's spiritual state improves, so does his physical well-being, and it is abundantly clear that what we are presented with is a demonstration of the Puritan theory of the elect, in which a whole shipload of men is drowned that one man may be saved.

In the popular mind this aspect of the book tends to be forgotten—what we remember is Crusoe's resourcefulness, his enterprising, middle-class spirit, which enables him to survive by profiting from adversity. This is the physical level of regeneration, the strength which emerges when a man is forcibly returned to a primitive stage of existence, the strength of maintaining a familiar relationship with the essentials of life: corn, bread, clay pots. But Crusoe remains throughout a civilized man, indeed a brilliant portrait of the English colonial mind, from whence the resourceful Yankee sprang, that eternally restless surveyor of the Farther Landscape. When the Puritans first arrived they lived in caves until they could build houses on the English plan, with boards laboriously fashioned. And Crusoe's first manufacture, once he is secure in his cave, is likewise a table and a chair, painfully fashioned, so that he may sit down to his meal like a proper Englishman, and not have to eat it squatting on his hams like a bloody savage. If the psychological burden of the book is Crusoe's increasing awareness and eventual acknowledgment of God's power and grace, the physical aspect concerns the increasing imposition of Crusoe's power over *his* appointed domain.

Though the wilderness is salvational, it is only so through providing an atmosphere of adversity, and Crusoe's (and Defoe's) attitude towards Nature is typically 18th-century. The abundance of the tropical island exists to be put to order, to serve mankind in shapely, Middle-Landscape ways. Characteristically, Crusoe continues to extend his orderly domain throughout the novel, until he has a good part of the island under control. It is here that we have an early equivalent of Crèvecoeur's diagram, with the conventional flow of progress from east to west. Thus, Crusoe first settles on the Eastern side of his island, the sea-side, where his ship originally foundered. He lives there because Providence has dictated it—because his stores, lugged from the ship, are necessarily stored there—and because he has a view of the open sea, from whence rescue must come. The Western side, on the other hand, faces the savage continent of South America (Trinidad, actually), and it is this side which represents danger—wildness. Yet it is here that Crusoe locates his little farm, in an Arcadian grove which he discovers soon after his religious awakening, where he keeps goats on the Virgilian model, regretfully returning each time to his Eastern home. Eventually he makes the dreadful discovery of the cannibals' feasting place, on the Western side also, and perilously close to his farm, and from that point on his Arcadia is a mixed blessing, threatened as it is by the absolute wildness of the West.

But it is the savages who eventually provide Crusoe with the human companion which he has so long desired, and in Friday he makes the discovery that the loathed cannibals close up are not so bad after all. Like Cooper's Chingachgook, who has an unpleasant habit of slicing off scalps, but otherwise is a pattern of nobility, Friday has an undeniable flaw, the mark of the man-beast. But, as his name suggests, he is a stage in Crusoe's atonement, whose natural, filial (Aenean) piety casts unfavorable reflections on Crusoe's own past attitude towards *his* father, and whose natural goodness and simplicity make Crusoe's attempts to convert him seem somewhat redundant if not ridiculous. Reflecting Defoe's attitude towards Nature, Friday may be interpreted as personified wildness, a salvational antithesis to Shakespeare's Caliban. If anything, Friday is closer to Ariel, and when mutineers land on the islands, he plays an Ariel-like role in leading them astray. Part and parcel of the notion of a salvational wildwood, Friday is the original of the many Noble Savages in American literature, he and his fur-clad, musket-toting Master providing the original pattern for that typical frontier pair isolated by Necessity—and Leslie Fiedler.

As we have seen, the Augustan literary triad established by

Virgil consists of the Eclogue (bucolic), the Georgic (didactic) and the Epic. The Eclogue emphasizes leisure and poetry and love; the Georgic, work, worship, production, security; the Epic, adventure, warfare, and the establishment of empire. If we regard Defoe's novel with this particular scheme in mind, *Robinson Crusoe* lies somewhere between Georgic and Epic, modified somewhat by the influence of Christian and Romance themes. Very little study has been made of the roots of the adventure story, the genre which Defoe helped to establish, and which, through Cooper's influence, became the chief literary means by which the Frontier was interpreted. But it seems obvious that the Epic is the ur-form, with various transmutations through the Romance and its counter-form, the Picaresque Novel, with elements of the Travel Narrative and Dryden's Heroic Drama added as well. The point is that the adventure story depends for its effects upon movement through open space, or struggles to escape closed space (hence the success of Scott's formula: pursuit, capture, escape), that the greatest available space is out-of-doors, and therefore the association of the adventure-hero with the epic-hero is inevitable—but misleading. For the adventure-hero, unlike the epic-hero, is a person of no great cosmic significance. He does not, that is to say, attain apotheosis, but only prospers on a more modest scale, surmounting obstacles and perhaps winning or marrying a fortune.

So it is with Robinson Crusoe. Despite the spiritual, salvational theme (a counterpart to apotheosis), Crusoe is very much an average man, for the most part dedicated to establishing his material well-being and ensuring his security from harm. Indeed, it is his averageness which makes his story so interesting: he fails as many times as he succeeds. And yet the *effect* of extending his domain over the island is imperial, and hence suggests the epic. Crusoe imports his own culture with him, like a typical colonizer, and insists on imposing it on Friday, who learns English rather than his Master learning Carib. Crusoe's rule is similarly imposed on the Spaniards who next come to his island, who are made to agree to a literal social contract recognizing him as "Governor."

593

Having been spiritually purified (reformed) through penitential isolation, Crusoe in stages becomes the ruler of his own world, progressively "civilizing" his island. In the beginning, forced to do all his own work, the techniques of which he renders in minute detail, Crusoe in effect is the central figure in a desert island Georgic, but as soon as a labor force is available, he moves over into the epic zone, and begins to rule and regulate "his" people. In time, one imagines, his little island would resemble Gibraltar—a hollowed-out outpost of empire in the Caribbean.

Warfare and travel, the two great epic (and adventure) themes are of minimal importance to *Robinson Crusoe*—though the hero does take longer getting to his island than most readers remember. The chief tensions are provided by the two great Puritan themes, the struggle with one's self and the struggle with adversity. These are also the great themes of tragedy, but are conducted here (as with the epic element) on a relatively low plane, and, moreover, are successfully terminated. What we have, in effect, is a Protestant Ethic version of the Georgic, where Work has a salvational as well as physical-survival aspect, the epic theme having been reduced to wilderness adversity, to the struggles of the hero to master himself and his environment. Again, the Arcadian element is virtually absent, and where present, is associated with great danger. Crusoe's salvation, both spiritual and physical, lies in work and hardship, not poetry and song, plentiful opportunities for which are provided by the wilderness (frontier) environment.

Like Shakespeare's wildwood folk, like Robin Hood, Crusoe is an outlaw and exile, but unlike them he does not represent wronged virtue in hiding. The wilderness for Crusoe is a penitential asylum, a place of spiritual isolation where he may discover his proper relationship to God and himself. The fun and games (and Maid Marian) associated with Sherwood Forest and the Forest of Arden are entirely missing, as is the Romance theme of gentle or noble birth. Crusoe is a middle-class man, who, despite his rebellion against his father, never really escapes his middle place in life. Even at the height of his rule on his island, he never classes himself as anything greater than "Governor," the zenith of middle-class, colonial aspiration. Contentment is his greatest joy, the snug sense of well-being that comes from being secure in his cave, all his goods (except his gunpowder) stored nearby. Like Crèvecoeur's Farmer, Defoe's Robinson Crusoe is a demonstration of the middle-classness of the Middle Landscape, the tendency of the frontier impulse to regard wildness not as an important thing in itself, but as a territory of adversity, a place where one improves oneself by "improving" the land, a place not so much of "retreat" as of militant advance—indeed, "frontier" was originally a military term, connoting the forefront of an advancing army, thus the farthest line of expanding empire.

Enter "wild Rousseau," for whom *Robinson Crusoe "sera le [livre] premier que lira mon Émile; seul il composera durant long-temps toute sa bibliothèque, et il y tiendra toujours une place distinguée."* It was not the wildness of the book which recommended it for Emile's education, but its pragmatic quality—the georgic quality as it were—but Rousseau nonetheless provided a romantic aura for the concept of "man alone," giving impetus to a latent emphasis in certain minor 18th-century English poets, a sort of Augustan underground which cherished notions of wildness and sensibility. The net result was Wordsworth's Child of Nature, the product of a spiritualized wildness which contributed greatly to the American literary concept of the frontier. But if Wordsworth absorbed Rousseau's ideas on education-in-nature, adding a certain mystic flavour derived from the German transcendentalists and populated his poems with wild children, idiots, and old leech gatherers, his concept of Nature seldom strays from the safe limits of the Middle Landscape, and his shepherds are too busy building stone walls to play pipes and write poetry. Wildness, for Wordsworth, has a rather park-like quality, and though he may thrill to more sublime aspects of nature, there is a quality of fright to his reaction. Thus his boy-rower flees the looming shadow-mountain, as Wordsworth himself was to flee the dark idea of Revolution and find shelter in the Establishment.

It was Scott and Byron who made literary capital out of the idea of wildness and outlawry, each contributing his share to the American concept of the Farther Landscape. Scott, who (as Peter Thorslev has shown us) in Marmion created a noble villain out of such various stuff as the Gothic Novel, Jacobean Tragedy, and Rake Rochester, had the dubious pleasure of seeing his creation come to life in Lord Byron, who proceeded to outwrite and outsell his creator with *Childe Harold* and *Manfred,* thereby establishing the Noble Outlaw as a permanent (though restless) fixture in romantic literature. Scott continued the tradition in his historical romances, and in such a character as Fergus MacIvor in *Waverly,* revealed his mixed feelings toward the type. In the Highlander chieftain are combined elements of natural wildness and political revolution (Jacobite counter-revolution), but Fergus, like Satan, is Lord of the North, and like Milton's Great Rebel, he is doomed to failure and ignominy. The putative "hero" of the story, the characteristically wavering Waverley, retires from playing at revolution to the life of a comfortable country squire, stolidly in the middle of the Middle Landscape, halfway between England and Establishment and the wild highlands of Scotland.

Byron, alone of the English Romantics, attempted to combine Satan with Prometheus—the bad and the good rebel—in an atmosphere of natural wildness and personal and political rebellion, not only in his poetry but in his own life as well. Stagy, melodramatic, and overdrawn to modern sensibilities, Byron's isolatos had a great effect on the direction of an emerging American literature, as much perhaps as did the inherited form of Scott's historical romances. Like most writers with a popular touch, Byron had a genius for absorbing and recombining current tastes and preferences, and a great deal of luck as well. It was as much his personal history as his literary creations which resulted in his sudden fame. Still, one cannot denigrate his accomplishment: Byron is singly responsible for popularizing the idea of the noble outlaw, in such a poem as *The Corsair* coupling that idea with natural wildness, on the one hand (the seacoast, and the sea itself), and with rebellion against repression (the Pasha) on the other. And he gave the image a tragic seal by dying in the struggle for Greek independence from Turkish rule, an outlaw and outcast from the English established morality.

Though elitist surely (this George had little truck with the georgic element), Byron elected open (collar) rebellion as a means of assuaging feelings of guilt (self-hatred) and social alienation ([m]other hatred), converting his Protestant-Puritan heritage, with its dual doctrines of damnation and election, into a form of militant Satanism. Convinced of his own black sinfulness, Byron turned it into an instrument of defiance, and in the end sacrificed himself in a revolution which he saw as an attempt to purify Greece, enabling her to return to a condition equivalent to the Golden Age. The type and symbol of the Romantic Revolutionary, Byron never knew who he was, and I have no time or space here even to block out the contrary aspects of his personality and poetry. But he is the original romantic rebel, combining qualities of wildness, revolution, elitism, eroticism, and nostalgia, whose loathing for the establishment was a complex derivation from his own deep, Calvinist sense of personal depravity.

His contrary is Carlyle, low- not high-born Scot, equally a son of puritanical Calvinism, but who emphasized the positive side, elevating the concept of the Elect to a doctrine of Transcendental hero worship, and who, in his quest for higher Truth, ended in the halls of the old Scandinavian Mythology, the realm of those rude, wild but sincere gods, Thor and Odin. As we shall see, his Transcendental Heroes had a profound effect on the particular direction which Byronism took in the American atmosphere of a frontier-oriented, anti-establishmentarian Transcendentalism. It suffices to point out here that where Byron's heroes are in defiance of systems, earthly or heavenly, all regarded as repressive of individual freedom, Carlyle's ideal hero is that old Elizabethan tragic concept personified, God's Minister, whose righteousness is evinced by victory (heroic not tragic drama), usually through the epic activity, Warfare. Thus his greatest (or at least his favorite) hero is Cromwell, his anti-hero, Napoleon, the one founded on truth, the other on falsehood, the both founders of Empire through Revolution.

James Fenimore Cooper, America's first popular novelist, and

597

in a sense the creator of the American literary landscape, American Pastoral, shared Byron's talent for creative *assemblage*. In Leatherstocking, that phantasm of the Farther Landscape, we find elements combined which evoke various aspects of wildness and outlawry: as outlaw-and-hunter, man-alone-in-the-woods, Leatherstocking is surely a mixture of Robin Hood and Robinson Crusoe, and as Christian Exemplar, Child of Nature, Moral Guide, and Pathfinder, his outlawry is screened through a Wordsworthian (not a Byronic) sieve. A political conservative and landowning squire, Cooper's politics, like his novels, are close to those of his literary master, Sir Walter Scott, and are a version of Jeffersonian agrarianism—land capitalism. It is therefore a testimony to his unique relationship to the pastoral ideal that he created the prototypal holy outlaw for America, providing a necessary, mythic link between the Good Hunter, Dan'l Boone, and the Bad Renegade, Simon Girty. A saintly outcast, Leatherstocking inhabits a Farther Landscape made possible by the historical fact of the Western wilderness, an ideal representative of the personal freedom spawned by that anarchic territory, and a figure who bridges the elitist principles of Jeffersonian agrarianism and its later equivalent, middle-class Populism.

At once a literary romantic and a political conservative, Cooper created in Leatherstocking a common-man, vernacular-speaking hero, who while flattering the evolving democratic prejudices of his age, was yet able to preserve certain elitist notions by personifying the Wordsworthian concept of natural nobility. A primitive, fundamentalist Christian and Child of Nature as well, whose best friend is a Noble Savage, Leatherstocking is a wilderness equivalent of Wordsworth's Middle-Landscape shepherds and leech-gatherers. In *The Pioneers,* the first of the Leatherstocking Tales, he becomes an outlaw, and he remains an outsider through the rest of the cycle, either by exile (as in *The Prairie*) or by choice. Natty exemplifies the idea that a dweller in the Farther Landscape is innately superior, morally and physically, to the dweller in the Middle Landscape. Most important, however, while Leatherstocking is exemplary, he is also a special case, an acknowledged creation of nostalgia, figment of a departed Golden Age—that dream which animates the far right and far left extremes of American politics. Like a good politician, Natty Bumppo has something for everybody.

The Farther Landscape which Natty inhabits is a wilderness of bygone times, not so much a place as an act of memory and imagination. Like most pastoral creations, Natty is an idealized fragment of an earlier, simpler, better time. Cooper's political conservatism is too tangled an issue to be unsnarled here, but it had the undeniable effect of making Leatherstocking both an admirable ideal and an anachronism. Natty was never relevant, or rather his relevance was always a matter of the past, against which the present moment always pales, for the past is shaped by the inhabitants of the present, who may heighten it and color it at will. Except for *The Pioneers,* where he drew on his childhood memories of the upstate New York wilderness, Cooper's Farther Landscape was an act of the imagination purely, and since he was a political (if not a politic) man, an act of politics as well.

The Leatherstocking Tales appear to be anything but political, set as they are in a wilderness far from society, but Cooper's persistent retreat to an ever-renewed (and ever-younger) wilderness was a Timon-like exile from a world in which he was more and more uncomfortable as a relic of Jeffersonian agrarianism in a turbulent Jacksonian democracy. Like Crèvecoeur's Wilderness and Shakespeare's Wildwood, Cooper's Woods was an asylum, a place where noble good men belong in an age dominated by petty bad men. It was Cooper's haven as much as Natty's, and the more America realized the goals of Jacksonian democracy, the farther back into the woods (and time) Cooper took his hero. Cooper's Farther Landscape was an interior territory as well, a wilderness equivalent of Virgil's spiritual terrain, wild not mild pastoral. It was a territory of the mind, in which Cooper could solace himself by voicing platitudes through the mouth of a man who never was in a place that never existed in a time that had long since passed.

Though an asylum, hence salvational, the Farther Landscape for Cooper is seldom a place of spiritual transformation. Despite his resemblance to Wordsworth's rustics, Natty is no pantheistic transcendentalist, but a conventional Christian, whose goodness is the result of his Moravian upbringing—it is institutional, not intuitional virtue. Though he is at home in the woods, being at home for Leatherstocking means being eternally vigilant, and his "woodcraft"—the Farther Landscape equivalent of Middle Landscape husbandry, "wild" georgics—is more or less the technics of survival. Cooper's wilderness is essentially a playing-field, where the Umpire is a severe but just Providence, and where the Game has a unique set of rules, quite different from those of the British Military Presence in America. The American wilderness is not the Playing Fields of Eton, nor is it a Sherwood or an Arden Forest, but a Darwinian arena, where Virtue unaided by Superior Skill is a goner. Here, Salvation is Survival. There is no concept of natural benevolence involved, only the understanding that a tough turf throws a man back on himself, resulting in a rugged self-reliance—pragmatic, resourceful, alert—in short, the ideal character for an epic hero. As we have seen in *Robinson Crusoe,* the Farther Landscape tends to border on epic terrain, the highlands where hover clouds of imperial glory.

Natty's real-life counterpart, Dan'l Boone, was something of a primitive land speculator, and Natty himself is essentially a realtor of the Farther Landscape, will he, nill he, assisting in its conversion to the first stages of the Middle Landscape—to Templeton. As his alias in *Last of the Mohicans* suggests, he is a Walking Gun, a free-lance (in D.H. Lawrence's word) "killer," dedicated to the extermination of bad Injuns—Mingos. As for the good Injuns (a minority of three), except for Hardheart in *The Prairie* (for reasons discussed below), they play the white man's game, Chingachgook being the original Uncle Tonto: he sees Templeton, as it were, and dies. Chingachgook, having died in *The Pioneers,* is doomed from the start (as Natty is outlawed). He is thereby "The Last of the Mohicans," his son Uncas having died in the second (so-named) of the series. Any way you want to look at it, for Cooper a Good Injun is a Doomed Injun.

Though an outlaw and gentle renegade, Leatherstocking is also a guide, thereby a reconciling agent, a symbol of wild-pastoral accommodation, like Tityrus a supporter of law and order and a respecter of authority, like Meliboeus accepting his exile stoically. Fiercely loyal to the memory of the Tory Effinghams, on whose vast estate, as a sort of "kept" forester, he lives until the Revolution and the coming of the somewhat-less-than-noble (slightly Whiggish) Judge Temple, Leatherstocking can only stand sadly by as his asylum is pillaged by the settlers. When he runs afoul of the Judge's new game laws, he can only escape to a still farther wilderness. He resents the intrusion of settlers, but he has served as scout and fellow Injun-killer with the frontier Army which made the woods safe for democracy, and though he grumbles and mumbles, he accepts the inevitable with a primitive Christian forbearance.

There is nothing in anything that Natty does and says (and Cooper speaks through him, as through a ventriloquist's dummy, woodenly) which suggests that there is any alternative to the remorseless westward march of civilization, that epical conquest of which he is the inadvertent but undeniable symbol. The one exception is the Great American Desert, the Prairie, which, for Cooper as for so many Americans of the 1820's, was a howling, impassable wilderness, fit only for savages—the Terminus of Empire. It is there that Natty pays his respects to Ultimate Authority (symbolized by the setting sun) by dying, a virtual personification of the frontier (imperial) impulse, providing the third volume of the original Leatherstocking Trilogy with a suitably epic (apotheotic) finale.

Natty, like the Noble Savage, is an unfavorable comment on those who follow him, whether rapacious, criminal backwoodsmen straight out of Crèvecoeur's diagram, like the Hutters and Bushes, or muddled land-scrapers like the piggish settlers in *The Pioneers,* and like the Savage he is doomed, while the others will be succeeded by a more stable, land-owning culture, the Jeffersonian-Crève-coeurean dream. Though a figment of the political imagination, Leatherstocking, like all such epic heroes and empire builders, is irrelevant to the problems of the present, and is significant only as a representative of a glorious past, from which one may draw strength or take bitter, nostalgic solace. He is, moreover, an evanescent phenomenon for all his wily courage and superhuman powers, like the New York wilderness itself, dependent on the stability of a pre-Revolutionary feudal aristocracy for his anarchic freedom, freedom which is contingent upon a species of servitude. Significantly, Natty turns outlaw only when his former way of life collides with the laws established by Judge Temple to protect the remaining game, and lights out for the Prairie to escape direct confrontation with the conditions of his "liberty." Though apparently a populist rebel fleeing the exploitation and restrictive legislation of the Eastern establishment, Natty is really nothing more than a feudal relic of the Effingham dynasty. To the very end, his chief loyalty is to the memory of his feudal master, as his talents throughout many of the Tales are in one way or another associated with the Army, a feudal, caste-ridden system. In Natty Bumppo, that is to say, we are very close to the "Good Man" of English literature, a norm posited by establishmentarian, reformational (not revolutionary) satire, which seems to spring up in time of turmoil and change, and is basically a nostalgic creation.

An early conservationist, and like most conservationists passionately conservative of the status quo, Cooper saw the depletion of the wilderness as an inevitable disaster, a consequence of national progress, perhaps well-meaning but always regrettable. As Davy Crockett was the tool of the Whigs, his backwoods heroics designed to draw populist support away from Andy Jackson, so Natty Bumppo was in some ways a vernacular creation of Jeffersonian (Virgilian) Democracy, a good, even saintly, uncommon common man, loyal to a land-based aristocracy. Leatherstocking was not, however, designed as a vote-getter, but as a reminder of the price of progress, whether Whig or Jacksonian-Democratic. Chiefly a literary and a psychological matter for Cooper, wildness was also a nostalgic buttress of his land-based conservatism, a political platform planted firmly in the middle of the Middle Landscape, with convenient views of Mount Vernon (to the Right) and Monticello (to the Left).

Though in many ways an exponent of Crèvecoeur's Jeffersonian diagram, Cooper took it one step further—following Defoe's lead, his Leatherstocking Tales commence where the *Letters* leave off, in the Farther Landscape. He is therefore responsible for the literary transference of the "spiritual" (i.e., imaginary) landscape from the Middle to the Farther zone in America, while yet preserving its Virgilian (conservative) aspects by mingling georgic values with the heroic element of American frontier enterprise. As Henry Nash Smith has pointed out, despite the appeal of Jefferson's agrarian idealism to Cooper and his contemporaries, no bucolic hero emerged in American popular literature. Given the heroic emphasis of the reigning literary models, the versions of rampant, Romantic individualism found in both Scott and Byron, this is hardly surprising. As in Crèvecoeur's *Letters,* the Middle Landscape is a relatively balanced area, cyclical less than linear, and it is the line which is the heroic figure. The Virgilian georgic, moreover, is a celebration of a people and a land, a folk emphasis, not the celebration of an individual, which is the function of the Epic. Cooper, again following the lead of Defoe, managed to combine all three forms in differing proportions, concocting the formula for American pastoral.

Perhaps the closest Cooper comes to the Virgilian georgic ideal is in *The Pioneers,* with its emphasis on the seasonal cycle and the necessity for social order. Leatherstocking at first is little more than one of Scott's local eccentrics, supplied for the sake of dramatic contrast, and though he eventually emerges as a central figure, it is as an outsider and an anachronism. Virtually a hermit, Natty is characterized as a quirky, querulous old man, and though still an excellent marksman, is given few opportunities to demonstrate his heroic nature. As a result, he closely resembles

Wordsworth's recluses, who inhabit the borders of the Georgian georgic scene. In *Last of the Mohicans,* by taking Natty back in time, and by placing him in his proper milieu as an army scout in the Farther Landscape, Cooper gives his creation full license for heroic activities. Where *Pioneers* is dominated by the circle—the georgic figure—suggested by the central symbol of Lake Otsego, *Mohicans* is dominated by the line of heroic endeavor, the rivers and streams, and finally the trail, which leads Leatherstocking into the heart of a savage wilderness in quest of the missing Monro sisters. Hardly pastoral in the Virgilian sense, *Mohicans* is nonetheless a version of wild pastoral, whose main themes are the bucolic ideals of friendship, loyalty, and love, and which stresses the wild georgic technics of wilderness survival: tracking, hunting, canoeing, killing. Though a restless representative of the heroic ideal, eternally in motion, Natty is not an epic hero, but a conventional hero of adventure. The epic role is reserved for him in *The Prairie.*

As Henry Nash Smith points out in his Introduction to *The Prairie* (Rinehart edition), Cooper tended to frame his novelistic action in dramatic terms—setting a scene, moving his characters into it, building to a confrontation, resolving the action, closing the scene, etc. As his many epigraphs from Shakespeare suggest, he was consciously forming his novel in the shape of a drama, and is therefore sparing in his choice of settings. From Natty's first appearance, all things conspire to elevate him to mythic stature, as a kind of Lear of the Prairies compounded with Ulysses at the end of his second voyage. Though the line of heroic endeavor is reduced to a series of sorties, and the movement is therefore reminiscent of *Pioneers,* Natty is here the central figure, a compound of Virgilian and Christian virtues—pious in both the Aenean and Christian (and Wordsworthian) sense, a stoic compound of courage and wisdom. It is in the wild pastoral setting of the Prairie, a wilderness area designed by Providence (and Cooper) to remain permanently Beyond, that Natty dies, elevated to Aenean apotheosis, like Aeneas a symbol of the imperial impulse. Significantly, the georgic theme is (mis)represented here by the

Ishmael Bush family, symbols of social disorder, who are driven back along the troubled trail they have come, emphasizing the ultimate inviolability of the Farther Landscape.

Cooper was wrong, but since it was the trans-Mississippi region which later became fixed in the popular consciousness as the trans-mundane, literary West, an artistic preserve closely approximating the epic arena, it is *The Prairie* and not *Last of the Mohicans* (despite the overwhelming popularity of the latter) which may be considered as having defined the Farther Landscape in the American mind. Since Cooper never saw the real Prairie, it was doubly a spiritual (pastoral) territory, a purely imagined and idealized zone, a scene of travels, adventure, and warfare, and as such a mythic threshold of Empire permanently held in a period of dynamic transition, a wild version of Keatsean "cold pastoral": "What men or gods are these? What maidens loth?/What mad pursuit? What struggle to escape?" In *Deerslayer* and *Path-finder,* Cooper returned Leatherstocking to the New York wilderness, the forests of the Eastern frontier, but it was the rolling, treeless prairie of the Great Desert which was The West for subsequent generations of Americans, long after The West was really downtown L.A.

The West also means for many Americans John Wayne, who, as the lineal descendent of Leatherstocking, represents as well a hardening of Natty's conservative implication into a varicose chauvinism, like the Know-Nothings an ugly aspect of American nativism, nursed by the myth of a rural, Protestant-Ethical America. For Cooper's territory expanded quickly to the schlock-epical arena of the pulpwood wilderness, the tawdry terrain of the Beadle Dime Empire, where it became an escapist asylum purely, though feeding populist prejudice by elevating Jesse James to holy outlaw stature, and helping Manifest Destiny along by depicting all Indians west of the Mississippi as a pack of degenerate sadists, granting a license to destroy the literal remnant of Cooper's Farther Landscape while preserving and maintaining its figurative counterpart until the movies could take it over. John Wayne is the end (though hardly the last) product of the process, receiving an Academy Award (O Pioneers! O Academe!) for a fleshy parody of himself as a one-eyed Odin of vigilante justice, but commanding popular attention (and popularity) by performing heroics on the latest frontier of Empire, a battle-ground presided over by the spirit of West-More-Land and imperiled by the slope-headed sons of Chink-a-gook.

But the West means many things to many people, for it is a wide enough territory to accommodate all, extending as far as the imagination may expand. Our woods are once again filled with Indians and Leatherstockings, dressed in beads and buckskins (or nothing at all) and searching for the love that passeth under-standing—and sometimes tolerance. For many young Americans, the woods still provide a salvational territory, whether for the utopians of Vermont and New Mexico or for the would-be guerrillas hidden in the High Sierra—along with the ghosts of Guevara and Bogart. Salvational, even evangelical pastoralism, whether psychic or political in orientation, is a strong force in Young America once again: "Woodstock" was but a latter-day version of camp-meeting, mass pastoral, or good vibrations in the woods. For this is Jonathan Edwards' territory, as much as Cooper's, and Transcendental Turf as well, where anarchy has a definitely anti-Virgilian, revolutionary ring. In the works of Thoreau, in particular, the Farther Landscape is at once wild and subversive, the rebellious green of seasonal and institu-tional change. Though he died without an heir, Thoreau has many children today.

Like these children, Thoreau squatted on Cooper's as well as Emerson's land, appropriating the spiritual landscape by turning it inside out, putting the furside inside and the skinside out, by internalizing the wildness, as when one devours a woodchuck raw. Where Nature for Cooper (and Leatherstocking) was a dangerous terrain, in which one learned the signs and survived, or didn't and died, where mind was a primitive calculating machine programmed for peril, for Thoreau it was a benign territory, where signs were symbols of a higher, spiritual truth, and mind was an intuitive resonator, a sort of inner witching-wand, vibrating to unseen, unheard, unfelt chords beyond the wall of Being. Character-istically, Cooper populated his landscape with fierce, treacherous, deadly savages, whereas for Thoreau the Indian was a wraith, a nostalgic compound of mist and woodsmoke, a good, red ghost haunting the green forests where once he hunted.

There is something evocative of Leatherstocking's situation in *The Pioneers* in Thoreau's choosing to live in a cabin in a clear-ing by a pond outside of town (though both Cooper and Thoreau were in debt to *Robinson Crusoe*), becoming a presiding spirit of the woods and a worshipper at the shrine of the great god Pan, the rumors of whose death were, according to Thoreau, highly exaggerated. Like Leatherstocking's retreat, Thoreau's was politically motivated, a protest against the materialistic, grasping spirit of American enterprise, but Thoreau was his own, not somebody else's creation, and where Cooper regarded Natty as a heroic but evanescent ideal, Thoreau insisted upon the Farther Landscape as a permanent, spiritual fact, which one could (and should) retreat to from time to time, to recreate one's soul—and reconsider the system in which we live.

With Cooper, Thoreau regarded wildness as a political idea, but not as a quiescent, nostalgic source of reactionary regret. Wildness for Thoreau was an ever-present, live radical root of psychic power, and the wilderness was a transformational, sacramental zone, one of those desert places of pure spirit. If, in Virgil's (and Crèvecoeur's) diagram, the Middle Landscape is invaded and controlled by the sphere of politics, if in Cooper's diagram, the Middle Landscape continually enroaches upon the Farther Landscape, bringing with it the Ax of the Backwoodsman, the Plow of the Settler, and the Sword of Temporal Justice, in Thor-eau's diagram, it is the Farther Landscape which does the in-vading, Thoreau like Young Lochinvar coming out of the West (or Left), the "wide Border" outside of town, to contest the claims of temporal law, particularly when they represent a rapacious materialism and an unjust State.

Whereas Leatherstocking keeps retreating West so as to live (and die) in the freedom zone denied the mass of men, Thoreau created his own private preserve of anarchic wildness in the East, and tried to serve—through his books and the example of his life—as a conduit of wilderness freedom, piping it right into town. Early on, we find him writing to his brother John in the elevated language of a Cooper (spiritualized) Indian (wild pastoral equivalent of the Virgilian shepherd), wrapping himself in that pattern of ideal accommodation with the wilderness spirit, for Thoreau felt a lifelong identification with the Red Man, even to the point of mystic union (evinced by his gift for ESPying arrowheads). Cooper created a Man of the Woods by getting his words' worth out of the legends of Dan'l Boone, creating a Child of Nature who was superior in woodcraft and virtue but noticeably lacking in intellect (which Yale drop-out Cooper distrusted anyway). Thoreau encountered Leatherstocking in the person of Alex Therien, was at first enchanted, but then went on, continuing his pursuit of the ghostly Red Man into the Farther Landscape, the elusive shade of Chingachgook that haunted Cooper's Woods, now Thoreau's by squatters' rights.

Significantly, Thoreau brought a book, not a gun, with him into the woods, *The Iliad,* chief of the classics which he so dearly loved for their simple, natural clarity, the work of an epic poet valued by the romantics (as Shakespeare was valued) for his antique closeness to Nature. Homer was "wild," like the Indian, but also an artist, a supreme poet, evidence of the transforming power of the imagination, the supremacy of the spirit over matter. Where Cooper, through Leatherstocking, made a distinction between the White and Red Man's "gifts," Thoreau sought to combine them, to install a brain in Cooper's Child and instill the spirit of Redness as well, hoping thereby to resurrect an ideal, heroic man for America, a wilderness version of the classical pattern, creating a "man with a cross," truly—a wild-pastoral Messiah—and Thoreau was his prophet, his John the Baptist.

In his photographs, like so many New Englanders of his generation, Thoreau even looked part-Indian, but beneath the calm eyes and prominent cheek- and nose-bones, there lurks a full and sensuous mouth, somewhat wryly slanted, which betrays the Byronic part. Like Byron, Thoreau associated personal and political rebellion with wildness (and himself and Byron with skunk-cabbage!), and, like the author of *Childe Harold,* he was his own best creation, with a flair for self-dramatization, if on a humbler, less cosmopolitan scale. Byronic also was Thoreau's conception of himself as a traveler, and though he made a sly joke about his journeys around Concord, it was clear that he regarded distance as a relative matter. Most of his writings are framed as literal as well as figurative trips—to Canada, Cape Cod, the Maine Woods, up the Merrimack—"Excursions" which were incursions also, spiritual, inner journeys into the territory of mind as well as pedestrian or boat trips into some unknown physical terrain.

Typically, Thoreau's wilderness manifesto is entitled "Walking," which suggests the difference between his mode of traveling and Byron's (which might be called "hurtling"), Childe Harold's "Pilgrimage" a species of high-speed transport between stage appearances at some well-known ruin or vista. Thoreau generally pictures himself as a "saunterer" or "sojourner" in space, both inner and outer. He has, moreover, none of Byron's stagy world-weariness, nor his romantic irony, his ability (particularly in *Don Juan*) to transcend his own limitations with a sardonic smile. Though Thoreau experienced from time to time that romantic (schizoid) sense of doubleness, the detachment of spirit from self which was such an important element of Transcendentalism, no irony or self-parody was ever involved. Thoreau's evangelism required a dead-serious center, a lodestone certainty that the Beyond, the Farther Landscape, was not an ever-elusive horizon, but THERE, a verifiable source of benevolent energy.

Like Emerson, Emerson's disciple was a disciple of Carlyle. Thoreau shared Carlyle's Calvinist sense of absolute righteousness, the elated sanctity of the Elect, with its concomitant impatience toward those who refuse to see his Light, nor did he keep that light under a bushel. His favorite mythic analogy for himself was Apollo, and he delighted in wrapping himself in an aureole glow (in his *Journal,* Thoreau dwelt at length on the "Thor" in his name) as a fellow sojourner on Olympus. *Walden* is a type of spiritual autobiography, but it lacks the essential element of repentance (even Ben Franklin included *that*), for Thoreau outdid Wordsworth in sublimity of egotism, presenting himself as a man without sin, without stain: plants which he "watered" thrived, land on which he "squatted" gained value thereby, for Thoreau was a veritable Johnny Appleseed of benign defecation, whose sh-t obviously did not st-nk. *Walden,* the most read of Thoreau's works, is often therefore the least understood, filled as it is with a sublime sense of well-being and certainty, a harmony which is a Transcendental equivalent (issuing from Self) of the Augustan pastoral peace, and lacking Thoreau's characteristic wandering in pursuit of the Farther Landscape. Indeed, *Walden* is set in the Middle Landscape, the pastoral center, and oozes from every pore with the rectitude of the Elect, the calm, inner "high" of the camp-meeting graduate. The spirit of the Pond itself dominates the book, clear and calm and cool and certain as a Spring morning or a lump of jade, casting a constant pastoral glory over all. No side trip is taken at Walden which does not bring Thoreau back home, his pockets loaded with certainties and slogans, and he returned to Concord at the end of his sojourn (like Frank Sinatra) with more in his baggage than when he left. "I have been to Walden Pond," says Thoreau, "and it works."

But when Thoreau left Walden, it was to take the first of his three voyages into Maine: the certainty of the book (like the environs of Concord) is a relative matter, for Thoreau did not leave off his restless wandering in pursuit of salvational wildness until he was too sick to move, his wanderlust clearly akin to the Byronic malaise. This restlessness, this continual thirst for wildness, is missing from Virgilian pastoral, the balanced, stable world of the Middle Landscape, where trouble not enlightenment is identified with "departure" (expulsion). In Thoreau as in Cooper (as in Defoe) the two are often confounded. Linear movement provides one half of the essential diagram, the lateral line of the far horizon providing the other, resulting in a "T"—as in "Thoreau." At the far end of Thoreau's perpendicular diagram lay the Maine Woods, and though Cooper's Prairie was its equivalent, the Prairie was Terminus (another "T") while Thoreau's Woods was its antithesis. Typically perverse, as Fussell has shown us, Thoreau throughout the *Maine Woods* insists on finding his "West" in the "East," an auroral wilderness which he associates with multiple dawning: of the sun, of mankind, and of the diviner glory of enlightenment. The Maine Woods was his Farther Landscape, imagined as a source instead of a final barrier, but, a source which did not so much corroborate as challenge his evangelical conviction of benevolent wildness, turning into a barrier after all, whose god-like Terminus was Ktaadn.

The line into Thoreau's Farther Landscape begins in the sunshine and blue skies of *A Week on the Concord and Merrimack,* the most purely (and consciously) Arcadian of Thoreau's works, but with several strategic departures from the Virgilian model, commencing with the linearism of the voyage itself. Though Thoreau's River Arcadia, like Virgil's pasteurized pasture, is a timeless place of natural beauty which inspires poetic thoughts and thoughts of poetry (and poems as well, a number of which are classically bucolic), it shares with Renaissance pastoral an emphasis on mutability, on the reminder that Death also dwells in Arcadia. Passing through the world of living men, the River also carries the voyagers past the reminders of another age, a world of Indian relics and *mementos mori,* which serve to link the River to all great rivers, and to the passage of time which rivers symbolize. These signs of a former way of life serve an additional function, enhancing the Indian-like quality of the brothers' voyage up the Merrimack in a boat painted the blue and green of Walden Pond: theirs is a life of simplicity set in wildness, a life of movement, of absolute freedom and ease, and though it is a spiritualized, hence idyllic (bucolic) existence, it is animated by a wild, Indian spirit, the emanation of the Farther not the Middle Landscape.

Everyone the travelers encounter is charitable and helpful, and even the water-mills along the way return their borrowed stream to the River without harming it, symbols of pastoral accommodation. Lying under the stars one night, listening to the martial rhythms of a militia drum, Thoreau attains a mystical epiphany, a vision of ultimate harmony and exaltation. This pervasive mood of harmony is summarized in the essay on Friendship, with its emphasis on shared but silent sympathies, an epitomized expression of the Transcendental mood. But the essay, like *A Week* itself, was written as a memorial to Thoreau's beloved brother, John, who had died shortly after the voyage was completed, and who seems also to have been in part the inspiration for the elegiac, indisputably pastoral poem, "Sympathy," which is at once a counterpoint and complement to the essays it prefaces. Similarly, the journey is accompanied by a change of seasons, from late Summer to early Autumn, a mood of greenness and growth followed by a mood of harvest and finality, the threshold of winter. A Thoreauvian version of bucolic pastoral, of Eclogue, *A Week* is devoted largely to the themes of natural beauty, poetry, and friendship, though not without a considerable emphasis on wildness, movement, and freedom, overshadowed throughout by a reminder that the only constant dweller in Arcadia wears a perpetual smile and carries a scythe.

In the Virgilian tradition, the "purely" pastoral Eclogue is contrasted to the didactic Georgic, but as in so many other respects, Thoreau does not hesitate to mix his modes. As he and his brother were schoolteachers for a while, so *A Week* is dominated by a pedagogical strain: the book is a virtual anthology, not only of Thoreau's poems and those of other poets he admires, living and long dead, but also of clippings and graftings and nosegays from his other reading, most of which are concerned with the ethics of action—morality—the highest didacticism of all. Where Virgil's pastoral poets inhabit a sort of Roman MacDowell Colony, the harmony of which is indebted to the fact of Empire, the State to which Tityrus makes his devotions, Thoreau's asylum (like Robin Hood's) is green with the spirit of anarchy. Though he is concerned throughout with the necessity of Duty (not, like Tityrus, made uneasy by it), his idea of Duty runs counter to the Aenean piety, for it is not based on fealty to the authority of Age or the State, but to oneself and Eternity. Nor is there, as in Virgil, any sharp division between the pastoral world and the world of law and order, the two being essentially one thing: "The Laws of Nature are the purest morality."

Throughout, Thoreau's preference is for what appear to be extreme alternatives, either the radicalism of the "Jewish peasant," Jesus Christ, or the conservatism of the ancient Brahmans, and he scorns the modern, intermediate spirit of "reform," which is but a liberalist equivalent of the meddlesome authority of the State. But apparent extremes are joined in the region of absolute (Natural) morality, Christianity being the most moral of spiritual religions, Brahman conservatism at base a legalistic system of morality, both therefore reflective of the Laws of Nature. In none of these ruminations is there any suggestion of a Virgilian (Middle Landscape) order emanating from some distant, secular, statist authority, but rather just the opposite. Whether appealing to the absolute laws of cyclical change, which is not really change at all (whence comes Eastern morality), or citing the radical example of Christ and Antigone, who oppose the arbitrary laws of the State with the strength of personal conviction, Thoreau constantly refutes the temporal rule of man-made laws, drawing on natural law for his sense of stability and order, and in a nutshell summarizes the argument of "Civil Disobedience": "To one who habitually endeavors to contemplate the true state of things, the political state can hardly be said to have any existence whatever."

"Contemplate" is the important word here, as elsewhere in Thoreau's work. What he shares with Virgilian pastoral is the spiritual emphasis, but raised to a higher, transcendent power, to the force of pure Platonic idealism. As the poem "The Inward Morning" suggests, set down as it is on the last day of the upward (outward) voyage, the journey has been chiefly an exploration of "the horizon of my mind," a yielding to that "singular yearning toward all wildness" in Thoreau's nature, but a testimony as well to the universal, natural order of which the mind is a paradigm. Though disorderly and random, reflecting a romantic love of

Aeolian Harps and Organic Principles, *A Week* is really a paean to Order—not the Virgilian, statist kind, but natural order, which is akin to artistic, poetic, or musical order, like the vision through the tumbler bottom a version of transcendental idealism: "A strain of music reminds me of a passage of the Vedas, and I associate with it the idea of infinite remoteness, as well as of beauty and serenity, for to the senses that is farthest from us which addresses the greatest depth within us."

This is the key to *A Week,* the meaning of the Farther Landscape, the "horizon of the mind," at once the line on which all lines of temporal perspective become vanishing points, windows into eternity, and the inner territory which they illumine. The "Excursion," as always, has been an "Incursion" as well, for the farther away one goes, the deeper into oneself one penetrates. Though the journey ends where it began, in Concord amidst the Middle Landscape of the Gilpin-like, picturesque "Grass-ground" River—the "dead" center of mild pastoral—the stress is on the outward bound voyage which ends in the freedom zone of "Unappropriated Land," the absolute source and center of "infinite remoteness," of wild pastoral. "Wildness" for Thoreau is not misrule, but a higher order—this is the meaning of his particular brand of anarchy—the ultimate implication of Emerson's diagram in *Nature,* which is the reverse of the Crèvecoeurean configuration. That is to say, if Nature is the source of Truth, then the farther into the landscape one penetrates, the closer one comes to Truth.

Again, as Fussell demonstrates, though Thoreau loved to play with the frontier metaphor of "West," his literal journeys were usually toward the East, at once a reflection of his interest in the Vedas (that "other Indian" culture) and an acknowledgment of the symbolic power of the dawn, with which he identified himself, whether as Apollo or Orpheus or simply as an early riser. Thoreau also identified himself with Thor, whom Carlyle associated with "Summer-heat," Thor being "the god of Peaceable Industry as well as Thunder. He is the Peasant's friend; his true henchman and attendant is Thialfi, *Manual Labour*. Thor himself engages in all manner of rough manual work, scorns no business for its plebeianism. . . . ." All of which brings us to *Walden,* which is a working out of a number of ideas set down in *A Week,* which was written while Thoreau was *at* Walden, chief among which is the thought that "The wilderness is near as well as dear to every man. . . . Our lives need the relief of such a background, where pine flourishes and the jay still screams." This is all part of loving the wild no less than the good, but *Walden* in many ways is not so much a perfected *Week* as its complement, as Virgil's *Georgics* are an extension and yet a contrast to the materials and mood of the *Eclogues.*

The difference between *Week* and *Walden* is signified by the difference between the Merrimack River and Walden Pond: the one is dominated by the figure of the line, the essential component of the Farther Landscape—heroic advance for Cooper, spiritual drifting for Thoreau; the other is dominated by the circle, the cyclical figure associated with the seasonal, georgic round. But as the georgic element is present along the banks of the River in *A Week,* the ethereal riverscape of the wild pastoral similarly invades *Walden,* spiritualizing it: the River empties into the Pond. Though Thoreau casts himself as a georgic Farmer, it is as a most unlikely Farmer, one who fishes most of the time, either in brooks, books, or ponds, and whose beans are filled with a divine afflatus.

Water was as important a thematic source as Woods were for Thoreau, and his major works all involve a watery background, whether the ocean (*Cape Cod*), ponds *(Walden)*, or rivers and streams (*Week, Maine Woods*). As Walden Pond was "God's Eye," water in general for Thoreau stood for the lens of Truth, an equivalent of his transforming water tumbler. Water was also important for Cooper ("Of the Wood and Wave"), again as ocean (*Red Rover*), lake (*Pioneers*), or river and stream *(Mohicans*), but it seldom had a spiritual, transcendental implication. The closest Cooper comes to Thoreau's vision is in the fishing scene in *The Pioneers,* where Leatherstocking by the light of a torch spears a giant salmon, his skill and selectivity in marked contrast (as

Henry Nash Smith has pointed out, in commenting on the transcendent implications of this passage) to the rapacious harvesting of fish by the greedy settlers. The use of the torch to illumine the depths is typical of Cooper's view of man's relation to Nature, artificial light being a prototypal emblem of intelligence, the torch itself a crude sort of frontier technology (as well as a glimmer of the forest fire which results from the settlers' "wasty ways").

But when Thoreau peers into the depths of River or Pond, the water is irradiated by the natural light of the Sun, and when he fishes at night it is without lantern or torch and with a metaphysical angle, a delicate instrument which registers the tug and flutter of invisible life in another world. This spiritual communication is the antithesis of Natty's fish-spear, which is thrust below the illuminated surface in a passage urgent with pure, linear, masculine power, impaling an equally powerful, equally phallic salmon. This physicalness and power is missing from *Walden,* whose fish are always a sort of glittering jewel brought up from beautiful depths, pieces of the Pond itself, and as such, transcendental, mystical symbols, evidence like the beautiful bug of a world beyond the mortal sphere.

As both *Walden* and *Week* are in debt to the pastoral mode, so they also share many qualities with Walton's *Angler,* including the angle of vision in which the piscatorial pastime expands into an encyclopedic array of loosely related meditations. Fish, those "fabulous inhabitants of another element," are central symbols in both books, their beauty reflecting the essential harmonies of Nature. Both works are essentially "wet" pastorals, blending the techniques of eclogue, georgic, and halieutic, substantiating the pagan and Christian (salvational) implication of pastoral with the pagan (generational) and Christian (regenerational) symbol of the Fish. Both Shepherd and Fisherman are dual symbols of Christianity, and of the two, it is the Fisherman who dominates *A Week* and *Walden,* the evangelical savior not the pastoral keeper of souls. Wildness is ever associated with evangelism, and Water as well, the one the source of prophetic inspiration, the other a symbol of baptism, of transformation.

Another Christian symbol of exultant resurrection is the crowing Cock, the image Thoreau selected as an emblem of himself in *Walden,* which he chose for its buoyant optimism, but which, like the glittering Bug and the iridescent Fish, has other connotations as well. At once a bird of dawn, of wild, Eastern origins, and a domestic, barnyard fowl, the crowing Cock is also a figure of exuberant egotism, thus a token of that peculiar pastoral blend of wildness and domesticity that is *Walden.* For like his version of Eclogue, Thoreau's version of Georgic reverses many of the Virgilian norms. Though set in the Middle Landscape, as Leo Marx has pointed out, it is at the farther end, where the Georgic circle is a "horizon bounded by woods," and though Thoreau's was a pastoral (spiritual) retreat, it is also a demonstration, a political act of secession by way of educating his fellow townsmen —and the world—didacticism of the highest sort. The emphases are surely Virgilian, for *Walden* is a virtual handbook of rough georgics, rendering with relish the details of primitive architecture and subsistence husbandry, all described against the backdrop of wildness, and set within a frame provided by the cyclical round of the seasons. The emphasis, moreover, is on the distinctly pastoral season, the summer months (which in the first, manuscript version dominated the book), the winter being not much more than a transition to the Springtime, with its rich oozings of growth and reformation.

A number of references in Thoreau's work to *Robinson Crusoe* suggest the original model for his sojourn at Walden (though, as I mentioned above, Leatherstocking provides another analogy), and like Defoe, Thoreau mingles epic elements with the georgic tradition, transforming the hoeing of beans into a mock battle with weeds, making frequent reference to the *Iliad* and Homer, witnessing an epical battle between ants, etc. Like Robinson Crusoe, Thoreau extends his dominion over the landscape, and borrowing, with a pun, from Cowper's poem on Alexander Selkirk, notes that he is "monarch of all I *survey,*" extending his literal survey to Walden Pond itself, converting the rumored bottomless mystery into a fathomed fact, from which he deduces one more Natural

617

Law: "the law of average." The Law of Average indeed dominates Walden Pond, as befits the Middle Landscape. Nature here is no adversary, but a benevolent ally, and Thoreau uses no fertilizer but the natural loam of long-fallow land. He puts a due, georgic emphasis on the value of hard work (scorning the lazy, improvident Irishmen who are his neighbors), and admires the zealous woodchopper, Alex Therien, for his energy. Though Wildness may abound in and about Walden, ferocity is absent, and the shy maniac, the Loon, is its chief representative, along with legions of muskrats and woodchucks, chickadees, phoebes, and blue jays. It is, by and large, a rather tame, Wordsworthian wildness.

Like Crèvecoeur's Farmer, Thoreau leads a life of simplicity and ease, enjoying the mild restraint of his own liberal laws, at harmony with the world about him, even (like the Farmer) living in close quarters with a colony of wasps. But the emphasis here is not on the Farmer as foundation of stable Empire—the Virgilian theme—but on that theme dear to Concord citizens, transcendental or otherwise, the Embattled Farmer, or Farmer as Rebel: "our only field known to fame [is the] Concord Battle Ground." It is in just such a field that Thoreau plants his beans, which were, as he is at pains to inform us, his claim to the agricultural fraternity, and, as such, his license to criticize the brotherhood. Thoreau, who professed to "love" the georgic type in *A Week,* now draws continual and unfavorable contrasts between his own farming habits and the daily lives of his fellow husbandmen in and about Concord, who are chained to their ox-cart ideas of material prosperity. Though he too hoes beans and harvests them, Thoreau puts manual labor and its profits into a proper perspective, less the be-and-end-all of existence than a means of subsistence—of survival—freeing him for more important labor.

His husbandry manuals are of a piece with his love of classics—Cato and Varro are favorite authorities—and part of his attack on his fellow farmers concerns their lack of traditional, natural piety, of respect for the earth that is such an important part of the Virgilian Georgic life. As Embattled Farmer, Thoreau tries to plant something more than beans in his field. Given the emphasis on books and matters of the soul, as well as pantheistic paeans to Nature reminiscent of Wordsworth's poetry, and scenes with Thoreau floating on his pond (like his favorite water lily, which labors not, nor does it, etc.), playing his flute and listening to the echoes rebound from the forest and hills, *Walden* is nothing if not a spiritualized Georgic, halfway to pure Eclogue.

Still, the quality of freedom is quite distinct from that in *A Week,* and lacks the impress of physical movement, the linear coefficient of the free-flowing play of mind. All things relate to the Pond and to the life on its banks. "Snug" is the word, with Thoreau bedded down in his little cabin while the squirrels play (fornicate?) under the floor, with Mother Nature rustling by on the way to the Pond, her basket of natural comestibles tucked under her arm, close to her ample bosom of benevolence. It is a very Hobbit-like burrow that Thoreau-as-Hermit occupies, and we are on our way towards John Burroughs as well, to say nothing of Thornton Burgess and Mother West Wind. "Certainty," that is another word, with never a doubt expressed, nor even the possibility of alternatives: close-worked and as tightly knit as his mortised and tendoned cabin, *Walden* is Thoreau's lath-and-plastered monument to transcendental certitude, a celebration of universal, natural benevolence. Small wonder this book is so dear to the academic sensibility, for one may spend hours by hours explicating Thoreau's puns, delineating his rhythmic compounds of theme and counter-theme, and relishing his puckish (Robin Goodfellowish) attacks on the plodding clods of middle-class farmers who pass his cabin in hours of darkness so as to be in Brighton by market-time.

It is easy to misread *Walden* (or misdirect the reader), to derive the impression that it is a closed system of harmonies, having to do with the salvation of self and society through an improved relation with the natural world. It is that, of course, and borrows much of its mythic force from the anchorite tradition, the salvational power of solitude and silence. And the political implication, derived from the idea of the Embattled Farmer, is rather subdued, reduced to a few, quick flashes suggestive but not insistent on deeper discontents: "the only true America is that country where you are at liberty to pursue such a mode of life as may enable you to do without [tea, and coffee, and meat every day], and where the state does not endeavor to compel you to sustain the slavery and war and other superfluous expenses which directly or indirectly result from the use of such things." We are here quite close, once again, to "Civil Disobedience," and a brief paragraph is devoted to the incident, but with barely a shrug of one shoulder. As a consequence, the antistatist aspect of Thoreau's version of Georgic is diminished, and is rather more latent than realized.

I think therefore that "Civil Disobedience" should be inserted somewhere in *Walden,* like a fiery eye of opal in the forehead of an otherwise smug and satisfied Buddha, a complement to those other two eyes, the "Lakes of Light," White Pond and Walden. Because it is in "Civil Disobedience" that the revolutionary potential of the apparently placid *Walden* is revealed, the power of individual liberty and of intuited, natural law concentrated in an open act of personal "nullification," as Emerson called it, an act which breaks Arcadia wide open, converting it into Sherwood Forest, no longer an Arden but a guerrilla den. The closest Thoreau ever came to playing at Robin Hood was the night he spent among fellow outlaws in the Concord Jail. As he is at pains to point out in that essay, the proper asylum for good men in bad times *is* a prison. Ever an advocate of freedom, Thoreau was willing to sacrifice his own when other men had none, a symbolic gesture against slavery, which he regarded as the ultimate insolence of the State, an absolute extension of arbitrary power, interior imperialism. More important, perhaps, Thoreau's night in jail, like Natty Bumppo's, points up the latent outlawry of his stay at Walden, which was a secession of one man, conceived in liberty, and dedicated to the test of whether that secession or any secession, so conceived, could long endure.

The drama of American political life may be seen as a contest between the Romantic principles of the Declaration of Independence, with its foundation in the concept of natural rights, and the Augustan principles of the Constitution, with its foundation in the rational, mechanistic formalism of the 18th century. The one is founded on a belief in the sanctity and perfectability of men, the other on their infinite capacity for mischief. Radicals usually take their stand on the principles of the Declaration (and its counterpart, the Bill of Rights), conservatives on the Constitution. In such disparate 19th-century novels as *The Pioneers,* John Neal's *Rachel Dyer,* Hawthorne's *Scarlet Letter,* Melville's *Billy Budd,* and Mark Twain's *Huckleberry Finn,* the essential issue is the contest between these opposing principles, often centered on the dramatic device of a trial (or moral decision), with the central figure at once a symbol of natural innocence (identified with an element of wildness) and civil disobedience. Thoreau, in his insistence on not paying his taxes, placed himself in this literary situation, participating in the American National Pastoral Dramatic Dilemma and acting out the lead role in its chief classical analogue (and his favorite tragedy), *Antigone.*

Concord was a lenient Creon, however, and the play turned into a comedy. Like Natty Bumppo, Henry was sprung, but as with the Leatherstocking Tales, the drama did not end with Thoreau's Huckleberry Finnale, which was not so much an ending as a beginning, a lighting out past Fair Haven Hill for the Territory beyond—not Walden Pond, for Thoreau had already been there, but the Maine Woods, which was Thoreau's main woods indeed. We tend to forget that at the end of *Walden,* Thoreau tells us that he left the Pond "for as good a reason as I went there." *Walden* works, as pond and book, because of secret springs, the inflow of spirituality from the pastoral landscape of the *Week,* a harmonious blending of the Farther and the Middle Landscape. The voyage in *A Week* carried Thoreau into "Unappropriated Land," but at either extremity lay a Concord, signifying the overall balance and harmony of the mild pastoral vision. But Walden Woods opened to the East, to an even farther landscape, those distant Maine Woods, which opened in turn to the

Dawn itself, not to an Apollonian Sun, but to a far wilder Eye, the single eye of Woden, God of Force, presiding deity of auroral origins, the unimpeded flow of raw, primitive, pulsating life.

When, in his last, dying year, Thoreau asked that the subtitle to *Walden,* "Life in the Woods," be removed, it was, I think, because he had decided that the *real* "Woods" was not the bordering forests of Walden, the *lucum conlucare* surrounding his pond-side temple to Pan. They were not, that is to say, Emerson's Woods, and they were something more than Cooper's. Since the first of his three trips into the Maine Woods (1846) took place before Thoreau began to write *Walden,* and the second (1853) before he commenced his final revision, his experiences there may well have had some effect on the shape which that book finally assumed. I think that in many ways they account for the symmetry and tightness of the mystic circle of *Walden,* and that the emphasis of Thoreau's version of georgic is reformational rather than revolutionary because Thoreau himself in a certain sense had staged a "retreat," as much from absolute wildness as from society. The Middle Landscape in *Walden,* like the Anglican *via media,* is less the product of absolute conviction than reliance on authority, not the State, not the Church, not even on the Bible or Emerson, but on the Classic verities. Homer not Woden is the God of Walden Pond, his antique purity and balance a refuge from the troublesome discoveries Thoreau had made in "Jötunheim, a distant dark chaotic land."

The Maine Woods lacks the paronomastic richness, the constant playing on words and with ideas which gives *Walden* its characteristic texture, being a relatively straightforward account of three tergiversational canoe trips into the Maine wilderness. It also lacks the pervasive certitude of *Walden,* nor are Thoreau's Maine voyages characterized by the buoyant spirit of Indian freedom which animates *A Week on the Concord and Merrimack.* They are in all senses Something Else, neither the Arcadian landscape of the *Week* nor the sweet wildness bordering the Garden of Walden Pond, but the Farthest Landscape itself, where wilderness has a distinctly howling quality about it. The Maine Woods is a territory which cannot be framed in the bottom of a tumbler, and thus accommodated to the pastoral vision. It is Thoreau's three voyages there which most closely correspond to Leo Marx's paradigmatic "retreat" (Thoreau at Walden having staged a strategic withdrawal), because it corresponds to that prototypal American genre, the romantic quest into the far (not the middle) distance. Whether intentionally or not, Thoreau's three journeys into the Maine Woods form an epical counterpart to the Eclogue of *A Week* and the Georgic of *Walden*.

Where the line in Thoreau's exploratory diagram in *A Week* suggests an advance of philosophical and ethical speculation, a leisurely, peripatetic movement dictated by the meanderings of a river, in *The Maine Woods* it for the first time resembles Cooper's heroic line of advance. What is missing, however, is the imperialistic connotation, and when we look very closely at Thoreau's Maine Woods it begins to resemble the erroneous terrain associated with the Quixotic, mock-heroic quest. Though the thrust of the Line is seldom qualified by the lengthy, planetary ruminations which characterize *A Week* and *Walden*, yet the powerful onward push of exploratory inquiry ends in a maze. The first of the three journeys, "Ktaadn," is thematic: though the goal of his endeavor is the summit of the mountain, Thoreau is ultimately baffled by the clouds shrouding the top.

Ultimate bafflement characterizes the other two quests after wildness also, and the dark, elusive Ktaadn looms over them, a wilderness Fujiyama. Wildness in the Maine Woods not only takes on a different quality from the benevolent, neo-Platonic spirituality suggested by the sacred grove of Walden Woods, but it is at once more savage and more evanescent—both frightening *and* fragile. Like Cooper's Indian, the Woods is a doomed adversary, and as Thoreau paddles up wilderness streams in search of Wildness, it literally floats past him downstream on the way to lumber mills. In his quest for the Moose—coefficient of Wildness—Thoreau learns most about the mysterious animal from the hunters who kill it for profit. And Joe Polis, the Indian guide from whom he hoped to discover wilderness secrets, turns out to be an imperfectly noble savage, his urbanization suggested by his surname—an etymology which Thoreau for once chooses to ignore. Still, the Woods retains much primeval force, as on the dark, tangled slopes of Ktaadn, a force which is plainly hostile to man's purposes. In one memorable episode, when his companion wanders off for a moment and is instantly lost to Thoreau and Joe Polis, Thoreau is seized by a primitive panic which suggests that the Great God is alive and well in Maine, rather than in the bucolic environs of Walden Pond.

When Thoreau returned from his last trip to Maine, in 1857, he wrote a friend concerning the trip: "It is a great satisfaction to find that your oldest convictions are permanent. With regard to essentials, I have never had occasion to change my mind." Insistence often suggests doubt, and in the same strain is Thoreau's declaration that "Ktaadn is there still, but much more surely my old conviction is there, resting with more than mountain breadth and weight on the world, the source still of fertilizing streams, and affording glorious views from its summit if I can get up to it again." The "if" is the telling conjunction, outweighing the several adjectives, and its counterpart in *The Maine Woods* is a detectable note of futility, a mood missing from *A Week* and *Walden*. If Thoreau's voyages into Maine were an equivalent of that characteristic American Romance-Epic form, the Quest, like Melville's quests the results are indeterminate.

Like Melville's failed questers, Thoreau was something of a Quixote, refusing to acknowledge aloud the futility of his search for benevolent Wildness, even when (as on Ktaadn) its antithesis confronted him full in the face, uprearing, black, shaggy, wet with primeval dew, reaching out with a most unfriendly grin to grant a chilly hug before disappearing like a mixture of woodsmoke and mist. Since his politics, his philosophy, and indeed his very life were based on an absolute conviction of the benevolent power of Wildness, the consequences of this dark challenge are interesting to trace. Though he reacted perhaps unconsciously to his experiences in the Maine Woods, they surely account for the reinforced stronghold of georgic pastoralism that is *Walden.* Equally important, they explain in part the explosive ferocity of Thoreau's defense of John Brown, the very language of which reveals a realignment of his pastoral perspective.

Following his last Maine voyage, Thoreau spent the last few years of his life writing a number of essays, revising such journal materials as he thought fitting for what was clearly to be his last will and testament. Among them is "Walking," his final manifesto of wilderness politics, an essay which at once testifies to Thoreau's continuing faith that Wildness is the "preservation of the World" and suggests that his experiences in Maine had indeed modified his expectations of "Wildness." Quixotic to the end, Thoreau responded to his experiences in Maine by radically changing his psychic, geopolitical orientation without any noticeable dampening of his enthusiasm for the quest, his conviction of the rightness of "natural" morality, shortly to be projected with terrific elan into the Ahab-like Captain John Brown.

In "Walking" Thoreau's belief in the salvational powers of wildness is expanded into a statement of evangelical faith, of "belief" in "the forest, and in the meadow, and in the night in which the corn grows." But, as Forest, Meadow, and Cornfield suggest, we are still in the Middle Landscape, not far off in the wild forests and raw clearings of Maine. Well, this is familiar enough territory, the pastoral "retreat" which we associate with Walden Woods, opening to "absolute freedom and wildness, as contrasted with a freedom and culture merely civil," but not so far as to entirely distance the sounds of Concord. Once again, it is to Natural Law that Thoreau pays his greatest allegiance, for "with regard to Nature I live a sort of border life, on the confines of a world into which I make occasional and transient forays only, and my patriotism and allegiance to the state into whose territories I seem to retreat are those of a moss-trooper," that is to say a Robin Goodfellow, or even Robin Hood. Fairies and spiritual felons alike need asylum, and, though in Thoreau's ideal world, "part will be tillage, but the greater part will be meadow and forest, not only serving an immediate use, but preparing a mould against a distant future."

"Walking" is testimony that the experience of the Maine Woods only strengthened Thoreau's faith in the Middle Landscape, that woodsy border between Arcadia and the Sabine Farm, that he had resolved the duality between savage and mild pastoral by forgetting the savage part. Where, one asks, are the Indians in these woods, this wild territory beyond the meadow and the village? There are none. They have silently folded their wigwams and faded away. Even more remarkable, this version of the Middle Landscape does not open to the East, to the regions of the rising Sun, but to the West, to the setting Sun which is ever tracing the path of Empire: "Every sunset which I witness inspires me with the desire to go to a West as distant and as fair as that into which the sun goes down. He appears to migrate westward daily, and tempts us to follow him. He is the Great Western Pioneer whom the nations follow." No longer the Indian, but the Great Western Pioneer is the hero now, Apollo as Noble Savage as Dan'l Boone.

The East, always before depicted as an opening vista, the source of Divine Illumination, the horizon of mystery, stands now for all that is familiar, dull, exhausted: "It is hard for me to believe that I shall find fair landscapes or sufficient wildness and freedom behind the eastern horizon." The Maine Woods, the Indian, the Primitive Past, all seem to have proved nothing more than a *pokelogan,* a cul-de-sac, ending at the blank wall of Ktaadn. It is now the Prairie, the Pioneer, the Future which holds the key to it All, evinced by the powerful westward tide of the People.

Westward, also, the Course of Empire. Thoreau associates wildness not only with the West ("another name for the Wild"), but with the imperial impulse as well: "The story of Romulus and Remus being suckled by a wolf is not a meaningless fable." Viewing a painted panorama of the Mississippi, with its unfolding mural of exploration and the relentless sprawl of civilization moving ever westward, Thoreau cannot but feel "that *this was the heroic age itself,* though we know it not, for the hero is commonly the simplest and obscurest of men." Simple and obscure—like the husbandman, the georgic ideal, the Farmer. "The callous palms of the laborer are conversant with finer tissues of self-respect and heroism, whose touch thrills the heart, than the languid fingers of idleness." Work is Worth, the familiar georgic motto, and the true hero follows his plow, the line of his furrow plotting the course of Empire.

This is not the Eastern Farmer, of course, hastening to market in the dawn darkness, but the Western, the Man with the Hoe who "displaces the Indian even because he redeems the meadow, and so makes himself stronger and in some respects more natural." The West makes an Odysseus of every plowman, and the Indian's role, as always, is to be displaced, to fade away like a reddish puff of smoke. As with Thoreau's laying about him in his bean-patch, this is epic agrarianism, hence "noble" labor, this occupation of the Farther Landscape, as American Georgic so frequently is: "The weapons with which we have gained our most important victories, which should be handed down as heirlooms from father to son, are not the sword and the lance, but the bushwack, the turf-cutter, the spade, and the bog hoe, rusted with the blood of many a meadow, and begrimed with the dust of many a hard-fought field." The New England Hector, the Embattled Farmer is newly relocated in the Western Reserve, the "landscape of the mind," next the Farther Landscape, ever retreating, as in Crèvecoeur's diagram. There is no talk now of Terminus, only of the westering urge of Empire that redeems both man and land, and it is the figure in the Middle, not the Farther, Landscape who is put upon the pedestal: Ishmael Bush Redeemed.

The answer, I think, for this remarkable shift in consciousness is not hard to find. There is such an intimate coupling of the idea of the West with the idea of an apotheotic Future for America, that the concluding epiphany in "Walking" is very much like the ending of *Walden,* at once secular and transcendent in implication. It is the crowing cock again, the bug in the woodwork, the fish from the pond. Or the Farmer in the Dell, the Embattled Farmer *redivivus,* gleaming out of the Great West in one of those cometary orbits, beard streaming, godlike, apotheotic—Woden, the quaternity sun-god of wisdom and poetry, agriculture and war. What redeemed Thoreau's faith in Empire and the imperial impulse was the Common Man as rebel, as guerrilla, and as Christ—as John Brown, Hero.

In the Westerner, John Brown, Thoreau at last found his proper Man, the heroic epitome of those other Borderers, those ideal dwellers in the margins of the Woods. And if this Man, this John Brown, came singing out of the Western Wilderness, then like an Aeolian harp, Thoreau's soul vibrated in sympathy. For this was no "John Farmer," this Farmer John, content to sit on his doorstep, to heed Thoreau's wild, pastoral flute, his Pan-pipe, by merely practicing "some new austerity." This Farmer John was the very personification of the *Walden* spirit, had not only "let his mind descend into his body and redeem it," but caused it to ignite there and expand, irradiating his whole being with the power of Truth. For, as Thoreau exulted, John Brown was indeed a Transcendentalist, the man he had been waiting for, his Messiah, and if he came, like Lochinvar, from out of the West, still his origins (like the Sun) were in the East, for he was Yankee Savior, a Life *with* Principle right to the very end—a Hero worthy of a Poet. Here was a Surveyor *deserving* of a Monarchy, whose heroic base-line sliced unhesitatingly into *Jötunheim,* whose very name resonated with saintly and fertile associations, as rich and warm and oozing with vitality as a railroad embankment in the early springtime.

As their spirit of worshipfulness should suggest, Thoreau's three essays (sermons, rather, or prophecies) on John Brown are filled with a Carlylean inspiration, the Carlyle who had seen the vitality of the Norsemen, the rude giantism, the exaggeration, the exuberant bragger and swag expanding once again as that "still other shape," the American Backwoodsman, the spirit of Odin

628

again returning to Earth, out of the Earth. This is also the Carlyle who celebrated the Hero as King in Cromwell, Cromwell the King as Commoner, and a pastoral commons at that, for, like John Brown, Cromwell had been a Farmer before he beat his plowshare into a sword. Cromwell, the Puritan King, was the original Embattled Farmer, a foretaste of those Puritan patriots of Concord Field.

"A man of rare common sense and directness of speech, as of action," is how Thoreau characterized John Brown, "a transcendentalist above all, a man of ideas and principles," whose purity of motive and dedication to truth irradiated all that he said, did, wrote. For even his style bespoke a simple eloquence, "simple as the discharge of a bullet from a rifle," a style impelled by the power of Truth and the urgency of conviction, and "a Sharp's rifle of infinitely surer and longer range." John Brown was not educated at Harvard: His Harvard and Yale was "the great university of the West, where he sedulously pursued the study of Liberty, for which he had early betrayed a fondness, and . . . finally commenced the public practice of Humanity in Kansas, as you know." The Practice of Humanity in this instance was guerrilla warfare, and where in *Walden* Thoreau shrank from the idea of murdering "any creature," man or (especially) beast, we now find him agreeing with John Brown's "peculiar doctrine that a man has a perfect right to interfere by force with the slaveholder in order to rescue the slave," even to the point of killing him, for to Thoreau a slaveholder's life was more shocking than his death.

It is a mistake to conceive of Thoreau as a pacifist, despite the Gandhian interpretation of "Civil Disobedience." As early as "The Service" Thoreau revealed a tendency to think of the spiritual in terms of the military life. "I do not wish to kill nor to be killed," he writes in "A Plea for Captain John Brown" (note the "Captaincy"), "but I can foresee circumstances in which both these things would be by me unavoidable," a stand which is only a further extension of his declaration in *Walden* that "there is never an instant's truce between virtue and vice." His objection to the Mexican War was to its purpose—its end—not the means themselves, and "We preserve the so-called peace of our community by deeds of petty violence every day ... [and] so we defend ourselves and our hen-roosts, and maintain slavery." But now the Sharp's rifles are in the right hands, that is to say the righteous hands, "for once ... employed in a righteous cause. The Tools [are] in the hands of one who [can] use them," claims Thoreau, paraphrasing Carlyle, who quotes Napoleon's *"La carrière ouverte aux talents."*

"The question," writes Thoreau, "is not about the weapon, but the spirit in which you use it," which is spirituality with a Yankee handle to it, a utilitarian notion, a morality based on simple expedience: "Is it not possible that an individual may be right and a government wrong?" This is it, the center of the thing, the question of liquid fire: "Treason! Where does such treason take its rise? ... High treason, when it is resistance to tyranny here below, has its origin in, and is first committed by, the power that makes and forever recreates man." The culprit is not the Christ before the bar, but the Governor who sends him out to die. "The power that establishes justice in the land" is not found behind the bench, but behind the plow—or a rifle. This is a power that Antaeus-like draws its strength from the earth, and like early (radical) Christianity it is a power that waxes rather than wanes in adversity: "He is more alive than he ever was. He has earned immortality. . . . He is no longer working in secret. He works in public, and in the clearest light that shines on this land," that "great awakening light" of evangelism which shines from out of the West.

If *The Maine Woods* was Thoreau's personal epic, a failed quest but a transforming experience, placing Thoreau's interior landscape firmly in the middle ground without altering his conviction of the essential Truth of wildness, which is Freedom, steadfastly anti-Virgilian because anti-statist, then John Brown was the incarnation of his faith, spiritualized Georgic itself. In an about-face which was absolutely consistent with his earlier position, though 180° in the opposite direction, Thoreau poured into John Brown all the power of his own love of freedom, seeing in him a gleam of hope for a nation that had seemed mired in the slough of his despair. As incarnation, John Brown is also apotheotic, providing Thoreau's lifelong quest with a suitable climax, a termination of epic which is less a celebration of the American Empire (Brown's crucifixion was hardly a spread-eagle affair) than a hope for a new order, a new revolution, which the emergence of John Brown seemed to promise.

Like Thoreau in the Concord Jail, John Brown was a participant in the prototypal American drama, standing with Natty Bumppo before Judge Temple, with Hester on the scaffold, floating with Huck and Jim on the raft, hanging silent and godlike beside Billy Budd. Behind John Brown (and all the rest) is the figure of Jesus Christ, "the Prince of Reformers and Radicals," standing before Pontius Pilate, and Antigone, "'having, like a criminal, done what is holy,'" before Creon, natural law defying the laws of the State. As Thoreau himself realized, the ending of the drama was necessarily apotheotic: "I see now that it was necessary that the bravest and humanest man in all the country should be hung. . . . Some eighteen hundred years ago Christ was crucified. . . . These are the two ends of a chain which is not without its links. He is not Old Brown any longer; he is an angel of light."

We can hear dimly in the background of this noble, impassioned, yet simple language the strains of "The Battle Hymn of the Republic," which was set to the tune of "John Brown's Body," itself set to the melody of a stirring revival hymn, Julia Ward Howe's version a celebration of the Militant Christ—returned at last with his fateful sword—and Abraham Lincoln, like John Brown a Titanic Farmer from out of the West, soon enough to meet his own martyrdom by the hand of one who, like John Brown, knew what he knew and did what he had to do. Lincoln's death was an epic and a tragic and an apotheotic climax also, marking the end of the American *Iliad* (as John Brown's death signaled its beginning), the Civil War, a poem which wrote itself, and which, while fulfilling Thoreau's desire that the slaves be freed, only did so by crushing his greater hope, by increasing the power of the State, evincing the final victory of Industrialism over the Agrarian Dream.

At the time, in his time, John Brown stood at the end of one process and at the beginning of another process and Thoreau was his prophet. Like Natty Bumppo, John Brown is a complex creation, not of a complex, troubled consciousness but of a complex, troubled era. (Are they not much the same thing?) Like Natty Bumppo, he looms up out of the anarchistic Frontier, not that backwoods utopia between civilization and the wilderness, but that political hell between slavery and free-soil territory — Bloody Kansas — the Border, the same troubled land that produced John Brown's counterpart, the Bushwhacker Quantrill and his guerrilla band, among them Jesse James, the American Robin Hood whose propensity for holding up trains was a prolongation of secession which got converted by the Dime Novel metempsychosis (and a psychosis it was) into populist heroics. For the Border Country is Populist Country too, and Jesse James and John Brown are brothers under the skin, Robin Hood and Christ the Prince of Radicals, symbols of violent decency and evangelical moral fervor. If, through the mystic bond of the Dime Novel, Natty Bumppo merged with Jesse James, then it was at a mystical ceremony, attended unawares by the citizens of Concord, that Thoreau caused his wild pastoralism to flow into John Brown, creating of that Embattled Farmer the image of righteous revolution, a living, breathing, fighting, and dying image of militant Transcendentalism, cast in the die of Puritan Cromwell, glorious refutation of the divinity of the State, champion of the Law of Average, which finds the greatest depth and width in the middle of all things, at the center of a Cross.

Unlike Cromwell, John Brown did not lead the victorious forces of virtue during the Civil War. That role was filled by a man named Ulysses, cast in the Aenean not the Cromwellean mold. The War brought on other reversals also. Certain of Thoreau's ideas in "Civil Disobedience" were similar to (even derived from) those of the evangelical radicals of the early 1840's, the "Come-

Outers," who denied authority to any agency other than individual conscience, and who, early on, wanted New England to secede from a Union which sanctioned slavery and its extension into the West by means of imperial expansion. As it turned out, the South seceded, filled with a similar conviction of righteousness — divinely sanctioned if not inspired — thus causing the War for the Union which incidentally freed the slaves. It was a War *for* Union which Lincoln's Ulysses captained, a War, like the Augustan campaign, to solidify the State, as the spread of Empire and the Mexican War had been *for* Union, a territorialist version of the Transcendentalist's vision of Many-in-One, indivisible, and founded on the secular, mechanistic harmonies of the Constitution, in which Daniel Webster, another defender of Union and arch-enemy of the Transcendentalists, placed his faith.

In all senses, then, the machine had won, and it was not long before Thoreau's beloved pastoral stream itself was the ravaged scene of industrialized, mechanized America, water no longer returned from her mills unsullied, but dark with corruption, like the country itself. Ulysses, like Augustus (like Aeneas) returned to rule, but the age of Ulysses was a Gilded Age, not a Golden Age, and an Age of Brass as well. For the North had won, and despite the righteousness of the cause, had won for the wrong reasons, Satan being ever the Lord of the North. And technology. And cannon. And mills. And secession — rebellion — and tyranny as well. For was it not the North that truly seceded — from the old, Jeffersonian Dream?

The thing is, there is no visible difference close up between Satan and Prometheus. What is different only becomes visible as we draw away in time. At the beginning even Carlyle had to admit that Cromwell and Napoleon appeared to be identical twins of righteous zeal. The party of wildness is ever the party of rebellion, of change, of regeneration, but it taps the powers of darkness by lighting a torch, the light making the dark even blacker. The other thing is: there is no absolute ideal possible here on earth, the Law of Averages being the Pyramid, not the Plane. The Augustan

633

peace was obtained at someone else's expense; the Jeffersonian dream was made possible by licensing the European nightmare and the Black Man's agony. Thus when men come down from the mountains bearing a handful of lightnings from Heaven, all Hell breaks loose. Had Thoreau not been so close to John Brown (in spirit, time, place—the classic unities) he might have seen the dark potential of rebellion, but his telescope was (like a Sharp's rifle) of a high power and was aimed at the middle of the mountain, the zone of wildness not savagery. Had he aimed it a little higher he would have recognized the Old Man for what he was, the Thunderer, not Woden but his Father, Thor.

"Weird" is the word, not much used by Thoreau.

Thoreau's plea for John Brown is a classic example of primitivist politics, and its indebtedness to Carlyle's doctrine of the Divine Hero, its insistence that the righteousness of the cause transcends the means used to implement that cause, brings us close to a militant form of mystical fascism, the seeds of which may be found in his own sense of divinity, his mystical identification with the Indian, his intense, evangelical conviction of personal rectitude, and his Romantic (elitist) individualism. (Perhaps Emerson knew more than he said when he characterized his disciple as the Napoleon of Concord.) Despite his retreat to the Middle Landscape from the frighteningly impersonal vision at the center of the Farther Landscape (the point where linear self vanishes), Thoreau persisted in reversing the statist implications of the georgic middle, in channeling his primitivist convictions through a version of secular evangelism, making of John Brown "an angel of light," which, in effect, was reminiscent of the elevation of Piers Plowman in the apotheotic climax of Langland's Lollard epic, but which emphasized the revolutionary not the other-worldly aspects of the Christian message, and—with the stress on agrarian simplicity, rather like a counter-revolution—the Puritan impulse.

Given the historical alternatives of political pastoralism in America, we are presented with the elitist tradition of Virgilian, (Virginian) statist, exclusivist, squirearchical agrarianism, or its

634

counterpart, anarchistic, demagogic, evangelical populism. Of the first, Jefferson is the chief proponent and representative; of the second, Thoreau and John Brown. The possibilities of Jeffersonian agrarianism died with the Civil War, though many of its attitudes still thrive in the rarefied, vacuum-packed atmosphere of the Academy (the Jeffersonian Bell Jar). Populism, the idealization of rural values, is still a powerful ideological and political force in America, though no longer confined to rural areas. At one extreme, Populism merges with Primitivism (on the far left as it were), the philosophical equivalent of the values of the Farther (wild) Landscape which I have attempted to describe and account for on the mythic plane above. At the other, it emerges as petty, small-business capitalism, with its psychotic terror of the centralization of financial power in large, urban combines, whether Railroads, Banks, or International Jewry. Primitivist, evangelical populism, with a concomitant worship of the Lowly (expectation of a new John Brown) is largely today the province of the Young, particularly the New Utopians, but also those factions of the New Left characterized by a dual tendency to romanticize revolution and spiritualize violence in the name of righteousness.

If Thoreau is at the source of primitivism as a political doctrine, then it is of interest perhaps to observe that in his, as in all mystical "systems" there is latent an essential fallacy. Primitivism, as an absolute ideology, posits the Wild as a source of the Good, and like all absolute ideologies, implies that the source is continuous, that that the Good increases in direct proportion to Wildness. Thoreau's voyages into Maine, especially his climb up Ktaadn, should have disabused him of his conviction concerning the benevolent source of wildness, but they did not. What he was apparently most impressed by was the singularly evanescent quality of wildness, its fragility in confrontation with the rude technology of loggers and hunters, a discovery singularly in harmony with Cooper's early conservationism. But where Cooper stoically accepted the march of civilization, regarding the Prairie as a barrier rather than a continuing source of goodness—a "preserve"

635

—Thoreau proposed the setting aside of large tracts of wilderness for the spiritual needs of the future generations.

Thoreau surely was responsible for the park system in America, his writings among the prime movers behind such conservationist activists as Frederick Law Olmsted and John Muir. In *Walden,* with its ideal of borderlands of wildness contingent to towns, we have the philosophical basis of such city oases as Central and Golden Gate Park. In *The Maine Woods* and in "Walking," we find the essential idea for the more recent concept of national wilderness preserves. But, given the essential continuousness implied in primitivism, a Park, of whatever extent, is merely a park, owing its very existence to the will of the State—as Natty's hunting preserve was but the outer fringe of the Effingham Royal Grant.

Parks, no matter how vast or how rugged, are no more than islands of wildness, surrounded by a sea of asphalt, and lack that quality of profoundness, endlessness, eternalness so important to the concept of "vernal impulse." A qualified wildness, a licensed wildness, is a Greenwood and an Arcadian wildness. A Walled-In Wildness. Walden becomes the Concord Jail, included in the vast hug of the State.

The Walden ideal, separated from the concept of primitive continuousness, becomes an Academic ideal, which is to say a Virgilian ideal: licensed (accredited) by the State, a walled-in park, tree-lined, georgic Georgian quadrangles celebrating the Holy Quaternity of God, Country, Yale, Me. None of this is what Thoreau meant, but if you start out from Walden, you end up with "Lake Innisfree," the "in-free!" of Tityrus. But to be in is not to be free. What one wants is not entrée, but outré: OUT. The Academy may be an asylum, a voluntary retreat, but it is not conducive to the outlaw impulse. Notably, when anarchy broke out there, its advocates were primitivist, romantic revolutionaries, latter-day Robin Hoods who thought that Ivy Walls were a pallisado to keep the State *out,* not the spirit of inquiry *in.* Some of them have since fled to other forests, still

636

pursuing the notion of wildwood autonomy, but no revolution ever started in the woods. One may retreat there to reform oneself, to reorder one's priorities, and one may hide there to sortie forth, but one is only one, surrounded at all times by "them," and liable to extirpation at a moment's notice. Without the sympathy of the countryside, guerrilla warfare, spiritual or otherwise, is a futile tactic. On the other hand, from the point of view of the State, parks are a very fine tactic indeed. Like campus quadrangles, they at once isolate and dissipate the wild energies of revolt. Parks are the modern equivalent of the Virgilian emphasis on getting the people back to the earth. Dynamite is customarily stored in a pastoral setting in little cabins with flimsy roofs and solid walls which very much resemble Thoreau's sturdy hut.

I should like to end as I began, with a paradigm of sorts. In a recent issue of the Sunday *New York Times,* which I read as I was bringing this ramble to an uncertain fate, there was a feature story concerning (to quote the informed metaphor of the title): "National Parks: A Report on the Range War at Generation Gap." by Robert A. Jones, which might have been subtitled: "Or, Thoreau's Chickens Come Home to Roost." The story is about the problems in the Yosemite National Park, one of the most beautiful of the Thoreau-inspired preserves in America, troubles brought about by the collision of aims and preferences of the Youth Cult and Middle America, the latter-day equivalents of wild and mild pastoral. The one pursues the Thoreauvian dream of a life of primitive simplicity in the wildwood, the other imports its orderly clutter, setting up a remote outpost of suburbia in the forest. The effect of this proximity is "wild," but not in the Thoreauvian sense, though the Yosemite National Park is just such a place as he recommended in *Maine Woods,* with the troublesome exception that everybody wants to be there at once, with hi-fi and pot, or pup-tent and chemical potty, with the result that the air, instead of being pure and undefiled, is full of shit.

What results is an equivalent of the result of ghetto-crowding, friction caused by the oblique compression along the fault-line

637

between the antagonistic principles of the Declaration of Independence and the Constitution: Individualism and Law and Order meet again, with violent consequences—again as in the *other* asylum, the ghetto—either spontaneous or licensed by the State, in either case generally coming from the Right side of Crèvecoeur's diagram, thus preserving "the so-called peace of our community by deeds of petty violence"—and some not so petty. Middle Americans still need Indians, and if it is their sons and daughters who wear the buckskins and beads, so be it. The solution, recommended by Robert Jones, is for the two classes of pastoralists to take up back-packing, to move farther out into the landscape, where there is enough room for everyone to be alone and do what he wants to do without disturbing the rest of the rest. But haven't we been out there before? And isn't this the solution that brought about the problem in the first place? The Garden, the Expulsion, and All?

Contributors

AILEEN WARD is Professor of English at Brandeis University. Her *John Keats: The Making of a Poet* was awarded the Duff Cooper Memorial Prize and National Book Award in Arts and Letters in 1964. She is working on a critical biography of William Blake. **JOHN SEELYE** teaches American literature at the University of Connecticut. He is author of *The True Adventures of Huckleberry Finn* (Northwestern University Press), excerpts of which appeared in *TriQuarterly* 16 and *The Kid*, a novel published in 1971 by Viking Press. **TODD GITLIN** was the third president of SDS and with Nanci Hollander he wrote *Uptown: Poor Whites in Chicago* (Harper & Row, 1970) and has contributed essays to *Ramparts, The Nation, Village Voice, Commonweal, Psychology Today* and many other periodicals. **HUGH FOX** teaches in the Department of American Thought and Language at Michigan State University. Four books of his are being published in 1972, including *Letters of an old Pro* (Venice) and *An Aesthetics for the Year 10,000* (Whitson). Mr. Fox edits *Ghost Dance Magazine*. **TRUMAN NELSON**'s first novel, *The Sin of the Prophet* was published in 1952 by Little Brown. Since then he has written five other books, most recently *The Torture of Mothers* and *The Right of Revolution*, both published by Beacon in 1968. **CARLOS FUENTES** was born in Mexico City in 1928. He is currently involved in politics there. His novels include *La Región más transparente* and *La muerte de Artemio Cruz*. *The Enemy: Words*, which appears in this issue of *TriQuarterly*, is the final chapter of *La nueva novela hispanoamericana*, a lengthy essay on the new Spanish-American novel. **TONY STONEBURNER** teaches at Denison University. He is an editor of *A Recognition of Austin Warren* (Ann Arbor, 1966) and *A Meeting of Poets & Theologians to Discuss Parable, Myth & Language* (Cambridge, 1968). **NOAM CHOMSKY** is the author of many books and articles on linguistics, philosophy, and contemporary affairs. His essay *Language and Freedom* in this issue of *TriQuarterly* first appeared as Volume I, No. 1 of *Abraxas* (Fall 1970) published at Southampton College, New York. The entire symposium, originally held at Loyola University in Chicago (from which Mr. Chomsky's article came) will be published by Warren & Breech, Inc. in their series *Studies in Contemporary Thought*. **ALLEN GROSSMAN** is the author of *Poetic Knowledge in the Early Yeats* and two volumes of verse, *A Harlot's Hire* and *The Recluse*. **HARRY LEVIN** is Irving Babbitt Professor of Comparative Literature at Harvard University. His most recent book is *The Myth of the Golden Age in the Renaissance*. His forthcoming collection of essays is entitled *Grounds for Comparison*. **DICK LOURIE** has two books, *Lies* (Radical America, 1971) and *Dream Telephone* (New Books, 1969). He is an editor of *Hanging Loose*. **MARGE PIERCY** has two novels published, *Going Down Fast* (Trident, 1969) and *Dance the Eagle to Sleep* (Doubleday, 1970). *Breaking Camp* (Wesleyan University Press, 1968) and *Hard Loving* (Wesleyan University Press, 1969) are her two volumes of poetry. **FREDERICK CREWS** has published books on Henry James, E. M. Forster, Nathaniel Hawthorne as well as *The Pooh Perplex* (1963). His piece in this issue of *TriQuarterly* is part of a book of essays on methodology. **LEO MARX** is William R. Kenan Professor of English and American Studies at Amherst College. His *The Machine in the Garden, Technology and the Pastoral*

Ideal in America was published by Oxford University Press in 1964. He has edited works by Hawthorne, Mark Twain and Thoreau. Two of his essays which relate to the article in this issue of *TriQuarterly* are "Pastoral Ideals and City Troubles" in *The Fitness of Man's Environment* (Smithsonian Annual II, Harper Colophon Books, 1968) and "American Institutions and Ecological Ideals" in *Science*, 27 November 1970. **CARL OGLESBY** was the fifth president of SDS and co-author of *Containment and Change* (Macmillan, 1967) as well as editor of *A New Left Reader* (Grove Press, 1971). **PAUL BUHLE** is editor of *Radical America*. He did his undergraduate work at the University of Illinois and his PhD at the University of Wisconsin. **SOL YURICK** has four books published and three more in the works. Among these are a book of short stories, a new history of the United States and an expansion of the essay in this issue of *TriQuarterly*. **KRYSTYNA DEVERT** was born in Warsaw and now lives in Cambridge, Massachusetts, where she is a doctoral candidate at Harvard in Education. She is active in the women's movement and is working on a book of feminist essays. **RAYMOND WILLIAMS** has published books on drama, culture and society, his latest book being *Modern Tragedy* published in 1966. He is now working on a book, *The Country and the City*. **CONOR CRUISE O'BRIEN**'s essay in this issue of *TriQuarterly* first appeared in *TriQuarterly* 4, then in a revised form in Macmillan's *In Excited Reverie*. Mr. O'Brien was counsellor for the Irish Embassy in Paris in the fifties and a United Nations delegate in the early sixties. His books include works on Parnell, Albert Camus and politics. **GEORGE ABBOTT WHITE** has taught in public and private schools as well as the Episcopal Theological School and Harvard University. He has had articles in many magazines, including *TriQuarterly*, and is currently working on a history of SDS with Paul Garver, as well as a critical biography of F. O. Matthiessen. **CHARLES NEWMAN** is author of two novels, *New Axis* (Houghton Mifflin) and *The Promisekeeper* (Simon & Schuster). He is currently working on *A Child's History of America* on the politics and culture of America in the sixties.